LIVING SPACES

Sustainable Building and Design

©1998 Könemann Verlagsgesellschaft mbH
Bonner Straße 126, D-50968 Cologne

Art Direction and Design: Peter Feierabend
Layout: Sabine Vonderstein
Project Coordinator: Kirsten E. Lehmann
Production Manager: Detlev Schaper
Reproduction: Omniascanners, Milan

Original title: Lebensräume

©1999 for the English Edition
Translation from German: Susan Bennett, Tanja Bridge,
Fiona Hulse, Stephen Hunter, Martin Pearce, Umasankar Sankarayya
English-language Editor: Allison McKechnie
Adaptation: Loren Abraham, Tom Fisher, Barbara Zeier
Managing Editor: Bettina Kaufmann
Assistant: Alex Morkramer
Production: Ursula Schümer
Reproduction: divis GmbH, Cologne
Printing and Binding: Mladinska knijga tiskarna d.d., Ljubljana

Printed in Slovenia

ISBN 3-89508-925-7

10 9 8 7 6 5 4 3 2 1

ÖKO TEST

LIVING SPACES

Sustainable Building and Design

Editor: Thomas Schmitz-Günther
Adaptation: Loren E. Abraham, Thomas A. Fisher

Photography: Karin Heßmann

Illustrations: Dietmar Lochner

KÖNEMANN

CONTENTS

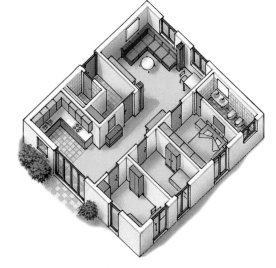

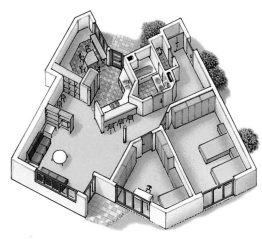

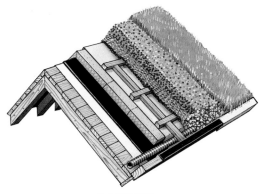

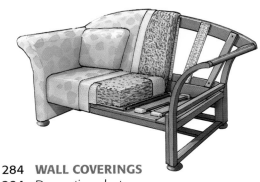

ECOLOGY, TECHNOLOGY

ECOLOGY, TECHNOLOGY AND BUILDING

Biologically correct building respects nature

The concept of ecologically friendly building is a fluid one, which is interpreted in somewhat different ways by builders, architects, engineers, ecologists and politicians. In general, biologically correct building describes a method of building which respects nature and biological processes. Other terms often used to describe ecologically appropriate building practices include Green Building,

Ecologists, however, believe that buildings should not only be energy efficient, but be made to last longer using materials whose manufacture has minimal impact on the environment. Toward this end considerable care and attention must be paid to the use of renewable raw materials, simpler technology that can be more easily repaired or replaced, as well as recycling. Obviously the use of components made from

Feeling at home
Arch.: D. Grünecke, Herdecke, Germany
Bright, well proportioned rooms and healthy, natural materials – just how everyone would like to live. Creating this sense of well-being is a primary aim of ecologically minded builders and designers. Attention is also paid to impact on the environment and to future generations. The building materials have been produced using as little energy as possible, and they contain little if any toxic materials that will make them dangerous or difficult to dispose of.

Building with natural materials for a healthy lifestyle

Harnessing technology to save energy

Sustainable Design and more loosely Organic Architecture.

For those with deeply ingrained ideas of what is biologically correct, Green Building means using natural materials to construct a building that places the health and general well-being of the occupants first. The most important criterion would probably be to choose only renewable materials (such as wood) that have not been treated with toxic, health threatening substances. Those whose primary aim is simply to conserve energy will have different priorities. Their main goal is to reduce the negative impact that the building has on the environment, and to decrease the amount of energy consumed and thereby the cost in both capital and environmental terms. It has been demonstrated that it would be possible to reduce energy consumption in buildings by more than 70% at a fairly modest cost. Advocates of energy conservation strategies promote increased building insulation values, airtight construction, superinsulated buildings, high-tech window glazings and many other energy efficient building technologies.

recycled materials is favored as long as their production and use does not require excessive energy nor create health risks due to inherent toxic substances. In addition, it is important that the materials, by and large, be recyclable or compostable (biodegradable with negligible harm to the earth). For urban ecologists, however, even these measures don't go far enough. They are particularly concerned about the way land is wastefully swallowed up by buildings and roads. Development should become more concentrated and efficient in terms of land use, and unnecessary roads should no longer be constructed. In addition, available buildings should be put to better use to cut down on the number of new buildings we need to construct. Accomplishing this will require a much more flexible approach to planning, land development and to living in general.

On the other hand, architects and engineers who specialize in designing for solar energy believe that all houses should be designed to abundantly receive and use the sun's energy. If all the energy generated by the sun were used to its full potential, buildings

could be transformed from energy guzzlers to energy producers. But in the past solar houses looked so plain and often distasteful, that many urban planners rejected them completely. They believe that new buildings must be integrated into the existing fabric of the town and surrounding countryside.

But wherever the emphasis is placed, there is complete agreement among all the protagonists that environmentally friendly building must not remain the privilege of the wealthy. On the contrary, every effort should be made to ensure that more and more people have access to housing that promotes health and is affordable both initially and in the long term.

For that purpose, it is the aim of this book to demonstrate that all these seemingly irreconcilable ideas can, nevertheless, be united.

For the publishers of two German ecologically minded magazines *ÖKO-TEST* and *ÖKO-HAUS,* construction methods must comply with the demands of ecology and the preservation of environmental as well as human health. They wish to present the reader with the findings obtained from carefully

examining a range of products and materials and to offer these as a basis for discussion among all those people interested in building or improving their home. Ultimately, every individual who has made the decision to build a home will discover what is most important for them. More and more of us are realizing the relevance of good insulation and of heating without squandering energy; the majority of families who are either building or renovating a house regard the use of healthy materials as paramount.

The environment and the way we live in it are inextricably linked. But even the experts don't have a complete grasp of everything that has to be taken into consideration when designing, constructing, and, indeed, living in buildings according to ecological and environmental principles. It is evident that guidance is very much needed.

Of course, we don't all have to move into cutting-edge, hi-tech homes designed by architects. It is rather the small things, the simple ideas and the principles that can inspire and guide even the less experienced that are important.

A low-energy house

Arch.: Hegedys & Haas, Graz, Austria
This house near Graz, Austria successfully combines elements of the quaint regional architecture with ecological building principles. The use of renewable raw materials such as wood conserves natural resources. Solar energy is well utilized through optimal orientation of the building with respect to the sun and by means of a high-tech solar collector array.

Less is more

SUSTAINABLE BUILDING

Sustainability means preserving the future

Sustainable building is the term most commonly used when describing building carried out according to sound ecological and environmental perspectives. The term Sustainable development was first defined in 1987 by the World Commission on Environment and Development as that "which meets the needs of the present without compromising the ability of future generations to meet their own needs."

Sustainable development means that any encroachment into the ecosystem must be done in such a manner that the survival of future generations is not threatened in any way. In simple terms this means that we should leave the world for our children a better place than we found it.

The notion of sustainability in building and urban development refers to the effects of buildings on the environment in all their phases from the production of building materials to the use of ecologically sound and non-toxic substances in building and finally to the eventual demolition of the buildings. It includes factors such as how much energy is produced during the process, and how waste is disposed of.

Sustainability is also taken into account during the planning of a house: How long can it continue to serve its purpose, before it will need to be converted or demolished? Above all, sustainability poses questions about the extent to which land is being exploited by the creation of new built-up areas and by the enormous increase in the volume of traffic which this has caused. The most important of these questions: How long can the ecological pressure from building and land development be tolerated?

Your dream home

Ninety percent of people dream of owning a home of their own, preferably a detached house in the country or at least in a semi-rural area. This holds true for every European nation and North America alike. But the patterns of ownership vary dramatically throughout the developed nations. In Ireland and Belgium most families are homeowners, but only 40% of Germans own the home they live in. In the United States 64% of nearly 100 million housing units are owner-occupied.

The amount of space available to each resident also varies widely. In Belgium and Britain there are two rooms or more per person, a fraction of the amount of space available per resident in Portugal and Italy. In the US the average is 2.2 rooms per dweller.

At the same time the trend toward one-person households should not be overlooked. Even though the population of the major European countries is stagnating, the number of single-person households rises every year. The number of single person households in the United States has grown to over 22 million or about 24% of all households. Finally, the pressures on the market for housing, to rent as well as to buy, increased in the 1990s as a result of the increasing numbers of people in the 20 – 35 age group. This age group accounts for nearly 25% of total households in the United States and the number of these renting is 50% greater than the number who own their home. For all these reasons, the demand for living space has risen quite considerably.

The construction of housing for rental, above all in the publicly financed sector, has almost come to a standstill since the 1980s, not only on account of the rise in building costs, but also because government subsidies in this sector have been drastically cut. In addition, over 2.5 million existing units have been torn down, abandoned or converted into luxury condominiums and office buildings (Miller, 1996). Detached or semi-detached houses are the most consumptive in terms of land requirements: For each square foot of living space, 11.77 square feet of land is taken up, if easements, lawns, driveways, garages, pathways and patios are included. Nature foots the

Houses near Graz, Austria
Single-family houses are the preferred form of accommodation. But such houses are ecologically sound only as long as land consumption is kept to a minimum.

bill for any move out of the town into the unspoiled surrounding countryside.

Each year in the United States about 1.3 million acres (526,000 ha) of rural land area is converted to urban development, rights-of-way, highways and airports. This is the equivalent of building a one-kilometer-wide road from New York to Los Angeles (Miller, 1996). For every square foot of hard surface created, the corresponding burden of absorbing runoff and pollutants is shifted to the surrounding undisturbed soil. For every tree bulldozed under the associated production of oxygen, removal of CO_2, transpiration of moisture, soil retention, and conversion of energy is eliminated forever.

In the future, housing developments are likely to arise in which most of the homeowners are of more or less the same age. Such housing developments will

go through clearly identifiable cycles: After countless children and teenagers have breathed life into these estates, density will drop quite considerably on their departure and a rise in the proportion of older people living there will become inevitable, until the process repeats itself. This development comes nowhere near the goal of creating compact communities with balanced multi-generational and mutually supportive neighborhoods. The alternative is not, however, a return to the construction of enormous housing developments such as took place in the 1960s; what is urgently needed instead is a well-conceived combination of high quality terraced houses and of low-rise multi-family structures.

A garden in miniature
Nature will foot the bill for any escape from the town into the country. But it is quite possible to enjoy the beauty that nature has to offer, even if space is at a premium.

SIZE OF HOUSEHOLDS IN THE UNITED STATES 1960–1995

Year	Average
1960	3.33
1970	3.14
1975	2.94
1980	2.76
1985	2.69
1990	2.63
1995	2.65

PERCENTAGE OF HOMEOWNERSHIP IN EUROPE AND THE US (1994)

	Total	Houses	Apartments
Europe	59	77	38
Belgium	66	78	27
Denmark	53	78	18
Germany	41	79	17
France	55	77	24
Greece	78	91	65
Great Britain	67	75	27
Ireland	81	85	6
Italy	70	83	64
Luxembourg	66	85	30
Holland	47	63	15
Portugal	61	67	51
Spain	79	85	76
United States	64	84	11

Source: eurostat, 1990 United States Census Data

HOUSEHOLDS ACCORDING TO NUMBER OF ROOMS (1988 IN %)
NUMBER OF ROOMS PER PERSON (1988)

	2 rooms	3–5 rooms	6 rooms	Rooms/person
Europe 12*	9	69	22	
Belgium	3	53	44	2.04
Germany	8	76	16	1.79
France	17	65	13	1.43
Italy	11	77	12	1.35
Luxembourg	3	47	50	1.85
Holland	5	61	34	1.79
Portugal	6	74	20	1.32
England	1	63	36	2.00
United States	4	51	17	2.24

* Combined total for 12 countries
Source: eurostat, 1990 US Census Data

The disastrous results of segregated land use and the failure of modern zoning laws

Modular housing development in Haarlem, Holland

Arch.: M. Janga, Haarlem
In recent years there has been a move toward physical segregation (zoning) of where people work, live, do their shopping and enjoy recreation. This remote separation of different components of people's lives is creating new problems.

The area of land taken up by commerce and industry has increased dramatically over the last few decades. As a result we have seen a growing trend toward segregating the various spaces associated with work and with other aspects of daily life. If an attempt were made to integrate all these spaces land utilization would be vastly improved and with a corresponding reduction in urban sprawl.

A mixed use development, where people can live, work, take care of their needs as consumers and enjoy recreation, works on the basic assumption that these various activities require parcels of land of identical size and buildings designed and constructed in a very similar way. In European towns in the Middle Ages all these functions flourished alongside each other. However, with the advent of industrialization and an increase in the specialization and centralization of labor, there came the need to develop areas solely for people to live in. Settlement expanded into the countryside and the established centers of population soon spread in all directions. Simultaneously

the confined space of town centers became overburdened by the increasing demands of the growing population and by the growth in traffic. Whenever industry saw the need to expand, it would move from the inner city out into the countryside. In most European countries this process followed roughly the same pattern.

In Britain suburban migration took place quite a long time ago – much to the detriment of the environment. Anyone able to afford it would move away to a fashionable and expensive residential district or to terraced suburbia, leaving the densely populated areas behind.

In the United States zoning laws enacted in the 1950s and 1960s have rigidly reinforced this same development pattern giving rise to endless suburbs surrounding its metropolitan areas characterized by legions of seemingly identical tract houses on spacious and finely manicured grass lots. The birth of the "Mega-mall" and of miles of unsightly commercial strips formed along collector roads rapidly followed.

Though it might have been interpreted subjectively as a return to nature, this form of migration destroys more than it conserves. The well-maintained garden with its neatly trimmed lawn will edge out wildlife and indigenous plants. At the same time distances are increasing, and commuter freeways, streets, power lines and a wide range of utilities are devouring more and more of the countryside as they spread almost uncontrollably destroying and dividing ecosystems and wildlife habitats.

More recently a wave of modernization has gained momentum, which is not entirely unwelcome. The centers of those older towns and disintegrating cities are gradually being redeveloped and refurbished. There is a renewed interest in living in the center of town once again, partly due to a concern for the time spent commuting long distances but also to widespread adoption of ecological ideals. This has required a relaxation of zoning laws, as well as an application of mixed-use and adaptive reuse concepts. The disadvantage is that this process of adapting old urban areas to current housing needs has significantly reduced the amount of living space available in older buildings because it replaces relatively small apartments with larger more typical home plans. This often displaces large quantities of lower income city dwellers who can no longer afford to remain in the

many gentrified neighborhoods. This causes still more migration from the towns and cities into the now aging suburbs and in turn from the suburbs to the surrounding countryside continuing the pattern of urban growth which is swallowing up the land.

2 PERCENTAGE OF DETACHED SINGLE-FAMILY HOMES VS. APARTMENTS IN MULTI-STORY BLOCKS AS A PROPORTION OF TOTAL AVAILABLE HOUSING (1994)		
	Houses	Apartments
Belgium	79	21
Denmark	59	41
Germany	39	61
France	58	42
Greece	48	52
Great Britain	82	18
Holland	68	32
Ireland	95	5
Italy	34	66
Luxembourg	68	32
Portugal	70	30
Spain	38	62
United States	67	33

Source: eurostat, 1990 US Census Data

Migration from the city does not necessarily improve quality of life

An historic town square

In Europe, there are many towns like Soest, Germany that have a historic central area, or one that has been restored, complete with a healthy infrastructure. Shopping, living and working are not separated, and neighborliness can still flourish.

Traffic congestion plagues our cities

The physical segregation of our working, living and shopping lives has been made possible and encouraged by technological advancements in transportation. The town of the past, built for pedestrians and for horse-drawn vehicles, first changed to a town built for trams and railways, and then, finally, to the city built for cars. But it was not merely in cities that the car became an inseparable part of our way of life: The growth of suburbia led to a loss of identity for those small villages and rural areas that had been quiet and peaceful.

Research has shown that over the past 100 years the amount of time we spend traveling may not have changed all that much, but the distances covered have increased continually. It is no longer unusual to travel 25 miles or more by car to get to work.

Similarly, the distances covered for shopping trips or to pursue leisure interests of various kinds have increased: Between 1960 and 1990 the distance traveled per person per year tripled, and the distance covered getting to work and going on a shopping trip doubled. The distance traveled to pursue leisure activities and to reach a holiday destination quadrupled over the same period.

In the United States the car is used for 86% of all trips. In nearly 75% of commuter trips the car carries only one person. Americans drive nearly two billion miles (three billion km) each year which is about the same distance traveled by all other countries combined (Miller, 1996). Between 1969 and 1990 travel by car in the US increased 22% to an average annual distance of 16,000 miles (24,000 km) per household (Brown, 1994).

The toll of this is quite frightening. Cars have become the greatest polluters of the environment. Despite the advent of the catalytic converter cars remain the prime source of air pollutants, according to German sources: 59% of the nitric oxide released, 47% of the suspended particulate matter and 70% of the carbon monoxide. According to a study published in 1997 traffic is responsible for as much as two-thirds of urban air pollution. Add to this large quantities of volatile organic compounds (VOCs) which cause ground level ozone and other greenhouse gasses which are in part responsible for global climate change. Most costly and alarming, perhaps, of all is the enormous quantity of land area devoured for highways, parking lots, and roads that are necessary to accommodate the increasing dependence on the automobile.

Each year auto accidents, worldwide, account for about 350,00 deaths and as many as 10 million serious injuries. In the US more Americans have been killed by car accidents than in all the country's wars, and car accidents cost Americans more than $350 billion annually (Miller, 1996). In addition, traffic jams cause untold stress and inconvenience to drivers and cost billions of dollars in lost time and delayed shipments of goods. In the US, one out of every six dollars spent and one sixth of all non-farm jobs are auto-related. In the past two decades the number of cars registered in the United States has increased 60%. Despite having only 4.7% of the world's population, the United States now has 35% of the world's cars and trucks. The number of new cars produced every day, worldwide, could form a line of traffic 375 miles long. Urban development and the changes in personal mobility feed off each other, and it is clear that unless building policy starts to take this into account the cancerous spread of traffic will never be brought effectively under control. In the final analysis, this task is the responsibility of politicians and regional planners. But ordinary people who are thinking of building a home of their own, in making their decisions, will directly influence general development and land use patterns. The question is whether we are going to continue to swallow up the countryside and allow traffic to increase in volume, or support the trend toward a more responsible approach to transportation needs and land use so that suburban sprawl can be curtailed.

To reject the idea of a "little place in the country" in favor of an apartment in an older, more centrally located building because you don't want to be dependent on a car is to make a very far-sighted and responsible choice.

A play street in Donaueschingen, Germany

It's not just children who are reclaiming the streets. Adults, too, can practice real neighborliness in traffic-free zones such as this. The fact that traffic is slowly strangling our cities to death is partly a result of how we locate and build our homes.

Urban development in the future

In the city of the future, anyone considering building their own home should consider these six principles as a guide:

- *Re-establish the balance between blending and segregating functional activities.* The likelihood of completely doing away with designated areas for highly specialized use, for example, for shopping, offices, manufacturing or recreation, is slight. Ideally such areas would be converted into a number of smaller areas, each with a variety of uses within a short distance of each other. In addition, developments should be planned and built on a smaller scale with the pedestrian in mind.
- *Maintain the balance between permanence and change.* In the wake of so much urban destruction resulting from road construction and uncontrolled development, it is increasingly vital to ensure that older buildings are used fully rather than simply putting up new ones. It is not just a question of conserving historical buildings, but also one of reusing land, such as brownfield sites formerly used by industry, and recycling valuable structures and their materials.
- *Use resources sparingly and effectively.* In the city of the future a complete break has to be made with the patterns of living, working, consuming and other day-to-day activities that increase the terrible and growing burden placed on the environment. Waste must be drastically reduced, and so must the amount of pollution. All discards should become raw materials for some other process.
- *Make business a servant to urban development.* The transition toward a service-based society and the democratic diffusion of all communications

technologies which decentralize work activities will contribute considerably to the reversal of modern zoning laws. Enlightened urban planning can greatly advance this goal by providing facilities for living and working in multi-use buildings.
- *Prevent exclusivity of all kinds.* People in low income groups, children and young people, the aged and the handicapped were not considered important in the urban development programs of the past largely conceived for the benefit of the middle-class and their cars. New ways of building and of living must serve the interests of these previously excluded groups with the same increased efforts as those being directed toward environmental protection.
- *Reverse the trend requiring ever greater mobility.* Whatever form economic and architectural evolution may take, there must be incentives to reduce personal mobility partly by avoiding wide dislocation of work and home. At the same time, a traffic system must also discourage individual habits and social tendencies which increase traffic congestion any further.

These six principles can be applied to almost every developed country in the world. In short, what is needed in towns and cities alike is a deliberate attempt to integrate diverse land uses and increase population density. For this reason it is important to note that in central urban areas around 10% of the space available is taken up by vacant and undeveloped sites; in the outlying areas of many cities this figure is as high as 60%.

What this means is that we have to learn to distinguish that vacant land between existing buildings

One house on top of another in Dortmund, Germany

Arch.: Planquadrat, Dortmund
A space-saving option that enables different purposes, such as living and shopping, to be combined: A home has been erected on the roof of an office – a haven of peace and tranquillity amidst all the noise and traffic of a large city.

Principles for the town of the future

which fulfills a vital ecological function or provides a local recreation area, from undeveloped sites which should be utilized in a carefully planned way including mixed-use development strategies.

Another means of reducing traffic is through preservation of existing parks and local amenities, rather than developing new ones in a remote location. Often it is possible to increase the functional floor area of existing buildings by adding additional floors making them taller or by constructing extensions. New developments on the edge of towns or in recycled inner-city industrial areas should be actively incorporated into any regional development plan which promotes mixed use. The unique character of each town should be carefully preserved and expressed. Peripheral developments should provide their own commercial/social centers with all the most important features essential to community and to an efficient and viable infrastructure.

Once shops and service facilities are available as a revitalized focal point of a village or community, the compulsion to travel into the city or to an out-of-town shopping center for everyday needs is reduced quite considerably.

Sustainable building in the city

What conclusions can therefore be drawn from these broad concepts about the town of the future and sustainable development, particularly by someone planning to build a house? First, where sustainability is concerned, the most important thing is to build energy-efficient, non-toxic houses. These aspects will be dealt with in great detail later. The following section will attempt to clarify just how this general approach to development can best be transferred to individual buildings.

First of all, a clear distinction must be drawn between a house built in the town and one built in the country. The former is very much constrained in its design by the need to optimize the available space, concentrate population and conserve resources. Therefore, the most viable option for development of urban areas is multi-family housing with increasingly higher densities as one approaches the population center. Other strategies include reducing sideyard setbacks on inner-city lots or, as is seen more often today, high-density, owner-occupied housing developments where buildings still have the appearance of detached single-family houses although they are attached. The benefit of this application of zoning requirements allows for much smaller land area per unit and lower costs and therefore higher value to the home buyer. If this approach is closely followed, even families with an average income will be able to afford a home of their own in the city. Ideally there should be a requirement that these developments reserve a small number of apartments as rentals. This would help to ensure that tenants of different ages and from different social strata would live together creating a more diverse community. In addition, parts of such buildings could be used for small businesses of various types. This mixed-use concept is quite feasible provided all stakeholders in the project including architect, developer, financier, building official and contractor combine their efforts and resources to make the project a success. Other important aspects of sustainable development include minimum destruction of existing vegetation, drainage patterns, topsoil and other topographical features, i.e., little or no restructuring of existing grades and preservation of existing trees.

Spaces surrounding the building need to be designed and laid out so as to encourage social intercourse.

Mixed utilization and polycentric development create a viable infrastructure

Terraced solar houses in Hamburg, Germany
Arch.: M. Dedekind, C. Gerth, Hamburg
The terraced house is popular in towns. Because it is compact it saves energy, but it can also be given a personal touch. Here, too, it is vital to ensure that the house faces south so that solar energy can be utilized to the full.

Housing must be made a priority

In the town the emphasis will continue to be on the building of apartment blocks. This is the only way to attain mixed use, and, at the same time, to retain as much of our natural environment as possible. It is important to design buildings that can be used in a variety of ways.

There should be play areas for children, as well as areas for open-air leisure activities; the number of roads should be kept to a minimum and motor cars and other traffic completely prohibited at least in some parts of the development. By incorporating a gradual transition from areas open to the general public (the road) to semi-private areas (the court-yard) to purely private gardens, the residents can plan and shape their day-to-day lives in many different ways. Some recent projects in the United States which address the full spectrum of sustainability principles include *Dewees Island,* a totally self-contained planned sustainable development off the coast of South Carolina and *Esperanza del Sol,* an inner-city infill development in Dallas, Texas. Other examples where local planning authorities have developed urban development plans addressing sustainability goals and incorporating many of the ideas presented here are Austin, Texas; Seattle, Washington; San Jose, California, and Minneapolis, Minnesota.

The next stage in the communal responsibility of homeowners is the collective decision to renounce the car as a means of transport, or at least to accept a drastic reduction in its use; instead there could be a generally acceptable car-sharing scheme. A reliable and attractive link to public transport systems is also an indispensable feature of communities planning such measures.

In an effort to create developments which are not exclusive, particularly ones which are intergenerational, flexibility of plan is paramount. For example, it must always be possible to transform a bedroom into a study with little trouble, or to convert the children's rooms into a separate apartment which can be rented after they grow up and leave home. A house or flat should be equally suitable for a family or for a group of people who have decided to share. In the past this flexibility was achieved by using interior walls that could be moved around. It is by no means unrealistic

Seseke Aue in Kamen, Germany

In this estate, architects and planners have succeeded in creating a careful mixture of private areas for the individual family as well as lawns and play areas easily accessible to the entire community.

to conceive of a form of building in which the static elements – the floors, the ceilings and load-bearing walls – are of permanent construction, whereas the rooms themselves are divided by easily movable partitions rather than immovable walls. But even walls and partitions designed to be portable take time and effort, and cost money to move; also floor coverings are bound to suffer quite considerably from such rearrangement. For these reasons efforts are now being made to design and fabricate rooms so that the utilities and lighting can be rearranged to suit a variety of specific purposes as needed. Such strategies, however flexible, clearly have their disadvantages. Standards and codes would have to be altered and all rooms would have to be the same size. Could people adapt their activities and social habits to this extent? Ultimately the surest way to conserve resources is to combine spaces and not to build unneeded space in the first place. Of the common maxim "reduce-reuse-recycle," reduce is quite clearly the best choice. It is also the most effective way to reduce costs.

The townhouse of the future will feature shared amenities

Sustainable building in the country

An estate designed along ecological principles in Erkheim, Germany

Arch.: K. Hartisch, Rosenheim, Germany
This is a model housing project, in which the detached houses are close together, and are surrounded by nature. The simply constructed building envelope is customized by extensions.

Houses in villages or small towns have different requirements when it comes to using space. Here there is no need to include large, green open spaces in the planning process, as is the case with new housing developments in towns. It is reasonable to assume that woods and fields are close at hand.

The classic type of home in the country tends to be a detached house rather than the terraced or semi-detached house typical of larger towns and cities. Out in the country a basement can be included as a part of the building, something which is often excluded for cost reasons in the city. Another aspect of living in the country is the growing preference for simple and traditional home designs and a reluctance to copy urban architecture in any form whatsoever. For example, in the US there is a popular resurgence of the

farmhouse style with its anachronistic porch or low sweeping verandah and other vernacular detailing.

Outbuildings have been, in the past, an essential part of many country houses and today they can still serve a useful purpose. Why not continue to use such buildings as a workshop or storage shed, instead of sacrificing valuable and more costly space in the house itself?

Even in the country, economical use should be made of the space available for building. For a housing development in the country this means that provision should be made for communal amenities, a village square, and a community center. This will in some ways compensate for an otherwise lack of direct social intercourse and of an efficient infrastructure typical of country life. An excellent example of this

vestibule or as an intermediate zone insulating the main building. The architecture encourages the owner to develop a courtyard, which can give the residents the feeling of being in a private garden, eliminating the need for extensive lawns and landscaping. Each owner enjoys a certain degree of privacy and feels close to nature. This courtyard space can be described as an open-air living room, providing an effect which normally requires a considerable amount of expense and a much larger plot of land. These compact buildings along with their various additions have a classic simplicity about them and have been reduced to the essentials of comfortable living: Though small, each house's plot is used efficiently and communal areas are an intrinsic feature of the architecture – here we find a basic concept for an efficient building design in a country setting which reflects the charm of its surroundings.

Even an economical use of building space allows for a sense of privacy

Privacy
Even in the smallest garden private spaces can be created by adding an extension, pergola or outbuilding. The ideal material for such structures is, of course, natural wood.

approach is the show estate "Das junge Dorf" (The young village) in Erkheim, Germany. Here a number of affordable houses for owner-occupancy have been built in such a way that each requires only a small building plot, but each owner also has a share in the generously proportioned communal areas. The wood houses, typically without a basement, have been designed to allow for considerable flexibility in how the livable space can be enlarged, whether through a shed or gable; a sunroom or conservatory: In this way each resident family can change its home according to its individual needs and financial situation, and can further adapt it as family circumstances change.

Sheds, store rooms, greenhouses and other heated or unheated ancillary spaces or outbuildings can readily serve as protection against bad weather, as a

The multi-generational home

As its name indicates, the multi-generational home is designed for several generations to live comfortably under the same roof. The ultimate aim is for elderly people in need of care to be able to live with their children and grandchildren. The situation in the home need not be static: When the children leave home, rooms originally planned for them can be handed over to the grandparents or put to another use.

In fact, the multi-generational home requires sensible and efficient long-term use of living space, which of course is a guiding principle of sustainable building. A family that has decided to build or buy such a home must ensure that the children's needs are placed above the parents' needs. There is a common belief that a home that is especially suitable for children is particularly costly to design and build, but with careful planning these extra costs can be avoided and a great deal achieved.

Children require sufficient space centrally located in the home where they can play and also do their homework without being too far from their parents. A spacious kitchen/dining area can best meet this purpose. In this way a separate dining room can be avoided, and the family will not have to move to a larger home as the children get older. The layout should allow for maximum flexibility so that there is always plenty of space for the children to improve or amuse themselves.

It is a good idea for each child to have a room of its own, because everyone needs privacy at some time.

Far more important than a generous amount of space (120 to 130 square feet is more than adequate) is a more or less square floorplan with few furnishings so that the child has plenty of space to move about and play. An abundance of natural light is important (preferably with a southern exposure); a sloped ceiling and roof angle which restricts sunlight should be avoided. Children also require a "natural" garden with trees, piles of stones and small rocks, and bushes, so that they can inexpensively enjoy outdoor play.

Careful planning is also essential when building a home which will meet the special needs of the elderly and the disabled. Architects should do their utmost to design buildings without obstacles such as steps or thresholds, unless they are completely unavoidable. In the United States the Americans with Disabilities Act, or ADA, makes it illegal to build any public buildings which in any way impair access or full use of the building by people with physical disabilities. In addition, any significant renovation to an existing building open to the public will also require that the entire building be brought in compliance with accessibility codes. Although smaller apartment buildings are often exempt, it is wise to build according to accessibility design standards whenever feasible.

Traditionally, the entrance to a house is raised slightly with steps leading up to it, mainly to prevent water from running into the house. The alternatives are to build a ramp with no greater than a 1:12 slope in front of the entrance to the house, or to install a drainage

A home adapted for the disabled in Erkheim, Germany

Arch.: K. Hartisch, Rosenheim/Baufritz, Erkheim/Allgäu, Germany

If several generations are to be accommodated under the same roof, ideally a separate entrance should be planned early on for access to the upper floor. The ground floor must be very easy to enter and the rooms designed in such a way that disabled people can also use the building.

system to carry the water away. Doors and corridors also require more thought: They must be wide enough for wheelchairs (at least 36 inches or 91.5 cm wide). If such factors are incorporated into a plan from the earliest stage, and if the number of doors is reduced to a minimum, building costs can be cut quite considerably. Anyone using a wheelchair or crutches, needs above all sufficient space to maneuver. There must be a minimum of three feet (91.5 cm) of space in front of cupboards and shelves, and at least 18 inches (45.5 cm) of space alongside toilets and washbasins. In addition, there should be an unobstructed area in each room equivalent to a five-foot (152.5 cm) diameter circle to allow a person in a wheelchair to turn around. In order to ensure that there are always enough options, floor plans need to be as flexible as possible. For example, a dining room and living room combined gives more space for other purposes. Another idea is to have a large bathroom (suitable for a disabled person) on the ground floor and a smaller than normal bathroom on an upper floor.

In addition to these basic requirements a house or flat suitable for a disabled person will also require attention to certain other details, some of which are, unfortunately, quite expensive. Window handles and light switches must be at a height that can be reached from a sitting position (i.e., 54 inches or 137 cm maximum). The range or stove and the kitchen sink should be fitted so that a person sitting in a wheelchair can use them including appropriate faucet levers. There must also be a kneespace beneath the washbasin for a wheelchair rather than a cabinet. A step-in shower should be avoided; instead the floor should be tiled continuously and sloped toward the drain. This is known as a flush-floor shower installation, and is more complicated and costly to install since it is not a standard off-the-shelf product, and because water containment is more difficult.

Sometimes specialized furnishings and installations will be called for, depending on the type and extent of the disability. There are, for example, adjustable-height kitchen cabinets, lever handles instead of round door knobs, special faucet and bathtub fittings, and various types of grab bars. Upholstered furniture and beds should be higher and firmer, because this will make it easier for those with limited mobility to stand up from a sitting or lying position. Single beds are simpler for a disabled person to cope with than full or king size beds.

How a multi-generational house can be developed in stages

Step by step, this family has put into practice its concept of how several generations can live together as a single unit. First the parents built their own living area as they wanted it (Phase 1); then the attic was converted into the children's rooms (Phase 2). The attic or a portion thereof could then be converted into a separate apartment (Phase 2a). The last stage is the building of an addition to the house designed to accommodate people with disabilities or aging parents (Phase 3).

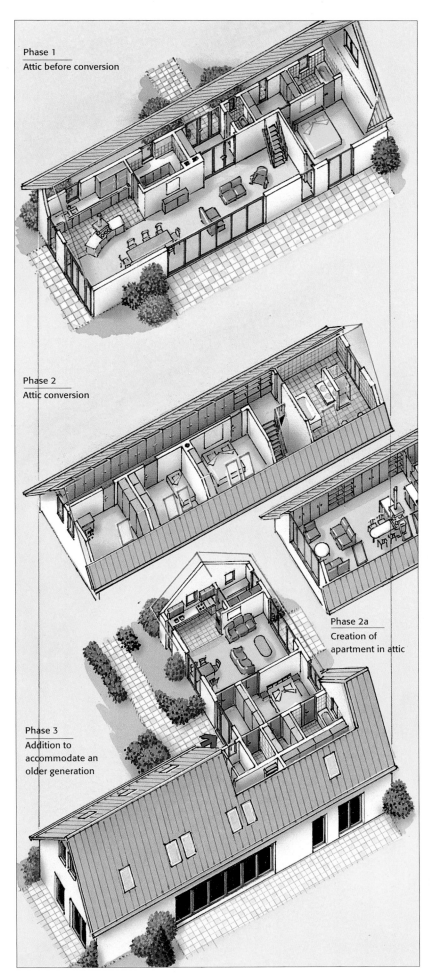

Phase 1
Attic before conversion

Phase 2
Attic conversion

Phase 2a
Creation of apartment in attic

Phase 3
Addition to accommodate an older generation

User-friendly design

A home suitable for a handicapped person is basically no
different from one built for anyone else with ease of use as a
priority. These large windows
offer a panoramic view and they
are easy for a wheelchair-bound
person to open. A firmer and
slightly elevated bed is easier to
get out of.

A flush-floor shower installation

This type of shower, without a
threshold, is just as convenient
for someone who is not disabled.
But since it is non-standard,
installing one creates several
technical problems. Grab bars
and a fold-away seat can be
installed later when needed.

An adjustable height washbasin

In a home suitable for disabled
people, the basin must be high
enough to allow wheelchair
access underneath it. Providing
an adjustable model allows the
maximum amount of flexibility
and comfort for all users.

Freedom to move about

An elderly or disabled person needs adequate room to maneuver and appreciates a house where there are no obstructions such as steps and doors. Modern home design aims to keep obstacles to a minimum.

A kitchen conversion for the disabled

Many details in this kitchen have been carefully thought out with an emphasis on technical solutions. The cupboards can be raised and lowered electrically, so that even when seated a handicapped person can reach everything. Space is provided so that a wheelchair can be pushed right under both the cooktop and sink.

There is little practical difference whether the home is being planned with children, the elderly or disabled persons in mind. Thus, it might make sense from the outset to allow for a small apartment within the home for the children to use initially, but which could later be used either by the parents or the grandparents with little alteration to the original layout. If the rooms are planned carefully and flexibly, and if most of them are designed for more than one purpose, the end result can be much more than just a dream house.

"Green" building for the community level

Despite the growing interest in ecologically sound living, it is hard to find examples of public buildings planned in accordance with ecologically and environmentally friendly standards, with efficient use of energy and sustainable construction methods. Ecological and environmental goals can best be achieved when an entire neighborhood is planned and constructed to incorporate an efficient transportation system, carefully laid out roads and open spaces with the same principles and goals in mind.

More and more people are showing an interest in conservation and environmentally friendly living, and are trying to put their ideals into practice. At the same time households are also becoming smaller and less "conventional" in terms of makeup. The nuclear family is no longer the norm. It is not surprising, then, that there is a trend toward living in groups and even planning and building a home as a community project. The desire to combat social isolation by living with a group of people who share common ideals, or by seeking new and better lifestyles, is reflected in the search for more efficient ways of building homes and developing communities.

Through a new development strategy known as "Co-housing" (Hanson, 1996) homeowners form a cooperative enterprise to develop their own housing project. Although it typically does not reduce development costs or shorten the process, it gives the ultimate residents control over almost all aspects of their home, and of their community services and organization. For example, they can determine whether and where automobile traffic will be allowed, what services and amenities will be provided by the homeowners' association and how much private and public open space will be afforded. They are involved in the design not only of their homes but also of the community as a whole.

It is always a good idea for architects and planners to consult the future residents when drawing up plans for new developments. The residents often come up with important ideas to ensure that the new development will function as a community rather than a collection of buildings.

This sort of planning phase can be quite lengthy and involves many pitfalls. Differences of opinion frequently come to the surface; and even before the first new home is completed, the original "team" may have changed considerably. Planning is always more difficult when many people are involved, but it is usually well worth the effort.

One example of a successful "green" community project is to be found in Romolenpolder in Haarlem, Holland. The community has managed to put several of the basic principles associated with sustainable planning and building into practice. There are around 1,000 people living in this development, some in

Everyone shares in decision making

The Romolenpolder development in Haarlem, Holland

This development, completed in 1990, is an excellent example of how to blend together people's different expectations of their community, and how various individual groups of society can live together in close proximity. This has been achieved through integral self-management of the community.

Romolenpolder: a "green" housing development

The level of personal involvement of the people living here can be seen in the shared responsibility for maintaining the gardens and in successful solid waste management, which has resulted in a drastic reduction in the amount of refuse generated.

their own homes and some in rented accommodation, and there is also a senior citizens' home integrated into the community.

The development has found room for a number of small-scale businesses, without sacrificing any of the principles associated with ecologically sound and environmentally healthy buildings, and there are several open spaces that have been allowed to remain in their natural state. But the most striking achievement is without any doubt the so-called "integral self-management."

In the earliest phase of the planning, the Haarlem city council organized meetings for all the people who would later live in the development. This gave the future residents a large element of control how the new development should be built and what should be done, above all, to cope with refuse disposal and to ensure that sufficient attention would be paid to laying out and maintaining parks and open spaces.

For both of these management tasks a system of self-administration was evolved. Certain members of the community were designated as the "refuse-disposal team," responsible for organizing an efficient method of sorting different kinds of waste and for finding the community a reliable pick-up service. In addition, the Romolenpolder residents took over responsibility for laying out and landscaping the entire development. Everything was done on a voluntary basis, with the city only granting a subsidy limited to the usual amount for covering the costs of refuse disposal. An outside architect acted in an advisory capacity until the project was completed.

Each inhabitant of the development has provided input regarding every aspect of the development and there is a high degree of communication between all the members of the Romolenpolder community, all of whom are prepared to do their part to make life even better for all the residents.

The recyclable house

A house built from recycled materials

Contractors: Blöcher, Lemgo, Germany
This half-timbered house built close to Lemgo was constructed entirely from old beams, used roof tiles and floorboards salvaged from houses that had been demolished. Clay bricks have been used for the external walls so that they can be used again, should this house ever have to be demolished.

Buildings account for many different kinds of environmental damage. Aside from the production of air pollutants as a result of energy consumption in buildings there is the staggering amount of waste generated on a daily basis by building occupants in the form of liquid wastes such as sewage sludge and garbage. The United States generates approximately 33% of the world's solid waste. The total volume of solid waste generated each year in the United States is an unbelievable 11 billion tons. Add to that the billions of tons which are generated from the wrecking and renovating of buildings and you begin to get a picture of the problem.

Obviously by reusing buildings rather than demolishing and building new ones, construction wastes can be significantly reduced. An alternative increasingly promoted by most environmental groups and many communities across the United States is the sorting and recycling of construction debris. The future recyclability of building materials, however, should be considered in the design stages. It is essential to avoid hazardous materials and materials which cannot be recycled or are difficult to separate and sort.

Restricting the choice of building materials to non-toxic, long-lasting, easily obtainable and also easily repairable materials facilitates planning and construction while producing a building that is less harmful to the environment over its life. It certainly makes sense

during the design phase to separate components that will require early replacement or servicing, such as interior decor, furnishings or technical equipment, from the more permanent and long-lasting materials used for the structure and shell of the building. It would, for example, be wise to install electrical wiring and other supply lines in designated chases or conduits with a means of easy access. This will make it

Back in business!

It is not just premium or antique building materials that should be used again. These humble drainpipes were carefully dismantled and are now waiting at the builders' supply store for the next user.

Consider the long term as you begin a building

simpler to re-wire the house or to replace pipes when the house has to be modernized or when additional plumbing connections are required.

Fitted carpets which are subject to wear and tear and require frequent replacement should not be adhered to the floor substrate: Rather, they should be laid loosely or with edge tack strips so that they can be removed easily. Ideally, the number of different materials should be kept to a minimum, and those that are used should be carefully selected to ensure that they contain as few toxic additives as possible. Consulting an independently obtained test report such as Material Safety Data (MSDS) information usually available from the manufacturer or supplier is recommended. Laminates and other composite materials should be avoided, since they are difficult to disassemble or recycle.

One should also begin to examine ways of incorporating recycled or reused materials from other buildings for various components, household fixtures and fittings. Old doors, salvaged windows, finish hardware and a wide variety of wood beams, posts, siding, flooring, interior wall paneling, etc., can be used if they are in reasonably good condition and fit the design and styling of the building.

Many building materials available today contain either pre-consumer or post-consumer recycled materials. Although there is not yet widespread agreement as to how recycled-content building materials should be defined, with a little research one can often find a suitable recycled-content replacement for a product which contains only virgin (not recycled) materials. In fact, it may not be long before every product bears a label with a relative environmental impact index so that we, the consumers, may make the best possible choice.

Reusing building materials is almost always far more valuable from an environmental standpoint, since they can be used again for their original purpose,

yielding the same value with little energy or material expenditure; or in some cases, an even greater value or value-added application is possible.

For example, it has often been the practice on building projects to use excavated earth for landscaping the site rather than hauling it away. Building rubble can quite easily be crushed and used instead of imported crushed rock as the foundation for a terrace or a path, or for drainage. Along different lines, roof tiles and concrete blocks can be pulverized and subsequently used in small quantities to manufacture similar products.

In a strict sense only natural building materials without synthetics, such as natural stone, wood, wood wool and wood fiber, clay, straw, flax, hemp and reeds can be considered as "globally recyclable." These materials can be produced without a great deal of energy and there are not as many problems with environmentally harmful byproducts or waste.

Waste can also be reduced on building sites. If the volume of waste can be reduced through more efficient use of materials, and through a concerted effort to recycle as much as possible by separating the wood, gypsum board, metal scrap and plastics from each other in different containers, it is then a relatively easy matter to persuade the building contractors to remove their waste from the site themselves. Because of a growing desire on the part of municipal authorities to promote construction waste recycling, a range of incentives and assistance can often be obtained locally toward this end. It is also often possible for the unused masonry and other surplus building materials to be returned to the suppliers by arrangement. Such an approach frequently reduces costs because of rapidly escalating tipping fees for disposal at the landfill, hauling costs, and the cost of the unused materials as well. If aggressively applied, measures like these should save as much as two-thirds of the cost of waste disposal.

Only natural building materials are environmentally friendly

Decorative wrought iron grillwork

A great many old fittings, such as these wrought iron railings, would cost a fortune if they were handcrafted today to the same high quality.

A wide choice

Dealers specializing in antique building materials offer a wide choice of antique doors, metal hardware, wood mouldings and often windows as well.

A touch of class

Antique building artifacts can create a certain style and bring a touch of class to your home.

BUILDING A HEALTHY HOME

House within a house

Design: P. Patt, Flamersfeld, Germany
This house blurs the boundaries between indoors and out. The building itself has been constructed within a huge glass envelope. The residents benefit from the generous light and sunshine coming in, and from the natural materials used such as wood and clay.

Most of us have very little idea just how much our living spaces affect our physical well-being. When talking about health in the context of houses, the main concern is the direct effect that the indoor environment has on those living in the house and whether they actually feel "healthy" in the normal sense of the word. Although it has become much more than just a "roof over one's head," a house is intended to fulfill quite basic human needs that can be defined very

precisely. Even such a vague concept as "comfort" can be expressed in numbers and statistics. If a house fails to meet these basic standards, the inhabitants will come to experience a general malaise or perhaps even fall seriously ill.

It is not only the failures of past building methods but also of our current common everyday building design and construction practices that dangerously compromise human health.

Criteria for a comfortable environment

Science has only recently been able to establish precisely the conditions which create a comfortable indoor environment. For example, the appropriate air temperature of a room will depend partly on the activity undertaken in the room, the clothing being worn and the approximate length of time spent in the room, and should ideally be between 64 and 75° F (18 and 24° C). The temperature of the air circulating in the room and the temperature of the surfaces enclosing the room, i.e. the walls, floor and ceiling, should never vary by more than 7° F (4° C). Relative atmospheric humidity should be between 40% and 60% (Levin, 1994), and the mean air circulation velocity should be below 4.91 feet per second, the speed sufficient to change the angle of the flame of a candle by 10 degrees.

Expressing comfort in these terms may seem relatively abstract. Yet they underlie conditions inside a building which are familiar to everyone: leaky windows, poorly insulated external walls that attract condensation, thermostats set too high in order to combat drafts and excessive moisture. All these factors have a detrimental effect on human health. For the most part strategies that are favorable in ecological terms because they reduce the amount of energy consumption – i.e., high efficiency heating and cooling systems, well insulated construction with adequate wind protection, etc. – will also contribute to the health and well-being of everyone using the building.

Scientists have found that the temperature we perceive is midway between room temperature and the temperature of the surrounding surfaces. Suppose a person using a particular room wants a "subjective" temperature of 68° F (20° C), which is generally considered a pleasant room temperature. In order to achieve the perception of that desired indoor temperature when the outside temperature is 14° F (10° C), the air inside a building with simple nine-and-a-half-inch-thick masonry walls would need to be heated to a temperature of over 74° F (23° C). In this case the inside wall surfaces would then reach a maximum of 62° F (17° C). The perceived temperature of 68° F (20° C) lies at the midpoint between 62 and 74° F (17 and 23° C). The difference in temperature will, however, not be a pleasant one for the occupants of the room. They will feel that the room is intolerably drafty. This is because of substantial convection caused by the cool exterior walls relative to the warmer room interior. But if this same house were to have four inches of cellulose insulation added, the temperature in the room could be maintained at 70° F (21° C), because the wall temperature would then only drop to 66 ° F (19° C).

This is why it is vital to make sure that windows and doors fit properly and have adequate weather-stripping to prevent air leakage. The technical term for this leaking is air infiltration. In the United States windows and doors must be tested and labeled for infiltration

in order to achieve certification. Other means of reducing undesirable drafts due to convection is by using windows with highly efficient glazing and by extensive use of surfaces with substantial thermal mass and good heat retention. Massive furniture and features such as masonry or plaster walls and stone floors also help to reduce temperature swings, i.e., the extent of fluctuation in room temperature.

Our health and well-being are also affected by the relative humidity of the rooms we live in. When relative humidity drops to below 30%, mucous membranes tend to dry up and electrostatic charges develop. Air humidity higher than 60% makes the room oppressive, fosters the growth of mildew and encourages mites. Where there is extreme sensitivity to certain airborne pollutants including mold and dust mite excretia, it has been suggested that relative humidity must be even more carefully controlled

within a range of 30–45% (Nevalainen, 1993). In a typical home there are many sources of humidity including showers, cooking, perspiration and even dampness found in basements. Therefore, well-built homes which are comparatively airtight usually have relative humidity levels which are too high, whereas older leaky (high air infiltration) homes often suffer from low relative humidity during the winter.

Although certain more porous materials may tend to regulate humidity levels to some extent, it is not practical to rely on building materials to control indoor humidity. It is important that buildings be properly ventilated, even though this can result in a loss of

A healthy environment
Designer: K. Becker, Möhr, Germany
This bio-solar house in the Eifel, Germany provides its lucky residents with a really healthy environment: The well-proportioned conservatory ensures that there is plenty of light and warmth, and heat-conserving materials have been used, keeping the temperature constant.

Living in a healthy environment

Arch.: M. Viktor-Ulmke, Construction: S. D. Sonnenhaus, Wettringen, Germany
Natural materials, efficient heat insulation, lots of light streaming through modern, air tight and efficient windows, adequate ventilation, a floor which discourages insect infestation and is warm to the feet – these are the factors that determine whether you feel really "at home" (opposite).

energy. We do not have any precise way of measuring indoor air quality in order to determine when excess pollutants require that the air be changed and we are often reluctant to open a door or window because of drafts and energy loss; and so rooms are often not adequately ventilated.

Light and air

Bertolt Brecht may have been correct when he said that "people can be struck down even by their homes." This is not only true in cases where toxic substances such as asbestos have been used in buildings, but also wherever superficial planning has ignored basic human needs.

In the 1920s, bacteriologist and public health pioneer Robert Koch criticized the gloomy tenements so common at the time because of their almost total exclusion of light, air and sunshine and the resulting negative impact this had on the occupants' health. Today it is well known that the absence of natural daylight can cause a genuine illness known as seasonal affective disorder or SAD, experienced by many people during winter months and particularly in more northern latitudes. Lack of adequate daylight in buildings has also been associated with elevated stress levels, and calcium deficiency which may be a contributing factor in cases of osteoporosis. In fact, phototherapy is recommended for many illnesses.

But ever since the oil crisis of the 1970s large windows in buildings have been blamed for wasteful energy loss, because the insulation they provide against heat loss is far less than that provided by a well-constructed wall or roof of a similar area. Even today apartment buildings are being built in which the units receive light only from the north or the east, which means, of course, that the sun will never shine directly into them. In addition, floorplan layouts frequently allow for large windows in the living room only, while the kitchen and dining area, where the children often do their homework and spend much of their time, only have electrical lighting. Since the turn of the century neighborhoods and house plans have been designed with far more concern for traffic access and neat gridlike rectilinear lot lines than with access to air and light and opening houses up to the sun! Prior to the advent of the ubiquitous electric light bulb, architects were necessarily more cognizant of the need for natural light in their buildings.

In many of the futuristic high-tech houses currently being built, provision for fresh air during the winter and frequently also during the summertime can be

guaranteed only by "artificial" means more common in an enormous office building, i.e., quite sophisticated mechanical ventilation systems. Healthy living is possible only in healthy surroundings. When the site for a new house is chosen, it is important to investigate subsoil characteristics (contaminated soil, natural radioactivity which can cause a serious indoor air pollutant known as radon gas, etc.) and other aspects of the immediate surroundings (traffic noise, hazardous emissions from nearby factories, power lines) that might have a negative effect on our health and well-being. Even a house situated in a relatively unpolluted area of a large city will only be truly healthy if the surrounding areas are found to have a sufficiently abundant oxygen supply.

Open-plan living

South-facing rooms that are built according to ecologically sound principles will make a home pleasant to live in. Here living, eating and working areas blend into one another.

Room to grow

It is not uncommon for the children's room to be given secondary importance in the interests of a more impressive living room. But the children do not necessarily need a large room to feel contented. What is more important is careful planning so that there is always suitable space for them to play and study.

Architecture that promotes health

The Kranichstein development in Darmstadt, Germany

A row of terraced houses will become less monotonous to the eye simply by incorporating a variety of materials into the houses, by breaking up areas with shrubs and plants, and by including different structural elements. The large open spaces outside the houses give people ample opportunity to interact with their neighbors.

The physical aspects of our environment which have a direct bearing on our health can be fairly precisely defined, but this is not necessarily the case when it comes to specifying the ideal design in terms of architectonic or esthetic criteria. These universal basic human needs are determined differently according to cultural heritage, social sphere and historical period. To a certain extent it may simply boil down to a question of taste. Within our culture, for example, quiet and privacy are eminently important factors. Most people want their own private, personal domain with freedom from interruptions, noise and obnoxious smells permeating from the outside world.

The inviolability of the individual's home could be considered as nothing less than a basic human right. Yet although this is a recognized fact, relatively little is done to ensure that it is observed. Quiet and privacy tend to be equated with large private estates situated out in the country, not an environmentally sound alternative, and in any case out of the financial reach of most people. It is, however, quite possible to achieve a sense of privacy and quiet in the most humble home by employing a variety of sound-attenuating strategies. Inside the home a sense of privacy can easily be fostered by doing away with ostentatiously furnished living rooms of enormous proportions in which no one can really feel "at home," and allocating the reclaimed space to other areas in the home.

The external design of a house is often based on traditional architecture modified to take into account the inherent characteristics of the building's surroundings – the vernacular style of the region. This takes into account the local climatic conditions while at the same time helping the new building blend in with the surrounding buildings and creating a harmonious environment. But there are, unfortunately,

has a more agreeable smell and natural textiles create a more pleasant atmosphere, in general making the residents feel at home.

It has recently been discovered that well-conceived design contributes quite significantly to a healthy living environment: This includes comfortable scale and proportion, clarity in the layout of the rooms, contrasts in lighting, variety in views, well landscaped surroundings and a return to traditional craftsmanship in all aspects of design and construction. Whoever lives in or enters the house should be able to feel the harmony within, yet the building should also be animated by contrasting color schemes and materials and by juxtaposition of shapes and forms with proper reverence for classical principles of proportion and perspective.

It is important to bear in mind, though, that function must ultimately determine the shape and layout of the individual rooms. It is simply ludicrous to include features such as bay windows, dormers, turrets, a sawtooth roof, terraces, canopies, ornamental gateways, splayed windows, balconies, columns and outside staircases for no particular reason or in a random fashion. "Embellishments" of this kind often destroy the esthetics of the building, and may even cause structural damage or unnecessary squandering of energy, because they impede efficient insulation and damp-proofing.

Modern building techniques have been considerably influenced by the flawed belief that "anything is possible." Just because something new is discovered does not make it a better idea. Modern building materials were developed through advances in the petrochemical industry at quite a considerable cost in terms of energy and environmental damage. But over time it has become apparent that many of these materials are unpredictable and even toxic.

Many modern building practices, too, have proved almost as disastrous as those they replaced. Many houses designed in the early part of the century to alleviate the depressing conditions in overcrowded, smoke-filled inner city tenements have turned out to be complete and utter failures. The enormous housing developments and high-rise tower blocks erected in the 1960s and 1970s which were intended to revolutionize housing were superseded in the next two decades by a monotonous low-rise row house culture: What they have in common is the atmosphere of total isolation they create, their barrenness, and their inability to adapt to social change. The advantages of rationalization were bought at the cost of quality and architectural attention to detail.

The injurious psychological effects of uninformed building and unsuitable or highly toxic building materials which can themselves present a health hazard are inextricably linked. In buildings erected in the 1960s and 1970s it was frequently impossible for social intercourse to evolve. The people living in the new developments had little or no opportunity for

Must healthy architecture be monotonous?

Ecological architecture is always in context with its surroundings

Even modern concepts are not always in accord with human needs

many architects who reject this more sustainable approach, because they seek to satisfy the short-sighted whims of clients who want to erect their "dream house" as an exact copy of some luxurious villa seen in Mallorca or perhaps a mountain retreat they admired in the Swiss Alps. Whether the occupants of such a house will ever really feel at home is questionable. Just as important as the style in which a house is built are the basic design, the color, the surface structure and the layout of the rooms. A building which responds to the local climate and evokes the rich history of the residents, which "sits well on the land" and expresses the warmth of natural materials in and of itself promotes a sense of well-being and serenity to its users. In practical terms it can be stated that natural materials such as wood are pleasing to the touch, natural stone imparts a feeling of security, paint free from chemical additives

The Kranichstein development in Darmstadt, Germany

This is an impressive example of a housing complex where no one feels isolated. The glass-covered public garden path linking the houses is an ideal place for neighbors to meet one another and for children to play safely.

The need for security and communication must be part of the overall design of buildings

any visual or social contact with the outside world; there were few open spaces such as gardens or playgrounds or they were so ill-situated as to inhibit their use. Grass, trees and plants were a rare sight. The buildings were often designed in such a way that it was difficult for anyone using them to feel any sense of warmth or security. In addition, the residents often found after a short time that their health was suffering. The developers and architects of these projects had simply ignored the basic human need for social contact which requires appropriate public and semi-private meeting and recreation areas as well as well conceived circulation to and from these spaces. Architects and planners had, it seemed, relied strictly on standardized forms of building based on questionable scientific data relating to ideal living conditions. Furthermore, it soon became apparent that these findings had been interpreted wrongly, resulting in buildings and communities which were not at all successful and did not create healthy environments. One important aspect which was completely overlooked was the intuitive sense of well-being that

is fostered by traditional forms of building, quite simply because they better harmonize with human nature and the human psyche.

The accepted norms in the field of publicly financed and subsidized housing were based on "scientifically valid" and well-intentioned definitions, such as a minimum size for a child's room or for a living room, and have certainly had an enduring effect on how houses have been constructed – with dire consequences.

One example would be a kitchen designed for preparing a meal in the smallest possible space. This may seem like a good idea, yet it fails to take into account the need to plan the kitchen as the room where a family tends to congregate. In this kitchen, cooking and conversation just cannot take place at the same time. The person doing the cooking is isolated from others in the home, and there is no chance of cozy gatherings in the kitchen at all. Architects must be reminded that they are dealing with humans who want a real home to live in. Only then will they create houses and other dwellings that are in complete harmony with the demands of our environment.

Poisons in the home

"Healthy" building is, of course, only possible if poisonous substances and materials are avoided. People living in industrialized countries are threatened everyday by a highly toxic cocktail made up of countless chemical and synthetic materials. To make matters worse, we still know very little about the precise effects they have on our health.

The European community is presently tackling this state of affairs through new guidelines on the use of biocides (chemicals capable of killing living organisms). These guidelines stipulate for the very first time that there will be very strict procedures governing the licensing of non-agricultural biocide products and their active ingredients. Such a procedure would affect insecticides, fungicides and pesticides used throughout the construction industry as well as leather, carpet, and wood preservatives. The aim is to lay down exact methods to be used for conducting the toxicological and ecological tests. Industry is far from happy about these guidelines, however, because toxic additives in wood preservatives and paints are big business, and if they are banned new alternatives would have to be found.

In the United States the situation lags far behind that of the European Community. Although some of the more dangerous chemicals such as PCBs, DDT, lead additives in paint, gasoline and solder, pentachlorophenol in wood preservatives, asbestos, and a few others have by now been banned, most building materials have few restrictions as to content. One exception is the United States requirement that building products containing formaldehyde bear a warning label. Unfortunately, in many cases, as with particle board and fiber board materials, alternatives are few and often difficult to obtain, not to mention more expensive.

A great many building materials, including paints and varnishes, impregnating agents, sealing compounds, concrete and plaster, have been "improved" over the last twenty years or so to make them easier to apply, quick-drying and water-resistant. Paints for example typically have dozens of additives such as mildewcides to prolong shelf life, carcinogenic compounds for opacity, anticoagulants, agents to improve flow, hardeners, plastic resins and various fillers.

Unfortunately, scientists failed to consider the possibility that these "helpful" materials could also endanger our health, in many cases quite considerably. Solvents, bonding agents and preservatives release toxic fumes and minute fibers into the air which irritate and injure the respiratory system. It becomes incumbent upon the consumer or builder to research the contents and their relative hazards (i.e., known or suspected carcinogen, known mutagen, etc).

Everyday items found in the home, such as furnishings, carpets and electrical equipment, can be harmful to our health as well. We come into contact with more and more chemicals all the time, and they are causing irreparable damage to our immune systems. Countless commonplace chemicals have the ability to mimic hormones such as estrogen or block the reception of critical hormones. These effects are being linked to the increasing occurance of infertility, breast cancer, prostate cancer, a wide range of birth defects and even incidents of attention disorders and other learning disabilities. The building industry is under no legal obligation to list all the substances contained in its products on product packaging. Thus the consumer finds it almost impossible to avoid harmful substances. Only those manufacturers with a firm belief in ecological principles state clearly what their products contain or more importantly make

efforts to eliminate ingredients known to be hazardous. The only legal obligation that manufacturers have at present is to state on the product's packaging whether it contains any chemicals included on a register of hazardous substances. Even if the container bears no warning whatsoever of any health hazards, it cannot be assumed that the product is completely safe. In some cases the product only contains very small amounts of a poisonous substance, so the manufacturer may not have to include it in the list; or they may have avoided the obligation to label the product by adding other substances.

Even those working in the building trade, who presumably have access to more extensive product information than the general public, do not, as a rule, really know what they are working with. The information they receive from manufacturers is generally confined to instructions on how to handle, use and store the product. In any case, the user is required to do a great deal of additional research in order to determine the specific hazards associated with any given substance.

The toxic home

Poisonous additives are very often unnecessary

Bonding agents or sealing compounds with warnings like these are best avoided. Non-toxic alternatives can always be found and they are just as easy to use.

How your house can make you sick

Harmful substances in buildings

A sick building

Arch.: O. Steeple, Hamburg, Germany
A short time after the publishers had moved into this new office building for the Gruner + Jahr Publishing House (opposite), many of the people working there complained of headaches and allergic reactions.

Using chemically treated wood can be avoided

Provided a number of basic rules are followed when a house is built, there is no need to use chemically treated wood: The eaves will protect the façade as long as they extend far enough, water drips on horizontal boards and using vertical battens will ensure that the water runs off more quickly and timbers are rested on metal "shoes" rather than coming into direct contact with the ground.

When a building is the cause of illness, the term generally used is building related illness (BRI), and if the cause cannot be established with absolute certainty, the term applied is sick building syndrome (SBS). More and more patients are complaining to their doctor of general malaise and often a variety of seemingly unexplainable symptoms such as chronic fatigue, burning eyes, dry coughs, headaches, attacks of dizziness, skin rash, loss of concentration, unusual tiredness, temporary loss of memory, depression or extreme irritability. Until only recently, many such people have been referred to a psychiatrist because no medical explanation could be found. Today, however, doctors would probably be considered negligent if they didn't consider possible environmental causes before making a diagnosis. An important indicator could be whether the symptoms lessen after leaving the workplace, whether there is a specific room or place where the patient feels especially ill, or whether there were any changes to the patients' environment such as redecorating their home or office just before their health worsened.

The medical world is taking increasing notice of BRI and SBS, as well as of other environmental illnesses such as multiple chemical sensitivity (MCS) and chronic fatigue syndrome (CFS), also known as Chronic Fatigue Immune Deficiency Syndrome (CFIDS). With these disorders the term syndrome is used to indicate a collection of apparently unrelated symptoms. Some experts believe that one office worker in five now suffers from illnesses of this kind. Occasionally the cause is traced to antiquated or poorly serviced air-conditioning or refrigeration equipment where contamination breeds highly toxic bacteria. The infamous example of this occurred at an American Legion Convention where hundreds of people became mysteriously and quite seriously ill. The illness became known as Legionnaire's disease even before the cause was traced to the hotel air conditioning system. In homes people with allergies are often made ill by the presence of dust, mold, and the products of dust mites which thrive in carpeting and bedding. These microscopic legions feed off of dead human skin cells discarded constantly by our bodies. It is virtually impossible to eliminate these creatures, so controlling them is the only solution. Other contaminants pervade our living environments including hosts of chemicals emitted by many building materials as well as furniture, cleaning products and toiletries. Almost everything we use, it seems, contains perfumes which are highly irritating to anyone suffering from MCS. These substances not only cause a number of different illnesses, they also compromise the immune system and make it easier for other illnesses to take hold. In fact, reactions to these pollutants for those with allergies or varying levels of chemical sensitivity are actually an indication of a malfunctioning or overactive immune system which is interpreting the presence of these substances as an invading pathogen to be attacked.

More is being learned each day about these disorders, but one thing is certain: The underlying cause is related to our increasing exposure to chemicals in the environment. So far little has been done to investigate the complex interrelationship between these chemical and biological pollutants and other environmental factors. Noise and unacceptably high ozone levels caused by automobiles certainly do have a detrimental effect on people, even when they are indoors. The most common air pollutant inside buildings, however, is tobacco smoke. Cigarette smoke contains more than 10,000 different substances that could cause health problems; these include formaldehyde, polycyclic hydrocarbons and nitrosamines.

Dangers inherent in wood preservatives

What concerns specialists in environmental medicine and toxicologists most of all, however, is the effect of chemical pesticides. Particularly notorious are two chemicals, pentachlorophenol (PCP) and lindane, both used as pesticides in wood preservatives and also to treat leather. PCP is now classified as highly carcinogenic, and in some countries including the United States its production has been prohibited. In Italy, however, it is still in frequent use. The results of exposure can include a breakdown in the immune system as well as the functioning of the kidneys and liver, and, in other cases, there have been instances of chloracne and dioxin-related birth defects. Lindane (gamma-HCH) causes neurological disorders, irritation of the mucous membranes and liver damage, and is concentrated in the fatty tissue; it is also under suspicion of being carcinogenic. Some authorities have concluded

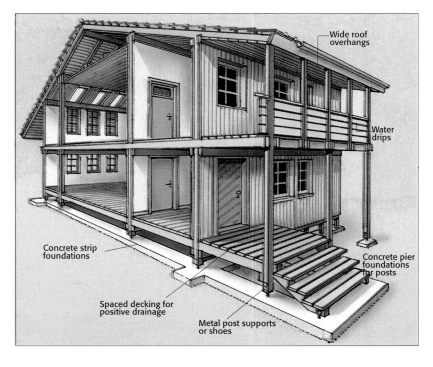

Wide roof overhangs

Water drips

Concrete strip foundations

Concrete pier foundations for posts

Spaced decking for positive drainage

Metal post supports or shoes

that as little as 1,000 ng/m³ (nanograms per cubic meter of air) can present a hazard.

A trial held in Frankfurt, Germany drew public attention to the dangers of wood preservatives in a legal battle regarding the use of products containing PCP or lindane in particular. The suspended sentence of one year for the negligent release of toxic substances drastically changed manufacturers' attitudes toward product liability. In other countries, too, it marked a significant change in attitudes toward the environmental pollution caused by chemicals in building materials. Today most treated lumber in the United States is pressure treated with chromated copper arsenate (CCA). Although this is considered much safer than many of the previous processes, CCA-treated wood does contain arsenic, so it should be used only when the wood will be in direct contact with the ground and when it is not located where it will come into direct contact with humans.

Pyrethroids, PCB and formaldehyde

The problem of PCP is one of dealing with the after-effects of chemicals used some time ago. The debate surrounding pyrethroids such as the widely used permethrin is even more crucial, because this controversial pesticide is still being used today. Formerly regarded as relatively harmless, it is used in wool carpets as a moth repellent, in insect sprays and in dog anti-flea powders. Pyrethroids are manmade derivatives of the natural substance pyrethrum found in chrysanthemum flowers. During processing, the potency of the pyrethrum is dramatically increased, so artificial pyrethroids are far more dangerous than they are in their natural form. If such substances are inhaled directly, they can cause serious poisoning. Even small amounts can become concentrated in the human body, and toxicologists believe they may cause irreversible damage to the nervous system and brain. Pyrethroids interfere with the neurochemistry within the brain and block the transfer of information,

A low-energy house in Drensteinfurt, Germany

Arch.: R. Wesson, Drensteinfurt
Carpets should be avoided or if used they should not be treated with moth repellent. There are many alternatives to fiberboard which may contain formaldehyde and other irritating chemicals.

leading to concentration problems and memory loss. As you might expect, the industry itself strongly denies this, and the manufacturers' team of experts discounts the possibility that these chemicals are dangerous in any way.

Polychlorinated biphenyls (PCBs) are similar to PCPs and are extremely difficult to dispose of, as they are organochlorine poisons. They were earlier used in the production of hydraulic fluids, as insulating fluid in transformers and the condensers for fluorescent tubes, as a fireproof coating for ceiling boards and as a softening agent in permanently elastic sealing compounds used to grout precast concrete slabs. PCBs once introduced are persistent ubiquitous toxins which reach a high level of concentration in the fatty tissues in humans and animals and they have been widely found in breastmilk. They attack the immune system and are both carcinogenic and mutagenic. They are known to cause birth defects and to inhibit brain development in the womb causing retarded mental and motor development, learning disabilities, hyperactivity and behavioral problems. Although the manufacture of PCBs has been prohibited since 1978, their persistent effects will unfortunately be felt for decades to come.

A government interdepartmental working party in Germany specified that remediation should be compulsory when the concentration rose above 3,000 ng PCB per cubic meter of air. While this was the acceptable level, the desirable level was set at 300 ng, only one tenth as much! However, these levels were not applicable in public buildings, such as schools, since the costs of the renovation would be astronomical. It was particularly difficult to clean up contaminated substances used for grouting, the so-called thiokol sealing compounds. At first it had been assumed that such highly contaminated sealing compounds had been used only in public buildings constructed principally from precast concrete slabs, but random inspection in Germany, for example, showed that private houses and apartments built between 1964 and 1975 were just as contaminated. The difference was that such buildings were mainly in large housing developments or in satellite communities where there were no interstitial spaces to contain the contaminants and therefore the residents were directly exposed to sealing compounds containing PCBs. In addition, the windows were also found to have been grouted with thiokol sealing compounds all of which resulted in high concentrations of PCBs.

Formaldehyde is another problem chemical. It is a colorless, pungent and poisonous gas used mainly in the manufacture of adhesives, as a binding agent in fiberboard and as a preservative in products containing a high percentage of water. Even in minute concentrations formaldehyde can cause severe eye and skin irritation and allergic reactions. It is very likely carcinogenic. Formaldehyde continues to be emitted long after the materials have been incorporated into

a building although less as time passes. In the United States building products containing formaldehyde are regulated only in that they must be labeled as such. Indoor air quality standards with respect to formaldehyde concentrations along with other pollutants such as volatile organic compounds (VOCs) have been established for public buildings in California and Washington state. The recommended maximum concentration of formaldehyde in a building is 0.1 ppm (parts per million). Emissions testing and reporting standards for specific materials such as carpeting and wood paneling are being developed with consensus from industry by the American Society of Testing Materials as well as individual industry groups. In some cases emissions data can even be obtained directly from the manufacturer upon request. The most dangerous formaldehyde emissions in the home are from veneered furniture and from the fiberboard paneling usually favored by the do-it-yourself enthusiast.

Some alternatives to fitted carpets

Wool fitted carpets frequently contain moth repellent, and should be avoided. Sisal can be used instead to give a room a more "natural" appearance.

A low-energy house in Braunschweig, Germany

Arch.: L. Gabriel, Oldenburg, Germany Living in healthy surroundings does not have to be expensive. Natural materials and generously proportioned design can reduce the price of a house considerably, as this example shows.

Toxic substances have no place in a the home

Solvents, fibers and radon

Corrugated asbestos roofing

What used to be a reasonably priced roofing material has turned out to be far more expensive to replace. Roofing made of corrugated asbestos or façades made of asbestos cement are the source of carcinogenic asbestos fibers. Boards made of asbestos are required to be disposed of as hazardous materials and cannot be simply thrown away like other refuse.

CFCs can be found almost everywhere

The most common hazard to health in the home is from volatile organic compounds, mainly solvents found in adhesives, varnishes, paints, paint thinners, and removers. These include toluene, xylene, acetone, methanol, methylethyl ketones (MEK), turpentine and ethylene glycol as well as CFCs to name only a few. There are also solvents that contribute to photochemical summer smog, and have a narcotic effect when inhaled in large quantities. Among the less serious symptoms of exposure to these toxins are headaches, a general feeling of malaise, and irritation of the mucous membranes. Toluene, for example, can cause damage to the nervous system and probably to the liver. Like xylene, it can be further contaminated by benzol, a strong carcinogen that can contribute to infertility. Among the most dangerous CFCs is dichlorethane, which is a skin irritant and a carcinogen extremely harmful to the liver and the kidneys. Another is dichloromethane, which is also considered to be a carcinogen. CFCs are commonly used as refrigerants, blowing agents in foam materials of various kinds and as propellants in aerosol cans.

Even solvents derived from natural dyes can be harmful to the health, but to a far lesser extent than those produced by the petrochemical industry. In addition to the health hazards posed by chemicals, carcinogenic asbestos fibers are a cause for concern. The asbestos fibers break off through weathering and cleaning, and even in areas designated as clean air zones levels of more than 50 asbestos fibers per cubic meter of air have been recorded. In areas of high concentration there can be as many as 1,000 fibers per cubic meter.

Between 1900 and 1986, asbestos was widely used in buildings in the United States for fireproofing, soundproofing, pipe and boiler insulation, as well as wall and ceiling decoration. In 1974, the United States banned all such uses of asbestos in buildings. The Asbestos Hazards Emergency Response Act, passed in 1986, required that all schools be inspected and submit plans for containment or removal of asbestos contamination by May 1989. In 1988, the United

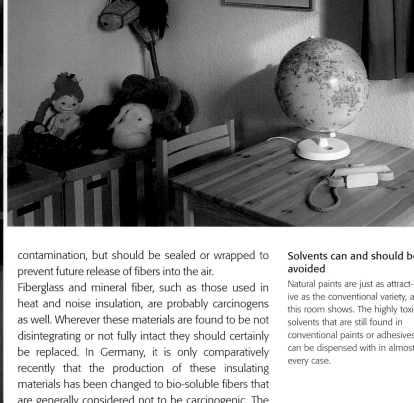

contamination, but should be sealed or wrapped to prevent future release of fibers into the air.

Fiberglass and mineral fiber, such as those used in heat and noise insulation, are probably carcinogens as well. Wherever these materials are found to be not disintegrating or not fully intact they should certainly be replaced. In Germany, it is only comparatively recently that the production of these insulating materials has been changed to bio-soluble fibers that are generally considered not to be carcinogenic. The mineral fiber matting and the imported products which are still in use should continue to be regarded as major health hazards.

A less well known danger is a radioactive gas called radon which emanates from natural uranium deposits in the earth. According to recent research findings there are almost 2,500 deaths a year from lung cancer in the old Federal states of Germany, for instance, caused by cancer resulting from exposure to radon. This means that it is second only to smoking as a cause of lung cancer.

Radiation protection agencies recommend a total clean-up of areas where the average readings over a lengthy period have been 250 Bq/cubic meter or more, and estimates that 1% of houses should be renovated completely. In parts of the United States renovation is compulsory in houses where levels reach 150 Bq/cubic meter. US Geological Survey maps can be obtained which indicate the prevalence of uranium deposits in certain areas; in addition, radon gas can be tested for in basements or below grade construction. Readings should also be taken to assess the level of pollution of the soil on which the buildings stand. Remediation methods typically consist of isolating air spaces between the subgrade earth and the occupied spaces and ventilating the air space mechanically.

Solvents can and should be avoided

Natural paints are just as attractive as the conventional variety, as this room shows. The highly toxic solvents that are still found in conventional paints or adhesives can be dispensed with in almost every case.

Danger lurks in the earth beneath our feet

States EPA estimated that 760,000 buildings – one of every seven commercial and public buildings in the United States (including 30,000 schools) – contain asbestos that presents a significant indoor environmental air quality hazard. Removal of asbestos from such buildings could cost $50–200 billion, with about $10 billion being spent by 1993.

Critics of asbestos removal have claimed that removal in most cases is quite unnecessary and that improper removal can release more asbestos fibers, thereby creating an imminent health hazard, than sealing off asbestos that is not crumbling. After much controversy and huge expenditures of money for asbestos removal, it is now generally agreed that asbestos should not be removed from buildings where it does not present an immediate danger of airborne fiber

Electrosmog (EMF), fungus, and Legionnaires' disease

The danger from EMF radiation

The development shown here lies immediately alongside an electric power line and, in the light of the possible risks established by scientific research, should not have been built where it now stands. The likelihood of contracting leukemia is twice as high for the residents of this development as it would be for someone living elsewhere.

An invisible threat of cancer

There is yet another potential danger to people's health caused by recent advances in technology – specifically from electromagnetic fields (EMF) around electric power lines, electrical appliances, and even from radio transmitters. Another term for all of this accumulated EMF radiation is electrosmog. It has been demonstrated that even at a distance of fifty meters (over 150 feet) from high voltage power transmission lines, the incidence of leukemia and of cerebral tumors is twice as high as for the rest of the population. It is important to draw a distinction between electrical fields and electromagnetic fields. An electrical field will be caused when an electric current is close at hand. Magnetic alternating fields, which are probably more likely to have quite a detrimental effect on our health, arise when an alternating current (AC) actually flows through a conductor, for example, in a motor,

transformer, video terminal, etc. One of the most insidious exposures to EMF radiation may be from an electric thermal blanket while in bed. There has, however, been very little research so far into the effects of EMF radiation on the human body. Even weak electromagnetic fields close to the head appear to bring about changes in the electrical activity of the brain. Patients who have been exposed in this fashion typically complain of insomnia, headaches and tiredness. The radio frequency waves sent out by radio transmitters or even by cellular telephones can, in some cases, create considerable warmth in the human body similar the process inside a microwave oven. Even with a relatively low dose exposure to EMF radiation, interference with the brain's normal electrical activity may cause nervous system malfunction and therefore be detrimental to one's health and cognitive abilities.

Mold fungus spores are, apart from mites and fleas, the most frequent cause of allergic reactions in the home. If the immune system is already weakened, there is a likelihood that internal organs, particularly the lungs, can be injured and that debilitating and possibly even fatal illness can result. Mold fungus spores develop as a result of excessive moisture due to inadequate ventilation and other building deficiencies such as poor insulation, air and water leakage, and thermal bridges. Basements are particularly common sources of mold spores because of problems with dampness; however, any cold surface where condensation occurs can support mold growth.

Another source of danger, especially for those with a weakened immune system, is posed by airborne bio-contaminants such as the *Legionella* bacteria, the cause of Legionaires' Disease, first identified at an American Legion Convention in Philadelphia in 1976. *Legionella* bacteria thrive in warm water where they are relatively innocuous to begin with. If, however, the contaminated water is sprayed into the surrounding air these bacteria become suspended and circulate in the air. When they are ultimately inhaled, they cause an infection not unlike influenza in its symptoms and which can develop into a severe, and often fatal form of pneumonia. These biocontaminants are typically spread by means of mechanical devices such as

humidifiers, badly maintained air-conditioners, refrigeration equipment and even hot tubs. The bacteria thrive in a temperature of between 30° C and 40° C, but require several days before attaining "a critical mass." For this reason it is imperative that little-used hot water pipes and antiquated water heaters are kept at an energy-saving temperature. Any refrigeration equipment should be carefully maintained or replaced.

Mould is not harmless
When mould thrives in a building, there is a significant risk to the health of the building occupants. This should not to be taken lightly. The products of mould can cause injury and irritation to the lungs, liver and kidneys as well as allergic reactions, skin ailments and cognitive problems.

Harmful bacteria and fungus spores

A breeding ground for *Legionella* bacteria
A jacuzzi can be great fun. But if it is tested infrequently or otherwise improperly maintained, the risks are great. The steam that is inhaled by those using it may well contain *Legionella* bacteria that can cause Legionnaires' disease, a serious and sometimes fatal respiratory infection.

NATURAL BUILDING

The ING Bank building in Amsterdam, Holland

Arch.: Ton Alberts, Amsterdam
The anthroposophical approach to building design rejects the use of right angles opting for patterns derived from nature. This style is a protest against the rational approach embodied in much of today's modern architecture. But this is not necessarily the same as building with nature in mind.

Natural building means building with respect for nature and it fulfills two basic requirements. First, building should adapt to all the existing conditions of the land. Secondly, the materials should, wherever possible, be obtained from renewable sources.

Building on the land in a natural setting

Historically our buildings were shaped primarily by the necessity to provide shelter for humans, animals or harvested crops often under the same roof. Utility

was made of the body heat of livestock and the protective buffering of sheds and outbuildings to insulate the living spaces.

The way a building was constructed was also determined by the local climate and the natural building materials available in the area. In high, cold mountains, eaves were extended to ensure that the wood exterior of the building was well protected from the incessant rain or snowstorms; houses in coastal regions were constructed with overhanging reed roofs to provide effective sheltering against the wind

was an abundance of coniferous trees to provide all the straight logs required, as in many parts of North America. In other regions where the forests consist mostly of knotty oaks the preference was for half-timbered houses. Wooden buildings would be protected from the wind and weather by shingles or clay tiles. Natural stone would frequently be employed to moderate the temperature inside the house by storing heat with its thermal mass. Windows would have folding shutters as a means of protection against severe winds and cold during inclement weather.

The process of industrialization has meant that traditional building methods have largely been superseded. Extremely strong and lightweight supporting structures, prefabricated and mass-produced components, a wide range of synthetic and engineered building materials, as well as centralized heating and ventilating systems, reliable electrical lighting and indoor plumbing have revolutionized the building industry. On the one hand, home building has become more democratic in the sense that owning a home is now within the reach of a great many more people than ever before. Another outcome of this revolution is that many people have far higher expectations regarding where and how they wish to live. Yet the introduction of modern standardized methods and materials means that homes are typically no longer built in sympathy with the environment nor responsive to the climatic conditions, and they include far fewer natural materials.

Many designers and architects have reacted to this trend by attempting to model their buildings after designs and principles found in nature. One example of this is the "anthroposophical" approach to building design seen in the ING Bank building in Amsterdam designed by Ton Alberts. In this style, just as they are seldom seen in nature, right angles are never used. Another example is the work of the artist and philosopher Friedensreich Hundertwasser. In both these cases the designs were rather too impractical to have much real impact, and had little effect other than registering a protest against current popular architectural styles. Still, there is a growing fascination with what has become known as "organic" architecture. From the earlier ground-breaking designs of Frank Lloyd Wright and avant garde work of the enigmatic Antonio Gaudí to the lesser known architects of today such as Bart Prince and Imre Makovecz, we get a glimpse of a more spiritual and time-honored expression of building in harmony with nature.

There are a great many other architects who firmly believe in environmental principles and design houses that attempt to mimic nature, even to create a kind of biotope. Although well intended, this approach can also be criticized because houses, by their very definition, represent an encroachment on nature, whether they are concealed beneath a grass covered roof or however many "natural" features they incorporate. Some baubiologists or "green"

Historically, a building's form tends to reflect the local climate and available building materials.

Modern building materials may be convenient, but they are not always the most suitable ones for the job

The revolt against the dominant non-sustainable building styles has not been taken seriously

and spray. In more humid regions skillfully devised ventilation systems were invented, and in hot areas thick stone or clay walls were found to offer the best protection against the heat and sun.

Depending on what natural resources could be found locally, buildings would typically be constructed of brick, stone or wood, with slate or wooden roofing. The number of floors and the dimensions of the rooms would usually depend on the size of the straight timbers that those building the house could lift into place. Log cabins would be built wherever there

Architect Hundertwasser's approach to building

Arch.: © Hundertwasser Architektur, Vienna, Austria

The artist and philosopher Friedensreich Hundertwasser has attempted to recreate an element of nature in his architectural designs, which are meant to give an impression of organic growth. While striking as a concept, his approach is somewhat fragmentary.

architects have gone so far as to propose "eco-developments" which spread out uncontrollably over the land eating up natural undeveloped countryside. Using this logic one might argue that an ecologically built single-family house "close to nature" is more environmentally benign than building the typical house or apartment building in today's developed urban areas. This is a very myopic and shortsighted view of ecology.

Historical approaches to designing and constructing buildings have generally provided the most economical and efficient solution to a particular building problem for that particular time, but today we have to adopt a different definition for efficiency.

Efficiency is really the cornerstone of sustainability. For a building to be considered sustainable it must be both energy and resource efficient. Therefore, efficiency means selecting from the wide variety of all possible materials, building systems and strategies those that are most likely to reduce energy consumption and usage of materials both during construction and for the life of the building and without making excessive use of non-renewable energy and other natural resources.

In modern terms, efficiency means achieving the greatest personal comfort and utility with the least possible depletion of natural resources

Details from one of Hundertwasser's designs

Color palettes, forms and non-technical details ostensibly take inspiration from nature, and include embellishments pleasant to the eye. Hundertwasser was the source of many new ideas in architecture, hence the fascination with his art. But ecological principles were not central to his approach.

It would be extremely unwise, therefore, simply to look back at past generations for inspiration and guidance. Today we have the technological expertise to more efficiently utilize all of the materials that are available to us and to find solutions to many of the challenges we face in our modern world as we try to live more safely, with greater health, and more in harmony with nature.

Choosing the best site

Topography invariably has a considerable influence on the local microclimate, and so is a major consideration when choosing a site for a new house. For example, the temperature in a hollow in which cold air accumulates could easily be 11° F (6° C) cooler than the terrain only a few hundred yards away, where the ground is level.

In a valley mists can considerably reduce the amount of solar energy available. The ideal site would be on a slope – preferably a south-facing one. A house standing in a slight depression typically requires much more energy than a house on level ground, however, if the house is on an exposed unsheltered site, it would require approximately 10% more energy

Using what nature supplies

The natural features
influence the microclimate
of a site

Opening outwards

The majority of windows in Scandinavia are fitted with casements which open outwards. In the United States only about 10–15% are of this type; however, the percentage is gradually increasing. Outswinging doors and windows are particularly effective in locations where the house is exposed to wind and rain. The positive wind pressure forces them more firmly against the frame compressing the weather-strip and thus prevent air leaks. The drawback is that they are harder to clean than windows which open inwards.

due to exposure to winds. Such an exposed site is in most cases unsuitable because of the increased energy needed for heating and cooling.

The ways in which the open spaces surrounding a building are landscaped can also reduce the loss of energy quite considerably. Trees and shrubs close to the building can offer considerable protection against the weather as well as shade from unwanted summer sun, and the excavated soil can often be used to construct a berm which can offer an effective means of diverting winds.

It is also important to remember that major openings, such as doors and windows, should not face into prevailing winds. Further energy savings can be achieved by installing the external doors so that they open outwards, as is common in Scandinavian countries. This allows the positive pressure of wind blowing against them to ensure the best possible seal against air leakage. Heat loss can be further reduced by lowering the level of the building, or by recessing parts of the building into a slope. This allows a positive interaction with the surrounding earth called thermal coupling. Because of the stored thermal energy in the ground, heat loss from the parts of a building in contact with it is appreciably lower on cold winter days than the loss from those areas directly exposed to the outside air.

One should remember that a building which totally ignores the sun's rays can require as much as 50% more energy to heat and cool than a similar building designed to take advantage of the sun's energy. In order to ensure the positive thermal effects of the sun it is important that the path of the sun and the angle of its rays be taken into account for the entire year. While the building design is still on the drawing board, it is vital to consider to what extent neighboring buildings will obstruct sunlight from the walls and particularly the windows of the building. On the other hand, it is also important that overhangs and other means are provided to shade the building from the direct sunlight during the summer or at other times when the building does not require heat.

Using local building materials

It might seem obvious that using natural materials is always a better option than using synthetic ones when it comes to building. This is not always the case, though. Natural materials are often to be found in very remote regions of the world and have to be transported over large distances to get them to where they are to be used. This common practice results in excessive expenditures of both capital and energy. Some examples of these materials are high-quality timber-land timber often harvested at great environmental cost, coir (coconut fiber), sisal, cork, latex, special resins and certain natural stones such as marble. In cases where these materials are used as a substitute for synthetic materials that require a large amount of energy to manufacture and also entail releases of pollutants which damage the environment, they should not be rejected out of hand. However, many of the materials mentioned above, such as tropical woods, should not be even considered, since the methods used in harvesting and processing them create considerable ecological problems primarily in lesser developed countries.

When we talk of "natural" materials, what we really mean is a return to *local* raw materials and, whenever possible, materials which can be regenerated. Following these precepts in a fundamental way throughout the world would certainly have different consequences in each land. In Portugal, for example, one traditional local material is cork, i. e., renewable material obtained from tree bark. In Egypt a favored locally obtained raw material is cotton. In the next section we will consider how these ideas may be applied to the building locale of the readers.

Earth-sheltered housing in Donaueschingen, Germany

Design: Archi Nova, Bönnigheim, Germany
Houses like this not only blend harmoniously with their surroundings, they also consume very little energy and limit exposure to the elements.

Earth-sheltered house in Dortmund, Germany

Arch.: PINK, Hoyerswerda, Germany
Although strange to look at, such houses provide optimal protection against energy loss.

Wood as a building material

A house in Erkheim,
Germany constructed
almost entirely of wood
This prefabricated house
proves that it is wrong to believe
that wooden houses must look
mass-produced, cheap and
uncomfortable.

Wood has been a building
material of choice for
thousands of years

The use of wood as a building material has quite a
long history; there are pile dwellings dating back
more than 5,000 years. In European countries such
as Sweden, Denmark and Norway, and in the USA,
wood is used in the majority of buildings, whereas in
the countries bordering the Mediterranean wood has
had only a very minor role in building. It must not be
forgotten, however, that wood is a natural and renewable material, and also has a very positive impact on
air quality by converting carbon dioxide, a greenhouse gas: It is actually, therefore, an environmentally
friendly building material.

In the United States forest reserves reached an all-
time low toward the end of the 1800s due to unrestricted clearing of land for agriculture and massive
logging to feed the enormous need for timber in the

growing urban and industrial centers. This resulted in
decimation of an estimated 85–90% of the old
growth forests. The subsequent awareness and alarm
at the vast squandering of this resource resulted in a
variety of public policy initiatives and incentives
implemented over the first half of the 20th century
which created protections for the remaining old
growth forests and promoted research, education
and development of a science of forest management. Since the early 1970s the concepts of sustainable forestry have been gaining favor gradually but
have only recently began to progress from the "sustainable yield" mentality, where the volume of timber
harvest cannot be greater than the rate at which it
can be replaced (and clear-cutting of large areas is
still allowed), to a more holistic emphasis on the

recreation and protection of ecosystems. In June 1993, the United States committed to achieving sustainable forest management by the year 2000.

A tactic gaining popularity in North America is monoculture operations feeding production of engineered composite wood fiber products such as oriented strand board (osb) used in sheathing and floor joists. The advantages of this practice is primarily in the improved efficiency of the manufacture of building materials in that little wood fiber is wasted. In fact, from one half to two thirds of the timber cut down is wasted in sawing, dimensioning, defecting, milling and culling. There are other advantages to these engineered composites. For example, whereas solid wood is not uniform in its structural properties because of grain direction and because of various defects such as knots, the corresponding engineered wood composite structural or framing members are homogenous in their structural properties and do not contain defects which reduce their resistance to loads

Engineered composite fiber products waste little timber

Pile dwellings on the shores of Lake Constance, Germany
This type of pile dwelling settlement has stood on the shores of Lake Constance for more than 5,000 years. These have been rebuilt to show how people used to live: Wooden houses stand the test of time.

Forests are vital for our climate
Forests protect our climate in many different ways, such as by slowing evaporation from the earth's surface and by taking in carbon dioxide from the air.

Living in a log cabin

Wood houses with thick wooden walls such as these may indeed be the coziest houses of all. The open-pored attribute of wood compensates for fluctuations in temperature and is healthy to live in, provided it has not been treated with toxic chemicals. But log cabins do have their disadvantages. The wood warps and gaps will quickly develop between the thick beams and the planks, thus creating the potential for drafts and heat loss.

Tropical woods are difficult to replace

and stresses. This reduction of wood waste produces a corresponding reduction in the amount of timber harvested. Still the practice of monoculture forestry does not protect any habitats or create the potential for self-sufficient ecosystems and is less preferable than well-managed and naturally diverse forests.

Not all woods are the same either. Though tropical woods are more easily worked, straighter and almost without any branches, and often more pleasing to look at and more weatherproof than most temperate woods, they are very slow-growing and very difficult to replace. In the United States some of the major users of tropical woods in the past have declared a moratorium on their use. But it should be noted that tropical timber has not been replaced by local woods for constructing window frames: There is a growing tendency to use synthetic materials that are harmful to the environment, such as PVC. Where wood windows are still popular such as in the United States and the Scandinavian countries, softwoods are typically transported long distances, for example from the US and Canadian Pacific Northwest to the window manufacturers in the central part of the continent.

Another distinct problem with using wood for building is that it is not always easy to tell from the type of wood whether it is a timber obtained locally using environmentally friendly methods, or imported timber that has been obtained at considerable cost in ecological terms. In spite of the continuous harm done to forests by environmental pollution, the actual number of trees in Western Europe and in the United States has in fact increased. In the United States forests cover about one third of the lower 48 states, however, only about two thirds of all United States forest land is classified as timberland – forests productive enough to grow commercially valuable trees.

Up until 1940 the United States was self sufficient in terms of timber consumption. Since that time, however, it has been a net importer of wood. Nevertheless, the United States is still the largest exporter of wood in the world. Even though the per capita consumption of wood products has actually decreased since 1900, a threefold increase in population since that time has resulted in the need for imported wood products, primarily from Canada. There has been little attempt to certify place of origin of imported stock; however, the importers themselves and large users typically have an accurate account of exactly what is being imported and from where. Once the product reaches the consumer, though, it is rarely possible to determine the place of origin of the particular timber used.

Guaranteed quality

There is quite a considerable amount of discussion about using some standardized method of indicating the origin and quality of timber. Some suggestions are limited to indication of the country of origin, others go so far as to propose a kind of "ecological certification." At an international level environmental organizations such as the Worldwide Fund for Nature (WWF) and Friends Of The Earth, various timber merchant organizations and research institutes such as the Forest Stewardship Council (FSC) have formulated minimum standards defining environmentally friendly forestry. Though the efforts of the above bodies are predominantly concentrated on developing a system of certification for tropical timbers harvested in a way that does little or no harm to the environment, the FSC is now turning its attention more and more toward the northern and boreal forests.

Though less than one percent of the wood on the market is currently certified, the number of certifying organizations is growing steadily. Their purpose is to provide objective third-party evaluation of timber sources and companies, enabling consumers to identify products whose harvesting does not contribute to the destruction of forests. The Rainforest Alliance is the largest timber certifier to date. Through its "Smart Wood" Certification Program, it certifies wood or wood products that come from either "sustainable" or "well-managed" forestry operations. Producers operating in strict adherence to "Smart Wood" requirements are classified as "sustainable" while sources that demonstrate a strong operational commitment to "Smart Wood" principles and guidelines are classified as "well-managed." Other wood certifiers include the Green Cross Certification (formerly Scientific Certification Systems), the Institute for Sustainable Forestry, the Rogue Institute for Ecology,

and the Soil Association of the U.K., as well as retailers such as Smith and Hawken.

As certification organizations proliferate, concerns over the consistency and credibility of their operations have grown. The Forest Stewardship Council (FSC) proposes to meet the ever growing need for a credible and unbiased mechanism to guarantee the authenticity of claims made by certifying organizations by establishing itself as an independent oversight and verification umbrella organization for independent timber certification programs to guard against false or misleading claims of sustainability. In so doing, the FSC hopes to support credible, third-party certification efforts by organizations in all countries and all types of forests.

The Tropical Forest Foundation (TFF) has established the Tropical Forest Management Recognition Program, designed to allow companies to voluntarily disclose confidential information regarding their suppliers to an expert review committee in order to achieve recognition for progress in obtaining their supply from sources moving toward sustainability. The review committee will evaluate companies for sustainability according to International Tropical Timber Organization (ITTO) guidelines and other accepted standards. Thus trees are to be felled only after careful selection and after conforming to sustainable forestry principles, fertilizers and insecticide sprays are banned or avoided, use of wood preservatives will be severely restricted. Which program or certification label is likely to establish itself as the standard remains to be seen. But what is clear is that the consumer needs to know the exact origin of the timber he or she is using and its impact on the environment. Above all, its production should not be hostile to the environment nor a threat to our health.

Certification labels and programs guarantee that the timber has been produced by sustainable or well-managed methods

Natural arboriculture

More and more forest owners are developing a sense of responsibility and are no longer practicing clear-cutting. They are also turning away from monoculture, but have introduced a system of rotation in accord with the natural processes of the forests. In many areas workhorses have been re-introduced to protect the forest floor from damage by the heavy equipment that would otherwise be used. In this way roads destructive to ecosystems and wildlife habitats can be avoided.

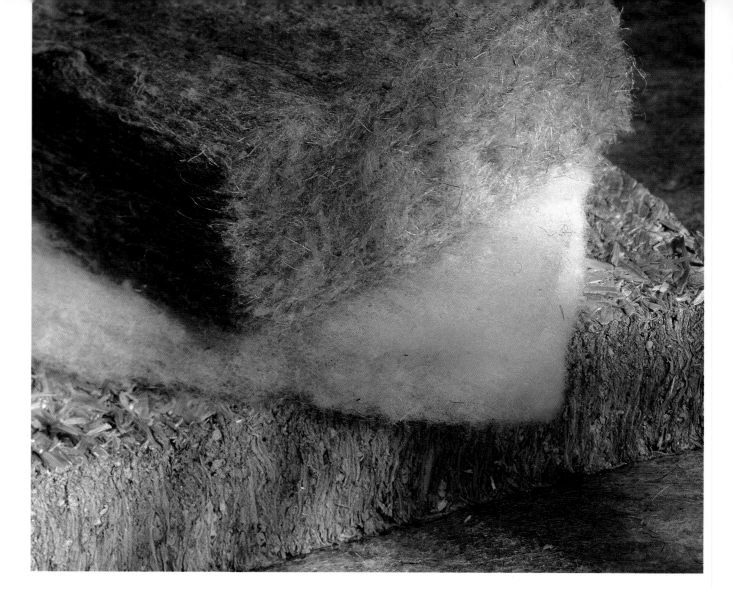

Other renewable materials

Building materials made from straw, flax and sheep's wool

Renewable raw materials are most suitable for building products. Agricultural products use fewer resources and many can replace fossil fuels.

Sheep wool is highly suitable as a non-synthetic floor covering and as insulating material. The world wool market is currently dominated by the enormous over-production in Australia and New Zealand. This wool is cheaper than most produced in Europe and the US. Wool, however, frequently contains a wide variety of chemical pesticides used during storage and transport. Nontoxic carpets that are classified as manufactured from pure virgin wool use the less objectionable pyrethroids (obtained from natural sources) for mothproofing.

Straw bale as a construction material is becoming increasingly popular in the semiarid regions of the American Southwest, Australia and New Zealand. It is also gaining increased use in Canada, California, New England and the American southeastern and mid-Atlantic regions as well. Solidity, a high thermal resistance (R-Value), low cost, and a nontoxic renewable source of grain agriculture make straw bales an environmentally responsible building material. It is usually locally available, inexpensive and long lasting. It is also an esthetically pleasing material, lending itself to soft curvature in building form, soft finishes and deep window recesses which speaks of substantiality. Straw has also been used to manufacture structural insulated panels (SIPs) as well. These straw building systems are ideal for the panelized rapid construction of the walls, roofs and floors of a house. In Britain it is now common to use straw boards for lightweight walls that do not require a reinforcing frame. Boards of

this kind also provide efficient insulation and possess good hygroscopic properties.

Water reeds have been used as a roofing material in North America for centuries. Native Americans were using reeds to thatch dwellings before the colonial era. Reed is now imported into the US from Asia in the form of window blinds, reed fences and interior panel systems. Today, however, thatchers such as British master thatcher Colin McGhee must import reed for American projects from Great Britain. Thatched roofs are long lasting (50 to 75 years) and highly insulating. In the northeast and mid-Atlantic regions of the US, the thatching reed genus *Phragmites* is considered an invasive foreign pest – in other words a weed. States such as Maryland have eradication programs using herbicides and burning when new growth shows in the spring. Other states such as New Jersey and Virginia have extensive marshland with acreage in wild reed marketed for commercial use. Clearly, reed as a building material is an untapped, easily renewable resource in America.

A cousin of the reed, bamboo, is also gaining increased use as a building material. In Asia, it is commonly used for structural building components and scaffolding. In America, attractive flooring systems are now available manufactured from bamboo.

Another renewable building material, flax has long been cultivated commercially in Europe, one reason being that it is indeed very simple to grow. Its seeds are used to manufacture linseed oil, an indispensable ingredient in linoleum flooring and in many paints, and its fibers are also used in the production of insulating materials.

In the US, the cultivation of hemp is still banned because of its close relation to the illegal Marijuana. In other European countries, particularly in France, the cultivation of industrial hemp is not restricted. Here, it is recognized as a valuable raw material for insulation and other building applications. Agricultural organizations in the US, particularly in Kentucky, are lobbying for a legalization of the industrial, non-intoxicating varieties with low THC content. Again, the main use will be in the manufacture of insulating materials; even the hard, wood-like parts of the hemp plant can be used as loose-fill insulation.

In Saxony-Anhalt, Germany recent experimental cultivation of willow has begun. Previously, willow had been grown in many regions of Europe in the Middle Ages as a dyer's raw material. The dye produced from this plant was later replaced by imported indigo and then by chemical dyes. In addition to its use as a dye for natural colors, willow produces a highly effective natural wood preservative.

Other organic building materials include a wide range of oils, resins and waxes. Examples of these are beeswax, natural resins or shellac, linseed oil and citrus oil. Also, naturally grown pigments and chalks are used in the production of nontoxic dyes and paints.

Bales of straw can be turned into building boards
Surplus straw can be used to make building boards, panels and used as insulation material.

Beeswax put to a good use
Beeswax is not only suited for making scented candles: Wood surfaces can be treated with it as well. It is also an ingredient in many natural chemical products.

Flax is really versatile
Flax is an easy-to-cultivate fiber used to make cloth and insulation materials. Flax seeds are also used to produce linseed oil, one of the basic ingredients of non-chemical finishes.

Bianco Sardo, granite, Sardinia

Jura yellow, marble, southern Germany

Daino Reate, marble, Italy

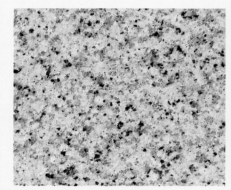
Bianco Cristal, granite, Spain

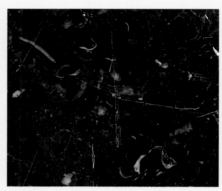
Nero Marquina, marble, Spain

Carra Ceoia, marble, Italy

Black slate, Norway

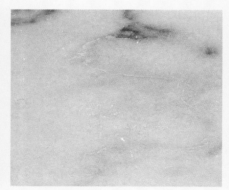
Estrawoz Rosa, marble, Portugal

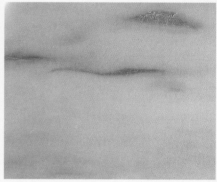
Marble, Portugal

Non-renewable natural building materials

In addition to organic renewable raw materials, minerals may be counted as natural building materials. An important example is natural stone. Hundreds of types of sandstone, limestone, granite, marble and slate are to be found all over the United States and Great Britain. For centuries these have been used to build walls, floors, foundations or for window and door surrounds. Today they are used as flooring material, façades, wall veneers and ornamentation, as well as for garden landscaping. For longevity, beauty and the health benefits of using nontoxic materials, stone is unequaled.

However, the quarrying of stone may come at an extremely high environmental cost involving waste runoff and mining pollution. Processing, finishing and transport of stone also consume large amounts of energy. The choice of locally available stone building products relieves this problem somewhat while also providing a market for a locally available building material.

In addition to the natural stone found in the United States and Great Britain, there are those imported from all over the world. The most popular is marble, followed by gabbro, both of which are used widely for façades. There are numerous kinds of slate, such as phyllite, highly prized for flooring, and roofing and schist used for wall facing. Quartzite, which is highly weather-resistant, and banded migmatite-gneiss are also used for decorative purposes. However, stone imported

Sarizzo Monte Rosa, granite, Italy

Ruhr sandstone, Germany

Shell marl, Germany

Solnhofner marble, Germany

Labrador Blue, Granite, Norway

Graphite, Norway

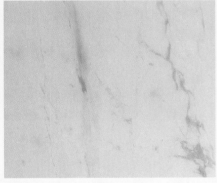
Marble, Greece

Trani marble, Italy

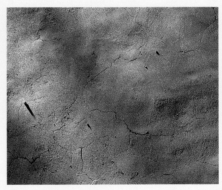
Clay, Germany

from exotic locations, even if it is quite reasonably priced, is expensive in ecological terms because of the cost of transporting it.

Clay, by contrast, has always been a traditional natural building material for both load-bearing and non-load-bearing wall systems and can be found all over the world. Bricks and structural clay or roofing tiles are produced by heating clay to a high temperature in kilns, and sand-lime bricks by using steam pressure to heat sand and quicklime. These wall materials cannot, strictly speaking, be regarded as "natural." Although they have natural ingredients, a considerable amount of petrochemical energy is required to produce them.

From all over the world

Marble, slate, granite or sandstone – natural stone rates among the most durable and healthy building materials. Stone has a long tradition in construction going back for centuries but only locally available material is really environmentally friendly.

Site considerations

Another important aspect of building in an environmentally responsible way is the regard for the land on which the building is to stand. Site sensitive design will include considering the ecology of the site, the slope and its directional orientation, water features and climatic characteristics, to name a few. An important goal will be to alter the environment as little as possible. When building, a certain amount of disruption is inevitable, yet we can lessen the degree to which we encroach upon natural systems. It is possible to retain and restore natural foliage, eco-systems, watercourses and natural features.

By incorporating foliage into façades and roofs we can relate the appearance of the building itself to its natural context. This restores foliage to built-up areas and improves the conditions around the building with moisture and temperature control while also protecting the surface of the building.

Other considerations may include gardens laid out according to organic and ecological principles. By keeping or planting indigenous plant species, an ecological habitat for local fauna and animal species is created as a natural, low-maintenance amenity. Additionally, small ponds or a microbiological sewage treatment plant will provide the ideal environment for aquatic and marsh species of plants and animals, at the same time creating a closer contact to nature.

Rainwater systems, rather than be fed directly into storm drains, can be designed to seep into the grounds around buildings. Storm water drainage systems are expensive investments for most communities. Alternatives that allow rainwater to be absorbed back into the site will be both less expensive and less ecologically damaging. The Village Green subdivision development in Davis, California is an excellent example of this. Rainwater can also be collected and stored in cisterns and used for other purposes around the home such as watering gardens and flushing toilets. This practice would not only reduce the capacity requirements on remote water delivery systems and

A house covered with climbing plants restores to nature much that it displaced

reservoirs, but would also save each homeowner money over time.

Making composting arrangements on site is also a way to maintain a fertile soil and the natural cycles in our environment. Human and food waste need not simply be thrown away. It can be turned directly into compost providing valuable humus for gardens and flower beds and thus become a contribution in the ecological cycle. The expensive septic and sewer systems may seem essential for the sanitary disposal of waste; however, commercially available systems can now be found to provide a safe, non-smelling ecological alternative. A composting toilet producing safe, valuable fertilizer has been developed to turn human waste and kitchen refuse into humus. When widespread, these systems will reduce or eliminate the need for enormous sewage plants that now produce vast quantities of toxic, difficult to dispose waste.

Everyone can make a valuable contribution to an ecological cycle in their everyday life

A nature lover's house in Dortmund, Germany

Arch.: N.Pangert, Hamm, Germany
The owner of this house contributes in a variety of ways to sustainability. Outside a blanket of climbing plants and grasses shields the home. The landscaping has also been allowed to remain natural. Rainwater is used for household purposes and a system of recycling is used.

A show house at the Documenta Urbana, Kassel, Germany

Climbing plants on the façades and a roof covered with grass and plants enhance the appearance of a house which would otherwise look quite ordinary. A modest contribution is made to bringing nature into the city again. A variety of birds build their nests, insects thrive here and the plants keep the building cool and humidified.

ENERGY-EFFICIENT BUILDING

House of Wood "Living in the Country," Dortmund, Germany

Arch.: Planquadrat, Dortmund
It need not be prohibitively expensive to build a house that requires very little energy. The compact design and efficient insulation make it feasible.

Energy use in buildings is arguably the most significant factor in terms of impact on the environment. In the United States 35% of all energy consumed is used by buildings – a whopping 29 quads (quadrillion Btus) each year. The amount used in residential buildings for space heating and cooling is over 7 quads generating 420 million tons of CO_2 and 9 million tons of other atmospheric pollutants (United States Environmental Protection Agency Report, 1993). Even in buildings using oil or gas for heating fuel, electricity is consumed also by pumps and fans which circulate the heat throughout the building. As much as 70% of this energy could be saved by aggressive application of energy conservation strategies such as better insulation, replacing windows, sealing air leaks, installing modern and more efficient heating and air conditioning systems, and landscaping designed

to provide barriers to winter winds and shade during the summer months. Most countries saw the distinct need to promote energy-efficiency in buildings after the oil embargo in the early 1970s created a worldwide energy crisis. Energy-efficiency was promoted in basically three ways:

- Regulations in the form of energy codes and design standards;
- Certification or labeling programs;
- Subsidies or tax incentives for investment in energy efficiency technologies.

Since 1972 regulations have been in effect in the United States governing design of buildings with regard to energy use. Modern energy-efficient building standards developed in the private sector by a number of groups, such as the American Society of Heating, Refrigerating and Air-conditioning Engineers (ASHRAE) now provide

standards for buildings which result in up to 40% less energy use than in buildings constructed prior to the 1970s.

To promote energy-efficiency still further, numerous certification and labeling systems have been developed such as the Energy Star® Home Program. This government program promotes voluntary partnerships with home builders to construct residences 30% more energy-efficient than the current Model Energy Code (MEC). A Canadian program designed to push home energy efficiency beyond the requirements of codes is the R-2000 Home Program. Directed toward the builder, R-2000 encourages the building of energy-efficient houses that are environmentally friendly and healthy to live in.

Energy consumption can be reduced simply by using increased insulation, without any need for expensive and sophisticated technology. Tried-and-true building materials and advanced building technology can be used to construct buildings that consume far less energy and will enhance the residents' quality of life.

Super-insulated house
Low-energy houses can be constructed according to a variety of designs. What matters most is the careful attention to detail.

EMISSION OF CO_2 IN VARIOUS COUNTRIES (1993 IN MILLION TONS)					
	Eur 15*	D	UK	S	US
Electric Power Utilities	940.3	326.0	191.7	8.3	800
Other Energy Sources	142.7	31.3	31.3	2.0	4
All Industrial Activities	555.5	158.6	74.2	11.5	30
Transportation	810.9	186.2	140.2	21.5	335
Residential Energy Use	665.2	206.8	121.6	9.7	260

* Combined total for 15 countries
Source: eurostat; 1990 United States Census Data

An energy-efficient housing project, Ingolstadt, Germany

Arch.: H. Eek, Göteburg, Sweden
This project completed by a Swedish architect in Bavaria is considered to be one of the best examples of such architecture because of its compact yet well articulated design as well as the careful use of open spaces.

A low-energy house in Sindelfingen, Germany

Wood is very suitable for building energy-efficient houses, as it is such an economical material in every sense. The thick layers of insulation material can be integrated into the design from the outset. Houses of this kind are strikingly different in appearance from the more conventional brick-and-mortar homes.

Super-insulated house

Even a conventional, solidly constructed house can be designed to be economical in its use of energy. The layers of insulation must be fixed to the outside walls and covered by a weather-resistant skin so that they are no longer visible. This will, of course, make the house a little more expensive but the additional expense will no doubt be worth it.

The low-energy house

The basic characteristic of a low-energy house is that it uses less energy for heating than the minimum established by local building regulations such as the Energy Star® Home which uses 30% less than codes allow. Regulations are continually being changed and so the term low-energy house is by no means a static concept. Above all, a low-energy house requires adequate thermal insulation in all the external sections of the building. The heat loss is mainly through the walls, windows, roof and, where there is one, through the basement. If, however, the attic has been converted into a room that has not been adequately insulated, the proportions of heat loss throughout the building would be different: The loss through the roof could be as much as 20%. Similarly, in other buildings where the basement is used quite extensively the heat loss could rise to 15%.

In a new building the heat losses described above are considerably lower, and can be reduced by using suitable material for efficient thermal insulation. Such insulation would be utilized even more in a low-energy house.

At this point a digression into the physics of building is unavoidable: Every material has its coefficient of thermal conduction which is denoted by its u-value (k-value is used for metric representation). This heat transmission coefficient describes the flow of warm air as the number of Btus (British thermal units) or watts (k-value) passing through a structural element in a building (such as a wall) with a surface area of 10.764 square feet (1 square meter) at a temperature difference of 1°F (°K used for metric k-value). The lower the

A low-energy house near Konstanz, Germany
Arch.: K. W. König, Überlingen, Germany
Anyone deciding to build a house requiring very little energy will want to make use of the energy that nature provides free of charge. This house has been constructed with one corner open to the sun's rays.

ENERGY LOSS % BY ENVELOPMENT COMPONENT

	Washington, DC	
	Typical House	MEC Standard Design
Walls	25	20
Windows	25	34
Foundation/ Base	21	16
Roof	9	8
Air Infiltration	20	22

	Denver, CO	
	Typical House	MEC Standard Design
Walls	17	16
Windows	22	30
Foundation/ Base	12	16
Roof	25	10
Air Infiltration	24	22

	Minneapolis, MN	
	Typical House	MEC Standard Design
Walls	19	16
Windows	24	35
Foundation/ Base	15	18
Roof	13	9
Air Infiltration	29	22

u-value, the less are the heat losses of the structural element. Therefore, in order to attain a specific total u-value the thickness of a particular material would be adjusted according to its heat loss coefficient. Another

Well shaded

Arch.: H. H. Stahmer, Möhnsen, Germany

An interesting example of how a house can be designed to look striking yet without losing its identity: The deep eaves or overhang protect the facades of the house. The architect has designed a house that requires very little energy and one which even draws substantial energy from solar technology and an efficient heat pump.

A house can draw its heat from various sources

Arch.: H. H. Stahmer, Möhnsen, Germany

The house shown here not only consumes very little energy, it even draws on solar energy and geothermal energy with its advanced heat pump technology.

value frequently used to label materials such as insulation is R-value which is exactly the reciprocal of the u-value. (U=1/R) For example, to attain an R-value of 20 for the outer walls required by today's low-energy house, the following materials would be required:

- 400 inches of concrete or
- 300 inches of porous brick or
- 7 inches of batt or cellulose insulation material.

In practice the preference is for a combination of different materials (stone, insulation material, plaster, wood). The u-value for such a wall can then only be computed by an expert. A low-energy house usually has thick external walls, windows with expensive high-performance glazing and a relatively complex and costly construction. But if all these features are included in the plans for a low-energy house before building starts, the extra costs can be reduced quite considerably. Heat transmission losses are generally caused by the air permeability of the building shell. Most drafts (air leakage) enter an older house through the attic and the windows, and most of the heat escapes in the same way. When a low-energy house is built, however, considerable attention is paid to ensuring that there are no such gaps and that the building is plastered correctly; it is also important to include windbreaks at all wall roof and floor joints in wood framed buildings.

The most serious problems with outdated heating systems are that they are not only inefficient, but also difficult to control and have a leaky or poorly insulated distribution system. A low-energy house, by contrast, will have an efficient modern heating system that will be extremely sensitive to changes in demand. All air distribution ducts will be properly sealed and insulated or in a hydronic system, hot water piping will be adequately insulated.

BUILDING INSULATION STANDARDS IN THE UNITED STATES

	Energy Loss % by Envelope Component	
	1979 National Model Energy (R) Guidelines u-value*	1989 Model Energy Code For Northern City u-value (R)
Walls	.09 (R11)	.053 (R19)
Roof	.05 (R20)	.033 (R30)
Floor (crawl space)	.09 (R11)	.04 (R25)
Floor (slab on grade)	NA	.5 (R2)
Windows	NA	.5 (R2)
Doors	NA	1.0 (R1)

*u-values are in Btu/square foot/hour/°F

A zero-energy house in Graz, Austria

Arch.: Hegedys & Haas, Graz

A step beyond the low-energy house is the zero-energy house. The house requires none of the conventional heating systems, and is heated entirely with solar energy, heat pumps or other renewable sources of energy. The gable on the right consists entirely of solar collectors.

The objectives of the ecologically-minded builder

The most important energy-saving measures in construction can be summed up as follows:

- Provide efficient thermal insulation for all external parts of the building, i.e. the walls, the windows, the roof and the basement;
- Avoid heat bridges and other energy leaks;
- Provide airtight building fabric; avoid heat loss through ventilation;
- Provide efficient heating systems with the lowest possible inertia;
- Provide adequate thermal mass especially if passive solar energy is utilized.

The entire concept is rejected by a great many ecologically minded builders. They argue that:

- efficient insulation can be achieved only with "unhealthy" synthetic materials;
- thick layers of insulation would probably exclude any possible benefit from warmth generated by solar energy;
- an airtight building is neither healthy nor comfortable, because a building has to breathe;
- heating must utilize only renewable materials (wood, solar energy) and systems with a high level of radiation (tiled stoves, underfloor heating, wall surface heating).

The attitude can best be summed up in a single sentence: Excessive technology is definitely unhealthy. Nevertheless, the argument is basically unsound for the following reasons:

- Insulation materials have been developed recently from renewable materials or from recycled products that comply fully with the requirements for their use in low-energy houses. Such materials may, however, require different building designs.
- While it may well be true that a certain amount of the heat from the sun is blocked, good thermal insulation will ensure that whatever solar energy is captured will be used more efficiently, because it comprises a greater proportion of the total energy required. In addition, modern technology (for example, transparent thermal insulation) will ensure that even if a building is highly insulated, solar energy can still be used passively.
- Drafts and heat leaks do not make the home comfortable and healthy. The exchange of humidity via fixed structural elements is minimal, insofar as there is no such thing as a wall that can breathe. Of course, efficient sealing of the building fabric requires more frequent and more thorough ventilation, and it is for this reason that a mechanical ventilation system such as a heat recovery ventilator (HRV), should be incorporated into the building from the outset.
- Heating systems that operate efficiently and react to changes in temperature swiftly can, in fact, run on renewable fuels (such as a gassified wood fired boiler system) or a combination of different fuels.

The advantage of modern heating systems is that they have a higher radiating capacity because their operating temperature is lower.

- The more efficiently a building has been insulated, the warmer will be the interior surfaces of the external walls and the shorter the time required for the room to reach a specific temperature.

Generally, the relative importance of various advantages will have to be weighed against the disadvantages of a given strategy. If the ultimate objective is to build a low-energy house incorporating all the most recent technological advances as well as doing right by the ecologically minded members of society, more money will have to be spent and more careful plans drawn up, before such ideals can be attained.

A low-energy house in Chiemsee, Germany

This house, designed for multiple occupancy, shows how to combine energy conservation strategies and solar energy. The less hot water and electricity that are required, the more worthwhile in terms of simple economics it will be to utilize solar energy.

It must be remembered that a single individual living in the United States, for example, consumes 121,000 kWh a year all activities combined. This equals over six times more primary energy than the total amount consumed by the average world citizen and eight times as much as would be acceptable in the long term in strict conformity with the principles of sustainability. Thus we do have sufficient reason to finally think about more drastic measures for saving energy.

A low-energy house
Arch.: P. Schorr, Vachendorf, Germany
From the exterior it is impossible to tell that this house has been constructed on a wooden foundation. The conservatory is an effective passive solar collector.

Recreating a traditional cottage

Arch.: M. Dedekind, Hamburg, Germany

Reeds have been used to thatch this house, which if built according to ancient methods is extremely energy-efficient. It was also built using structural elements from an old house that had been demolished.

A bio-solar envelope house

Designer: K. Becker, Höhr, Germany

This house has been built with an outer envelope of patented steel girders and with a non-load-bearing inner house. Although it requires very little energy, energy consumption could be reduced even further if the rear walls of the barrel-shaped building are bermed or "earth-sheltered." Light and fresh air come into the house through the glass structure at the entrance. This house was awarded a prize in 1997 for providing a particularly healthy environment for its occupants.

A multi-functional container

Design: Transferzentrum für angepaßte Technologien, Rheine, Germany

The idea for constructing this "eco-container" originated from the architect's desire to combine a number of small units in a wooden-framed structure for different uses, including an office, studio, living area and storeroom. The separate containers are arranged according to a modular pattern and can be positioned as required either next to or on top of each other, depending on characteristics of the site. Here, the upper containers are reached by an outside steel staircase.

A low-energy house in Darmstadt-Kranichstein, Germany

Making a building energy-efficient doesn't mean you have to limit the design possibilities. It is quite possible for the architect to incorporate something rather eye-catching for a distinctive image.

Building shapes and heat loss or gain

A/V Ratio

The ratio of external surface area to volume (A/V ratio) of a house determines, to a great extent, its energy efficiency or "energy index." A bungalow constructed with several wings will use twice as much energy as a multi-family building with the same amount of enclosed space.

The external structural elements are the greatest contributors to the heat losses and gains (thermal loads) of a building. This means that the more compact the house, the more energy efficient it will be. Therefore it is important to make sure that all the available space within the house is well used and necessary for the functional needs of the occupants. How can rooms best be laid out so that none of the available space is wasted? Can rooms be subdivided or joined together later, if the needs of the occupants change?

Questions like these must be asked at the planning stage to ensure that all space is used efficiently, and thus reduce the amount of heating and cooling energy the building will require.

Depending on the shape of the house, the outer shell can be made more compact without sacrificing building volume. A geometrically compact shape such as a half sphere, a half cylinder, or a cube, has the lowest heat loss because it has a small surface area in relation to volume. The igloo is the most efficient building

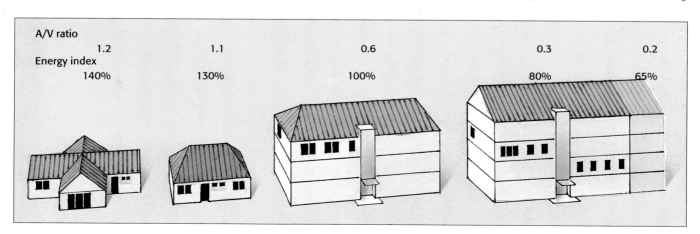

A/V ratio	1.2	1.1	0.6	0.3	0.2
Energy index	140%	130%	100%	80%	65%

Terraced housing in Drensteinfurt, Germany

Arch.: R. Weißen, Drensteinfurt
Nestled close to one another with their compact design, these eco-houses will provide little cause for concern about energy consumption (opposite).

An L-shaped bungalow in Witten, Germany

This was considered the "dream" house of the 1960s when oil was cheap. The low almost flat roof is reminiscent of an Italian Villa and the two wings of the house are set at a right angle to afford privacy. Nowadays it is widely known that this unnecessarily large external surface area will result in excessive heat loss.

shape in terms of energy consumption, so from that standpoint a dome might be considered the ideal shape for a building.

In comparison with a single-story house with a gradually sloping roof, a perfectly square three-story house of identical volume will require a surface area which is 44% less. All those decorative features which are so popular today, such as small turrets, dormers, bay windows or balconies, though they are intended to make the appearance more attractive to the eye, increase the surface area of the building while the volume of the building remains the same and thus decrease the efficiency of the surface-to-volume ratio. To make matters even worse, these embellishments have the same effect as the fins on a radiator in that they conduct heat away from the building at a significantly greater rate than a smooth wall.

Efficient thermal insulation is difficult if the building has been constructed in several angled wings rather than a compact shape. In fact, it is difficult to optimize a contorted building shape for a given climate in terms of taking into account the direction and angle of solar radiation and prevailing wind patterns. Climate-responsive building design takes these into account in determining solar orientation and window arrangement. Nevertheless, a compact shape for a building need not be uninteresting. Unheated extensions such as conservatories, balconies, outbuildings, and large, high-quality windows (windows having NFRC certification in the US and a tested u-value of less than 0.35) and features such as outdoor terraces, overhangs or eaves for protection from

unwanted sun and wind as well as grass and vines on the outer walls and the roof, will all make the building more attractive improve energy-efficiency.

A detached single-family house usually cannot be considered ideal as an energy-saving type of building for the above reasons. In such a house the ratio of external surface area to volume (A/V ratio) is on average about 2:3 or 0.71, whereas a house standing in the middle of a row of terraced houses would have an A/V ratio of less than 1:2 or 0.45. In fact, the lower the A/V ratio the greater the energy-efficiency. Building more compact houses brings distinct advantages not only in terms of saving space, but also in terms of conserving energy.

Housing development in Hamburg, Germany

Arch.: M. Dedekind, C. Gerth, Hamburg
This model low-cost housing with a massive double envelope construction is a superb example of a compact building form. Note the creative positioning of the solar panels!

A passive housing development in Wiesbaden, Germany

Arch.: Rasch & Partner, Darmstadt, Germany

This model experimental passive building was intended to be a demonstration of innovative construction techniques for future energy-efficient buildings of this type. The units were constructed for 2500 DM per square meter (about $140 per square foot).

First all-passive building

Arch.: Bott, Stuttgart & Ridder, Berlin, & Westermeyer, Darmstadt, Germany
This housing complex was the first example of passive house construction in Germany and stands on the site of a former army barracks. It demonstrates that energy-efficiency need not be prohibitively expensive.

Passive house, active energy savings

The "passive" house

The most highly sophisticated form of low-energy house makes use of a passive, rather than active, heating system. This type of house often uses less than 4.75 KBtu/square foot (15 kWh/square meter) of annual heating energy. The average annual heating energy consumption in residential buildings in the US is about 28.5 KBtu/square foot (90 kWh/square meter) according to US Energy Information Administration (EIA) reports. The term "passive" is used because the building requires very little heating energy and a much smaller active heating system to meet its heating requirements. Here's how it works:

- by using the natural body heat of the occupants and heat emitted by electrical appliances, for example, refrigerators, hot water heater, range, computers, etc. (30%);
- by utilizing a heat recovery ventilation system (HRV) to recapture and recirculate warm air (28%);
- by harnessing passive solar energy (25%).

Frequently the value of the heat generated within a building is underestimated. A person engaged in a sedentary occupation (such as reading) will release

around 100 watts into the space around them; this will increase to around 150 watts for light activity (such as typing) and to 250 watts for strenuous physical activity. A computer releases 150 watts of thermal energy, a copier as much as 1,300 watts, and household appliances such as the electric range, interior lights and refrigerator in a household of four will release about 3.16 KBtu/square foot (10 kWh/square meter) of surplus heat per day. It is sometimes said that a single light bulb could heat a whole house, and this is not that far from the truth in a passive house.

The heat from the sun penetrating the windows of a passive house will be reduced in absolute terms by the use of glass with high insulating properties – by highly-efficient R-8 (0.13 u-value) super-glazing, as it is called. However, with more standard R3–4 (0.33–0.25 u-value) high quality low-e windows, the sun can contribute significantly toward the total heating requirements in a house with poor to moderately good thermal insulation. Even in a climate with frequently overcast skies the annual thermal energy in this way is potentially 6.3 KBtu/square foot (20 kWh/square meter) which is nearly the total heating energy requirement.

In passive houses, every attempt is made to use as few and as efficient electrical appliances as possible, and to install plumbing fixtures and systems that conserve water. According to readings taken inside passive houses, the total energy consumption of such houses can be as low as 4.75 KBtu/square foot (15 kWh/square meter) for domestic heating, 2.2 KBtu/square foot (7 kWh/square meter) for heating water and 3.16 KBtu/square foot (10 kWh/square meter) for domestic appliances. Some of these houses are designed to use only renewable energy sources such as photovoltaic and wind power and thus remain totally independent of conventional fossil fuel sources of energy. In the case of these zero-energy houses solar technology is usually used for producing domestic hot water and also for generating electricity.

SOLAR ARCHITECTURE

The sun is the most important source of the earth's energy, radiating a continuous flow of energy equal to 1,353 watts for each square meter of the earth's atmosphere. In fact, the solar energy striking the surface of the earth at any given moment is estimated to be 10,000 times the world's energy requirements. All renewable energy, whether it is converted from wind or water, or from decomposing organic material, comes originally from the sun. Even fossil fuels are in fact nothing other than the sun's energy that has been converted by living processes and stored beneath the earth's crust.

The aim of solar architecture is to harness the sun both actively and passively. Passive heating is accomplished by several different techniques. In direct gain buildings, one side of the building, elongated if possible, is deliberately oriented to the south, and large windows on the south side accept the sun's electromagnetic energy. In indirect gain systems the glass collector area is a greenhouse, sunroom or conservatory attached to the building to be heated.

Active solar energy, on the other hand, includes a much more intensive use of technology in a variety of fields depending on the function of the system. Some

"O sole mio:" a house that incorporates interesting wooden elements, Klagenfurt, Austria

Arch.: M. Thun, Milan, Italy in collaboration with the "Europäisches Designdepot," Klagenfurt, Austria
This building is the work of the highly gifted architect Matteo Thun. Its enormous glass front faces due south, but allows for solar control by means of moving wooden slats.

of these technologies include transparent thermal insulation and both thermal (such as solar hot water heating systems) as well as photovoltaic (PV) collectors as an electrical power source.

Solar architecture is an attractive and progressive way of creating the energy that is required in a building, and if skillfully applied it need not result in buildings that all look the same; instead it can be fitted to a wide variety of architectural structures. This approach is just one among many strategies for optimizing our planet's resources to meet the energy requirements of a building.

Solar architecture optimizes our planet's resources

The building's orientation

The passive energy derived from the sun would typically align the roof ridge from east to west so that the house faces south and receives direct sunlight. The roof pitch will then be oriented correctly for fitting the solar collectors or solar cells. It is often desirable to elongate the building so that the south-facing facade is longer than the east and west facades. A house that features windows that open to the south and has few windows to the north uses about 30% less energy than a building with no particular orientation to the sun. Large windows should be fitted in the south-facing side of the house so that sunlight and the resulting

A house near Graz, Austria

Arch.: Hegedys & Haas, Graz
This home (opposite) has a transparent center to which the two wings of the building have been connected. The solidly constructed ground floor serves as a reliable, high-capacity thermal storage medium.

A home near Konstanz, Germany

Arch.: K. W. König, Überlingen, Germany
Solar collectors are an essential feature of a solar house, even if they may sometimes be quite small in area.

heat from the sun's rays can penetrate well into the building during the months when heating is required. Overhangs or eaves, extending balconies or sunshades will provide sufficient protection from the sun in the summer, when the sun is at its highest.

Unfortunately, residential development plans are often drawn up in such a way that they do not permit the building front to face south. More often than not buildings are constructed to fit the way the land parcels have been laid out, or to fit in with the topographical characteristics of the terrain. If at all possible, it is worth the effort to try to persuade the developers and the local planning department to make an exception. It is still acceptable for the southern orientation to deviate by a maximum of 20° from due south which reduces the solar energy available by only about 5%. In this case it is especially vital to ensure that there are no neighboring buildings, hedges or trees to obstruct the sun's rays.

As a rule the total window area on the south side of the building should be at least 20% but usually not more than 60% of the total wall area. When the glass to wall area is more than 60%, the energy lost through the extra panes of glass will exceed the energy gained from the extra sunlight unless one installs advanced high-efficiency windows. In this case elaborate sunshades or mechanical ventilation systems to prevent overheating would be needed, which would substantially increase building costs.

Buildings designed to use direct gain passive solar heating in this way consume less energy for heating; they are also more economical in terms of lighting energy requirements. Less artificial lighting not only means lower electricity bills. The occupants of the building feel much better because of the natural, full-spectrum light.

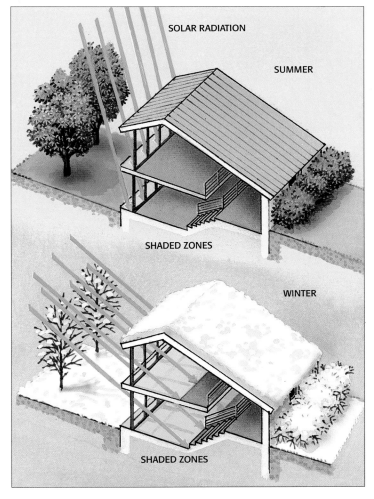

Passive solar shading and penetration

It is vital to construct the building in such a way that the sun's rays can penetrate well inside in winter, but shade is provided by roof overhangs and deciduous trees in summer.

Indirect gain solar spaces:
the pros and cons

**A private house in
Dortmund, Germany**

Arch.: U. Drahtler, Dortmund
A conservatory is considered to
be the height of luxury, providing
sun and a plant-filled haven
throughout the year. A well-
planned conservatory can
improve heat distribution inside
the house, though sometimes
quite the opposite happens.

When solar energy is trapped by means of ancillary spaces such as a sunroom, greenhouse or conservatory or even a glazed entrance foyer and then somehow stored and transfered to the main building, this is known as an indirect gain passive solar design. To gain the best result the glass used must always be very efficient and of high quality. It is often wise to consider using glazing with a high solar heat gain coefficient (SHGC) if there are horizontal glazed surfaces which receive direct sun during the summer or late in the day when the temperature has peaked. The construction should also have an appropriate amount of thermal mass which can be a stone or concrete floor and a masonry wall between the sunroom and the main building.

If these rules are observed, the loss of energy through a wall that is moderately insulated can be reduced by as much as 20% by adding the sunroom. This would of course be far more expensive than insulating the wall more efficiently, but the advantages are that the amount of living space can be increased in the warmer months. A disadvantage is that such a space will almost inevitably reduce the amount of direct light falling on the windows behind

A house in Flamersfeld, Germany
Design: P. Patt, Flamersfeld
This house has been laid out with great care: There are large areas of glass in the rooms which are most lived in, whereas the bathrooms, store rooms and bedrooms are on the north side, where the building is less open to the sun.

it. Another problem created by a conservatory is the difficulty of ventilating the rooms adjoining it.

If the conservatory is used as an extra room during the winter months it will have to be heated – thus using valuable energy. This is because the glass walls of the conservatory cannot feasibly be brought up to the insulating capabilities of an opaque wall and therefore will always allow more energy to escape than conventional walls. In designing the sunroom or conservatory it is important to ensure that it can be thoroughly ventilated and well shaded from the sun by some means during the summer months.

The layout of buildings

An important aspect of orienting the building to face south is a satisfactory layout of the interior rooms. The living room, kitchen and other areas where people usually spend a lot of time during the day should ideally be oriented toward the south, whereas the bedrooms, bathrooms and rooms used for other purposes, as well as stairwells and store rooms, should, as a rule, be oriented to the north. On the north side the area taken up by windows should not be more than 10% of the facade area except in regions where the summer climate tends to be very hot, and good natural ventilation is required throughout the building.

By using this approach the lesser used rooms provide a kind of thermal buffer for the other heated living spaces. The north face of the building being more closed, will not receive nearly as much light, but then

less natural light is needed in the rooms on that side. The one exception to this rule is the need for good morning light in the bedrooms. For this reason, they should, if possible, be located on the east side of the house or, if not, they could be provided with clerestory windows which face east or skylights with an eastern exposure.

A house with a sunroom in Erkheim, Germany
Here, the glass-enclosed room can be closed off from the main building by its own doors so that heat is not dissipated during winter through the large expanses of glass.

A feeling of well-being

Solid walls will store both heat and cold. When it is hot outside on a summer's day, the walls keep the house pleasantly cool. In winter they will retain the heat longer than a lightly constructed building, moderating temperature fluctuations inside.

Natural stone flooring

Floors of natural stone are another way of providing adequate thermal mass inside the house. They look good, they are indestructible, and they maintain a pleasant temperature inside the house.

Terracotta flooring

This eye-catching alternative adds a sense of luxury to the house and is ideal with under-floor heating. But as a thermal storage medium it is somewhat inferior to natural stone.

Thermal storage

The passive solar energy harnessed in a solar house will not be of full benefit to the occupants unless certain materials used inside the building retain heat well and are properly located. These surfaces are known as thermal mass and they should be used in proportion with the amount of southfacing glazed area. In this way the building will be able to take in surplus heat and then release it gradually and as required later in the day when the temperature drops. Thus, use of non-renewable energy for heating the building can be further reduced and over-heating from the surplus heat is avoided. Natural stone floors and thick inside walls made of sand-stone or limestone containing calcite, for example, will help to balance the room temperature. These types of stone heat up slowly while warmed by the sun's rays and retain the heat long after the sun has set. As a result the rooms are more healthful and more comfortable.

If heat-retaining materials are not used, the ambient room temperature tends to become very unpleasant. Provided that the thermal insulation is adequate, a solar house will then become overheated. Because of its gradual intake and release of heat energy, thermal mass also serves to moderate fluctuations in tempera-ture and helps make a room cooler and more pleasant during the summer. At night the air entering through the open windows cools the surfaces, removing the stored heat and restoring the capacity to remove heat from the building during the day. This is one reason why buildings in southern Europe are predominantly built out of thick, heavy stone, and you seldom see a building constructed of wood.

The disadvantage of natural stone floor tiles or other types of ceramic tile flooring is their high thermal conductivity. This explains why they feel cool to bare feet, even if the room itself is warm. Ordinarily, such floors are laid in combination with an underfloor heating system.

People who like to walk around barefoot or who pre-fer wood, carpeted or cork floors should construct their house so that the heat is stored in the walls or ceilings. It would make no sense to build a solar house entirely from wood, because wood doesn't store heat efficiently. The house should be con-structed from stone combined with other suitable materials. The half-timbered house, as historically constructed, is ideal, and the basic materials can be combined with clay. Alternatively, a light and solid construction can be used together, for example by constructing a light wood outer envelope and having a solidly built interior. The advantages and disadvan-tages of the various construction methods will be discussed later.

Exposed stonework

Natural stone interior walls, left exposed and uncovered, suit some surroundings and add a sense of luxury. This type of wall is ideal for internal walls, but if used as an outer wall heat loss can be a problem. Materials which are good thermal storage mediums unfortunately tend to be poor insulators.

Thermal mass evens out temperature swings

Harnessing solar energy

Tracking the sun

Arch.: Terhorst & Terhorst, Rheine, Germany
This solar house actually revolves so that its open side always faces or "tracks" the sun. Solar collectors provide a major proportion of its energy.

A solar house can also use active or high-tech approaches even if it has not been designed as a passive solar house. However, using solar energy passively always makes better economic sense than employing various high-tech active solar strategies. First, however, it is essential to understand the difference between thermal active solar energy systems (known as collectors) which generate heat, and photovoltaic solar energy systems (known as modules or arrays) which generate electricity.

The technical problems once associated with heating hot water by means of solar collectors are now a thing of the past. These devices have been refined until today they are very nearly faultless and require little maintenance. Moreover, they are so inexpensive that the solar energy harnessed will soon pay for itself in reduced utility cost, especially if subsidies are available from government programs or utilities. A solar energy system consisting of collectors with an area of between 55 and 80 square feet (5 and 7 square meters) would typically provide approximately 65% of the hot water requirements for a family of four. The annual savings on heating costs could run into hundreds of dollars or pounds as the case may be.

The big snag, of course, is that solar energy is not really an economically sound proposition for heating a detached house. The reason is quite simple: When the sun is providing most of the heat, actual requirements are at their lowest. What would be required is a storage medium with an enormous capacity of at the very least 70 cubic feet in order to accumulate sufficient heat from the sun during the winter months. The cost of such a system would be almost prohibitive, even if one took into account only the cost of the additional space required. In fact, a storage system of this size would be viable only if it served an entire housing development and used newer concentrating high-temperature collector systems.

On every roof

Solar collectors can fit almost any roof, provided that the times when the roof is shaded are minimized. In most cases they can be fitted to a house that is already built.

Electricity for this house in Cologne, Germany comes from photovoltaic collectors

Arch.: Böttger Architekten, Cologne

Solar collectors that harness electricity from sunlight are called photovoltaic collectors. They operate quite differently from thermal solar collectors, which convert solar energy into heat. At present, however, they are not an economical alternative. This group of collectors in Cologne won a special prize in 1996 for the best photovoltaic system. It consists of 16 modules with an output of 1,100 kWh a year. This amount covers one tenth of the annual electricity used in the architect's office (an area of approximately 2,750 square feet or 250 square meters). Systems such as this are very expensive at present, but future mass production and improvement in technology could reduce the price considerably.

In addition to the widely used hot water storage systems there are also air collectors. Air is a relatively poor thermal conductor, but is easily transported when hot. There are collectors that can be fixed to the side or roof of a house. The air that is heated is transferred from them through conduits into the floors, and heats up way similar to the ancient Roman hypocaust. But the problem of heat storage is an even more insurmountable one in this case.

Using photovoltaic modules for converting and storing energy from the sun is a different proposition altogether. The energy stored in such a system in the form of direct current (DC) electricity is stored in batteries so that it can be utilized effectively throughout the year for various home energy requirements, but capturing the solar power is not very economical. With a collector of around 200 square feet on the roof it should be possible to generate enough solar power to meet up to half (about 2 kilowatts) of the electrical requirements of a family of four. But such a system would cost about $15,000 or about $7.50/watt for the complete system and would require over 25 years to pay for itself.

The situation is quite different when the local electrical utility decides to invest in distributed PV power generation in lieu of building new power plants or in order to build smaller power plants. An example of this is the Sacramento Municipal Utility District (SMUD), who installed residential PV systems totaling 640 kilowatts in 1993 at no cost to the customer as part of a multi-faceted distributed power strategy following the decommissioning of a nuclear power plant. Large-scale distributed power production certainly could solve the problem of expense to the individual consumer both by reducing the cost of delivering power and by reducing the system cost through higher production rates, but unless government funded R&D, technology transfer and subsidy programs are expanded little is likely to be achieved.

Thermal solar collector array in a garden

When the collectors cannot be placed on the roof for esthetic reasons or because the roof faces the wrong way, they can be set up in the garden, as has been done here in Bavaria.

Transparent thermal insulation

Turned toward the sun

*Arch.: M. Viktor-Ulmke, Construction:
S. D. Sonnenhaus, Ing. Gesellschaft,
Wettringen, Germany*
This zero-energy house is
designed as a four-sided polygon.
It faces due south, allowing both
heat and light to enter the building. The living area is on two
levels. The huge storage system
on the roof ensures that the heat
trapped in the collectors can be
released when needed.

**Solar energy means
independence**

Transparent thermal insulation combines solar energy
technology and passive solar strategies. This system
operates by fitting a collector on the building so that
the wall directly behind the insulation will be heated.
The most important structural elements are minute
capillaries made of acrylic glass (plexiglas or poly-
methylmethacrylate) or polycarbonate. Recent experiments have been carried out with cellulose as well.
Whatever the material, the solar radiation is efficiently
transmitted to a black facade. This enormous wall
mass heats up and gradually releases the heat into the
interior of the building.

Simultaneously, the fiberlike elements for the transparent thermal energy transfer medium provide an
insulating effect to ensure that as little heat as possible
can escape to the exterior of the building. The elements are protected on the outside by a pane of poly-
methylmethacrylate or glass, and a sunshade (a white
roller blind) keeps the heat out in summer. At present,
scientists are trying to develop a sunshade that will
automatically change color when the outside temperature increases so that the mechanically operated blind
will no longer be necessary.

There is a great deal to be gained from this system. In a
multiple dwelling erected in Freiburg, Germany it has
been possible to save more than 22% of the energy
required during the period in which the building has to
be heated than would be possible in a building with
conventional thermal insulation. By replacing the normally used capillary tubes with acrylic glass bubbles
many companies have made the transparent thermal
insulation system less expensive than before. But
although prices have fallen overall, this system still
cannot be regarded as truly economical.

There are two further problems with transparent thermal insulation: The insulation has to be shaded in
some way during periods when heating is not
required, and an efficient control system needs to be
developed. Transparent thermal insulation is a more
economical proposition where an older building has
to be brought up to date, but cannot have any windows fitted to the south-facing side, or where an office
building has a completely glazed façade, in which
case it can be used in the spandrel panels.

In the case of private dwellings the question of exterior esthetics and compatibility with a given architectural style must also be considered. The smooth,
somewhat "clinical" outer surface may not be in
keeping with the surrounding buildings, and it may
even contradict building regulations.

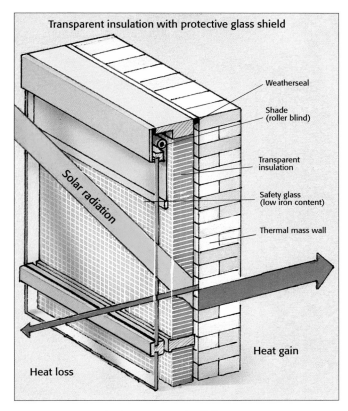

Transparent insulation with protective glass shield

Solar radiation

Weatherseal

Shade (roller blind)

Transparent insulation

Safety glass (low iron content)

Thermal mass wall

Heat gain

Heat loss

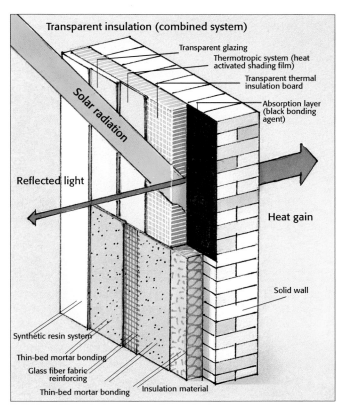

Transparent insulation (combined system)

Solar radiation

Transparent glazing

Thermotropic system (heat activated shading film)

Transparent thermal insulation board

Absorption layer (black bonding agent)

Reflected light

Heat gain

Solid wall

Synthetic resin system

Thin-bed mortar bonding

Glass fiber fabric reinforcing

Thin-bed mortar bonding

Insulation material

Zero-energy and plus-energy buildings

A passive house heated with solar energy that generates its own electricity by means of modules or from other renewable sources of energy so that no external energy source is required is called a zero-energy house. Such buildings derive no energy whatsoever from the burning of fossil fuels or from nuclear power plants. It is, however, perfectly acceptable for a passively heated house with any type of renewable energy power source to feed excess energy at various times into the grid and then to draw on it again when needed, always provided that this "account" is not "in the red." By contrast there are plus-energy houses which generate more energy than they use throughout the year. This has been accomplished by using highly efficient thermal insulation, a considerable amount of passive solar energy and a carefully planned layout of rooms. A solar collector measuring

approximately 350 square feet (31.5 square meters) for domestic hot water and a photovoltaic system of about 420 square feet (38.6 square meters) are sufficient to meet four-fifths of the building's energy requirements, and so only 1.1 kWh/square foot (11 kWh/square meter) of extra energy from alternative sources is required. In Old Snowmass, Colorado energy experts Hunter and Amory Lovins built a passively heated, superinsulated and partially earth-sheltered home. This building which also houses the research center for the Rocky Mountain Institute gets 99% of its space and water heating needs from passive and active solar systems and it receives 95% of its daytime electrical energy from PV systems. It uses less than one tenth the normal amount of electricity and less than one half the usual amount of water for a building its size.

Transparent thermal insulation

These diagrams show two different approaches to utilizing the heat of the sun to the best possible effect. On the left is the more complex system with glazing and a sunshade for summer. The system on the right has been integrated into a conventional thermal insulation system. Shading is not required and the heat intake is via the difference in the reflection of the sun's rays during the summer. Future developments will include some kind of heat-sensitive reflecting layer.

A self-sufficient house

Development: Fraunhofer Institut für Solare Energiesysteme ISE, Freiburg, Germany
This house in Freiburg can produce all the energy it requires without recourse to other sources. All forms of solar energy collection have been combined in a radical way to show what might be achieved. The orientation of the house is perfect, there are both thermal and photovoltaic collectors, transparent thermal insulation has been installed, and there is even a solar hydrogen plant to provide fuel for the cooktop and there are fuel cells for the remaining energy requirements.

BUILDINGS TO STAND THE TEST OF TIME

Restoration is good for the environment

Bulldozers are a thing of the past. Today the main aim of the urban planner is to retain town centers with all the history they have to tell. But their intention is not solely motivated by a fervent belief in ecological principles: They also want to avoid, above all, anything that might tear out the heart of the community. But it is not only the picture-postcard half-timbered houses or the buildings of historic worth that should be saved. Many of the housing projects and buildings erected during the early post-war years that, at first glance, look as though they should be razed to the ground, can be adapted to today's standards and made attractive. This approach is ecologically friendly and saves precious natural resources, and is preferable to demolition and erecting completely new buildings. If it is impossible to avoid demolishing older buildings, such demolition should be carefully organized and planned so that the undamaged parts of the structure can be preserved and reused. As a matter of principle one should keep in mind that any process of redevelopment should avoid any building's unnecessary alterations or damage to the underlying structure and fabric of the building, because this will inevitably increase redevelopment costs quite substantially.

The dimensions and proportions of the old building should also be retained: Any form of reconstruction or renovation which takes only the future owner's interest into account will most probably compromise the esthetics of the building. For example, the small divided windows typical of half-timbered houses and their folding shutters are critical to maintaining the integrity of that particular style of building. Should a new owner, seeking perhaps to let in more light, tear out and replace them with large windows with undivided panes of glass, this would completely change the look of the house, destroying the historical character. Though they may not provide as much natural light, these "old-fashioned" windows are critical elements to preserve, and will look far more acceptable than an enormous pane of glass. The old front door, the wrought iron fittings, the hand-carved staircase and all the other details should be retained as far as possible as well. Such things are far too valuable in an historic and esthetic sense, and there are few skilled craftsmen left to reproduce such works of art. There are a great many examples showing how little care and thought has gone into redevelopment. Part of the reason for this could be the shortage of skilled craftsmen, but another reason is the total disregard for the elementary principles involved when thermal insulation is improperly installed into an old building. It is apparent that many of the firms engaged in redeveloping and renovating have not been made fully aware of the need to save energy and to avoid moisture problems where none have previously existed. According to report on building damage published by

the German government the most serious building deficit (13%) is the incidence of dry rot after old single-paned windows have been replaced with double-glazed ones. Another common problem is that flat roofs that have been renovated tend to leak again very quickly (11%), the damage to sloping roofs, on the other hand, tends to be linked with the growing fashion for converting attics to living space (10%). There is also an increase in the conversion of basements into useful rooms of various kinds, and this has no doubt contributed to the high proportion of problematic alterations to those parts of the building which are in direct contact with the ground (9%). Again, it is improper installation of insulation, inadequate or improperly located air barriers, and inadequate damp proofing that are at fault. In nearly 8% of renovations, thermal insulation was not installed correctly.

Frequently, when problems surface, only the symptoms are addressed, and no attempt is undertaken to find the real cause of the damage to the building. It is for this reason that expert advice should be sought and no attempt be made to start repair work and improvements to the building without first drawing up a detailed plan which addresses potential moisture problems. The first step is to have a survey of the entire building completed, preferably by an architect or qualified surveyor specializing in the renovation of older buildings. The expert eye will immediately locate structural damage as well as dampness in the cellar or basement, or signs of damage from termites. The expert will know which walls can be moved and which ones must remain where they are, and he will be able to identify the parts of the building where energy is being lost or otherwise wasted. Finally, as-built drawings as well as a comprehensive repair and renovation plan can be drawn up. By following this approach, the owner of the house can reduce costs quite considerably by recognizing immediately where a professional will be imperative and where the skilled amateur might assist in the work.

Anyone living in an older house or apartment built prior to the 1940s is quite probably living in a reasonably healthy environment because up until that time predominantly natural building materials were used, and buildings usually did not suffer from indoor air quality problems because they were not at all airtight. An important exception to this, however, would be the widespread use of lead paint. Toward the end of the 1950s the era started when everything had to be labor-saving and low-maintenance. Thus, we saw the advent of insulating foam, mineral fibers, gloss paints and varnishes, plastic window frames – and, of course, all the attendant problems that are still with us. Restoration can very often be a boon for the environment in so far as the undesirable materials and qualities of a building can be removed.

A house with a history
Old houses frequently have many stories to tell. Their façades lend character to the surroundings. Yet it is not just their maintenance that is expensive; frequently they waste large amounts of energy or they may contain toxic substances dangerous to human health. This makes restoration more expensive. But the maintenance of the historical structure is worth the effort, as can be seen from this old building in Dortmund, Germany.

The condition of older buildings in the United States

The housing stock in the United States in total amounts to approximately 110 million units today, with 35% in multiple dwellings; 25% is more than fifty years old. About 10% or 11 million units of housing lie vacant; 68% are single-family buildings of some sort and 32% multiple unit. It is estimated that an investment of over $700 billion would be needed to renovate and repair the existing aging housing stock. The greatest need for expenditures in renovations are for buildings built after 1945 and before 1970. To house the "baby boom" huge volumes of housing were built at very low cost and often with inferior materials and sub-standard workmanship. In addition, these buildings were not subject to the 1972 National Fire Code which required multi-story buildings to be fitted with automatic fire protection systems, nor were they subject to modern energy codes. One other factor is the National Historic Preservation Act passed in the 1970s which established the National Register of Historic Sites and significant tax credits for investments in renovating buildings which were placed on the Register. When the tax credits were dropped in the late 1980s, the interest in historic preservation diminished greatly because meeting the demands of the Historic Preservation Requirements for maintaining the historic character of the buildings often added great expense. However, buildings which were built in the 1970s are also in need of substantial repairs. One reason is that many of the energy conservation methods employed at that time caused severe damage to the building envelope, or air quality problems which have resulted in the phenomenon known as Sick Building Syndrome. Significant problems also surfaced due to the use of new fenestration (window) systems especially in "curtainwall" building types.

Apart from the need for wide-ranging maintenance work the insulation of the buildings has to be improved. The generously proportioned and stuccoed town houses built at the turn of the century with thick external walls do in general conform to modern requirements. By contrast the houses erected in the 1920s had far thinner walls. Even though concrete was being used more and more in the construction of cellars, adequate damp proofing tended to be the exception rather than the rule. Post-war buildings erected in the 1950s have, in the main, extremely thin external walls well below the norms for thermal insulation and soundproofing. On buildings erected in the 1960s and the 1970s damage to concrete occurs more frequently, mainly as a result of poor-quality reinforcement, and there are also problems with moisture and with heat bridges on balconies. Buildings erected during the next two decades now have problems with prefabricated concrete elements and the incorrect fitting of what were at that time completely new insulation systems, all resulting in serious structural damage.

Older buildings are often in need of substantial repairs

A reflection of the times
War, destruction and crises are mirrored in the age of the buildings; but we can also read the reconstruction and economic prosperity in the buildings around us.

PROPORTION OF HOUSING ACCORDING TO PERIOD OF COMPLETION (AS OF 1990)

	Before 1918	1918–45	1946–70	After 1970
Europe	26	19	39	16
Belgium	33	21	37	8
DK	24	19	32	25
Germany	27	23	37	13
Spain	-	14	42	44
France	40	11	37	12
Italy	25	26	46	3
Netherlands	29	12	42	16
UK	27	19	32	22
United States	NA	19*	39	40

*Before 1945
Source: eurostat, 1990 United States Census Data

The magnificent 1920s

At the beginning of the century buildings were really solidly built, as can be seen from this garden estate in the Ruhr area. Cheaper and lesser quality construction did start in the 1920s, but most buildings erected during this period at least were given massive walls and, in general, architecture perfectly suited to its surroundings. But basements of such buildings are, almost without exception, damp. Renovation tends to concentrate primarily on the plumbing, the windows, attic improvements, and roof insulation.

A shortage of housing

Most of the housing in Germany was erected after the war. It was above all in the 1950s that poor-quality materials were utilized. Walls were too thin and so houses built during this period wasted a great deal of energy. The most important repair work, however, is the installation of better insulation for the external walls and the roof.

More money than good sense

The 1960s enjoyed the emergence of an economic boom, and, in Germany, more and more people fulfilled their dream of owning a bungalow. Yet the style of building so admired while on vacation abroad was hardly suited to central Europe: A flat roof would soon start to leak and let in cold draught, the walls were far too flimsy, and the huge windows squandered a lot of energy. The wonderful new and impressive-looking home soon became a white elephant.

The solution depends on the type of construction

The use of prefabricated concrete was popular in the 1970s because buildings could be built more quickly and cheaply. But the concrete was often poorly reinforced, and sealants made with toxic substances were typically used in the expansion joints between the concrete sections. More and more use was made of hazardous materials such as asbestos fireproofing and insulation. There were also heat bridges causing energy loss and moisture problems in many of the buildings. All of these factors contributed to serious problems in this type of housing.

Refurbishing historical buildings and half-timbered houses

Historical buildings need special care

In Germany, there are approximately two million buildings under a preservation order according to German government estimates. This figure includes sculptures and ruins, and the actual number of such buildings is more likely to be between one million and one and a half million. 40% of these buildings of architectural importance located in the old Federal states and 90% of them in eastern Germany are in chronic need of repair. The number of half-timbered buildings is estimated to be two million, and of these 79% were built before 1870. Only 3% of them were erected after 1919. There are no half-timbered

applying multiple layers of plaster and various different types of coatings over the woodwork. Another improper solution is to simply fill and grout the cracks and joints between the woodwork and the plaster with silicone. In many cases, the thermal insulation is also installed incorrectly, which makes the problem worse. Behind any façade that has been improperly insulated and the exterior skin sealed in some way, wood rot is inevitable.

Half-timbered buildings and those under a preservation order have one feature in common: Whatever is done to improve the building and to repair it must

The sheer beauty of half-timbering

Half-timbered houses such as these in Minden are not so difficult to restore, because they are erected in separate units. Nonetheless, great skill and considerable knowledge of building traditions are essential. The insulation and façade restoration are particularly difficult and painstaking. But insulation of this type is very expensive. Recently a triple-layer thermal insulation material made of wood fiber boards has been developed and it has been found that it is highly efficient at retaining moisture inside the insulation and releasing it inwards. Such material has been found to be ideal for half-timbered buildings.

houses in the United States but a number of timber-frame structures (similar to half-timber but with the structure built completely interior to the exterior cladding, usually of wood boards) built from 1636 up to the late 1800s exist. According to government statistics, the average life span of a conventionally built stud house is about 75 years, whereas the life span of a timber-frame house is at least 300 years.

Damage to half-timbered and timber-frame houses is due mainly to a lack of maintenance or improper care of the substance of the building and to so-called "experiments" with modern materials and methods. For example, a frequent mistake is the attempt to weather-proof a façade by means of resurfacing and

Bad workmanship and ignorance can cause a lot of damage

not in any way have a detrimental effect on the physical appearance of the building. This in itself adds to the problems, particularly when thermal insulation has to be installed. External thermal insulation of any kind is virtually out of the question, because the façade with its decorative surface and exposed timbers would be hidden. There are now, it is true, all kinds of cornices, stucco work and façade moldings made of plastic and even, more recently, of recycled materials, which can be used to restore or rather to imitate the look of the original façade by application over the new layer of insulation. However, this approach does not really have much in common with the true principles of historical building preservation

and certainly not with ecological building. In such a situation all that can be done is to install insulation inside the building. It demands careful detailing and painstaking installation, however, or condensation could occur resulting in damage to the structure of the building and problems with mold and mildew inside the building. It is for this reason that biological building materials come into their own. They can frequently be used for internal insulation without installation of a moisture barrier. A moisture barrier is usually used to prevent entry of moisture from the exterior causing condensation somewhere in the wall cavity. In renovation projects, however, there is no general rule, and so the architect must search for the best solution for each individual case. Furthermore, it is almost impossible to install a totally impervious moisture barrier, because there are so many gaps in the joists and floors of a half-timbered building. If the timbers are to be repaired, it is advisable to adhere to the local traditions and use either clay filling or small bricks. The addition of the internal insulation material must cover the timbers preventing a thermal bridge. The best answer might well be to use a mixture of straw and clay, of which one of the most useful properties is its ability to absorb moisture and to release it: It has the added advantage that it does not clash with the wood. A further method is to nail light insulating boards made of wood-wool or wood fiber onto lath-work and then to pack the spaces with mortar, taking care to ensure that a capillary connection will still remain to the outside allowing moisture to escape. A firm in Celle, Germany specializes in insulation for half-timbered buildings and has developed a material consisting of clay, straw, cork, and diatomite. This mixture can be sprayed in thin layers or molded into thicker strips and compressed behind the timbering. Within three weeks the mixture is as solid as a rock. The material has the same properties of absorption and diffusion as the existing clay or brick, and can, for this reason, lie directly on the surface that is to be insulated without a moisture barrier. Determining which method is finally chosen will depend on the particular building and has to be thoroughly reviewed by the architect. If the interior of the building is generously proportioned without a large number of separate rooms, having numerous openings and galleries, ventilation will be more efficient and less moisture will penetrate and therefore damage the walls and the structure of the building.

Decorative façades

The façades of this house erected in Münster in the 1870s are the work of a genuine artist and they cannot possibly be insulated from the outside. Even insulation on the inside could have disastrous consequences if not executed with expert knowledge and skill.

The right method of insulation has to be considered carefully

There are probably two million half-timbered buildings in Germany, all bearing witness to a long tradition of craftsmanship. The house shown here with its magnificent gable is to be seen in Schieder-Schwalenberg. But because no more half-timbered buildings have been erected for many years, there is hardly anyone with the skills and experience to ensure upkeep. It is for this reason that irreparable damage can be done to buildings of this type; less work will have a disastrous effect on its entire structure including the interior.

retain the walls. Once the beams have been sawn through, for example to build a staircase, the entire structure of the building could change shape considerably and be undermined. The same would happen if diagonal struts were removed: Their purpose is to stabilize the frame construction consisting of timber pillars and beams. The struts are often sawn through out of ignorance in order to fit larger windows. In addition, it is very important to heed the warnings against removing old filling material entirely from the timber, as is all too frequently recommended. Over the passage of time the filling has taken over a load-bearing function, and if it were to be removed, the beams would very likely give way under the weight that they alone have to bear as a result. It is likely that the building would then break apart. Once the new timbers have come to rest, it is probable that the newly installed stonework will no longer fit properly.

In fact, modern concrete blocks should never be placed between the wooden beams. This particular material is, no doubt, an excellent insulator and can easily be cut to the correct shape. But aerated concrete absorbs water, unless it is completely protected even from a driving rain. This is extremely difficult to do, because there are so many gaps between the beams. The water is transported to the edges of the beams, which then start to rot. The best solution is to use stones for the backfilling. A thinner second wall of aerated concrete behind the thin frame wall will not ruin the wall's appearance, nor will it cause any problems with the building's equilibrium. Again, there must be a mortar layer between the external wall and the backfilling, or, alternatively, adequate ventilation of the entire building façade so that any condensation might dissipate. The unfortunate truth is that most attempts to restore a half-timbered building are disastrous. Instead of seasoned oak timbers new softwoods are very often used. They are usually not given a chance to dry out properly and will continue to contract and warp, thus causing cracks and subsidence. Sometimes there are even cases of rotting and diseased woodwork being covered over with boards and paint without any effort to find and remove the cause. Measures such as these merely create the illusion of stability in the building, and sooner or later such superficial and careless work will have a disastrous effect on the entire structure. And it is by no means just the interior insulation that needs the utmost care and expert planning: The incorrect external insulation

The most common mistakes while repairing a half-timbered building

While repairs and improvements are being carried out, what is often overlooked is that the interior walls in a half-timbered building also serve structural and load-bearing functions, even though the timbers themselves have a relatively small cross-section. If walls are removed to "modernize" the interior or to combine several rooms into one, the beams may start to sag or the walls to buckle, because the timbering has started to move. What is also frequently overlooked is that the function of the wall-to-wall beams is to stiffen and

Skilled craftsmanship is essential

of a half-timbered building can do irreparable damage as well. If the easy way out is taken by covering the façades with cladding or plastic bricks, the woodwork will simply disintegrate.

In Germany people were frowned on for many years if they did not live in a "real" brick house. Even as early as in the Biedermeier period there were types of cladding that imitated stonework. After the Second World War damaged half-timbers would very often disappear behind thick layers of cement facing: It is, therefore, hardly surprising that the primary timbers and the supporting columns would start to rot within a few years. This resulted from the application of materials such as imitation tiles and asbestos cement boards, if they were applied to the original façade without any ventilation. The moisture remains on the wall, the wood rots and will be eaten away by wood ticks and borers. Builders' merchants, too, sell a wide range of materials manufactured explicitly, so it seems, with the intention of simplifying the process of disfiguring any building of historical or architectural importance that might be in need of repair. Just some examples of pseudo-historical kitsch now available are imitation window muntin bars, bull's eye glass usually placed where they do not belong, cast aluminum and fiberglass doors made to look like real wood, faux copper guttering and lamps with scroll mountings. It is quite evident, therefore, that we need to be reminded of the value of skilled craftsmen. A great many architects and civil engineers have never learned that conservation and building are inseparable, and so it is essential to seek advice from experts who have the necessary experience and knowledge.

Healthy surroundings

Buildings of clay, such as this half-timbered house, can be very healthy to live in. At the same time a house like this is the embodiment of the best traditions of sustainability, because it has been constructed using local natural and renewable materials. For this reason expert restoration is certainly worthwhile.

Following the traditional methods

It is the responsibility of certain young craftsmen today to gain the necessary skill and knowledge to ensure the preservation of the ancient art of building half-timbered houses so that it is not lost. The walls of this house in Kescheid are being repaired with a mixture of clay and straw, as was the tradition when the house was originally erected.

Applying straw to a timber frame

Straw matting is an excellent means of insulation and a base for plasterwork. But walls of this type rarely meet with today's requirements as far as adequate insulation is concerned.

Best obtained on site

Clay suitable for house building is often to be found on the site itself. But if the excavated material is unsuitable, there are always companies specializing in the various earth materials.

A romantic street corner
These houses in Minden (above) and in Hattingen (left) have a particular charm and are an expression of romantic traditions in Germany. Tourists find them particularly appealing.

Kitsch and false economy

It is an unfortunate fact that there are too many examples like this one of how not to restore old buildings. The old wagon wheels are merely kitsch and the windows (below) are in very bad taste in that they are historically out of place as is the gallery in the renovated barn structure in the background. The façade cladding is not only an example of lack of taste but of false economy as well (right): The work has not been done expertly and the timbering beneath the cladding will be seriously damaged, ultimately causing considerable expense to correct the problem.

Remediation of moisture problems

Damage caused by moisture is a serious and recurring problem in older buildings. Leaky roofs, poor roof drainage, wall cracks and bad insulation all can allow unwanted moisture to gain access. Problems can also be caused by moisture saturation. This can occur in the foundation or basement walls and any walls in direct contact with the ground. Renovation and repairs are likely to be exceedingly difficult and expensive. Walls can absorb as much moisture from the subsoil as they do rain or ground water. Even the smallest capillary in a wall will transport water upwards and cause damage to the ends of wood rafters or beams embedded in or bearing on the wall. Over the years, the footings of buildings have been protected from moisture by various means. From around the turn of the century up until the present

made to the cellar, and damp-proofing plaster to be applied to the outside surfaces of the walls, or new, tightly closing windows fitted, the evaporation process would be stopped and the resulting accumulation of moisture would start to do its damage. Enormous stains would then appear on the walls indicating the extent of moisture penetration. At this point the only cure is to excavate the entire perimeter of the building and undertake measures to damp-proof the walls from the outside. Of course any structural damage already done would have to be repaired. The most suitable material for accomplishing this, despite its limitations, is cement grout. Other materials which can be used include a variety of bitumen-based damp-proofing products which are painted on, or a variety of plastic or bitumen membranes usually referred to as a water stop and a material called bentonite which chemically reacts with water and seals any cracks when exposed to it. None of these materials is ecologically acceptable, but they are better able to accommodate movement of older stone or brick foundation walls than cement grout, which becomes brittle and will lose its integrity once the wall settles or shifts to any degree. At the same time it is advisable to attend to the thermal insulation in this part of the building by improving the perimeter insulation. Suitable materials in this case include expanded glass, a waterproof insulating material manufactured from recycled glass fixed to the building with bitumen, or rigid fiberglass sheet insulation both of which do not lose their insulating properties when saturated, as batt or open cell foam insulation would do. Once the excavation has been completed, a layer consisting of ballast or gravel is required for drainage and to prevent water collecting close to the walls. There are also new drainage membranes which are made of EPDM rubber or PVC (not recommended for ecological reasons) which are designed specifically for this purpose. The rate of absorption or seepage through a wall is proportionate to the force of hydrostatic pressure, which can be extremely great unless there is good continuous vertical drainage at the face of the wall to alleviate it.

In order to insulate and thus protect the basement floor and the foundation walls against rising moisture, the walls must be lifted up meter by meter or horizontal sawcuts made above the affected area. A metal or plastic water stop membrane, or a bitumen layer must then be inserted into these narrow gaps. If the gaps in the walls are fairly sizable it is safer to use special machinery to insert high-quality steel sheets. The alternative to the lengthy and expensive method of splitting the walls is to use the injection method. Special chemicals, or sometimes paraffin oils, are injected through carefully drilled holes in the walls so that the capillaries are filled, thus forming a zone into which water will be unable to penetrate. This method is not known to be harmful to health or to the

Damp-proofing a cellar

Moisture rising from the subsoil presents a danger to a great many buildings. Unless measures are undertaken to stop rising moisture, the walls will probably weaken and rot. Water from the surrounding soil makes the cellar damp. If this room is to be used for anything other than storing provisions, drainage is essential as well as insulation of the exterior cellar walls (perimeter insulation).

time it has been common to apply a portland cement plaster facing called parging to protect wall surfaces. Historically, cellar floors were left unprotected from subsurface water, and as a result moisture did penetrate the building which was the best way for people to store their provisions. The moisture was prevented from spreading upwards into other parts of the building by constructing high wall bases (sometimes called a watertable) so that the floor joists would be well above the level of the topsoil. In this way there would be enough room for moisture to evaporate, particularly as the cellar would be continually ventilated by the unglazed windows. Later, it became the practice to apply damp-proofing onto many walls, normally of roofing felt, or sheets made of lead or tiles. The cellar floor, however, still remained damp. If building improvements of some kind were later

environment, but some experts still doubt whether it can be effective. In addition, it will not work with uneven or extremely damp stone masonry. Damp-proofing from inside, for example by means of a specially formulated wet-use plaster, will make the wall look dry, but the moisture will nevertheless continue to rise in the wall until it finds a surface on which it can evaporate. The moisture will ultimately end up precisely where it is least wanted.

Problems with 1950s buildings

Environmentally harmful and unhealthy materials such as polystyrene foam and mineral fibers have been used pervasively for insulation. Today environmentally benign materials such as cellulose from wood by-products and recycled paper, and other renewable materials such as reeds or cork can be used for this purpose. When it is not necessary to preserve the existing building façade which is inadequately insulated in its original form, it is possible to build a new façade in front of the original. As little as four and a half inches of added insulation will attain a u-value of 0.05 (k-value of 0.30) or less for the walls — a completely acceptable heat-loss coefficient for a rehabilitated older building.

A recurring problem with post-war buildings is the water leakage through the built-up roofing typically used on a flat roof. It is now considered preferable to erect a conventional sloped roof on top of the old roof structure including the desired amount of added

insulation, instead of trying to repair the existing roof. But this is extremely expensive and may not be feasible due to structural limitations. Problems may also arise if the entire estate consists of houses with flat roofs: The new roof might infringe on the other buildings' access to natural light or it might simply look out of place. For these reasons a better solution may actually be to grass over the roof. A specially developed drainage membrane needs to be laid down before laying the grass which resolves any water leakage problems previously present. The membrane itself is shielded from damage caused by ultraviolet (UV) radiation by the natural vegetation which also insulates and keeps the building cooler during the summer by reflecting most of the light and heat from the sun. The green roof will also contribute considerably to the local micro-environment by converting CO_2, manufacturing oxygen, reducing runoff and reducing the ambient local temperature in areas with lots of paved surfaces. Depending on the climate, there may be a requirement for a thicker layer of growing medium (lightweight soil) to protect the grass planted. It is also important to have the design reviewed for structural soundness before going ahead with a green roof project. A recently completed corporate eco-office building for The Gap in San Bruno, California was given an undulating green roof evoking the surrounding landscape. The green roof feature was estimated to reduce the building's annual operating and energy costs by $28,000 and will pay for itself in eleven years.

Green roofs restore natural vegetation to our cities

Boldness in design pays off
The frontage of this low-energy house before and after its renovation: All that shows externally that the old building has been improved quite drastically is the newly designed stairwell. The old house stands in a part of the city which contains several large residences and its outer wall, cellar and roof were treated with thick insulating material. A new ventilation system complete with heat recovery was also installed. As can be seen, there are huge windows glazed with heat-absorbing glass letting in even more light than before.

More light

This is the same house from the garden which opens out even more to the sun. Very few alterations were necessary to create a totally different impression of the building. The attic gable has a bigger area of glass than before. The old balcony was an enormous heat bridge and was removed completely and replaced by a freestanding extension to provide extra space for sitting in the open. The solar collector on the roof is a good advertisement for a sensible approach to sourcing energy.

A better use for gables

In nearly all older buildings there is almost certainly space beneath the gables which could be put to better use. This means the house can offer more accommodation without the need for more land. The sloping walls do not always convey a feeling of being confined, provided that there is enough light. But there are several important rules to follow when a roof extension is being carried out. In particular, special attention must be paid to the structure of the building, access and roof insulation.

House on a house

Arch.: A. Mense, B. Bürger, Basta Baubüro, Dortmund, Germany
The height of this building has not been altered, but nevertheless an entire apartment has been constructed in the roof, with space for a small family.

Windproofing is very important.

Arch.: A. Mense, B. Bürger, Basta Baubüro, Dortmund, Germany
This house in Bochum, Germany (opposite) shows very clearly the work involved in building a roof extension; the floor will have to be re-laid with special attention paid to soundproofing. When larger roof windows are to be installed, framing the new openings will have to be dealt with as well. Among other tasks, increased insulation will have to be laid between the rafters. Most important of all is proper sealing and windproofing, which is the function of the coated kraft paper. The last step is to lay battens over the sealed insulating layer for attachment of the interior cladding panels made of plaster board or wood.

Roof conversion

The easiest way to gain more space in a house without making structural alterations is to convert an attic or any other unused space in the space just below the roof structure. On the face of it, this seems quite simple, and so is frequently tackled without expert advice or help. Basically, there is no reason why you should not go at it alone, provided you stick to a few basic rules. First, it is important to check that the roof structure is sound, whether there has been any water damage to the wood members, and whether there are any infestations of pests. If rafters are in need of repair, it is worth remembering from the outset that they are not likely to be deep enough for modern insulating materials. For this reason the boards for reinforcing them should be longer and wider than the rafters themselves; another approach is to enlarge the rafters with lathing.

It is difficult to make a roof really watertight unless it is first completely stripped so that the battens can be removed. Undamaged roof tiles should be set aside for use on the new roof. Next, foil-backed plaster board with the lowest possible resistance to vapor diffusion, or impregnated wood fiber boarding must be fixed over the rafters so that the roof will be effectively protected against driving rain and snow. It is wise to lay this sheathing between the rafters before the roof is replaced, even though it will involve far more work. Next, the tiled roof can be replaced, vented with laths on the outside, and the insulating material put into position on the inside between the rafters.

It is vital to ensure that this part of the building is absolutely windproof without interfering in any way with the diffusion of water vapor. The best way of tackling this is to install a wind stop made of kraft paper or sheeting made of some kind of breathable material. It has to be laid very carefully and fixed with adhesive to the places where it joins the gable end wall, the floor and the jamb wall, as well as to all openings such as the roof windows, chimney, ventilating ducts and aerial so that the gaps are completely sealed. One has to keep in mind that the windproofing will not be very efficient if it has to be broken for wiring, heating pipes and other connections.

A second conduit for these features should run between the windproofing and the inside of the outside wall: The best materials for this would be gypsum plaster board or fibrous plaster sheet or wood. This conduit can also be filled with insulating material. The advantage of this procedure is that if all the voids are filled with insulation there will be no air spaces where condensation can occur.

The lighting used in the new rooms under the roof must be adequate. If roof windows are to be installed, the glass should have an area of at least 25% of the total of the room area subtracted from the total area of the roof on account of the sloping roof. Another method of calculating the minimum glass area is to set it at no less than one-eighth of the total area of the space. More recently, larger roof windows have become available which can be extended to form a small roof balcony. Yet another alternative for admitting light and ventilation is the addition of roof dormers, but the disadvantage of them is that they may need some planning or design approvals. They are also more expensive, and involve more work. A tradesperson will probably also be needed to carefully seal the transitions between the dormers and the roof on the outside of the building.

A stairway can add excitement

Arch.: B. Heidbrede, Schwerte, Germany

In most cases, a new staircase will have to be part of an extension to the roof, because the old steps were far too narrow and steep. This photo shows how modern materials can be used effectively to provide a solution that blends in well with the surroundings and allows more light into the new room.

Spacious and open

Arch.: B. Heidbrede, Schwerte, Germany

The photographs show how an attic has successfully been converted and carefully integrated into an existing dwelling. The split-level design enhances the alterations still further. This renovation proves that improvements to an older building do not necessarily involve drastic structural changes. The main beam resting on slim metal columns supports the roof, and together with the newly constructed balcony creates more space in what was a small room. The large expanses of glass let generous amounts of light into the room.

Arch.: B. Heidbrede, Schwerte, Germany

Amazing old barn door

Dealers in antique fittings stock a wide range of parts from old buildings. A new house can be fitted with a beautiful old door to give it more character.

Still useful somewhere

These old windows can still be put to good use. They can serve as combination windows, or as box-type windows, or they could be used for an unheated conservatory, shed or summer house.

Historical building materials

For many centuries it was taken for granted that any new building being constructed should make use of materials salvaged from the demolition or destruction of older buildings. It was not until fairly recently that this form of recycling fell out of fashion. But there is now a gradual return to traditional ideas, prompted by both ecological and economic motives, as well as by the realization that the character of a building can be enhanced or restored to what it once was.

Landfills are becoming full and new locations are difficult to establish, especially near an urban area. Environmental costs of maintaining these sites is skyrocketing and therefore the costs to the consumer for refuse collection and disposal is growing at a rapid rate. In the United States most construction debris must be taken to designated landfills and higher tipping fees may apply. For this reason more and more contractors are beginning to sort and recycle the debris from building and demolition projects. In addition, companies to buy and sell the recycled materials are springing up all over. These companies generally restrict themselves to sorting wood, metals, plastics and minerals, which are then pulverized and treated and redirected to an end user.

In some areas pulverized bricks and powdered concrete have started to replace gravel as material for road foundations. Another reason for this change is that high-quality gravel has become more and more expensive. Wood doors, windows and beams are frequently ground up in a "wood hog" and turned into hardboard while metals are melted down. Doing so wastes a significant amount of the inherent value of many older building components which still have useful life left in them. Recycling structural elements such as old roof tiles, oak beams, doors, windows and flooring was for a long time something that only interested the do-it-yourself enthusiast. But over the last few years more and more firms have started to specialize in salvaging and reselling specific structural elements and fixtures or even in reconstructing entire buildings for reuse.

Intricately carved old doors, beautifully made box bay windows with forged brass handles, antique wall tiles and glazed terracotta floors, iron shutter fastenings and delicately carved staircases, sandstone moldings and beams, are all valuable testimony to the skills of craftsmen as well as of great historical and architectural value. They can all add a great deal to the appearance of almost any compatible building and are essential if a property is to be properly restored to its former glory. In the United States, every community of any size has its building salvage yards and one or two architectural antique stores packed with old fireplace mantels, wood columns, terracotta relief panels, cornices, arch window sashes, leaded glass panels, marble wainscot, etc. which can still serve their purpose.

From the first guidebook on recycling of building materials, GREBE, recycling of old building parts has become a ubiquitous if not mainstream business. It is not a lucrative activity for contractors on tight commercial construction budgets or schedules, so the movement is basically fueled by the small scale entrepreneur who specializes in rehabilitating older residential and multi-family buildings or the skilled do-it-youselfer working on his or her "This Old (Dream) House" renovation.

On the other hand, building codes make no allowances for putting these used materials back into service nor do they exclude such practices. The building must meet codes whether built of new or old materials, and one is expected to know what can or cannot "fly" with the local building inspector. A good example of a reused component which will not meet modern day codes is an older balcony railing which might typically have been constructed at a 2–3 foot height and with openings greater than the smaller than 6 inches requirement of today's codes regarding railings. If the railing happens to be a Chippendale style railing on an exterior balcony, adding the additional six inches of height will destroy the classical design quality and therefore render the railing useless for its original application. It can be used, for example, on a roof edge, where there will be no occupancy and there is no requirement for a railing but where an architecturally decorative railing will satisfy the classical design intent.

The historical value of true craftsmanship

Door hardware, locks and handles from old buildings and even the beautifully finished doors of an old country house can be used in a new building or in one being returned to its former glory. Old roof tiles and carefully cleaned bricks can be used to repair an existing roof or wall or to construct new ones.

COST-EFFECTIVE BUILDING

Building with reused material

Construction: Blöcher Co., Lemgo, Germany

This former farmhouse was carefully dismantled and then re-erected near Lemgo, thus saving the new occupant a fortune in building materials.

It might sound strange, but the least important consideration when building an ecologically sound house is the initial cost of the enterprise. Usually projects of this kind are associated with higher costs. Yet in the long run, sticking to ecologically sound principles usually brings enormous savings.

The basic principle behind environmentally sound building is, above all, restraint in the use of all types of resources. A considerable amount of money can be saved in this way. When building plans are drawn up, it is important to concentrate on the most essential aspects of the house and leave out any unnecessary embellishments. After all, building according to ecological principles is not meant to be a pursuit for the wealthy, but an example of socially responsible behavior for everyone to follow.

Ecology is economical

The cost of the land may take up 50% of the cost of a new building, so it's important to keep this down. In the United States and Canada, prime locations near a large urban area can be priced at about $700,000 for a ¼ acre building site, and even the average building site in a municipality with schools and services can cost from $50,000 to over $100,000. Two of the basic rules of ecologically sound building are to reduce the amount of land needed to build a house and to place houses closer to each other. These measures not only reduce the impact of the buildings on the environment, but they have now become an economic necessity. Most people just cannot afford to buy big plots. One can easily see, therefore, that the law of supply and demand does have a remarkable effect on the environment: Whenever natural resources such as water, soil or air get too expensive the market begins to exert its regulatory force by compelling us to be more thrifty.

Costs can also be reduced greatly by saving space inside a house. Entrance halls, stairwells and similar features often take up about 20% of the entire floor area. These circulation areas can easily be eliminated if they are integrated into other spaces such as the shared living space used by all the occupants: The entrance hall, for example, could be a dining area, and the staircase to the upper story could be integrated into the living room. An open-plan kitchen flowing into the living/dining room eliminates the need for a partition wall and creates extra space. Open-plan houses bring considerable savings in terms of walls, doors, plaster or gypsum board, wallpaper and painting. Savings of this kind mean the house can be built on a smaller plot, and they often make it a much cozier place to live in.

If the plans for a house are drawn up to allow for subsequent additions or attic conversions, the homeowner will not end up paying as much later on for wall openings, reinforcement of the building's structure, complicated roof configurations or extensions of supply lines. If the finished space is not divided up physically into separate spaces for specific purposes, later conversions may actually become quite unnecessary since the space can then be put to different uses as needs change. A building that is designed and constructed simply and compactly is

Economy in ecological construction

Arch.: D. Grünecke, Herdecke, Germany

An development near Wetter, Germany completed in accordance with ecological principles. The terraced houses are an economical form of building, since the floorplan has been kept simple and the whole design keeps to the basics. The cost was $100/square foot.

not only going to consume far less energy, it will also be more economical to build.

For example, if a house is planned as an L-shaped building it will require 25% more perimeter wall area than a square one. The additional walls would cost about $11/square foot based on a national average of residential construction costs (Means Residential Cost Data, 1997), not including the added energy consumption required because of the additional thermal losses through these walls. A wall projection measuring just five feet would cost about $3,000 for a two-story house, and a bay window with an opening size of about 10×6 ft would cost at least another $3,000. The fewer corners a building has, and the fewer projections and breaks in its perimeter, the lower the building costs and the heating bills. There is also less likelihood of mistakes and subsequent structural or moisture problems as a result of a complicated design.

Building close together

Arch.: Büro Brucker, Stuttgart, Germany

The left photograph shows an example of ecological principles put to work in a city, where space is always at a premium. Money has been saved and environmental damage limited, because less building land is used.

A compact floorplan is important

From the very start of planning process it is wise to think about how to reduce costs. Sprawling houses with several wings will not only cost more, they will use more energy. Open floorplans with a minimum of permanent interior walls make a building more flexible to use and adapt in the future and it will save on building costs as well.

Economy of wood

Arch.: J. Gabriel, Oldenburg, Germany

These ecologically built wood sided slab-on-grade houses near Braunschweig, Germany – an example of cost-effective construction – were built at a cost of less than $125/square foot. One strategy which resulted in a great deal of the savings was the considerable amount of prefabrication of wall sections in the local millwork shops. In addition, all the homes share a central heating plant housed in the shed in the center of the photograph.

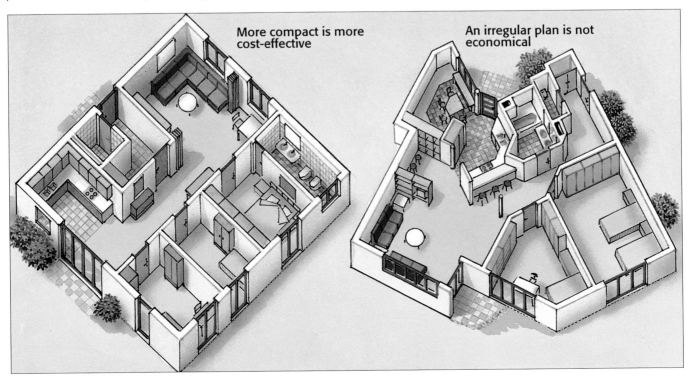

More compact is more cost-effective

An irregular plan is not economical

Applying ecological principles sensibly

A kitchen with movable appliances

Why does it always have to be a built-in custom kitchen? The space will certainly be put to better use, but you cannot always take the kitchen with you when you move. If the next owner doesn't like it, it could well end up on the scrapheap. Unattached electrical appliances can be moved around and used in different combinations, and the kitchen can grow and be added to as family finances improve.

Thinking ecologically eliminates waste

Sandy limestone is an ideal choice for the surfaces of interior walls because it's good at storing heat and balancing room temperature. In many locations it may be cheaper than bricks, and, if the walls are just plastered or even left completely bare, savings could amount to as much as $0.50–1.00/square foot of wall. At the same time the walls will be able to moderate the temperature in the room more effectively improving comfort and saving energy.

The bathroom is one of the most expensive rooms in the house. If it is tiled only where absolutely necessary (cut the total area to be tiled by 200 square feet), it is possible to save as much as $2,000. The bathroom walls will be able to absorb moisture better and dissipate it more efficiently, if they are not completely tiled over. Wood paneling instead of tiles would also create savings. The room will be far healthier, provided that the air is allowed to circulate behind the wood.

Custom fabricated kitchens with built-in appliances are extremely popular, but it's far less expensive to equip the kitchen with standard cabinets or even movable fixtures and freestanding appliances. This will cost up to one-third less than a custom built-in kitchen, and it will be far easier to change the layout

of the room later, or convert it for use by an elderly or disabled person. The money that has been saved by not installing a fitted kitchen is better invested in energy-saving kitchen appliances.

The heating system is a further example of the close relationship between "green" building and saving money. A gas-fired system creates less pollution and uses energy more efficiently than oil-fired heating. Gas also works out cheaper in the long term, mainly because the oil and the boiler have to be separated physically from each other, whereas the gas boiler requires very little space. In areas where piped natural gas is not available, one may be tempted to install electrical heating equipment, but except for advanced heat pump systems, electrical heating is by far the worst from an energy standpoint. The cost to operate an electric radiant heating system can easily be twice that of a natural gas or LP gas furnace.

Moreover a gas-fired (or LP) system can quite easily be installed indoors under the roof, and systems which vent through the sidewall will also save the expense of a flue. One should also consider locating the system near a solar hot water system which can be used as a preheat system for a hydronic (hot water) heating system.

High-efficiency heating systems with a modern type of condensing boiler will use 15% less energy than a conventional gas-fired system, and as much as 20% less than with an oil-fired system. A modern central-heating system of this type will cost more than the conventional system, but this initial higher outlay will easily pay for itself over the years.

Underfloor heating which has advantages in terms of comfort, costs about 30–40% more than a conventional hydronic heating system with various types of radiators. This money can be put to better use, because such heating tends to be less responsive when temperatures outside change abruptly and some argue that it is not compatible with ecological building principles and may cause problems for those suffering from allergies or multiple chemical sensitivities. By far the worst choice of heating system for allergy sufferers, however, is a forced-air heating system which creates turbulence and considerable amounts of particulate pollutants in the air.

Simply constructed panel radiators have a higher radiating capacity than ribbed radiators or fin-tube radiators, and are recommended for health reasons as well. They are also often less expensive.

Careful planning of each stage of the building will not only save money, but create opportunities for improving the indoor environment and therefore the occupants' health as well. It makes sense to put the bathroom, kitchen and central heating system either stacked one above the other or adjacent to one another. This shortens the required supply lines for water, electricity and gas considerably and hot water standing in the pipes will not cool down so quickly. In the same way electrical wiring should be laid as economically as possible. Although electrical codes require most walls to have receptacles, they are not necessary for every single wall, and one should run power to as few of the walls as possible.

Keep bathroom tiling to a minimum

It is better to avoid tiling the bathroom from floor to ceiling. This allows the walls to help absorb and regulate the high humidity common in the bathroom. The only areas that should be tiled are those likely to be splashed with water. Not only will you save money, you'll find that the environment in the bathroom will be more tolerable.

An unplastered cast brick wall

Calcareous aggregate bricks (below right) require much less energy to make than clay bricks, and are far cheaper. For interior walls they are excellent at storing heat and balancing the room temperature.

Revealing the beauty of brick

Bricks are particularly good at regulating the level of humidity in a room. At the same time they create a warm and homey atmosphere. A wall like this is best left unplastered.

Wood is worth every penny

Building with wood can save money

If you're thinking about building a new house you obviously want to save money wherever possible, and this is where wood can have the edge on other materials, especially as it is also a renewable material and therefore ecologically sound. The materials for a wooden house are on average 10% cheaper than those for a house built with other materials. With wooden walls, the insulation material can fill up the entire wall structure, so the exterior wall of a wood construction will be two-thirds thinner than a typical solid masonry wall with the identical heat loss coefficient.

In practical terms this will mean that the identical floor area will offer 10% more space for the occupants on each floor. Modern computer-assisted manufacturing

wall and roof sheathing, and the interior ceilings and wall skin, all rigidly attached to the framing, to be an integral part of the structure and contribute to the overall strength and stability of the shell. The primary advantage is that relatively little expensive solid wood is required for any of the framing: Instead, composite oriented strand board (chipboard) or OSB is used for the sheathing panels. A further advantage is that a detailed cutting plan is completed first so that the framing members can be pre-cut and produced more efficiently in terms of both time and wasted material. After the structural elements have been cut and assembled in the fabricator's shop, a building can be erected on site in a relatively short time and, of course,

Wood is not just for detached houses

For a long time building regulations prohibited the erection of multi-story wooden buildings in Germany. But this development in Sulzbach-Rosenberg is a clear demonstration of how ecological principles can be incorporated into such buildings without sacrificing safety or comfort. This particular compact building type costs less than $140/square foot.

techniques enable even quite small lumber firms to pre-cut or prefabricate the various wood components, which will reduce construction time and further increase savings. In Leipzig, Germany, for example, 20 small lumber yards combined forces to complete a development made up of 149 units of terraced housing for families with young children and with limited finances. The entire project was directed by ecological principles of saving on resources and energy, and so priority was given to installing state-of-the-art heating and air-conditioning systems in all the houses. The price of the structural elements of the buildings was considerably reduced because a wood frame construction developed and tested in the United States was used for the project. This type of system known as a "stress skin" structural system relies on the exterior

Wood frame construction saves resources and energy

with less cost. The average construction cost for a wood frame low-energy house, excluding land, in the United States is about $150/square foot. By comparison, wood framed detached houses classified as low energy houses with state-of-the-art heating can be obtained in Germany for about $140/square foot (DM 2,000/square meter). In eastern Germany there is a firm offering a comfortable wood framed house with a small solar energy collector and rainwater plant for a mere $125/square foot (DM 1,800/square meter). In fact, eastern Germany is a flourishing market for less expensive and quickly erected housing, and this has even overcome the initial antipathy toward light construction: In 1995, 25% of the detached and semi-detached houses erected in eastern Germany were made of wood. Most building codes in the

An eco-house using resource efficient wood materials

Arch.: D. Pohlmann, Kiefen, Germany
Here is one of the very first houses to be built on ecological principles. It was copied in great numbers by numerous companies specializing in high-quality housing. The wood frame structure allows for a variety of floorplans by virtue of its modular design. At the same time costs are kept low through wise use of standard parts and prefabricated components.

A large development of wood frame houses

In eastern Germany there is little prejudice against wood frame buildings as exists in western Germany. This example was built in accordance with ecological principles and consists of several hundred apartment blocks and terraced row houses, all wood framed. The emphasis is on low-cost housing for families with small children.

United States allow construction of wood frame buildings for residential use to be as high as three stories if built of one-hour rated fire-resistant construction or two stories otherwise. In order to construct buildings of more than three stories with a wood structural system, a heavy timber frame (Type IV fire-resistant construction) is required. There are also limitations on allowable total floor area depending on whether or not the building is provided with an automatic fire protection system (sprinklers).

Pilot projects in various German cities have proved that it is possible to build large blocks of apartments according to environmentally friendly methods using the American wood frame system of construction; the projects showed that prices could be kept as low as about $125/square foot (DM 1,800/square meter) or less. In addition, new wood materials have meanwhile been developed in the United States that are easy to manufacture using a highly automated mass-production process and that combine durability and high quality with small cross-sections meaning less material and less weight. In this way wood frame building components can be made more affordable and more resource efficient.

It has now become possible to manufacture composite wood timbers using oriented strand technologies, similar to OSB panels, from wood shavings or alternatively high strength beams from thin veneers called laminated veneer lumber (LVL) that are nearly as strong as steel I-beams, and that can be utilized to construct an extremely well-insulated wood frame with relatively lightweight and thin walls.

New wooden materials

Stacked wood strips provide novel materials

Walls, roof cladding and ceilings can now be prefabricated from wooden panels without the use of adhesives. Thin wooden strips or boards are stacked on top of each other to form thicker boards and then fastened together. Inexpensive small dimension lumber which might otherwise be scrap can thus be made to serve a variety of useful purposes as structural or non-structural elements.

Suspended brick decking

Using the type of brick shown here a roof deck which also provides a finish ceiling can be completed without reinforced concrete elements. The bricks are also "green" building materials.

Prefabricated components

Modular construction reduces costs

Pre-assembled components and structural elements are common in wood houses, but they can also be used in traditional brick-and-mortar homes. For example, ceilings and floors made of environmentally friendly bricks or aerated concrete have recently been made available ready-made in Europe. More use is being made of complete wall sections wide and high enough for a single room that can be fitted together in the factory from bricks according to individual plans for a given building. A number of firms make prefab wall panels as well as complete gable ends from aerated concrete or lime-sand brick. These are manufactured according to the customer's specifications so they can be assembled on site to produce rooms of the correct dimensions. The advantages of these new types of wall sections are that they are relatively inexpensive, they do not cause thermal bridges, and, in contrast to concrete, they have a better coefficient of vapor diffusion. There are also pre-assembled units for shutter boxes and lintels. There are even special rabbeted wall bricks for windows and some already prepared for wiring. Ten-foot chimney sections made of lightweight concrete with a built-in ceramic flue can be stacked on top of each other to reach whatever height is required.

There is a tendency when solid construction is concerned to favor large bricks and components that have to be moved into position with special machinery and lifting gear. In fact, almost 80% of the work on a building site is devoted to erecting the external walls, and only 20% to the staircases, floors, ceilings and chimney. New types of super-size building block made from sandy limestone with lightweight aggregate called "big blocks," have a face area of 18 square feet and can save approximately 500 work-hours per house, i.e., 60% of the labor required. Bricklaying in the old sense of the word is no longer necessary: The blocks just have to be joined with a thin layer of mortar, which even an unskilled person can do. Furthermore, the thermal insulation is better. Not all of these developments are sensible, however, as has been demonstrated very well by the slab construction approach to building which created many unforeseen problems. This also is true when manufacturers produce and sell prefabricated systems that have been made with a total disregard for ecological principles. There are, for example, prefabricated balconies made from aluminum, which is by no means environmentally friendly, pre-assembled staircases that do not meet building codes and standards, and pre-manufactured dormer windows made of plastic and light metal that will not hold up and really should be constructed in a more conventional way. On the other hand, the new wave in technology in wall construction has also been shown by a German firm, Baufritz, which developed a "technology block" for a project called "Rosenheim Haus" that is, in fact, a single wall module inside a two-story wood framed house. The wall contains the entire heating system, the air-conditioning, plumbing, solar hot water system, electrical wiring, central vac system, and, as an option, a wall safe. When an entire house has to be modernized or a section repaired, it is not very different from exchanging one car engine for another: The entire module is removed and lowered to the ground and then repaired, or a different module is installed to replace the old one. As the demand grows, mass production of walls of this type with all services pre-installed could make them more affordable.

Prefabricated brick building sections

Bricks can also be used in the manufacture of large construction components that can be erected quickly and easily. This is illustrated here by this solid brick roof section (left) and floor section (below), both of which will save considerable time and money.

A wall with pre-installed services

This idea is certainly worth imitating. The walls for this house in southern Germany contain all the wiring and plumbing required for the heating, the kitchen, the bathroom and the toilets. In this way careful design will result in extremely short supply lines. The wall with pre-installed services is like a drawer that can be slid down into the wooden frame for installation and slid out again for repairs which can be completed easily and quickly without the need to re-plaster.

Doing it yourself

The owners did it all themselves: Gelsenkirchen, Germany

During the International Building Exhibition (IBA) in the Ruhr region of Germany a wide range of experimental houses were erected. They also included a number of developments which were finished off by the occupants themselves in small and well-organized groups.

Whatever the future occupants of a house can do themselves will save money. As much as 30% of the building costs can be eliminated by tackling tasks that do not really require a professional. Here, a breakdown of the potential savings is possible:

- Basement   40–60%
- Exterior walls   20–40%
- Interior walls   20–40%
- Painting and wallpapering   50–80%
- Roof insulation   40%
- Floor coverings   25%
- Plumbing and laying tile   20%
- Heating system   10%
- Electrical wiring   40%
- Staircase fabrication   10%
- Door installation   15%
- Window installation   20%

Don't overestimate your own skills

But do-it-yourself enthusiasts have to remember not to overestimate their capabilities. Anyone deciding to give a helping hand on the building site has to have a great deal of time to spare and must also be physically fit, apart from having the basic knowledge and skills required around the site. A lack of professional guidance at the beginning often leads to mistakes later. These could result in structural damage or endless delays in the project. Ultimately, attempts to save money in this way could have the opposite effect.

An example of how future owner-occupiers can help complete the work themselves is a cooperative housing project. The concept of cooperative housing projects built by the residents themselves is certainly not new. There are hundreds of such communities throughout the United States among Shaker, Mennonite, Hudderite, Amish and numerous other groups tied together by close religious and social bonds. The oldest housing projects in the United States still occupied are the Pueblos of New Mexico made up of adobe multi-family structures built hundreds of years ago by native Americans around a tightly knit and lasting social structure.

There is, however, a renewed interest in this type of cooperative community and quite often these modern examples embrace ecological or sustainable building principles. Several examples of more recent cooperative developments or co-housing projects in the Pacific Northwest include the following: The Winslow Co-housing community on Bainbridge Island, Washington was completed in 1991. Its 30 housing units are tightly clustered on 4.8 acres about an open pedestrian street. Parking of automobiles is restricted to a single landscaped area on the edge of the property. It offers residents a 5,000 square-foot commons building. The total project budget was about $4.1 million.

The Cardiff Place community completed in 1993 is in Victoria, the provincial capital of British Columbia, also known as the city of gardens. Cardiff Place is located only 15 blocks from the inner harbor and walking distance to shopping and schools located near the city's center. Its residents share a renovated turn-of-the-century mansion and a new four-story apartment building with a total of 17 apartments totaling 16,000 square feet and a 2,600 square-foot commons for a total investment of $2.3 million.

Habitat for Humanity, an organization in the United States which marshals community resources and volunteer labor to provide low-cost housing to those who could not otherwise afford to own their own home, requires every new homeowner to put in a certain amount of their own time in completing the construction of their dream home. This requirement is commonly referred to as sweat equity and it not only gives homeowners the pride and satisfaction of having helped to build a home for themselves, but it also gives them the ability to customize certain details which would otherwise not be possible in a low-cost home.

Another progressive approach to doing it yourself, co-operative building, or co-housing, has a distinct set of advantages, including centralized planning, control, and coordination to name a few. Better discounts can be obtained by purchasing large quantities and settling bills more quickly. Resources can be shared and each member can be provided with the materials and tools that will be required at a reduced cost. By working in groups community spirit will be fostered and the members of the association will work together to ensure that the project follows established ecological guidelines and is completed to everyone's satisfaction.

With the benefit of expert guidance
The future homeowners were never left to their own devices. The planning, organization and purchase of materials was under the expert guidance of skilled craftsmen and there was always professional advice on hand.

All together now!
From the erection of the building shell to the interior work, each house was completed by the members of the group. Each member helped the others, thus keeping costs to a minimum.

THE BASICS

THE BASICS

Not built on sand

The fabric of a house reveals a lot about the construction method. Once the house has been finished, the plastering or the cladding will cover the walls completely. With the wood-frame construction method (above) several kinds of load transfering strategies are possible, because the weight of the building is borne by a large number of relatively closely spaced system of supporting members. The interior walls are also typically load-bearing.

This chapter will explain just what thermal insulation, sound insulation, fire protection and other concepts mean. You will also find out how to critically evaluate whether a building material is environmentally friendly or not.

Building structure

Structural engineering is the science of building stability. The architect or civil engineer is responsible for making the calculations required to ensure that all the components in a building will be able to bear an anticipated load to ensure the safety of those using the building and the stability of the building itself. The first thing to consider is the very nature of the soil on which the foundations will be laid. When there is a deep layer of sand and substrata allowing water to flow freely, special preparations must be made before building can begin. Depending upon local building codes, a strip footing foundation of unreinforced

concrete beneath the load-bearing walls positioned just below the lowest floor of the building may in some cases be adequate. This foundation must reach a frost-proof depth of between 12 and 54 or more inches (30–135 cm) beneath the surface of the site depending on local climate conditions. You will have to check local building codes to determine what the required depth is for a particular location. If a building is to have a basement, the foundation depth below the basement floor will normally be no more than 24 inches (60 cm). If subsoil is not sound, it may be necessary to use a steel-reinforced foundation raft which will distribute the load more evenly. The purpose of the steel reinforcement, even in the case of ceilings and floors, or of lintels over doors and windows, whether of concrete or of stone, is to provide resistance to tensile stress or strength in bending. The load creates pressure on the top surface of the component and a tensile force downwards. Mineral materials are very well able to resist the pressure of

A wood post-and-beam structure

The wood post-and-beam structure is completely different. There are relatively few supports so that the walls between them need have no "prescribed" position.

compressive force, but are typically not able to withstand very much tensile stress. In the case of steel the opposite is true, which is why a combination of materials is preferable. In this way the materials each lend their strengths to the composite material overcoming the weaknesses of the other. The walls constructed of stone, steel or wooden piles have to transfer the loads from the structure on to the foundations. This applies to the "load-bearing walls" as opposed to the "nonstructural walls" which merely subdivide areas within the building. Nonstructural walls can be moved to a different position or removed completely at any given time, whereas the slightest alteration to a load-bearing wall needs careful review. Beams, ties and extra supporting members may have to be added to accept the load previously borne by the wall. In a timber-frame building and a half-timbered house the interior walls frequently are also load-bearing and can only serve their purpose in the structure of the building if they are left intact. Thus, alterations should never be undertaken without expert advice from an architect or structural engineer.

Dropping in the walls

Arch.: A. Mense, B. Bürger, Basta Baubüro, Dortmund, Germany

Timber panels are convenient because they allow entire walls to be prefabricated and assembled very quickly. But one has to bear in mind that these panels do have a load-bearing function, like that of precast concrete in other types of building.

THERMAL INSULATION

Thermal insulation is one of the most important features of a well-designed house and, as far as building physics is concerned, one of the most critical issues for that branch of applied science.

Scientific background

Heat is the oscillating movement of the molecules within a particular substance, and it increases as the temperature rises. Thermal conduction is said to occur whenever a strongly oscillating molecule transfers energy to the colder adjacent molecule and, in turn, causes it to oscillate. Thermal conduction takes place within all materials and between all materials next to each other, but its intensity varies. This is why heat loss can never be totally prevented, but only reduced. Dense, heavy materials such as iron are good at conducting heat, but light, porous materials such as wool are poor thermal conductors. Air is a very poor thermal conductor as well; this is why it is possible to reduce the thermal conductivity of a dense material by increasing its porosity or creating tiny pockets of air, and thus enhancing its insulating properties. Water conducts heat 25 times better than air. This is one reason why moisture must be prevented from reaching insulating materials; if it did it would reduce the efficiency of most types of insulation. Many inert gases such as argon and krypton gas are even poorer thermal conductors than air, and so they are frequently used between panes of insulating glass to improve their insulating value. How efficient a substance is at conducting heat depends on the size and distribution of the pores. They should be as small as possible, and evenly distributed.

The coefficient of thermal conductivity λ for every material is given in Btu/sq. ft./h/°F/in. – i.e., the value of λ is the flow of energy in Btu that will pass in one hour through one square foot of material with a thickness of one inch, when the temperature difference between the two surfaces of the material is 1°. In metric representation, this would be given as λ = W/sq. m./h/°K/m. – watts/square meter of surface/hour/°Kelvin temperature difference/meter of thickness.

The lower the value of λ, the lower the thermal conductivity of the material: This means that less energy can flow through the material. If the English representation of thermal conductivity is used, the value of λ for copper is 2724, for concrete 12, for light honeycomb bricks 1.4, for wood 0.78–1.78 and polyurethane foam 0.16. These data can be used to calculate the heat transmission – the u-value – for each separate structural element consisting of various components. To illustrate, a simple cavity wall might be made up of several different materials: the exterior plaster, the stone, the interior plaster and the mortar used to bond the stones together. Complicated calculations have to be made concerning the value of λ and the thickness of each material layer as well as the resistance of the enclosed layers of air and the transitional resistance between the surfaces of the wall and the outside or inside air. The size of the u-value denotes the flow of heat in Btus per hour passing through a structural element such as a wall – measuring 1 square foot at a temperature difference of 1°. The u-value of the exterior structural elements – that is the walls, the roof and the floor above the basement or crawl space – impacts the health and well-being of the occupants as well as the amount of

A solid multi-layered wall construction

This shows the exterior wall of a new house in Hamburg, Germany. The wall appears to have been designed and built very competently: On the inside hard and heavy calcium silicate bricks provide thermal mass and also serve a load-bearing purpose. The next layer is a well proportioned, permeable layer of insulating material. On the outside the clinker bricks will protect the façade against the elements for a long time to come.

Roof insulation using wood fiber materials

The best escape route for energy is the roof, unless it is insulated. Normally it will be insulated between the rafters. But this Austrian house demonstrates clearly that the insulation can consist of fiberboards made from softwoods laid on top of the rafters. The insulation consists of several layers of boards with different degrees of hardness. Some are impregnated as additional moisture protection. The roof battens will then be fastened so that the clay roof tiles can be put in place.

energy that is lost by the building envelope. It would be a mistake, however, to overlook poor quality windows determining heat loss through the walls. Whatever encloses a space in the building but has poor thermal conductivity (good insulating value) will increase the comfort of people in the room and save energy. As a rule of thumb the following assumption can be made: u-value × 20 = gallons of oil/square foot/year (k-value × 10 = liters/square meter), which means that if the u-value of a specific structural element is multiplied by 20, the product is the annual loss of heating energy through the element in gallons of oil. Thus, the lower the u-value, the less energy will be lost. This coefficient can be kept as low as possible by increasing the thickness of each layer of material. But there are obviously limits to this solution: A reinforced concrete wall would have to be several yards thick to comply with current thermal insulation requirements. What is done instead is to make the building materials more porous and thus lighter creating millions of tiny air spaces. This can be seen in

- exterior walls: 0.08; LEH 0.035
- windows: 0.53; LEH 0.26
- roof: 0.035; LEH 0.026
- basement ceiling: 0.11; LEH 0.053

a variety of building materials such as certain types of aerated concrete brick in common use today. But this reduces the compressive strength or load-bearing capacity of the material and can therefore compromise the structural integrity of a load-bearing wall.

A third alternative is to use building materials that are not quite such good insulators but which possess excellent load-bearing qualities in combination with light materials which are in turn excellent insulators. Note: A maximum u-value has been specified for a number of structural elements (see box, left). The second u-value is that established for a low-energy house (LEH) of no more than two complete floors.

To convert u-values to R-values use the formula: $1/R =$ u-value. To determine the k-value or metric equivalent stipulated in the regulation, multiply by 5.68.

This wall will retain heat

This cavity wall is an ideal method of constructing this structural element. The insulating material has already been fixed to the load-bearing wall with special fasteners. Then, the protecting outside wall is erected. In this way thermal bridges between the inside and the outside of the building will be prevented.

Thermal bridges

The u-value of a structural element should be as homogeneous as possible so that thermal bridges are avoided. A thermal bridge is created in a specific area of a surface, such as a wall, where more heat loss occurs than through the rest of that surface. Heat always tries to find the path of least resistance. Reinforcing between the concrete and brick of a brick wall forms a thermal bridge. A concrete window lintel or a concrete floor extending right up to an exterior wall will form a thermal bridge which must be alleviated by providing additional insulation; otherwise large amounts of heat can escape. Wherever there is a dado, for example, or where a concrete foundation wall meets with a façade, or there is a parapet on a flat roof there will inevitably be thermal bridges. In all such cases the best solution is a continuous layer of external insulation if feasible.

Thermal bridges don't just allow energy to escape; they can also cause damage to the structure of a building. Water from the moisture-laden air of the building interior will condense at or near such bridges and it will sooner damage the structure. Another problem related to thermal bridges is the difference in expansion and contraction from one side of the material to the other. The greater the differences in temperature the greater the stress which can result in stress cracks in the plaster, mortar or concrete. Thermal bridges can also affect the health and comfort of the occupants, because they cause convection or

drafts. The larger the "gap" in the insulation, the stronger the draft. Thermal bridges are common at structural elements that jut out of the building, such as cantilevered balconies and roof overhangs. When the base of a balcony is anchored to the wall, it is nearly impossible to separate the elements thermally. Energy is always going to escape outwards. This is why so many 1970s buildings have suffered considerable structural damage. Fortunately the tendency is now to construct the balcony as an entirely separate structural element positioned, as it were, outside the building's thermal envelope.

A further example can be found where interior walls meet exterior ones and where there is interior wall insulation. This system is frequently used when a building listed on the historical register is being renovated because it is necessary to install wedge-shaped insulating material at the cross-walls to prevent the formation of mold in the corners.

Thermal bridges cannot be prevented at the corners of a building because at these points the area of interior wall absorbing the heat is smaller than the exterior wall area which is actively losing heat. Suppose it was a question of a wall in an older building constructed of 10-inch-thick perforated bricks and plastered on both sides (u = 0.25 Btu/square foot/° F), the results of the ensuing calculations would be as follows. Assuming that the outside temperature is 14° F (-10° C) and the room temperature is 68° F

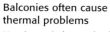

Balconies often cause thermal problems

Here is a typical example of a thermal bridge: The balconies on the right have been cast in one piece together with the concrete floor. As a result, the heat inside the room will escape to the outside of the building at the points where the balcony connects much like the fins on a radiator. More energy will be used, the corners of the room will become damp from condensation, and mold will soon spread. The balconies on the left do not cause such problems. They have been isolated from the shell of the building and thus have no contact with the warmer inside sections of the building.

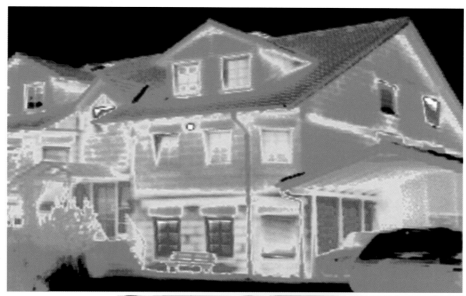

The thermal bridges can be made visible

This house has a well-insulated roof, but the dark blue patches in the thermograph are a warning that in the surface connecting the gable wall and the windows no air barrier has been installed (red). On the upper story the façade cladding offers good thermal protection, but the apparently uninsulated walls and the enormous French windows on the ground floor allow a high amount of heat to escape.

(20° C), the temperature of the wall would be approximately 57° F (14° C), which is really unpleasantly low. In the corners the temperature would be as low as 41° F (5° C), and serious structural damage is inevitable. Even in a wall built to comply with government insulation standards the temperature in the corners will still drop to 55° F (13° C), or so, which is 9° F (5° C) below the temperature on the rest of the wall. If a cupboard were to be placed here, it would stop the air from circulating and causing the humidity condensing on the colder surface to evaporate rather than accumulate. The outcome would be a serious accumulation of condensation resulting in the formation of mold in the corner. But efficient thermal insulation can lessen the temperature differential in the corners to between 2° and 4° F. Thermal bridges are often quite small. For example, tiny lumps of mortar inside a cavity wall, through-bolts, and even mortar joints between lightweight walls set using mortar that is too thick can, in fact, all be thermal bridges to a greater or lesser degree. Sometimes a wall structure is weakened by radiator niches or electrical receptacle boxes which will also create thermal bridges that have to be countered with additional insulation. Poorly installed insulation, the metal anchoring between a façade and the supporting wall, or long, continuous window sills without any form of insulation provide more examples of how easy it can be to overlook potential thermal bridges, even if the building is otherwise well insulated.

Thermal bridges can be located by photographing the exterior walls with a special technique know as infrared thermography. The bridges will be brightly colored, yellow or red areas, while the well-insulated structural elements will be dark blue or mauve. Thermographic photographs are only useful in identifying thermal bridges if they are taken during the colder part of the year, when the heating is on.

Problems can occur at the base of a wall

When a low-energy house is built, even the smallest detail is important. There has to be adequate insulation at the sill of every wall where the floor connects, otherwise there will be serious structural damage.

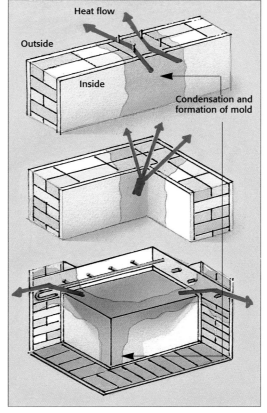

This is where the mold starts

Wherever heat escapes more rapidly through a weak point in the structure of a building, condensation will occur leading to constant dampness. This provides ideal conditions for mold to thrive. Frequently the type of mold will indicate the cause. These examples, from top to bottom, show an uninsulated reinforced concrete column in a brick wall, the corner of a building with a relatively thin wall, and a reinforced concrete ceiling connection to an exterior wall uninsulated on the outside.

Testing for air leakage

The type of fan shown here is used in the blower-door test. The equipment is set up at the front door, all the windows are closed and as a partial vacuum is created the loss in pressure is measured. If the test seems to indicate an excessive pressure loss, the sites can be localized by using special tracer smoke.

Draftproofing and windproofing

Leaky parts of the building shell or areas where gaps allow air to move freely into or out of the building can have the same effect as thermal bridges. Until quite recently it was the windows that created most problems in this regard. But if windows are well made and meet industry standards or bear NFRC certification they will be sufficiently airtight. Then, of course, they must be installed correctly with the shim spaces properly insulated and the air barrier made to overlap the edge of the frame. The weakest section in a modern building with solid as opposed to framed walls is the roof, whereas with a timber or wood frame building, the problem can be virtually anywhere. Even if there is a gap only 1 millimeter wide and 1 meter long in a structural element with an area of 1 square meter, the effects of the thermal insulation will be reduced by a factor of 5, with a pressure difference of 30 pascal (wind pressure coefficient of 2). Close to the gap the effectiveness of any insulation will disappear completely, even without any perceptible draft in the room: Energy is wasted considerably and moisture starts to accumulate. For quite some time very little was undertaken to deal with the problems of draft- and windproofing, but now there is much discussion about new standards that will efficiently regulate the air permeability of structural elements and connections between them. The façade of a solidly constructed building is made windproof by plastering (e.g., stucco). But great care is needed to ensure that even the penetrations in the interior plasterwork, such as those for electrical receptacles, are adequately run into the plaster: If this isn't done skillfully, problems are almost certain to develop. When dealing with drafts and wind, frequently it is not a question of whether a gap is continuous in the sense that you can see right through from inside to outside. The damage is already done if there are leaky sections in the external and internal insulating course allowing the air blowing in from outside to spread into and through the structural element and ultimately into the building in a completely different place from where it first entered from the outside.

Airtight need not mean stuffy

These photographs show the correct way to windproof a roof and keep out moisture. The vapor diffusion ability of the roof will not be in any way diminished as long as you stick to sturdy but permeable or natural materials.

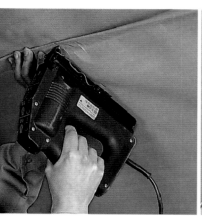

Even when the internal air barrier in the roof or wall framing (where it may also serve as a moisture barrier) does serve its purpose, any leakage in the exterior weather proofing (siding or sheathing), or the roof underlay will allow air to penetrate into the insulating material and will thus reduce the effectiveness of the insulation. Essentially, good insulation relies on air that remains where it is in the insulating material. Clearly, then, it is very important to ensure that the air barrier is carefully installed, which means that the layers of sheeting must overlap generously and be fixed to each other with special adhesive tape made of butyl rubber, or, when paper is used, with a special adhesive. Packing tape, carpet tape, or particularly thin aluminum tape are not very likely to remain in place for more than a year and so are totally unsuitable. Nor should the sheeting be too thin. Cheap polyethylene film will tear too easily and so is best avoided. In any case, cheap polyethylene film is not really defensible in an ecological sense. First and foremost, it is synthetic, even though polyethylene itself is, comparatively, more environmentally friendly than most other synthetics.

The main objection to barriers of this kind, though, is that they inhibit moisture diffusion from the building interior quite considerably and so do very little to enhance the quality of the air in the building. Here, the term used is "moisture barrier" rather than "vapor barrier," and it is frequently utilized in ecological building because it does have suitable vapor diffusion characteristics. High-quality woven polyester films of this type have minute pores to allow vapor diffusion. A more ecologically acceptable solution is to be found in special wood fiber sheeting or kraft paper for the moisture barrier and air barrier on the inside, and impregnated wood fiberboard for a heavy-duty roof underlay on the exterior.

A number of other basic rules must be followed to ensure a draft-free building. The real problems can occur at the transitions between solid and lightweight structural elements such as between a sloping roof and brickwork of the gables or the solidly built wall. An answer might be to lay expanded metal lath before plastering to avoid any gaps. Another recurring problem is created by the number of penetrations that necessarily must occur for vents, flues and chimneys. Where an opening is absolutely necessary, such as when waste pipe vents or a chimney have to be installed, it is absolutely vital to ensure that there is careful windproofing all around the opening. Any unnecessary openings are best avoided. This means

that the practice of running wiring along the rafters and then through the air barrier is better avoided. It would be far more sensible to lay the wiring along the inside of the gable end wall or along the interior walls. If, for some reason, it is necessary to run wiring on the underside of a sloping roof, it should be taken horizontally below the inside of the windproofing. This method is especially recommended for wooden buildings in order to prevent undermining the efficiency of the insulation.

It is also important to make sure whenever possible that there will be enough space for the air barrier itself to be moved, should this ever become necessary. Ventilation pipes and other essential openings should never run too close to the walls, otherwise they will be difficult to repair or move.

Keeping out the winter chill

In the past most windows fitted poorly and let in drafts. This was not only bad for people's health but wasted too much energy. Today windows fit much better, are better insulators, seal out air and moisture and generally contribute to health and comfort.

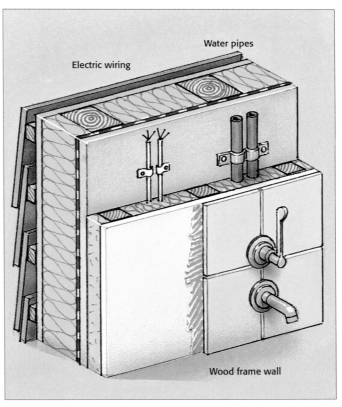

Electric wiring

Water pipes

Wood frame wall

Plumbing and wiring a wooden building

Wood frame buildings are particularly hard to windproof, because they are not usually plastered over. If the air barrier has to be penetrated for the electrical wiring and plumbing to be installed, avoiding air leakage will be even harder. It is a good idea to have a special raceway for wires and pipes, and to improve acoustic control by installing special insulating material around the piping.

MOISTURE PROBLEMS

There are many possible causes of moisture in a house. In a new building a considerable amount of moisture is simply contained in the building materials themselves. For example, moisture from the mixing water used with the cementitious building materials such as concrete, mortar, screed and plaster will take some time to evaporate. This is partly because this moisture is necessary for cement to cure and the curing process can actually continue over a period of years. In the case of bricks water will continue to be released for about 12 months, and for concrete or limestone bricks it could take as long three years. Wood, painted walls, drywall, and many other materials also experience a drying-out period after construction is completed. For these reasons, it is advisable to consider a building "flush out" when construction is nearly complete to aid in removing this moisture more quickly as well as other air pollutants being released from the newly installed building materials. This source of dampness and humidity is more of a nuisance than a real problem, but dampness can also cause or result from structural damage. Damage can be done by condensing

moisture, sometimes called sweating, caused by thermal bridges, air leakage or inadequate insulation. Once the surface begins to sweat, mold will appear and soon begin to spread. This sweating can also occur inside the wall or roof structure. Salty deposits may result from minerals leaching from building materials and may also weaken the structure and the effectiveness of the insulation. As the mold spreads, other pests may gain a foothold. Water can also penetrate into the walls of the building wherever there is insufficient damp-proofing. The moisture may originate from burst water pipes, damaged gutters, or most commonly from the soil. If there is no damp course or water stop in the foundation walls, moisture will begin to rise.

What causes a wall to sweat?

It is not always easy to tell whether a house has too much humidity or moisture in the air. People tend to think there is a problem only when they can actually see water collecting or condensing, and by that time it may be too late to do anything about it.

The amount of moisture in the air depends on its temperature. The higher the temperature, the more moisture the air will be able to hold. One cubic meter of air at a temperature of 32 °F (0 °C) can absorb 4.8 g of water; at 0 °F (-20 °C) the amount drops to 0.9 g, and at 86 °F (30 °C) it increases to 30.4 g (about 1 oz.).

It is the temperature at which the air is saturated and condensation begins. The dew point depends, therefore, on the air temperature and relative humidity (the amount of moisture in the air relative to the maximum amount the air can hold represented as a percentage). At an air temperature of 72° F (22° C) and a relative humidity of 70% the dew point will be 61.3° F (16.3° C). A temperature drop of 11° F (6° C) will cause condensation to occur.

The atmospheric moisture in a house mostly originates from the kitchen and bathroom. The people in a room also give off water from respiration and perspiration. For example, a person will give off about 60 g of water vapor per hour while sleeping, about 100 g while doing light physical activity, and as much as 300 g during more strenuous activity. A typical shower will produce 1,700 g of water vapor and a fully loaded washing machine 6,000 g. A family of four can release as much as 4 gallons (15 liters) of water into the air each day.

Humidity can make you sick

The high humidity has caused condensation on the surface of the cold mirror. If this cold point was a thermal bridge in a wall that was constantly damp, mold would very soon form.

A lot of data but all the same problem

As the temperature of the air fluctuates, so too does its capacity to hold moisture. At 86° F (30° C), it can absorb three times as much moisture as air of 50° F (10° C), see top table. The relative humidity also depends on the temperature in the air. The amount of water that produces a relative humidity of 80% at a temperature of 68° F (20° C) will, at 50° F (10° F), exceed the saturation limit (center). The lower table shows the critical relationship. A difference of just a few degrees, for example between the air inside the room and the exterior wall or windowpane, can cause condensation when the relative atmospheric humidity is high. At a temperature of 75° F (24° C) and with a relative atmospheric humidity of 70 %, which is not uncommon in the kitchen, the dew point (the point at which condensation forms) is as low as 64.8° F (18.2° C).

THE AIR CAN ABSORB THE FOLLOWING AMOUNTS OF WATER AT A GIVEN TEMPERATURE

Air temperature °F	4	14	32	50	68	86	104
Saturation in g/cubic meter	0.9	2.2	4.8	9.4	17.3	30.4	50.2

RELATIONSHIP BETWEEN AMOUNT OF WATER AND RELATIVE HUMIDITY

Water vapor in g/cubic meter with relative moisture saturation 100%

Air temp °F	30%	40%	50%	60%	70%	80%	90%	100%
60.8	4.1	5.5	6.9	8.2	9.6	11.0	12.3	13.7
68	5.2	6.9	8.6	10.4	12.1	13.8	15.6	17.3

RELATIONSHIP BETWEEN DEW POINT TEMPERATURE, AIR TEMPERATURE AND RELATIVE ATMOSPHERIC HUMIDITY

Dew point temperature with a relative atmospheric humidity of

Air temp °F	30%	40%	50%	60%	70%	80%	90%
84.4	8.8	13.1	16.6	19.5	22.0	24.2	26.2
78.8	7.1	11.4	14.8	17.6	20.1	22.3	24.2
75.2	5.4	9.6	12.9	15.8	18.2	20.3	22.3
71.6	3.6	7.8	11.1	13.9	16.3	18.4	20.3
68	1.9	6.0	9.3	12.0	14.4	16.4	18.3
64.4	0.2	4.2	7.4	10.1	12.5	14.5	16.3
60.8	-1.4	2.4	5.6	8.2	10.5	12.6	14.4

Mold on the walls

Don't let mold take hold

In the past when we did not have washing machines, showers or even inside toilets, the only significant source of humidity was cooking and people themselves. In addition, windows and the buildings themselves were usually leaky and allowed the moisture to dissipate quickly. Condensation, if it formed on the single glazing at all, would quickly evaporate. Today with so many conveniences and our efforts to be more comfortable and energy-efficient, we have created three direct causes of condensation and the resulting mold in our buildings:

- thermal bridges;
- inadequate ventilation;
- surfaces that do not absorb moisture well.

Time for drastic action

It is risky to ignore mold as it is a serious health hazard. There are several causes for the dampness that allows mold to thrive (from top to bottom): The roof is not adequately weatherproofed and the ceiling has become damp; there is a thermal bridge on the wall or ceiling causing moisture to condense; there is poor insulation between the ground and the building and so condensation again leads to development of mold on the basement walls.

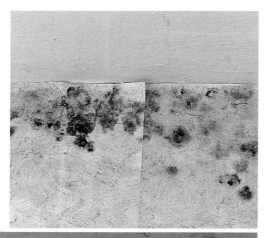

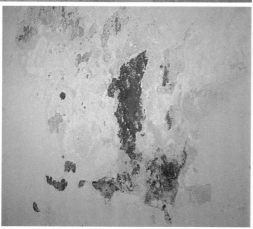

The mold spores can only settle and multiply if there is dampness and organic material for them to thrive on. Wallpaper, wood and paint all provide an ideal breeding ground. Moisture condenses on cold areas such as thermal bridges, and the higher the atmospheric pressure, the quicker this will occur. Unfortunately, thermal bridges can never be entirely prevented, and so something else has to be done to reduce humidity. All that is needed, in most cases, is adequate ventilation. In winter the colder air outside the building contains far less moisture than the air inside, so ventilation will ensure that the damp air is drawn out of the room.

The best method is to ventilate the rooms very quickly during the day for about two to four minutes three times a day so that the air is completely exchanged without giving the interior walls and the furniture any time to cool down. Another alternative is a mechanical ventilation system such as a heat recovery ventilator (HRV). The most important thing, however, is to create sporadic moisture "sinks," or surfaces which act like a sponge and absorb water vapor during periods of high humidity and then release it again when humidity levels drop without causing any moisture damage. Many ecologically acceptable materials do just this. They include wood, clay, gypsum, lime plaster, bricks, as well as various floor coverings and furniture coverings made of natural fiber. Glass, metals, plastics, and painted surfaces do not have this property and their use should be restricted. Mold has to be dealt with immediately, because it presents a serious health hazard. It is not wise to use harsh fungicides based on chlorinated compounds or cleaners which contain chlorine, because they are harmful to health. It is better to use terpene or alcohol-based cleaners, or a solution of 5% acetic acid. Alternatively, make a paste with baking soda and water and scrub with a hard bristled brush. The affected surfaces must not be painted with latex paint; use either a whitewash or a mineral paint, which will help prevent the mold from reappearing.

Sweating walls

Most of the surface moisture or condensation will be removed from the interior of the building by evaporation, but about 2% of the moisture will travel through the walls to the exterior surface of the building. This process is called vapor diffusion and it occurs because the vapor pressure inside the building is higher than on the outside as a result of human activity. The walls can resist this pressure to a certain extent, and this resistance can be calculated. The coefficient that is arrived at, m, indicates the amount of resistance of a material to the diffusion of moisture from inside the building. For organic insulating materials, cellulose for example, the value of μ is 1, indicating a low resistance to diffusion; for a brick wall the value of μ is 8, of concrete 70 and polystyrene 100. So the higher the value of μ the greater the resistance to diffusion.

But diffusion cannot and should not be totally eliminated. Water vapor diffusion does no harm to the structure, provided that the moisture can easily find a path through the wall and escape to the outside. This is why the thermal conductivity coefficient values decrease toward the exterior side of the wall.

It is also important to place the material most impervious to the water vapor on the inside of the wall and the materials most likely to be adversely affected by vapor diffusion on the exterior side: Any moisture that permeates through the inner surfaces of the wall will then be dissipated more effectively.

If condensation does accumulate in significant quantities somewhere in the structure of a house, damage is inevitable. As already stated, this damage will mostly occur at the thermal bridges, but could also affect a much larger area or translate to a completely different location in cases where vapor barriers are improperly located, are not continuous or where there are voids inside the wall allowing the moisture to flow elsewhere.

Vapor diffusing through a wall will condense when it reaches a surface whose temperature at that location is at or below the dew point. The dew point of a particular element in the wall section, therefore, should be at a point where the condensing water can cause no damage, because it can easily be dissipated outwards. For this reason, it is not at all advisable to cover the outside surface of a wall with paint or with

vapor-retarding synthetic resin. The protection offered by such treatment against driving rain is not likely to last that long, whereas the damage caused by preventing diffusion and trapping moisture inside the wall will be very costly and difficult to deal with. The insulating materials, then, should absorb and diffuse moisture without reducing their overall efficiency. This is why damp-proofing and closed-cell insulating materials such as polystyrene and polyurethane are best avoided both inside and outside a building.

Good ventilation is vital

Unless a room is adequately ventilated, steam and high humidity will not dissipate. The moisture has to be exhausted particularly in the kitchen and bathroom as they tend to steam up quickly. In summer nobody will mind if the windows are wide open, but in winter you want to lose as little heat as possible. One solution is a quick, short burst of ventilation at various times during the day. This is an acceptable means of ventilating a space because it is not the air that makes the room warm, but the walls as they dissipate heat. It is therefore all right to ventilate a room thoroughly, as long as the walls are not allowed to cool down.

Why insulating properly is so problematic

If the vapor barrier has not been located correctly (left), moisture will penetrate into the wall structure and the plaster will begin to flake. In winter the wall might even split, when the moisture freezes. The stresses of differential temperature is considerably lower with exterior wall insulation than with interior insulation (right). Thus the number of cracks will be fewer and the wall will remain sound far longer. In addition, the dew point and the freezing point of the exterior wall insulation are within the layer of insulating material. This will prevent condensation and the resulting structural damage to the wall.

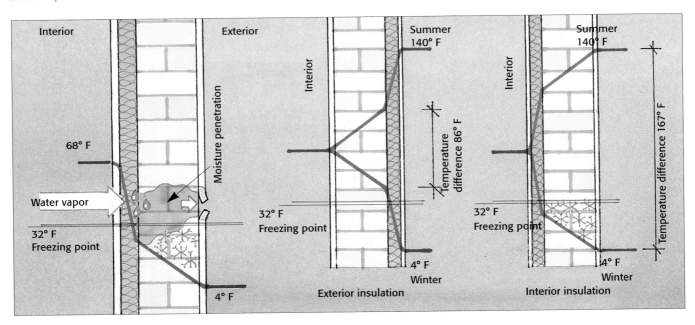

ACOUSTIC CONTROL

Noise reduction can reduce stress and improve your health

Excessive noise puts a strain on everyone's nerves and is the most common cause of arguments between neighbors. Traffic noise and other city sounds are cited by most people as the reason they'd most like to move out to the country. Noise is not only irritating; it's a health hazard. It can damage your hearing, and you cannot sleep or relax properly if subjected to excessive noise, which can result in all sorts of health problems. Soundproofing means protecting your health as well as your peace of mind.

Sound levels are measured in dB(A) (the A-weighted decibel scale), a logarithmic scale which indicates in relative terms, the ratio of the amount of power emitted by two sources and equal to 10 times the logarithm of that ratio. In other words dB(A) are used to

clock. When the noise level reaches 40 dB(A), the noise of a subdued conversation, work requiring a certain amount of concentration is still possible. But at 50 dB(A), the noise of traffic in a residential area, the noise level starts to become annoying. Over 60 dB(A), the noise created by a vacuum cleaner three feet away, the noise is really difficult to bear. Over 70 dB(A), which is about the level of people talking loudly, those within earshot begin to get irritated. And once 80 dB(A) is reached – loud traffic – listeners find it difficult to concentrate or to complete a simple task. Over 90 dB(A), the noise of a door being slammed shut, we are approaching the level at which noise becomes a health hazard. An electric saw produces 100 dB(A). The sound of a pneumatic drill at a

The noise in a disco
Most people know that disco music can do damage to your hearing. But those who are constantly exposed to loud noise are in greater danger than occasional party animals. The human body cannot rest properly unless the surroundings are reasonably quiet.

describe the sound pressure level: If the sound pressure is increased tenfold, our level of subjective sensitivity will double, thus the amount will increase by 10 dB(A). If the sound level is increased from 30 to 50 dB(A), the sound pressure has increased a hundredfold and the noise, judged subjectively, has quadrupled. At 120 dB(A), equivalent to the noise of a low-flying jet, the pain threshold for humans has been reached, and the level is 1,012-fold, or one billion times 1 dB(A).

The human ear cannot perceive noises below 10 dB(A). A noise up to 25 dB(A), such as that produced by drizzle, will be registered as quite pleasant and restful. At a level of 30 dB(A) the noise starts to get irritating – that would be the noise of a humming refrigerator or the ticking of an old-fashioned alarm

level of 110 dB(A) is the level at which people's auditory system is at risk not to mention their mental health. Constant exposure to high levels of noise is known to cause significant stress in people.

For this reason soundproofing is important not only in a rented apartment but in any household. It's always advisable to make concerted efforts to maintain peace and privacy, particularly if you have teenage children. The building standards and regulations governing acoustic control are somewhat limited. Typically they limit noise levels with respect to such installations as piping, but they are regarded as inadequate by many experts.

The greatest noise hazards are:
- air-transmitted sound from voices, music, general kinds of noise, etc.;

- impact sound caused for example by people walking across a floor, a door slamming, water flowing through a drainpipe, etc.;
- external noise, noise from outside the building.

Air-transmitted sound

The best protection against air-transmitted sound and general noise is a thick and solidly constructed wall or ceiling. The sound waves will then, at least partly, be reflected, and it will also be more difficult for them to cause vibration because the power of the sound is absorbed by the mass of the wall or ceiling. Thick, solidly constructed walls will in this way deaden or attenuate sound. For this reason lighter buildings such as a wood frame house are typically poorly soundproofed. One solution is to install heavy materials in the ceilings to increase the mass and therefore the sound absorbing properties of the room. Soft materials such as carpets, wall coverings, furniture, and acoustic ceiling boards also absorb air-transmitted sound. This phenomenon is termed acoustic absorption and in the process the sound waves are transformed into heat. The caveat here is that very often soft materials which are good from an acoustic control standpoint are not so good from an indoor air quality standpoint.

Impact sound

Concrete slab or other solid floor structures tend to be very good conductors of impact sound. One way of combatting such noise is by using soft, fibrous materials that will absorb the energy of the sound waves. In apartment buildings impact sound can be combatted using a floating layer of insulation. The decking is covered with a layer of insulating material, usually of rigid mineral fiber or insulation board; other suitable materials are panels of cork or coir, a fiber made from coconut husks. This elastic surface is then covered with a layer of plaster or concrete, to provide a durable floor substrate and adding mass. When this is being done, it is important to ensure that the concrete does not come in direct contact with the walls: If it did, thermal bridges would be created. The floor can then be laid on the topping. The same method can also be used when it is desirable to use a dry material in lieu of the plaster or concrete. In this case the decking can be covered with a sound insulating layer of wood fiberboard or coir panels, which is then covered by the floor substrate or by a loose layer of floor battens; the actual finish floor is then laid on top of this. A similar procedure can be applied in a wood frame building. In this case, wood fiberboard or coir panels provide the acoustical separation between the battens on which the floor is to be laid and the floor joists. The joist

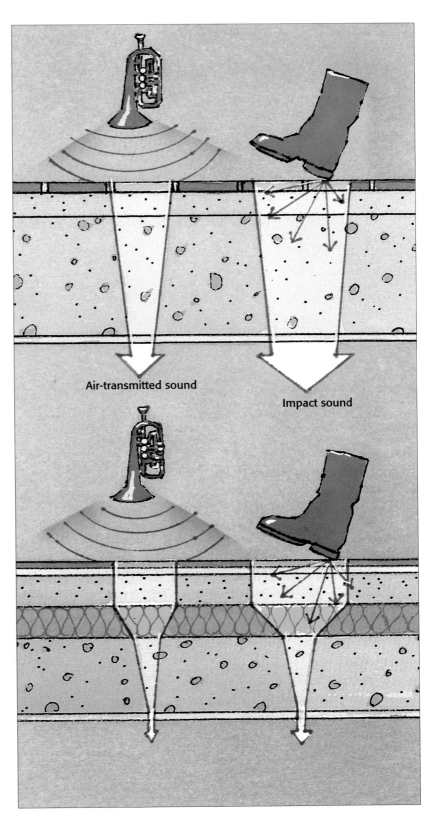

Air-transmitted sound

Impact sound

Both hard and soft materials can be used to control noise

Air-transmitted sound, such as loud music, and impact sound caused by walking up and down or by knocking, are dealt with in totally different ways. Air-transmitted sound is best combated with thick, massive walls and ceilings to absorb sound energy, whereas impact sound can best be reduced by soft insulating layers. This is why it's best to combine both hard and soft layers for effective acoustic control.

A floating floor

In a solid construction it's customary to use a floating layer for soundproofing. This requires that great care be taken to ensure that the floor plaster does not come into contact with the walls or the ceilings of the building and thus avoiding both thermal and acoustic bridges. Instead, concrete, gypcrete or plaster is poured on top of an elastic insulating layer and protected from the walls by an offset.

Wood frame buildings need effective noise control

In a wooden building the best strategy for reducing air-transmitted sound is to increase the mass of floors and walls. An example shown here is to set a layer of brick pavers, i.e., solid clay bricks (above) below the floor in the joist spaces. The attenuation of noise from pipes will be improved by wrapping them with coir strips. This can be finished with grout or cement leveling the surface and filling in all the gaps (left). The soft fiberboard will insulate against the sound of footsteps.

spaces between the floor and the ceiling can be filled with brick paves or clay tile for example in order to provide mass to further attenuate vibration. This additional load must, of course, be included when the building loads are being calculated for structural design. Any remaining gaps must also be filled with a light insulating material in order to eliminate reverberation inside any hollow space within that would tend to magnify the noise. Thin partition walls can be soundproofed similarly. In this case the wall is constructed of two separate wall panels, usually of gypsum board over some type of framing, which are not in any way connected to each other. Between them there should be a layer of soft, fibrous insulating material, such as fiberboard made from recycled paper, and a heavy (roofing) felt or wool matting. An existing wall or ceiling with poor sound insulating characteristics can be insulated by simply adding a new wall in front the wall or a new ceiling just below the existing ceiling. The cavity is filled with sound insulating material as before, but the

new wall itself must not be attached to the structure from which the acoustic isolation is desired: Any contact would result in acoustic bridges and thus sound transmission.

One can easily obtain low-noise plumbing fixtures, piping, and pipe fittings and there are also other methods which can reduce the amount of noise from this source to a minimum. For example, the inside of the pipe brackets can be lined with corrugated rubber or foam strips to prevent the noise and vibration from the pipes from being transferred to the walls and vice versa. When plumbing is installed inside a wall, the pipes should be wrapped with insulating material before the wall is finished off. The bathtub or shower pan should always be separated from the adjacent wall structure and the gaps then grouted or caulked. The heating and air-conditioning ducts are typically installed with duct liners which reduce noise but they should also be completely wrapped with foil backed insulation as well.

As a rule insulating materials that function well as acoustic insulation tend to be good thermal insulating materials as well. This casts a very different light on the additional costs of increased insulation for acoustic control, since the expenditure would have been spent on thermal insulation anyway. However, this does not necessarily apply in the opposite direction. Insulating panels made of polystyrene or of polyurethane are extremely poor sound insulators.

External noise reduction

The most important aspect of adequate noise protection from external sources such as street traffic, airplanes and weather, is high-quality windows which have low air leakage. For examples, windows made in the United States should have been tested to meet NWWDA Grade 60 requirements. Old windows do not always have to be replaced in a building on a busy street. Sometimes it's enough to add or replace weather-stripping and caulk any gaps around the frames. Another strategy is to reglaze the windows with heavier sound deadening glass (usually 4mm) or to add a storm panel glazed with this glass.

Reducing the noise from pipes
Heating and water pipes should be well insulated against sound transfer at minimal cost. This is standard practice in new buildings. In most cases it's enough just to wrap the pipes with soft materials, particularly at the brackets where vibrations could be transferred to the structure.

Acoustic isolation
The shower can be made less of a source of noise pollution as well by separating it from the surrounding walls and filling the hollow spaces with soft material up to the height of the wainscot.

Street noise
The table shows the noise nuisance on the outside of a building in different traffic conditions. At an approximate noise level of 54 dB(A) or more acoustic control strategies are imperative.

NOISE LEVEL IN FRONT OF BUILDINGS IN VARIOUS TRAFFIC CONDITIONS

Type of road	Traffic volume (vehicles/day)	Acceptable noise level in dB(A) Distance to middle of road in meters				
		10	50	100	500	1000
Freeways and freeway frontage roads	100,000	–	–	75	64	59
	10,000	–	70	65	54	49
Federal and state highways	50,000	–	–	70	59	54
	5000	73	65	61	50	45
Main thoroughfares and collector streets	20,000	–	67	63	52	46
	2000	66	57	53	42	–
Residential streets	5000	67	58	54	43	–
	500	57	48	44	–	–

FIRE PROTECTION

In the United States building materials are classified as combustible or not combustible and building codes allow for five types of fire-resistant construction depending upon the building use and its desired size. Non-combustible materials can be used in all types of construction whereas combustible materials may only be used in Types III-V. Materials are further rated as to their resistance to fire as determined by the "Standard Fire Test" developed by Underwriters Laboratory and required in ASTM (American Society of Testing Materials) Standard E119. The resulting rating is expressed in hours, as the time that the material or assembly can withstand exposure to and resist the spread of fire. A door able to inhibit the spread of fire for 90 minutes would be labeled as a 1½-hour fire-resistant door. Because the requirements for doors and windows are less than the surrounding wall this door would be suitable for installation in a 2-hour fire separation wall. Other tests classify materials as to their "flame spread" (ability to remain burning when flame is removed) and "smoke produced" which is a

crucial factor in determining the immediate threat to life caused by a burning material during a fire. Materials which have a flame spread and smoke produced rating of less than 25 are labeled Class A and are considered relatively safe materials. In this test a piece of oak hardwood by comparison would have a flame spread rating of 100. Any residential multi-family structure (R1) four stories high must be Type III One Hour Fire-Resistant construction or Type IV Heavy Timber. A building over four stories requires that it be built of Type I or Type II non-combustible materials. Generally, low-rise buildings of three stories or less can be of light wood frame (Type V) construction with 1-hour fire-resistant exterior walls and structural frame. This requires fireproofing usually by applying 2 layers of ⅝ inch gypsum wall board to both sides of a wall, or by using fire-treated lumber.

Structural components such as the wall, ceilings, beams, ventilating ducts and fire doors are also divided into fire-resistance classes. Depending on whether the structural element will resist a fully raging fire for 30, 60, 90 or 120 minutes, load-bearing

elements are placed in the fire-resistance class of 60, 90, or 120. A load-bearing wall must not collapse during the allotted period of time and must also prevent fire, smoke, or high temperatures from reaching the other side. According to state building regulations there are strict rules on the fire classification for a particular structural element. The interior compartment walls in apartments of a two-story house must have a classification of 30, the building walls have to comply with the requirements for classification 30 as structural elements as well.

The fire-resistance of a structure can often be improved if it is made up of several different materials. In this way the disadvantages of a "normal flammable" material can very well be compensated for by combining it with a variety of other materials manufactured from non-flammable materials. It is impossible, for example, to attain the 90 minutes specifications solely with wooden materials. But if a wood-framed building is clad on the outside with several layers of gypsum wallboards, attaining 90 minutes will not be a problem.

In private homes fire-resistant doors are compulsory only between the house and the basement or other rooms where heating equipment is installed, and between the house and the garage. Fire doors are also classified according to how long they resist a fire: FD 30 or 30 minute fire-resistant doors are flame-retarding and doors of FD 90 or higher are fireproof. Fire protection doors must be self-closing, which means that a door-closing device with a fusible link which will close by itself in case of fire is compulsory. Escape routes via fire stairs are frequently compulsory in the case of private wood frame dwellings and should never be replaced by a fire escape, which is more difficult to use in an emergency. It is preferable to install the stairs as a separate entrance to the upper story, because it will later be easier to separate this section of the building and to rent it out if desired. Fire protection equipment such as smoke alarms and fire extinguishers need no further discussion here. Nevertheless, it is important to point out that extinguishers containing halon gas should not be used at all. These gases which are frequently used because they do not damage computers and electronic equipment, do far more damage to the ozone layer than even CFCs and moves are afoot to have them banned completely.

The European Union Commission is trying to standardize the regulations for all European countries. However, some fire experts believe too little attention has been paid to testing smoke and its toxicity as in the American system. In the United States the new fire codes are having a very positive effect. Deaths due to fires in buildings are down from 16,000 in 1975 to less than 4,000 deaths in 1995.

A combination of materials improves fire-resistance

Strict fire regulations ensure that devastating fires are much rarer than in the past

THE ENERGY CONTENT OF BUILDING MATERIALS

The amount of energy used to manufacture and process a building material, or its "embodied energy," is one of the most important criteria when evaluating that material for its environmental acceptability. The building industry is one of the largest consumers of our natural resources for the materials with which to build, and, consequently, one of the prime perpetrators of environmental damage. A major part of this flow of resources, and thus of the environmental damage, results from the manufacture of a product, starting with the extraction of the raw materials and ending with the finished product. This applies particularly to metals, highly finished products and for complex technology intensive systems. Although this method of evaluating a material is far less thorough and exacting than a full "Life Cycle Assessment" or LCA, as discussed in the first section of this book, it is nevertheless a valuable and fairly quick method for making comparisons of one product or material over another. The portion of a product's embodied energy which comprises energy generated by non-renewable fossil fuels at all stages of production, transport, and processing is known as "gray" energy. The gray energy that goes into a building material in turn determines to a large extent, the amount of air pollution caused during its production through the emission of carbon dioxide and of other pollutants.

It is very difficult to assess the amount of gray energy used up by a product, and even the technical literature is sometimes not much help. For example the "electricity mix" or the fuel sources used by power stations to generate electricity differ widely. In France nuclear power is the most significant source of energy, in Sweden it is hydro-electricity and in Eastern Europe it is coal. The same diversity applies to the United States from region to region. Even the type of coal used can have significant impact on the resulting emissions. For this reason the Energy Information Agency publishes figures for power plant emissions from one part of the United States to another so that the specific emissions related to electricity use can be estimated for any area. This makes it possible to calculate the environmental damage due to the embodied energy of a specific product or material.

Again, there are variations in how efficiently the primary energy is used. The conditions under which the same building material is produced also vary considerably from country to country. Aging manufacturing plants may operate far less efficiently and require more energy, raw materials may have to be transported over dramatically varying distances. In spite of all these variables there is still enough statistical evidence to enable environmentally friendly builders to differentiate between building materials that are extracted using environmentally acceptable and environmentally hazardous methods.

Enough energy to melt steel

It takes energy to produce every kind of building material: energy for extraction, processing and finishing, and for transporting it to its destination. This embodied energy can be expressed in kilowatt hours per ton or per cubic meter.

"Green" building means choosing materials that require the least energy to manufacture and transport

Despite the difficulties in establishing how much energy has been used in the manufacture of a certain material, it is still important for builders and architects to take this factor into account when planning a building, and to obtain as much information as possible about different materials.

By way of illustration the list given here contains the energy component in the production of a number of building materials in kWh/cubic meter. The examples have been deliberately selected to show the possibility of alternatives:

- lightweight bricks   700
- limestone   350
- bonded resin plaster   3300
- limestone plaster   1100
- structural steel   57,000
- building timber   180
- hardboard (formaldehyde bonded)   2000
- MDF – medium density fiberboard   1400
- polystyrene insulating materials   450
- cellulose insulating materials   50

There are currently projects in progress attempting to incorporate the findings on the energy component of a wide range of materials into a number of CAD programs. Architects would then be able to integrate such programs into their building plans. At the press of a key professionals would have immediate access to information on the broader environmental advantages and disadvantages of constructing a building in different ways and using different materials.

THE USE OF PVC IN THE BUILDING INDUSTRY

Nowadays there is a growing demand for PVC in the building industry. Worldwide about 15 million tons of PVC are produced annually, or, to put it into perspective, 16% of all synthetics. A highly energetic and powerful lobby of PVC manufacturers and union representatives is continually trying to convince the general public that PVC is an environmentally friendly building material.

In recent years, PVC has been the subject of heated debate over the health and environmental effects of its manufacture. The environmental group Greenpeace considers PVC to be a serious hazard to human and ecological health. PVC has been banned or scheduled for phasing out in numerous cities, states and certain countries including Australia and Switzerland. New medical research indicates disturbing health risks caused by the many necessary additives

PVC is not OK

PVC seems to be used more and more in building, particularly in places where it cannot be seen. It is widely used to make pipes, conduits and toilet cisterns. Both the manufacture and the disposal of this plastic are extremely harmful to the environment, despite the manufacturers' statements to the contrary.

used in the manufacture of PVC. Some of these findings include the following substances:

- Plasticisers commonly used in large amounts in PVC are suspected of posing numerous health hazards. Phthalate plasticisers are the most commonly used type. High temperatures, such as those found in cars left in the sun, can cause the evaporation of plasticisers into the air rapidly. They also tend to off-gas normally at a gradually declining rate over the life of the product and they may readily be absorbed through the skin by direct contact. They are believed to cause damage to the immune system, central nervous system and reproductive organs. Moreover, such substances, in particular DEHP (Dil-2-ethylhexylphthalat), are believed to be carcinogenic. Research has found that as much as one-third of all household dust may consist of various plasticisers, and in a particular study 20% of the air samples taken exceeded the recommended exposure limits considerably.

- PVC requires the addition of stabilizers. Lead compounds are the most often used PVC heat stabilizers. When used for waste water piping, lead can leach out of the product contaminating the environment. Cadmium, a toxic metal, is widely used as a stabilizer in PVC but is more costly then lead. In the United States very little lead is currently being used in PVC. Tin and aluminum stabilizers are used instead. PVC also contains flame-retardants containing substances which are known to be health hazards, and in some cases antimony compounds which are also known carcinogens.

- Possibly the most serious problem presented by PVC, however, is the creation of highly toxic fumes containing dioxins, corrosive hydrochloric acid and highly toxic airborne lead or cadmium when PVC is burned. Due to its chemical contents it can quickly cause incapacitation and ultimately death or severe lasting injuries.

It is for these reasons that several communities in the United States and elsewhere have passed legislation severely restricting the use of PVC in the building industry. They are, however, mostly at the community level with the exception of a regional Great Lakes Area initiative. It is clear that in approximately 90% of the instances where PVC is used in construction, it could be replaced with other, less hazardous materials. PVC is usually chosen because of its low cost initially, however its replacement and repair costs over time may actually make it a more expensive alternative. Alternatives to rigid PVC include high density polyethylene, fired clay, concrete and polypropylene for pipes and related fittings.

Linoleum, tile and wood flooring, wood or aluminum clad wood windows, wood or wood composite siding and jute backed carpets are all readily available and reasonably priced alternatives.

Many of the more recently built buildings have a high PVC content, so when they are eventually demolished it is likely to prove very difficult to recycle all this PVC. Furthermore, the actual recycling of PVC from an environmental standpoint may not make sense at all. In order to reclaim the materials it requires careful, sorting and large amounts of energy to regrind and remelt the product. The new material is still far inferior from a performance standpoint and therefore will be used to manufacture low-grade materials such as park benches, or lawn chairs. Other research intended to break the polymer down into its basic parts for re-polymerization is currently attracting a lot of intention but it too is extremely energy intensive. Probably the best option at the present time is to do our utmost to avoid this potentially dangerous and harmful material.

PVC is harmful to the environment and, in case of fire, presents a considerable health hazard

Not a pleasant sight

PVC windows are capturing more and more of the market. It is estimated that 90% of the windows installed in the UK are now made of PVC. The price and the ease of maintenance are in their favor, as is the wide range of shapes and sizes. They are, however, a great source of danger in case of a fire and they are not historically accurate in appearance nor are they esthetically pleasing.

Not the best thing underfoot

PVC is becoming less popular as a floor covering. As far as the consumer is concerned the worst thing about PVC on the floor is that it doesn't look good and is not very durable. But it is important to know that PVC floor coverings can emit toxic substances, mostly phthalate; they often contain lead or cadmium and are a major health hazard in a fire.

THE FIRST STEPS TOWARD OWNING YOUR OWN HOME

Ecological design

Arch.: Professor T. Spiegelhalter, Freiburg, Germany

The compact shape of this house and the materials used reveal the ecological principles underlying its design. Unfortunately, very few architects have much experience in ecological and environmentally friendly construction methods, and their training up till now barely touches on the subject.

Buying a house is the most expensive undertaking most families will make. Careful planning and inquiry before taking the plunge will make this investment a good one. Should you buy an existing house or build a new one? If building your own, should you use the services of an architect or a building contractor? Can you be your own contractor? Where can you get the best advice? What should you look out for when buying land to build on? Who is liable if the construction work is shoddy? What are the advantages and disadvantages of the various construction techniques? How can you recognize construction faults/damage?

Getting started

If you are to build or buy a house, or have a renovation or additions made to your present home, expert advice will help you avert expensive oversights and prevent any unnecessary mistakes. The preferred choice is to use an architect at least in the preliminary phases. Another option is to put everything from the planning stage onwards to the final completion of the building in the hands of a single design/building contractor. Unfortunately, this involves certain risks as there will be quite a lot of your resources at stake and no clear definition of your building plans. Nonetheless, a building contractor may help you select pre-designed plans from a catalog, although much flexibility in taking advantage of your site or building unique spaces will be lost. Another option is to use a construction manager who will oversee the project as an advisor, estimator, construction director and team member with you and your architect.

An individual design

*Arch.: Professor T. Spiegelhalter,
Freiburg, Germany*

This home in Breisach, Germany
(see right and below) was made
entirely from recycled materials.
The highly original design bears
clear hallmarks of its well-known
architect, who has a strong
commitment to ecological
methods. However, one has to
question whether people would
be comfortable living permanently in such an odd-looking
home, and whether it would
really be practical.

The architect's role

An architect will be an invaluable assistant in translating all of your wishes, magazine cutouts and rough sketches into a dwelling that perfectly suits you and your budget. He or she will understand how to best utilize the site, use structural, mechanical and material systems and conform to current building codes. An architect can provide guidance in selecting construction professionals as he or she will be familiar with many local builders. Architects are also trained and adept at discovering creative opportunities that can make your home unique, tasteful and inspiring.

When choosing an architect, be sure to visit more than one firm, call references and visit a recent project or two. Many architects will express a willingness to consider an ecological approach to design and building. However, it is helpful to find one experienced with the challenges of solar design, energy-efficiency features, non-toxic construction, building with environmentally benign materials and site sensitive planning. Generally speaking, an architect who is a member of the local American Institute of Architects (AIA) chapter and who is active in the AIA Committee on the Environment (COTE) will be a good choice.

At present, architects specializing in ecological construction methods are not very common in the US. Working with one via the internet and the telephone via long distance may be possible if you cannot find someone suitable locally.

Architect's fees vary from region to region and from the degree of services you negotiate. Plan on spending 10% to 15% of the building construction cost on architectural services for design, bidding and construction administration of your contract with a contractor. If you have retained an architect to design and draw up plans for your dwelling, it is advisable to keep him or her involved in observing and monitoring the construction of the building. Of course, limited services can be obtained from an architect either for a set fee or on an hourly consulting basis.

Using a building contractor

Unless you plan to build your house yourself, you will need a good contractor to organize the complex construction process, build the home, and supervise the many subcontractors that will be used. And unless your builder is also a designer, you will need to provide him or her with plans of exactly how you want your future home to be constructed inside and out. The more detailed and specific these plans are, the more accurately the cost can be estimated and the clearer your agreement with the contractor will be. As with architects, be sure to interview several builders, talk to their clients and visit their projects

A skillful architect is of invaluable help in supervising construction work

to get an idea which builder will be best suited to the project you have in mind. A builder who is a member of the National Association of Home Builders (NAHB) will have a professional outlook. Contractors should be bonded, their employees insured and they should seek to build you as much as can be had for your budget with quality workmanship and materials. Since you are striving to build in an ecologically intelligent way, they should be somewhat informed in this regard or at the very least open to doing things in a different way than they may have built in the past.

Choosing a builder can involve negotiating a price with one who you like and has a good reputation, or by requesting bids from several to find the lowest price. The bidding process must be handled very carefully with identical and detailed information given to each bidding contractor to have a common factor by which you can actually compare them. In both cases, you may contract for a set price or on a time and materials basis with an amount not to be exceeded.

A popular alternative is to purchase a turn-key home package where a builder will have you choose from several house plans he builds and tailor it to your needs with cost adjustments. Unfortunately this process does not lend itself to incorporating green building features unless the builder specializes in providing energy-efficient housing using environmentally friendly construction methods. Contractors that use an Energy Star rating are required to meet federal standards for energy-efficiency. Still this type of home design does not lend itself to best use of the site, the sun, the local foliage and the uniqueness and individual values of the buyer.

Ecology is not outdated

Arch.: Professor T. Spiegelhalter, Freiburg, Germany

The solar panels on this small apartment building were placed on the roof in such a way that they contribute to the design of the building as an independent element and also provide shade. Structural elements are deliberately placed in full view rather than modestly hidden away.

Prefabricated houses running on solar energy

Arch.: R. Disch, Freiburg, Germany
The *Övolution* passive house is mass-produced by the largest German manufacturer of prefabricated houses. It features a high degree of active and passive use of solar energy and also optimal heat insulation properties. This system of construction demonstrates that even large manufacturers of prefabricated houses have recognized the trend toward ecological methods.

No longer production-line items

Today prefabricated houses are so individually designed that you cannot tell from looking at them that they are factory assembled.

Made of wood

These prefabricated houses have many ecological advantages, for example their above-average thermal insulation characteristics.

Prefabricated housing

Buying a prefabricated house means you get an all-in-one package. Occasionally, the manufacturer working together with a developer can even offer plots of building land, though in most cases the owner or the builders have to find their own. Today many suppliers of prefabricated homes offer a high degree of variety and individual choice as well as the security of fixed costs. Prefabricated houses can also be put up much quicker than traditional houses. Most of them are wooden structures, and this has led several ecologically oriented firms to move into this sector of the construction industry.

Although they all advertise their products from an ecological point of view, most prefabricated house suppliers are still careless in their choice of materials. Chipboard containing formaldehyde or isocyanate, and mineral fibers which pose a possible health risk and are still standard items. This is especially true of the segment of the prefabricated housing market known as *modular homes* which are extremely affordable but cheaply built homes which are usually trucked to the building site in one (single-wide) or two (double-wide) sections. Most of these homes are located in special developments sometimes known as "trailer parks" because zoning restrictions in most areas do not allow their construction in other residential neighborhoods. The lots are minuscule and conditions cramped. These neighborhoods have a high transience rate but are often chosen by seniors living on fixed incomes who are forced to reduce their living expenses and by first time home buyers who hope to move up to a "normal" neighborhood as quickly as possible. Unfortunately the living conditions in such housing is far from healthy and although high population densities make for efficient land use, the environmental damage done in developing these sites is usually considerable. Modular homes are typically flimsy, very energy-inefficient, have many serious indoor air quality problems and therefore have very little to offer those intending to build an ecologically friendly and healthy home.

Despite these problems, a number of particularly innovative pioneers of ecological methods are involved in this sector of the construction industry. These are mostly small firms that were already committed to the search for ecological solutions well before conventional firms began to identify the market potential of this field. For example, many of the log home fabricators which are enjoying a resurgent market are certifying their logs as harvested from sustainable or well-managed timber stands.

Increasingly, easily standardized construction methods are tempting small firms to build complete houses. Modern computer technology enables the advantages of individual planning to be combined with the use of largely prefabricated construction techniques. In many of the prefabricated components of such housing structural insulated panels (SIP) provide a high level of insulation and therefore an energy-efficient structure.

A number of smaller firms provide environmentally friendly products to make the most of prefabricated construction techniques

Building material suppliers and stores

Conventional building suppliers generally show little awareness of the problems posed by building materials which are environmentally harmful or potentially hazardous to health, or the ecological impact and sources of building materials. In addition, traditional do-it-yourself stores offer virtually no advice to those planning to build their homes in accord with ecological priciples. However, in many countries do-it-yourself Eco-stores have opened whose aim it is to offer both quality products and an advisory service. They can provide extensive advice on how to handle the materials involved – some of which require considerable care and expertise – and can also supply information on ecologically-minded architects and craftspeople.

The market for Green and non-toxic building materials is only just developing in the US. In Germany many do-it-yourself stores have opened a "shop within a shop" offering ecological products and there are even building supply stores specializing in eco-building materials. In the United States this is still limited to a small group of locally owned businesses in certain areas. The exceptions are several large chain building materials stores which have begun focusing on sustainable wood resources. For example the Home Depot offers a "smart wood" program which provides a certified sustainably harvested alternative for certain framing, moulding, and panel products. In addition, there are a number of catalog distributors of various "green" products such as Green Goods a supplier of renewable energy systems and components, energy-efficient appliances and water conservation devices.

A wide selection

The times when ecological self-service stores in Germany led a marginal existence are over. Stores of this kind are growing ever larger, the range of products is getting ever wider and sales are soaring, so much so that conventional chains of self-service stores have now "discovered" ecological products.

Construction financing

There are few financial decisions more important than those regarding the purchase of a family residence. A substantial portion of our incomes often goes toward housing expenses. Housing costs have skyrocketed over the past decade but our salaries have not kept pace with these rising costs. Therefore, home mortgage financing should be approached with as much knowledge as possible.

One of the greatest incentives to own one's home is the availability of mortgage interest tax deductions from personal income tax. In some cases the resulting savings on your tax liability may offset a significant part of the mortgage payments particularly in the early years of the loan when the proportion of the payment going toward interest is greatest. Of course everyone would also like to build up equity in their home to improve their net worth and borrowing capability and in most cases rising property values combined with the steady reduction of principal on the loan have this result. However, if you are building or buying your first home or even your second, obtaining financing can be a daunting and sometimes lengthy process. It can also be costly depending on the type and length of the loan, the amount being financed and the fees required by the particular institution or bank.

In the United States there is a variety of government insured mortgage programs designed to favor certain individuals who meet the given requirements whether it be low income, veteran, farmer, or first-time home-owner. This type of loan is often easier to obtain, allows a lower downpayment or, in some cases, a more favorable rate of interest. These insured loan programs include FHA (Federal Home Administration), VA (Veteran's Administration) and FmHA (Farmers' Home Administration). It is always advisable to consider financial planning considerations such as children's education, investment and savings strategies and retirement when making a decision about the type of loan most suitable for your individual needs. In addition, there is also a wide variety of mortgage loan types from which to choose. Some of the many options available include:

- *Fixed-rate conventional mortgage*
  This is the most commonly utilized mortgage in America. Borrowers are guaranteed a set interest rate and loan payments (principal and interest) for the life of the loan which will assist in long-term budgeting. The interest rate will almost always be higher than the beginning interest rate of an adjustable rate mortgage (ARM).

- *Adjustable-rate mortgage (ARM)*

  An adjustable (or variable) rate mortgage has an interest rate with the potential to change during the life of the loan. The interest rate may change as frequently as quarterly or as infrequently as once a year or once every 3 to 5 years and is usually tied to an outside indicator or index. A commonly used ARM index is the One Year Treasury Index, a weekly average yield of US Treasury Securities adjusted to a constant maturity of one year. To encourage their use, ARMs are almost always offered at interest rates below fixed-rate mortgages.

- *Construction loans*

  Typically written for terms of 6 to 12 months, construction loans provide the borrower with the funds (minus the downpayment) to construct a home. Monies are periodically advanced to pay for the various stages of construction. The borrower is usually charged interest only on the advanced funds. Lenders periodically inspect the building site to ensure the actual construction agrees with the borrower's submitted plans and the funds being advanced. Once the construction phase is finished, some loan plans automatically convert to a permanent mortgage either at a fixed or adjustable rate.

With any type of home financing, it is a good idea to consult a tax specialist such as an accountant or an attorney regarding the tax advantages of the various options. Receiving professional advice regarding which particular loan will offer you the best tax advantage can be well worth the price of a consultation.

MORTGAGE INTEREST RATS FOR THE UNITED STATES 1980–1995

Year	80	82	85	88	90	92	95
FHA	13.44	15.30	12.24	10.49	10.17	8.46	8.18
Conventional New Home	13.95	15.79	12.28	10.30	10.08	8.43	8.05
Conventional Exist. Home	13.95	15.82	12.29	10.31	10.08	8.43	8.05

Sources: Board of Governors of the Federal Reserve System, Federal Reserve Monthly, and Annual Statistical Digest; FHA Insured, Secondary Market

OWNER-OCCUPIED HOUSES AND APARTMENTS FOR WHICH A MORTGAGE EXISTS (1993 FIGURES)

Belgium	62%
Denmark	90%
Greece	15%
Spain	26%
France	48%
The Netherlands	77%
Portugal	14%
Great Britain	68%
United States	42%

source: eurostat; US Federal Reserve Balance Sheets for the US Economy

Rich or poor?
The further south you go in Europe the smaller the proportion of mortgage-funded purchases. However, the investment sums required in the Mediterranean area are generally smaller.

Get out of my light ...
as the philosopher Diogenes said to Alexander the Great. Like Diogenes, modern construction researchers dwell under drum-shaped roofs as they debate the importance of solar energy construction methods. These conference and exhibition halls are located on what was once the site of a colliery.

Subsidies give solar technology a boost

Arch.: Hegedys & Haus of Graz, Austria
Without federal subsidies, the sort of thoroughgoing exploitation of solar energy evinced by this zero energy consumption house in Graz would be too expensive.

Incentives for the building technologies of the future

Financial incentives for use of renewable energy in the United States

Today there is significant federal money being spent every year on R&D, business technology transfer, partnerships between government labs and industry (CRADAs), upgrades to public buildings, education and public awareness and numerous high visibility case studies and pilot projects.

As the 1998 fiscal year came to a close, Congress made DOEs involvement in the Million Solar Roofs Initiative "official." In addition to authorizing the Initiative, Congress budgeted $1.5 million to support its activities. The money will be used to overcome implementation obstacles and support partnerships.

1998 was a year of unbridled growth for the solar energy industry. The Solar Energy Industries Association (SEIA) reported that over 25,000 solar pool heating systems, 6,000 solar water heating systems, and 3,000 solar electric systems were installed in the United States. In addition, five new solar manufacturing facilities came on-line in California, Delaware, Massachusetts, Ohio, and Virginia. According to the Worldwatch Institute, the sale of photovoltaic cells expanded more than 40% in 1997. Solar power is now the world's second fastest growing energy source next to wind power. Much of the recent growth in solar sales can be attributed to major solar rooftop programs initiated in the United States, Europe, and Japan (Worldwatch Report, 1998).

Federal programs such as the Department of Energy's Million Solar Roofs Initiative and the President's Climate Change Action Plan, the EPA's Energy Star Homes and Green Lights Programs, are designed to promote renewable energy systems and energy-efficiency though a variety of grants, subsidies and tax incentives to institutional as well as residential customers primarily in partnership with other governmental and private organizations and at the local level. Some examples of the many programs include:

- The New York State Energy Research and Development Authority (NYSERDA) has $1 million available to support grid-connected photovoltaics (PV) projects aimed at stimulating the PV market in the state of New York. NYSERDA's goals are to gain experience in installing and operating the systems in the residential market. The New York State legislature has also recently enacted an income tax credit for homeowners who install PV systems. The credit is equal to 25 % of the total cost and installation of the system.

- The Renewable Energy Resources Program is a state grant program administered by the Illinois Department of Commerce and Community Affairs (DCCA) to facilitate the use of renewable energy resources. Qualifying technologies include solar, wind, energy crops, biomass and some small hydropower.

- The Colorado Governor's Office of Energy Conservation (OEC) has been working to educate the public about photovoltaic system financing and maintains a list entitled "Colorado Lenders and Brokers Who Finance Photovoltaic-powered Homes." This has been and will continue to be distributed to potential PV system owners to help them more easily identify sources of financing.

- The State of Vermont has pledged to add 1000 solar energy systems to roofs around the state by 2010. In addition to current domestic hot water marketing efforts with Solar Works, it is estimated that Vermont currently has 300 solar installations on its buildings.
- The California Renewable Energy Marketing Board (REMB) released a report pointing out that an increasing number of California utilities are investing in green power. As of next year, California will have 55 new renewable projects operating in the state.
- The US. Department of Energy (DOE) recently announced that it had awarded $1.4 million in grant money to 17 renewable energy projects in 15 US. States and Territories. The 17 projects focus on applications of renewable energy for remote energy needs. The purpose of the grants is to demonstrate that cost-effective, modular technologies are reliable, easy to operate and easy to maintain.

In addition, a number of states have recently passed "net metering" legislation which generally requires utilities to credit homeowners and small businesses that generate a portion of their own electricity from renewable sources such as wind, solar or small-scale hydro at the same price they are paying for power. For example, in New Hampshire, the state's net metering law allows customers who are generating 25 kW or less of renewable energy to interconnect with a single electric meter that will run backwards when the customer is producing more power than needed. Credits earned during a given month will be carried over to the customer's next monthly bill. Other states which have passed net metering legislation include Maine, New Mexico, and California, which also allows a property tax exemption for solar energy systems. The California legislature determined that net metering encourages private investment in renewable energy sources and helps stimulate economic growth in the state.

A variety of programs offers grants and tax incentives

Subsidies for many different projects

A huge variety of subsidies for ecological construction are available, whether for solar hot water, photovoltaic, or wind energy systems (far right). Other countries, such as Germany, even subsidize the costs of adding greenery to façades (right) or planting courtyards (below).

THE BUILDING SITE

The house must be adapted to the location

Design options for a new house are limited by the chosen location and situation of the building site and by the prevailing building regulations. Development costs are a factor which is often overlooked, and obligations provided for in the deed or abstract can occasionally lead to unpleasant surprises.

Location

The choice between an urban, suburban or rural location is the first and possibly the most important choice most homeowners will make. To choose to live in the city you may be able to do without a car since schools, shopping, cinemas, restaurants, and so on are all within easy reach by foot or by public transportation. On the other hand, a rural setting provides more open space and greater opportunities for children to play, security is not as great an issue and you

do not have your neighbors living on top of you. On the other hand, a car will be indispensable for most trips. Good plots of building land inside a city are rare and you may have to pay up to a third or more of the total construction cost for the land alone. Land costs vary tremendously from one area to the next. While one may find a suitable rural site for less than $10,000 per acre of land, it is not uncommon in a choice inner-city location to pay over $50,000 for a small one-quarter acre site. The end result is you might pay the same for a five-acre site in the country near a large city as you would for a postage stamp sized lot within the city. Other considerations include property taxes, available utilities such as gas, sewer and water, quality of schools, etc.

An ideal location for an ecologically friendly house would be a south-facing hillside. But if it is in a central location the price may be high to begin with and a

Extreme situations

The views from such a hilltop location may be breathtaking, and if the house faces south or southeast it is ideal for exploiting solar energy, but building in such locations, or on hillsides, can lead to a number of costly problems not to mention the danger of mudslides or subsidence.

Flooding

Ill-considered building developments in flood plain areas and the resulting destruction of property in flood years are having bitter consequences for the inhabitants: Ever more serious flooding of the Rhine, Elbe and Neckar are a serious problem for the local populations shown here and for the Mississippi River Valley inhabitants in the United States in recent years of high water.

hillside situation also means higher construction costs and more ongoing maintenance. Before you buy a plot of land on which to build you should consider the following questions:

- Is there evidence of pollution as the result of any previous use of the site, for example as a landfill or some other industrial use?
- Does the site receive enough sunshine or is it in the shade of neighboring buildings, or trees? – Is there any danger of flooding from nearby rivers or water draining down the hillside? – Is the level of ground water so high that expensive foundations will have to be built?
- Is there a problem with ambient noise from nearby streets or other sources? – Particularly, is there noise in the direction in which you will wish to open the house up to the sun or which is near the garden or patio?
- Is the site exposed to harsh winter winds? – Does it benefit from cool summer breezes?
- Are there any public or private development plans for the immediate vicinity which will restrict views, solar access, make the area noisier or in some other way detract from the future use of the site?
- What are the subsurface soils? – Will they support conventional foundations?
- Are there particularly attractive or unattractive views?
- Is access to the building site easy or difficult?

When checking for any polluted areas on or near the site the local planning authorities can help. They will generally be aware of any Superfund sites (EPA identified sites which are mandated for cleanup and restoration) and they may even keep a listing of other contaminated sites of lesser hazard. Alternatively, one might ask the neighbors what the site was used for in the past. One should also determine whether there are any restrictions on the way the land can be used or whether there has been intensive farming including heavy use of pesticides, in which case planting a garden may be problematical.

Protection from Groundwater

Building a basement in an area with a high water table require special construction and high expenditures. One might very well decide they can do without the basement after all.

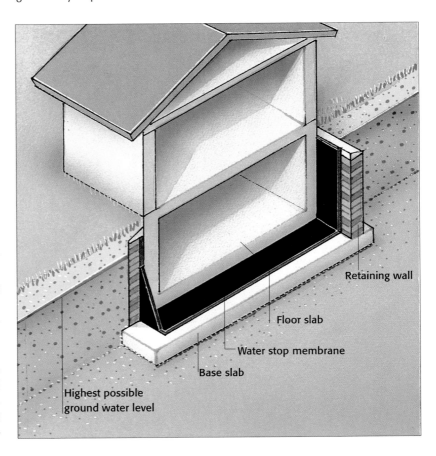

Retaining wall

Floor slab

Water stop membrane

Base slab

Highest possible ground water level

Urban development plan and building regulations

In order to receive federal tax dollars for various purposes all cities, municipalities or counties in the United States must submit five-year development plans periodically. These plans include such aspects as land use, infrastructure expansion, watershed protection, air water emissions, etc. In larger metropolitan areas where there are numerous such governing bodies with their individual plans, there are sometimes supervisory planning councils which coordinate and blend these development plans at the respective boundaries. As a means of implementing these development plans and also regulating land development, each governing body develops its own zoning ordinance which specifies such things as the

Corner sites can cost extra
If you buy a corner site you may find yourself having to pay higher development costs or street assessments.

minimum lot size, boundary setbacks, maximum floor areas, maximum permissible number of floors, required greenspaces, etc., for each zoning designation (for example, single-family, multiple residential or commercial as specified in the applicable land use plan). There may also be architectural design guidelines or regulations which specify maximum heights of buildings, the slope of the roof, and perhaps even the direction of the roof ridge (i.e., whether the house's gable end or eaves is facing the street). Also covered may be rules governing colors and materials to be used for external design, the appearance of the roof, whether the façade has to be plastered, etc.

In order to proceed with construction in almost all parts of the United States one must obtain a building permit. This usually requires that plans be submitted to the municipal building inspection or building safety department for review to determine that the requirements of all applicable building codes and zoning ordinances have been met. In the case of the architectural design regulations or rules governing historic districts, these are often administered separately by an empowered Architectural Review Board (ARB), but not always. If one wishes to circumvent some aspect of the zoning ordinance, it is usually necessary to apply for a variance to the municipal or city planning and zoning department which would then be subject to a vote by the city council, county board or other local governing body.

A critical aspect of the zoning regulation are the various lot setbacks and height restrictions. These determine the actual "building window" or the three-dimensional space within the boundaries and setbacks that the building can occupy. The size of the building may also be limited by floor area limitations depending on zoning designation and location.

In built-up areas where almost all neighboring plots of land have had houses on them for many years, many cities also have established historical districts which are governed by requirements that seek to preserve the fabric, quality and materials of a neighborhood or district for posterity. In such cases the external design of any new house must be in harmony with existing buildings, subject to review by a appointed historical review or architectural review board. It is advisable, then, to make a preliminary planning application in which you submit rough sketches of the intended building to find out whether the house would be acceptable in its intended form. This should be done long before one sets about designing in earnest.

Billions invested below ground
Sewer systems, water, gas and electricity supply lines do not come cheap. Billions are invested in these underground utilities, and anyone building a new home will have to contribute to these development costs.

Land development (provision of access and connections to utilities)

Usually included in the price of the lot in a newly developed neighborhood, which the land developer would typically bear, are all of the costs and fees of providing access to the plot via roads and paths, of gas, water and sewage connections, and sometimes also a proportion of the costs for a playground. These costs can constitute a major expense, and do inflate the price of the land significantly in heavily populated areas. If one is disposed to undertake development alone, these costs must be taken into account. It is customary for costs of public utilities and roads to be in the form of assessments made against the land owner. Thus, when purchasing a pre-existing property it is advisable to ensure that there are no such development costs outstanding. The utilities available also determine the kind of heating fuel which can be used. For example, if there is to be no gas pipeline in the neighborhood, it hardly makes sense to opt for gas central heating.

In rural areas with larger building lots, it is not usually cost effective to lay pipelines over several miles to each individual house, and thus each house must rely on its own well, rainwater collection system, septic systems, wood or biomass generators for heating and perhaps solar arrays for electricity. In particularly remote areas it may even be unfeasible to hook up to the electric grid or phone wires. These houses are referred to as "off-the-grid." Since they must be totally self-reliant it is even more important that they be as energy-efficient as possible and that the site allow for renewable energy sources such as PV systems or wind generators.

Not by accident or individual whim

The development plan (below) gives an inkling of the detailed planning that has to be done before construction can begin. The example of the German city, Tiefenbronn, shows local authority's ecological requirements for "the city of the future." Low energy construction methods are specified, flat garage roofs must be planted to receive planned permission, cultivated areas must use indigenous vegetation, and the use of rainwater to flush toilets is recommended.

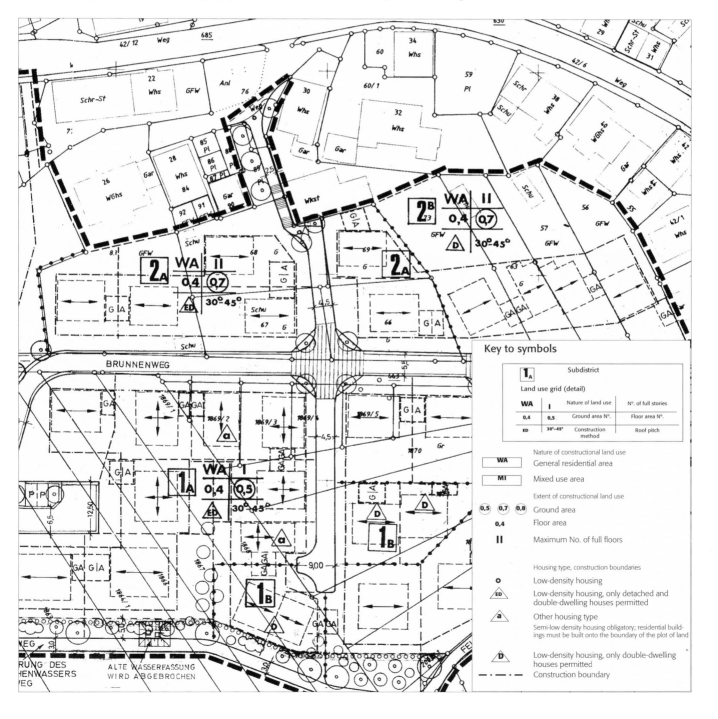

Biological sewage treatment facilities

Smell the roses

Who would have thought that sewage was being treated here? Innovative subsurface-flow wetlands, also called microbial rock plant filters, are soil-less, and utilize a gravel medium to anchor plants. Wastewater flows through the gravel and is not visible at the surface. This type of sewage treatment facility bears more resemblance to a flower garden than to a foul-smelling cesspool. Despite this, the authorities are often suspicious of this kind of biological sewage treatment.

In all new developments storm sewers for rain water and surface runoff is separate from the sanitary sewer collection system. Approximately 1,200 United States cities still have older combined septic and storm sewers. Here, the problem is that rains often cause these systems to overflow, discharging untreated sewage into lakes and streams. In 1989 the EPA found that more than 66% of conventional sewage treatment plants in the United States have either water quality or public health problems. But recently numerous safe and effective as well as environmentally sound alternatives have emerged for the localized treatment of sewage wastes. If we

consider natural systems present in nature which have the function of removing waste materials from water we find an incredibly effective model for our own sewage treatment – the wetlands or marshes. Natural wetlands have a huge capacity to cleanse and restore. They can be used to treat sewage from urban sources if not already overwhelmed with pollutants or destroyed by development. For this reason natural wetlands have been protected for a number of years in the United States.

A low-tech and relatively inexpensive alternative to traditional waste treatment plants is the use of artificial or constructed wetlands. One such example which has been proven effective is in Arcata, California where the sewage from a town of 17,000 residents is treated naturally by 155 acres of wetlands constructed on land which was previously used as a landfill. Completed in 1974, the project cost $3 million less than the estimated cost of a conventional plant. In addition, the artificial marshes provide a bird sanctuary and habitat for thousands of otters, birds and other marine animals. The location is a city park and focal point for tourists and for civic pride. Over 150 other cities and towns have since implemented natural or artificial wetland sewage treatment.

Such low-cost and ecologically based methods are even feasible for neighborhoods of ecologically minded residents such as a co-housing project or eco-development. Many communities allow for use of biological sewage treatment approaches which commonly include the surface-flow and the subsurface-flow wetland. Surface flow wetlands, also called wastewater lagoons, usually use a tiered system of ponds with wetland plants to treat wastewater. Subsurface-flow wetlands, also called microbial rock plant filters, are soil-less, and utilize a gravel medium to anchor plants. Wastewater flows through the gravel and is not visible at the surface. Effluent from both types of privately installed systems currently are only used for irrigation or other similar graywater uses, however, as experience and controls are improved they may actually become potable water sources in the end.

Registrar of deeds

In addition to the regional land-use plan, the local registrar of deeds and abstracts is quite an important source of information which should always be consulted before purchasing any prospective building lot. Apart from detailed information on existing financial commitments, you can also learn about past owners and transactions, purchase options, rights of way and other easements. These can mean, for example, that a neighbor has a right of access to his land via your land, or that a water or gas pipeline has been laid under your land, significantly restricting the use to which it can be put.

Regulations governing the use of land

Fences are not a solution for disputes

Disputes between neighbors cannot be solved by putting up high fences. Arguments about noise and lot boundaries keep the courts in business. Legal provisions are designed to keep such disputes to a minimum.

There is no waste in natural ecosystems

Plant sewage treatment facilities can treat normal household sewage leaving no residue, while enriching the natural environment at the same time because in natural systems everything becomes food for some other organism. Only synthetic chemicals are sometimes beyond their capability to remove. In conventional sewage treatment plants everything becomes a waste product in need of disposal.

CONTRACTS AND LIABILITY

Liability for construction work is considerable

The various legal issues relating to construction and drawing up the necessary ironclad agreements with contractors and/or architects are very complicated and can only be touched briefly in a book of this kind. Standard forms of agreement have been developed by the American Institute of Architects and can be obtained by contacting the local chapter AIA office in your area. It is relatively easy to abbreviate or customize these standard forms to individual needs. When establishing these agreements between owner and architect and between owner and contractor, it is important that the document clearly establishes who is responsible for what, how the fees are to be established and how invoices for payments to the contractor are to be certified. For example, if you are billed for work that is not completed or is not completed satisfactorily, some means of determining this and correcting the problem before payment is made should be outlined in the agreement. Often the architect provides this certification; however, it can be performed by any suitable inspection agency. It is usually in the owner's interests to establish the full amounts to be paid up front or by "lump sum" rather than by the "time plus materials" method. The

He who digs a pit for others ...
Barricades and other safety measures do not exempt the builder/owner of liability. The risk of someone accidentally falling into the excavations requires adequate insurance.

Excavation
It is all too easy to damage pipelines during construction work if the backhoe operator is careless. This kind of risk is also covered by insurance.

architect or the contractor would always prefer to be able to charge for whatever work is ultimately required but this is not feasible in most situations for the owner who is limited to a specific amount in terms of financing. Often a suitable compromise may be an hourly fee with a "not-to-exceed" cap on the total fees. Contractors, on the other hand, are used to bidding the total cost of the project at the beginning provided there are detailed plans for the contractor's estimate. If a total sum is agreed upon, it is usually a good idea to avoid changes in the plan, because this will give the contractor an opportunity to make up for any shortfall resulting from something he may have overlooked in his estimate.

Mortgage lenders always require a title or abstract search by a licensed title company and title insurance just in case the investigation fails to uncover some glitch or abnormality which could affect their interests. Even if one is paying cash, it is a good idea to pay for these things if only for peace of mind. Given the large sums of money that are usually at stake it is usually best to consult with an attorney before drawing up papers or before signing any agreement.

Insurance

During the construction phase certain insurance policies are a must. Generally, contractors are required to pay workmen's compensation insurance for each of their employees so that they will continue to receive an income in the event of an injury on the job. Another is builder's risk insurance. This provides coverage if anyone is injured or anything is damaged on the construction site, for example, if someone falls into an excavation hole or a pile of building materials falls on your neighbor's car. Liability coverage should be provided for not less than one million dollars. In the event that you secure assistance from friends or neighbors you must be certain that your existing insurance will provide for liability if they are injured; in any case, they should sign a release stating that you are not responsible for any injuries that might befall them.

Architects and contractors frequently carry insurance which cover omissions or errors in the performance of their work which ultimately cause damage or loss of value to the premises. Be sure to ask them whether they have this coverage. In addition, contractors may be bonded up to a certain value for a given project so that the owner will be fully reimbursed if the contractor fails to perform the work properly.

If, however, excavations are flooded or a storm destroys a newly-constructed roof, temporary construction or builder's risk insurance should include this. Fire damage could also be included, but another option is to take out homeowner's insurance, covering the finished house at the earliest possible date. In some cases this means that you will also be covered during the construction phase at no extra expense.

Usually homeowners insure themselves not only against fire but also against storm damage and flooding as a result of burst pipes. This is known as comprehensive homeowner's policy, and banks normally insist on such a policy before they will grant a mortgage. Before obtaining such insurance it is certainly worth comparing prices, as it is not unusual for the premiums charged by different companies to vary by as much as 50–100%. In some regions storm and gale insurance also provides coverage against earthquakes and flooding (overflowing rivers, etc.) If the building is in a designated flood plain, special flood insurance will normally be required. Always read the policy carefully to determine what is and what is not covered. To avoid any under-insurance you should declare any special characteristics such as underfloor heating, and also notify the insurance company of any subsequent remodeling or improvements. In addition, retain plans and photos of all sides of all buildings.

When the house is finished, liability insurance will again be required to provide coverage against such accidents as someone slipping on an icy path or being hit by a falling roof tile. If you are an owner-occupier, personal liability insurance may be adequate, but in the case of rented premises, house- and landowner's liability insurance should be underwritten. Again a standard minimum for such insurance is $1 million but may be much higher.

Direct insurers who provide policies directly rather than through an independent agent or broker often offer particularly favorable terms. On the other hand, insurance brokers are not tied to one insurance company and can select the most favorable policies for their clients.

No Trespassing!

Anything that is forbidden is twice as much fun and just as dangerous. Therefore, particular care must be taken to prevent unauthorized access, especially by children and teenagers, to construction sites.

THE REAL ESTATE MARKET

Older houses have many advantages

Older buildings have style

If you buy an older house you will normally pay less than for a new home and will have a more convenient location. And of course older houses often have more character and style. There is a downside however...

There are many advantages to purchasing an existing home. You will generally have to pay less than for a new ready-to-occupy property, and will be able to move in after a brief period for renovation and remodeling. Additionally, you do not have to bear the interest charges during a lengthy construction period while simultaneously continuing to pay rent on your current accommodation. Furthermore, you will be able to assess the maturely developed residential area and its associated local infrastructure, factors which are decisive to the value of a house.

The United States real estate market has been less volatile in recent years, however during the 1980s

Extra space
Arch.: B. Heidbreide, Schwerte, Germany
If space is short you can generally build an addition and at the same time add ecological features such as a sun room. However, it is advisable to check if your plan is permissible prior to purchase.

property values increased by a factor of 3.6. Real estate values appreciated a whopping 76% from 1979–1981, 37% from 1981–1984 and 48% from 1984–1989. In the ten years from 1985 to 1995 rents have increased a total of 42% with an annual increase of only 3–5% or roughly the rate of inflation for that period. Even though some tax benefits for acquiring your own home have been discontinued in recent times, and the overheated market cooled off during the early 1990s, real estate still represents a fairly good capital investment and owning a home remains the goal of almost all renters.

However, an old proverb says: "Anyone with more money than sense buys an old house and fixes it up." This is true in two different ways. First, you have to accept the property in its existing state, since any major renovation will be more expensive than comparable work on a new structure. Second, it is difficult for laymen to correctly evaluate the structural state or infrastructure of a house and thus the need for the required expenditures on immediate improvements or ongoing maintenance work.

Points to clear up before purchase

In view of the above considerations, it is highly advisable to have an accredited building expert look at the property. The address of such an expert can usually be obtained from the local Chamber of Commerce, a property appraisal firm, or in some cases a prospective lender. If you are already working with an architect you can often rely on him or her along with various consultants they might recommend. They will be able to carry out a survey to determine any identifiable structural defects, code problems or inadequate heating, plumbing or electrical systems and calculate the actual value of the property less the estimated cost of repair work. Depending on the area and work to be done, this will cost around $50–100 per hour, and is money well spent as it gives you a stronger position when negotiating the purchase price.

When evaluating the building there are many important factors to consider apart from the date of construction and the superficial appearance of the building's interior. If at all possible you should also find out in detail what building materials were used both when the house was originally constructed and during any subsequent renovation or remodeling work. This will enable you to estimate how soon major maintenance work may be required. Information about date of construction and subsequent work can sometimes be obtained from the local building inspection department for as long back as they retain building permit applications. Another source of such information is the public library, especially if the house has historical significance. The building's

Extra living space underneath the roof

Arch.: B. Heidbreide, Schwerte, Germany

The popular trend of turning the attic space into a useable living area is not always feasible. Thus it is a good idea to check that there are no legal or structural impediments before you buy.

energy consumption status is also of great importance. Usually the local utilities can provide such information although you may need permission from the previous occupants to get it.

Before purchasing the house it also makes sense to check with the planning authorities and with specialists whether any intended changes are technically feasible and would, in fact, receive permission. In the case of an owner-occupied apartment not only the planning authorities but also other adjacent owners will have a say if supporting elements are to be removed or alterations undertaken which affect any externally visible parts of the building. If purchasing the property through a real estate agent you should determine who pays the agent's fee, and you should be suspicious if the realtor wants to sell a financing package at the same time. In the United States, it is generally advisable only to do business with licensed real estate agents who are also members of a local chapter of the National Association of Realtors.

What work needs doing when?

Beauty is a passing thing

Today, a building which lasts 100 years is considered more than adequate. However, historic structures from bygone ages show that they can of course survive much longer than that. But not all structural elements last the same length of time so one should have a general idea of the life expectancy desired before selecting the materials and methods.

Buildings require maintenance work at roughly predictable intervals

Even if you can move into an old house with minimal initial refurbishment, it is important to get as precise an idea as possible of what work will need to be completed in the medium and long term as well. Buildings and grounds require more or less intensive maintenance work at roughly predictable intervals. Some examples are given below:

- painting of external windows and doors – every 5 to 10 years;
- painting of façades, chimney pots, roof gutters and drainage pipes, wallpapering and interior painting, carpeting, renewal of silicone sealant – at least every 10 to 15 years;
- tar paper or shingle roofs, external stucco, exposed or attic insulation, vinyl windows, window blinds and roller shutters, heating systems – every 20 to 30 years or so;
- water pipes and electrical installations, linoleum flooring, tiles, light wooden or plaster board partition walls – 25 to 40 years or less;
- wooden windows and external doors, cast iron railings, radiators, porches, eave brackets – 30 to 50 years or less;
- tile and slate roofing, softwood window ledges and floors – 50 to 60 years;
- hardwood roof structures, floor sill plates – 80 to 100 years.

How can I uncover structural damage?

Whether or not you have any expert building knowledge you can get a rough idea whether there are serious structural defects in an old house by looking for the following:

- Damp walls in the basement due to inadequate damp-proofing. This can lead to damage to structural elements supporting the main floor, for example due to rusting steel beams or rotting floor joists. Diagnosis is very simple: Look out for a musty odor or damp patches on the wall. It will cost a lot to rectify this problem.
- Cracks on the façade are a warning sign, and may be due to movement of structural elements (subsidence, structural defects). Other possible causes of cracks are the use of unsuitable materials, while thermal bridges and water damage can cause cracks and subsequent spalling of plaster. In all cases, the cause of any cracks should be carefully investigated.
- In the roof area poorly sealed joints and missing roof tiles are common, and can often lead to damage to the wooden roof structure due to moisture damage, dry rot, or infestation by insects. A simple screwdriver test can determine whether the wood of the roof structure is still capable of bearing weight. If the screwdriver will remain firmly fixed in the wood without causing any crumbling of the

wood when the screwdriver is withdrawn, then the rafters are still sound.

- Binding structural elements in the masonry are also a weak point in which rot often occurs, and are difficult to gain access to. When converting the attic area, faulty sealing of the structure can also lead to structural damage, but it may require a specialist to determine this.
- On the roof, the chimney flue tiles are particularly exposed to the elements and can easily become unstable. It's hard to tell whether this has happened without taking a closer look. However, it's dangerous to get up on a roof, and this should be left to a professional. Large deposits of soot can build up in wide old chimneys, sometimes falling out of the fireplace. Installing a steel or ceramic chimney flue will eradicate this problem.
- Flat roofs, roof terraces and balconies often suffer from defective sealing and poor drainage. A lack of gradient, warped sheet metal and blocked drains all lead to frequent puddles from which moisture can penetrate the building's structure. On balconies rusting steel beams are the most frequent problem, and they can be identified by flaking on the underside. The cause may be either thermal bridges or defective sealing.
- Internal walls should be carefully checked for cracks and damp patches which can be signs of structural damage. Blistering under flaking plaster may, however, be harmless if it is due to poorly plastered lath. Patches of mildew in corners and on internal walls connecting to external walls are signs of inadequate air sealing or moisture proofing of the external walls.

- Wooden joist floors often exhibit damage to the bearing ends. This can only be reliably determined by taking the floor surface up. This is particularly awkward if the underside of the wooden joist floor is faced with plaster or drywall, in which case making good the damage without destroying the ceiling is a time-consuming and expensive business.
- Windows and doors can be tested for tightness of seal by simply using a strip of paper. If the door is closed on the strip and the strip can then easily be pulled out, the door is not tight. If you are uncertain how to judge a structure, and a large investment is at stake, it is advisable to turn to a professional for advice and have a further assessment done with the aid of infra-red thermograph imaging and a blower door test. Opening up walls or ceilings at the key points cited above, or expert acoustic analysis will provide more precise information.

Due for replacement
Electrical wiring almost always needs replacement when renovating a structure. Safety regulations have become ever stricter, and old services and wiring were not designed to meet modern requirements.

Trouble areas
When viewing a house these areas should be examined with particular care, for they are the places where problems are most often detected in older buildings, or where they are particularly expensive to correct.

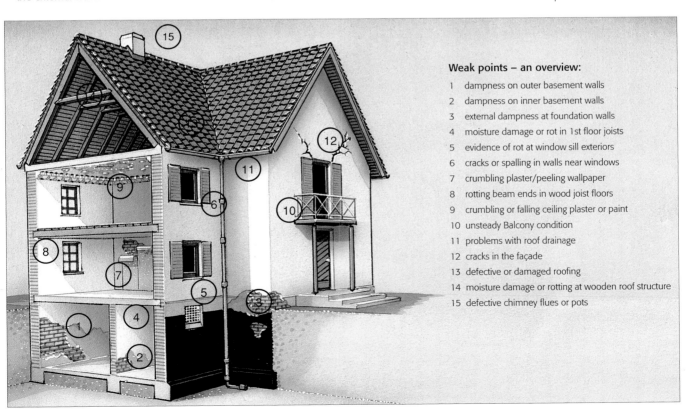

Weak points – an overview:

1 dampness on outer basement walls
2 dampness on inner basement walls
3 external dampness at foundation walls
4 moisture damage or rot in 1st floor joists
5 evidence of rot at window sill exteriors
6 cracks or spalling in walls near windows
7 crumbling plaster/peeling wallpaper
8 rotting beam ends in wood joist floors
9 crumbling or falling ceiling plaster or paint
10 unsteady Balcony condition
11 problems with roof drainage
12 cracks in the façade
13 defective or damaged roofing
14 moisture damage or rotting at wooden roof structure
15 defective chimney flues or pots

THE BUILDING SHELL

THE BUILDING SHELL

Whether it's a traditional brick-and-mortar construction or wood frame construction makes a big difference to the finished house. Although a house with a wood frame or post-and-beam skeleton cannot be distinguished from a masonry wall house from the inside once it has been plastered, the feeling of living in one can be quite different.

Wall construction

The essential distinctions relating to the shell are between internal and external walls, and between bearing and non-bearing walls. These distinctions can be clearly seen as we look beneath the surface. Internal walls chiefly have the function of separating

insulation. Due to the wide range of possible designs and climatic conditions, no attempt is being made here to specify the degrees of thickness of the necessary wall and insulating material required for constructing a low-energy house or a passive house or to comply with the various energy codes.

The type of building method and availability of materials locally obviously plays a large part in deciding what materials to use. In the postwar years prefabricated construction methods largely supplanted traditional building methods. These new systems generally produced poor results, so traditional methods are in many areas now undergoing a renaissance, though in many cases using totally new building materials. Accordingly, whether one builds using solid masonry construction

The naked structure
The underlying framework reveals what type of construction is being used: In this case the load-bearing structure is made of wood.

spaces. As a result, they are normally a good deal thinner than external walls and are used to provide soundproofing, thermal zone separation and, to a lesser extent, to control atmospheric humidity. External walls, on the other hand, provide protection from the elements to the living areas and generally also support the floors and the roof.

As a result the main influence on the design of external walls is the ever growing demand for thermal

methods, i.e., using stone or other mineral building materials, or with a lightweight design using lumber or wood-based materials, is not purely a matter of taste.

In most cases, building codes have permitted only wood frame construction systems for one- or two-story buildings, and it is only recently that some regions have relaxed their regulations. By using fire-treated lumber and or fireproofing walls with multiple layers of gypsum wallboard three- and four-story

High in the air

Not only the roof, but the entire house can be constructed of wood. However, in certain cases building codes may prohibit this.

One stone on top of another

In Germany, as in most European countries, the preferred construction method is masonry walls of brick or stone. For most people these materials are synonymous with durability and quality.

buildings may be constructed in most locations. This is in response to examples from around the world of lumber construction methods being used safely and successfully in densely populated multi-story residential buildings. Additionally, both masonry and wood construction methods have been shown to each have their own specific disadvantages. For this reason hybrid construction methods can often satisfy the desire for a structure which has not only good heat insulating and heat storage properties, but is also attractive and comfortable to live in. Solid or masonry wall construction and wood frame houses don't have to look different. With many wood buildings, the outer lumber paneling can be stuccoed, which makes it resistant to fire and gives it the look of a half-timbered building. On the other hand, a solid masonry house may also be finished with wood siding or a wooden curtain wall façade.

Innovative architecture
Arch.: B. Heidbrede, Schwerte, Germany
In Germany wooden houses tend to have a poor image, as a lot of people associate them with impermanence or shoddy building methods. However, they can be quite beautiful.

Houses built of wood are warmer
Arch.: B. Heidbrede, Schwerte, Germany
Houses with light wooden frameworks can be better insulated and are easier to convert. On the downside, they often have poor sound insulation and do not store heat very well.

Pros and cons of solid and lightweight building methods

Stone or brick is favored for building in most European countries

If you're building a house, one of the first things you have to decide is which building method to use. It is this, rather than the shape of the building or the size of the rooms, that is the decisive factor in the preliminary planning and construction phases. Depending on whether a solid masonry or wood frame construction is chosen, different contractors will usually be required, possibly different vendors, and the details and construction processes will also be entirely different.

Solid stone or brick masonry construction is the dominant construction method in Britain. This may be done using traditional brickwork, energy-efficient sand lime bricks or alternatively with the new lightweight building blocks. Another method for building more rapidly is using precast concrete load-bearing components such as oversize block or precast "tilt-up" panels. Single-wythe and multi-wythe versions are possible using most of these methods. The chief advantages of the solid masonry construction method are the following:

- long lifetime and fairly infrequent maintenance and repair;
- good soundproofing;
- good thermal storage allowing less inside temperature fluctuation;
- better protection against summer heat;
- better draftproofing.

Solid-construction houses are more stable

Prefabricated house exhibition, Wuppertal, Germany
Stone or brick houses require less maintenance and provide better protection from summer heat. However, they cost more to build and are often plagued with moisture problems initially and may be unhealthy to live in.

The main disadvantages of solid masonry construction methods include the following:

- longer construction time;
- higher labor costs – comparatively small prefabricated element;
- risk of wall damage from building moisture;
- more energy involved in production of building materials;
- good thermal insulation properties can generally only be achieved by using layers of insulating material (usually foam) inside or sandwiched between walls;
- higher cost of adding extensions, remodeling and demolition.

In the United States nearly 90% of residential construction is built using some form of wood structure. Even so-called brick houses are usually wood frame buildings with a brick veneer for appearance only, in that the brick (or stone) veneers in these homes serve no structural purpose. Building with wood has been popular from the earliest colonial times due to the readily available timber resources in most regions. Some exceptions to this are the Southwestern United States where adobe walls have been used historically and certain areas where clay brick has been preferred because of local soils which made this material readily available. But today the transportability of building materials as well as the higher labor costs have made wood frame buildings the norm in these areas as well. As masonry construction has become less used, skilled masons have become more scarce and the costs of building with brick and stone have increased even further.

The most important advantages of wood construction include the following:

- the raw materials used mostly consist of renewable resources;
- comparatively simple and highly effective methods of thermal insulation are possible;
- rapid modular construction of houses makes savings possible;
- healthier and simpler dry construction methods are employed;
- greater flexibility and variety are possible due to ease of adding on, remodeling, conversions, etc.

The main disadvantages of wood construction are:

- high degree of craftsmanship necessary to ensure a durable, long-lasting structure;
- greater degree of regular maintenance necessary;
- soundproofing and protection from summer heat require greater effort and expense;
- complicated layered construction can mean higher probability of errors in construction;
- often inadequate draftproofing and moisture problems in walls;
- variable quality of lumber, inadequate drying sometimes leads to shrinkage and warpage;
- frequent use of toxic treating materials which may pose health hazards.

A range of hybrid construction techniques exists in order to combine the various advantages of the different materials and methods. The classical example is the half-lumbered house with lumber supporting elements and clay or cob infilling and ceilings. Its high capacity to absorb moisture makes clay an ideal complement to lumber. Other mineral infills frequently lead to problems with building moisture due to their lack of hygroscopic properties.

Other hybrid construction methods include:

- post-and-beam construction with clay or sand lime brick wall infilling;
- wood joist floors with brick tile infilling;
- solid construction framework combined with lightweight construction non-bearing internal walls;
- reinforced concrete frame with lightweight construction for external and internal walls;
- solid core structure (e.g., stairwell, bathrooms, etc.) supporting cantilevered floors and roof surrounded by lightweight construction dividing and enclosing the living areas.

Hybrid construction methods combine the advantages of both lightweight and solid construction

Methods for building solid construction houses

White walls

Arch.: B. Heidbrede, Schwerte, Germany

It is impossible to tell from the exterior what lies behind this white façade. The outer wall may conceal a thick layer of insulating material, a second internal wall, double wythe walls to improve heat storage, or perhaps just a single massive brick wall.

In western countries including the United States and Canada, the following types of solid-wall construction methods are used:

- the monolithic wall;
- the single-wythe wall with an external thermal insulation layer;
- the brick wall with a curtain wall façade (with or without additional thermal insulation);
- the double-whyte brick wall plus either ventilation or cavity insulation;
- double-wythe masonry wall with concrete masonry interior and brick exterior skin with or without an air space;
- single- or double-wythe wall "furred out" and insulated on the interior side;
- precast concrete "tilt-up panels" (not commonly used in residential).

The simplest wall structure is the single-wythe brick wall, generally plastered on both sides. It is made from a single material and is the quickest to build. This cheap and traditional construction method has another advantage in that not a lot can go wrong, and on top of this, the plaster coating means that the structure is well sealed from an air leakage standpoint. The disadvantage, though, is that it is not possible to achieve adequate thermal insulation for most temperate climates with an external wall of feasible thickness. This means that in new buildings, especially those built to ecological specifications, an additional thermal insulation layer is necessary. If insulation is applied directly to the brickwork using a technique commonly known

A single wall does not offer enough protection

as thermoskin, a composite thermal insulation system, an additional procedure and a consequent increase in construction costs is involved. A further problem is that if work is not done correctly, thermal bridges can form, leading to structural damage. It is also extremely difficult to seal this type of exterior skin from water leakage and moisture problems in the wall very often result. Because of this it is advisable to contract a specialist firm for this sort of work. Additionally, this thermal insulation layer is fitted to the exterior of the wall for structural reasons. The advantage of this construction method is that the supporting shell is insulated and protected from the elements, and the brickwork can perform its thermal storage function efficiently since it is situated inside the insulating shell of the building.

Unfortunately, few insulating materials can satisfy all the demands made of them. Firstly, they must be able to withstand the extreme conditions to which the exterior of the building will be exposed. Thus they must be coated with a protective layer of plaster, and must not cause cracks under mechanical stress. Secondly, they must be safe both in terms of composition and manufacture, while also possessing all the necessary structural qualities, such as the capacity to efficiently diffuse water vapor.

An alternative method, involving less use of insulating materials, is the heat insulating curtain wall façade. This involves protecting the insulating layer from the elements via external paneling or facing which is attached to the brickwork. Possible facing materials include natural stone slabs, fiber cement panels, brick tiling units, plaster-coated wooden building materials such as lightweight wood wool panels, standard wood siding or wood composite panels (e.g., chipboard, plywood, etc.). Aluminum sheets, plastic panels or special glass, on the other hand, are ecologically questionable, though the latter product can safely be used in combination with transparent heat insulating materials.

Although not commonly used for residential buildings in the United States, this system of construction is frequently used on large commercial structures, where the side of the house exposed to the elements is protected using wood shingles, slate tiles or sheet metal. It exists in both ventilated and unventilated versions. Behind ventilated curtain wall façades there is a cavity approximately 4 cm thick with openings at the base of the façade and under the eaves to allow air to circulate. This air-filled cavity ensures that moisture can escape from the structure. Another advantage of this cavity is that it provides a "pressure drop" area of low pressure where moisture driven by high wind pressure through the exterior outer skin will be allowed to drain harmlessly away so that the inner wall is thereby well protected from any moisture penetration.

In the unventilated version the cavity between the brickwork and the curtain wall is filled with insulating material. In this case the material used for the curtain wall should have very good diffusion properties to prevent moisture damage. A further problem with curtain wall façades is their anchoring. It has been found that the customary wire stays cause problems by acting as thermal bridges. This problem can be avoided by using wooden battens, but these may not be as durable.

A form of solid construction which was very common during the early part of the century in the United States is the double-wythe wall. This too involves external protection against the elements in the form of hard, durable clinker bricks or facing brick. This hard outer shell is not, however, attached to the supporting wall. Because of this, thermal bridges cannot form. In this method, too, the whole of the supporting structure is protected either by an air space or by insulating material in the cavity, allowing the interior wythe to perform its heat storing function effectively.

This construction method is a relatively simple way of producing walls with high levels of thermal insulation. However, the danger of structural damage due to shoddy workmanship is greater than with a single-wythe method since the outer wall will hide the evidence if insufficient thermal insulating material has been installed or there are gaps. Double-wythe walls also come in ventilated and unventilated variants. In the unventilated type, the so-called cavity insulation method, easily-worked, moisture-resistant insulating materials such as Perlite or cork can be used, to improve the heat insulating properties of old buildings.

Double-wythe walls provide better thermal and sound insulation

Brick constructions
Modern porous bricks are used at this construction site but openings for windows and the roof also play a focal point.

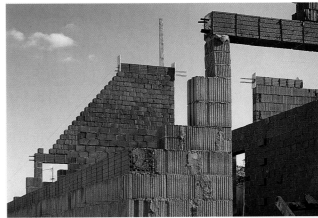

Good thermal insulation
Solid single-wythe walls can be constructed with expanded concrete. These walls provide excellent thermal insulation without being too thick.

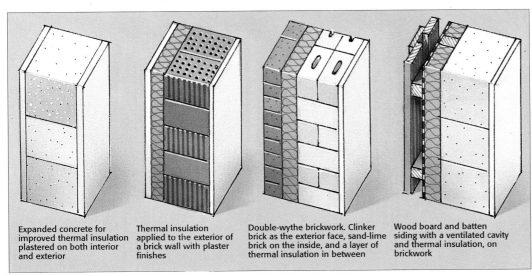

| Expanded concrete for improved thermal insulation plastered on both interior and exterior | Thermal insulation applied to the exterior of a brick wall with plaster finishes | Double-wythe brickwork. Clinker brick as the exterior face, sand-lime brick on the inside, and a layer of thermal insulation in between | Wood board and batten siding with a ventilated cavity and thermal insulation, on brickwork |

Wall structures
The diagram shows four solid-wall construction options you can choose from including a single-wythe wall with or without a composite thermal insulation system, a double-wythe wall and a wood façade curtain wall.

Construction methods using wood

A half-timbered house in modern style

Arch.: B. Heidbrede, Schwerte, Germany

It used to be a common wood construction method, but the half-timbered house is rarely built today nowadays. Despite the solid construction walls, it is the wood frame that performs the load-bearing role.

From solid wooden blocks to slender wooden pillars

There are four main lumber construction methods:
- the log cabin construction method;
- the wood frame construction method;
- the stress-skin panel construction method;
- the post-and-beam construction method.

The main difference between these methods lies in the supporting wooden structural elements, and in practice there is quite a good deal of overlap between these four types of lumber construction.

The most traditional style of wooden house, the log cabin is currently enjoying a modest renaissance in the United States and elsewhere. For a long time this age-old construction method was completely out of favor, mainly because in this type of structure the wooden wall was continually expanding and contracting, causing gaps and movement in the external wall as its moisture content changed from summer to winter. This meant that log houses were subject to continual drafts whistling through the gaps between the logs, making the rooms uncomfortable to live in. On top of this, walls made of heavy logs are not exactly cheap. However, solutions to these problems have now been found. To ensure higher levels of thermal insulation, a double-wythe construction method has been adopted with the heavy log wall on the outside. Furthermore, the logs are now no thicker than they need

to be for load-bearing purposes, generally around 4-5 inches (10-12 cm). Cellulose or wood chips, neither of which are very expensive, are often used for thermal insulation. Another useful material is expanded clay, a substance that compensates for the movement of the log walls. When coupled with a special paper glued to the inner side of the external log wall plus sealing strips between the logs, this structure has good draftproofing properties.

New products regularly come onto the market which can replace expensive logs while still allowing solid wood construction. Examples of these are stave lumber walls where 3–4 inch thick tongue-and-groove boards are stacked much like a log wall construction, cross logs or wooden strip wall units.

However, the most popular method of wood construction is the wood frame house. This system consists of a skeleton of 2x4 or larger wood framing members, or studs, spaced at 16 inches on center with an exterior and interior wall sheathing material to provide lateral stability. Similarly floors are typically constructed with 2x10 joists with a tongue-and-groove plywood or particle board subfloor on top and wood or metal bridging to provide lateral stability. Roofs are framed with either 2x-rafters or increasingly prefabricated wood trusses made with 2x-lumber and

An economical building method

Arch.: I. Gabriel, Oldenburg, Germany
The stress-skin panel construction method allows a high degree of prefabrication, thus making construction fast and economical, as in the case of this small ecological development in Germany.

An advantage of wood frame construction is the ability to standardize and prefabricate parts

Building on a grid system offers flexibly

Arch.: Künkeler & Bornemann, Schwerte, Germany
The post-and-beam wood construction method provides the means for a wide range of individual variations. Although everything revolves around a given structural framework or grid, it makes no difference to the structure what arrangement of doors, windows or rooms there is within this framework.

again an exterior plywood or OSB sheathing and interior ceiling finish usually gypsum wall board to provide the lateral strength. The advantage of the wood frame construction method over the very similar post-and-beam technique is its high degree of standardization and prefabrication and therefore lower material and labor costs. This standardization not only cuts down on construction time, but within certain limitations, almost any shape of building is possible; the interior walls perform supporting functions, and the spaces between all the exterior framing members can easily be filled with insulating material.

Prefabricated houses, on the other hand, are still constructed mostly from factory assembled wall and roof sections. They were developed with the aim of producing the largest possible individual components in the workshop, which are then simply assembled at the construction site in a very short time and mostly with unskilled labor. The technical term for this type of construction system is "stress skin panel" construction. With this method the sheathing materials such as exterior grade plywood or oriented strand board (OSB) which are the "skin" play a vitally important structural role, and only the frame and sheathing as a

Only as a synergistic whole can the loads be supported

Arch.: A. Mense, B. Bürger, Basta Baubüro, Dortmund, Germany

With stress-skin panel construction it is the sum of all the structural elements as a whole that bears the load. All of the components are prefabricated in the workshop and then assembled on site. This kind of house can be built very rapidly, but it is difficult to change later on.

composite whole are strong enough to bear the structural loads both vertical and lateral, a fact that can make subsequent remodeling or revisions rather difficult. The components are already fitted with thermal insulation and frequently even the electrical wiring and plumbing are pre-installed, so the possibilities for adding on are quite limited.

With the post-and-beam construction method, the wood framework of supporting columns and floor beams, floor joists and roof beams can only be made from certain wood species and in addition must be graded for structural applications. The primary difference here is that the structural frame takes on the whole load-bearing function, while internal and external walls can be freely installed into the predetermined framework. The much greater distance between supports as compared to the similar half-timbered construction method is made possible by the use of structurally stronger solid, or sometimes laminated wood beams.

The advantage of the post-and-beam construction method over the wood frame construction method, apart from the greater freedom of design, is the fact that thermal insulation can be completely separated from the supporting structure and is typically applied to the building's exterior. This leads to an overall improvement in the structure's energy-efficiency, and a great deal more flexibility down the road.

At a glance

The opposite page gives an overview of a variety of construction methods using wood.

Longer spans

The post-and-beam construction method makes possible longer spans between the supporting members, so that larger structures with unobstructed rooms are possible. Furthermore, the thermal insulation can be fitted outside the supporting structure, providing better energy-efficiency and comfort.

Rustic living

Perhaps the most traditional type of wooden house, the log cabin, is experiencing something of a renaissance. However, construction methods have been greatly refined, as modern tastes do not fancy icy winds whistling through the rooms.

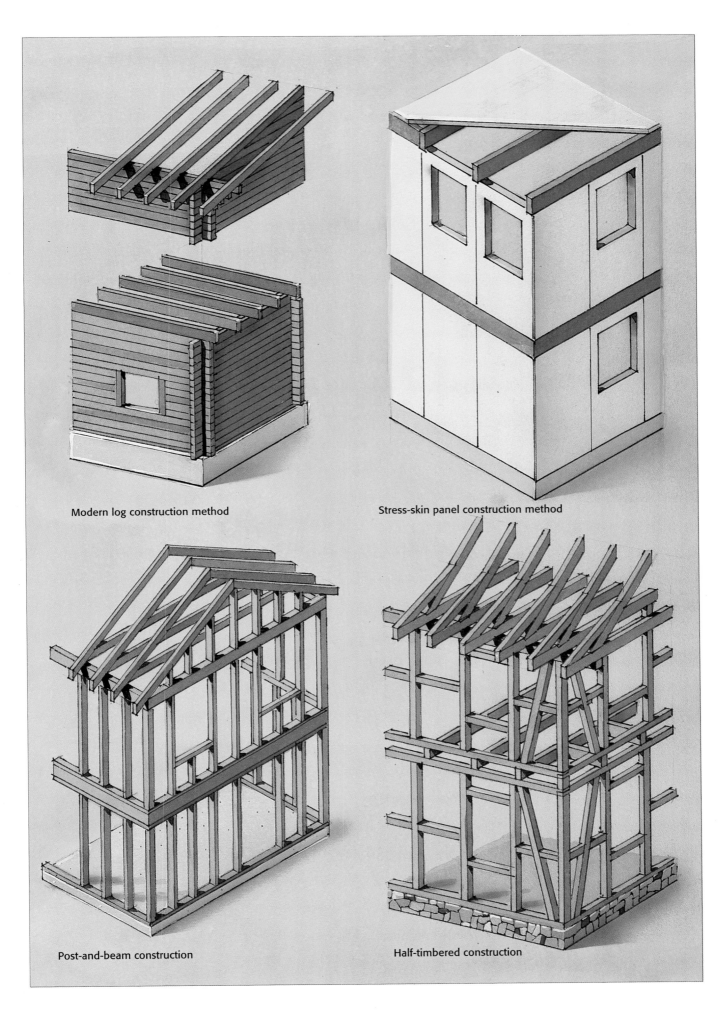

Modern log construction method

Stress-skin panel construction method

Post-and-beam construction

Half-timbered construction

Hybrid construction methods

Hybrid construction methods are frequently used

The half-timbered house is a classic example of hybrid construction. In this type of structure the wooden framework bears the entire load and the infill stone, brickwork or other earthen material is used purely as protection from the elements and to provide thermal storage. Due to major problems in providing modern levels of thermal insulation, draftproofing and the ability of the building shell to readily convey building moisture from the building interior to the outside, the classic half-timbered house is rarely constructed today. However, modern clay building materials can be used effectively, since they are better at regulating the exchange of building moisture than most of the other conventional wall materials.

However, other types of lightweight (wood) structures are frequently seen, where the walls and floors are deliberately infilled with heavy materials such as clay, sand lime brick or concrete blocks in order to add mass to the structure for thermal storage or soundproofing.

In the case of the reinforced concrete frame construction method, which is more often employed for commercial and institutional buildings than for residential ones, the steel reinforced floors and supporting walls (or in some cases columns and beams) take on the entire load-bearing function. While some of the other installations such as stairwells, fire separation walls and bathroom facilities may also be built with reinforced

concrete or block walls, the other non-supporting walls, including external ones, may be built using lightweight dry construction methods such as wood frame walls.

A more frequent arrangement for the walls which separate the individual units of terraced houses (multi-family row-houses) is to be of solid masonry or concrete construction, providing greater protection from fire, while the external and internal walls are of lightweight wood construction. Additionally, some of the new structural wood building components such as glulam, LVL and OSB lend themselves to combinations with solid construction materials due to their rigidity and good acoustic properties.

The third hybrid construction method mentioned here is a composite shell technique which combines elements of prefabricated panel systems and cast-in place concrete construction. This involves on-site assembly, often by a single person, of prefabricated hollow wooden or polystyrene wall modules, which have insulation, wiring and plumbing, and in some cases even windows and doors pre-installed. Then, when the whole house has been assembled, the cavities in the walls and floors are filled with poured concrete. The advantage of this technique is the high degree of prefabrication and potential do-it-yourself assembly combined with the advantages of a solid construction, allowing whole structures to be erected quickly and economically. The disadvantage is the building materials used, which have poor absorbency and are ecologically questionable. Additionally, the concrete construction means that subsequent alterations are extremely difficult if not impossible.

In contrast, there is still another hybrid technique which can be recommended both from structural and ecological points of view. This is a method whereby at the center of the building a solid construction core is erected consisting of bathrooms, staircase, kitchen, larder, laundry room, central heating plant and other services. All of the cooler, moisture- and noise-producing rooms are concentrated in this area. The walls around this central core can be fitted with pre-installed HVAC, plumbing and wiring and thereby function as heaters. In winter, they can be designed to be heated by direct sunshine and store the heat for release to the building interior whenever needed, while in summer they can be left in shade so as to absorb heat from the building keeping it cooler. Around this solid construction core the living areas are constructed using wood construction methods, so that better thermal insulation and the pleasant ambiance of a wooden building are combined.

Inner value

Arch.: Gruppe 3, Graz, Austria
This settlement in Austria is particularly desirable from an ecological standpoint. A solid construction core is surrounded by a lightweight wood structure providing good thermal insulation. The solid wall core contains the stairwell, kitchen, bathroom and also the laundry room.

A combined construction method gives better results

Arch.: Miggelt Co., Unna, Germany
A rare sight these days: This half-timbered house combines a wood supporting frame with brick infill panels in a single wall.

Dividing walls and floors

Arch.: Alte Windkunst, Herzogenrath, Germany

One of the most widespread mixed-construction methods is exemplified by this house in Germany. The walls dividing separate living quarters as well as the floors are of solid construction, while the external walls and non-load-bearing walls are of lightweight construction.

Principles of mixed construction

Either a solid construction core surrounded by lightweight construction, or solid construction load-bearing structures, provide the most ecologically desirable mixed-construction methods. The solid walls store thermal energy, provide sound insulation and protection against fire, while the lightweight parts provide better thermal insulation and a more pleasant living environment.

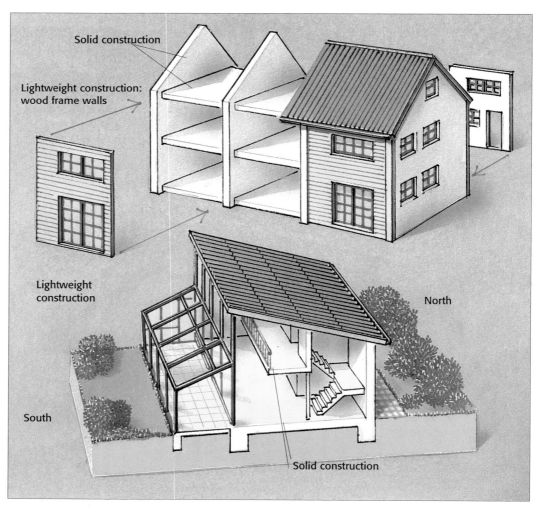

Solid construction

Lightweight construction:
wood frame walls

Lightweight
construction

North

South

Solid construction

Upstairs downstairs

Arch.: M. Dedekind, C. Gerth, Hamburg, Germany

In this model ecological social housing development in Hamburg the lower story is made of double-wythe brickwork while in the upper story only the dividing walls are of solid construction.

Prize winner

Arch.: Büro Brucker, Stuttgart, Germany

This prize-winning ecological settlement is a model of efficient use of space, which helps to keep costs down. Here, too, the dividing walls and floors are of solid construction while the outer walls are made of wood stress-skin panels.

ROOF CONSTRUCTION

The roof structure is almost always made of wood. Because of this, all the problems previously mentioned concerning draftproofing and the ease with which insulating materials can be installed apply in this case. An exception to this would be the flat roof, where for reasons previously mentioned, the best option is for the roof to be covered with live grass in keeping with ecological principles.

The most common roof design is still the gable roof, while the hip roof, false hip roof, the shed roof, mansard and the gambrel roof are all also widespread, and in more recent times roof types such as the transverse roof and the barrel roof have all become increasingly fashionable.

Roofscape

A view across the rooftops of Tübingen reveals a great variety of different roof designs and roofing materials. This is one of the most environmentally committed municipalities in Germany, and here even the majority of older buildings are required to have thermal insulation.

Roof insulation

With a pitched roof thermal insulation can basically take one of the following forms:
- insulation at the roof plane itself;
- insulation directly above the ceiling of the upper floor in cases where the attic has not been converted into living space.

Depending on the material used, the local climatic conditions and also the chosen design, the thickness of the insulating material required typically varies between 10 inches (R25) and 12 inches (R30) of fiberglass batt or 8–10 inches of stabilized cellulose insulation for a low-energy house, and between 12 inches (R30) and 16 inches (R40) or 10–14 inches

of cellulose for a passive house. Insulation can be fitted on top of, between and underneath the rafters. Both ventilated and unventilated designs are possible, though unventilated designs are becoming more common, with the insulating material occupying the entire space between the rafters.

Another recent innovation is the use of wood "I" joists, some times referred to as "TJI's" from the manufacturer who first developed them in the United States. These engineered composite structural members consist of a laminated wood top and bottom chord with a thin OSB web giving it the shape of an "I" beam section. They are commonly used for sloped roof applications to function as rafters. These sections make it possible, easily and inexpensively, to have larger rafter cross-sections without loss of stability and with practically no thermal bridges. Using this component to construct a roof for a detached house can result in a structural weight as little as 176.4 pounds (80 kg).

Insulation on top of the rafters is more common in mountainous regions. It is usually seen in post-and-beam buildings where it lends itself to a more rustic look since the rafters are visible from the living space. Either wood paneling or decking material such as a cedar or pine tongue-and-groove beaded board are fitted between or over the rafters. These are visible from inside the space, and can be either painted or clear finished on the interior surface. A moisture barrier is then laid on top of the panels or decking, and on top of this the thermal insulation material is laid. Softboard panels which are joined by a tongue-and-groove arrangement are available for this purpose.

Other paneling materials such as a cellulose and jute composite or cork can also be used. It is recommended that one install an extra under-roof panel for additional durability and insulating characteristics and over that the roof battens and counter battens, then finally the roof cladding itself, which may be shingles, brick tiles, standing seam metal or some other roofing material available. This method of construction has the disadvantage that the connections at the eaves and gable end are technically difficult, making draftproofing an awkward business. Furthermore, this kind of roof is much thicker overall and has a bulkier appearance. Furthermore, plumbing and wiring must be run completely through the inside of the roof structure quite often necessitating leaving it exposed to the interior side. The chief advantage, however, is that all structural components are very well protected underneath the heat insulating layer and thermal bridges are completely eliminated.

Thermal insulation beneath the rafters is uncommon because it takes up too much potentially useful living space in the attic area. However, it is sometimes used when renovating old buildings where the roof is still sound and has a shallow pitch allowing sufficient

room to stand after the insulating material has been fitted. A commonly used method for increasing the thickness of insulating material in this case, is to insulate both between the rafters *and* under the rafters. You can then include an interstitial chase for wiring and plumbing between the draftproofing and the interior finish material.

To accomplish this you would attach a secondary supporting structure of cross framing for the ceiling panels onto the rafters. All plumbing and wiring can then be fitted inside the insulated and airtight roof within this 1½ to 3½ inch cavity, which will later also be filled with insulating material such as blown-in cellulose. Thus you can achieve a well-sealed structure free of thermal bridges.

Another important aspect of attic insulation is the question of protection against summer heat. Roofs which receive direct sunlight during the day will typically result in uncomfortably high temperatures in attic living spaces. Lightweight roof structures also allow this overheating to occur more rapidly as opposed to massive structures which tend to absorb the heat during the day and release it at night, when it can be removed effectively by ventilating the area. The caveat here, however, is that thermal insulation properties are known to decrease as the insulating material becomes more dense, and the best compromise between winter thermal insulation and summer protection from heat appears to be the use of softboard insulating decking board along with a radiant barrier and adequate ventilation. Still another means of reducing overheating in summer might be to construct a solid roof made of concrete or prefabricated tiling components.

Wool for warmth

When developing the loft area, inter-rafter insulation is normally used. In this case wool is the insulating material. The internal draftproofing seal is also critical.

Types of roofs

The gable and hip roof are the most widespread types of roof in the United States.

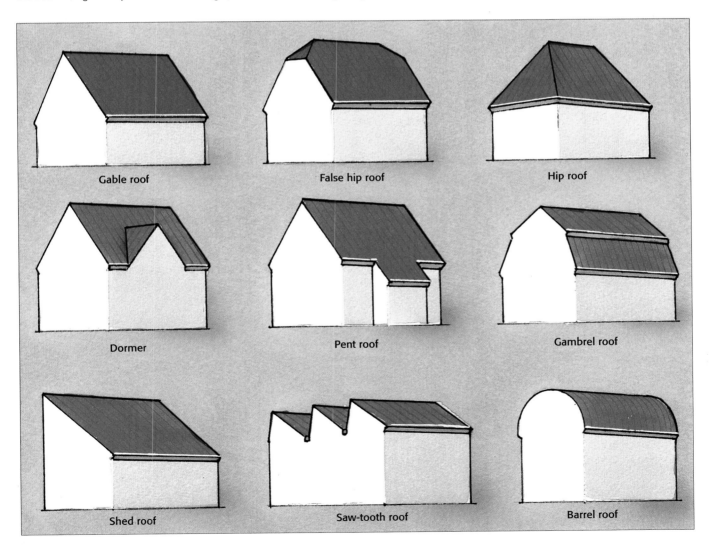

Gable roof

False hip roof

Hip roof

Dormer

Pent roof

Gambrel roof

Shed roof

Saw-tooth roof

Barrel roof

Sheet material for roofing underlays

As mentioned above, the roof cladding must always be ventilated to allow condensation which occurs on the underside of roof tiles or other materials, as well as any rain or snow which may penetrate, to evaporate. This is normally done by fitting vertical counter battens underneath the roofing or tile battens. Special perforated tiles can also provide sufficient ventilation. The insulating layer must also be protected against condensation, driving rain and drifting snow. This can be done by fitting plastic sheeting or a secondary roofing to the upper side of the insulating layer. Depending on the location it is most common to use a layer of asphalt impregnated building paper or an underlay made of polyethylene sheeting specially designed for this purpose. This is economical, light, waterproof and robust, but it does have a high level of resistance to moisture diffusion and is thus ineffective in allowing moisture from inside the building to escape. This means that the underlay must itself be ventilated, and this will have the effect of reducing the insulating value of the roof. This in turn defeats the goal of filling, if possible, the entire space between the rafters with insulating material (full rafter insulation) since the required thicknesses of insulating material can otherwise only be achieved at a great deal of extra expense and effort.

The capacity to draw off moisture is measured in terms of the so-called s_d value. The smaller this value for the diffusion-equivalent cavity thickness, the better diffusion is. Polyethylene sheets have an s_d value of 80 or more, and asphalt paper, which is still widely used, also has a poor s_d value of greater than 50. In the case of full rafter insulation the underlay should have an s_d value of well below 1, and the s_d value must at the very least be lower than that of the underlying insulating layer. To this end, new types of sheeting such as plastic-coated polyester fabric are now widely available. These materials are quite similar to modern weatherproof clothing in that the fabric has micropores that prevent moisture from penetrating while at the same time allowing water vapor to escape. However, they are less than ideal from an ecological point of view due to their high content of halogen-organic flame retardants and PVC or polyurethane coatings, leading to high levels of pollutant emissions in case of fire. The disposal or recycling of such materials is also problematical. A better solution is the use of special polyethylene-coated sheathing felt, which has a relatively low synthetic content and less associated environmental impact.

The best solution of all, however, is probably a solid under-roof layer made of impregnated softboard panels. These must be fitted carefully to make sure they are airtight, while also contributing to the insulation of the structure as a whole and protecting it against summer heat. A further advantage of this form of paneling is that it provides a walkable surface, making the roof readily accessible and thus greatly simplifying the roofer's job. Until recently, bitumen was almost always the impregnating material, and this contains a number of different hazardous substances. However, as the paneling is far away from the interior living spaces it does not pose an indoor health hazard to the occupants of the building. However, boards impregnated with latex are now available and present a better option. Special hardboard panels are also available for this purpose.

Solid enough to walk on

Here, underroof sheathing made of impregnated softboard provides good protection against drafts. These panels also make life easier for the roofer because they can be walked on.

Airtight

Indoors a layer of special blue paper provides draftproofing. Because the paper should not be torn wires are laid between the battens, screwed to the gypsum board panels.

Breather paper

The breather paper laid below the roof's external cladding permits ventilation and lets water vapor escape. A moisture barrier here would endanger the roof structure.

In addition, the interior of the structure must be protected via a moisture barrier which has the additional requirement of providing the necessary draftproofing. In the past, insulating material lined with completely vapor-tight aluminum foil has been used, but this is no longer recommended. Apart from the large amounts of energy required to produce aluminum, the risk of damage during installation, resulting in an imperfect seal, is fairly high. In fact, all in all, a completely vapor-tight foil is structurally highly undesirable because it prevents the diffusion of high humidity which may be present in the attic area through the roof to the outside. On top of this, ungrounded aluminum foil can act as a giant receptor for hazardous EMF radiation.

As a rule thin PE or (less often) PVC foil is used for this purpose, and the environmentally friendlier polyethylene is in widespread use. However, its s_d value of three is fairly high, and a long-term draftproof seal can only be achieved by using compressible strips. The acknowledged wisdom in the construction industry is that the s_d value or the vapor diffusion resistance, m, must be higher indoors than out so that the moisture can be drawn to the outside, but this principle breaks down in the case of a structure with an overall design which is open to diffusion, or where there is no obstacle to moisture moving in either direction. Ecological insulating materials made of organic fiber can temporarily absorb a small amount of moisture without endangering the wooden structure, before releasing it again.

For this reason it is advisable to have a moisture barrier of special kraft paper with a fabric ply that makes it relatively tear resistant. Kraft paper can be used with non-toxic adhesives and is also easy to repair. Another alternative, which does however require more work to install, is to use boards made of various wood fiber products or gypsum wall board which are firmly attached at all abutments and joints. These cannot, however, form the innermost wall surface because a layer for plumbing and wiring has to be installed in order to make the structure properly draftproof. The advantage of this system is its extra stability and also the greater protection it offers against summer heat.

Roof insulation methods

The diagrams show three different methods which can be used to insulate a wood roof structure. The first shows a traditional European tile roof construction method. The second method provides a greater degree of insulation while still providing the necessary ventilation. It also provides the roofer a firm surface for walking on. The third method shows a completely external insulation method which eliminates any thermal bridges inherent in the other two while also allowing the beauty of the wood structure to be exposed on the interior side. Although these diagrams are shown with a tile roof cladding material, these methods can be used just as easily with slate or composite tiles or wood shingles.

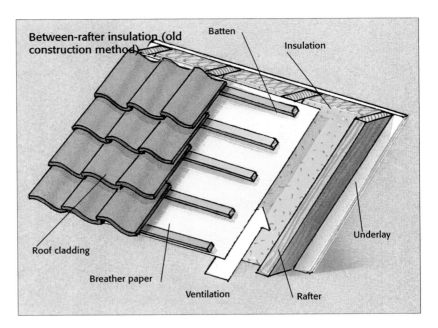

Between-rafter insulation (old construction method)

Batten · Insulation · Underlay · Rafter · Ventilation · Breather paper · Roof cladding

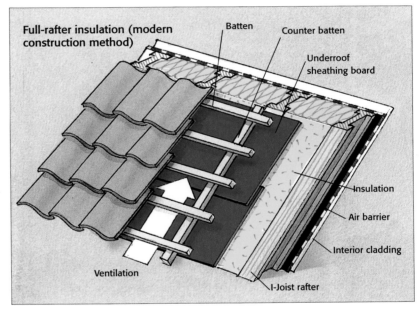

Full-rafter insulation (modern construction method)

Batten · Counter batten · Underroof sheathing board · Insulation · Air barrier · Interior cladding · I-Joist rafter · Ventilation

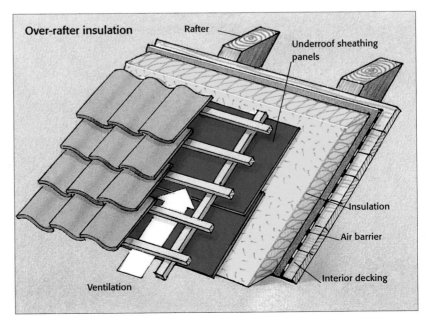

Over-rafter insulation

Rafter · Underroof sheathing panels · Insulation · Air barrier · Interior decking · Ventilation

CEILING/FLOOR CONSTRUCTION

The main requirement for the construction of intermediate floors, apart from structural engineering considerations, is soundproofing. Since the floor usually separates different apartments, or rooms designated for different purposes (e.g., living rooms and bedrooms), it's essential to mitigate both impact noise as well as airborne noise.

A further important consideration, in cases where the temperature levels in the adjacent floors are very different, is thermal insulation. Ceilings in houses which are adjacent to unfinished attic spaces or to the outdoors should have a u-value of no more than 0.05 (R20), while floors over unheated basements or in contact with the ground should have a maximum u-value of 0.09 (R11). The corresponding recommended values for low-energy houses respectively are 0.033 (R30) and 0.053 (R19). Finally, floors and ceilings also play an important role in thermal storage.

Floors and ceilings in solid construction houses

The vast majority of floors are made of reinforced concrete, the advantages of which are its low cost, practically universal applicability and, due to its high mass, good thermal storage characteristics if the design of the building is such that this can be properly exploited. Furthermore, there are few alternatives which are better from an acoustical standpoint. However, it should be noted that concrete has relatively poor thermal insulating properties.

Of course, thermal insulating properties are not always needed in intermediate floors, and basement floors and ceilings adjacent to unheated areas can easily be fitted with additional insulating material. On the other hand, in the past concrete floors have been responsible for a large proportion of the thermal bridges that very often cause major problems. These occur mainly in projecting structural elements such as balconies, as well as in cases where no additional thermal insulation has been provided to the outside of the building's structure.

A further disadvantage of concrete floors is that concrete has minimal capacity to absorb water. In certain cases, a layer of plaster on the underside of a concrete intermediate floor can help to control humidity levels. Moreover, subsequent alterations to concrete structures involve considerable effort and expense, not to mention that the use of a high proportion of cement is not ecologically ideal. Therefore, structural

Open and visible
The mezzanine gallery in this detached house (opposite) reveals the functions of the intermediate floor: The supporting wall does not just carry the weight of the furniture and occupants; it should also serve to effectively separate living space.

brick tile floors are currently gaining in popularity. Some of the prefabricated brick floor systems currently available are as easy to work as concrete floors, offering both speed of installation and relatively long spans (distances between supports) possible.

Also widely available are prefabricated brick flooring units which can span between reinforced concrete, steel or wooden floor joists and then be covered with a finish coat of grout, cement or gypcrete. In wooden

structures this provides the required mass for thermal storage. However, they do not play any significant structural role in that the loads must always be transferred to the supporting floor joists and beams. The advantages of such brick floor systems include a lower level of moisture being released into the building than from poured concrete floors, their superior thermal insulation and high moisture absorption properties as compared to concrete, and also their more desirable ecological profile. On the other hand, they offer a less

Sound insulation for a wooden floor
A heavy material such as the limestone used here provides a wooden structure with sound insulation. Dry subflooring is laid over it. In contrast, in a solid structure a layer of soft material below the subfloor provides the sound insulation.

Natural insulating material
Cork and coconut panels can be laid underneath the flooring to provide natural sound insulation. It is important that the floor is floating so that it prevents the transmission of sound.

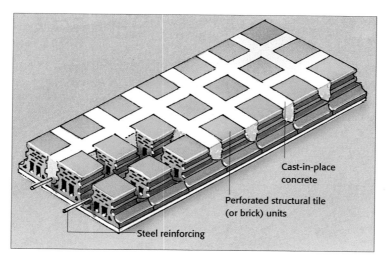

Solid construction floor designs

Solid wooden floorboards can be screwed to floor battens laid on sound insulating coconut matting. The gaps between the battens are filled with insulating material. Brick or natural stone tiles are placed on a layer of floating floor substrate separated from the supporting layer by insulating matting. With underfloor heating it is also important to make sure the heating pipes are well insulated from below.

Pre-fabricated brick floor

Instead of the usual concrete floor a prefabricated brick floor may be used. These are lighter and provide better thermal insulation and a better living environment. They also speed up construction because they are delivered ready to install.

Cast-in-place concrete

Perforated structural tile (or brick) units

Steel reinforcing

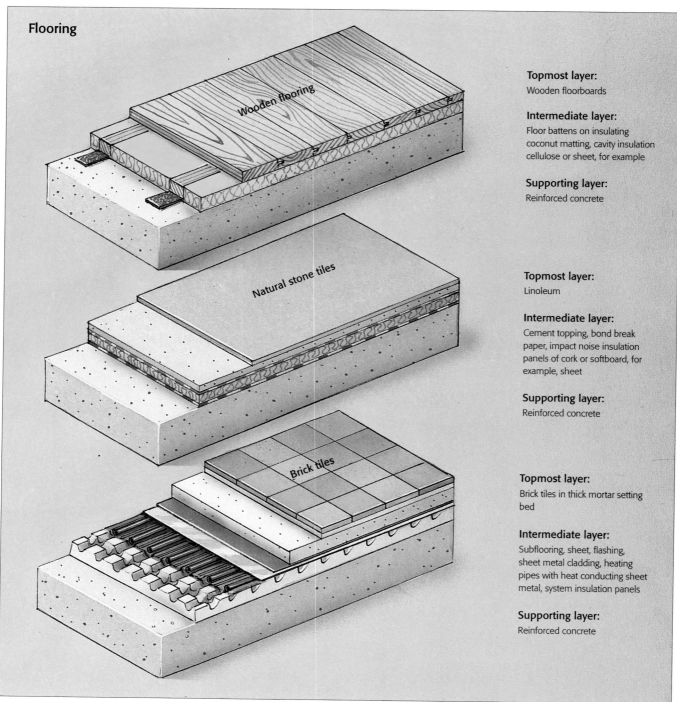

Flooring

Wooden flooring

Topmost layer:
Wooden floorboards

Intermediate layer:
Floor battens on insulating coconut matting, cavity insulation cellulose or sheet, for example

Supporting layer:
Reinforced concrete

Natural stone tiles

Topmost layer:
Linoleum

Intermediate layer:
Cement topping, bond break paper, impact noise insulation panels of cork or softboard, for example, sheet

Supporting layer:
Reinforced concrete

Brick tiles

Topmost layer:
Brick tiles in thick mortar setting bed

Intermediate layer:
Subflooring, sheet, flashing, sheet metal cladding, heating pipes with heat conducting sheet metal, system insulation panels

Supporting layer:
Reinforced concrete

effective resistance to sound transfer, and their load-bearing properties are not quite as good.

A third alternative is prefabricated reinforced expanded (lightweight) concrete decking. These are equally easy to lay and their heat insulating properties are not a problem. They also pose no problem in terms of thermal bridges. However, the soundproofing capacity of this lighter material is mediocre at best. Whereas solid construction ceilings provide effective protection against airborne noise, in the case of the expanded concrete modules, they tend to transmit impact and structure-borne sound to a greater extent. Accordingly, special precautions have to be taken to combat noise. The flooring must be laid so that it "floats" over the structural floor below. One way to do this is to put down a layer of resilient impact absorbing sound insulation over which a 1 to 1½ inch layer of cement or grout is poured. The edges of the top cement are isolated from the surrounding walls by placement of lateral strips of a compressible material to ensure that vibrations will not be transferred to the walls. A more ecologically favorable option, and one that is easier to do on your own, is to lay resilient moisture proof strips such as EPDM rubber onto the concrete floor over which wood sleepers can be laid. A sound insulating material is then placed between the sleepers and the finish (or a wood subfloor) can be laid over all of this. It is again desirable to isolate this top floor material from the surrounding walls to prevent transfer of vibration.

The inside story

It is rare to see the interior of a wooden structure laid bare as it is here in this old wooden floor. It starkly reveals how little original separating structure there actually is, and how important it is to insulate properly if you don't want to hear everything going on next door.

Massive construction in wood buildings

In general, construction methods using wood provide poorer soundproofing, though the use of more massive wood products can improve the situation. The amplification of sound in hollow spaces is the same principle that is at work inside a drum or piano and it can be reduced by the use of generous quantities of soft insulating materials, which have the added benefit of providing added thermal insulation. In order to dampen impact and structure-borne sound, elastic materials such as coir (coconut fiber) strips can be used for acoustic separation of individual construction elements. However, with wooden structures you must take great care to ensure that sound bridges are not created since the great majority of joints are nailed or screwed together, and a single nail hammered through a layer of impact soundproofing can destroy the entire soundproofing effect. The basic principles of "floating" interior surfaces over resilient sound absorbing layers apply equally here. Essentially, the use of more massive building materials means that the intermediate floors will not only provide better soundproofing but also that the wooden structure will have a greater thermal storage capacity. Historically, this has been accomplished by the clay infill panels of half-timbered structures. Gravel was also sometimes added to wood joist ceilings, though this has less mass. Today a material known as loam brick (brick made from a clay and sandy soil) is the best choice as a dry filling to be placed between floor joists due to its high mass moisture-absorbing properties which make it an ideal companion for wood. Rather than installing it in the joist spaces it can simply

Layer upon layer – there is no other way to efficient insulation

Wooden construction floor designs

The ideal floor design shown at the top comes at the expense of a good deal of headroom: Wooden subflooring boards are laid on floor joists and then covered with a layer of heavy material such as brick, limestone or concrete blocks to provide mass for thermal storage and sound attenuation. On top of the stone or brick a layer of impact sound insulation is laid, and on top of this a floating layer in the form of OSB (chipboard) or gypsum fiberboard. On top of this a finish floor such as parquet, linoleum or tiles may be laid. The floor design in the middle has far less mass and offers correspondingly poor sound insulation. Individual insulation mats help prevent sound amplification, while insulation against impact noise is provided by resilient layers such as cork strips fitted on the joists. The lower of the three examples incorporates limestone blocks into a structurally complex false floor but has the advantage that it takes up less headroom.

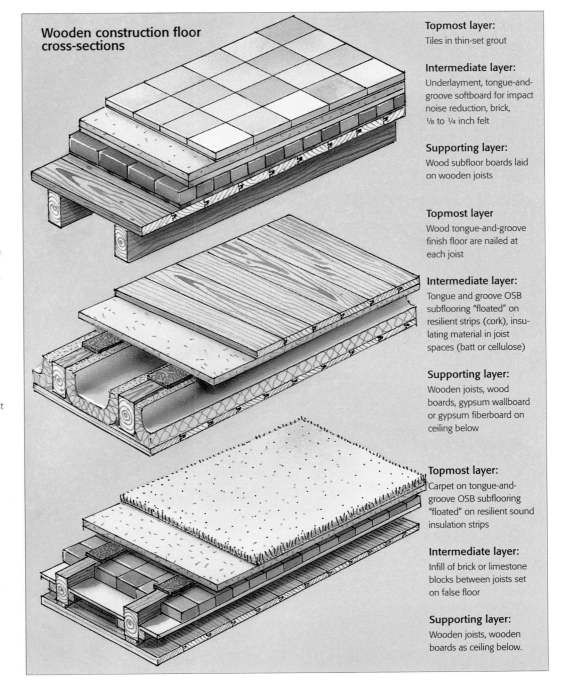

Wooden construction floor cross-sections

Topmost layer:
Tiles in thin-set grout

Intermediate layer:
Underlayment, tongue-and-groove softboard for impact noise reduction, brick, 1/8 to 1/4 inch felt

Supporting layer:
Wood subfloor boards laid on wooden joists

Topmost layer
Wood tongue-and-groove finish floor are nailed at each joist

Intermediate layer:
Tongue and groove OSB subflooring "floated" on resilient strips (cork), insulating material in joist spaces (batt or cellulose)

Supporting layer:
Wooden joists, wood boards, gypsum wallboard or gypsum fiberboard on ceiling below

Topmost layer:
Carpet on tongue-and-groove OSB subflooring "floated" on resilient sound insulation strips

Intermediate layer:
Infill of brick or limestone blocks between joists set on false floor

Supporting layer:
Wooden joists, wooden boards as ceiling below.

Exposed beams

Arch.: M. Thun, Milan, Italy, in collaboration with the "Europäische Designdepot," Klagenfurt, Austria
When structural elements such as ceiling joists, supporting beams and columns are left exposed, as in this ecological designer house (opposite), the load-bearing structure becomes an integral part of the interior design.

A unique structural design

Designer: P. Patt, Flamersfeld, Germany
Wood roof structures need not always have parallel beams. This example of an envelope low-energy house demonstrates a radial beam design which modern materials make possible with stronger, more compact profiles.

be laid on a classic false floor. This is, however, a very awkward and time-consuming job. Alternatively, it can be laid over an exposed joist floor, although this makes the construction fairly thick and consequently reduces ceiling height. A much more economical alternative is to use paving tiles, but as these are usually made of concrete they are less desirable from an ecological standpoint.

Another way of adding mass to a lightweight floor construction is to use the hollow brick tile units mentioned previously, which can be suspended between the wood joists. Filling with a mineral material, preferably something heavy like expanded clay, is another good way of improving the properties of a wood joist floor. Extreme care should be taken to

lay a separating layer, for example of oil impregnated paper; otherwise insulating material may crumble and fall from the ceiling into the rooms below due to the constant vibration.

An advantage of wooden floor construction methods is that they have a little give, and thus are kinder to the joints and spine of those walking on them than the more rigid concrete floors. On the other hand, wood varies in volume as it takes up or loses moisture, often leading to mysterious creaking and groaning sounds in the building, and sometimes causing cracks and fissures to form. However, this should not lead to any structural problems provided these properties of timber have been taken into account during construction.

MINERAL BUILDING MATERIALS

The base substances for mineral building materials such as clay, loam, sand, gravel and other types of rock are literally all around us, and they have been used for building for a very long time. It makes sense to use those materials in the areas where they are easily obtained, and accordingly their use is, as a rule, highly localized. Mining or quarrying can lead to quite substantial environmental damage to the surrounding area, and, in addition, processing these raw materials into the finished building materials often requires large amounts of energy (for example in firing bricks) and can involve a variety of hazardous industrial processes.

Base materials

Cement is a hydraulic binding agent for mortar, concrete, grout and a variety of structural elements such as paving stones, curbstones, shaped stones, storm drainpipes, fiber cement products, lightweight building blocks and many wall building materials. Cement

plants for example. They are ground up and fired at a temperature of 2,732° F (1,500° C), in some areas using toxic waste or used tires as fuel. This practice can lead to the production of hazardous substances such as dioxins and furans which may escape into the atmosphere if safety precautions are inadequate. Moreover, this manufacturing process regularly leads to emissions into the surrounding environment of toxic dust and heavy metals such as thallium and mercury. Furthermore, the high firing temperature means that cement is an energy-intensive construction material. The total energy requirement for the production of cement is 2,900 Btus/lb. or about 5.8 million Btus/ton. Cement also contains between 20 and 200 mg/kg of chromium. This, in particular the highly toxic chromium VI, can cause eczema if it comes into contact with the skin. Cement with a chromium VI content greater than 2 ppm (so-called chromate-rich cement), should be avoided. Cement is also highly alkaline and can cause skin irritation. It has been demonstrated that

Cement, lime, clay and gypsum – the basic materials from which building blocks are made

Available in abundance
The raw materials for most mineral building products are abundant and they can be extracted locally, which reduces the energy necessary to transport them. Extraction, however, does not come without an environmental price. The best solution of all, therefore, is to use recycled materials whenever possible.

has the property, when finely ground, of becoming rock-hard through a chemical reaction when water is added. The purest form of cement, known as Portland cement, has the following constituents:
- 64% caustic lime (CaO);
- 20% silicic acid (SiO_2);
- 5% aluminum oxide (Al_2O_3);
- 2.5% hematite (Fe_2O_3);
- 8.5% others, for example calcium sulfate, blast furnace slag, flue ash, oil shale, limestone dust, trass, bentonite and so on.

These constituents are mostly obtained from limestone, clay and marl (calcareous clay for making brick) quarries, while some others are the residue of industrial processes, at steelworks and coal-fired power

Iron Portland, blast-furnace and certain other cement types contain elevated levels of radioactivity.
Despite its shortcomings, cement is indispensable for many building purposes. In addition, it is less energy intensive than structural steel and it has extremely good thermal storage characteristics. It should, however, be used sparingly, and alternatives such as brick and wood should be considered. On a positive note, concrete is not difficult to dispose of and it can be recycled to a certain extent.
Lime is also the bonding agent for plaster, mortar and lime-sand brick. It is reduced to caustic lime (CaO) by baking limestone, which is chiefly obtained by quarrying, at a temperature of 1,652° F (900° C) and then grinding it to a fine powder. The baked lime becomes

slaked lime with the addition of water. This process, referred to as calcination, releases a great deal of heat, then cures over a long period of time taking up carbon dioxide from the atmosphere, and once again becomes limestone. Unslaked lime is a strongly alkaline corrosive agent but has low radioactivity. Lime has good absorption properties, binds acid from atmospheric pollutants and has a disinfectant quality. Accordingly, it is particularly suitable for plaster, and is not difficult to reuse or dispose of provided it does not contain any harmful additives.

Gypsum is a bonding agent used mostly in interior applications for plaster, stucco work, gypsum wallboard, reinforced plaster decking, and grout. It is obtained either from naturally occurring calcium sulfate deposits (gypsum rock or anhydrite gypsum) or as an industrial byproduct of flue gas desulfurization (FGS gypsum) by extracting the water from the rock at temperatures of between 212° and 572° F (100° and 300° C). If water is then added again it solidifies, and 40–75% of its volume is porous. This porosity ensures good moisture buffering. Gypsum also has good fire retardant properties. Synthetic gypsum obtained from phosphoric acid production is banned as a building material in some countries due to its high levels of heavy metals, radioactivity and other pollutants. In contrast, various studies have shown that FGS gypsum contains few hazardous constituents, and has a lower heavy metal content than naturally occurring gypsum. For this reason FGS gypsum should be the preferred option when it is available. Another increasing trend by a number of United States manufacturers of gypsum products, is the use of recycled gypsum content in their products. This is especially true in acoustical "lay-in" ceiling tiles. The recycled gypsum

used is generally obtained from post-industrial and construction waste recycling efforts.

When clay (which consists largely of aluminum silicate, the weathering products of feldspar, plus quartz and mica), is mixed with sand and coarse clay, loam is produced. This material can be used, unfired, as infill in walls and floors, and also as a binding agent in mortar, plaster or grout. Alternatively, it may be mixed with clay and fired to produce brick for masonry bricks, roof tiles, floor tiles or other building components as well as stoneware. Clay is obtained from quarries, and unlike the raw materials for cement must not contain any lime. Deposits of the raw material are widespread but despite this the process of obtaining it from quarries inevitably leads to damage to the natural environment similar to that mentioned above regarding the open-pit mining of gypsum. Unrestricted reuse of loam is possible, while fired brick can only be reused to a limited extent (downcycling), and disposal of loam is not difficult at all.

Brick

Brick is made from a blend of loam and clay, most recently with admixtures of materials that add porosity, such as sawdust and cellulose (the *Unipor* system) or polystyrene beads (the *poroton* system). The composite mixture is then extruded as a continuous billet from a die which determines the shape and perforations of the subsequent brick. The billet is sliced into the final shape and the unfired brick is then predried in a drying chamber which is heated by excess heat from the kiln, and is then fired for nearly three hours at a temperature of 1,500 to 2,200 °F (800 to 1,200° C) in a tunnel kiln. As the composite

Necessary exploitation or rape of the countryside?

The mining of mineral building materials is not always environmentally damaging, but it can often involve widespread destruction of the landscape. The deciding factor is the relative scarcity of the material involved: The more limited the deposits are, the greater the likelihood that environmental considerations will be set aside. Lengthy transport distances worsen the ecological costs further. Perhaps the most important factor is what is done after the deposit has been exhausted: Sensitive restoration of the surrounding countryside is possible in virtually all cases.

bakes, tiny cavities form which give the finished product additional heat insulating properties. However, the process does involve the emission of benzol and styrol in the case of composites containing polystyrene, or of phenol and formaldehyde where cellulose has been added.

These toxic byproducts must be extracted, like other waste gases, by suitable filters, a wide variety of studies have shown that it is highly improbable that

today consist of little more than a thin brickwork lattice. And as we saw above, the same period has seen increasing use of added materials designed to increase porosity. These developments have of course always involved a compromise between the need to ensure that the bricks retain sufficient load-bearing capacity and the desire, on the other hand, to improve thermal insulating properties by adding as much air as possible to the brick. Some bricks are now so advanced in this respect that traditional single-wythe external walls can be erected in less harsh climates without the need for additional insulation.

The latest innovation is honeycomb brick, which after a lengthy and costly development period is now being manufactured at an eastern German brickwork. In this type of brick the brick ribs between the hexagonal holes are no more than two to three millimeters thick. To achieve this, particularly fine clay is used, and the finest of cellulose fibers are employed to add porosity. Special drying and firing techniques prevent the fragile structure from deforming or cracking. Honeycomb brick makes possible thermal insulation values as good as those of expanded concrete and the use of this kind of brick will mean that traditional brick-on-brick construction methods without additional thermal insulation will still be possible.

Solid brick is found today only in the form of clinker brick, fired at high temperatures, which is still used to provide very high levels of durability for pavers, facework and chimney brick. In order to promote the use of brick in double-wythe masonry structures, Germany, for example, has established a brick bearing the trademark "double-wythe construction using brick."

Fired from clay

Some traditional brick kilns are still in use (see below), but in modern brickwork production is almost completely automatic. Here, the freshly fired bricks are emerging from the kiln to be packed onto pallets by machine (see right picture).

the finished brick will contain any of them. The porosity-inducing materials mostly come from the recycling of paper, sawmill byproducts and polystyrene from industrial waste. In principle, it is possible to use other industrial waste by-products to add porosity to bricks, for example, fine sewage sludge derived from sewage treatment plants. Research from a pilot project showed that the use of this kind of additive does not increase the heavy metal content. Nevertheless it may be some time before manufacturers embrace such radical concepts.

Brick has been in use for 5,000 years

In recent times this ancient wall building material, which has been in use throughout the world for over 5,000 years, has undergone considerable evolution as ever lighter types of brick with improved thermal insulation properties have been developed. The past 40 years have seen the replacement of solid brick by ever-more perforated types of brick, so that many

- Porous vertically perforated brick: thermal conductivity λ 1.4 (honeycomb brick λ 0.8) (Btu/hr/ft.²/°F/in.) – density 44 lb./ft.³ – embodied energy 1,000 Btu/lb. or 43,000 Btu/ft.³
- Light vertically perforated brick: thermal conductivity λ 3.1 (Btu/hr/ft.²/°F/in.) – density 62 lb./ft.³ – embodied energy 1,300 Btu/lb. or 82,000 Btu/ft.³
- Masonry brick: thermal conductivity λ 4.7 (Btu/hr/ft.²/°F/in.) – density 100 lb./ft.³ – embodied energy 1,200 Btu/lb. or 116,000 Btu/ft.³
- Clinker brick: thermal conductivity λ 6.7 (Btu/hr/ft.²/°F/in.) – density 125 lb./ft.³ – embodied energy 460 Btu/lb. or 58,000 Btu/ft.³

Ever more perforations

The evolution of the brick is outlined in the illustration on the facing page. Originally they were formed by hand from mud or clay (1), while later they were hand-shaped in molds (2). By the turn of the century they began to be made by machine (3). To make them lighter and improve their heat insulating properties the first perforations were then introduced (4), and hard clinker bricks without perforations (5) were reserved for specially demanding applications. Then bricks were not only given more and more perforations, they had extra ingredients added to increase their porosity (6). Plan brick with the thickness of a wall (7) does not require any masonry mortar, being laid by the thin bed procedure. The most recent development is the honeycomb brick (8).

1. Solid earthen brick

2. Hand-formed molded brick

3. Machine-formed brick

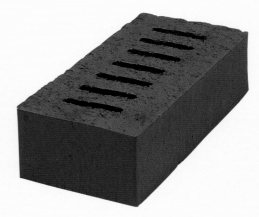

4. Perforated brick

5. Wall facing brick

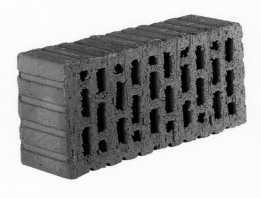

6. Lightweight vertically perforated brick

7. Plan brick

8. Honeycomb brick

Loam building materials

Loam has excellent moisture regulating and heat storage properties and ensures a pleasant living environment. Hitherto its use for load-bearing purposes has not been permitted. In Germany, however, licensing procedures for a variety of types of loam brick are currently in progress. It is suitable as infill brickwork for wooden structures or for non-supporting interior walls. Unfortunately loam brick is not widely available outside of Germany and its use in the United States is limited to a small number of cases of owner-built homes where the loam or earth is usually mixed with straw and water, formed into bricks which are allowed to dry in the sun. In the Southwest United States these mud bricks, or adobe, have been long used, initially by native American tribes. Adobe construction is also native to Latin America, and East Anglia (England) where they are known as "clay lump" houses. Loam remains hygroscopic after drying, and shrinks as it dries, which can lead to cracks making

Earth and wood
Earth, a mixture of clay and sandy soil, is suitable for walls in non-supporting structures, in particular as the infilling material in wooden houses, where its humidity regulating properties come into play.

Aggregates
Because clay cracks easily and has a poor thermal capacity, it is mixed with aggregates such as chopped straw or sawdust.

A wide range
Modern earthen building products are largely standardized, allowing for efficient construction. They include clay or loam building blocks, premixed clay content plaster and construction panels. Straw matting is used as a plaster base while also providing thermal insulation.

reworking necessary. To stabilize the mixture, lime, cement and bitumen are added. With traditional wet working it requires several weeks in a warm environment to dry out, and because of this the current trend is toward dry loam construction work, using previously air-dried loam building materials. Loam does not have good heat insulating properties. Even lightweight loam products including organic or other heat insulating materials do not allow exterior walls of normal strength to be built without the need for additional insulating material such as reed, softwood fiber or mineral fill

material. Also commonly used is the rammed earth method where local earth is dug from the site and rammed into wooden forms in successive layers.

For a long time loam or earth was known only as a do-it-yourself excavated material, or as an unfired, air-dried or sun-dried type of green brick, but over the last five years a number of German manufacturers have begun the mass production of loam-based building materials. For example, lime brick with added wood fragments for improved durability are available, and also lightweight loam bricks with added straw, Perlite,

Imagination set free

Earthen building materials allow imaginative wall designs because they are slow to dry. Homebuilders with artistic ambitions can use earth as a means of self-expression. These rounded shapes are a typical example.

expanded clay or cork for improved thermal insulation. Ready-mixed lightweight loams for traditional working with the rammed earth method or for working with

- lightweight loam (earth): thermal conductivity λ 2.1 (Btu/hr/ft.²/°F/in.) – density 50 lb./ft.³ – embodied energy 60 Btu/lb. or 3,000 Btu/ft.³
- cob (earth and straw mixture): thermal conductivity λ 4.9 (Btu/hr/ft.²/°F/in.) – density 87 lb./ft.³ – embodied energy 30 Btu/lb. or 2,000 Btu/ft.³

modern plastering machines, reduce the risks involved. These risks include poor resistance to shear loads (such as earthquakes, susceptibility to rising damp from the ground, and to a certain extent susceptibility to driving rain when used as an external wall material). Recently, building boards made of lightweight loam plus jute fabric, using reed as a stabilizer, have come on to the market in Germany, for use, like standard building panels, in interior construction work. It is hopeful that these types of products will soon be available in North American markets and the UK.

Green house in Rheine, Germany

Arch.: N. Elbeshausen, Rheine
Earthen structures have a tradition going back thousands of years. However, earth still has a part in the most modern of structures.

Speeding things up

Even relatively heavy lime sand bricks are now being produced in larger sizes, speeding up construction. They are laid on a thin bed of mortar rather than by the traditional technique.

Perforated lime sand bricks and facing bricks

Lime sand bricks are also perforated, though not so much in order to improve thermal insulation as to make them lighter and easier to work with. Unfortunately they are not widely available.

Lime sand brick

Caustic lime (8%) and quartz sand (92%) were first mixed together by a process patented in 1880. Water is added to the mixture, which is subsequently formed into green bricks in block machines and hardened in autoclaves for four to eight hours at a temperature of around 392° F (200° C). During this process silicic acid is released from the sand and combines with the slaked lime to form crystalline compounds which hold the sand together. Neither the manufacture nor the use in construction involve hazardous emissions, the final product is completely free of pollutants and its energy content is much lower than that of conventional brick. Lime sand bricks are comparatively dense and thus are very suitable for thermal storage and soundproofing.

They also come in larger sizes which can be used in conjunction with thin-bed mortar joining or unmortared butt joints. The weight of the oversized versions makes them difficult for the bricklayer to handle, however, and thus it is advisable to use mechanical lifting equipment. Their moisture absorption is only a quarter of the conventional brick, but in combination with plaster it is sufficient for interior use. An added advantage is that lime sand brick is about one-third the cost of normal brick.

Lime sand brick has very poor heat insulating properties. It can be used for external walls only in combination with additional thermal insulation, whether by

- Perforated lime sand brick: thermal conductivity λ 4.9 (Btu/hr.ft.²/°F/in.) – density 87 lb./ft.³ – embodied energy 400 Btu/lb. or 34,000 Btu/ft.³
- Lime sand facing brick: thermal conductivity λ 7.6 (Btu/hr.ft.²/°F/in.) – density 125 lb./ft.³ – embodied energy 400 Btu/lb. or 48,000 Btu/ft.³

means of an externally fitted composite system, which generally involves the use of ecologically questionable materials, or by a double-wythe structure, as is customary in northern climates. This type of structure allows very good insulation levels to be achieved at a reasonable price. Here, in particular, the price advantage of lime sand brick over normal brick comes into play, as well as its significantly lower embodied energy.

Lightweight concrete blocks

Lightweight concrete building blocks are made from cement plus a light granular material such as pumice stone, perlite or expanded clay, with the addition of water. While the ecological reservations about the use of cement have already been noted above on a number of occasions, the additives used to produce a lightweight option (pumice, expanded clay) should be viewed very differently.

Naturally occurring pumice is a porous volcanic rock. Because its extraction often involves damage to the natural environment, and since the deposits are limited, the future of this raw material is unclear. Furthermore, naturally occurring pumice frequently has a high level of radioactivity. However, small quantities of pumice slag are produced as a byproduct of steel production. On the other hand, concrete building blocks containing pumice have the lowest primary energy content of any walling material.

Expanded clay is manufactured through a number of procedures involving the foaming and subsequent firing of clay, a manufacturing process that uses a relatively large amount of energy. Pumice and expanded clay lightweight concrete building blocks both have very good thermal insulating properties and have the best soundproofing qualities of any single-wythe construction method. Their manufacturers were pioneers in the development of large walling components.

Lateral pointing is sometimes done using a jointing system which saves on mortar. There are also reinforced lightweight concrete building components such as wall and roof panels, prefabricated gables, ceiling units, lintels and shutter boxes. A problem with these, however, is that they usually contain 30% cement as the bonding agent.

Lightweight lime sand bricks are available only in Germany, and even there only recently. Like normal lime sand bricks they are manufactured using the autoclave process but instead of the fly ash or sand component expanded clay is added which accounts for 90% of the volume of the end product. Currently the only manufacturer of this product is in northern Bavaria, Germany. Lightweight lime sand brick has properties similar to lightweight concrete building blocks, only the less environmentally questionable lime is used as the bonding agent rather than cement.

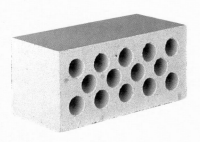

Perforated lime sand brick

Standard Lime sand brick

Lime sand facing brick with perforations

Lightweight lime sand brick is available as super-size building blocks one-third the height of a story, or even as individually prefabricated large building units, both of which make for considerable savings over traditional solid construction methods.

Expanded concrete typically consists of a mixture of

- 50–60% quartz sand
- 20–30% cement
- 10–20% lime and
- small quantities of gypsum or anhydrite.

Water is then added to this mixture with the addition of 0.1% aluminum powder or paste. The aluminum initiates a chemical reaction which produces countless air bubbles in the mix and causes a fivefold increase in volume. The concrete is then cut into shape when it is just half-set and finally hardened in an autoclave at a temperature of around 356° F (180° C).

The evenly-distributed air bubbles lead to a building material with the lowest weight per unit volume of any walling stone or brick, making it easy to work with even in large sizes. Its thermal insulating properties are easily the best of all walling materials, though conversely its soundproofing capacity is the poorest.

The building blocks can easily be sawn into shape and laid with sparing use of adhesive mortar without the risk of producing thermal bridges. However, the fine dust produced by the sawing may be a health hazard and workers should certainly wear a respirator. With steel reinforcement, the material can be used to make prefabricated lintels, roof and floor panels and also wall sections.

Expanded concrete is highly hygroscopic and must be coated with a water-resistant plaster, which usually contains a proportion of synthetic materials, since normal plaster for indoor use does not stick without the use of an undercoat containing some type of plastic resin. The main ecological objection to expanded concrete is its relatively high cement content.

- Lightweight concrete: thermal conductivity λ 1.0 (Btu/hr/ft.^{2}/°F/in.) – density 37 lb./ft.^{3} – embodied energy 500 Btu/lb. or 19,000 Btu/ft.^{3} (expanded clay concrete); 400 Btu/lb. or 15,400 Btu/ft.^{3} (pumice concrete)
- Lightweight lime sand brick: thermal conductivity λ 0.9 (Btu/hr/ft.^{2}/°F/in.) – density 37 lb./ft.^{3} – embodied energy 1,000 Btu/lb. or 39,000 Btu/ft.^{3}
- Expanded concrete: thermal conductivity λ 0.8 (Btu/hr/ft.^{2}/°F/in.) – density 22 lb./ft.^{3} – embodied energy 1,800 Btu/lb. or 39,000 Btu/ft.^{3}

Expanded concrete masonry block

Expanded concrete facing units

Concrete, grout and mortar

Concrete, a mixture of cement and sand, gravel or crushed stone, has been used as a building material since Roman times. However, it was not until the 1960s that it developed into one of the most important of all building materials. Concrete can be cast into almost any shape and, by varying the ingredients, can perform a wide variety of functions. Due to its high compressive strength and water resistance it is indispensable in some areas even in ecological construction, for example, as a foundation material.

Mortar provides the bond

Traditional bricklaying is a skill that must be thoroughly mastered, because the wall will be able to bear the required loads only if it is absolutely plumb. Mortar provides a durable bonding agent for the bricks.

Steel reinforcing gives concrete its tensile strength

Concrete's high degree of compressive strength makes it ideal for foundations. Steel reinforcing of a variety of gauges and configurations provides the necessary tensile strength and in the case of this floor, to prevent the concrete from cracking.

When reinforced with steel it can withstand both high compressive loads and tensile stresses and is thus the preferred material for free-span ceilings, girders and lintels. However, under some circumstances the embedded steel can act as what is known as a "Faraday" shield, which can serve to intensify or in some cases exclude electromagnetic (EMF) radiation.

Concrete also has good thermal storage and sound-proofing properties. On the downside, it has the worst thermal insulating properties of any mineral building material, it can only absorb minimal amounts of moisture and it tends to resist vapor diffusion. However, adding pumice, expanded clay, expanded shale (Perlite) or polystyrene improves the thermal insulating properties of lightweight concrete. When the cement contains fly ash (blast-furnace slag), or when naturally occurring pumice is used, higher levels of radioactivity may have to be taken into account. Chromate-rich cement can also cause contact dermatitis. A wide range of additives and admixtures are available, many of which pose health hazards or lead to the release of various pollutants. Among these are chemicals which accelerate or retard curing, increase strength, workability or plasticity, improve bonds to reinforcing or adjoining materials, add coloration, resist fungus or insects and other desirable effects. These additives include chemicals such as calcium chloride, polyacrylates, saccharose, silicates and other pozzolans, formates, fatty acids, mineral oils, cellulose ether and many other substances of known or unknown toxicity, and sometimes also salts of wood resins and tensides with skin irritating or corrosive effects. Although these additives provide convenience, they are not really necessary and it is strongly recommended that they be avoided.

A cement topping or setting bed is sometimes referred to as grout and is applied wet, screeded level and then allowed to harden forming a smooth and continuous base on which the final flooring can be laid. The grout is either applied directly to the subfloor or substrate material or onto bond-break layer (e.g. oil paper), or else it can be "floated" on a layer of insulation material. The most common material for this purpose is portland cement or grout. This is a fine-grained (< 8 mm) concrete to which, when necessary, additional water or a fluidifier is added to make it especially runny (self-leveling), facilitating the laying of a completely smooth and even finish floor surface. There are also anhydrite or gypsum versions called gypcrete. Cement grout is a good heat conductor and thus is particularly suitable for use in conjunction with underfloor heating systems. However, it is normal practice for cement topping materials to contain considerable quantities of synthetic additives, among them the environmentally unfriendly PVC, and also solvents. This means that smaller quantities of water are needed, thus reducing the drying and setting time, but synthetic additives also lead to potential health hazards and ecological concerns.

An alternative option, particularly for renovating old houses, when the weight of the cement setting bed must not be too great, is melted asphalt. This consists chiefly of bitumen plus an added aggregate material, and is applied hot. The manufacture of this material requires a lot of energy and furthermore bitumen is a byproduct of crude oil refining and is a

fresh mortar remains workable for as long as possible after delivery to the construction site, but sets rapidly when applied to the brickwork, chemical additives have to be used. Particularly hazardous is epoxy resin mortar, which is very strong and hard-wearing, but contains the carcinogen epichlorhydrine, and can lead to allergies and also eye irritation. Also worth mentioning is the use of fly ash in concrete which can be used to replace a large percentage of the aggregate and up to 30 % of the cement without any negative effect on structural properties.

- Concrete: thermal conductivity λ 12.0 (Btu/hr/ft.^{2}/°F/in.) – density 144 lb./ft.^{3} – embodied energy 340 Btu/lb. or 48,000 Btu/ft.^{3}
- Reinforced concrete: density 150 lb./ft.^{3} – embodied energy 1,200 Btu/lb. or 179,000 Btu/ft.^{3}
- Concrete grout: density 150 lb./ft.^{3} – embodied energy 1,200 Btu/lb. or 179,000 Btu/ft.^{3}
- Melted asphalt topping: density 57 lb./ft.^{3} – embodied energy 3,400 Btu/lb. or 188,000 Btu/ft.^{3}
- Cement mortar: density 125 lb./ft.^{3} – embodied energy 230 Btu/lb. or 29,000 Btu/ft.^{3}
- Fly ash concrete: density 100–115 lb./ft.^{3} – embodied en. 875–1,000 Btu/lb. or 100,000 Btu/ft.^{3}

Brick by brick

The mortar must be suitable for the brick or stone being used. For example, if typical masonry mortar is used for external walls made of expanded stone, thermal bridges will result. Lightweight building materials require a lightweight mortar or thin-set mortar. Here, masonry mortar is being used with lime sand brick.

suspected carcinogen. But this suspected carcinogenic effect applies only to certain types of bitumen made from bituminous coal tar and also to mixtures of tar components and crack bitumen, which contain considerable quantities of polycyclic aromatic hydrocarbons. In contrast pure, carefully distilled bitumen is not believed to contain any hazardous components. Bitumen's classification is under review. According to advisory centers for the use of asphalt the categorization "carcinogenic" only applies to vapor and aerosol containing polycyclic aromatic hydrocarbons, which can be produced when working with hot bitumen. However, after normal ventilation and when allowing the usual period between laying the melted asphalt and occupying the home, independent research has found that concentrations of polycyclic aromatic hydrocarbons are at normal ambient levels.

Mortar consists of a bonding agent such as cement and lime, plus aggregates, usually sand, plus, in most cases, various chemical and in certain cases thermal insulating additives. As bricklaying involves regular skin contact with building materials, the risk posed by chromate-rich cement and by the general irritant effect of alkaline substances should once again be noted. A rough distinction is made between normal bricklaying mortar and lightweight bricklaying mortar, which should be used when laying the lightweight insulating building blocks, where the use of normal mortar would lead to the formation of significant thermal bridges. There is also facing wall mortar, which is used for solid filling of facing wall brickwork in double-wythe construction and is designed for the clinkers and facing bricks used there. In order to ensure that

Screeding provides smooth surfaces

The concrete substrate on which the finish floor is to be laid are still smoothed by hand with a long level bar or screed. In order to ensure a smooth and absolutely even surface a thin layer of topping cement is sometimes poured over the slab and screeded flat.

Scratched finish

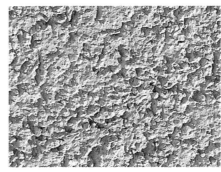
Disc finish

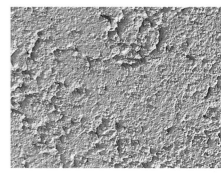
Float finish

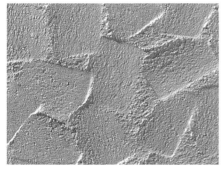
Antique finish

Trowel finish

Rustic finish

Plaster

Different plaster finishes

Depending on the different application and application techniques used, the same materials can produce a wide range of different plaster finishes. For example, a trowel can be used to produce patterns, scrapers and brushes can be used to form a smooth surface or produce swirling, criss-cross, or striated patterns. The applied plaster can also be left unsmoothed in order to give a rustic effect. Special rollers or the use of coarse aggregates can produce fluted or worm finishes.

Plaster: exterior cladding, wall surface and decorative element

A distinction is made between indoor and outdoor plaster, also sometimes referred to as stucco. While exterior plaster generally consists of lime or cement plus sand and various additives, indoors the less durable gypsum is the most common bonding agent. The high cement content of exterior plaster makes the wall surface watertight but also resists diffusion of vapor through the wall. The same essentially applies to resin plaster, though the use of silicon resins will make it less resistive to diffusion. As moisture moving through the wall reaches the plaster it can adsorb into the plaster, and vapor pressure will cause spalling of the plaster surface on the outside of the wall. Other types of exterior finishes which very well can be substituted for plaster consist of various thermoset resins such as fiber-reinforced polyester, methyl methacryl resins, epoxy resins and polyurethane resins which involve somewhat environmentally questionable manufacturing processes. In these processes toxic isocyanates and carcinogenic epichlorhydrine gases are used and quite often released into the atmosphere. In addition, they are non-recyclable and pose a disposal problem later on, since thermoset synthetics cannot be remelted. Preservatives are usually added to silicon resins because their organic component encourages the growth of fungi and algae. Whether these chemicals are actually emitted by the plaster has not yet been investigated.

Resin systems have the distinct advantage that even thin coats remain flexible and crack-free, and can be pigmented almost any color you like, while mineral plasters must be painted as a separate operation.

Despite this, traditional lime and sand plaster is usually preferable since it can absorb and release moisture, while the lime also acts as a disinfectant resisting fungal growth. Cement plaster can contain the toxic chromium VI, considered to be the cause of 90% of all cases of bricklayer's eczema. Plasters with a high chromate content must, therefore, bear a warning label. Exterior plastering can also be applied with the addition of the environmentally questionable polystyrene or, preferably, perlite to provide added thermal insulation. Indoor plaster generally contains gypsum which, due to its porous nature, has very good moisture-buffering properties. Gypsum plaster is also easy to work with because it sticks to a variety of different bases better than lime cement plaster. Indoor plaster too can be mixed with resin, to make it easier to clean, for example, but this should generally be avoided for the reasons mentioned earlier.

Loam plaster is becoming more and more popular because of its positive impact on the indoor climate. In recent years it has become increasingly fashionable to leave the walls free of wallpaper and apply a variety of decorative or textured plaster finishes. To make the plaster stick better, in particular to sandy base surfaces, a liquid plastic- or cellulose-based undercoat or bonding coat must first be applied. Where the base surface has large cracks or is made of a different material, in particular wood or metal, a plaster lath must be used, which may consist of plastic webbing, reed matting or metal netting. A clean application and long-term protection of edges and corners are ensured by plaster beads which are generally made

Multi-colored stone finish

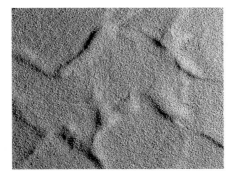
Antique finish

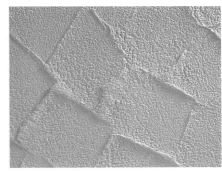
Antique finish

Worm finish

Scraped finish

Disc finish

of aluminum or galvanized steel. These beads require a lot of energy to make, and they are sometimes coated with PVC which makes them ecologically questionable.

- Resin plaster: density 81 lb./ft.³ – embodied energy 3,900 Btu/lb. or 319,000 Btu/ft.³
- Lime cement plaster: density 116 lb./ft.³ – embodied energy 1,200 Btu/lb. or 135,000 Btu/ft.³
- Gypsum plaster: density 45 lb./ft.³ – embodied energy 1,600 Btu/lb. or 72,000 Btu/ft.³

Building panels

The most common mineral building panels used for interior work are gypsum wallboard and gypsum fiber wallboard. Gypsum wallboard typically consists of a gypsum core covered with a heavy paper skin which provides the necessary tensile and flexural strength. The boards normally measure 48×96×½ inches or 48×144×½ inches. They are chiefly used for wall and ceiling paneling, and also for prefabricated walls. They are also available, with glass fiber reinforcement for walls where movement is suspected to occur, as fireproofing panels in heavier thicknesses (commonly 2 layers of ⅝ inch provides 1-hour fire-resistance), and are available impregnated with moisture repellent for wet-use applications such as bathrooms. These products often also contain a fungicide. Independent research indicates that gypsum plaster board is not treated with halogen-organic preservatives, and

it does not contain significant levels of radioactivity or heavy metals. The same also goes for gypsum fiber wallboards, which consist of a homogeneous composite of gypsum and cellulose fibers derived from recycled paper, which, with the addition of water, is pressed under high pressure into boards. They are more robust than gypsum plaster board and like gypsum plaster board are available in ceiling-height

panels, as well as in a smaller and lighter one-man do-it-yourself size. Gypsum fiber wallboards are also suitable for use in humid rooms such as bathrooms, laundries, etc., without any additives, and can be used as fireproof paneling by applying multiple layers.

- Gypsum plaster board: density 45 lb./ft.³ – embodied energy 1,600 Btu/lb. or 72,500 Btu/ft.³
- Gypsum fiber wallboard: density 56 lb./ft.³ – embodied energy 1,500 Btu/lb. or 82,000 Btu/ft.³

Light and robust
Gypsum board is ideal for interior construction work, used either in its paper lined form or reinforced with cellulose fiber extra bending durability. Gypsum plaster board is mostly used for ceilings and walls, however, there are also gypsum flooring panels as well (left).

Long-term impact resistance
Fiber reinforced gypsum board is more durable than ordinary gypsum wallboard and is suitable for dry flooring applications. However, a double thickness of board is recommended. Manufacturers supply two-ply boards ready glued as well as thicker tongue-and-groove board for this purpose.

WOODEN BUILDING MATERIALS

Wood – a warm, flexible, breathing material

Wood has been used as a building material since pre-historic times, and until well into the eighteenth century most houses in Europe were made of wood. In central Europe oak, beech, elm, ash, fir and spruce have been the dominant species for millennia.

Due to the lack of open communication in the timber industry today, however, it is rather difficult to know whether a spruce log or an oak board is derived from Canadian clear felling, Scandinavian monoculture or ecologically sustainable forestry in Switzerland. Currently the predominant timber used for building comes from coniferous trees, which are preferred because of their straightness and relative economy while hardwoods, despite a wide range of possible applications, are used almost exclusively for furniture, veneer, flooring, wood paneling, and musical instruments. Low grade hardwood may also be used for shipping containers and pallets.

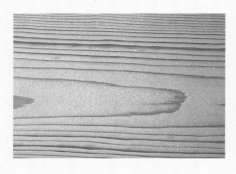

- **Spruce/fir:** evenly colored yellowish-white coniferous wood, goes a brownish color with age; can be used as lumber, for windows, flooring, façades, doors, gates, furniture, batten boards, particle board, lightweight wood wool panels; hardness 12, weight sitka spruce: 27 lb./cubic foot (433 kg/cubic meter), fir: 34 lb./cubic foot (545 kg/cubic meter); a softwood, low durability, good elasticity, low shrinkage, low weather resistance.

- **Larch/hemlock:** reddish to ruddy-brown coniferous wood with prominent grain; can be used for doors, gates, windows, concrete formwork, in wood foundations and hydraulic engineering, for stairs, flooring, paneling and furniture; hardness 19, weight 30 lb./cubic foot (481 kg/cubic meter); high resin content, good durability and elasticity, moderate shrinkage, resistant to chemicals and weather and durable under water.

- **Oak/red oak:** coarse-pored yellowish-brown to reddish-brown deciduous wood, darkens markedly with age; used for construction work, civil and hydraulic engineering, doors, flooring, veneer, furniture and tools, and also indoors for wall and ceiling paneling; hardness 40, weight 35 lb./cubic foot (561 kg/cubic meter); excellent durability and springiness, minimal shrinkage, good moisture resistance and underwater durability.

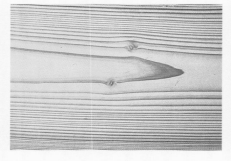

- **Pine/southern pine:** yellowish to reddish coniferous wood with prominent grain, darkens with age; used as wall and floor framing, for windows, doors, flooring, stairs, furniture and particle board; hardness 20, weight western white pine: 28 lb./cubic foot (450 kg/cubic meter), southern pine: 35 lb./cubic foot (561 kg/cubic meter); good durability and springiness, hardens with age, low shrinkage, weather-resistant, susceptible to blue stain.

- **Douglas fir (Oregon pine):** yellowish to ruddy-brown coniferous wood with prominent grain; can be used for wall and floor framing, external façades, balconies, doors, windows, stairs, flooring and furniture; hardness 20, weight 34 lb./cubic foot (545 kg/cubic meter); good durability and springiness, moderate shrinkage, good weather resistance.

- **Beech:** fine-pored deciduous wood yellowish to reddish in color, (hornbeam gray-white in color), no grain markings; can be used for furniture, stairs, parquet, wood block flooring, wood-based materials, plywood, veneer, particle board and batten board; hardness 34, weight 47 lb./cubic foot (561 kg/cubic meter); very durable and tough, resistant to abrasion, high shrinkage, very susceptible to moisture.

Indigenous types of wood

The following overview outlines the appearance, uses and properties of common types of indigenous European and North American wood species used in the construction industry. Their range of uses is determined chiefly by their structural properties, hardness, susceptibility to moisture and their capacity to withstand the elements. The hardness of a wood is measured by the Brinell hardness test expressed as N/mm². The higher the hardness number, the harder the wood. High hardness numbers mean the wood is suitable for flooring and for load-bearing purposes. Care should be taken when working with wood, since wood dust is a suspected carcinogen, with the exception of beech and oak dust, which have the more hazardous classification of being known carcinogens in animal research.

- **Ash:** coarse-pored whitish deciduous wood with brown heart, prominent grain; can be used for veneer, stairs, flooring, furniture, baseball bats and ladders; hardness 38, weight 41 lb./cubic foot (657 kg/cubic meter); very tough and elastic, very resistant to abrasion and chemicals, moderate shrinkage, moderately weather-resistant.

- **Elm:** coarse-pored yellow to dark brown prominent grained deciduous wood; used chiefly for indoor work as wall or ceiling paneling and flooring, and also for furniture; hardness 29, weight 41 lb./cubic foot (660 kg/cubic meter); very elastic and tough, easy to bend, moderate shrinkage and weather resistance.

- **Alder:** fine-pored reddish-white to ruddy brown deciduous wood, fine grained; can be used for furniture, battens, tool handles and for strapping; hardness 17, weight 34 lb./cubic foot (550 kg/cubic meter), relatively soft, minimal elasticity, tends to split, minimal weather resistance, but durable under water.

- **Maple:** fine-pored deciduous wood, almost white in color, minimal grain; can be used for veneer, furniture, flooring, stairs, tool handles and household appliances; hardness 27, weight 44 lb./cubic foot (705 kg/cubic meter); elastic, tough, moderate shrinkage, but somewhat susceptible to moisture.

- **Chestnut:** coarse-pored, greenish-brown deciduous wood with prominent grain, darkens markedly to brown with age; used for parquet, plywood and fiberboard, furniture and wood turning; hardness 18, weight 37 lb./cubic foot (600 kg/cubic meter); a relatively soft and not very elastic wood, moderate shrinkage, very weather-sensitive, often spiral-grained and unsound.

- **Robinia:** a rare, coarse-pored greenish-yellow deciduous wood, darkens to brown with age, prominent grain; can be used as piling wood, in hydraulic engineering, for garden furniture, tool handles or as turning wood; hardness 48, weight 47 lb./cubic foot (750 kg/cubic meter); extremely hard and tough, high degree of bending possible, almost no shrinkage, very water-resistant, grows very twisted and multi-branched.

Structural lumber preservation

Chemicals are not needed to preserve wood

In the United States there is no requirement for lumber to be treated with a preservative with the exception of NWWDA certified exterior wood windows (National Wood Window and Door Manufacturers Association). However, lumber which comes in contact with the ground or foundation is typical "green" or treated lumber. It has increasingly been recognized that the use of wood preservatives in indoor areas probably does more harm than good, and that there is almost always a structural solution that makes chemical treatment unnecessary.

Historically, a variety of methods have been used to ensure that wooden structural elements do not remain in contact with moisture for too long. Among these measures are the use of protective roof over-

horizontal wooden surfaces exposed to the elements, cannot be protected in the long term even by chemical means. For limited periods, unacceptably high levels of humidity can be reached as a result of the use of inadequately seasoned building lumber. Although the use of lumber with a water content of up to 35% is permitted under certain circumstances, this should be avoided on safety grounds and due to the wood's tendency to shrink, crack or warp as it dries out. After construction, wood will dry out over a given period, and if this period is less than three to six months then fungal attack should not be a problem. Inadequately seasoned wood can always dry out well if it is part of a structure which is subject to diffusion or ventilation allowing evaporation to occur.

Shoes keep the feet dry

Wooden beams do not rot if they are protected from ground moisture by metal "shoes" that prevent the moisture from getting to the wood (right).

Overhangs keep the rain off the wood

A roof that projects well beyond the walls below protects the wood from rain (far right). However, on the side of prevailing weather and wind, where driving rain is most likely, this will not be sufficient.

hangs, water drips and beveled edges (watersheds) on wooden parts exposed to the elements, good sealing of roofs, stilts for beams to eliminate contact with the soil, adequate ventilation and the avoidance of thermal bridges.

Fungi that can attack lumber require a wood moisture content of 20 to 25% in order to thrive. These levels of moisture will not be reached in indoor areas, even when they are unheated, provided there are no major construction defects. This also applies to rooms where high levels of humidity are produced, such as kitchens and bathrooms. The important factor is always long-term humidity: The occasional spilt bucket of water has little effect. Major construction defects such as a leaking roof, structural faults leading to the condensation of copious amounts of water, or

Woodworm and termites, on the other hand, require no more than 9–12% moisture content. This level can easily occur in unheated areas and in external wood. In this case it is vital that infestation by these pests is prevented by making the outer shell of the house insect-proof. In the case of ventilated wood façades, this can be achieved by fitting wire mesh that prevents the termite from flying in and laying its eggs. Shuttering, for example with interlocking tongue-and-groove boards, is also insect-resistant. However, cracks in the large visible beams, e.g. of half-timbered houses, can provide opportunities for insects to lay their eggs. In this case the wood preservation standard assumes that the attack will be noticed in good time and combated, so that preventative chemical wood preservation will not be necessary.

Chemical wood preservation

Only a small percentage of building lumber is treated. Very few wood species are sufficiently permeable for consistent penetration and desired retention of preservative treating solutions. If you decide to use a wood preservative anyway, you will be confronted with a confusing array of different wood preservation products. The highly toxic substances Pentachlorphenol (PCP) and Lindane are no longer in use today; all commercially pressure treated lumber should conform to standards established by the American Wood Preservers' Association. Chemical preservatives can be applied using either pressure or dip processes. About 95% of treated wood including most framing lumber is treated by pressure which forces greater penetration into the pores of the wood. The most

chemicals and water soluble salts. Solvent soluble chemicals are the most environmentally damaging because they require VOCs as carriers which are highly flammable, and also highly toxic. They will leach out over time and can therefore pose a distinct threat of groundwater contamination. The most commonly used water soluble salts are ammoniacal copper arsenate (ACA) and chromated copper arsenate (CCA) which leave a greenish tint, hence the term "green lumber."

Facilities which use these chemicals for wood treating typically recycle their treating water; however, spills do occur and soils around them usually contain an accumulation of these salts and groundwater may become contaminated. Furthermore, the surface of the treated

Watersheds

To avoid damage to wood, water must always be able to run off rapidly rather than forming puddles. Because of this all wooden parts should slope downwards and outwards. This is known as a watershed (right).

Water Drip

The grooves on the underside of a projecting wood profile ensure that the water drips away quickly rather than running back toward the building and forming a film that remains on the wood for a longer period (far right).

common method is the full-cell process where the wood is subjected to a vacuum just before treating resulting in maximum retention of the preservative. The degree of protection depends on the type and strength or concentration of the treating solution, depth of penetration, retention, proportion of heartwood to sapwood, and moisture content at the time of treating. Retention is measured in pounds of chemical retained per cubic foot (pcf) of wood. Framing lumber treated with chromated copper arsenate, for example, is required to have .25 pcf retention of the chemical for above grade applications, .40 pcf for ground contact and .60 pcf for below grade foundations.

Although there are dozens of chemicals commonly used for commercial treating they fall into three basic categories: oily preservatives, solvent-soluble organic

wood contains white arsenic powder which can cling to skin and clothing if handled. Arsenic compounds are highly toxic, and some are carcinogenic and capable of causing genetic damage. Anyone handling lumber treated with these metallic salts should wash their hands and clothing thoroughly afterward. This applies particularly to arsenic compounds, chromate and salts containing fluorine. Chromates can cause eczema, and also liver, kidney and circulatory disorders. Fluorine compounds tend to give off gases that are corrosive and irritating to the skin. Wood impregnated by the boiler pressure method is normally classified as hazardous waste and must be disposed of separately. Commercial treating of wood also requires a fair amount of energy to power the pressure treating and for the added transportation to and from the facility.

Alternative wood preservation methods with minimal toxicity

Naturally occurring chemicals

Boron salts such as borax or boracic acid are preferable as wood preservatives. Their toxicity to humans is minimal, and they do not give off harmful gases. They also do little harm to the environment, and because of this borates are contained in a wide variety of detergents. However, in large quantities they can be toxic to plants and fish, and also disrupt composting. However, they are regarded as "relatively harmless," and thus wood treated with them is not classified as toxic waste. The disadvantage of borates is that they will easily leach out of wood reducing their long term effectiveness. In order to bond them to wood, they are either mixed in with scumble or a protective coating is painted over the wood to prevent leaching.

The energy content is a further factor that tips the balance in favor of using more gentle wood preservatives in that most conventional pressure treating processes require 15 times as much energy.

An old wood preservation ingredient has recently been rediscovered: a plant called *Reseda luteola*. Resedas, mainly used in the past as a blue textile dye, but long since replaced by indigo, and then later by chemical dyes, were once used as a wood preservative, and are now once again available for this purpose. In northern Europe a clay known as Swedish red was used traditionally to treat wood, and this is now also available in other countries. However, it has a naturally high lead content and can thus only be recommended with reservations.

If, despite all precautions, wood does become infested by insects, the recommended method of combating the infestation is the hot-air method. This involves heating the affected area for several hours with hot air blowers until the core of the wood reaches a temperature of 130° F (55° C) for at least one hour. This will be sufficient to kill any worm, insect or egg. However, to avoid damaging the wood

- Borax: embodied energy content 184,000 Btu/ft.³
- Petrochemical pesticides: embodied energy content 2,955,000 Btu/ft.³

its surface temperature should not exceed 180° F (80° C) during the procedure. This procedure has the added advantage of thoroughly drying out the wood. The energy content, as given above, is a further factor demonstrating the ecological advantages of more gentle wood preservatives.

Reseda glaze protects and decorates

In eastern Germany some buildings are now being restored using a non-toxic wood preservative glaze derived from the plant *Reseda luteola*.

An unobtrusive plant

For centuries *Reseda luteola* was used to dye textiles. Now this virtually forgotten plant is making a successful comeback as a wood preservative.

Swedish red

This naturally occurring red mineral wood preservative comes from Sweden, where it was used traditionally to protect wooden houses. It is now available in various other countries.

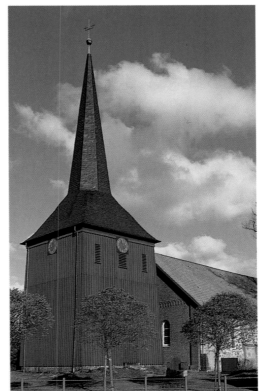

Traditional red preservative

The wooden façade of the building below and the church tower to the left have been treated with traditional Swedish red to protect against weathering and pest attack. Unfortunately, though, this mineral wood preservative has a relatively high lead content and thus cannot be recommended unreservedly.

Wood fiber building materials

Until only recently wooden building materials consisted either of solid wood or composite wood products such as particle board or plywood, and today these composite wood materials are still the most prevalent. Solid wood is still in common use for load-bearing beams, framing lumber, wood trim and battens, and a wide range of solid wood panels are available for siding and for interior paneling. In contrast, particle board and fiberboard are used for applications where strength and durability and often esthetics are not so important.

However, the simple equation, solid wood = strong, composite wood products = weak, no longer applies. The current generation of composite wood products including glulam, laminated veneer lumber and oriented strand members can be used for load-bearing purposes, and even has superior structural properties by and large as compared to solid heartwood. Structural properties of wood include such things as modulus of elasticity (stiffness as a beam), tensile strength (strength in bending parallel to grain), or sheer strength (ability to resist point loads across the grain), and compressive strength (resistance to crushing both parallel and perpendicular to the grain). The superior structural properties of composite wood stem from the obvious fact that there are natural limits to the length and thickness of solid lumber beams, which also have a tendency to warp or crack. Besides, solid wood always has defects such as knots and

New structural wood products are often preferable to steel

uneven grain. Thus long, clear beams are scarce and correspondingly expensive.

The new generation of composites allows builders to avoid these disadvantages and also means that lower grade wood can be used for high-grade applications. Composites are generally made by taking small sections of timber and cut-off pieces from standard sawmill operations and bonding them together. The individual pieces may be thin planks, strips and veneers, or even coarse wood chips. Although these products are made up primarily of wood, they may have completely different properties from solid wood of the same species. Furthermore, they make possible a variety of shapes which are not available in solid wood or sawn lumber, and they can also bear greater loads using more slender sections. In fact, in many cases they are capable of replacing not only solid wood but even steel, where the applicable loads could not have been borne by solid wood members.

At the same time these new composite wood products retain all the positive properties of wood, for example its moisture absorption capacity and warmth, pleasant odor and tactile qualities. A disadvantage, though, is that the adhesives used are generally phenolic formaldehyde resins or polyurethanes (isocyanates). However, since these adhesives constitute a relatively small proportion of the product in comparison to particle board, for example, and the joint surfaces are small, little formaldehyde gas is given off. No significant emissions of toxic isocyanates have been detected from these wood products because the isocyanates are almost totally cross-linked (chemically bonded) during the manufacturing process. It is a potentially hazardous environment to the workers making the product, however.

Currently, the most widely used structural wood product is glulam, which is made by bonding wooden planks between ¼ and 1½ inches thick to form composite sections under intense pressure, after first finger-joining the abutting ends of the strips. This enables beams with spans of up to 100 feet and up to 6 feet in depth to be manufactured. The wood used for this purpose is typically spruce; however, some hemlock and douglas fir are used as well. Glulam beams can achieve significantly greater load-bearing capacity than solid wood beams of the same thickness.

Laminated board is produced by a similar principle and is used to make very long, slender sections. Debarked relatively small softwood timber is sorted, cut to shape and glued together with a phenolic resin adhesive. This produces very strong beams of a relatively low weight. This product is used to make double-T or I-beams, which are used as rafters or as frames for wall paneling.

Another wood composite, laminated veneer lumber (LVL), is produced from sheets of veneer approximately ¼ inches thick and up to 8 feet long, which are bonded with a structural adhesive under intense heat and pressure in a continuous feed dye and using a radio frequency generator to cure the adhesive as it passes through the dye. The strips are arranged so that they lie as flush as possible to each other with the grain running in the same direction. This material is extruded in a continuously long section which is then cut to length producing beams of any desired length measuring up to 10 inches wide and 18 inches deep. LVL has significantly higher flexural, compressive and shear strength than solid wood, and is commonly used for columns, headers, joists and beams.

Another interesting product is a modular building panel system fabricated from small dimension boards. The system, developed by Professor Julius Natterer of Switzerland, utilizes multiple seasoned spruce boards placed edgewise next to each other and nailed together. This produces solid flat units of any desired width which can be used for the load-bearing structure of floors, walls and roofs, and can later be left exposed, insulated or sided over. Because they do not contain adhesives the units do not emit any chemical substances, and compared with other wooden products they provide very good acoustic insulation as well as protection against fire and summer heat. These solid units require a minimum of structural height, as a spanning distance of almost 16 feet can be achieved in living areas with a piled board ceiling only 4½ inches thick.

Wooden block panels are made in a completely different way. They consist of between three and seven

Wood structural panels

Another solid lumber construction system produced from glued-together wooden battens, offering log cabin quality without the usual problems associated with this type of structure.

Composite wood building modules

Thin boards nailed together produce thick structural units from which walls, floors or stairs can be cut (see left and below). These solid wood products, which are held together without any potentially hazardous glues, combine all the positive qualities of wood with a high degree of durability and lateral rigidity.

wood plies, depending on the application, glued crosswise at set intervals, providing a high degree of strength and rigidity. In addition, thanks to the generous wall cavity, adequate thermal insulation and diffusion are easily achieved.

- Construction lumber: thermal conductivity λ 0.9 (Btu/hr/ft.²/°F/in.) – density 31 lb./ft.³ – embodied energy 560 Btu/lb. or 17,000 Btu/ft.³
- Laminated board: thermal conductivity λ 1.39 (Btu/hr/ft.²/°F/in.) – density 37 lb./ft.³ – embodied energy 5,700 Btu/lb. or 213,000 Btu/ft.³

Particle board

Particle board is made up mainly of softwood from sawmill waste and manufacturing by-products and other residue. Particle board may also contain some beech and oak or other hardwoods, which are beneficial for technical reasons. The process was invented during the 1940s. The wood is first chipped by machine and then mixed with 7% adhesive. After this stage the wood is hot pressed, generally in flat presses, but for special applications such as interior doors also in extruding machines. Particle board is especially suitable for indoor construction work, for flooring and for furniture and cabinet manufacture. Its main disadvantage stems from the fact that it is not capable of performing load-bearing functions and has particularly low flexural strength. However, worst of all from an environmental and health point of view, particle board is the most serious source of indoor air pollutants, particularly formaldehyde. The pollutants derive from the adhesives used to make the particle board, chiefly urea-formaldehyde resins with high formaldehyde emissions, and also weather-resistant phenol formaldehyde resins with lower formaldehyde emissions but the additional risk of phenol gas emissions.

Formaldehyde, which is a pungent and allergenic gas that is strongly suspected of being carcinogenic, does not completely harden during the particle board production process, and as a result the residue is given off by the board as gas. This can also happen if the particle board is at some point later attacked by moisture. According to the current guidelines by the US Environmental Protection Agency (EPA) and the requirements of the department of Housing and Urban Development (HUD) as well as the American National Standards Institute (ANSI), formaldehyde emissions from particle board used in construction cannot exceed 0.3 ppm per cubic meter of air. However, Washington state public building requirements and, to cite a European example, the German hazardous materials directive are more restrictive with an emissions limit of 0.1 ppm.

According to most governmental agencies, this sort of concentration is considered rather harmless. However, meeting this requirement does not generally guarantee that, under specific living conditions, the air in a room actually does contain no more than 0.1 ppm formaldehyde. If a small space is packed with a large amount of particle board, for example, as may sometimes be found in children's bedrooms, or if the particle board is bare or has a lot of holes or notches in it, then the guideline value may indeed be exceeded to some extent.

Formaldehyde-free particle board can be found in the form of boards where isocyanates are used as the bonding agent. These are predominantly MDI boards using diphenylmethane-4.4-diisocyanate. Isocyanates are produced by a particularly dangerous and very energetic chlorine chemistry process, involving a chemical reaction between the highly toxic phosgene and a number of carcinogenic aromatic amines. If isocyanate is given off as gas – and this has not yet been proven in the case of particle board – amines are rapidly formed again, and, on combustion, prussic acid. Polymeric MDI is very strongly suspected of being carcinogenic.

Cement- or magnesite-bonded particle board, the so-called inorganic bonded particle board, does not pose a health hazard. Although it is considered less desirable from an ecological point of view cement is used to color the board gray, while magnesite colors it yellow. Magnesite consists chiefly of magnesium carbonate, and the biggest deposits of it are to be found in the Balkans and Turkey, where they are extracted by open-pit mining.

Inorganic bonded particle board is very heavy and thus is not suitable for many applications. An exception to this are lightweight wood wool boards, which are nearly always bonded using magnesite. Due to their better thermal insulating effect they are often used as sheathing in walls and ceilings, and due to their rough surface they are ideally suited as a base for plaster and as acoustic board. Particle board marked V 100 G contains wood preservatives.

- Urea formaldehyde-bonded particle board: thermal conductivity λ 0.90 (Btu/hr/ft.²/°F/in.) – density 41 lb./ft.³ – embodied energy 4,800 Btu/lb. or 193,300 Btu/ft.³
- Isocyanate-bonded particle board: thermal conductivity λ 1.18 (Btu/hr/ft.²/°F/in.) – density 50 lb./ft.³ – embodied energy 5,800 Btu/lb. or 290,000 Btu/ft.³
- Cement-bonded particle board: thermal conductivity λ 1.39 (Btu/hr/ft.²/°F/in.) – density 78 lb./ft.³ – embodied energy 3,600 Btu/lb. or 280,000 Btu/ft.³
- Lightweight wood wool boards: thermal conductivity λ 0.62 (Btu/hr/ft.²/°F/in.) – density 31 lb./ft.³ – embodied energy 3,710 Btu/lb. or 116,000 Btu/ft.³

OSB does less harm

Second generation particle board consists of highly robust, low-formaldehyde boards made of glued laminated wood shavings. These engineered OSB boards can be used both for interior construction work and for structural sheathing.

Chips provide solidity

Low-emission OSB board is particularly valued for structural jobs in ecological wood housebuilding. This innovation provides high quality at a reasonable price.

Other wooden building boards

Striking wooden flooring

OSB board is increasingly used for flooring, as in this house. All it requires is to be treated with resin oil. The striking patterns of large wood shavings provide a novel design touch.

OSB – a new generation of waferboard

No noise transmission

Soft fiberboard is also used for flooring, where it provides thermal and sound insulation

Plywood is used for high-grade applications such as furniture-making, but also as paneling for natural wood interiors and even for exterior siding. It is made from at least three layers of wooden veneer glued with the grain running at right angles to each other and often made from tropical woods such as luan. Plywood is very strong and also has good flexural strength. A sub-category of plywood is stave-core plywood, where there is a core of solid wooden strips glued between two eternal layers of veneer. Once again, the main problem is the adhesive used, which for most interior grade plywood is urea formaldehyde. However, due to the slender glue joints, emissions are much less than for particle-board and only increase if the surface is broken by large numbers of holes or notches. An even better choice with plywood is to use exterior grade plywood which uses melamine formaldehyde adhesives and which has far lower emissions than interior grade plywood.

A fairly recent development that can be recommended without reservations is OSB, or oriented strand board, which combines the strength of plywood with the low cost of particle-board. This material is made chiefly from low-grade timber, often aspen, poplar or other fast growing pulpwood trees. Long, thin wooden shavings (ca. 0.6 × 65 mm) are dried, arranged in parallel, coated with glue and then glued together in three layers with phenol formaldehyde adhesives. The longitudinal or horizontal arrangement of the individual layers of strands allows greater strength and higher permissible structural stresses than with conventional particle-board. OSB also retains its shape very well. It has a rather low glue content (2–3%) and the formaldehyde emission levels are correspondingly low. Thus it can be used indoors in moderate quantities. It is particularly suitable for use on wood construction as external sheathing which bears part of the load, or for sub-flooring. Another useful wood fiber material is fiberboards which can be

further divided into low density and medium density fiberboard (MDF). The former is widely used as an insulated sheathing material while MDF is typically used for casework and furniture. Fiberboards are dried for several days at 120–190° C after processing and finally formed into boards by high-pressure rollers with the addition of similar adhesives to those used in particle-board. In recent years non-hazardous lignin has been used increasingly as a bonding agent for fiberboard. Lignin is largely a byproduct of cellulose production. Industrial wood fiber byproducts such as sawdust are often used to make fiberboard along with pulpwood, paper and sawmill wastes.

An alternative to particle board and fiberboard is a wheat-straw particle board made by Naturall Fibre Boards of Minneapolis, Kansas. Their 4 x 8 (1200 mm × 2400 mm) panels come in 1/8 inch (3 mm), ¼ inch (6 mm), and ½ inch (13 mm) thicknesses and with various surface veneers. The product which uses Norwegian manufacturing technology, consists of wheat straw chopped and bound with an MDI (non-formaldehyde) resin. It is lighter than conventional particle board and has greater tensile strength. It is reported to be priced comparably to particle board in the mid United States. Similar products made of flax straw are being manufactured in Canada. Availability of these alternatives to wood particle board may be somewhat limited presently but it is expected that more will start appearing in other areas.

- Plywood: thermal conductivity λ 0.80 (Btu/hr./ft.²/°F/in.) – density 34 lb./ft.³ – embodied energy 11,300 Btu/lb.
- Hard fiberboard: thermal conductivity λ 0.31 (Btu/hr./ft.²/°F/in.) – density 19 lb./ft.³ – embodied energy 7,200 Btu/lb.
- Soft fiberboard: thermal conductivity λ 0.31 (Btu/hr./ft.²/°F/in.) – density 19 lb./ft.³ – embodied energy 7,200 Btu/lb.

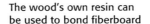

The wood's own resin can be used to bond fiberboard

Ideal for walls
Soft fiberboard is particularly suitable for the thermal and sound insulation of walls (photographs top and right). The boards can simply be pressed onto the existing wall using mortar as the bonding agent.

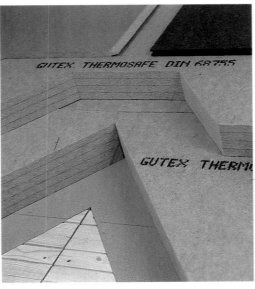

Between the rafters
When boards are fitted between rafters, gaps can be hard to avoid (see left picture).

Soft fiber for insulation
Soft fiber insulating board is favored for use in the roof structure (far left). It provides good phase shifting so that the loft area does not become unpleasantly hot.

INSULATING MATERIALS

Synthetic insulating materials raise a lot of issues

Choosing the insulation for your building is one of the most important decisions to be made relative to the environmental impact of the building because insulation reduces energy consumption. The most efficient insulating materials are those made of synthetic substances but their manufacture involves an environmentally damaging chain of processes generally requiring a great deal of energy. Various mineral insulating materials typically create potential health hazards and can also consume a great deal of energy when produced. There are, however, many alternatives available today and in most cases it is quite possible to avoid using materials that are environmentally damaging or which create health hazards either in their manufacture or their installation.

Synthetic insulating materials

The most common synthetic insulating material is polystyrene foam. This form of expanded polystyrene is produced from ethylene, a natural gas component, and benzene, which is derived from petroleum.

Foam for expedience

Do-it-yourself polyurethane in aerosol cans for on-site foaming is very handy and easy to use, making it highly popular for sealing windows and doors, However, its manufacture is environmentally unfriendly and it poses significant health risks.

Foam for warmth

Expanded polystyrene insulating panels are particularly effective for the insulation of walls. However, this material is also ecologically undesirable.

Foam for durability

Extruded polystyrene insulating panels are watertight and thus particularly suitable for use in foundations and parts in contact with the ground. Here too, though, environmentally friendlier alternatives exist.

Expanded polystyrene foam uses pentane as a blowing agent and is open-celled in structure, while extruded polystyrene foam is forced through a nozzle or dye by a propellant gas and has a closed-cell, vapor-resistant structure with higher compressive strength, making it suitable for use in humid environments or where exposed to moisture. In the past ozone-damaging CFCs were used as the propellant for extruded polystyrene, but production in Europe and in North America has now almost completely switched to partially halogenated HCFCs. HCFC-141b is slated for phase-out by December 31, 2002, and HCFC-142b by 2020. While HCFCs are only 5% to 11% as damaging to ozone as CFCs because they do not last as long in the atmosphere, they are almost as damaging while they are, and HCFCs are significant greenhouse gases and contribute to global warming.

Styrene, a powerful nerve toxin which is also suspected of being carcinogenic and causing genetic damage, can be released both during and after manufacture and when the product is exposed to heat. Because of this, polystyrene should be held for two months after manufacture and before it is used. During production and throughout its lifetime it can emit pentane, which contributes to smog and global warming.

In addition, polystyrene foams are usually treated with brominated fire retardants which release toxic gases when exposed to flames. Expanded polystyrene is typically used in composite wall systems such as structural insulated panels (SIPs), or in multi-wythe masonry walls where it is used between the interior and exterior wythes. It is also often used as underslab insulation, and polystyrene beads are often used as a lightweight additive for heat insulating plasters or as masonry fill insulation in concrete block.

Polyurethane board as well as polyurethane resin sold in containers for on-site foaming, are produced by adding catalysts and propellant gas to isocyanates. A hard, closed-cell foaming material is produced which has similar applications to extruded polystyrene, but is also suitable for the insulation of pitched roofs. The unmixed polyurethane resin for on-site foaming is a two-component product which is sprayed under pressure into cavities, where it expands and then hardens. It can also be used for sealing around window and door frames and for filling crevices and joints. Significant quantities of isocyanate are released when foaming materials are used on-site, and if exposed to fire, the highly toxic prussic acid is produced. As with Polystyrene, Polyurethane is treated with fire retardants, and these too produce toxic gases in a fire. To manufacture isocyanate, a precursor of polyisocyanurate and polyurethane insulation, two chlorine-based chemical intermediates are used: phosgene and propylene chlorohydrin. Citing pollution problems, a number of environmental groups, including

The birthplace of all synthetics – an oil refinery

Greenpeace, are calling for the phase-out of most industrial uses of chlorine.

A less harmful product has recently been introduced in Europe consisting of insulating blankets made of pure polyester fibers of the type used in clothing. Fire retardants and pesticides are not necessary for this product since polyester is not flammable and quite impervious to insects. In addition, polyester fiber blankets are safe to work with, and as it is made from a single resin product it can easily be recycled and it can also be made from recycled materials. Furthermore, it has particularly good insulating properties. However, it cannot absorb moisture and is produced from petrochemicals, thus requiring higher levels of manufacturing energy than insulating blankets made of natural fiber.

Note: The value λ thermal conductivity is given in Btu/hr/ft.²/°F/in. – i.e., Btu per hour per square foot per degree Fahrenheit per inch. The metric equivalent of Watts per meter per degree Kelvin can be obtained by multiplying the value given by the value 0.144228.

- Expanded polystyrene: thermal conductivity λ 0.28 (Btu/hr/ft.²/°F/in.) – R-value 3.61/in. – density 1.2 lb./ft.³ – embodied energy 35,000 Btu/lb. or 43,000 Btu/ft.³
- Extruded polystyrene: thermal conductivity λ 0.19 (Btu/hr/ft.²/°F/in.) – R-value 5.15/in. – density 1.9 lb./ft.³ – embodied energy 44,000 Btu/lb. or 82,100 Btu/ft.³
- Polyurethane board: thermal conductivity λ 0.17 (Btu/hr/ft.²/°F/in.) – R-value 5.8/in. – density 2.5 lb./ft.³ – embodied energy 290,000 Btu/lb. or 116,000 Btu/ft.³
- Polyurethane foam (field applied): thermal conductivity λ 0.16 (Btu/hr/ft.²/°F/in.) – R-value 6.27/in. – density 1.9 lb./ft.³ – embodied energy 52,000 Btu/lb. or 97,000 Btu/ft.³

Super-insulating made easy
The most efficient insulating panels are made from polyurethane. They provide almost twice as much insulating value per inch as other insulating materials. Nevertheless, the material remains ecologically questionable.

Synthetic fiber for allergy sufferers
Recently polyester insulating batts have come on to the market. This material has many desirable properties, one of which is that it does not cause allergies, On the downside, it is derived 100% from petrochemicals.

Mineral fibers

Mineral fiber insulating materials are the most widely used insulating products with a wide range of applications including roof insulation, cavity wall insulation and a variety of composite systems. Worldwide sales of these products amount to around $170 billion. Mineral fiber insulating materials are produced by melting the mineral-based substances at about 1,500 °C and then centrifuging, blowing or extruding them. Recycled glass or glass raw materials such as quartzite are used for the manufacture of glass wool, and greenstone for the manufacture of rock wool. The fibers are bonded with up to 10% phenolic formaldehyde resin which subsequently hardens to form bakelite. Recent research has revealed that they have a minimal content of soluble formaldehyde, and during a fire toxic phenols can be released. Mineral fibers have good insulating properties and are non-combustible. Unfortunately, they typically contain hazardous fibers which can be inhaled and carried into the lungs. It is those

and also some governments have decided to treat fiberglass glass and rock wool as carcinogenic substances similar to asbestos fibers. In Germany, for example, government contracts will only be awarded to projects which do not use fiberglass glass or rock-wool. In addition, renovation work is strongly recommended for all buildings in which mineral fibers are not completely separated from living areas. On the other hand, if rock wool or fiberglass batts are laid correctly behind a moisture barrier they do not pose a hazard to health except during alterations or rebuilding. A series of recent technical articles about the carcinogenicity of glass fibers has been damaging to the image of the fiberglass industry, as has the requirement for cancer warning labels in the United States.

As a result, insulating material manufacturers have been forced to develop new products. The most significant new fiberglass product to address the health concern about glass fibers is Owens Corning's

Fiberglass — controversial market-share leader

Stone or glass

Either gray basalt (stone wool) or yellow-colored silicate and recycled glass (glass wool) provide the base material for mineral wool insulating material (far left). Stone and glass wool are virtually identical as far as their technical properties are concerned, but stone wool fibers are particularly long-lasting and thus raise more of a health concern.

Mineral fiber for efficient cavity insulation

Mineral fiber can also be used for cavity insulation of double-shell structures. Its resistance to the elements means that this kind of insulation will retain its insulating properties until the building is demolished. However, the fibers can then pose a problem.

fibers greater than 5 micrometers in length and less than 3 micrometers in diameter which are of greatest concern. Larger diameter fibers will typically not enter the lungs. When laying mineral fiber batts, levels of up to 200,000 fibers per cubic meter of air can be reached.

The health hazard posed by rock wool and fiberglass insulation has been the subject of heated debate among experts for many years. Animal experiments showed these materials to be clearly carcinogenic. Although no proven cases of human cancer caused by mineral fibers have been recorded, many experts

Miraflex™ fiber which has fibers that are much stronger and less brittle and thereby reducing the health risk. Also, this type of fiberglass contains no chemical binders or dyes, whatsoever, so there should be no offgassing. In order to assess these products without the need for painstaking animal experiments, new methods of evaluation have been developed which define the health hazard posed by a mineral fiber in terms of the length of time it persists in the human body: The more rapidly it breaks down in the lungs, the lower the risk it poses. The level of biodegradability is determined by the fiber's content of certain minerals, from which the so-called "carcinogenicity index" (CI) can be calculated. A CI figure of at least 40 is advisable, with fibers exceeding this figure classified as non-carcinogenic.

However, research has revealed that some mineral fibers with very low CI figures break down rapidly in the lungs, and as a result the CI formula is the subject of controversy. Research also indicates that some of the new fiberglass insulating materials actually do break down in the body far more quickly than the older products. While a conventional glass fiber has a half-life in the lung of 150–200 days, for these new products the figure is less than 20 days. Figures for newer rock wool, which poses particularly serious problems due to its aluminum content, have been reduced to between 20 and 60 days, as opposed to 300 for the previous products.

In 1997 the German Hazardous Materials Committee ruled that a specific animal experiment should be required in addition to the CI formula as definite proof of a material's safety. This involves a so-called intratracheal test whereby fibers in suspension are injected into rats' lungs. If the half-life of the fibers is 40 days or less in the animals' lungs then they are classified as non-carcinogenic. However, according to current knowledge this figure can only be achieved by CI 40 fibers. Some European countries have switched virtually all their production to new biodegradable or CI 40 products, which are labeled as such. But in many other European countries absolutely nothing is being done. The British health authorities, on the other hand, have declared that they do not regard mineral fibers as posing any risk of cancer.

At the end of 1997 the European Union Harmonization Committee ruled against the German CI 40 regulation. Their ruling was that materials can only be freed from suspicion of being carcinogenic by animal experimentation. To this end a short-term inhalation experiment was authorized, but some experts believe it is not strict enough. According to leading figures on Germany's Hazardous Materials Committee, even asbestos could pass this test, which means, in effect, that this now binding instrument for all member states of the European Union is quite inadequate to protect against the health hazards involved. It even gives the all-clear to mineral fiber insulating materials that have previously been recognized as hazardous. However, a significant detraction regarding mineral fiber insulating is their inability to absorb moisture; when they become wet their insulating properties are markedly reduced. The phenolic formaldehyde binder used in most of these products also presents a health risk. Furthermore, their recycling potential is limited. They are sometimes made with an aluminum foil backing which completely blocks moisture diffusion.

Fiberglass cladding
Rigid fiberglass insulation sheets are particularly suitable for insulating the external walls of larger buildings, because the material is not flammable.

Not recommended
Reasonably priced insulating batts and insulating wedges are available for the highly popular insulation. However, you should not work with these products without any protection against the carcinogenic fibers. Anyone installing them should at least wear a face mask.

An efficient system
Wall cavity insulation is especially well protected from the elements and is considered a particularly efficient system.

- Fiberglass: thermal conductivity λ 0.28 (Btu/hr./ft.²/°F/in.) — R-value 3.52/in. — density 1.6 lb./ft.³ — embodied energy 15,000 Btu/lb. or 24,000 Btu/ft.³
- Rock wool: thermal conductivity λ 0.29 — R-value 3.43/in. — density 2.5 lb./ft.³ — embodied energy 6,000 Btu/lb. or 14,000 Btu/ft.³

ecological concern, and, in addition, hazardous dust may be produced when working them. Wearing a respirator mask is, therefore, highly recommended to prevent any damage to the applicator's health.

Expanded clay is produced through a series of processes taking place in rotary kilns at a temperature of 2,192° C, which involves swelling the clay and then firing and fusing the clay beads. This makes expanded clay extremely water-resistant and gives it a high degree of compressive strength.

Another mineral insulating material, expanded clay, has a similar range of applications to vermiculite and perlite, presents minimal environmental concern, and poses no known health hazard. However, it has significantly poorer heat insulating properties, and correspondingly better thermal storage capacity. The practice of adding heavy oil can lead to the escape of pollutants during the manufacturing process. There is also no indication that expanded clay possesses any increased radioactivity.

Cellular glass is produced from recycled glass or from glass raw materials such as quartz sand or feldspar. Carbon is then added to the molten glass at a temperature of about 1,800° F, and the resulting CO_2 produced causes the glass to expand while simultaneously producing hydrogen sulfide. Cellular glass is a watertight, closed-cell, moisture-resistant and fire-retardant insulating material with high compressive strength and good insulating properties. It is particularly suitable for external insulation in contact with the soil (perimeter insulation) or for insulating flat or cultivated (green) roofs. It is also available for wall or pitched roof insulation but is not recommended for use in such applications due to its resistance to vapor diffusion. Cutting it can result in quite unpleasant odors due to the hydrogen sulfide content, but the material is otherwise harmless.

Other mineral insulating materials

Perlite and vermiculite insulating materials are produced by heating the base material (volcanic perlite rock or mica schist) to around 1,800° F. This causes the chemically bonded water to escape rapidly, and the material then expands to about 15 times its original volume. These granulates are used mainly as loose-fill insulation for floors, cavity insulation in concrete masonry and as a lightweight aggregate for mortar, plaster, concrete or building blocks. They are environmentally benign, and the suspicion that expanded Perlite might in some cases contain radioactive properties has not been confirmed. These materials are non-combustible and chemically inert. However, they are sometimes treated with bitumen or silicone to make them water-repellent, which is of

Red earth – not just for the flowerpot

Expanded clay resembles the materials used for hydroponics. It is produced from swollen clay minerals and is used as an aggregate for lightweight building blocks as well as a loose-fill insulating material.

Rarely used but ecologically desirable: expanded clay and cellular glass

Lightweight stone

Perlite is produced by grinding up a certain volcanic rock and heating it so that the water it contains causes the granules to swell up. It is a popular loose-fill insulating material. Cellular glass (right of picture) is produced by adding carbon to glass. It is a particularly water-resistant insulating material.

Apart from its high primary energy content, the chief ecological disadvantage of cellular glass is that it is generally used in conjunction with bitumen. Bitumen is a waste product from the refining of crude oil and is considered to be a probable carcinogen. Its constituents vary to a great extent, with the main concern being the polycyclic aromatic hydrocarbons, which may be released during the hot application of bitumen. The proportion of polycyclic aromatic hydrocarbons can vary by a factor of 10, and according to manufacturers' figures pure, carefully extracted bitumen is entirely free of pollutants. However, it should certainly be avoided for use indoors, and when working with it outdoors health and safety (OSHA) regulations should be strictly observed and precautions taken to avoid inhalation and contact with the skin. In any case, the use of cellular glass indoors is not common.

Note: The value λ thermal conductivity is given in Btu/hr/ft.^{2}/°F/in. — i.e., Btu per hour per square foot per degree Fahrenheit per inch. The metric equivalent of Watts per meter per degree Kelvin can be obtained by multiplying the value given by the value 0.144228.

- Perlite: thermal conductivity λ 0.35 — R-value 2.88/in. — density 6 lb./ft.^{3} — embodied energy 4,000 Btu/lb. or 22,000 Btu/ft.^{3}
- Expanded clay: thermal conductivity λ 0.69 — R-value 1.44/in. — density 18.7 lb./ft.^{3} — embodied energy 2,000 Btu/lb. or 29,000 Btu/ft.^{3}
- Cellular glass: thermal conductivity λ 0.35 — R-value 2.88/in. — density 8 lb./ft.^{3} — embodied energy 18,000 Btu/lb. or 155,000 Btu/ft.^{3}

Expanded clay for leveling floors

Expanded clay beads can be used to level uneven floors in old buildings, while at the same time providing added insulation. This loose-fill material can bear loads, and is also used in new wooden houses to provide some added mass to floors.

Cellular glass for the roof

Cellular glass insulating slabs can simultaneously seal and insulate flat roofs, and the robust panels are strong enough to walk on.

Perlite for cavity wall insulation

Perlite makes a good loose-fill insulating material for wall cavities. It is capable of bearing loads, and is thus also suitable for floors.

Laying cellular glass

Bitumen is used to bond and seal cellular glass slabs. However, bitumen can pose a health hazard under certain circumstances and should, therefore, only be worked with outdoors.

Cellulose insulating materials

Made from recycled newspapers

Only old newspapers, not glossy magazines, can be used to make cellulose insulating material. It comes both in loose-fill and spray-on forms or as panels for the do-it-yourself enthusiast. The cellulose is mixed with various additives to protect against mold and act as fire retardants.

Recycled paper is an excellent insulating material

Cellulose is the leading organic insulating material. In the US as well as Scandinavia it has reached a market share of 25–30%. Cellulose is probably the best example of recycled material used as an insulation material. Most cellulose insulation is approximately 80% post-consumer recycled newspaper by weight — the remaining 20% consists of fire retardant chemicals or in some cases, acrylic binders. The use of lower-density cellulose is increasing where the material is produced by breaking down the individual fibers — a process called "fiberizing" which makes them fluffier. Many manufacturers are switching to this process from the hammermill process because it results in an improved product which creates less dust,

has a slightly higher R-value and is more resource efficient.

Cellulose insulation is usually either blown into attics or existing wall cavities (loose-fill) or sprayed into wall or roof cavities to form a dense, fibrous blanket completely filling the void and providing the required level of insulation. Once sprayed in place it can easily be trimmed flush with the wall surface. It can also be injected into vertical panels, though in this case the same density cannot be reached. Because its insulating properties depend on the application being carried out correctly, installation of cellulose insulation should only be done by licensed insulation contractors. Loose-fill cellulose, on the other hand, can be applied by do-it-yourself

A view behind the scenes

For the sake of this picture, a normally invisible process is exposed by the use of a glass panel. If the cellulose is sprayed in correctly there should be no gaps or cavities left, and the fibrous material is so elastic that it follows the vibrations of the rafters.

Directly onto the wall

Slightly dampened cellulose can be sprayed directly on the wall, but this method does not allow such thicknesses of insulating material to be achieved. The procedure is most suited to partition walls. Effective respiratory equipment should be worn while doing this.

homeowners, and the equipment can usually be borrowed or rented from the retailer.

Cellulose insulation has excellent vapor diffusion properties, is very good at completely filling cavities, has very good thermal insulation and absorption properties but low compressive strength. It shows very favorable behavior in fire. On top of this, it is the least costly of the non-synthetic insulating materials. However, large amounts of dust are produced when working with it, so applicators should wear respirator masks. During application, levels of up to 8 million fibers/cubic meter of air have been measured. These fibers are less biodegradable than some of the new fiberglass materials but research carried out to date has not revealed any evidence that organic fibers have any carcinogenic effect. In any case, once the cellulose has been installed behind an airtight seal it can no longer pose a health risk. The printers' ink in recycled newsprint, which at one time contained lead, no longer presents a health risk since lead has been replaced by other materials. The only possible exception is cellulose products from eastern Europe which may contain high levels of heavy metals.

Borates are added to the cellulose material by a variety of processes, for example, by damp spraying or by swing-hammer pulverizers. Because they do not readily bind they have to form a relatively high proportion of the overall mass – between 18% and 25%. If a wood frame house is insulated with cellulose, as much as a ton of borates may be included in the insulation content. Although boric salts are not considered a health risk and have a minor impact on the environment, in these quantities they make composting of the material unfeasible. Because of this some manufacturers are experimenting with alternative additives as fire retardants. Theoretically, phosphates should be particularly suited to this purpose.

For a number of years cellulose has also been available in the form of an insulation or sheathing board. In the United States the most widely used example of this is "Homosote™." These boards can be applied in wall cavities or to the interior or exterior side of the wall framing as a continuous insulating layer. They are simple to install and produce far less dust, are economical and ideal for indoor construction. On the downside, they are relatively difficult to cut and can be easily damaged. As with other insulation materials it is advisable to wear respirator masks when working with them.

- Cellulose – loose-fill: thermal conductivity λ 0.29 – embodied energy 2,200 Btu/lb. or 5,000 Btu/ft.³
- Cellulose – sprayed on: thermal conductivity λ 0.27 – embodied energy 1,300 Btu/lb. or 5,000 Btu/ft.³

Seamless cavity insulation

Cellulose is ideal for filling cavities in walls, floors or roofs. The material is sprayed in under pressure and forms a seamless cushion. The work should always be carried out by a reputable insulation contractor.

A simple procedure

After spraying on the cellulose it is smoothed out and wall board can then be applied. This procedure can be done very quickly, but the health consequences of the large numbers of fibers released into the air is as yet unknown and care should always be taken.

For the floor too

The simplest application of cellulose is as loose-fill floor insulation. It is really important to get the density of the cellulose just right, so this should only be done by an insulation contractor, which will also take full responsibility for the safety of their workers.

Other wood-based insulating materials

Wood fiberboard has been discussed previously. It should preferably be bonded using only the resin contained in the wood itself, but a certain proportion of low-formaldehyde white glue (casein) can be tolerated, as tests have not revealed high formaldehyde levels in any of the insulating boards investigated. Fiberboard panels are suitable for indoor construction work, and in particular for thermal and acoustic insulation of floors, and can also be used for the above-rafter insulation that is so popular in Alpine regions. Their ecological drawback is their relatively high primary energy content.

In Europe a new insulation system has recently been developed using wood fiberboard panels, which are also used as part of a composite heat insulation

requires little energy to manufacture and contains ecologically harmless preservatives which pose no known health hazard. However, its installation is not easy and it is chiefly suitable for prefabricated structural components. Even more recently, sprayed-on planing chip insulating material has come onto the European market.

Flax and hemp insulating materials

An alternative which can be thoroughly recommended for between-rafter insulation and lightweight structures is insulating batts made of flax fiber. These insulating batts are made from fibers that are too coarse for linen textiles and have thus previously been considered as waste. Small amounts of borates

Wood in abundance

In Germany only a small proportion of trees are used for commercial purposes. Most wood simply rots on the forest floor. Thinner branches and trunks left behind when trees are felled would be ideal for wood fiberboard.

system. This system involves bonding three boards of different thicknesses plus an integral plaster or other surface finish.

A more traditional alternative is lightweight wood wool paneling, which has also been discussed earlier. This material consists of wood wool and planing chips made from cutting waste bonded with magnesium carbonate (magnesite) or portland cement. Because of its relatively limited heat insulating properties it is arguable whether it really can be regarded as an insulating material at all, but in any case it is used in a variety of composite systems along with other insulating materials for indoor construction and external wall paneling.

A recent novelty in Europe is an insulating material completely made of planing chips bonded only with an environmentally friendly mixture of whey and soda. Roofs or walls are filled with the material and it is then packed down by using a special automatic climbing vibrator. This insulating material

(4%) and soluble glass are also added. Flax has been cultivated for hundreds of years. It is easy to grow, requiring neither fertilization nor insecticides, and it can be cultivated on marginal land. The European Union is currently trying to promote its cultivation. The insulating batts it produces have very good insulating properties, are easy to work with and require little primary energy. However, some flax products include polyester as a reinforcing fiber, making later recycling a problem.

Thus far, hemp insulating material has not been authorized for use in most countries and is used on a purely experimental basis. In the past hemp was an indigenous crop, but its cultivation was banned in a high number of countries because of its use as an illegal drug. Recently its cultivation has been allowed in certain areas, though the raw material has hitherto chiefly come from Mexico and France. Like flax, hemp is extremely easy to cultivate, requiring neither fertilization nor pesticides,

Flax: plant of the future

Flax is enjoying a renaissance. It requires no fertilization and no tending, making it ideal for extensive organic farming methods. The long, soft fibers can be used to make textiles, while the shorter fibers make an excellent insulating material.

A replacement for synthetic foam

Flax rope was traditionally used to plug gaps, for example between windows and walls. Today it is used as a substitute for polyurethane foam.

and it even does very well in poor soil. It is fast-growing and the woody parts as well as the fibers can be used. Like flax, the fibers can be worked into insulating batts, and the woody parts can be ground and used as loose-fill insulation or as an aggregate for insulating plaster or lightweight mortar. Since the substance has natural fungicidal and antibacterial properties there is generally no need for it to be impregnated with anything other than a fire retardant.

Note to box below: The value λ thermal conductivity is given in Btu/hr/ft.²/°F/in. – i.e., Btu per hour per square foot per degree Fahrenheit per inch.

Wood and flax

In Europe wood and flax fibers offer the best renewable sources of insulating material. Softwood fiberboard, woven flax insulation batts and rope have already undergone successful trials.

- Wood fiberboard panels: thermal conductivity λ 0.35 — R-value 2.9/in. — density 19 lb./ft.³ — embodied energy 7,200 Btu/lb. or 135,000 Btu/ft.³
- Lightweight wood wool panels: thermal conductivity λ 0.35 — R-value 2.9/in. — density 31 lb./ft.³ — embodied energy 3,700 Btu/lb. or 116,000 Btu/ft.³
- Flax fiber panels: thermal conductivity λ 0.28 — R-value 3.61/in. — density 1.6 lb./ft.³ — embodied energy 1,900 Btu/lb. or 3,000 Btu/ft.³

Other insulating products made from indigenous renewable raw materials

Wool: kind to the skin
Lambswool is an excellent insulating material and kind to the skin. However, the wool must be treated for moths, and this can only be done using chemicals which threaten human health.

Indigenous organic insulating materials

Other organic insulating materials can only be given a qualified recommendation. For example, reed or lambswool, though in theory entirely indigenous to most parts of North America and Europe, are in fact typically imported from remote locations. Therefore, the long-distance transport adds to the total embodied energy of these materials, making them questionable from an environmental point of view. In addition, significant quantities of indigenous reeds grow in wetland areas which are mostly in protected conservation areas and thus cannot be used.

Reed has a long tradition as a building material. For instance, thin reed mats were used in the past as a plaster lath in wood joist floors. The thicker versions available today are suitable for lightweight insulating panels, can readily be plastered with lime plaster or loam and are mostly used for external wall insulation. Reed is naturally moisture-resistant and is also a natural fire retardant due to its high silicic acid content, and thus does not need to be treated

chemically. The reed straws are laid parallel to each other and are then mechanically pressed and fastened with galvanized iron wire to form solid but flexible boards between 2 and 10 cm thick. Some experts believe that the wire used can act as an aerial, strengthening electromagnetic radiation. Furthermore, it does not have particularly good insulation properties.

Lambswool insulating materials have rapidly gained a significant market share in countries, such as Germany, since their introduction in 1992. They have a very positive image with consumers and this has led even mainstream companies to become involved in their production. The raw material is mostly imported from New Zealand and Australia. However, in those countries sheep-dipping is still standard practice, while the long-distance transport, though not making prices prohibitive, is a further negative factor from an ecological point of view. For these reasons, a number of European manufacturers have turned to wool produced in Austria or Britain more recently.

Reed is in short supply
Natural supplies of reed are scarce and are often found in nature conservation areas. An increase in demand in the construction sector could make the cultivation of Chinese reed feasible.

Lambswool has excellent insulating properties, is gentle on the skin and is a natural fire retardant. It is also the most breathable natural fiber and can absorb up to 40% of its total weight in moisture, storing it within the fibers and releasing it by evaporation. However, it must be protected against moth attack, generally by the use of the halogen-organic compounds contained in the standard moth retardants. Although these compounds are relatively harmless to people, as products of chlorine chemistry they are eschewed as an environmental alternative. Toxic pyrethroids may also be used, though this hasn't yet been conclusively proved. A frequently used method is impregnation with boron salts, but this is only effective against moths in the long term if they are fixated in the fibers by a process such as latexing, which detracts from the product's insulating properties. Because wool is very pliable and thus difficult to install, polyester reinforcing fiber is added to increase its rigidity, and the synthetic fiber content of the final product may be as high as 20%, making later recycling problematic. When using lower-grade recycled lambswool, high airborne dust or fiber levels can result.

Many of the substances used to protect wool against moth attack are ecologically questionable

- Lambswool blankets or batts: thermal conductivity λ 0.28 — R-value 3.61/in. — density 1.6 lb./ft.³ — embodied energy 5,000 Btu/ft.³ or 3,400 Btu/lb.

External wall insulation using reed
Reed matting is very resistant to rotting and provides an excellent substrate for plaster, making it ideal for insulating masonry external walls.

Loam construction with reed
Reed matting is used traditionally in loam construction. This wood structure is infilled using loam brick and then insulated with reed inside and out.

Undemanding producers
Sheep require little tending and their habits contribute to the conservation of the countryside. However, most wool for insulation purposes is imported from countries where it is produced under ecologically questionable practices.

Pleasant to handle
Wool batts are pleasant to handle but not necessarily easy to work with, because without reinforcing fiber it is too soft and floppy. The reinforcing fiber is normally synthetic and can constitute as much as 20% of the product.

Insulating materials made from imported renewable raw materials

Cork insulation

The bark of the cork oak has by now a long tradition as an ecologically friendly insulating material. It is available either in the form of granules or pressed into boards using its own resin as a bonding agent.

Protective board

Expanded cork board has good insulating properties and is popular in some areas for external wall and floor insulation. This normally involves installing several layers of board in order to achieve the desired insulation value.

When seeking alternatives to polystyrene or mineral fibers, renewable raw materials produced in distant countries should generally not be at the top of the list. The reasons for that and the individual properties of a selected number of important renewable raw materials, such as cork, coconut fibers and cotton, are discussed in this chapter.

Compared with cellulose and lambswool, a traditional natural insulating material, cork, has lost popularity in recent times. The raw material, which is the bark of the cork oak, is found in greatest abundance in Portugal, Spain and North Africa, where subsequent processing also generally takes place, and not always under ideal conditions from an environmental or technical point of view. Additionally, the long transport distance adds to the total embodied energy. Small quantities of cork insulating material are produced in Germany from recycled bottle corks, leading to an end product which initially strongly reeks of wine. In general, supplies of cork are very limited, though planting cork oak forests in arid areas could remedy this situation in the long term.

Granulated cork can also be used for cavity insulation of double-shell brickwork and as loose-fill insulation for ceilings and floors, and as a lightweight additive for loam products, etc. However, it is not ideal for internal wall or pitched roof insulation because when the material settles major thermal bridges are formed, and when alterations or repairs are carried out it will trickle out like sand.

Cork has good compressive strength and retains its shape very well, and even better insulation is achieved by the use of baked/agglomerated cork produced by steam-heating cork granulate to a temperature of around 380° C, without any additives but using the cork's own resin content as the bonding agent. If higher temperatures are reached, for example, in order to dissolve the lower resin content of low-grade cork, carcinogenic benzoapyrene can be produced. The boards can be used for indoor construction work or for façade insulation. They provide extremely good sound insulation, but are rather difficult to plaster.

Coconut fiber blankets or batts are traditionally used chiefly for sound insulation, and rather less frequently for thermal insulation. More recently, however, coconut matting has been developed specially for use in pitched roofs. Although coconut fibers are a byproduct of the Far Eastern coconut harvest, they do have to be pre-processed and transported over a long distance. They are flexible, extremely tough, rot-resistant, have antibacterial properties, and can be made water-resistant by the addition of soluble glass or latex. In addition, environmentally friendly ammonium sulfate can be used as a fire retardant. The thermal conductivity of coconut fiber, however, is mediocre at best. Coconut fiber is available only in limited quantities, and its use should preferably be limited to the Far Eastern countries where the coconut is cultivated.

Cotton is available both for insulating matting and as a spray-in material like cellulose. It has similar

very limited number of producers supplying high-end cotton for the textile industry. Environmentally damaging materials are used when processing cotton, particularly when washing and bleaching it. Dust and fibers are also given off, though not to the same extent as in the processing of cellulose.

- Cork board: thermal conductivity λ 0.31 — R-value 3.21/in. — density 7 lb./ft.³ — embodied energy 43,000 Btu/ft.³ or 6,300 Btu/lb.

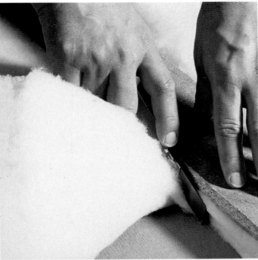

properties to lambswool, but does not have to be protected from moth attack, and small quantities of borates suffice as fire retardants. Arguments against its use are the highly environmentally unfriendly production methods used during its cultivation, and also the fairly long transport distances involved. On the other hand, cotton typically does not contain any residual traces of the sprays which are used liberally during cultivation, and therefore it does not pose a health risk to users of the final product.

Furthermore, there is currently a significant surplus of cotton on the world market, and its use as an insulating material would be able to convert this surplus into long-lasting products. Pesticide-free cultivation is possible, but is practiced only by a

Cotton cladding for warmth

Cotton is almost always grown and harvested under ecologically questionable conditions, damaging the image of cotton insulating materials. However, they do have good insulating properties and are easy to work with. And after all, everyone has a few cotton T-shirts in a drawer somewhere, without worrying about their origins.

Easy to work with

Cork insulating board is very easy to saw to the desired shape (far left). However, plaster does not adhere to it very well, so one either has to apply an additional plaster base coat to the insulating layer or use an expensive specially formulated plaster with resin additives.

Very resistant

The bark of the coconut is regarded as a waste product in the countries where it is cultivated. However, the fiber obtained from it is very strong and resistant to the elements. Its main use is as floor insulation against impact noise or, as in this case, as cavity insulation.

ROOFING

Concrete roofing tiles

A wide range of concrete roofing tiles are available today. They are less expensive than clay roofing tiles and also very durable, but not necessarily an ideal choice from an ecological point of view.

Clay roofing tiles have been in use for thousands of years

Most roofing materials have a long tradition. While in many European regions as well as the American Southwest, houses with clay tile roofs predominate, and the traditional color of the tiles is red, there are also areas where slate has been the roofing of choice. Wood shakes used to be prevalent in many wooded and mountain regions, while thatched roofs were common primarily on the North Sea and Baltic coasts, and flat roofs in hot Mediterranean regions. Today a colorful variety of roof types is generally found wherever building regulations permit.

Clay and concrete roofing tiles

Clay roofing tiles have been in use for over 4,000 years. Their great strength is that they can rapidly absorb moisture and just as rapidly they can give it off again. One result of this is that it is difficult for moss to become established on this type of roof. We commonly distinguish, according to the method of manufacture, between pressed roofing tiles, such as interlocking tiles, convex and concave tiles on the one hand, and extruded roofing tiles such as single-lap tiles or hollow pantiles on the other. Another advantage of a tiled roof is in the ability of individually laid tiles to move, enabling them to absorb movements of the roof structure as well as expansion and contraction of the roof itself, thus preventing stresses from building up. Traditional roofing tiles are widely available in an enormous range of shapes, sizes and colors. The classic single-lap tile alone is available in more than ten different shapes. As a rule the tiles consist of a mixture of clay and loess clay which is fired at around 1652° F (900° C). Depending on the particular type of clay used, roofing tiles can have very different appearances even before the addition of any coloring agent. Pure clay tiles are fired at a higher temperature of around 2192° F (1,200° C). They are particularly light and are often used on registered historic buildings.

The range of colors is increased by the use of slip or treated clay slurry which is applied to the tile

before firing. This produces brown to black coloration or patterns. Other colors can be produced by the use of glazes. However, since glaze must be applied to the tile after firing, and the tile then fired again at a high temperature, this greatly increases the amount of energy involved in producing the tile. A result of this is that glazed tiles cost nearly three times as much as unglazed ones. Even without this additional glazing process, firing tiles requires a good deal of energy, and this is their one drawback from an ecological point of view. Disposing of roofing tiles, on the other hand, does not pose any problem.

Concrete roofing tiles consist of sand, cement and iron-oxide based colored pigments. Visually they can barely be distinguished from clay roofing tiles, but they are generally larger, with only about a hundred being required to cover one standard roofing square or about 100 square feet of roof. In many areas they have even grown more popular than clay tiles. The main reason for this is that, at a significantly lower price, they provide excellent

long-term quality, frost protection and increased resistance to breakage. Concrete roofing tiles also require less energy to manufacture than clay tiles, drying in eight hours at a temperature of just 140° F (60° C) and then hardening over a period of four weeks without the need for any further energy. Its content of cement (less desirable from an environmental standpoint for reasons explained earlier) is limited to 20%.

Clay roofing tiles

The range of different shapes and colors of traditional clay roofing tiles is unsurpassed. The light natural nuances of color alone, a result of variations in the constituents of the earthen raw materials, make for a warm and natural roofing material.

- Clay roofing tiles: density 112 lb./ft.^{3} — embodied energy 1,200 Btu/lb. or 135,000 Btu/ft.^{3}
- Concrete roofing tiles: density 144 lb./ft.^{3} — embodied energy 300 Btu/lb. or 48,000 Btu/ft.^{3}

A natural slate façade

In some regions the use of slate as a roofing material has a long tradition and, as in the case of this historic building in Germany, it is sometimes also used for exterior siding.

Unusually durable

Natural slate roofs like these are particularly weather-resistant and long-lasting (right).

A black roofscape

In some regions the traditional color of roofing is black, and building regulations prevent the use of other colors. However, this is not the natural color in all cases: Besides slate, fiber cement and dark-colored roofing tiles are also in use here (far right).

Slate and fiber reinforced cement tiles

Natural stone roofing tiles also have a long tradition. For example, in Switzerland and Provence, southern France, sandstone roofing tiles are widespread, while in western Germany and Belgium roofs and façades of natural slate are frequently seen. They are laid on top of each other often in a fish-scale pattern and then nailed to the roof structure, making for a particularly durable and weather-resistant roof. The stone is a silicated and dehydrated clay shale, and must be free of iron pyrites, lime, clay, bitumen and coal. Natural slate is weather-resistant, watertight, frost-resistant and heat-resistant.

Slate tiles are perforable, making them easy to lay. With a minimum lifetime of 100 years, slate roofs are exceptionally durable.

Slate is a fine grained argillaceous metamorphic rock which splits easily into slabs. The material is normally quarried and its preparation is labor-intensive. As a natural stone its initial production requires very little energy, and in areas where it is available locally it is a very suitable building material. Natural deposits of top-quality slate have long been exhausted, for example, in Germany, requiring that it be imported from Spain and Portugal.

The long-distance transport involved increases the amount of energy needed to produce the slate, and that added to its labor-intensive production makes slate a very expensive roofing material. Laying slate also requires relatively great overlap, resulting in a proportionately larger quantity of slate tiles to cover a given roof.

In Europe a substitute material which has been available for some time is commonly known as schieferite. This is made from a blend of around 70% slate granules, a mineral filler of calcium carbonate and using polyester resin as the bonding agent. It has a similar external appearance to natural slate and can be laid in a similar fashion.

Unlike other slate imitations, schieferite is slate-colored all the way through, and exposed edges are not lighter in color. However, it is not as durable as the natural product and the high proportion of resin makes it less ecologically desirable and disposal is more problematic.

Since 1945 an increasingly widespread successor to natural slate has been fiber-reinforced cement tile. While asbestos cement tiles were available until the late 1980s, and in some other countries until they were banned in the early 1990s, a similar tile product has been marketed using cellulose or synthetic fibers as reinforcing. The most commonly used replacements for asbestos are polyacryl nitrite fibers (PAN, brand name Dralon™) and polyvinyl acetate fibers (PVA). These do not pose a known health hazard, but do derive from environmentally questionable manufacturing processes. In

Laid with large overlaps
The slate tiles lie on top of each other like protective fish scales, resulting in an attractive and extremely durable albeit fairly expensive roofing solution.

coated with an acrylic coating or laminate to provide coloring and UV stabilization. When they are ready they can be cut to produce roofing and siding tiles as well as panels in a wide variety of sizes. The material is weather-resistant, light, easy to work with and, as far as can be determined at this stage, has a very long lifetime.

However, recycling of a composite material such as this, containing synthetic fibers and coatings, is practically impossible, and its hazardous waste disposal status is as yet unclear. Furthermore, the high cement content is a problem from an environmental point of view. Corrugated fiber reinforced

Fiber reinforced cement roofing
Until the 1980s fiber reinforced cement roofing tiles contained asbestos. The large, cheap corrugated boards, which were very popular for sheds and other makeshift buildings, now release carcinogenic fibers in considerable quantities (far left).

addition, these tiles typically have a cement content of about 85% and they are rather complex to manufacture. The natural or synthetic fibers are mixed with cement and water to form a paste which is sprayed on in successive one millimeter-thick layers. The fibers' bulk allows the individual layers to mat together, giving the relatively thin tiles an extremely high degree of impact resistance, and a strength which is significantly superior, for example, to that of asbestos cement board. The sheet material or felt produced in this fashion is then pressed together, and hardens over a period of four weeks with no additional energy required. The boards are generally

cement panels are manufactured in the same way and the felt is corrugated while still soft by drawing a vacuum. It is generally left uncoated. Old corrugated board made of asbestos cement tends to deteriorate badly and is the main contributor in the release of 500 tons of asbestos fibers annually in Germany alone. The extent of its use in the United States is unknown.

- Fiber reinforced cement roofing: density 125 lb./ft.^{3} — embodied energy 3,100 Btu/lb. or 386,000 Btu/ft.^{3}

Asphalt roofing
A black roof may also be made of asphalt roof shingles (left).

Other roofing materials

Asphalt shingle roofing

Roofing shingles made of asphalt are economical and easy to adapt to any shape of roof, as in this unusual home. However, the result is not as durable as other roofing materials.

Reed and straw thatch roofing has been widely used throughout the world since the Sumerians adopted it around 5000 BC for construction of their homes. Although reed and long stalked straw are in decline, they can still be used in a sustainable fashion and are ecologically desirable provided the raw material is available in adequate quantities near the site where it is to be used. Specialist skill is needed to thatch roofs, but when it is done correctly thatch provides a comfortable and relatively durable roof offering a fair degree of thermal insulation. In addition, the moist peripheral areas provide a useful habitat for small animals. Thatch is far preferable to rattan and bamboo which are usually not harvested in a sustainable fashion and must be obtained from distant locations. Rattan is obtained from a tropical palm

plant and bamboo from places such as China where its clearing threatens the habitat of the giant Panda.

The wood shingle and shake roofs often seen in Alpine countries and increasingly in the United States are generally made of larch or cedar. Hand-split shakes are preferred rather than sawn shingles because they are far more durable. Wood roofing must have a sufficiently steep pitch to allow water to drain rapidly before it can damage the wood.

The most commonly used roofing material today is asphalt shingles which consist of glass fiber matting bonded with bitumen plus various synthetic additives as stabilizers or emulsifiers. The surface is protected against UV radiation by application of a pigmented mineral aggregate and it may have a gray, blue, green, red or brown coloration. This type of roofing is laid over a rigid underlay, usually consisting of asphalt impregnated roofing felt over plywood or OSB roof sheathing on a wood frame structure of some kind. It is fastened with galvanized roofing nails or staples. It is very economical, has an average lifetime of 15 to 20 years and can be shaped and cut at will, making it particularly suitable for flashing and unusual roof shapes. On the other hand, bitumen is considered to be potentially carcinogenic, largely due to potential emissions of polycyclic aromatic hydrocarbons which can occur at high temperatures during summer. Bitumen is also environmentally dubious because its blend of ingredients means it cannot be recycled in any way.

Metal roofing, most commonly associated with church roofs, has recently become increasingly

Thatched roof

Thatching a roof is something of a dying art. Reed, once available in great quantities, has become more scarce as a result of intensive agricultural methods and conservation of wetland areas.

fashionable for residential buildings, and even more so for small commercial buildings. In the southeastern areas of the United States, however, it has historically been the predominant roofing material. It is particularly suitable in creating the curved shaped roofs many post-modern architects are so fond of. The production of metal involves relatively large amounts of energy and results in a variety of negative environmental impacts both during extraction of the metal ore and when smelting. However, the primary energy content per cubic meter does paint a somewhat misleading picture given that metal is used in relatively thin sheets which are usually formed in a cold rolling process. Most metals can readily be recycled and often contain a high recycled material content. Nevertheless, environmentally conscious builders should consider its use carefully, because, for example, steel and aluminum sheets often receive a factory applied synthetic coating of polyester acrylate, polyurethane, PVC (plastisol) or fluorocarbon finish to protect them from corrosion and weathering.

Copper roofing, which is typically applied unfinished, quickly forms a protective layer of dark-brown copper oxide, and after about 10 years the distinctive green patina of copper sulfate or copper carbonate forms. Copper is resistant to mortar but can be corroded by hydrogen sulfide, the oxygen in water or by ammonia. Conversely, in moist conditions copper electrolyzes base metals such as iron, zinc or aluminum due to a galvanic reaction, so care should be taken when combining it with other materials to avoid any direct contact between them. Metallic copper is non-toxic, but copper ions in drinking water are not, and pose a hazard to small children, while copper salts cause vomiting and can lead to inflammation of the digestive tract.

Zinc forms a corrosion-inhibiting layer of carbonate via contact with atmospheric carbonic acid. It is susceptible to acids and bases, and thus to air pollution, but overall does not readily corrode and has good longevity. However, it does undergo a comparatively large amount of thermal expansion and contraction and thus should only be soldered to a limited extent and fitted with so-called sliding seams. Paint sticks poorly to zinc but is generally unnecessary in any case. A variety of pollutants are produced during the manufacture of zinc, but zinc is relatively non-toxic to humans.

Aluminum is protected against corrosion by a gray oxide layer, but is susceptible to attack by airborne salt near the coast, cement mortar, acids and bases, and also by green wood and wood softboard. However, overall it has good anti-corrosion properties, good durability and good tensile strength. The manufacturing process requires a great deal of energy, 75% of which takes the form of the electrical current used for electrolysis. Manufacture also involves the production of highly toxic fluoride compounds and large amounts of other solid wastes.

Wood shingle
Today larch shingle roofing is hardly ever found except on historic buildings such as this one.

- Aluminum sheet: density 169 lb./ft.³ — embodied energy 109,000 Btu/lb. or 18,358,000 Btu/ft.³
- Titanium zinc sheet: density 449 lb./ft.³ — embodied energy 39,000 Btu/lb. or 17,488,000 Btu/ft.³
- Copper sheet: density 556 lb./ft.³ — embodied energy 24,000 Btu/lb. or 13,430,000 Btu/ft.³
- Steel sheet: density 490 lb./ft.³ — embodied energy 11,000 Btu/lb. or 5,507,000 Btu/ft.³

100% wood
This new home in Germany's Black Forest not only has an all-wooden structure, but the roof is clad with wood shingles. To protect them from rot they must be hand-split along the grain, making this kind of roofing expensive.

Copper has a long tradition
Over the years copper roofing develops a green patina that protects the metal. Copper roofs are extremely durable and long lived.

A modern zinc roof
Zinc forms a gray patina, but it may be coated with special paints. Zinc is economical and very resistant to corrosion. Its drawback is that it expands greatly at high temperatures. Therefore, it should be installed either in overlapping fashion or with sliding seams which allow plenty of movement.

A new copper roof

Initially copper forms a corrosion-resistant brown coating of copper oxide, and the characteristic green patina only forms slowly over a number of years. Copper can cause decomposition of base metals so care should be taken to avoid any contact between dissimilar metals.

Modern corrugated sheet metal

Aluminum roof sheeting is generally coated with synthetic materials such as polyester, acrylates or PVC. These materials require particularly large amounts of energy to produce and often involve high releases of VOCs.

offer a long-term solution to the problem, and any improvement is more apparent than real.

The only way of effectively rendering such roofs safe is to carefully remove the asbestos cement boards. This job should not be attempted by do-it-yourself enthusiasts: A firm specializing in the removal of asbestos should be called in. The asbestos fiberboards should if possible be stored separately at rubbish dumps. Boards should be removed as soon as possible rather than waiting until they have begun to degrade due to weathering, because by then they will have released large quantities of fibers. Since the maximum longevity of asbestos cement board is 50 years, it will present a large scale hazardous waste disposal problem from the turn of the century onwards.

Flat roofs

In warm countries flat roofs have long been traditional since their greater thermal capacity means that they typically provide better protection against summer heat. However, in more temperate climates they only enjoyed a brief period of popularity. Since no reliable and satisfactory solution to the chronic problems of water leakage could be found, by the 1980s flat roofs had fallen almost entirely out of favor for private residential buildings.

Flat roofs have to be made relatively watertight rather than merely providing a rain screen and allowing water to run off. A distinction is made between the single-shell warm roof, where the surface is directly above the rooms below, and the double-shell cold roof, where there is a ventilated cavity between the roof and the uppermost ceiling, effectively forming a completely rectilinear attic area. Thermal insulation is generally provided above the roof substructure, which is in turn protected by a waterproofing membrane of some kind. There should be a vapor barrier below this as well since there is considerable vapor pressure from below due to the ceiling plane being the warmest surface. This vapor barrier can be dispensed

A poor outlook

Flat roofs are very susceptible to leaking and must be checked regularly, particularly when they are in continual use as in the case of roof terraces like this.

Replacement of asbestos cement roofs

In Germany alone about 1.3 billion square meters of roof and façade surfaces were clad with asbestos cement board, about a quarter thereof with uncoated products. Although this problem exists in other European countries it is not considered a major problem in the United States. Weathering of these surfaces has led to the release of considerable quantities of carcinogenic asbestos fibers. Coating of these roof surfaces is often attempted on the grounds that this will render the roofs safe. However, this coating approach is inadvisable, since the preliminary removal of deposited materials such as moss and the like leads to the release of millions of asbestos fibers. Due to the associated health hazard this procedure is banned in Germany under the Hazardous Substances Regulations. Even when completed coating does not

The warm roof

With warm roofs the layer of insulation is on the outside and serves to protect the structure. Today it is the most common design of flat roofs. A layer of gravel protects the waterproof sheeting from becoming brittle due to the effects of heat and UV radiation. However, such protection is often not enough, and roof cultivation (green or planted roof) provides much better protection.

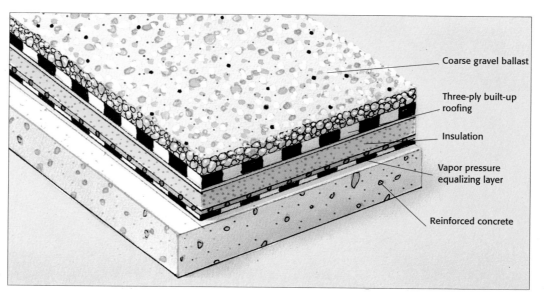

Coarse gravel ballast

Three-ply built-up roofing

Insulation

Vapor pressure equalizing layer

Reinforced concrete

with in the case of reinforced concrete ceilings more than 4 inches (10 cm) thick.

In the case of the inverted roof, the insulation is placed above the water seal. A watertight, closed-cell material such as glass foam or rigid fiberglass should be used for this purpose.

The waterproofing membrane has in the past generally been built-up roofing consisting of a series of layers of asphalt roofing felt or bitumen impregnated jute fabric and old textiles, laminated by application of hot liquid asphalt which is applied at around 360° F (182° C), at which temperatures carcinogenic polycyclic aromatic hydrocarbons are released in significant quantities and pose a health risk to workers. The edge seal generally involves use of metal flashing also wet mopped or bedded in asphalt sealants. Increasingly today a single continuous EPDM (synthetic rubber) membrane is used in lieu of the built-up system to provide a longer lasting and more reliable watertight seal. Individual sheets which come in long rolls are sealed in place using highly toxic solvents which fuse the pieces together. Sealing materials on flat roofs are subject to extreme stresses for all of the reasons set out below:

- They often have to repel not only rain and humidity but also standing water as in a ponding roof design (for evaporative cooling) or when the drains and overflow scuppers become blocked;
- Penetrations through the roof for chimneys, antennas and plumbing vents or air ventilation ducts are difficult to adequately flash and seal;
- Temperature differentials of up to 120° F (48° C) from day to night and of over 180° F (82° C) from summer to winter lead to considerable stresses due to expansion and contraction of materials;
- UV radiation causes the waterproof sheeting to decompose over time;
- Vapor pressure from inside the building must be completely repelled.

To provide much better protection against heat, wind and UV radiation flat roofs are almost

always covered with a layer of gravel ballast. In the case of inverted roofs the ballast ensures that the external insulation does not float up or blow away for some reason. If there is to be roof access, flagstones or concrete pavers are frequently laid on a gravel underlay.

Leisure areas on the roof

A roof terrace with a few tubs of flowers can readily be upgraded to a roof garden where you can relax and escape from the hustle and bustle of the city streets below. However, it is important to carefully check the roof's load-bearing capacity and seals.

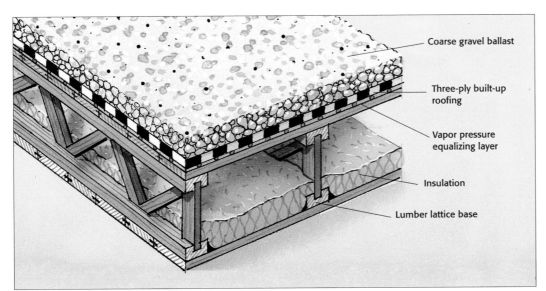

Coarse gravel ballast

Three-ply built-up roofing

Vapor pressure equalizing layer

Insulation

Lumber lattice base

The cold roof

This type of roof design is less popular than it used to be. It involves the use of an unheated space between the roof and ceiling below, and has the advantage that the thermal insulation can readily be improved by spraying in additional insulating material.

Roof gardens and green roofs

Roof cultivation on a large scale could significantly improve city micro-climates

Instead of gravel, the outer surface of a flat roof can be protected just as well by turning it into a cultivated area or green roof. Not only does this combat temperature variations better than gravel, it also has a whole range of other advantages:

- Thicker roof structure leads to better sound and thermal insulation;
- Improvement to the surrounding microclimate due to the much cooler roof surface and the moisture given off by plants;
- Increased thermal mass thereby stabilizing indoor temperature swings;
- Absorption of dust and pollutants;
- Retention of 50–70% of rain water and resulting reduction in site run-off;

prevents long-term moisture retention, but it is possible to plant roofs with pitches of up to 40°. With pitches over 25°, though, erosion of the soil substrate must be checked by the use of special matting and crossbeams to provide protection against shearing stresses. Do-it-yourself roof gardens are only really advisable for smaller roofs such as those of carports, sheds or summer houses, while planting the roofs of larger structures should be left to specialist firms because errors in the execution of the work can lead to major structural damage, and structural design must be carefully planned.

A vital feature for the functioning of a roof garden is the root retention membrane which prevents the underlying roof cladding from being damaged over

Grassed-roof homes
Architect: D. Grünecke, Herdecke, Germany
In heavily populated residential areas, having plants on roofs provides a natural touch and improves the microclimate by lowering temperatures and increasing humidity levels.

The root retention membrane must meet exacting requirements

- Plants provide habitat for small mammals and birds;
- More esthetically pleasing.

A clear distinction should be made between intensively and extensively planted roofs. While intensively planted roofs require a 24-inch-deep substrate or growing medium, place an increased load-bearing burden on the structure and require constant care and upkeep, an extensively planted roof garden with a substrate as little as 4 inches in depth is quite feasible depending on the climate, and is, moreover, largely maintenance-free.

Roofs with a slight pitch can also be planted. A pitch of 7° to 10° is ideal, in fact, because it actually

time by plant roots. Some systems also use a sophisticated design for this membrane to allow for improved drainage. The drainage membranes consist typically of many small molded bumps covered by a filter fabric to prevent the soil medium from filling in the spaces between the bumps. Because this membrane provides a second complete and watertight layer of roof cladding with its own drainage, it ensures the long-term sealing even of the most problematic flat roofs. This protective membrane should be approved after installation by a qualified inspector.

However, the materials employed in the roof retention and drainage membranes are not without their ecological drawbacks. Most of them consist either of

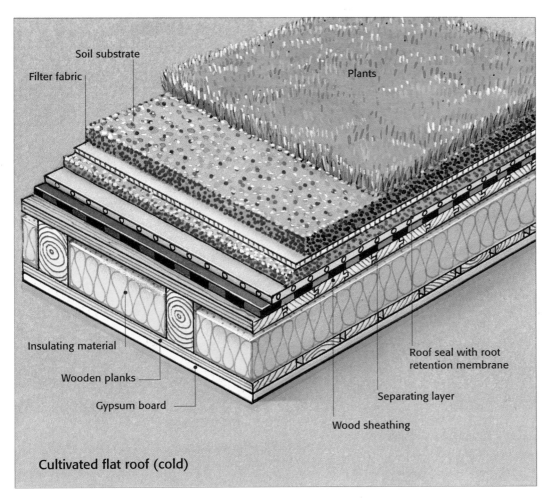

Soil substrate

Filter fabric

Plants

Insulating material

Wooden planks

Gypsum board

Roof seal with root
retention membrane

Separating layer

Wood sheathing

Cultivated flat roof (cold)

**A flat cultivated roof need
not be difficult to seal**

With a cultivated roof the roof
seal is of particular importance. It
must be root-resistant so that the
roof plants cannot damage it.

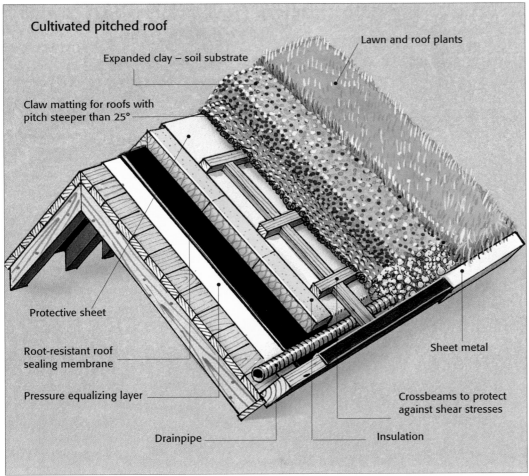

Cultivated pitched roof

Expanded clay – soil substrate

Lawn and roof plants

Claw matting for roofs with
pitch steeper than 25°

Protective sheet

Root-resistant roof
sealing membrane

Pressure equalizing layer

Drainpipe

Insulation

Crossbeams to protect
against shear stresses

Sheet metal

**Pitched roofs can also be
cultivated**

Roofs with pitches of up to 40°
can be cultivated. When they are
steeper than 25° they require
protection against shearing to
prevent the soil substrate from
slipping, and there must also be a
drainpipe along the eaves.

A touch of nature

Roof cultivation goes a small way to compensate for the vegetation which is destroyed by a housing development.

An extreme habitat

Even though many plants can do rather well well in a roof garden, it remains an extreme and harsh habitat. During droughts it may turn brown and dusty, if only temporarily.

environmentally damaging PVC or of bitumen with arsenic or copper additives to repel the plant roots. PVC and arsenic-impregnated layers should be rejected out of hand. Protective sheets with copper inlays are a more acceptable alternative, although a lot of energy goes into producing them. The potential health hazard posed by some of the ingredients of bitumen membranes must also be taken into account. Membranes made of polyethylene, EPDM synthetic rubber or plastomer bitumen are also available. Polyethylene sheets cannot be bonded to each other and are thus less suitable from a technical point of view, while EPDM sheet is fairly expensive and working

with it involves the use of environmentally damaging solvents. A better option is plastomer bitumen, a blend of bitumen and elastic synthetic materials. This is fairly easy to install, but is only suitable for smaller roofs because the sheets are prone to shrinkage.

Suppliers of roof garden systems sell a complete package from drainage to planting, and from the soil medium substrate to vegetation matting. These packages include a variety of mainly synthetic materials which are supposed to guarantee the success of the planting. However, many of these materials are completely unnecessary. For example, a thin substrate for the plant layer can be made from materials such as locally obtained loam, sand and expanded clay or lava. Instead of synthetic matting, jute fabric or burlap can be used to ensure not only that the substrate holds together but also to guarantee a well connected carpet of roots.

Other important factors are the drainage of the roof garden and also protection against mechanical damage and improvement of stress equalization via the use of protective felt layers between the root retention membrane and the other individual layers of the roof structure. Occasionally the root retention layer is incompatible with the roof cladding material.

The roof always remains an extremely harsh habitat for plants, and good plant cover does not always develop immediately even if you do your own planting rather than relying on natural plant colonization. The most suitable plants are succulents, as well as such dry habitat plants such as lavender, sage, daisies, phlox and chives, and various indigenous grasses. Moss, lichen, rose of Sharon, yarrow and other plants will generally colonize the roof of their own accord.

Luxuriant vegetation

Depending on the thickness of the soil substrate, a variety of different plant species can flourish on a cultivated roof. They may be planted or seed may be sown, while some species will colonize the roof of their own accord.

Succulents

Succulents do particularly well on an extensively planted roof. They can store water in their fleshy leaves, enabling them to survive long periods of dry weather.

OVERVIEW OF PLANTS SUITABLE FOR ROOF CULTIVATION

Plants for extensive roof cultivation

- **Water-storing succulents:**

Sedum species: (over 300 species in widespread use) e.g. *Sedum spectabile* – showy stonecrop, *Sedum spurium* – dragon's blood, *Sedum acre L., Sedum album L., Sedum roseum, Sedum spathafolium var. purpurium, Sedum stoloniferum*

Sempervivum species (over 40 species and 350 cultivars) commonly hens and chicks or houseleeks: *Sempervivum borissovae, Sempervivum nevadense, Sempervivum tectorum L.*

Kalanchoe species (Christmas Cactus), e.g. *Kalanchoe mangini, millotii, Kalanchoe rhombopilosa*

Crassula species (over 250 species): e.g. *Crassula obligua, Crassula muscosa monstrose, Crassula perforata* (shrub)

Graptopetulum species – commonly moss rose: e.g. *Graptopetulum bellum, Graptopetulum macdougalii*

Other succulents: *Monanthes muralis, Monanthes polyphylla, Oxalis succulenta, Rosularia chrysanthe, Peperomia L.*

- **Supplementary species:**

Garden herbs such as chives, dillweed, *Sage Galium odoratum* – sweet woodruff, bedstraw, *Lamium maculatum* – spotted deadnettle, *Thymus pseudolanuginosus* – wooly thyme, *Nepeta x faassenii* - catmint, *Stachys lanata* – lambs' ears

Perennials including: *Veronica pectinata* – blue wooly speedwell, *Penstemon* species – beardtongue, *Linum perenne var. Lewisii* – blue flax or perennial flax, *Aurinia saxatile* – basket of gold (mustard family), *Achillea L.* – yarrow, and others including varieties of daisies, lavender, phlox

- **Grasses for ground cover:**

Festuca arvadinacea – tall fescue, *Buchloe dactryloides* – buffalo grass, *Calamagrostis acutiflora* – "Karl Foerster" feather reed grass, *Miscanthus sinensis* – maidenhair grass, *Polygonum affine* – himalayan fleeceflower (member of the buckwheat family)

- **Species that colonize of their own accord:**

Various members of the mustard family, clover, rose of Sharon, plantain lily (hosta species), chickweed and a variety of mosses and lichens

FAÇADE DESIGN

A solar façade

Cladding a façade with solar panels, as in this Heidelberg office building, not only looks attractive, it also utilizes the solar energy striking the walls.

Plants can be used to protect and embellish the front of a house

The façade or the exterior walls, moldings and window and door openings determine the style and character of a house. If you do not feel that the external wall provides a satisfactory finish surface for the building exterior, the façade can be supplemented by additional elements. For example, a exterior curtain wall may be employed to provide both protection and a more esthetically pleasing appearance, while also providing additional thermal insulation. Recent technological developments have also made it possible for such walls to actively store energy. Of course, the most economical way of decorating a façade is to add plants and flowers such as climbing vines, but certain rules should be followed to ensure that this does not lead to unexpected additional expense later on.

Siding materials

Cladding façades with siding boards, shingles or panels is an accepted and common procedure. The siding protects the inner walls from the elements,

while the ventilation behind the finish siding material improves thermal insulation in both summer and winter and provides a way for moisture which penetrates the exterior surface to run off. Generally any material that can be used for roofing can also be used for façades. Traditionally, wood shingle and slate tiles were in widespread use, and in some areas lead can be found as a wall cladding on older houses. Although not generally popular as a siding in the United States, asbestos panels have been used to clad many building exteriors in Europe.

A very acceptable alternative is clay or ceramic tile, while natural stone cladding, which is often used for office buildings, can also be suitable depending on its availability near the site. In contrast, siding made of aluminum, PVC and high density fiberboard (typically referred to by its product name — Masonite™), all very popular siding materials since the early 1970s, are for the most part undesirable from an ecological and health point of view.

Wood siding, which is becoming fashionable once again, can also be recommended. A type in widespread use is the simple board-and-batten siding consisting of vertical overlapping planks normally fitted over a ventilation cavity. This involves less risk of moisture retention than with horizontal siding, which should always be installed with a weather drip on the external edge to prevent moisture lingering between the overlapping boards. When using solid wood siding, a transparent or semi-transparent stain or similar wood-preservative treatment is advisable (see previous section on wood preservatives). If the siding is to be painted it should definitely be back-primed prior to installation. However redwood and cedar can also be left uncoated and allowed to weather naturally. In this case it will quickly turn a dull gray in color giving the building a very rustic appearance.

A curtain wall can also be used to protect the thermal insulation from the elements, and is particularly suitable in the case of soft insulating material which cannot be plastered or stuccoed. At the same time it allows you to give the wall whatever outward appearance you desire. The curtain wall must be ventilated to allow any condensation to evaporate. The ventilation openings can then be fitted with screen cloth to make it insect-proof. When installing a curtain wall for this purpose you should take care to ensure that any metal fastenings attaching the insulating material to the underlying masonry wall do not lead to thermal bridges, it may be preferable to use wood or plastic fasteners.

Solar façades

Architects specializing in solar buildings often do not stop at façades which passively protect the structure against heat loss, they have developed methods of making them actively contribute to the building heating demands by collecting and/or storing solar energy. This is sometimes referred to as transparent insulation, which acts as a kind of solar collector, but rather than heating water or air it directly heats the wall behind it. An example of this is a "trombe wall" where the exterior glass is placed in front of a thermal storage wall, usually of masonry. Sometimes the storage material is a container which a phase change material such as eutectic salts. By undergoing a phase change at the appropriate temperature, this material greatly increases its storage capacity. An alternative is to fit photovoltaic cells to the façade. A number of manufacturers are already specializing in solar façades, whose elegant black glass panels are particularly suitable for office and administrative buildings. Furthermore, in this type of construction costly wall cladding is already the norm, so that part of the costs of the solar panels would be met by savings made on exterior cladding materials that are being replaced with the solar panels.

Wood siding
Architect: I. Gabriel, Oldenburg, Germany
The patterns and texture of the façade of this low-energy building adds interest to an otherwise plain building design.

Slate shingles
A durable cladding of natural slate can be particularly resistant to the elements as well as very attractive.

Wood shingle siding
Today it is very rare for a house-front to be clad with small, hand-split shingles. This type of cladding is very durable, however, in addition to being elegant.

Silverlace vine grows rapidly

Silverlace vine requires a climbing aid to scale any wall, but its extremely fast rate of growth means that it can rapidly scale a building façade. Because of this it needs to be regularly cut back to prevent it from becoming too heavy or offering too large a surface area to the wind.

Use of climbing plants on façades

Cultivating plants on the façade is an ideal way both of adding interest to an otherwise unremarkable housefront and also improving it from an environmental standpoint. It not only provides a habitat and an indispensable food source for a wide variety of different animals but it also performs quite a number of useful functions for the residents. The plants increase the local atmospheric humidity, provide shade and filter out dust. In addition, they can protect the façade from driving rain and prevent the formation of cracks due to excessive thermal stresses. According to some (admittedly disputed) research, they also provide a certain degree of climate control in both summer and winter. For example, a 5–10% improvement in thermal insulation has been observed, which is chiefly due to dampening of wind pressure and the formation of a cushion of air in the vegetation.

Growing plants on the front of a house can bring a touch of nature into the most cramped city center environments. If done correctly, virtually all buildings can be planted in some shape or form without any risk to the structure of the building. Manufacturers of trellises and similar equipment have gained much experience in recent years with this application and there have also been some scientific advances in this area. Growing plants on building façades is still very much

Plants can protect façades, but they can also do a lot of damage

Ivy

Ivy is the classic clinging vine. It can completely cover the façade of a house, especially in the shaded areas. However, ivy takes a long time to grow and does not thrive well on every kind of façade.

regarded as a do-it-yourself measure requiring little capital outlay. However, seeking cheap solutions here may be costly: If you choose the wrong climbing plants they may end up doing a lot of damage to the walls, particularly to the underlying brickwork.

A distinction should be made between trellis climbing and clinging plants. While plants that need a trellis or other climbing assistance are easy to keep off areas where they are not wanted, clinging plants, the plants typically selected as a low-cost solution, are more difficult to control. Among these are the root climbers like ivy *(Hedera helix)*, trumpet vines *(Campsis radicans)* and climbing hydrangea. Then there are the contact climbers such as Virginia creeper *(Parthenocissus quinquefolia)*. They have adhesive pads which produce a secretion creating an initial bond with the surface, and this is followed by the proliferation of tendrils which can anchor themselves in the tiniest fissure or surface irregularity. No damage is typically done to the surface being colonized by contact climbers. However, this type of climber cannot grow on surfaces that are too smooth, those painted a dark color causing excessive heat, or those treated with weed killers.

Root climbers produce shoot-like roots, generally no more than 2.5 to 3 inches in length, which can splay out and anchor themselves in the tiniest surface crack. Ivy prefers moist, shady areas but can also grow in bright, sunlit spots provided the surface on which it is growing is not a smooth one such as stone, glass or metal.

If the surface is broken or irregular, the photophobic ivy roots grow into it and become feed roots. Therefore, when using root climbers the underlying plaster must be absolutely free of cracks. Ivy establishes its roots in moist wall joints and old plaster, and this can even lead to structural cracks since old 20-foot ivy plants can produce shoots with a diameter of 4 inches (10 cm). This risk of structural cracks is greater in the case of multi-wythe wall structures, and the weight of the plants can become so great that the load-bearing capacity of the wall may actually be exceeded.

The moist and crumbly plaster beneath window ledges often poses a particular problem, and type 2 portland cement plaster should be used in such areas. The roots of both trumpet vines and ivy can penetrate synthetic coatings that form a film, while ivy can also destroy synthetic resin cladding materials. Clinging vines should not be grown over any surface that needs regular painting or other maintenance.

Virginia creeper

Virginia creeper does particularly well on the south side of buildings. In the summer it will protect the façade from excessive heat, while it sheds its leaves in the fall so that the winter sun can bring a little warmth to the walls. Its splendid colors in the fall are an added attraction.

The following types of surfaces should be left free of clinging plants (reasons given in brackets):

- half-timbered or wood siding surfaces (wood preservation treatment, need for renovation work, fungal attack);
- curtain walls (load-bearing capacity, risk of structural cracks);
- structures subject to cracks (risk of structural cracks);
- wall paint containing synthetic materials (risk of root penetration);
- resin plaster (need for renovation work);
- composite insulated panel systems (load-bearing capacity);
- porous thermal insulating plaster (load-bearing capacity);
- weathered brickwork (risk of cracking, risk of root penetration);
- metal siding (need for renovation work).

Trellis climbing plants

Trellis climbing plants are those creepers that require some form of framework in order to climb the wall structure. Certain types of wall structures, and also very high ones, may not be able to support the weight of a trellis. Another potential problem which should be carefully checked before attaching a trellis is whether they are tensile loads caused by wind. Creepers or twining plants such as Clematis, silverlace vine *(Polygonym aubertii)*, morning glory *(Ipomoea tricolor)*, climbing honeysuckle *(Lonicera* species), Bougainvillea species or Wisteria *(Wisteria floribunda* or *W. sinensis)*, to name a few, anchor their shoots by winding movements around vertical wires, string or laths. The climbing aid should not be thicker than 2 inches and should have a rounded cross-section. However, laths should not be too thin either or they will be broken by the winding action of the plants over the course of the years. The gap between the trellis and the wall should be between 4 and 6 inches to allow the plants to grow to a suitable girth. In the case of Bougainvillea, the gap should be even greater, about eight inches, since Bougainvillea can grow a stem with a diameter of 6 to 7 inches within ten years. This naturally makes cultivation a lot more expensive,

One size does not fit all

Different types of climbing aids are required for different plants. Creepers such as Silverlace vine prefer vertical wires, while spreading climbers such as the climbing rose need horizontal battens. Only clinging vines such as English Ivy or Trumpet Vine are indifferent to the type of support provided since they do not need any help. Twining plants like clematis, on the other hand, always require a trellis.

since the greater the gap the more extensive the fastenings must be. The lateral gap between wires or strings should be around 12 inches in order to allow a dense, even coverage of plant growth. Metal chains are inadvisable as climbing aids since species such as silverlace vine, which grow thick woody stems, will initially grow through the relatively small chain links and consequently become deformed as they grow larger. Similarly, care should be taken to prevent the plants growing into fastening fixtures or suspensions. Creepers should not be allowed to reach gutter height because they can slowly crush the gutter over the course of the years, eventually tearing it from its anchoring. Fast growing varieties like silverlace vine must regularly be kept in check to prevent them growing into shutter boxes or loft space or overrunning the gutter.

Twining plants develop touch-sensitive gripping organs which anchor themselves preferentially on grid-like climbing aids. Twining plants include most varieties of vine, the clematis, gourds and the popular morning glory.

The individual laths on a trellis should have a diameter of between ¼ inch and one inch depending on the plant, the trellis grid size should be between four and 12 inches, and the gap between the trellis

and the wall should be between 2 and 6 inches. Along with industrially produced wire trellises, simple welded wire mesh makes a good climbing aid, but as a rule roof batten frameworks are too thick.

Lichens and certain spreading climbers are not genuine climbing plants because they need human help in order to climb. They are capable, however, of attaching themselves to largely horizontal supports via side shoots, spines or thorns. The best known plants of this type are the climbing rose (*Rosa* species) and the yellow-flowered winter jasmine or the bridal jasmine (*Jasimum polyanthum*). In the wild their long stems intertwine with other plants and with each other to form thick, impenetrable undergrowth. They require a good deal of care and attention in the form of regular pruning, rearranging and refastening to the trellis. Ideal support for this type of plant is provided by wires which are arranged horizontally on the wall at an interval of about 16 inches, while the vertical trellis supports should be at an interval of a good 20 inches to make them easier to tend. Again the gap between the wall and the trellis should be 6 inches if the plants are intended to grow between the climbing aid and the wall, or it can be attached directly to the wall surface if they are to be tied to the trellis.

have led to contamination of drinking water with asbestos fibers. PVC is mostly used only for the smaller service mains.

Sewage pipes

Today PVC pipes are almost always used for interior plumbing, because they were much lighter and easier to work with than the older cast-iron pipes. In addition, the cast-iron pipes suffer from mineral build-up and corrosion and are insufficiently flexible. Finally PVC is far less expensive than any alternative. A distinction is made between gray pipes and molded parts for carrying hot water, and green (or sometimes orange) pipes made of a somewhat tougher type of PVC for carrying away the cooled sewage. However, although PVC pipes have clear advantages, the material is undesirable from an ecological point of view as has been explained in the text earlier. They do not pose a problem in case of fire, but they are not as durable as traditional materials, and they are difficult to dispose of.

An inexpensive new generation of sleeveless stoneware pipes has recently been developed in Britain. They are fitted with collars made of environmentally neutral polypropylene which provides a certain degree of tolerance, so that the pipes can compensate for settling to a certain extent. The environmentally friendly stoneware used is manufactured by means of an energy-saving quick-firing process. The pipes are very smooth and comparatively light, and the collar system involves little waste of materials because leftover lengths of pipe can be reused. Its availability may be limited in North America at this time; however, similar products may be introduced here as well.

- PVC pipe: embodied energy: c. 2,500,000 Btu/square foot
- Stoneware pipe: embodied energy: c. 315,000 Btu/square foot

Roof drainage

It is also inadvisable to use cheap PVC roof gutters, if only because they are very unsightly. In addition, PVC becomes extremely brittle at low temperatures, so it is not really suitable for roof guttering or external drainpipes. Zinc or copper pipes are easy to install, but are expensive and require a great deal of energy to manufacture. On the other hand, zinc is very durable and long-lasting and has long been used for this purpose. Indeed, its use is often mandatory on listed buildings. Copper, on the other hand, cannot be used in conjunction with base metals like iron, zinc or aluminum because of severe corrosion from galvanic reaction. For new buildings the best solution from an ecological point of view is the use of galvanized steel gutters and drainpipes.

WASTEWATER SYSTEMS

Decorative

Roof drainage can play a decorative as well as functional role.

For a long time very little attention was paid to wastewater systems with the "out of sight, out of mind" principle in effect. The public sanitary sewer system largely dates from around the turn of the century and was traditionally constructed from stoneware and cast-iron pipes or in some cases clay and concrete tiles. Decades of neglect have resulted in far reaching damage to this system arising from leaks, tree roots, soil settlement and earth tremors and pipe breakage has become increasingly widespread. Replacement sewage pipes are usually made of fiber-reinforced cement, which has higher tensile strength than concrete and is less brittle than stoneware. Asbestos cement was also used at one stage, and this may

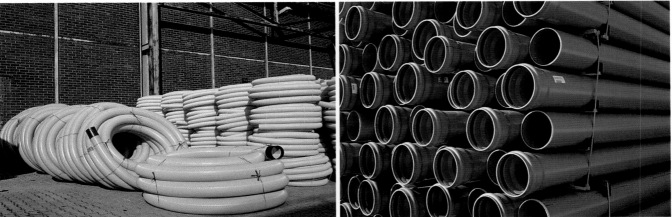

PVC should be avoided
Civil engineering firms' store rooms are piled high with PVC pipes. They have become nearly universal for all residential waste-water systems, but they have serious ecological drawbacks.

A stoneware renaissance
Stoneware pipes went out of fashion some time ago because they were so awkward to work with. However, a new generation of environmentally friendly and economical stoneware piping is now available, providing a practical alternative to PVC. They are fitted with sleeves made of environmentally benign polypropylene, making them much easier to install.

INTERNAL BUILDING

INTERNAL BUILDING COMPONENTS

Doors and windows, or fenestration, are the openings in the building shell which provide access for air and light and of course people, to the interior of the building. To perform their function and maintain an adequate weathertight envelope, they must be manufactured to close tolerances and maintain a good seal when closed. They must therefore meet high quality standards and be constructed of durable materials. The staircases, too, are one of the most challenging parts of a structure because they must satisfy special safety requirements and yet be comfortable to use.

Stairs

Stairs can be dangerous: In the United States alone there are some 5,000 accidents a day on stairs with over 3,000 deaths a year resulting from falls. Often the condition of the stairs themselves is responsible. But this is not because the owner refuses to repair the well-worn steps and the loose banisters. In many cases it is because the stairs were badly built in the first place.

The pressures on design-orientated contemporaries to come up with more ambitious versions of these at times rather boring features are great and can be at the expense of safety considerations. Home interior magazines also support this foolish tendency by publishing pictures of stairs without any railings which are not even allowable under building codes. Sometimes they even show banisters with so few vertical rails that children could easily slide through them and fall.

In order to ensure banisters are safe for small children most building codes in the United States require that nothing larger than a four-inch-diameter sphere (smaller than a baby's head) can pass through any railing. This is to prevent children from squeezing their heads through and getting stuck. The banister rail must typically be 42 inches above the floor and 32 inches above the tread nosing of the stair. Banisters should not have any horizontal railings which could be used by children as a sort of ladder to climb over them. Finally, the steps must be sealed off by the railings so that there is no area for children to step on and play on the outer side of the stairs.

But stairs can also provide adults with unpleasant surprises. For example, a winding stair that has steps that wind too sharply, thereby reducing the space on which to place one's foot, presents a hazard as well as being extremely uncomfortable. The step should be at least 10 inches wide to enable people to place their feet on it safely. Steps that are too high can also be difficult to climb; they should not be more than 9 inches high, with 7 inches being an ideal height. As a rule of thumb, the height of two steps and the depth of one step

should total about 24 to 26 inches. A safe, comfortable staircase therefore requires a lot of space and careful planning. The layout of the stairs, i.e., single flight, two flights with an intermediate landing, winding, spiral, will largely be determined by the layout of the floors being connected as well as the available space. The width of the steps and the provision of comfortable

landings will also depend on the amount of space available, the age of the user, the frequency of use and the applicable building codes. However, in regularly used areas, steps must be at least 32 inches wide or, bearing in mind that furniture will have to be carried up them, preferably at least 40 inches wide. A single, straight flight of steps usually appears awkward and steep but is much easier for carrying up furniture than

Ample clearances

The two staircases could hardly be more spacious and user-friendly. However, successful designs like these are rare in apartment buildings.

Compared with other designs spiral staircases take up the least space, but from a structural engineering point of view they must meet exacting standards.

Various stair designs

A comparison of some of the most popular staircase configurations: It is easy to see just how much space each type requires. This helps to decide which type would best suit the floorplan in question. But one thing must never be forgotten: U-shaped stairs with high banisters or spiral stairs should have a diameter of at least 7 feet 6 inches so that large pieces of furniture can easily be carried up and down them.

a U-shaped two flight stair. If they are not open on at least one side the stairs will tend to feel very cramped. A winding staircase with a wide stairwell usually feels much more comfortable to use.

If the individual steps differ in height there is a significant risk of tripping and the stair will feel very uncomfortable. This occasionally happens with old steps where some have worn more than others, or as a result of renovations. In the case of the latter, new floor coverings are placed on top of old with the effect that the first and last steps are either higher or lower than the others. The body, however, instinctively memorizes movement sequences and "expects" each step be the same height.

Specific design errors also regularly come to light with stairs: banging one's head on the ceiling while climbing a staircase because the distance to the ceiling fails to comply with the minimum of 80 inches; or searching in vain for a light switch, because there isn't any where you would expect it. Occasionally designers fail to take bulky or unwieldy furniture into consideration, let alone an ambulance service carrying a sick or injured person on a stretcher. As a result, especially in new buildings, it is impossible to carry large items of furniture up winding staircases. Spiral staircases with harp-like railings should have a diameter of about 7 feet.

Attic conversions to create additional living space can pose special problems because there is usually no permanent staircase to the attic. It is likely to have

been supplied only with makeshift pull-out stairs or a ladder which has generally only had occasional use prior to its conversion to living space. This often means that there is little space available for a proper staircase. One popular solution is the use of an especially narrow and steep stair known as a "ship's ladder." Although they require far less space, they are inherently hazardous and often have unsteady steps with little room for feet. They are available cheaply from many do-it-yourself stores even though they are typically only allowed for access to a storage area or as an emergency egress and not for use in key living areas. These stairs can often lead to falls and if they were to occur in a rented accommodation, the landlord could certainly be held liable.

Soundproofing is another key consideration when it comes to stairs. In apartment buildings which house several families stairs can be an obvious source of complaints and, therefore, the use of heavier building materials such as cast-in-place or prefabricated concrete is advisable. The surfaces of the steps on the stringers, the newel or the wall as well as the surfaces of the stringers should always be fitted with an acoustic break which will significantly reduce the noise transmission of a wooden staircase. An appropriate ecological material to use would be locally grown hardwood because of its durability. Hardwood stairs fashioned from oak can last some 80 to 100 years. Do not under any circumstances be tempted to use thin softwood steps.

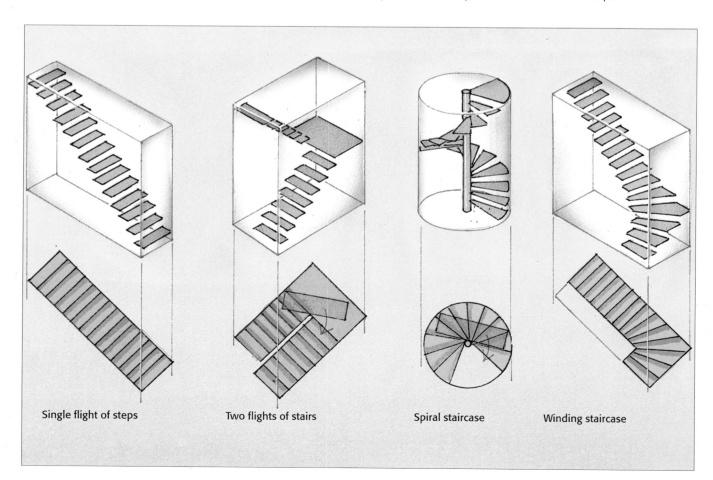

| Single flight of steps | Two flights of stairs | Spiral staircase | Winding staircase |

WINDOWS

Tiffany glass windows
A beautiful stained glass window like this is rarely seen anymore, partly because a single pane on an outside wall is no longer viable from a construction point of view. However, it can still be used for decorative purposes as an internal decorative glazing layer.

The term window comes from the old Gaelic word "windeye" or "eye to the wind." They provide the source of light and air but can also present a weakness in the building thermal envelope. In order to protect the house against heat loss, or against noise or burglary they must meet exacting standards. Windows can bring in solar warmth but must also protect from excessive heat gain in the summer. The size of the windows usually depends on the surface area of the exterior wall. A rule of thumb is that windows should comprise roughly a third of the wall in order to guarantee sufficient light. However, this can very well be adjusted to suit the room's function and position in order to open rooms to the sun and make north-facing adjoining rooms weatherproof. A desirable window to floor area ratio might be 15–20% – 12 to 15 square feet of window for every 100 square feet of total living space.

Window glazing and energy conservation

Windows can be the weakest point in the building shell

Rapid progress has been made over recent years in reducing the amount of heat loss through windows. Thirty years ago ordinary single pane windows would on average have a heat transmission coefficient or u-value of about 1 Btu/square foot/°F. Today, with the introduction of insulated low-emittance (low-e) glass this has fallen to 0.35 for a standard low-energy window and as low as 0.15 for a "super window."

These are called "super windows" because elaborate advances in glazing technology provide multiple air spaces and multiple low-e glazing layers with krypton gas fill as well as a low conductance glass edge design, and in most cases polyurethane foam insulation injected into the hollow frame profiles. Low-e insulating glass is typically filled with an inert gas such as argon or krypton and has an extremely thin transparent coating of multiple metal (silver oxide) layers added to the inner pane to reflect the infrared energy back inside. Another type of low-e glass designed for use in hot climates places the selective low-e coating on the inside of the outer pane to reject radiant energy primarily from outside the building.

Unfortunately, only half the windows installed each year in the United States today have an insulating value better than standard clear double-pane insulated glazing with a u-value of about 0.49. All Energy Star® qualifying windows, doors and skylights must bear a label from the National Fenestration Rating Council (NFRC). NFRC is a non-profit collaborative of manufacturers, builders, designers, government officials, utilities and consumers which provides unbiased energy performance ratings for window, doors and skylights. In order to obtain an NFRC label, window manufacturers must have their products independently tested and they must have a combined window unit u-value no greater than 0.5.

Solar heat gain through glass is easily obtained

South-facing windows can help gain rather than lose energy in the winter, but they should be provided with energy-efficient insulated glazing.

In hot climates where cooling costs are typically more of a concern than heating costs, the insulating value of windows is not as important as the ability to block heat gain. Up until recently the solar heat transmission properties of glazings were similar enough that they didn't figure into window energy ratings. But today's windows can have selective glazings that control heat loss in winter, or block solar heat gain in summer. Previously the NFRC label provided the u-value or thermal insulating performance of a particular window and the solar heat gain coefficient (SHGC) – the ability to reject unwanted heat gain. The solar heat gain coefficient is the fraction of the total incident light energy which enters the building through the window as heat gain. The lower the number the better the performance: For example, while a typical dual pane window might have a u-value of 0.49 and a SHGC of 0.58, a low-energy window with low-e argon filled glass would have a u-value of 0.30 and a SHGC of 0.44 and a similar window with a selective glazing for a cooling climate would have a u-value of 0.29 and SHGC of 0.31.

This labeling system, however, proved confusing to most consumers who did not understand the terminology or the numbering system, and it did not take into consideration the aspect of air leakage (infiltration), which is very important in determining a window's overall performance. In response to this, the NFRC has developed a new window-rating system that considers solar heat gain in addition to u-value and air leakage. With the new system in place, NFRC ratings will include two numbers between 0 and 70 that reflect annual heating and cooling performance. The numbers, which represent the Fenestration Heating Ratio

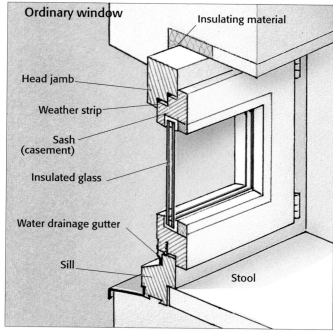

Ordinary window

Insulating material

Head jamb

Weather strip

Sash (casement)

Insulated glass

Water drainage gutter

Sill

Stool

Energy saving glass

This "Superhouse" in Gelsen-kirchen, Germany has huge glass areas. Potential energy loss is contained thanks to modern high tech super glazing having an extremely low u-value. In this case the windows are almost as well insulated as the wall.

Various window construction details in comparison

The ordinary window (opposite, right) has the narrowest frame and is the least complicated in its construction. But both frame and sash must be energy-efficient. The multiple-sash window (below) on the other hand, actually incorporates two sash each separately weather-stripped in a well-insulated frame profile. Both sash operate as one and are only rarely separated for cleaning. This "belt and suspenders" system results in very little heat loss through the glass and frame crack. The box window (bottom right) comprises two completely separate ordinary windows which must be opened individually. These windows are each good insulators and have the combined effect of very good acoustical control.

(FHR) and the Fenestration Cooling Ratio (FCR), indicate the percentage of annual household heating or cooling energy the window will save compared to a worst-case window with single glazing and an aluminum frame. Unlike the previous ratings, the higher the number in either category, the greater the savings. For example, an FHR 20 window adds 20% less to the home's heating bill than a worst-case window; an FCR 20 window adds 20% less to the cooling bill. FHR and FCR can't be used to perform

energy-load calculations. They are meant only as a tool for comparing windows.

According to the NFRC, a typical wood or PVC double-pane window would rate at around FHR 20 and FCR 10, while a more efficient window with low-e, argon gas fill and low-conductance spacers might have an FHR of 35 and an FCR between 20 and 35, depending on the selective low-e coating. Whether you choose high heating or cooling numbers will entirely depend on your climate.

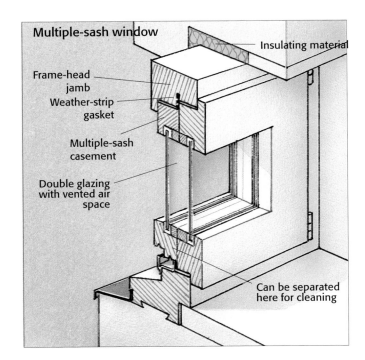

Multiple-sash window

- Insulating material
- Frame-head jamb
- Weather-strip gasket
- Multiple-sash casement
- Double glazing with vented air space
- Can be separated here for cleaning

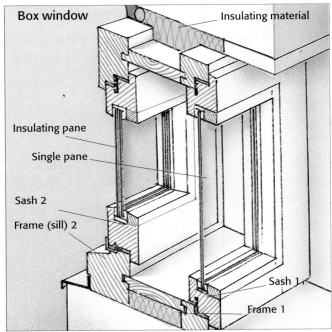

Box window

- Insulating material
- Insulating pane
- Single pane
- Sash 2
- Frame (sill) 2
- Sash 1
- Frame 1

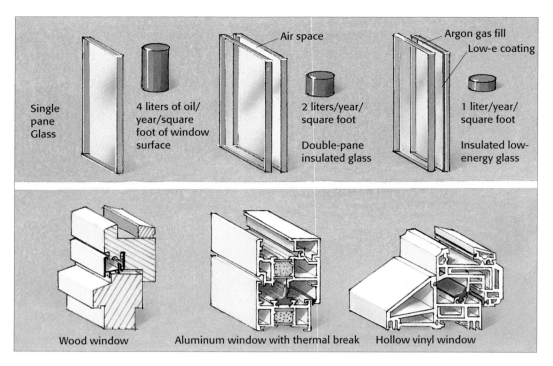

Single pane Glass

4 liters of oil/ year/square foot of window surface

Air space

2 liters/year/ square foot

Double-pane insulated glass

Argon gas fill

Low-e coating

1 liter/year/ square foot

Insulated low-energy glass

Wood window

Aluminum window with thermal break

Hollow vinyl window

Window profiles

These cross-section detail show the construction of wood, extruded aluminum and extruded PVC window profiles. Wood is the best insulator of these materials, aluminum is the most durable and PVC is the least costly. The aluminum and PVC chambers can be filled with an insulating foam to reduce the energy lost through the frame. However, this adds considerable expense and is environmentally questionable. The diagram (top) showing the three most common types of glass shows the available technological advances made in energy-efficient glazing.

Window frames, materials

Frames are the weakest points of a window. The frame can take up to a third of the opening in the wall so it is hardly worth investing in expensive high performance glazing when installing small windows because all the heat conserved by the glazing may be quickly lost through the frame. In addition, when the difference between the insulating value of the glass and frame are great, condensation occurs at the edge of the glass which can cause water damage to surrounding surfaces. To combat this, the range of super windows available today use frames with insulated profiles made from polyurethane or a composite sandwich construction comprising wood and polyurethane which, from an environmental point of view, is hardly a satisfactory solution.

In the US more environmentally friendly systems have been developed by the United States Department of Energy Windows and Glazing Research Program at Lawrence Berkeley National Laboratory. The range of materials available for frame and sash profiles comprise locally grown and tropical woods such as mahogany and teak, as well as aluminum and plastic, primarily PVC. In terms of market share in the US, PVC windows still enjoy the greatest market share with about 40%, followed by wood and clad wood windows with 35% and aluminum with some 20%. The most ecologically sound option would be windows manufactured with locally grown wood. However, it is nearly impossible to find the quality and performance demanded by a low-energy house from a locally made

Tropical wood

In light of the prevailing destruction of tropical rainforests, windows fashioned from tropical hardwoods cannot be recommended although, technically, they are a more suitable option than most other materials (bottom left). Anyone who already has such frames should try to preserve this valuable material by, for example, replacing the single pane or insulated double glazing with low-e or advanced superglazings if possible.

Opening out

This Scandinavian window product offers a more elegant alternative: Windows that open out are easier to lock but awkward to clean. Most casements windows sold in North America are crank out windows similar to this one.

window fabricator or millwork company. Another disadvantage of using unclad wood windows is that they require painting about every five years whereas clad wood windows may go 25 years or more without repainting. Also, wood has a better insulating capability than many of the other comparable materials. The primary energy requirement in producing simple wood windows is about one-tenth that of comparable plastic windows and about 40 times less than aluminum windows. When making the frames, it is especially important to use only properly dried and stored wood with a maximum moisture content of 19% and to ensure that the corner joints of the sash are strong and durable. The exterior color should not be too dark because in the summer the amount of heat absorbed can generate surface temperatures of up to 200° F or more and thereby affect the life of the paint. Tropical woods, particularly meranti, mahogany and teak, have established themselves as a materials of choice with many high-end window fabricators because they are particularly hard and weather-resistant, offer a rich and elegant appearance and do not necessarily require a protective coat of paint. But in view of the prevailing exploitation of tropical forests they should be avoided unless the particular source can be certified as sustainable by organizations such as the Rainforest Alliance's "Smart Wood" program or The Tropical Forest Foundation (TFF). In any case the long distances covered in transporting the wood also tip the balance to locally sourced raw materials. Nevertheless, any existing or salvaged window frames made from tropical woods should certainly be reconditioned and upgraded with heat conservation glazing if possible.

Extruded aluminum has been a popular window material in the past because it has a long useful life with minimal maintenance costs. It does, however, require a great deal of energy to produce, and can't be considered an ecologically sound alternative. Besides, aluminum windows are among the worst from an energy conservation standpoint. Even if they are fitted with insulated double pane glass the average aluminum window has a u-value of about 0.60 and therefore does not meet minimum requirements for NFRC certification. Alternatively, there are aluminum-clad wood windows which combine the low maintenance of aluminum with the thermal insulating and esthetic advantages of wood. Plastic windows are predominantly made of extruded PVC and to a lesser degree polyolefins and polyurethane. They are typically reinforced with aluminum or steel sections placed in the hollow chambers to overcome the high expansion and contraction properties of plastic as well as its tendency to deform under high temperature conditions. PVC and polyolefins have a comparable insulating value to that of wood. Polyurethane is the most effective with an insulating value three times better than that of wood.

Both PVC and PU involve manufacturing processes which have severe environmental impact, however. In

order to extrude PVC window profiles heavy metals such as cadmium, tin and lead are used as heat stabilizers. Although PVC windows will not burn when exposed to flames, they give off highly toxic smoke containing dioxins. Some of the larger PVC window manufacturers do offer recycling opportunities for old PVC windows, but at most only half of the returned plastic finds its way into new products. In the United States the problem of how to deal with used PVC remains a waste management problem for local solid waste authorities.

The joint between the window sash or frame profile and the glass must be absolutely weathertight and the traditional linseed oil glazing putty adequate for this purpose. In manufacturing sealed insulated glass units, mostly polybutylene and silicon sealants are used. The joint between the glass is typically sealed with either liquid silicone or extruded EPDM or flexible plastic gaskets or glazing beads. While silicon and extruded gaskets made of silicon-rubber or neoprene stem from an environmentally damaging production process, sealants based on ethylene-propylene-polymer rubber are an environmentally friendly alternative. Often not enough attention has been paid to the gap between the window frame itself and the wall which is susceptible to movement of the building structure. But proper sealing here is crucial to minimize air leakage and keep the building free from drafts.

Plastic windows

Modern extruded PVC windows are available in a vast range of designs including imitations of old-style windows. Nevertheless, for ecological and health reasons they are not the best choice.

Window types

The oldest window is the casement which was first used in medieval times and consists of a frame with one or more sash which pivot on a vertical axis or "casement" inward or outward. A derivation of the casement window is the awning window which pivots on a horizontal axis. These windows were popular in Great Britain and in the United States during the 1950s and 1960s and are still used today; they usually open outward. When they open inward they pivot at the bottom and are called "hopper" windows. These are not very popular because during a rain shower water can come in and they are also more difficult to seal.

The advantage of casements and awnings which open outward is that when winds press against the window the window is sealed even more tightly against the weather-strip reducing the potential for air and water leakage. However, the open window can be damaged in high winds, so typically some kind of securing mechanism is necessary. Still another type of window which was recently introduced in the United States is the "tilt-turn" window which can pivot either vertically like a casement or horizontally similar to a hopper window. Both operations are performed with a single lever handle. This window also has a vent position where the window is pivoted in just slightly to allow ventilation. These windows are typically more expensive because of the complicated hardware mechanism, but they are very weathertight.

The most popular window in the United States since colonial times has been the double hung window. This type of window has two sash which operate independently by sliding up and down in a grooved frame called jamb. Thus ventilation can be provided both at the top and at the bottom of the opening. The window is secured in a closed position by one or more latches but is difficult to seal against air and water leakage and also more subject to forced entry by burglars. A close relative of the double hung window is the single hung window in which the top sash is stationary and only the lower sash operates.

Dual sash or layered windows consist of two individual sash which are installed directly behind one another and fastened together by a latch. These windows are only separated if they need to be cleaned. Box windows, on the other hand, consist of two separate window units whose frames are connected by means of a 6-inch wide extension jamb. Both casements are designed to open separately – one inward and the other out. These types of windows can be combined with energy-efficient glazings and offer better heat insulation and certainly better soundproofing than ordinary windows.

Divided-lite windows where the sash consists of numerous panes of glass divided by muntin bars, are important stylistic features of many older buildings. Unfortunately, true divided-lite (TDL) windows are difficult to seal and if they are constructed with insulated glass the muntins must typically be wider than required for single pane glass resulting in less daylight. They are also very expensive. There are, however, "simulated" divided-lite (SDL) windows where artificial muntin bars are attached in various ways to the outer pane and in some cases to the inner pane as well.

It can be worthwhile to update old wooden windows by replacing the existing single glazed panes with insulating glass having a low-emissivity coating. When considering this option one must be certain that the sash profile and the window hardware are strong enough to carry the extra weight. If the existing window is too weak or you would prefer to keep the true divided-lite (TDL) construction, it can, in some cases, be left as a single pane TDL sash and turned into a layered window with energy-efficient glass added on the interior side. Cellar windows, which do not necessarily have to be transparent, can be fitted with light-transmissive acrylic-foam panels and are as effective as insulating glass.

User-friendly and bright
Box windows provide excellent soundproofing. Although recessed deeply into the wall they can still provide lots of light. They are also quite easy to use.

Skylights

Since the boom in loft conversions skylights or roof windows built into the sloping roof of a building have replaced dormer windows. They come either as awning style hinged windows which open outward or center-pivot windows where the sash pivots at the center of the frame opening inward and outward at the same time. They typically offer the same degree of heat insulation as normal windows and are available with the same range of glazing options and with wood, plastic-clad or metal-clad wood or extruded aluminum which is the least desirable from an energy and environmental standpoint. As they follow the line of the sloping roofs, skylights must be able to withstand significant structural loads, for example, from high winds, hail, and accumulating snow.

But they must also meet more demanding requirements in the summer because of the greater amount of incident solar radiation. Hence manufacturers of high quality skylights have introduced a variety of spe-

cial heat-reflective shades and blinds. Most of them feature some form of reflective metal lining or coating – similar to that in low-emissivity glass. The most effective of these is a rolling shade located on the external side of the window – which reflects much of the infrared energy before it strikes the window. There is also a new film called "Cloudgel™" which can be added to skylight glazing and which becomes more opaque to light when a certain temperature is reached. Other less effective options include blinds and shades with reflective properties located to the inside of the glass. Skylights provide lofts with more light than conventional attic windows and the total skylight area should, as a rule, equal at least one-eighth or more of the usable floor area of the room.

To improve air circulation in the converted attic space, it is advisable to install two or more smaller windows on opposing sides of the roof rather than using one large single window.

Roof balcony

This innovative dual-sash skylight can be folded out into a roof balcony (top left). This particular design can only be built into sloping roofs where the bottom of the skylight is aligned with the floor level of the attic (i.e., without a knee-wall).

Roof windows

In line with the current trend toward attic conversions, the traditional dormer windows of the past have given way to modern skylights and roof windows (above). They require special protection against wind and snow, however.

Beautiful craftsmanship

These beautiful historical box windows are worth retaining the old craftsmanship and updating the sash with new insulated low-e glazing.

Privacy and protection from the sun

If curtains are not quite your style, then window shutters, roller blinds and folding shutters are all options which offer the same functions. In the summer they also offer protection from unwanted sunlight – especially important for south-facing buildings to prevent overheating. Specially insulated roller blinds or shutters also enable night-time heat insulation while retaining the benefit of sunlight during the day.

Heat loss around the perimeter of windows can be avoided

Installation

The preferred window installation method from an environmental standpoint is the use of shims to level and plumb the window in the opening and screws or installation clips for securing the window directly to the surrounding wall material. These allow for better alignment, and if necessary in the future, easier removal for replacement purposes. The gaps between the frame and the exterior wall can then be filled with insulation such as batts made of cotton, hemp or flax and then filled with an elastic, cork-based filler which swells up to seal the gaps. Where the walls have been insulated with exterior insulation board, it is advisable to install the window flush with the insulation material. If necessary for the application of the external siding, exterior extension jambs or casings can be added. Insulation material must also be installed beneath the exterior side of the window sill to prevent air leakage at this point. A good strategy for installing "superwindows," which do not have polyurethane fill in the frame profile, is to allow the exterior insulation material to overlap the window frame itself, effectively blocking heat loss at this weak point. Another serious source of heat loss in skylights is around the perimeter of the exterior glass bead or retainer against which little can be done. This is the greatest cause of excessive condensation on the interior of the skylight glazing which is often mistake for water leakage.

Window hardware

Window hardware and trim are available in an assortment of styles ranging from contemporary to traditional. After the window has passed its prime and is taken out of service, the trim and hardware are often still in good condition and can be given a new lease on life. When it comes to security against break-ins, it is best to choose from a range of lockable handles, or multiple-point locking mechanisms which usually feature sliding button shaped protrusions which securely lock the sash and frame while at the same time drawing them more tightly together. A good option are lever handles made of steel or aluminum. Traditional handles made from brass or nickel silver, alloys of copper, zinc and nickel may be a problem for those with allergic sensitivities. From an environmental and durability standpoint, plastic hardware options, primarily made of nylon, polycarbonate or ABS, is not recommended.

Window shutters, blinds and awnings

There are a number of possibilities open to anyone just wanting a "quick fix" solution to preventing heat loss or alternatively heat gain through windows: folding shutters, venetian blinds or rolling shutters for the outside; roller blinds, venetian blinds, thermal shades and curtains for the inside. Curtains are only useful if the material is thick enough, an overhead valance is pro-

vided and they do not extend beyond the plane of the radiators or air supply registers. The distance to the pane must be no more than 4 inches. Less than this will allow a convective loop to defeat the added insulating value of the curtain. Roller blinds and venetian blinds should seal off as much space around the window as possible and there are a range of specially insulated varieties available. Another option is to apply heat reflective or low-e films directly onto the window pane or to fit roller shades between the panes.

The amount of heat saved (or excluded) by these measures depends on the quality of the window itself as well as the specific thermal and optical properties of the material used. When using the above-mentioned methods with insulated windows, the following reduction in heat loss in winter can be expected:

- Curtains   4–8%
- Roller blinds between the glass panes   10–30%
- External venetian blind   4–8%
- Wooden roller blind   20–40%
- Folding shutters   25–50%

Roller blinds on the outside of windows are more commonly used in Europe than in the US. Most of these products have drawbacks which offset the potential energy saved. Only recently a new type of roller blind has been developed which offers excellent soundproofing and heat conservation properties.

They are made from light or porous concrete which offer a load-bearing function or made of lightweight panels of hardwood or wood wool in non-load-bearing version. They are, however, covered with questionable insulating materials such as polystyrene and mineral wool. During the summer the insulating properties of roller blinds or folding shutters become less important than the need for good sun-screening. The following list shows by approximately how much each type of barrier can reduce solar heat gain:

- Indoor venetian blind   40–60%
- Roller blinds, reflective   45–65%
- Roller blind between panes, reflective   50–70%
- Window pane film   40–75%
- External venetian blind   70–80%
- Roller blinds   50–70%
- Folding shutters   60–80%
- Awning   45–65%

Balconies, overhangs, attached porches and verandahs, etc. can offer as much shade as roller blinds or folding shutters but because they are permanently fixed they do not allow for much flexibility.

Another advantage of roller blinds and folding shutters is that they can also help to soundproof and burglar-proof the home. Heavier wooden roller blinds can be operated by means of motorized operators or automatic electronic controls.

Protection from the sun is best achieved outside the window

As a protective measure against solar heat gain, roller blinds and awnings on the outside of the window offer the best protection. Reflective coatings can be added which increase their efficiency. Venetian blinds allow better control the amount of light coming in. Optional electronic controls offer the ability to automatically open and close blinds based on desired shading and inclement weather conditions.

Gates

While in the past it was only the land holding aristocrats who could boast a gate at the entrance of their estate, it seems that many more property owners today seek to seal off their plots with such a device. Modern entry gates can be composed from a wide variety of materials, mainly steel, aluminum or tropical woods and are typically surrounded by a metal frame. Such a gate is very costly, in energy terms, to produce. However, if you are determined to have a gate, although they really are more symbolic than useful, it is better to use locally harvested wood; this way you can ensure that the energy consumption of a long distance transport will not be added to the relatively high primary energy content.

Garage doors are usually steel and are either configured as a single pivoting panel, or rolling sectional panels, the latter bearing similarities to a roller blind construction. As garages are increasingly attached to homes or are used as occasionally heated storage or hobby rooms, it may be a good idea to consider insulating this door, at little extra cost.

Front doors

Front doors have to be able to endure wet weather, frost and heat. They should resist heat loss and noise transmission, keep burglars at bay and yet have an inviting and welcoming look. As many customers do not believe that traditional doors can satisfy all these criteria, hardware stores have embraced metal and composite plastic doors which are filled with undesirable foam-insulating materials. These doors should be avoided on ecological grounds. The preferred option is a solid wood doors of which there are still many options from which to choose.

There is a significant difference, however, between a solid wood door and one with a solid wood frame enclosing panels of wood, glass or other materials. A solid wood door made from, for example, three to five layers of cross-banded (alternating grain direction) laminated wood plies is certainly stable, and can provide reasonably good thermal insulating properties (0.25–0.46 u-value depending on thickness), and soundproofing (STC 29–32 depending on thickness). If you take two solid wooden planks and stick a thick board made of cork or hardwood inside then you can improve thermal insulation and soundproofing by about 33%. If the door is to have a glass panel for light then either insulated glass or an double-pane acrylic glazing – to prevent too much heat escaping – would be the best bet. A solid door is stable on its own and does not actually require a frame, however, in the interests of increased security against break-ins, it can be further strengthened by means of a steel band. Panel doors are not quite as sturdy, but then they are often not as expensive as solid doors. The strength depends on the quality and wood species used.

DOORS

Outside looking in

Front doors can be inviting or imposing: These multi-paned windows give onlookers a full view to the inside – something most people would only desire in a door to the back garden.

According to an old Danish proverb, doors have by far the toughest job in the house. Not only do they have to shield the entrance from drafts and cold, they must also be able to fend off any unwelcome visitors while presenting a warm and inviting face to prospective guests. Doors must, therefore, provide the residents with a sense of security – and the most ecologically sound option is a solid wood door.

In lieu of solid wood, very often particleboard or fiberboard panels are used as a core material with a wood veneer overlay. Panel doors do not appear as substantial as their solid wood counterparts but certainly allow for more creativity in the profiles used as well as the number and configuration of panels. The infill panels can "move" in this kind of construction and usually will not warp or buckle.

In principle, tropical hardwood is far superior in meeting a front door's demanding requirements but at the moment it is difficult to obtain these woods from forests managed according to sustainable principles.

There are many temperate woods which can be obtained from local sources which are suitable for a front door, particularly, oak and, to a lesser extent, larch, fir and pine. It is important to determine whether the door in question has been treated with chemical preservatives. Such chemicals typically pose a significant health risk and should be avoided. Alternatively, doors treated with borax compounds are less of a problem but they are rarely used because they can be washed out easily. Wood protection is in most cases unnecessary if the front door is protected against bad weather by a porch or a wide overhang.

Variety

Beautiful, handcrafted front doors come in an endless variety of forms and can greatly influence the style of the house. Doors made of solid wood can withstand harsh weather as well as provide resistance against the intrusion of uninvited guests.

Safe and secure

Thick steel deadbolts, sturdy escutcheons and smooth hard surfaces can help to keep a burglar at bay – and add to the occupants' feeling of security.

Something to suit every taste

Inside doors made of wood are preferable because they are beneficial to indoor climate and create a warm and pleasant atmosphere. An endless variety of raised panel doors consisting of individual panels set in a wood surround of stiles and rails are available. In addition, flush veneer-core doors can be an ecologically sound choice, although they are not as durable.

Security of front doors

Roughly half of all break-ins occur through the front door of houses and apartments. The classic method: Screw off the cover and open the lock with a pipe wrench. The cover, therefore, should be screwed on from the inside and should be as smooth and as flush as possible to the escutcheon plate in order to make it difficult to get a good grasp with any type of tool.

The cylinder lock should be fully recessed behind the escutcheon because if it sticks out it can be easily grasped with a tool and screwed or twisted off. Although it still may be possible to remove the lock with special tools, this can be prevented by buying a special cover to fit over the lock.

Double cylinder locks where a key is required to open the door either from the outside or inside are also available so that even if a burglar gains entry elsewhere they will be unable to exit with your belongings through the door. This practice is not allowed in some locations because of the possible entrapment of occupants in a fire or emergency situation and should be considered carefully if there are small children in the house. in addition to the standard lockset, a second steel deadbolt latch is often used to better secure the door to the frame and surrounding wall and to ensure that the door cannot be levered out of the frame. In this case however the burglar will normally try to circumvent the hinge connections of the door so a deadbolt is only added security if special security hinges are provided as well.

A refinement of a standard deadbolt includes hook bolts which swing into place in the associated strike plate offering greater protection against removal by circumventing the hinges and levering the door out that side. There are also multi-point locks which usually have two or three deadbolts or hookbolts along the lock stile or bolts which go up into the head and down into the sill of the door frame. Finally, the ultimate security devices for doors include a rather hefty armor bar, which stretches across the width of the door, or a diagonal steel bar which engages a steel plate on the inside face of the door and a similar plate mounted in the floor. This latter device is especially popular in urban apartment buildings where break-ins are a regular occurrence. The door itself should always be as sturdy as possible or the locks will be useless.

Interior doors

Although steel doors are considered very durable, wood interior doors are preferable both for a better indoor climate and because they are more economical and resource efficient. Stability is not such a key factor here and raised panel doors are the best alternative. The panels are not necessarily made of solid wood – even if that were the best option. For instance, veneered wood fiber core panels are adequate and may be more resource efficient; however, be certain that they do not contain formaldehyde or isocyanates.

Dividing and bringing together

Generous French doors like these add flexibility to interior room layouts. When closed, they create smaller self-contained spaces. When open, two rooms can become one.

Hollow core wood doors are flush doors with a core made of finger-jointed softwood edgebanding and an inner stiffener consisting of corrugated cardboard and a crossbanded plywood veneer overlay on both sides. They are very economical to produce but not very durable. Less advisable are the solid core flush doors with a particle board core. As always, it is necessary to ensure that they do not contain urea formaldehyde adhesives or binders. The protective finish of interior doors can be limited to waxes, vegetable oils or a coat of natural paint.

Special doors, such as fire doors, are made of either steel or wood lined with steel and are filled with non-flammable insulation material, usually mineral fibers. Older fire doors usually contain asbestos, which can be released if there is any corrosion. Fire doors are only effective when they are closed and must therefore be installed with an automatic closing mechanism.

Stylish handles

These door handles crafted by a carpenter in Oetzen, Germany are made of fine woods such as olive and plumwood, oak, hornbeam and robinia. The surfaces have been finished with a vegetable oil.

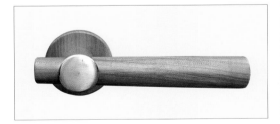
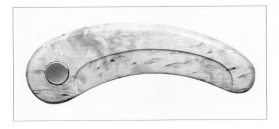

INTERIOR DESIGN

INTERIOR DESIGN

While the structural aspects of house building are mostly left to construction firms, many people who have houses built decide to do the interior decorating themselves. One reason is most certainly to save the costs that professional interior decorators would add to the initial expense of construction and materials. In addition, most people feel fairly confident when it comes to choosing paint, wallpaper or floor coverings for their home. Manufacturers have responded by offering a large range of ready-to-use products, though their quality and environmental friendliness often leave much to be desired.

Floor coverings

A large majority of floors in living areas are covered with carpets. Among the other common floor coverings, synthetic materials are still dominant, particularly PVC, but their popularity is declining all the time. Over the last few years, there has been a constant upward trend in the use of hardwood floors. This is partly the result of the development of parquet flooring, which allows wooden floors to be laid more easily and cheaply especially by the do-it-yourself homeowner. Linoleum has also seen a steady comeback in recent years after having fallen completely out of fashion for a while. Ceramic tile has always had its place in the bathroom and kitchen, but are also coming to be used more frequently in living areas along with quarry tile. This trend may be linked to the increasing installation of underfloor heating systems.

Mineral floor coverings

Ceramic tiles have, of course, been used as floor covering since ancient times. They have the advantage of retaining heat during the winter and staying cool in summer. In the fifteenth century Italian Faience mosaic tiles, Spanish majolica, and Delft tiles from the Netherlands became desirable

decorative items for major buildings. In the eighteenth and nineteenth centuries it became fashionable to use them to decorate walls and roofs, especially in Spain and France. Only at the end of the nineteenth century were tiles first mass produced on an industrial scale.

Tiles are made of clay mixed with kaolin, quartz, chalk and feldspar, pressed in a mold (dust-pressed process) or extruded (plastic process) and then fired at high temperatures. The end product is either harder or more porous, depending on the proportions of the ingredients in the mix and the temperature at which it is fired. Porcelain as well as stoneware tiles are suitable for all floors inside and out, including bathrooms. They have white or colored biscuit and are fired at temperatures of around 2,192° F (1,200° C). Some stoneware tiles are unglazed, others are glazed during the firing procedure. Because they are watertight, they are frost-resistant even when unglazed. Stoneware tiles make up the majority of the market. A considerable proportion of stoneware tiles are made in large plates which are wire cut and fired at over 2,192° F (1,200° C), then split up into individual tiles after firing. They are particularly well suited as floor coverings for patios, balconies and other areas subject to heavy wear.

By contrast, whiteware or porcelain tiles are fired at lower temperatures of about 1,832° F (1,000° C). They have pure white biscuit and finer pores, are more porous and can absorb water. Whiteware tiles are always glazed, mostly in a second firing, and are used in bathrooms, usually as wall coverings. They are also laid on floors in living areas, but are not frost-resistant and are, therefore, completely unsuitable for use outdoors.

Tiles are glazed with a mixture of quartz and other perfectly safe minerals. However, a variety of metal pigments are added to produce many shades, and the toxic metal lead, which is used occasionally, is supposed to give tiles a particularly shiny finish. As long as it is bound in the glaze no health problems

Ancient wall decoration
Tiles were also used for decorating walls, as this mosaic in Seville, Spain shows.

Historic tiles
Tiles have been favorite floor coverings for thousands of years, particularly in sunny southern Europe. They can also be esthetically appealing, as is beautifully demonstrated by this building in Seville, Spain.

Secondhand tiles

Terracotta tiles can now be purchased secondhand from building salvage companies and architectural antique dealers. Secondhand tiles give a room a very special ambience. The vivid patina gives each tile an individual appearance.

Warm red tones

Terracotta floors (top right) are manufactured in a relatively low-energy process and have beneficial effects on the climate of the room. Their natural, individual character gives this apartment a unique atmosphere.

The ecological building materials trade recommends terracotta for living areas

will arise, but it becomes dangerous if the glaze is damaged and poisonous lead dust inhaled. Ceramics of this type are therefore not suitable as floor coverings.

In the early 1980s there was a lot of controversy about ceramic tiles because some were contaminated with radioactivity. The clay was sometimes mixed with radioactive red mud, a waste product from aluminum production, while uranium was used in the manufacture of red, yellow and brown tones in glazes. Tiles of this kind are no longer made.

Stoneware tiles are divided into four groups according to their durability, as expressed by the abrasion resistance of the glaze. Tiles which belong to the least resilient Group I are generally only adequate for bathrooms, as long as no one walks on them in outdoor shoes. Otherwise, they are not at all suitable as floor coverings.

The ecological building materials trade recommends coarse ceramic terracotta or quarry tiles for high traffic living areas in particular. They consist of pure clay, are fired in a less energy intensive process at temperatures of around 1,652° F (900° C), and can be treated with silicon, though it is better to

use natural waxes and oils. Terracotta is an open-pored natural material that promotes a balanced microclimate within a room. It is manufactured in Europe, mainly in Tuscany, and its typical red color is due to the high iron content of the clay pits there. Handmade terracotta tiles are also produced in various colors in France and Spain. Terracotta is less well suited for bathrooms because urine or shower gel can quickly cause unpleasant stains.

Natural stone floor coverings are another good alternative. Marble and granite are particularly appropriate in the bathroom. Thanks to their classic appearance they will not go out of fashion as quickly as tiles, and are more stable and less slippery. They are indestructible in living areas, and are particularly suitable for areas exposed to plenty of wear and tear near entrances, and on corridors and staircases. However, they are considerably more expensive than ceramic tile, even though they contain little primary energy. Often, however, they are imported from distant countries because of an unusual or particularly appealing coloration or pattern. This practice mitigates severely their ecological advantages.

Synthetic floor coverings

Warm on the feet

Cork floors are pleasantly warm for the feet and very good sound insulators as well. This natural material is also very hard-wearing and durable making cork floors ideal for children's rooms.

Nearly half of all uncarpeted floors are finished with PVC resilient floor coverings either in sheet or tile form. Apart from the well-known problems caused by their manufacture and disposal, PVC floor coverings can release significant quantities of plasticizers which are predominantly estrogenic compounds believed to cause damage to endocrine system development in fetuses and children. In addition, the phthalates such as DEHP and DBP (dibutyl phthalate) are known respiratory irritants and allergens. It is still not clear, though, whether PVC floors also give off the plasticizer chlorinated paraffin, which damages the liver and is a suspected carcinogen. If PVC is burned poisonous dioxins may be released, causing toxic smoke and dangerous contamination of the whole building.

By comparison with ceramics, or even wood, PVC is not very durable. In many buildings there are still floors installed prior to 1982 of vinyl asbestos tile.

PVC is out, linoleum's in

Dangerous asbestos fibers can be released when these floor coverings are removed, and, therefore, only asbestos remediation firms should be retained for its removal. Rubber floors are a less worrying alternative. For the most part they consist of synthetic rubber, styrene-butadiene rubber (SBR). Natural rubber, which has between 3 and 50% synthetic materials added to it to improve its performance, is also used, but somewhat less often.

The seemingly indestructible industrial looking "studded" floors produced by a large Italian tire company have proved their worth in many commercial and public buildings. However, they cannot be recommended unreservedly if they contain high levels of SBR. Toxic nitrosamines are released during the production of SBR and, in addition, the material cannot be recycled. Furthermore, SBR sometimes gives off vinylcyclohexene, which is converted by the human body into a substance suspected of causing cancer.

Floor coverings made of a polyolefin, specifically a mixture of polyethylene and polypropylene, are relative newcomers to the market. According to information provided by the manufacturers, they contain no flame retardants or plasticizers. Thermoplastics produced on an industrial scale can be recycled, but not without degrading the material and altering its properties. If necessary, they should be limited to suitable applications such as areas that frequently get wet.

Cork and linoleum

Natural cork is molded into floor tiles under pressure and heat with the addition of synthetic or natural resins. Their attractiveness, durability, and noise and heat insulating properties make cork tiles popular floor coverings. However, the surface is often coated with waxes, lacquers and in some cases PVC. Some cork tiles are coated on both sides and have characteristics comparable to those of plastic floor coverings. These coatings and the adhesives used in laying cork tiles often contain so many harmful materials that they may cause chemically sensitive people to develop allergic reactions, nervous or respiratory problems. Sealants are particularly unnecessary when cork tiles are laid because any moisture will penetrate the joints between the tiles and cause them to swell up. It is possible to obtain uncoated cork tiles, which are then treated only with natural oils and waxes after laying in order to seal the surface.

After its heyday in the 1940s and 1950s, linoleum fell almost completely out of use, but it has enjoyed a successful comeback in the last few years. This classic floor covering is an almost completely pure natural material consisting of cork and wood flour, which are combined with a mixture of linseed oil and colophony (known as linoleum cement), pigments and chalk filler on a fabric backing made of jute. Linoleum comes in many colors and marbled patterns, and can also meet modern, highly expressive esthetic design requirements with a range of colorful mosaic-like patterns. However, the fuse wire that joins the pieces of these "patchworks" is made of PVC. Nevertheless, linoleum is robust, warm to the feet, absorbs noise, and complements underfloor heating systems. Since its electrostatic charge is low, it does not affect computers, so it is now being used in many offices. This covering is also suited to all domestic areas except the bathroom because it is not compatible with constantly wet conditions. A fresh linoleum floor gives off aldehydes as the linseed oil oxidizes. Aldehydes not only smell bad; they also irritate the mucous membranes and apparantly can have narcotic effects. The reason this problem is so severe is that the linoleum manufacturers have cut down their production times, and the material is no longer stored long enough in dry conditions before being sold to allow the off-gassing of these compounds. As protection against unpleasant odors, the producers cover the linoleum with a layer of polyacrylate, or sometimes PVC. This layer is also intended to prevent dust being trodden into the porous material during building work. It may reduce the odor, but it also seals the material and reduces its porosity. For this reason it is far better to ask for unsealed linoleum or scrub off the coating with an alcohol-based cleaner. After this the linoleum needs approximately three weeks in a well ventilated room to air fully.

Ideal for public buildings

Floors made of rubber are durable and easy to care for. Their understated appearance is ideal for public places, such as schools and hospitals.

No longer uncool

Linoleum is currently going through a renaissance in homes and offices. This natural floor covering made of cork, linseed oil and jute is again being sold in many modern colors and marbled patterns to suit every taste. It is warm for the feet, robust and, unlike synthetic floors, does not build up electrostatic charges. This makes linoleum a suitable floor covering for offices because it does not adversely affect computers.

Wooden floor coverings

Wood floors combine many advantages

Wooden floor coverings are enjoying increased popularity. They are warm to the feet, pleasant to the touch, are more resilient than stone or tile floors and therefore better for backs. They also have a positive influence on the room micro-climate, and do they not build up electrostatic charges. As a renewable raw material, wood offers a great variety of grain patterns, textures and natural colors, which provide ample flexibility for the designer. In particular, floors made of hardwoods are quite durable and long-lasting and can be refurbished by sanding and then refinishing.

One particularly hard-wearing type of wood floor, which is often used for industrial floors, is fabricated industrial wood block. Blocks of end-cut southern yellow pine, gum, douglas fir, larch, oak or beech usually from two to four inches thick. They are laid in asphalt mastic (bitumen) or synthetic resin adhesives. and are typically grouted with bituminous filler. The blocks are provided with metal or wood splines and assembled into strips of up to eight feet in length. After installation, the floor is sanded and usually waxed and polished; however, they can be left natural. Because of the tendency of this type of floor to expand and contract with changes in humidity, a one inch expansion space should be provided all around, at walls, columns, thresholds and other permanent fixtures. One drawback of industrial

wood block flooring is that the solvents in the synthetic resins or hydrocarbons in the bitumen may off-gas and contaminate the surrounding air. Because of this, you should choose your grouting with care.

Other types of wood flooring include strip flooring, plank flooring and parquet flooring. Previously, only long, wide floorboards and short, narrow parquet pieces were available, both of which were difficult for amateurs to work with. Today there are shorter laminated sections and pre-assembled parquet components provided with tongue-and-groove joints and in a large selection of solid woods which can be laid by the moderately skilled amateur. Plank flooring is typically 22 mm thick and three to eight inches wide in regular or random widths (colonial flooring) which means it can be refinished many times and last for over a hundred years. These flooring materials are laid either on sleepers 12 inches apart or more commonly on an underlayment of fiberboard. In cases where the floor is laid over a concrete slab on grade, it is necessary to install a vapor barrier to prevent moisture from rising into the wood flooring. The boards are either fixed with adhesives (not recommended because of VOC emissions), screwed down, or fastened with concealed nails driven through the tongue with a special floor nailing tool. The surface is sanded, sometimes several times, and either sealed and varnished or, preferably, treated with oils and waxes. In certain circumstances it makes sense to use hot wax on floors subject to particularly heavy wear. A dust mask should be worn during sanding as protection against potentially carcinogenic dust, particularly from beech and oak.

Because this involves lots of work, floor manufacturers have come up with a time saving version of parquet tile: Industrially manufactured prefinished square or rectangular tiles which are provided with a tongue-and-groove and topped with a thin laminate of wood veneer providing the parquet pattern. The parquet tiles are factory finished and can be used immediately after laying. Most parquet tiles consists of several layers,

Popular parquet paneling
Because it is easy to lay and care for, and gives a pleasant atmosphere to living areas, parquet paneling is enjoying increasing popularity. However, the adhesives between the layers of wood can give off unhealthy fumes and if the sealing is too thick it can have negative effects on the room climate.

Coping with heavy loads
Wood block is suitable even for industrial uses. Because its upper surface is all end-grain wood, it is extremely durable and scarcely shows wear and tear under the most strenuous abuse.

Fiberboard + plastic = laminate

Laminated floors have unfortunately become popular in recent years. They may look natural, but they are anything but. Superficially similar to parquet paneling, they consist mainly of a transparent plastic surface, through which a photograph of a wood or stone floor can be seen. This is adhered to a low-grade fiberboard substrate. A floor of this kind can quite easily gain an electrostatic charge.

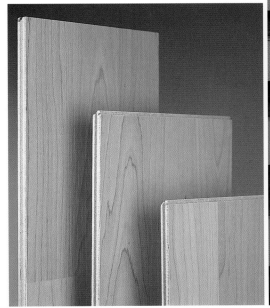

which similar to plywood provides a more stable material which will not warp or cup the way real parquet sometimes does. It is also much easier to lay, and as no sanding is required it does not fill the house with dust, and it is an ideal product for the do-it-yourself enthusiast. Furthermore, parquet tiles are generally less expensive than real parquet flooring.

The main drawback, however, is that the top veneer of solid wood is usually less than 4 mm thick, and can only be sanded two to four times at most, which limits its life span. Parquet tiles must always be fixed with an adhesive, and most conventional ones have solvents that produce hazardous VOC emissions. That is why low-VOC dispersion adhesives are recommended for this purpose. Dispersion adhesives contain only small quantities of solvents, but can release plasticizers over a long period of time, for example, ethylene glycol, which can cause respiratory and eye irritation as well as possible kidney damage. Unfortunately, floor adhesives based on natural resins are suitable only for linoleum and carpets, and not for laying parquet.

Parquet tile is laid on an underlay, usually of fiberboard or chipboard, but occasionally plywood. According to research significant quantities of formaldehyde can off-gas from three-quarters of the underlayment products on the market. It was also found that, in many cases, prefinished parquet developed qualities similar to those of plastic floorings because of the thick layer of finish. The wood also loses its porosity quality, which

has a positive effect on the air in the room, and it can even build up slight electrostatic charges. Fortunately unfinished parquet floor tiles, which can be impregnated with oils and waxes just like real parquet, is also available. A sealed and varnished floor is less sensitive to dirt and easier to clean with a mop or a damp cloth. On the other hand, scratches are easier to repair in an oiled or waxed floor, but care is time-consuming. If you want a smooth, shiny surface. the parquet has to be cleaned and waxed regularly. It can be cleaned with soap and water, but water must never be allowed to stand on it, because this will leave stains. In the past parquet was waxed, not sealed and varnished, and was still very durable. There are 300-year-old intarsia parquet floors in existence that are cleaned thoroughly with soapy water just once a year and are still in fine condition. The fact that floors like this show their age is by no means a disadvantage.

Laminated wood-strip flooring products, similar in construction and installation to the parquet tile products have come onto the market recently. They consist of a low-grade composite board, a length of paper printed with a wood pattern and a thick layer of clear plastic topcoat. Although they are extolled as indestructible, they are very easily damaged by objects with sharp edges and sand. It goes without saying that they cannot be sanded or refurbished in any way so their life-expectancy is on the order of carpet or vinyl flooring.

Proverbially durable

Thick, solid cottage floorboards are extraordinarily durable. They can be sanded down again and again, are resistant to almost anything you can throw at them, and give a room a sense of history, particularly when they have been aged by time.

Carpets

The pleasures of walking barefoot on a cozy carpet have convinced us: In 1990 alone about 1.1 billion square yards (900 million square meters) of broadloom carpet were produced in the United States alone. It is estimated that this represents 46% of the world's total production. Carpets are very good at absorbing noise, they are warm and comfortable to your feet and they are a good non-slip surface for walking. In addition, they reduce stress on joints and are ideal if you have small children. However, they also provide a suitable habitat for dust mites, the scourge of allergy sufferers everywhere.

Elaborate wool patterns

Sheep's wool carpets are produced in many patterns. The trend toward natural lifestyles has increased sales of wool carpets, but they are often treated with moth repellents.

Most carpets are made of synthetic fibers

There has been a great deal of discussion about carpets, and not just because the vast majority of them are composed of man-made fibers. Whereas in the 1950s carpets were mainly made from wool fibers today in the United States about 80% of all carpets are made from nylon fibers, and in 1990 wool represented only one percent of the total production. Other synthetic materials used include polyester, olefin (polyethylene) and recycled PET (terepthalate). Natural fibers used in carpets include sheep's wool, cotton mix weaves, goats wool, coconut and sisal to a lesser extent. In the United States 95% of carpet products are tufted carpets. In this process the pile fibers (yarn) are stitched into a backing made of polypropylene weave, polyester fleece or, occasionally, jute. Other processes used include weaving, carpet-knitting, in-fusion bonding, and custom tufting. Nylon is

derived from benzene a known carcinogen. Apart from the fact that they are derived from petroleum and are very difficult to dispose of, carpets made from synthetic fibers also cause a great deal of static buildup.

Textile floor coverings are also rather controversial, mainly because of their backing. Most carpets have both a primary and secondary backing to prevent loss and fuzzing and to provide dimensional stability, resilience and comfort. The primary backing is usually made of polypropylene and the secondary backing can be an SBR latex laminated to a fabric, jute, or a synthetic foam cushion which may be hazardous to health and to the environment. The foam is usually synthetic rubber (SBR latex), and less often polyurethane or foamed PVC. The contaminants released may include carcinogenic nitrosamines, carbamates, 4-phenylcyclohexene or 4-PC (residual monomers, accelerators and age resistors in SBR latex), allergenic phthalates (plasticizers in PVC), formaldehyde and problematic solvents such as xylene, ethylbenzene or trichloromethane (from the adhesive used to fix the fibers). The generally inexpensive woven fleece carpets, present a special case. For the most part, they are made of an unbacked synthetic-fiber fleece which is bonded by heating or with a synthetic resin.

The trend toward more natural furnishings in the home and a noticeable drop in prices helped sales of sheep's wool to grow strongly in the 1980s.

Rugs of dubious origins

Most hand-knotted rugs are suspected of being produced under exploitative conditions or by child labor. Do not let these magnificent items tempt you unless the manufacturer can prove that they have been produced under acceptable conditions, which of course will also drive up the price.

Carpet backings may release carcinogenic substances

Valuable items

Rugs produced by socially responsible and eco-friendly methods improve the appearance of any room, but more and more traditional and environmentally sustainable natural dyes are being replaced by harmful chemical products in the countries where they are produced.

Unreliable certification schemes

Ecological certification schemes for carpets, such as these, cannot be recommended without reservation because they allow the use of moth repellents.

However, at the same time the public became aware that these carpets were typically treated with the moth repellent, pyrethrin, an insecticide that can cause damage to the central nervous system. Carpets often are required to be treated in order to qualify for the relevant certification labels, such as the Wool Stamp administered by the European Carpet Association.

Individual manufacturers do produce carpets without this controversial moth repellent, partly in response to demand from their customers. In fact, moth repellent in carpets is not really necessary. The German company Donautufting, for example, produces a wool carpet that satisfies even strict ecological testing criteria; they have never had any problems with moths even in the warehouses where they keep their large stock.

Problems can also arise from the various methods used to lay carpets. Although in most private residences carpets are stretched between tack strips at the edges or with carpet tape, problematic adhesives are very often used in public buildings. The preferred method is the environmentally friendly, but more difficult stretching method, though this is only possible with carpets that have fabric backings. Usually carpets are stretched over a separate carpet cushion made of bonded urethane.

A major advantage of the stretching method is that a new carpet can simply be attached to the fastenings already in place. The other advantage, of course, is the absence of any adhesives along with their attendant VOC and chemical emissions.

Natural fiber floor coverings made of flax, coconut and sisal can be hard-wearing alternatives to wool and manmade fibers. They do not require chemical treatment to protect them against insects, which hardly bother them at all. They perform well in all parts of the home, except wet areas, and form a porous surface. However, carpets made of sisal are particularly sensitive to soiling from greasy dirt.

The alternative: coconut and sisal

Carpets made of coconut and sisal may not be as luxurious as wool carpets, but these natural materials are much more durable, and are not contaminated with nor do they emit toxic substances. They are the best alternatives for a healthy atmosphere in the home. The many examples on the opposite page show the large selection of colors and designs available.

Laying floors

To keep contamination down floors should be fastened mechanically

When laying floors of all kinds a mechanical fastening is preferable to adhesives made from synthetic or natural resins. As a rule this makes it easier to repair and replace the floor, and contamination by chemical substances is kept to a minimum. It is recommended that wood floors be nailed or screwed down, carpets stretched between tack strips, and floor tiles laid in a mortar bed. When laying tiles, it is necessary to distinguish between thin-bed mortars and cements, or lime cement mortars, which harden by a process of hydraulic setting, i.e. a chemical reaction.

Tile adhesives, or thin-bed mortars, contain a resin dissolved in water that hardens as the water evaporates. They have mineral ingredients such as chalk, calcite, mica or clay added to them. There are also combinations of the two types of mortar, cement mortars with artificial additives such as synthetic rubber, or epoxy resins and mortars with additives made from natural resins, such as dammar or rubber milk. The adhesives recommended for carpets, linoleum, cork tiles and wood parquet tiles are low-VOC dispersion adhesives with a solvent content well under 5%. These solvents are usually either propylene glycol (less toxic) or ethylene glycol (more toxic) and they are usually considered relatively harmless to human health. Formaldehyde is sometimes used as a preservative in adhesives with a high water content. The most problematic chemicals in these dispersion adhesives are plasticizers made from synthetic resins in the ethylene glycol and glycol ester groups. They evaporate over a long period of time and can irritate the skin and eyes and cause damage to the kidneys and nervous system. Apart from this, most synthetic resins release acrylates, which can have allergenic effects. The most frequently

Floor adhesives contain problematic solvents and plasticizers

used synthetic resin adhesive is polyvinyl acetate (PVA), which can also be manufactured without solvents or plasticizers. Solvent-free dispersions have sufficient adhesive power only for foam-backed carpets. Natural resin-based dispersions are recommended, but can contain up to 10% solvents, mostly turpentine or mineral spirits.

Solvent adhesives containing 20–50% solvents give off aromatic hydrocarbons, such as toluene and xylol, which can cause severe damage to health and to the environment. Much the same is true of reaction adhesives and adhesive mortars containing epoxy resins or polyurethane. They sometimes release epichlorhydrin monomers, which are skin irritants and allergenic, or toxic isocyanates which are absorbed through the skin.

Caring for floors

Waxes made from natural beeswax and carnauba wax are suitable for wood and cork floors. Vegetable oils, mainly linseed oil, and natural solvents such as citrus oil are added to them to improve their performance. Depending on their wax content, they are classified as hard waxes, balsamic waxes or wax solutions. Linoleum is typically cleaned simply with soap and water.

All waxes should be used as sparingly as possible so that they do not leave a greasy layer on the floor. It is important that cloths soaked in linseed oil are hung out to dry, or kept in a sealed metal container. There is a danger of spontaneous combustion if they are left lying around.

Vacuum cleaners are generally suspected of blowing out nearly as much smaller particulate dust as they pick up, which causes distinct problems for allergy

Instinctive problem-solving
Tile-laying requires a good eye and experience, especially if the room is not perfectly rectangular. Tile adhesives look superficially like normal mortar, but hold ceramic tiles firmly to the floor.

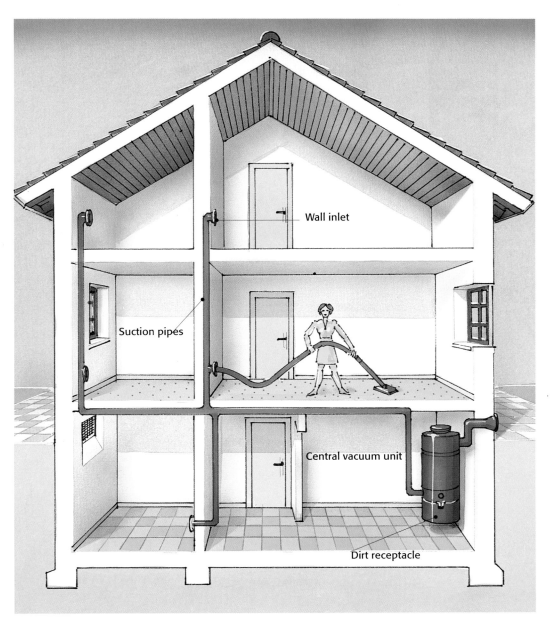

Wall inlet

Suction pipes

Central vacuum unit

Dirt receptacle

Central vacuum systems: healthy and practical

Instead of pushing the vacuum cleaner all around the house blowing fine dust out at the same time as you suck it up, it is worth considering a central vacuum system in a new house. The power unit and dust filter (illustrated below) are located in the basement or a utility room and discharge air to the outside of the house. The filter is cleaned several times in a year. A hose is simply attached to an inlet in each room. The inlets are linked to a high-performance power unit via a system of ducts, as shown in the diagram (left).

sufferers using them. This is why high-quality vacuum cleaners are fitted with hepa-filters which are claimed to retain particles down to an extremely small size. But research showed that these expensive vacuum cleaners, which are particularly targeted at allergy sufferers, have many shortcomings. On the one hand, they do not live up to their promises never to leak fine dust. On the other, their hepa-filters are mostly made of mineral fibers which are suspected carcinogens, which can be blown out into a room in the air-flow.

Another even better alternative is the central vacuum system. This system uses a central power unit and filter which are installed permanently in the house, usually in the garage or basement because of noise. A system of pipes is installed within the walls with inlets in the hallways and larger rooms where a separate nozzle with a long hose can be fitted. This increases the product's service life because the delicate motor and the dust bag do not have to be carried round the whole house, and vacuuming is therefore more comfortable because you only have to carry the hose. The motor is usually much more powerful than a standard portable unit and can therefore clean better. The debris laden air which is sucked in is not passed through a dust bag, but into a cyclone type settling chamber, filtered and vented to the outside. The dust bin can be emptied periodically and the filter can be disposed of or in some cases cleaned and reused. For these reasons a central vacuum system should cause allergy sufferers few problems. Installation of a central vacuum system (costing at least $2,000) is only really worthwhile in an existing structure if extensive building work is being undertaken. In new construction where carpets are to be included, it is a very worthwhile amenity.

WALL COVERINGS

these wall and ceiling finishes. Decorative plasters have to be distinguished from the fine mineral plasters used to create special surface effects with methods such as "skimming," in which the plaster is applied and shaped with a trowel or brush before drying to give a variety of textural effects. Resins are often added to "improve" these products, but unfortunately they actually degrade their physical properties.

Apart from the fine mineral plasters, there are also decorative plasters containing colored minerals, mainly quartz granules and various coarse grades of mica. These minerals are applied onto finished plaster with wallpaper paste made of non-hazardous methylcellulose which is harmless from an environmental and health point of view. These decorative plasters are used mostly in public buildings as robust hard-wearing surface finishes to provide both visual and tactile interest.

Products made of fine marble aggregate, lime, cement and titanium dioxide (whitener) are used to obtain surfaces similar to marble. They are mixed with water and linseed oil, and applied with a trowel. The surface can also be polished with wax to make it waterproof and glossy.

In Europe textile wall plasters are also becoming more widely used. They come originally from Japan, from where most of them are imported. They are normally sprayed onto the wall with compressed air using a spray gun or applied directly with a trowel. They consist primarily of natural fibers, such as cotton in various colors.

Jute and viscose fibers, as well as various mineral substances, are employed to create particular hues or textured effects. Methylcellulose and even potato starch are used as binders. These methods can be used to produce an amazing variety of patterns, colors and surface textures on walls without going to a lot of trouble.

These so-called "fluid wallpapers" or decorative plasters pose no known health problems and are to be recommended for their beneficial effects on the indoor environment within a building. They are sold either as powders to be mixed with water, or ready-mixed by the manufacturer according to the color and texture desired. It is easy to repair small dents or tears by simply filling them in. It is even possible to recycle them: Textile wall coverings can be removed from the wall by spraying it with water and put up again on a wall at a new location with a little fresh paste. There are also less-desirable wall coverings made with polystyrene particles to give textured finishes, and synthetic fibers and resins as binding agents. These fluid wallpapers cause problems during production and disposal, and their emissions of solvents and lack of absorbency can cause air quality problems and do not have positive effects on the climate in a room.

Plaster instead of wallpaper

Decorative mineral-based plasters are increasingly being used as internal wall coverings. Their permeable surfaces are healthier than wallpaper, which is often sealed by application of paint.

The simple, plastered interior wall seems to be making a comeback, whereas the use of wallpaper with multi-colored patterns is on the decline. Historically, patterned wallpapers were first developed in Europe and are descended from devotional pictures and the pictorial tapestries of the middle ages which imitated paintings.

Today, patterned wallpaper is hung mainly in children's rooms, while the rest of the home is primarily painted in subdued mono-colors. This "wave of white" has brought with it several new innovations: colored borders added to walls with home-made stencils and "faux-finishing" techniques imitating the look of marbles, or other rich materials.

Decorative plasters

Plasters made from minerals, cotton, and linseed oil

From here it is only a short step to reducing the use of wallpaper altogether in favor of plaster, and sales of decorative plasters are indeed rising. It is possible to create individual wall designs with

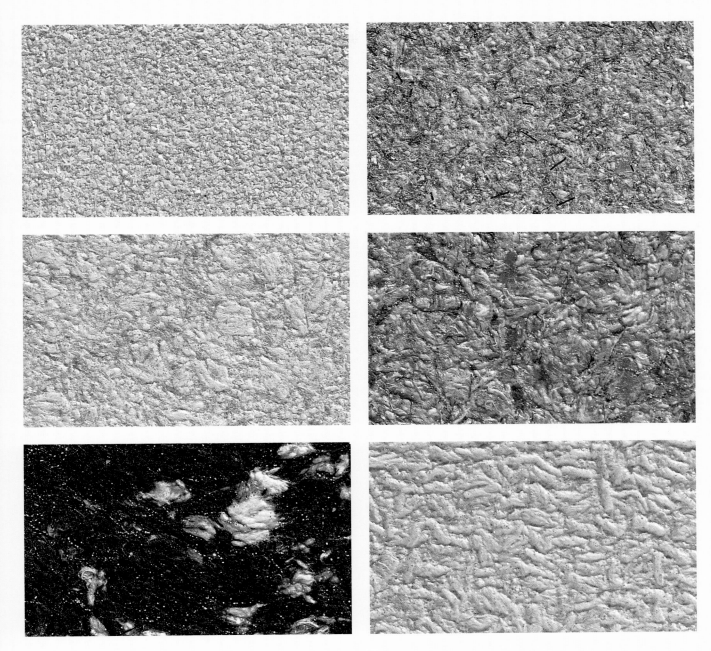

Textile wall covering

This cotton-based textile covering is simply sprayed onto the wall. A variety of pigments and the addition of mica and similar substances are used to good effect to give these "fluid wallpapers" highly individual surface finishes with soft and natural transitions. This ecologically friendly wall decoration can even be recycled.

Amazing effects

These mineral decorative plasters display not only the most amazing color effects – they are also interesting to touch. They consist mainly of various coarse grades of mica or quartz sands, and are applied with wallpaper paste which is completely harmless to one's health. In addition, they are very durable.

Stenciling instead of wallpaper

Artist: Henrike Müller, Gut Horbell, Cologne, Germany

If you do not like plaster or wallpaper, you can decorate walls without resorting to patterned wallpapers by using stencils.

Paper wall coverings

Thanks to their absorbency, wall coverings made of paper and cellulose or textiles can help balance the humidity of a room. Paper wall coverings are now mostly made from recycled paper. Paper-based wall coverings consist of cellulose, wood pulp, additives, fillers, pigments used to color the base paper, and printing inks. Sometimes they are passed through embossing rollers to give them a textured finish. Formaldehyde used to be added to improve their resistance to tearing when wet, but this is no longer the practice. However, it is not possible to rule out contamination with heavy metals in printing inks. These wallpapers do not present a health hazard, but there can be problems with their disposal. In addition, significant solvent residues in heavily printed papers and specialty papers with high proportions of synthetic fibers may affect the air quality in a room. There is really no need for fungicides to be added, and people should be discouraged from buying papers treated this way.

Textile wall coverings consist of natural or synthetic fibers bonded onto a paper base. Synthetic resin adhesives may be used in this process and reduce absorbency. Recommended natural fiber products include cotton, jute, linen, sisal, silk, and even grasses.

Wool is also available, but is usually impregnated with moth repellents. Static electricity can build up in synthetic fibers.

Glass fiber wallpapers are seldom used in North America but are increasingly popular in Europe. They are fireproof and offer interesting textures, for example wishbone patterns, which means they are of particular interest in public areas, such as hotels or offices. However, when they are hung they can release mineral fibers which can cause skin irritations. Apart from this, synthetic resin is used to bind the fibers onto the paper base in most of these wallpapers and is bad for indoor air quality.

Plastic wallpapers should be rejected on principle. Recently, textured wallpapers made of plastics have become particularly popular. Commonly known as vinyl wallpapers, they are usually made from environmentally damaging PVC. Thermal insulation wall coverings with polystyrene or polyurethane coatings are now also available. The plastics reduce the diffusion properties of the wall and can lead to condensation. For this reason these wallpapers are almost always given a fungicidal coating to prevent mold growth. PVC can also emit plasticizers (allergenic phthalates and chlorinated paraffin, which

Glass fiber wallpapers are bad for indoor air quality

Plastic wallpapers emit hazardous substances

may cause liver damage), and gives off extremely toxic dioxins in a fire. Plastic wallpapers specially intended to clean room air have come onto the market in recent years. They are coated with activated carbon and are intended to prevent poisonous substances such as PCB or PCP being released from heavily contaminated (wooden) walls into internal rooms. The activated carbon in these products is, therefore, used as a sink which is supposed to collect the contaminants. Apart from the fact that the use of these wall coverings involves a conscious decision to reduce the wall's diffusion capability, these temporary pollutant depots also cause problems when they are replaced and disposed of. We do not know how long these wallpapers will retain their absorbency. Thorough cleaning to remove the causes of the contamination would be a better solution.

Wallpaper paste consists mostly of methylcellulose, which poses no health dangers, but derives from the chlorine industry and is therefore rejected by many manufacturers of natural products. They use pastes made of starches which are not quite so easy to use, primarily because it takes longer for the starch to have an adhesive effect. For particularly heavy wallpapers there are special pastes with dispersion adhesives based on polyvinyl acetate, acrylate, polyurethane or natural resins added to them. Adhesives of this kind are not recommended due to the solvents they generally contain and the residual monomers they may give off at some point, as well as the large surface area from which they can emit air pollutants. In any case, it is not even necessary to use them under normal circumstances.

Plastic wallpaper coated with activated carbon collects poisonous substances, such as PCB

Wallpaper paste – harmless but a product of the chlorine industry

A variety of wallpapers

Printed patterned wallpapers, colored textile wall coverings or textured wall coverings with lots of plastics of different kinds of wallpaper that all contain contaminants. The simplest and best option is possibly woodchip wallpaper, preferably made of recycled paper; however, it is not commonly available in the United States.

JOINT SEALANTS

Joint sealants are used to seal the joints between various parts of a building, often between different materials, and provide lasting protection against moisture, air infiltration and dust. For example, there are connecting joints between components such as windows, doors or metal reinforcements and masonry. Today these joints are sealed mostly with in-situ foams made of polyurethane, caulking of various kinds or in some cases, impervious adhesive tape. In the case of in-situ polyurethane, these two-part products give off short-term toxic emissions of isocyanates as well as dangerous long-term by-products during decomposition. CFCs used to be used as foaming agents, but today mixtures of hydrofluorocarbons (HFCs) and butane are used. These do not damage the ozone layer, but are associated with global warming. For these reasons these foams are not recommended. The same is true of urea-formaldehyde-based in-situ foams (UF-foams), which give off allergenic form-aldehyde fumes and can also swell later due to the effects of dampness. It is better to fill joints with textile gaskets made of jute or cotton and sealed with cork paste. Coconut fibers can also be effective pressed into the gaps around windows and doors.

There are also elastic joints between the structural elements of a building, especially in prefabricated concrete buildings. The individual pieces of cladding and the reinforced concrete skeleton onto which they are attached expand at different rates as the temperature changes. Air leakage and rain water may enter if the materials filling the cavities do not remain adequately elastic. These joints are usually sealed with polysulfides, also known as polymethylene tetra-sulfides, which retain their properties over time. They are mostly two-part products derived from chlorine industry processes. They are known to contain toxic lead and antimony compounds as hardening agents, allergenic phthalates as plasticizers and chlorinated paraffin, which are suspected carcinogens. Highly poisonous polychlorinated biphenyls (PCBs) were once used as plasticizers, and sometimes caused considerable contamination of the air inside buildings. They are no longer in use today, but may still be found in older buildings.

The joint sealants most widely used by amateurs and professionals are polysiloxanes, generally known

Sealants – necessary but not always harmless

Chlorine-based caulking
No modern bathroom is without silicone caulking. The walls behind the bathtub and the basin have to be protected from splashed water, but all the liquid sealants currently available are derived from the chlorine indus-try, and also have fungicides added to them.

as silicones. They are used principally in bathrooms as grouting between bathtubs and tiled walls, but also as sealants for window glazing and around window frames on the exterior of a wall. Silicones are produced from silicium and methyl chloride in an energy-intensive process. They are waterproof, highly heat-resistant and very durable, with a service life of approximately 20 years. They cannot be coated with paint or lacquer and are therefore produced in many colors in order to match surrounding surfaces. They form a skin within ten minutes and harden completely within two days. Some quick curing silicones harden sufficiently within two hours of application. During hardening, also known as curing, various chemicals are released into the air. The most common one is acetic acid, which is environmentally acceptable but has a pungent smell and can irritate the eyes, mucous membranes and respiratory system. Enclosed spaces therefore need to be ventilated thoroughly during its application. Also, acetic acid attacks shiny metals, marble, cement and plaster. Alternatives to silicones include acrylic latex caulk, acrylic/silicone blends and neutral reacting oxime emulsions, which need longer to harden, and are not as strong in resisting mechanical loads. Many silicones are supplemented with fungicides, and pesticides based on neurotoxic tributyltin or organic arsenic compounds. These are known to weaken the immune system, have damaging genetic effects and are suspected of causing cancer. For this reason silicones, particularly products intended for use in bathrooms, should not be smoothed down with unprotected fingers, but with a teaspoon dipped in liquid dish soap.

Acrylic sealants are not as abrasion-resistant as silicones, but they can be painted. They are suitable for use on concrete, stone and metal surfaces. They only release water and no chemicals as they harden. However, most acrylic sealants cannot be used in bathrooms because they adhere poorly to smooth surfaces.

Putty made of linseed oil and chalk is hardly used any more today, but it is good to remember that very little primary energy is used in its manufacture. Oil putty can be coated without the slightest problem, and can even be composted, but cannot be used in multiple glazing, while its elasticity leaves much to be desired over the long term.

The recommended means of sealing joints in internal vapor barriers in wooden buildings and roofs are pre-formed foam strips. These are typically self-adhesive, pre-compressed strips of polyurethane foam which can be used to fasten together and windproof the layers of polyethylene sheeting, and seal the connections between the sheeting and the structural members, walls, floors or plaster work. Pre-formed foam strips expand after a certain time and can be relied upon to close any gaps and provide a

Cork sealant

There is no need to use harmful in-situ foams in the joints between windows and walls. There is now an environmentally friendly gasket system made of flax fibers and a self-hardening cork paste which works very well for this purpose.

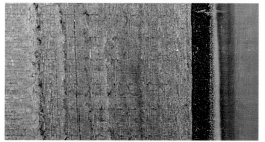

Never smooth silicone with your fingers

Most silicone-based sealants contain anti-bacterial or fungicidal agents which are harmful to health. Therefore you should never smooth them with your fingers, but with a spoon or a plastic scraper like the one illustrated.

Pre-formed foam strips feel the squeeze

Compressed foam strips are used to seal joints in wood frame construction. They can be pressed very thin, but expand of their own accord and have an adhesive surface, which means they are very good for sealing elastic joints.

barrier to wind. However, the material used is ecologically questionable. The same effect can be achieved in a more environmentally benign way by using special rosin papers and adhesives or expanded metal embedded in the plaster work.

- In-situ urethane foams: embodied energy 13,000 Btu/ft.^{3} (130 kWh/m^3)
- In-situ PUR foams: embodied energy 110,000 Btu/ft.^{3} (1,140 kWh/m^3)

SURFACE COATINGS

Conventional paints are being improved from an environmental and health standpoint

Since the areas within buildings which are coated with paints, enamels and stains, are great compared to any other material or finish, attention has focused on their environmental and health impacts. Manufacturers of "natural" and "hypo-allergenic" paints have succeeded in steadily gaining market share with their products in many countries in recent years. This, combined with lower emissions standards required by the Clean Air Act Amendments passed in the United States in 1990, has caused conventional paint manufacturers to reformulate and improve their products from a health and environmental standpoint. Many new products have been introduced by larger United States paint manufacturers in recent years which are touted as environmentally friendly because of their reformulation as a "low-VOC" or "non-VOC" paint. However, one look at the MSDS (Material Safety Data Sheet) information provided by the manufacturers shows that the long list of toxic additives, preservatives, fungicides, mildewcides, drying agents, emulsifiers, etc., remain. In addition, it is important to note that the VOC content published in the manufacturers' literature applies to unpigmented white paint only so unless you want only white walls, you really don't know what you are getting.

The debate about natural paints

Presently, solvents used in natural paints are coming under attack by conventional product manufacturers. A test carried out by the Swiss Federal Office for the Environment, Forestry and Agriculture found that natural resin oil paints produced more air

Pigments used in natural paints

Brown and red earth, white chalk, ground stones and sulfur compounds provide the range of colors used in natural enamels. Artificial ingredients, such as pure white titanium oxide, are only used in a few products.

emissions and were more eco-toxic than normal acrylic enamels. However, it is very difficult to give a final judgment in this area. Work on a comprehensive evaluation of this question is currently being undertaken by various state agencies, the US Environmental Protection Agency (US Environmental Protection Agency (EPA), National Paint and Coating Association (NPCA), and authorities in the European Union.

In fact, enamels and paints produced from natural raw materials and by natural methods typically contain higher levels of solvents than conventionally made products. According to some tests, on average four times as many terpenes are found in "eco-houses" as in conventional houses. In some cases, terpene concentrations may even be several hundred times the average. Terpenes are vegetable based aromatic solvents commonly used by industry in perfumes. Natural paint manufacturers use them in their products as solvents. In the environment they contribute to the formation of the photochemical oxidants (ground level ozone) which cause "summer smog." Many of these substances, such as turpentine oils and citrus peel oils are potentially allergenic. Even if they have a fragrance which most users find pleasant, they can still harm those with a chemical sensitivity to them. Unlike conventional products, they usually cause no long-term damage and their intense smell is usually enough to warn off people who are sensitive to them. Turpentine oils can cause headaches and breathing difficulties. Also, some turpentine oil fumes are thought to have a narcotic effect, which means that rooms must be ventilated thoroughly if they are used. Delta-3-carene, a component of balsamic

turpentine oil extracted from the sap of living pine trees, is criticized harshly for causing an allergic skin disease common among painters.

In contrast to Scandinavian and east European pine trees, wood from Portugal or Spain naturally contains little delta-3-carene. This allows the manufacturers to keep levels of this harmful substance below the detection threshold of 0.1% vol. A number of tests nevertheless found individual products to contain high levels of delta-3-carene. Turpentine oils also have very high levels of alpha-pinenes, which irritate the eyes and mucous membranes in the nose and throat, and can damage kidney functioning.

The possible carcinogenic effects of citrus terpenes, which are extracted from orange peel, are currently being investigated in Europe. D,l-limonene is derived from lemon and citrus oils and is released in large quantities when an orange is peeled. A particularly thorough study of the effects of limonene has indicated that it has no carcinogenic effects on humans and does not cause genetic damage, but there is no doubt about its irritating effects on skin or its strong odor.

Anyone who is unaffected by these solvents will usually not have problems with natural paints. The positive difference between them and conventional products is that the contents of natural paints are stated in full on the packaging, so allergy sufferers can easily find out whether they contain substances which may cause problems. With conventional paint products, consumers must request MSDS information from the retailer or manufacturer and determine the potential health risks of each hazardous ingredient on their own. MSDS sheets are required in the United States under Occupational Health and Safety (OSHA) regulations, for any product which contains substances known or suspected of being carcinogens, mutagens, or posing other significant health risks.

On the other hand, the human immune system has had thousands of years to adjust to some of the resins and aromatic organic compounds found in terpenes. They also tend to break down more quickly in the environment than most synthetic products. However, they need more time to evaporate from natural paints than synthetic solvents because they are less volatile.

On these grounds, some of the natural paint manufacturers have switched over to using isoaliphatic compounds such as propylene glycol instead of terpenes. They are regarded as the healthiest solvents and are used in cosmetics and medicines as well as in food processing. They contain less than 0.01% harmful aromatics and only tiny amounts of other harmful chemicals. Until now, isoaliphatic compounds have only been produced from petroleum. Other manufacturers say that this discredits their use as ingredients in natural paints. At the moment attempts are being made to produce isoaliphatic compounds from linseed oil.

Due to the inherently long drying time of natural paints chemical drying agents, or siccatives, have to be

Gentle tones

Whether in enamels or paints, natural pigments have strong but soothing tones.

Natural paints are controversial, particularly because their solvents have such strong odors

added. Manufacturers have switched to relatively less toxic cobalt-zirconium siccatives, but these are also thought to be carcinogenic if they are inhaled as dust. This can happen, for example, when a enameled surface is sanded down later. In this case, the person doing the work must take adequate precautions.

The products made by natural paint manufacturers have so far made hardly any impression on professional decorators because they generally are not as easy to apply and they do not perform well enough for professional purposes. Decorators particularly dislike their long drying time, which makes professional work extremely difficult and time consuming. Nevertheless, the eco-paints have largely overcome their growing pains with respect to covering ability (opacity) and ease of use. Natural paints even have the advantage over conventional ones in that they do not crack or bubble as readily because of their greater toughness.

Glazed walls

Natural colors, which can occasionally have slight variations of shade, are particularly suitable for glazing walls, a technique currently very much in fashion. It involves using a variety of techniques to paint on top of an initial undercoat without covering it entirely using translucent or transparent finishes. Flowing transitions can be accomplished with great success.

Ingredients of natural paints

Natural paints consist mainly of binding agents such as oils, resins or waxes, solvents and pigments. They require smaller amounts of fillers and additives such as thickeners, siccatives, adhesion promoters, and curing agents. The sometimes controversial solvents in natural paints have already been discussed in detail above.

The most important binding agent is linseed oil, which is the main ingredient in most natural paints. It is obtained from flax plants, which it is believed have been cultivated for nearly 8,000 years. The principal areas of cultivation are found in South America, North America, Europe, Russia and India. It combines well with other raw materials used in paints and adheres strongly to any surface. Thanks to their high water absorbency and expansive capacity, linseed oil paints always stay elastic and provide a flexible protective coating.

Another quite common ingredient, tung oil, is obtained from the walnut-like seeds of the tung tree, which are cultivated mainly in Japan, India, Florida and Zimbabwe. Tung oil commonly provided the basis for the beautiful Chinese art of lacquering and today is used mainly to make sure that linseed oil dries more quickly. In addition, it is used in marine applications for watertight fast-drying enamels.

Although safflower oil tends to be better known as a cooking oil, it is also commonly used in paints to prevent yellowing. The safflower originated in Persia and is grown today in India, North Africa and North America. Most vegetable resins in natural paints come from trees. The most important of these resins is colophony, which is obtained from the coniferous trees of the northern hemisphere. It gives a full, shiny finish to the paint, but remains tacky, which is why it has to be combined with self-drying oils. Larch resin can help to make paints smooth, giving them a bright, silky shine. The larch tree is widely found in Europe, Asia and North America. Dammar is the resin of the dammar tree, which grows in Sumatra, the Philippines and Malaysia. It develops high strength and elasticity, remains clear and transparent, and does not yellow with age.

Of the animal resins, the most frequently used is shellac, which is produced by the Asian lac insect from the sap of the fig tree, and propolis, which is made from tree resins by bees as putty for repairing damage to bee hives.

Acacia rubber, also known as gum arabic, is used as a thickener and adhesive. It is made from the dried excretions of various acacia trees which grow in Africa, India and Australia. Natural rubber comes from the *Hevea brasiliensis*, rubber tree, which originated in Brazil, but is now also cultivated in Malaysia, Indonesia, Thailand and Sri Lanka.

Various vegetable and citrus oils form the basis for natural paints

Ingredients of natural paints

Oils, resins and waxes are the basic ingredients of natural paints. They protect surfaces, sometimes permeating deep into the wood, act as hardeners and help the paint to dry. Other ingredients are used as thickening agents or give surfaces the desired gloss.

Plants are a source for color

Many natural paints contain vegetable pigments. Some are obtained from exotic plants, such as sandalwood, oak apples, alcanet roots or dragon's blood gum. Common indigenous plants like safflower also provide pigments. The disadvantage is that these colors can fade.

Waxes are used as binding agents and give normally glossy enamels a silky matte finish. The most important is beeswax, which was used in ancient times for protecting frescos. Carnauba wax comes from the Brazilian carnauba palm and covers the tree's fan-like leaves. Its hardening qualities increase the mechanical load-bearing capacity of soft waxes. Candelilla is the juice of a Mexican spurge variety used to impregnate surfaces and make them waterproof. Japan wax is obtained by boiling the fruit of the Japanese wax tree and protects surfaces against wetness. Casein makes up roughly 80% of the protein in cow's milk and is obtained from milk using enzymes. It is also used as a binding agent in wall paints (lime-casein paints), an additive to rubber dispersions, a clear finish and also as an adhesive.

Earth is used to produce red and brown pigments, and various stones are ground to powders for the other colors, except ultramarine blue and green, which are made from sodium sulfide and clay or chrome oxide. Natural Syrian asphalt is typically used for deep black, and white pigments are made from chalk, talc and titanium dioxide, the production of which requires recycled dilute acid. Talc is also a filler with a matte effect that very much improves adhesion. Titanium dioxide is a carcinogen when inhaled as airborne dust.

Apart from larch resin, castor oils are used as plasticizers. They are obtained from the seeds of the Christ-palm or *Ricinus communalis,* which is grown mainly in Brazil, India, China and Russia. Clay is used as a thickening agent and also provides

for good distribution of pigments. Soya lecithin is used as a surfactant to reduce the surface tension of oils. Siliceous earth from California, France, Australia and Germany is used as a filler which lightens colors and speeds up drying times. Methylcellulose made from wood fibers increases viscosity and ensures that the finish remains permeable to gases. Borax from natural deposits in California, Egypt or Iran is the salt of boric acid and is used as a disinfectant and wood-preservative. Bergamot oil from southern Italy is pressed from the peel of the fruit of the bergamot tree and is used to scent various coatings.

Colorfast minerals

Pigments obtained from minerals do not fade with age. Natural earth gives brown or red tones. The original materials used in some pigments are rare and valuable, such as smalt, blue glass, or natural, green sulfur compounds which are added to paints as fine powders.

Dispersion paints

Depending on the kind of binding agent used, wall paints are classified as one of the following:
- mineral paints (enamels);
- casein paints (temperas);
- distempers;
- dispersion paints (latex).

The easiest wall paints to use are dispersion paints, sometimes called latex paints. They are well suited to painting interior walls, stick well to plaster and wood, and can be wiped and even washed. They contain natural or synthetic resins dispersed finely in a watery solution. The binding agents used in synthetic resin products are mainly acrylates or styrenes, the production of which is damaging to the environment. The most frequently used natural resin is dammar, while natural and synthetic latex are used relatively seldom. Most paints depend for their radiant white color on titanium dioxide. Its production produces dilute

Dispersion paints contain solvents as well as water

hydrocarbon compounds (e.g. isothiazole), which irritate the skin and are known to have damaging effects on the central nervous system. Synthetic resin dispersions also contain small quantities of plasticizers, which give off dimethylphthalate (DMP) fumes. DMP can be a health hazard and was found in a fifth of all conventional paints. Finally, a quarter of these dispersion paints were found to contain residual monomers of styrene, which is strongly suspected of being a carcinogen. As a rule, paints which only need to stand up to light demands require fewer chemicals than products intended to withstand regular washing or scouring. Natural resin dispersions often contain linseed oil, which does have a tendency to yellow over time and may show where light does not fall on it evenly. This can be a serious problem from an appearance standpoint especially in rooms with direct sun striking certain

A quick roll

Dispersion paints are the classic interior paints. They can easily be applied with a roller. Even if the pigments are dissolved in water, they are not 100% environment friendly. Silica based mineral paints are better, but should not be applied directly onto plaster.

acid, which presents waste disposal problems. Since 1993 the EU has only allowed this white pigment to be made by means of a low-residue process, and, after enormous expenditures on research, it is now possible to use recycled dilute acid in its manufacture.

Although most dispersion paints are dissolved in water, they require small amounts of solvents to serve as thinners and promote adequate dispersion of the solid ingredients. The solvent content of synthetic resin dispersion paints is roughly 1–5%, and can be even higher in natural resin dispersions. Glycol ethers, which are possibly hazardous according to a National Paint and Coating Association (NPCA) report in 1982, or aromatic oxides, which are suspected of causing cancer, were found in a quarter of all synthetic resin dispersions. Furthermore, half of all synthetic resin dispersion paints contained preservatives such as formaldehyde or halogenated

surfaces. Furthermore, as mentioned earlier, if these paints are used, the room has to be ventilated thoroughly during and after painting in order to let the solvents evaporate and be exhausted to the outside. If the room is not ventilated adequately, the solvents which evaporate can be adsorbed on any nearby porous surfaces or in the air circulation ducts where it will continue to pollute the indoor environment and create obnoxious odors for a long time to come.

Other wall paints

An alternative to dispersion paints is the use of distempers, which contain no contaminants and are very environmentally sustainable, but are rarely used anymore. They consist of methyl cellulose, chalk, talc and water, and do not employ titanium dioxide which is known to be environmentally damaging. It

A long tradition of paints

The best alternative to dispersion paints are casein paints made of milk protein, borax and lime. They give pleasant, matte white as well as colored surfaces. Casein paints have been used for hundreds of years. The paintings on this page were created using tempera paints which are casein paints mixed with linseed oil.

is possible to apply them to almost any surface, but they have to be washed off before a new coat is painted on because otherwise the previous layer of distemper will simply become loose from the substrate and wrap around the roller. This of course, means that layers of old paint do not build up on top of one another, retaining more and more contaminants and reducing the diffusion characteristics of the wall surface.

The best alternative to dispersion paints are probably casein paints. They contain the protein found in milk (casein) as a binder and typically use lime as a pigment and filler rather than titanium dioxide. Lime has the added advantage of a disinfectant effect that successfully retards growth of mold and other bio-contaminants. Borax is also frequently used for breaking down the casein. Lime-casein paints emulsified with linseed oil lacquer are known as tempera paints. Even pure white lime-casein paints containing

titanium dioxide give a room a pleasantly soft and gentler ambiance compared to dispersion paints with their hard contrasts. Casein paints can be used both indoors and out. Their durability can be judged from the ancient techniques of fresco painting, or, for example, the paintings on the ceiling of the St. Michaels Kirche in Hildesheim, Germany, which have lasted for eight hundred years. Casein paints are open-pored, they have good diffusion properties and can be disposed of easily. It is recommended that consumers never buy ready-mixed casein paints because they contain preservatives. Rather they should buy the powder form and mix the paint with water themselves. Casein paints can be applied on top of dispersion paints and they can also be painted over with dispersion paints.

Mineral paints which include both distempers and silicate paints can be applied to natural stone or lime plasters indoors and out without any problems,

Not necessary

The paint on this exterior wood-work has to be reapplied every couple of years. Synthetic resin enamels are particularly sensitive and easily develop small cracks. If good wood protection and suit-able woods, such as larch, are used, it is sometimes possible to do without paint completely.

- Water-based acrylic latex (dispersion) paint, white: embodied energy 6,000 Btu/ft.³ (64 kWh/m³)
- Clay mineral paint, white: embodied energy 4,000 Btu/ft.³ (41 kWh/m³)

They contain potash water glass as a binding agent, which is made from quartz sand and potash in a relatively environmentally sustainable process. Chalk and other alkaline pigments are employed to color silicate paints. There is no need for preservatives in these paints because of their alkalinity. However, they must never come into contact with the skin or eyes during application. Silicate paints are often thinned with synthetic resin dispersions in order to make them easier to work with, and as a result can have undesirable attributes including unpleasant odors, long drying times and off-gassing of hazardous substances.

Cheerful colors

Enamels and wood stains provide a touch of color, indoors and out. Cheerful colors cause no damage whatsoever to either the environment or your health provided you use natural products.

but not as a topcoat over existing dispersion paint work. Distempers in this category consist of slaked lime and water, in which the lime acts as both a (weak) binder and a pigment, and titanium dioxide is not required. They have disinfectant properties and are somewhat moisture-resistant, but they also have a tendency to run easily. They can be applied to most materials except gypsum plaster and gypsum fiberboards, and they are particularly well suited to clay plaster. Distempers are quite often mixed with linseed oil or water glass, a viscous solution of sodium silicate, to increase their abrasion resistance to some degree.

Silicate paints are prized above all as traditional exterior paints. They are particularly long-lasting and weatherproof, but are open-pored and diffusive. As paints naturally resistant to moisture, fungi and fire, they can also be used on all interior mineral surfaces.

Enamels

Enamels are used for coating wood, metal, plastic and mineral materials. By comparison with wall paints, they contain more binding agents, i.e. resins, that form a film. As a result they have to contain more solvents to make the binding agents easier to paint with. There are fundamental distinctions between natural and synthetic enamels, and between enamels which contain solvents, epoxies and dispersion, or water-based acrylic enamels.

The most important enamels to contain solvents are the alkyd resin enamels, with solvent contents of 20–50%, and nitrocellulose enamel, which contains up to 70% solvents. Alkyd resins are polyesters made from natural linseed oils and synthetic carboxylic or phthalic acids. Most traditional decorators' enamel is of this type. If alkyd resins are mixed with aldehyde resins they form acidic hardening systems, which are used mainly in millwork finishing.

The binding agent in nitrocellulose enamel is nitrocellulose (celluloid), a plastic made from wood fibers treated with acids. Nitrocellulose enamels are particularly quick to dry and give a good surface finish, but contain more solvents than other products. Their use is therefore declining rapidly in central Europe.

By contrast, the high solids paints, as they are termed, are becoming more and more prominent. High solids paints are synthetic resin enamels with solvent contents reduced to 10–25% and large proportions of binding agents and pigments. High solids containing less than 15% solvents can be labeled with environmental quality marks, such as the German *Blauer Engel* (Blue Angel), as "low-pollutant enamels" if they contain no aromatics, other solvents which damage unborn children, or heavy metal pigments.

Reaction coatings consist of two components, which harden together in a chemical process. The most widely distributed are polyurethane-based finishes, which are often used for parquet paneling, but there are also retain coatings based on unsaturated polyesters, epoxy resins, and formaldehyde resins. Reaction coatings can contain up to 50% solvents. Particular problems are caused by the emission of residual monomers, in particular, irritant, allergenic isocyanates, the neurotoxin styrene and carcinogenic epichlorhydrin. Appropriate information has to be given on the packaging of retain coatings containing epoxies and isocyanates.

In water-based acrylic enamels the binding agents are distributed finely in water. The binding agents used are mainly acrylic resins (styrene-acrylate-copolymers) because they mix well with water. Even if they are labeled as "low-solvent," they contain up to 16% solvents, mostly glycols and alcohols. Products misleadingly labeled as "solvent-free" or "no-VOC" can contain up to 3% solvents and as already mentioned this is normally applicable only to an unpigmented product. High solids enamels containing less than 10% solvents qualify for the *Blauer Engel,* provided they meet the other conditions mentioned. High solids enamels are gradually becoming standard in Germany because they are generally viewed as more eco-friendly than other products and they offer more durability than standard dispersion paints.

In fact, investigations have shown that residual monomer fumes can also evaporate from the binding agents in water-based acrylic enamels. A third of the enamels tested released problematic styrene into room air, while an allergenic acrylate was given off by others. Apart from this, there are also problems with solvents in water-based enamels, even if they are less severe than those associated with other types. VOCs released in the manufacture and application of various enamels are a sever environmental problem. After transport they are the second largest source of the volatile organic compounds

Low-VOC paints are becoming the standard

Solvents in enamel are bad for our health and cause low-level air pollution

Conventional enamels
Most conventional enamels are made from petroleum products. Depending on the type and application, they contain varying quantities of solvents, almost all of which present health hazards. Enamels used in the building trade are a major source of volatile organic compounds (VOCs) which cause low-level air pollution (smog).

(VOCs) that cause photochemical smog. Moreover, they all have narcotic effects similar to those of alcohol and cause damage to the liver and kidneys over the long term.

The solvents used most often are mineral spirits or terpentine, which, apart from relatively harmless aliphatic hydrocarbons, sometimes contains aromatic hydrocarbons, such as benzene, toluene and xylene. Benzene is undoubtedly carcinogenic, toluene is a neurotoxin and has damaging effects on fetuses, xylene causes poor concentration, disrupts the sense of balance and is also suspected of causing harm to unborn children. In Austria the use of enamel with an aromatic content of greater than 5% has been banned since 1996. As tests carried out by the German consumer magazine *ÖKO-TEST* have shown, there is no reason to expect normal do-it-yourself products to contain such high levels of dangerous aromatics, but a third of all enamels were found to contain more than 0.1 mg/kg. The solvents used in water-based paints are usually glycols and ethylene glycols. Ethyl glycols and methyl glycols used to be employed in most products, but have been used less often since it was discovered that these solvents can interfere with endocrine development in unborn children and may cause birth defects. Less harmful substitutes have been prescribed by law in Germany since 1992. These are often butyl glycol and propylene glycol. These substances are not entirely harmless, however. Butyl glycol is known to cause vomiting, headaches, abdominal pains and general feelings of ill health. In tests on animals it caused red blood cells to decompose, the main consequence of which was damage to fetuses. Propylene glycol evaporates from paints for a very long time and then forms aggressive "free radicals," which can cause skin aging and damage to joints. Propylene glycol, however, is not toxic. Enamels can also off-gas or leach out plasticizers, particularly phthalates, which are characterized by their persistence in the environment

Many substances commonly found in paint solvents are extremely toxic

Misleading signals
Some environmental quality labels, such as the German *Blauer Engel* (Blue Angel), may indicate particularly low-solvent lacquers or stains, which are therefore less damaging to the health. However, this label is only awarded to conventional products, not natural paints.

Colorful borders
Furniture can be creatively decorated with natural paints.

and may have toxic effects which we still do not know about. Water-based paints can also contain preservatives, and biocides which inhibit mold growth. These are often skin-irritant formaldehyde derivatives or unhealthy halogenated hydrocarbons, such as isothiazole. The contamination of enamel paints with toxic heavy metals was once mainly due to pigments, the yellow and red tones of which were often created with lead or cadmium. Other metals used are chromium oxide, strontium chromate, zinc chromate, cobalt, copper and cuprous oxide.

Today these pigments have been replaced with iron oxides and azo dyes. Some azo dyes are viewed as carcinogens if they can be split up into aromatic amines. Heavy metals are also found as siccatives in enamels and stop them from staying tacky. Poisonous lead was used for this purpose in the past, but now cobalt compounds are used for the most part. There is currently much debate in expert circles about how dangerous cobalt compounds are. What is certain is that these substances produce dust which is suspected of causing cancer when the lacquer is sanded down. These siccatives are also found in natural paints.

There are two possible methods of stripping coatings: either an alkaline bath, in which case a specialist firm should be entrusted with deleaching; or an old-fashioned mechanical method which produces no lacquer dust: scraping them off with a special knife. Many people use hot-air guns, but this is not to be recommended because dangerous gases are released.

The contents of natural paints vary widely, as described in detail above. What they all have in common is that the binding agents and most of the solvents originate in regenerative raw materials.

However, most natural paints contain relatively large quantities of solvents. *ÖKO-TEST* also found aromatic residues in some products containing petroleum-based solvents known as aliphatic compounds.

- Water-based acrylic enamel, white: embodied energy 13,000 Btu/ft.^{3} (130 kWh/m^3)
- Solvent-based alkyd enamel, white: embodied energy 17,000 Btu/ft.^{3} (180 kWh/m^3)
- Solvent-based natural resin-oil enamel, white: embodied energy 10,000 Btu/ft.^{3} (100 kWh/m^3)

Clear varnishes

Varnishes have similar qualities to lacquers and enamels. They are often uncolored, or only lightly tinted, and allow the grain of wood, for example, to be seen. They are very thin liquids, permeate the surface of the material, usually wood, and only form a thin coating. This means the texture of the material is not obliterated and its diffusivity is retained. Varnishes contain far fewer binding agents than enamel or lacquer, but still up to 40% solvents. Clear finishes are also produced as dispersions in water (such as water-based polyurethanes) with an average residual solvent content of approximately 10%.

HOME TECHNOLOGY

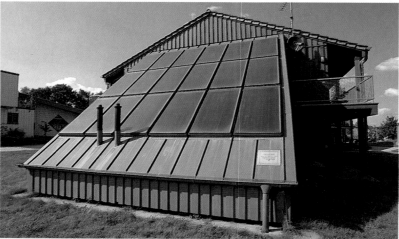

HOME TECHNOLOGY

High tech or low tech?

Technology should be as simple as possible so that the initial capital outlay and return on investment are in proportion to each other. Installing a rainwater harvesting system starts to pay for itself from the very first day. But if you want a system that will give you water heated to exacting requirements and at all times, more investment and effort is required. You'll certainly need to employ an engineer to install a solar system such as the one pictured here.

The proportion of the cost of building taken up by home technologies and systems has risen constantly during this century and is now around 25%. Behind this alarming increase lies an excessive demand for comfort – as, for example, the use of air-conditioning systems in temperate climates – and the loss of knowledge about building adapted to nature. The shortcomings in buildings that are unsuited to the local climatic conditions are simply compensated for by various energy-intensive home technologies such as heating and cooling systems. Frequently, substantial interests come into play, such as those of the electric utility, which in many locations is compelled to favor ecologically unsound electrical heating and lighting systems and ineffective heat pumps.

The disadvantages of such a disproportionate use of technology range from the financial burden associated with the high consumption of resources and the increasing alienation of people from their own living spaces. The most damaging, however, are the resulting effects on human health due to air pollution, EMF (electro-magnetic field) pollution and global warming, which accompany many electrical appliances and technological comforts we have grown dependent on. Legionnaires' disease, for example, can arise from poorly maintained or improperly designed air-conditioners and hot water appliances. Fungal spores and other allergy-exacerbating substances also collect and are promulgated by forced air heating and air-conditioning systems. In fact, it is difficult for many planners to combine environmentally friendly methods of building with an appropriate use of home technology – in other words creating an environment that is neither too spartan nor too wasteful of resources. The idealization of primitive wood-fired systems is contrasted with the other extreme of an overzealous use of technology in the so-called "smart house" as a utopian vision of the future. Thus, electronically controlled rolling shutters become "necessary" so that the "solar house" does not overheat, as do air-conditioning systems with heat recovery so that the very last bit of energy loss can be in some way compensated for. It is not usually questioned whether these investments will ever pay off and whether the desired effect could be achieved by more simple or less technologically advanced means.

Unfortunately, little money is being spent on sensible, energy-saving home technology that uses fewer resources. There is to a great extent a lack of minimum standards, reasonable guidelines and clear priorities have yet to be established as to which technical appliances should be included in an environmentally friendly house and what can be left to individual preference. Environmentally sensible and appropriate technologies, such as solar heating and rainwater harvesting systems, should always be simple, so that they are easily maintained, do not interfere with other required systems and do not quickly become obsolete. Modern heating systems should be laid out in such a way that individual components, such as the circulating pumps, do not nullify the savings gained from the use of advanced technology elsewhere due to inefficiency or improper sizing.

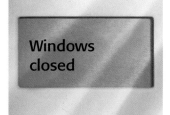

Garage door open

Windows closed

Highly advanced controls

The three switches on the far left are an example of the most modern control mechanisms. The display screen at the top shows, for example, the temperature and whether any windows are open – two examples of typical displays are given to the right of the switches. The middle of the three switches is a room temperature control, and at the bottom are special switches to create different lighting effects. A motion detector (bottom center) can be used to switch lights on when needed, or as part of an alarm system. The switches (below) can be used to raise or lower all shutters in the house at the same time.

Smart houses?

Few people who are building their own houses consider putting in electronic controls. Not many homeowners feel the need to have shutters that lower automatically, lamps that switch on by themselves and heating systems that can be controlled by telephone. Somehow the idea of a high-tech or "smart house" strikes most of us as soulless and rather irrelevant to our lives.

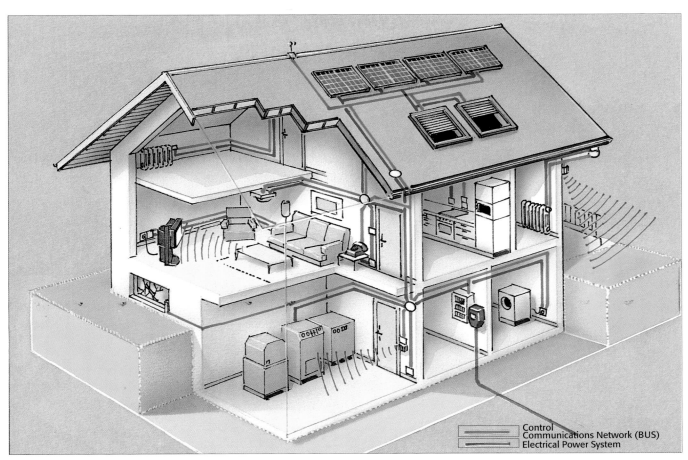

	Control
	Communications Network (BUS)
	Electrical Power System

HEATING AND WARM WATER

Straight from the faucet

Hot water on demand is one of the additional benefits of a modern heating system. Typically about 12% of the energy used in a home goes to heat water.

Until the early 1900s individual fireplaces, room heaters, chimneys and tiled stoves were the favored means of heating a home. Hot water for baths and cleaning was usually produced separately, but using the same sources of heat. Later central heating plants became common, but primarily using steam or convective air distribution methods. By the 1950s, hydronic central heating systems which use hot water as the delivery vehicle had become the most widely accepted method, at least in those locations where heating is needed for at least one-third of the year. Since that time forced air-heating systems have become more popular because of the need to easily

integrate mechanical air-conditioning with central heating and distribution systems. In 1993, 44% of all homes in the United States had central air conditioning. The predominance of forced air heating is an unfortunate development because hydronic heating systems which provide radiant heat are far more compatible with ecological principles and more comfortable as well. In modern hydronic heating systems it is possible to produce hot water for heating and domestic hot water by the same system. This results not merely in greater comfort – hot water is available at any time – but also clearly improves the use of energy as compared to individual isolated systems. Furthermore, hydronic systems have far fewer system losses than do forced air systems and are therefore more efficient.

The efficiency of central heating plants has improved dramatically during the last 20 years. While boilers and furnaces produced in the 1970s still had efficiency levels of only 80%, by the 1980s levels of 90% were common, and now gas condensing boilers have efficiency levels of over 105%. The situation regarding emissions has also changed drastically: Solid fuels such as coal, which contain high levels of sulfur dioxide, are rarely used anymore, and oil fired boilers are becoming far more scarce as well with the exception of larger public buildings where they still provide supplemental heat on the coldest winter days. In addition, where heating oil is concerned, improved technology has also helped reduce the sulfur content and the resulting emissions.

Gas is naturally low in sulfur and produces little soot. In 1993 48 million or 50% of all homes in the United States used natural gas as compared to only 11 million or 27% in 1950. In addition 4% of all homes used bottled LP gas with only 13% using fuel oil, 5% using wood and less than .05% using coal. Regular servicing of all installations and legally required inspections, together with a constant tightening of standards, have resulted in a clear increase in the performance of heating systems.

In the meantime, it has become obvious to many that electric heating is in most cases not an environmentally sensible alternative and only appears to be environmentally friendly. It is true that electric heating does not produce any harmful substances in the owner's building, and that the investment costs are initially lower for the individual consumer. But at the power plant three times as much energy needs to be invested to generate sufficient energy for heating, causing a correspondingly high level of harmful environmental emissions; or if the source is atomic energy, radioactive wastes are created which will remain dangerous for thousands of years. In addition, it is roughly twice as costly to produce hot water or heat with electricity than with gas or oil. The situation is somewhat different in countries such as Norway, and in very selective parts of North America where power is produced mainly from renewable sources such as hydro-electric dams, but, in principle, this high-quality form of energy should not be squandered for such uses as space heating which can be more efficiently accomplished with local sources of energy including solar energy.

The process of choosing the most environmentally sensible heating system and heating fuel depends on the immediate conditions including climate, site geography, local ordinances and codes, availability of fuels, building size and type, financial means, etc. While wood-fired heating such as a wood burning stove or furnace, possibly combined with a solar heating system of some type, may be the correct alternative in the countryside where piped natural gas is unavailable and firewood is plentiful, the optimal system for an urban single-family house is usually gas heating. Here, too, combining an energy-efficient furnace with a solar energy system is usually the most optimal. In apartment buildings, multiple-unit housing and self-contained communities featuring low-energy homes, it may well be advisable, instead of using many individual heating systems, to make use of a centralized heat source in the form of a communal cogeneration plant which simultaneously produces hot water for heating and electrical power and which therefore makes optimum use of one or more energy sources.

Cogeneration – a more efficient way to produce heat and electrical power

Cogeneration is the production of two or more forms of useful energy from one fuel-burning installation. For example, when electricity is produced in a power plant, tremendous quantities of heat are used to produce steam which powers a turbine which in turn runs a generator that produces electricity. More than

Cogeneration plants utilize energy more efficiently

half of the primary energy used is wasted either in the form of heat which passes unused up the smokestack or heat which is removed from the steam in the condensing stage of the loop and which is usually dissipated into the surrounding air or a nearby lake or river. Cogeneration allows much of these losses to be avoided and is appropriate wherever facilities with substantial energy requirements for both heat and electricity are located close to each other. As the distance between the cogeneration plant and the users of its thermal energy increases, so does the capital cost of the system and the losses the system will suffer.

An excellent example of a mutually beneficial cogeneration arrangement exists in Bayport, Minnesota, where a coal-fired power plant operated by the electric utility Northern States Power supplies

Cogeneration of heat and power

Many modern small power plants produce more than just electricity: The waste heat is reclaimed for heating purposes. This means that almost all of the energy from oil or gas can be effectively utilized. Cogeneration plants such as Senertec in Schweinfurt, Germany can now be as small as an ordinary domestic heating system.

Eco-hotel in Hamburg

A small cogeneration plant (below) is used to heat, and supply the electricity for Ökotel in Hamburg, Germany (above), an hotel built an accord with ecological principles.

thermal energy to the adjacent 3.5 million square foot industrial facility of Andersen Windows which is the largest window manufacturing plant in the world. Andersen Windows use this steam for space heating and for generating compressed air to power their manufacturing equipment. In return they provide a substantial amount of waste wood fiber material in the form of sawdust to the power plant. This material, which would otherwise have to go to a landfill or be burned in less efficient boilers is pumped pneumatically to the power plant where it fuels the coal fires.

For consumers, using heat produced externally has the advantage of requiring less investment. They avoid the space and capital costs of boilers, flues, and in some cases heat storage and fuel tanks. They also typically have lower maintenance costs.

Often cogeneration is combined with district heating and cooling systems. These systems produce thermal energy, which is used to generate electricity and steam or hot water which is distributed to buildings through a network of insulated pipes, providing space heating, domestic hot water, cooling from absorption chillers, or industrial process energy. The plant may also produce chilled water which can be used for cooling buildings. The electricity generated is typically used on-site or may be fed back into the utility grid to provide revenues. This particular kind of cogeneration results in system efficiencies as high as 75% – about

twice the efficiency of a conventional power plant that produces only electricity!

Small cogeneration systems are even more flexible and losses within the network can be kept to a minimum because the heat energy typically gained has only short distances to travel. For example, in 1990 the city of San Jose, California, developed a smaller 1,500 kilowatt cogeneration facility which supplies electricity, heat, and chilled water to the San Jose Convention Center and the adjacent main library, and the adjacent 350-room Hilton Hotel, a total of about 1.5 million square feet (140,000 square meters). The cogeneration system consists of a single natural-gas-fueled reciprocating engine and generator, a 310-ton (281-metric-ton) absorption chiller, and a heat exchanger which produces hot water. The cogeneration system saves about $480,000 in utility bills annually, compared to the previous heating, ventilating, and air-conditioning system and operates about 90% of the time. The facility sells excess electricity to Pacific Gas and Electric Company (PG&E), the local utility, during off-peak hours, producing an additional $34,400 of revenue in 1994. With this added income, the payback has been 2.5 years for the city, producing an attractive 40% return on investment.

Cogeneration plants can be scaled up or down to produce greatly varying levels of capacity, and can replace a conventional heating system in a larger building or numerous individual systems in a small residential development. In very small cogeneration systems the "power plant" may be a normal internal combustion engine powered by diesel or gas such as a conventional truck, car or even motorcycle engine. Another type of cogeneration system gaining in popularity in the United States because of extremely low environmental emissions, is the fuel cell power plant. In 1996 there were 65 installed systems, many in demonstration programs involving utilities and end users seeking to become familiar with this promising technology.

Fueled by pipeline natural gas or propane, the ONSI PC25 fuel cell power plant can simultaneously produce 200 kW of electric power and more than 700,000 Btu per hour of thermal power. It has been installed in cogeneration systems for hospitals, hotels, and boiler plants. This system is ideal in facilities where electric power reliability is a higher priority than low-cost power such as in hospitals. The major drawback to widespread application of this technology up until now has been its high initial price – about $3,000 per kW. The price is expected to drop to about $1,500 per kW by the turn of the century, expanding the range of cost-effective applications.

The optimal conditions for the use of small communal cogeneration plants are in manufacturing facilities where continuous process heat is required. Applications also exist in facilities such as public swimming pools, hospitals, laundries and sewage treatment plants where the continuous demand for heat is certain. Alternatively, a consistently high demand for refrigeration such as in a cold-storage warehouse can also be efficiently provided by a cogeneration system coupled with an absorption refrigeration system. The investments for these installations pay for themselves very quickly, particularly when the electricity generated can be used to reduce peak electric demand loads.

In situations where a group of residential dwellings are to be supplied, its annual operating time must be at least 4,500 hours or more than 50% of the time in order for the system to operate economically. In addition, the capacity of such a communal cogeneration plant should be about 20–30% of the annual peak heating energy demand. This will typically produce 60–80% of the required domestic hot water demand, and the additional capacity during the peak demand in winter can be provided by a supplemental conventional boiler.

There are now very small cogeneration plants available which, producing 46,000 Btu per hour of heating capacity and 5.5 kilowatts of electrical power, may be feasible for supplying a smaller multiple dwelling or several single-family homes. A distinct advantage of these ultra-compact cogeneration units is that, being equipped with several motors, they can be more flexible in reacting to the normal increases and decreases in energy demand inherent in a residential application by running only the required number motors. They are, however, relatively more expensive per unit of power output than larger communal cogeneration modules but then again larger units are only economical to run if the required heating output is at least 200 kilowatts or more. This would correspond to the requirements of about 20 individual dwellings in a moderate climate. It is also a good idea to thoroughly insulate the buildings being supplied in order to minimize the fluctuations in heating demand.

Although the utilities are required to buy back power generated by such cogeneration systems connected to the grid, the buy-back rate is somewhat lower than the normal rate paid for electrical power. For this reason it is to the operators' advantage to use as high a proportion as possible of the generated electricity (over 60% in the case of a residential project) for their own needs. The individual residences, then, no longer obtain their electricity from the electric utility but from the operators of the communal cogeneration plant. Should the residents choose to form their own operating company further savings can be obtained. However, this would normally require special permits, licensing or approvals from the Public Utility Commission or other local authorities. Even though such "small operators" are on an equal footing with the electrical utilities, in legal terms, they are dependent on them because of the occasional need for supplemental power which can only be supplied from the utility's grid.

Less residue

Less residue is produced when burning natural gas in contrast to fuel oil. The exhaust fumes also contain less sulfur and therefore far less aggressive sulfur dioxide, which causes acid rain.

Modern gas-fired boilers can be placed almost anywhere

Modern gas boilers do not necessarily need a separate space of their own in the basement and they take up very little room. They are also much safer than in the past.

Oil or gas heating?

Natural gas – the cleanest form of fossile-fuel energy

The decision whether to heat with oil or gas normally depends on whether natural gas is available as a piped supply. If so, this is the cleanest form of fossil-fuel energy in environmental terms, even if one takes into account the rather unfortunate fact that nearly a third is lost from pipes or burned off as waste during the extraction and distribution of natural gas.

Bottled gas or LP (liquid propane) gas is produced from crude oil in refineries. It contains a little more sulfur than natural gas and is considerably more expensive. LP gas is still lower in pollutants than oil and also has the advantage that gas-fired boilers are more efficient than oil-fired ones. It is also possible to use the more advanced condensing technology which will partly compensate for the increased cost. Configuring a heating system to use bottled gas instead of oil is certainly more cost-effective if it is eventually connected to a natural gas pipeline.

However, older systems and individual gas-fired unit heaters often waste up to 40% of the energy either through incomplete combustion or in the form of waste heat which goes up the flue. In poorly insulated water heaters, energy consumed to maintain the water temperature can be as much as 30% or more of the energy required to heat the water in the first place. They also use up additional energy by constantly switching on and off, and each time they start up they produce high levels of pollutants because of incomplete combustion. Antiquated furnaces and water heaters with pilot lights also score very badly from an

environmental point of view. The pilot light alone consumes up to 3,500 cubic feet of gas annually.

Reasonable consumption levels in a hydronic or hot water radiant heating system depend on the proper setting of the supply-side water temperature – the temperature of the water leaving the boiler on its way to the radiators. The return pipe temperature is the temperature of the water before it re-enters the boiler. The greater the energy requirements of the building and the smaller the combined surface area of the radiators, the higher the temperature level must be in the supply and return pipes. While the supply-side temperature in the 1980s was usually 120° F and that of the return 100° F, this ratio tends to be about 100/85 in the most advanced heating systems. In modern low-temperature systems, oil and gas-fired boilers use roughly equal amounts of energy, but the levels of pollutants emitted by gas systems are always lower.

Due to the low temperature level, however, the exhaust gases are also cooler, so they sometimes will begin condensing in the flue. If you renovate your system to run at low temperatures, you usually have to replace the flue as well – usually the draft of the flue is improved by inserting a double wall stainless steel tube – so that the new heating system will not cause excessive carbon build-up. There is, however, a considerable difference between oil and gas in the best and most advanced heating systems which feature condensing boilers. Oil-fired condensing boilers are far more expensive, so gas is ultimately the best choice.

Schematic diagram of a condensing boiler

Condensing boilers make optimal use of the combustion heat because the flue gases are directed through a larger heat exchanger extending into the flue outlet. Latent heat in the form of water vapor in the exhaust gases condenses and the resulting heat is used to preheat water before entering the main heat exchanger inside the combustion chamber. The flue of a condensing boiler is, however, different from an ordinary flue. Because of the lower temperatures it can be made of plastic pipe.

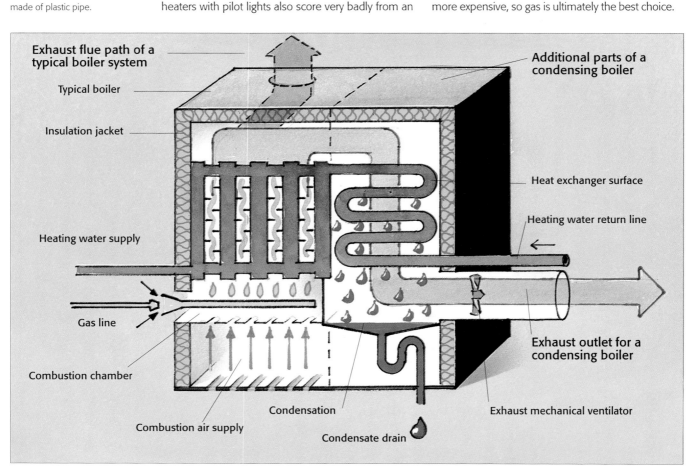

Exhaust flue path of a typical boiler system

Typical boiler

Insulation jacket

Heating water supply

Gas line

Combustion chamber

Combustion air supply

Condensation

Condensate drain

Additional parts of a condensing boiler

Heat exchanger surface

Heating water return line

Exhaust outlet for a condensing boiler

Exhaust mechanical ventilator

Condensing boiler technology

The best heating boilers operate by using condensing boiler technology which reclaims heat from the exhaust gases. This can lead to efficiency levels of over 105% AFUE (annual fuel utilization efficiency) although this sounds like a physical impossibility. Up until about 20 years ago, boiler manufacturers were still convinced that waste gases had to be hot when they left the flue so that the flue and boiler would not be damaged by the condensing steam and the aggressive by-product sulfuric acid. Therefore, they did not consider the heat escaping through the flue – in the case of heating gas, 11% of the primary energy – to be viable in terms of the available energy for heating. So they invented the upper and lower calorific values. Whatever escaped from the flue was the upper calorific value and was omitted from the calculations. What was left, the lower calorific value, was defined as being 100% of the energy available for heating, even though this was really only about 89% of the total.

Modern heat exchangers draw the heat out of the waste gases and cool it down to the point where the steam in it condenses. The condensation, which is only moderately acidic due to the low level of sulfur content in the gas, flows into the condensate drain. The additional heat reclaimed from this process is used to preheat the water.

In new buildings, the cool waste gas is not a problem for flues as they typically vent through the sidewall or they may be installed in the attic; they do not require a brick chimney, simply a short waste pipe made of a synthetic material, stainless steel, aluminum or ceramics. The best systems of all are those in which the combustion or intake air is drawn in from outside into the combustion chamber through a liner which wraps around the exhaust pipe. This preheats the combustion air while at the same time cooling the exhaust gases further which improves the efficiency of the system even more. If, on the other hand, the condensing boiler is set up in the basement, perhaps during the course of a renovation of the heating system, it will require the installation of a special exhaust system.

A wide range of condensing boilers are currently available, and it is difficult for the layperson to compare the quality and corresponding costs of the various products. Even if a particular system promises to deliver a better energy yield, an inefficient circulating pump motor can cause higher electricity use and therefore a higher net energy consumption.

A good condensing boiler should have as little exhaust, radiant and start-up losses as possible. This will be determined mostly by the boiler water temperature, the proper sizing and utilization of the boiler and the level of insulation in the unit. The standard AFUE efficiency rating should be a good method of comparison. The determination of this value is based on Department of Energy requirements, industry standards set by ASTM (American Society of Testing Materials) and the manufacturers themselves.

A lot of useful information can be gleaned from the data which the manufacturers are required to provide. These data concern the level of efficiency of the boiler, its partial load behavior and standby losses, which are generally low. The level of efficiency of the boiler should amount to over 101% AFUE on an average of a high (180/140) and low (100/80) supply/return temperature level. The burners should operate on either a multi-step or a modulating (pulse combustion) basis. A single step burner, particularly during the transitional stage, runs on a "stop and go" basis like a car in a traffic jam, and this consequently leads to higher standby losses, a poorer use of energy and increased waste gases. In contrast, a multi-step or modulating system is far more efficient and can even compensate for a lower boiler efficiency.

Appliances with a low water content have to be protected against overheating. Here, a device known as a minimum flow switch prevents the boiler from starting to boil. That is good for the system, but not for the environment or the electricity bill, as the circulating pump has to run constantly. But a minimum flow switch does not have to cause a negative impact on electricity consumption if the system has a variable speed motor which can adapt to the demand.

Unnecessary electricity is also consumed if the heat exchangers are undersized or if the transfer valve has an excessively high level of electrical resistance. This can create a loss of line pressure which the pump has to compensate for. If the loss is higher than 10 millibar/kW of the boiler's performance, the system will not be economical to run. Nonetheless, condensing boiler systems are the best choice wherever it is possible to connect to a natural gas supply.

Integrated into the living space

Modern gas boilers do not need a boiler room. They can easily be integrated into the living space, whether the bathroom or kitchen. Condensing boilers are best installed beneath the roof. That means a short flue can be used both to discharge the waste air and draw in the combustion air.

Reliable supply

Many people prefer fuel oil because they think it provides a more reliable supply than energy sources such as gas that rely on pipe networks. In addition, oil is generally cheaper. But using oil as a heating fuel requires expenditures for boiler rooms and oil tanks, which are not needed for gas heating.

Heat pumps

If the manufacturers' promises are to be believed, the heat pump is about to make a triumphant comeback. At the time of the oil crisis there had been a strong increase in sales of heat pumps which rely on electrical power rather than fossil fuels; electric utilities since the 1970s have promoted their use particularly in milder climates where the systems are most efficient. As of 1993, 9% of all households in the United States, or about 9.7 million homes, used a heat pump as the primary heating equipment. Whereas earlier heat pumps had many technical shortcomings

Earth, air and water

Heat pumps obtain their heat from the surrounding environment and, by using electric power, raise it to the necessary temperature. When heat is gained from the surrounding air, the technology is less effective than when it is gained from the ground or water. The latter options, however, are distinctly more expensive.

Heating with electricity?

Heat pumps are mainly criticized because the electricity needed to operate them is usually not produced in an environmentally friendly way. They can be recommended without reservation where the electricity comes from renewable sources such as solar cells, wind or hydroelectric energy.

Schematic diagram of a heat pump

A heat pump (opposite) uses temperature differences in the surrounding environment in order to extract heat from an area of lower temperature to one of higher temperature. For example, in winter the earth, ground water, deeper parts of the water in a pond and the air itself are warmer than the surrounding temperature. The heat pump (opposite, bottom) extracts this heat and feeds it into the heating system. For cooling the process is consequently reversed.

these technical flaws have now been corrected and efficiencies have been improved. Heat pumps work in principle similarly to a refrigerator or air-conditioner in that they transfer heat from an area of lower temperature to one of higher temperature. They also have the ability to reverse the process and provide cooling in addition to heating.

There are basically three types: air-to-air, water-to-water and ground-to-water, or groundsource, heat pumps. The manufacturers claim that heat pumps produce 40–50% less of the greenhouse gas CO_2 than oil or gas-fired heating systems. In fact, it has been demonstrated that air-to-air systems commonly used in single and two-family houses produce about

the same CO_2 emissions as a conventional oil-fired central heating system and, therefore, lag far behind a modern gas-fired condensing boiler system. However, if groundsource or watersource systems are used, the end result is somewhat better.

Of course, the ecological balance of heat pumps depends not only on the preceding generation of electricity, but on how efficient the system is. In terms of heating energy heat pumps can be compared based on a COP coefficient (coefficient of performance) rating, which is the ratio of heat energy produced to the electrical energy input. Today air-to-air heat pumps approach a COP of 3.0. In practical use, however, the manufacturers' claims can seldom be achieved. In fact, the efficiency of heat pumps is dramatically reduced when the temperature outside falls. Below temperatures of 37° F, they stop working altogether. Heat pumps, therefore, require the addition of a conventional heating source such as an electric resistance coil or a separate gas furnace as a backup, calling into question how economical they really are. Another method of rating heat pumps is the HSPF (heating seasonal performance factor). HSPF measures how many Btus of heat are provided by the heat pump as a ratio to the watts used to operate it. The HSPF accounts for some decline of performance as the weather gets colder but it does not include the effect of backup electric resistance heating. Efficient heat pumps have an HSPF in the 7.5 to 8.5 range. When considering the efficiency of a heat pump for cooling it must be compared to other available systems in terms of its SEER (seasonal energy-efficient ratio). SEER is similar to HSPF, except that it measures the ratio of heat *extracted* to watts of input energy. An efficient heat pump has a SEER of 8 to 10 as compared to SEER's of 10 to 13 for newer absorption cooling systems.

Water-to-water and groundsource heat pumps can actually achieve a COP of 4.0 or even higher, in other words they can produce energy equaling up to four times the amount of electricity used and they are largely unaffected by a drop in outside air temperature. But the high initial investment costs to install these systems create very long payback periods with respect to the operational savings. Experts have calculated that heat pumps increase heating costs overall by about 20–30%. In the United States there are currently no subsidies at the federal level; however, some states and many electric utilities still offer such programs. Heat pumps are a much more realistic option in houses which only have a very limited energy requirement, such as, zero-energy or passive houses which only require heating a few days out of the year. In addition, one could use electricity from a photovoltaic array for driving the heat pump, thus creating an entirely clean and environmetally friendly solution.

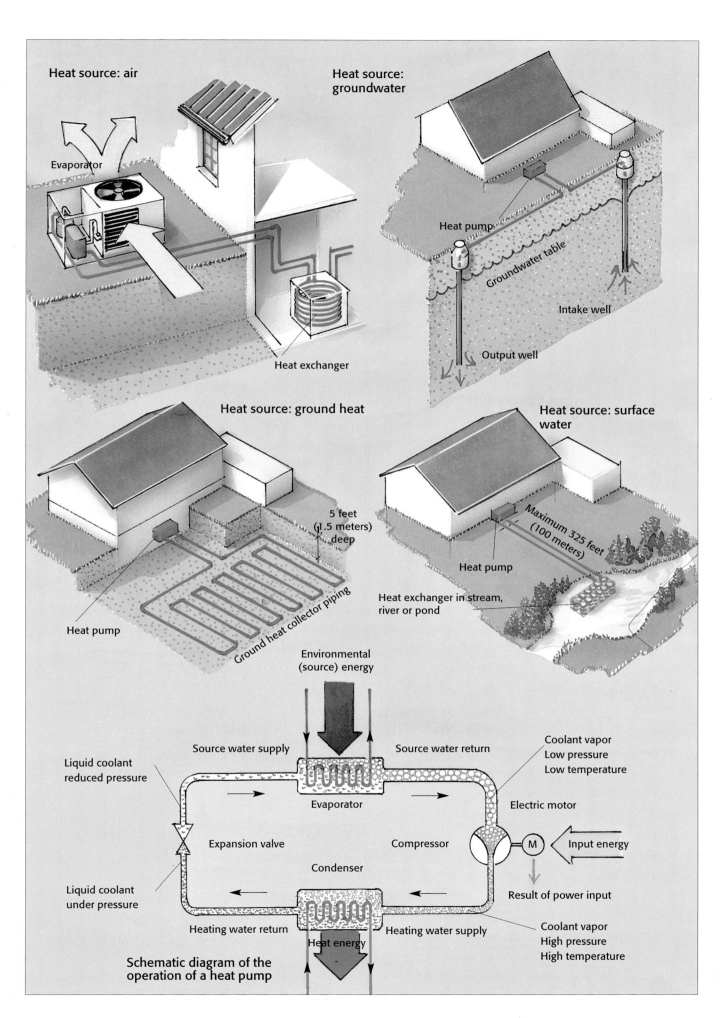

Heat source: air

Evaporator

Heat exchanger

Heat source: groundwater

Heat pump

Groundwater table

Intake well

Output well

Heat source: ground heat

Heat pump

5 feet
(1.5 meters)
deep

Ground heat collector piping

Heat source: surface water

Heat pump

Maximum 325 feet
(100 meters)

Heat exchanger in stream,
river or pond

Environmental
(source) energy

Liquid coolant
reduced pressure

Source water supply

Source water return

Coolant vapor
Low pressure
Low temperature

Expansion valve

Evaporator

Compressor

Electric motor

M

Input energy

Condenser

Result of power input

Liquid coolant
under pressure

Heating water return

Heating water supply

Coolant vapor
High pressure
High temperature

Heat energy

Schematic diagram of the
operation of a heat pump

Wood-fired heating

Firewood is readily
available

Wood was the original heating fuel used by the indigenous peoples of North America. Although the number of homes heated with wood declined dramatically in mid-century, many homeowners turned to wood heating in the 1970s when there were concerns about the price and security of supply of conventional heating fuels. For example, in the United States nearly 5% of homes (about 5.3 million) use wood as the primary heating fuel, up from only 1.7% in 1970. In Canada, more than 6% or about 400,000 of all single-family dwellings use wood for heating; in addition, over 950,000, or 14%, use it as a supplementary heating fuel. There have been major advances in wood burning over the past five years which have made wood burning safer, more effective, efficient and more convenient than ever before.

Traditional fireplaces cause
air pollution

As recently as 1980, most serious wood burning was done with basement wood furnaces or simple black wood stoves. Now, the majority of new wood heating installations are attractive stoves and advanced technology fireplaces located in main living areas which are able to provide most or all of the heat for the home, if properly installed.

A wood fire is not just very pleasant to look at, but burning wood can be considered environmentally friendly because wood is a renewable energy resource. Add to this the fact that advanced wood combustion technologies mean more heat and less smoke from the fuel you burn.

But there are problems with many wood heating installations. Many older systems still in use pose serious environmental hazards both to outside air quality and to indoor air quality because of smoke spillage. This is why there are restrictions on burning wood in many places. In North America appliances approved by the Canadian Standards Association or US Environmental Protection Agency performance standards are becoming the norm. At the same time emission standards for wood burning appliances are becoming much more stringent and the manufacturers themselves are making significant improvements. For example, some have made a commitment to keep within a limit of 1.6 g carbon monoxide per cubic meter of used air while at the same time raising the efficiency rating by 10%. Depending on the type of appliance, it now actually lies between 75 and 85%. Nonetheless, the emissions of even the best wood stoves are still significantly higher than the levels in modern oil and gas-fired heating systems. You can, however, control the amount of smoke released as a result of wood heating in a number of ways:

- Select an appliance that is approved by the US Environmental Protection Agency (EPA). These certified clean-burning appliances reduce smoke

Warm and pleasant

A fireplace like this allows you to enjoy the flickering flames through the expansive glass doors, just like an open fire. Without the doors, it would be impossible to stoke the fire, and a vent which is usually operable also allows good control of the combustion air feeding the fire.

emissions by as much as 90% compared to conventional appliances.

- Select a properly-sized appliance and, in the case of a stove or fireplace, locate it in the main living area to make the most effective use of the heat it produces.
- Use a modern chimney matched to your appliance.
- Avoid smoldering fires by using the proper burning techniques.
- Use seasoned firewood that is split to the right size for your appliance.
- Make your house more energy-efficient so you will use less fuel to heat it and less associated emissions.

Advanced technology wood stoves are relatively expensive and typically unfeasible when operated in parallel with other systems. It is also very difficult to produce hot water with these systems, and a wood-burning stove combined with electrically heated hot water is an inferior combination from an environmental point of view. In order for wood-fired central heating systems to

meet the basic heating requirements of a house, a high degree of maintenance and a lot of personal time for their operation is often required which is incompatible for anything other than a rural environment.

Conventional fireplaces, though popular, tend to produce an unpleasantly dry environment and are a source of smoke and dust. While the fireplace rapidly warms the adjacent room, most of the heat passes unused up the chimney, and the other peripheral rooms may become uncomfortably cold. Once the fire has gone out the heat rapidly dissipates unless ample thermal storage has been provided.

Fireplaces are now becoming available which contain a lining of heat-storing tiles or stones, which is a novel improvement, and heat circulating fireplaces have been available for some time. Nevertheless, open fireplaces will never be energy-efficient in relative terms and they are not suitable for people with allergies and other sensitivities.

Natural and beautiful

A fireplace like this one not only enhances the living space, it is a work of art in its own right. But there is also an obligation: The fireplace must be designed to burn cleanly so that the neighbors do not have to put up with the smoke and pollutants billowing from the chimney.

Modern or rustic

Every fireplace has the potential to be unique and can be designed to fit in with the style of the home. The photos on these pages show stylish fireplaces that have been designed to burn cleanly and efficiently.

Easily and quickly installed

Wood-burning stoves need only to be connected to a chimney, so they can be installed in short order. This is probably why they are very popular among consumers. Less expensive, though also usually less efficient models, are available in most do-it-yourself building supply stores.

Advanced wood-fired heating technology

Long-lasting thermal storage

Tiled stoves store heat in their long circuitous heat extraction channels and then pleasantly and gradually release it mainly in the form of radiant heat. This makes them particularly comfortable sources of warmth. However, they need quite a long time to warm up, and of course with these units there are no flickering flames to enjoy.

Over the past decade, researchers and designers have developed technologies that can reduce the amount of smoke and other pollutants produced by wood burning appliances. Most of these technologies are aimed at burning off the smoke before it leaves the firebox which is not a very easy task. To burn, the smoke must simultaneously be at a high temperature, have adequate oxygen available, and have enough time to burn before being cooled.

Three general categories of technologies are in use:

- Advanced combustion systems create the conditions necessary to burn the combustible gases without the use of catalysts. This is primarily accomplished by increasing firebox insulation to keep temperatures high, using devices to reflect heat back into the firebox and create the gas turbulence needed for complete combustion. This

provides a longer route for the escaping gases which will then burn longer before being cooled. They also employ heated secondary air supplies to ensure that enough oxygen is present.

- Catalytic combustion appliances use a catalyst to effect a reaction during combustion but without being consumed in the process. The catalyst is a coated ceramic honeycomb through which the exhaust gas is drawn. The catalytic coating lowers the ignition temperature of the gases as they pass through allowing these appliances to operate at lower temperatures while still burning cleanly.
- Densified Pellet Technology uses pellets made of sawdust or other biomass waste which are compressed to about 6 mm (¼ inch) in diameter and 25 mm (1 inch) long. Pressure and heat binds the pellets together without the need for additives.

Pellet-burning appliances have a hopper which holds at least 40 lb. of fuel and an auger which moves the pellets into the combustion chamber. These pellets burn very cleanly because they are fed into the combustion chamber at the best rate mixed with the right amount of air. These systems generally have lower emissions than conventional firewood appliances.

Using these technologies a higher quality of combustion and longer combustion times can be achieved, so that the appliance does not need to be refilled as often. The manufacturers of these products are incorporating an afterburner into their newer appliances and they are using increasingly sophisticated systems to direct the air exactly where it is needed.

Some innovative manufacturers even use sensors, such as the l-tube familiar in automobiles, which measure pollutants in the waste gases and operate air flaps that open and close automatically. If damp wood or even rubbish is about to be burned, these sensors indicate that there is a fault in the system. When rubbish, varnished wood and similar materials are burned they can release toxic substances such as dioxins and furans which will also be present in the ashes. Even when newspaper and cardboard packaging is burned to start the fire the level of pollution rises. Firewood must always be seasoned and will preferably have been stored for at least two or three years. Wood-fired central heating boilers produce less waste gas emissions and provide more even combustion than smaller fireplaces or stoves.

Individualized tiled stoves

Custom built-in tiled stoves do not necessarily require tiles on the outside, even though tiles are an optimal way of transferring the radiant heat. Individually shaped and plastered heaters can be fashioned to fit better into more contemporary homes.

Use only well-seasoned firewood

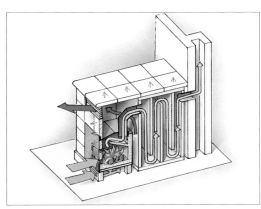

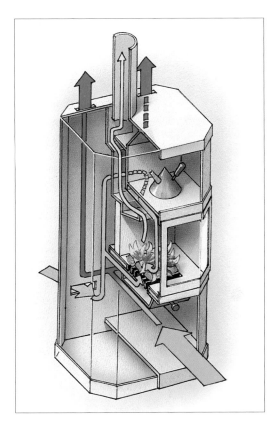

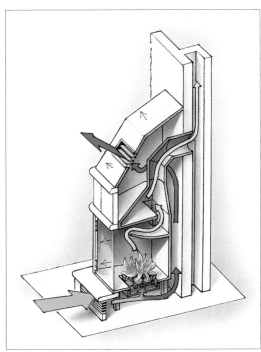

Schematic diagrams: heat circulating fireplace, traditional tiled stove, and a modern wood-burning stove

This built-in heat-circulating fireplace (left) heats air drawn from the room and returns it to the room by convection, some heat can be stored in the masonry chimney behind. By venting the exhaust gases through a circuitous labyrinth of tiled chambers the tiled stove (top) can store great quantities of heat and then slowly radiate the heat into the room. The inexpensive wood-burning stove (far left) heats up rapidly, and its metal housing which may be decorated with tiles can store little heat. While it is burning it provides heat to the surrounding space by radiation and also through surface conduction which then circulates by convection of the room air.

Tiled stoves

There is a centuries-long tradition of tiled stoves in central Europe. Genuine tiled stoves are individual pieces of craftsmanship with which an entire house would be heated. While in the past many historical tiled stoves were converted to more convenient gas heating, in the meantime new stoves are being built almost exclusively for burning wood. Tiled stoves are particularly suitable for low-energy houses that only infrequently require limited heating. They often require only about two logs at a time. While most heaters are too big to be particularly economical on fuel, smaller tiled stoves or masonry heaters (these are stoves built on the same principle, but without tiles and a somewhat differently constructed combustion chamber) match up very well both on economical and ecological grounds. However, tiled stoves have their own problems: They take a long time to heat up and are rather difficult to adjust to abrupt changes in heating demand. In tiled stoves, the hot combustion air is directed through seemingly endless passages, known as heat exchange channels, lined with fireclay tiles. During the course of this process, this massive hulk gradually heats up and can store the heat for a long time.

Anyone who comes home late and would like to warm up a little before going to bed will very likely drop off to sleep before a tiled stove has heated up. For the same reason it is not possible for this type of stove to react quickly when temperatures rise or fall during the course of the day – for example, due to passive solar gain through windows. The only way to get rid of this excess heat is literally to throw it out by opening a window and ventilating the room. In addition, low-energy houses should be built airtight. For that reason, both the combustion air and the exhaust air has to be piped to and away from the tiled stove in a sealed system.

This hand-crafted heating system is suitable for energy-efficient homes

Every built-in tiled stove is a unique piece of craftsmanship. In principle, the heating performance is enough for a low-energy house. But if these heaters are combined with a conventional heating system, this can turn out to be rather expensive.

These classical designs are more for homebodies
Wood-fired tiled stoves need a long time to reach the correct temperature, so they are not a good choice for people who are away from home all day and only want to heat up the house briefly in the evening.

Areas around the heating flaps that are not air-tight are, unfortunately, unavoidable due to the limits of the design. Perhaps the most serious drawback of this type of radiant heating system is the difficulty in producing hot water. The traditional "water pockets" in tiled stoves are totally inadequate for modern purposes.

There is also the question of how to heat water in summer. Additional electrical bath heaters or tankless demand water heaters can be installed for this purpose, but they are undesirable from an environmental point of view. Having to install a second system driven by oil or liquid gas merely to heat water is a nuisance for those who have already made an investment equal to the price of a new car. One possible environmentally friendly solution to this problem which has emerged recently is to combine tiled stoves and solar domestic hot water systems. Here, the hot water is initially provided by the solar energy and is collected in a well insulated storage tank. In the winter, heated coils in the tiled stove take on the task of reheating the water. In this way hot water from renewable energy sources can be enjoyed all year long. Despite this, there can be bottlenecks during winter months and during the transitional seasons.

A tiled stove is certainly an attractive feature in any house, and many are prepared to accept some of these drawbacks as a result. Making the tiled stove a central focal point is a good idea for more than merely esthetic reasons: It should be centrally located so that it can heat as many rooms as possible and its radiant heat can be more effectively conveyed throughout the home. Tiled stoves are popular mainly because they give off warmth in the form of radiant heat which is more comfortable and healthy. The proportion of heat that is radiant,

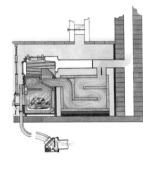

A limited supply of hot water
A tiled stove with a water chamber can furnish hot water but only in small quantities and when the heater is in use.

nearly 90%, is unequaled by most other wood burning appliances. There is no doubt that ceramic tiled stoves also produce an excellent distribution of heat – even for conventional heating systems. For that reason, fireplaces are often "dressed up" with a couple of tiles in order to create a false association in the purchaser's mind.

Hybrid solar/wood systems can provide heating and hot water all year-round
This new system promises to deliver renewable energy all year round, using the sun in summer and wood-fired heating in winter. The main difficulties occur during the transitional periods, when its reliability may suffer.

Surface heating

Surface heating systems which provide mainly radiant heat work on the same principle as the old-fashioned tiled stove and the ancient hypocaust heating systems first employed by the Romans. The most familiar type of surface heating is underfloor heating, but wall heating is also available.

Radiation or convection

The most common underfloor heating system is hydronic, i.e., it uses hot water as the heat transfer medium. In this system, the hot water, driven by a mechanical pump, flows through pipes made of copper or more commonly today a synthetic material such as high density polypropylene. These tubes are laid beneath the floor in a spiral or snaking path. The variation referred to as a radiant floor is a particularly

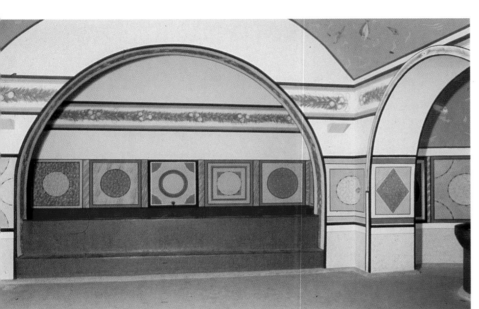

Blast from the past

This Roman hypocaust heating system, which is almost 2,000 years old, works on the same principle as many modern eco-friendly heating systems.

flat type of construction containing a thin layer of mesh made up of a network of thin water pipes or in some cases an electric resistance heating element.

Underfloor heating can be divided into wet and dry applied systems. In wet systems, the pipes are arranged directly above the sub-floor with concrete or a liquid gypsum variation called gypcrete poured over. In the dry systems, insulation panels with raised guides are put down. The water pipes are then laid in the guides, which also facilitate bending the pipes into the correct shape. To improve heat transfer, another layer of floor is usually laid or poured over it. In this case dry gypsum floor panels may be laid between and over the pipes, or gypcrete may be poured in place as in the wet system. While all types of floor coverings are theoretically suitable for underfloor heating, ceramic surfaces or natural stone floors are generally used because they transfer heat better. Carpets that are to be used on top of underfloor heating systems have to have a special label to show that they are able to withstand the higher temperatures, and a special heat-resistant adhesive must be used. Wood floors should be approved for this application by the manufacturer and may have a

tendency to dry out and shrink, creating gaps or causing an uneven floor surface.

Provided the correct surface temperature is maintained, however, underfloor heating should guarantee a pleasant room climate. It provides a high proportion of radiant heat, keeping the floor cozy and warm without making the room overly hot and stifling. Due to the radiant heat, the room air temperature can be kept at a relatively low 65° F (19° C) without being perceived as unpleasant. This is because the higher the temperature of the surrounding surfaces, the lower the air temperature itself should be. Large radiant surface systems, such as this, provide an excellent delivery mechanism for energy-saving low temperature and condensing boilers.

On the other hand, underfloor heating systems also have some disadvantages. If the insulation layer between the heating system and the ground or an unheated basement below is too thin, which was frequently the case in older systems, it can result in enormous heat losses. According to independent studies, by the end of the 1980s houses with underfloor heating were still using up to 50% more energy than similar houses with conventional radiators. Frequently the temperature of the underfloor heating was too high, creating surface temperatures of above 75° F (22° C). At temperatures over 80° F (27° C) the heat is considered to be unpleasant, and can contribute to varicose veins. In addition, at higher temperatures fine dust is carried upwards by the rising warm air, and this can cause problems for people with allergies.

There is one general shortcoming of all underfloor and radiant wall heating systems: They tend to react very sluggishly to fluctuations in demand. In winter, if heat is suddenly gained through the large glass surfaces of a solar house, the room can easily overheat. Then windows are flung open and the solar gain is allowed to escape. It has become more popular recently to install underfloor heating systems with several zones, making it possible to regulate the heat in individual rooms more quickly and only where needed. Underfloor

Schematic diagrams of baseboard radiators, hypocausts and radiant wall heating systems

The basic idea is always the same: The heat should be radiated from as large a wall surface as possible, and not just from one small radiator. This type of heating is preferable because it creates a more pleasant and healthy environment. In the most common type, baseboard radiators, a "fin-tube" pipe produces hot air at 140–170° F (60–76° C) which, because of the design, is not just radiated to the room directly but is also carried up the wall behind and heats it evenly. Modern hypocausts are best installed in new buildings. For this, there are special masonry blocks with perforations that provide adequate air passages on the inside so that the hot air produced by the fin-tube pipes can rise through them. A similar system can be used in buildings which are being retrofitted. Here, a plaster or gypsum board sheet is mounted a few inches out from the wall creating an air space through which the hot air circulates. Radiant wall heating systems, in contrast, are similar to underfloor heating systems: Networks of pipes are installed inside the wall under a plaster finish and hot water circulates through them.

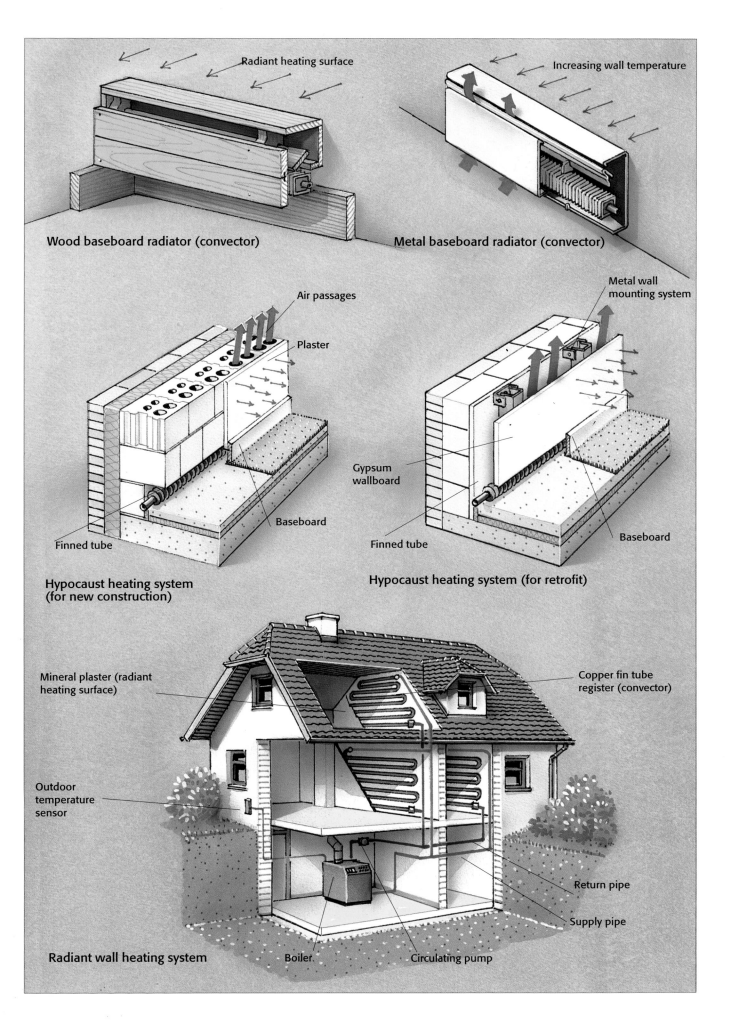

Radiant heating surface

Wood baseboard radiator (convector)

Increasing wall temperature

Metal baseboard radiator (convector)

Air passages

Plaster

Finned tube

Baseboard

Hypocaust heating system
(for new construction)

Metal wall
mounting system

Gypsum
wallboard

Finned tube

Baseboard

Hypocaust heating system (for retrofit)

Mineral plaster (radiant
heating surface)

Copper fin tube
register (convector)

Outdoor
temperature
sensor

Return pipe

Supply pipe

Radiant wall heating system

Boiler

Circulating pump

heating may not be the best choice, therefore, in a light wood frame building because of the limited thermal mass and the resulting tendency for greater temperature fluctuations. These types of heating systems are really more suited to concrete or masonry buildings with relatively large thermal mass.

Much the same is true of radiant wall heating systems, though they have some additional peculiarities. While the energy losses on interior walls are lower than those of underfloor heating systems, they require thicker walls thus creating smaller living spaces within. They also greatly reduce the available wall space for windows, doors, pictures and cabinetry. The most suitable walls are those which do not have doors or windows; however, to avoid a buildup of heat they cannot be used for cabinets or pictures either. In many systems you cannot even pound a nail in the wall for fear of damaging the water piping.

In addition, they take up a high proportion of space: For a 200 square foot room, a wall heating surface of nearly 120 square feet is required. Because of the unavoidable energy losses and the structural difficulties, it is not recommended that one install radiant wall heating systems in exterior walls. On the other hand, the exterior walls are classically the "cold" walls, unless the house is very well insulated.

In addition to hot-water wall heating systems, there are also warm-air wall heating systems similar to ancient Roman hypocausts. Hypocausts were used mainly in large public baths. Hot air circulated by convection in a double-layered floor or in clay pipes or hollow chambers in the walls. Similarly, in modern systems warm air moves either between the wall and a layer of plaster in front of it. Alternatively, special bricks with wide air passages may be used.

The hot air usually comes from a type of baseboard convector similar to standard fin-tube baseboard radiators in modern hydronic systems. They consist of a copper pipe surrounded by a large number of fins and with relatively hot water (170–190° F/76–88° C) passing through it. This creates a strong convection current, meaning that hot air rises and cold air is drawn in at the bottom. The hot air passes along the wall and heats it and the plaster layer, or moves through the air passages in the bricks. However, because of the water temperature required, it is not easy to combine this system with low temperature boiler systems. Closed air passages can be supplied quite well with hot air from wood-burning fireplaces. On the other hand, the wall heating system using a layer of plaster is the least sluggish of all surface heating systems and is comparable to normal radiators in terms of adjustability. This system is also available as a non-load-bearing wall which heats on both sides and correspondingly reduces wall thickness.

Underfloor heating

Underfloor heating produces a particularly pleasant heat. If it is set at too high a temperature, however, the rising air current raises dust which can cause problems for people with allergies. In addition, underfloor heating has to be well insulated below so that little heat is lost in this way. A top layer of concrete or gypcrete flooring is generally poured over the pipe network that has been laid on the subfloor.

Wall heating

This modern hypocaust heating system is very unobtrusive.

Ideal for the bathroom
These contemporary tube-type radiators not only heat the bathroom, they can also be used to hold and dry towels.

Modern tube-type radiators
Modern tube-type radiators work on the same principle as the time-honored cast-iron radiators of yesterday and they produce a large proportion of radiant heat. Unlike panel heaters, they can be architecturally adapted to suit the layout of the room.

Radiators

The most common type of radiators are generally baseboard radiators. They have the advantage of a potentially high heating performance combined with low weight and low water content. They are also the cheapest of all hydronic heating systems. There are also wall convectors which generally have several tiers of fin tubes stacked one above the other inside a metal housing which is open at the base and top to allow convection. Such radiators only produce about 20–30% radiant heat, however. In addition, dust gathers between the fins inside the convectors, and this is very difficult to remove.

It is better to use simple panel radiators without fin tubes. They also have a low water content and are, therefore, from the point of view of control engineering, considered to be "rapid" systems. At the same time, the proportion of radiant heat produced is more than 60%. Due to the lower temperatures (110–140° F/43–60° C) they can easily be combined with low-temperature or condensing boilers. They are particularly suitable for well-insulated houses with low-energy requirements. In the past, free-standing radiators made of cast-iron or steel were mainly used. They had a large mass and large water content. This made them difficult to regulate, though on the other hand they had a fairly high proportion of radiant heat at about 40%. Today they are typically found only in older buildings.

Modern tube-type radiators are similarly constructed of individual horizontal or vertical elements. They are made up of steel pipes and are appealing from an esthetic point of view. Although they have less mass and water content than the old-fashioned cast-iron radiators, equally high proportions of radiant heat can be achieved when they are arranged properly. Tube-type radiators are often installed in bathrooms.

Tips for correct heating

Lowering room temperature saves up to 6% off heating bills for each 2° F of reduction

Regulators are important
In many countries individual radiators have to be fitted with thermostats as a safety precaution. The heating system as a whole is regulated by a thermostat for each zone as well as an outside temperature sensor.

- It is often wise to consider replacing a boiler that is more than 10 to 15 years old before major repairs become necessary.
- The heating system should not be too big. Very large systems are more likely to operate on a constant "stop and go" basis. If the level of thermal insulation in the house has been improved, the energy requirements and arrangement of the heating system should be adjusted accordingly to avoid any waste of energy.
- All pipes that convey hot water should be insulated, usually with a 1-inch-thick insulating layer. This is not necessary in interior walls between heated rooms.
- Radiators must be fitted with thermostats. An outside thermometer is also advisable to regulate the entire system properly.
- Heavy curtains and furniture should never be placed in front of radiators. The thermostats must not be covered either.
- Radiator niches should be insulated particularly well.

- Air which becomes trapped in radiators has to be bled regularly – especially if the radiator starts to make a "glug" sound.
- Lowering the room temperature by 2° F can save up to 6% of heating energy.

Heating water

The proportion of energy used to provide hot water for the kitchen, shower and bathroom used to be very low when compared to the energy required for heating. However, in recent years it has increased because of various conservation measures and constantly rising standards for comfort. Nowadays, each person in a typical Western household probably uses around 8 gallons (30 liters) of hot water at 115° F (46° C) daily. In 1991, the proportion of the entire domestic energy consumption used for heating was about 76.5%, with 12% being used to prepare hot water; the rest was accounted for by lighting and equipment and provided mainly by electricity. So heating and hot water are required in a ratio of about 6:1. In low-energy houses, the proportion of hot water is even higher, with annual heating energy consumption levels of 6,000 kWh compared to hot water requirements of 2,000 kWh, in other words a ratio of 3:1.

There are basically two systems available for heating water: storage and tankless or point-of-use water heaters. Both of these types of systems are available with either electricity or natural gas (or LP gas) as the energy source. Given a choice gas will always be the most sensible alternative. A $425 electric water heater can cost $5,900 in operating costs over its 13-year life, compared to about $2,900 for a comparable natural gas water heater.

Usually the most economical way to heat water is by installing an energy-efficient condensing boiler system which includes a domestic hot water heating loop. This requires a separate storage tank for the hot water but the heat itself is generated by the central boiler. Even if a stand-alone hot water is used it becomes necessary to combat the main problem inherent in these systems: the energy losses due to the need to maintain a large volume of water at the desired temperature. Obviously these losses can be kept to a minimum by reducing the temperature set point on the system. Another means is to ensure that the tank itself is well insulated. Finally, the pipes can be responsible for significant losses so they must be well insulated, and the overall distance the hot water must travel to the point of use and back to the tank should be kept to a minimum. This can be accomplished in the planning stage by centralizing the hot water appliances and fixtures as much as possible – making bathrooms, laundry rooms and kitchen adjacent each other and near the water heater and stacking them above one another from floor to floor. This will also save considerably on installation costs.

Insulating heating pipes is vital
So that less heat is lost during distribution, heating pipes must be well insulated, usually with specially fabricated sleeves made of foam rubber or mineral fibers. But there are more natural ways of doing this: These heating pipes are insulated with pipe insulation made with sheep's wool.

If the tap is a long way from the tank, a lot of cold water will be wasted when the tap is turned on. This is why a continuous circulating water circuit that always contains hot water is sometimes installed. But this takes up additional pump energy and, even where the pipes are well insulated, causes unnecessary losses.

Unnecessarily long pipe distances also pose health problems. This is because harmful *Legionella* bacteria can spread in seldom-used sections of the hot water supply network. Although there were only 1,615 reported cases in the United States in 1994, it is estimated that thousands of people die annually of this infection, since it cannot be treated with ordinary antibiotics. Conditions for *Legionella* bacteria are most favorable at temperatures between 90–110° F (32–43° C), but they increase at such a slow pace that they do not normally reach a "critical mass." They typically breed in disused hot water pipes, rarely used boilers and also cooling towers and air-conditioning systems where warm water is left standing. There they multiply in the chalky and sludgy deposits where they are not washed away. The only effective means of combating them in hot water pipes is to flush out rarely used pipes once a month with water heated to 160° F (71° C) or designing systems to avoid water standing in pipes for any length of time.

Health warning

There's nothing more relaxing than a soak in a whirlpool bath. But the danger of Legionnaires' disease means you need to take extra care that they are properly cleaned on a regular basis and functioning properly.

Solar systems for heating domestic water

A typical sight

In some parts of Europe, solar panels are an integral part of the urban landscape. They can be installed on almost any roof without detracting from its appearance. In certain areas, subsidies are available making it possible for the installation to pay for itself in only a few years.

Solar water heating systems absorb solar radiation and transfer the heat to storage, usually in the form of a water tank. In domestic hot water systems, the energy collected is then used to heat potable water directly or by a heat exchanger. The energy savings of a solar system can easily be predicted on an annual basis, but because of variations in climate and sunlight availability, the savings at any given hour, day or month of the year are unpredictable. Besides saving energy costs, other benefits of solar water heaters may include: increased capacity due to a larger storage tank; no pollution; and increased reliability, since it is unlikely that both the solar and

backup systems will be down at the same time. The location of solar collectors used for water heating is important. On the continental United States, for example, collectors should be rotated within 30° of true or solar south. In addition, a tilt angle (up from the horizontal) equal to the local latitude maximizes year-round solar gains and is usually appropriate for solar water heating; however, a tilt angle equal to the latitude *minus* 15° will maximize summer solar gains, but reduce winter gains and a tilt angle of latitude *plus* 15° maximizes winter gain and produces a solar energy production that is more uniform throughout the year. It is generally best to mount the collectors

on a pitched roof as close to the optimal orientation as possible in order to reduce installed cost and improve esthetics.

Studies have shown that, depending on the type of construction and quality, a typical solar collector can produce between 100,000 and 230,000 Btus/square foot annually (gross heat production). Taking into account normal heat losses and availability of sunlight, a solar domestic hot water system can produce 40–60% of the hot water requirements of the typical home. Some high temperature concentrating systems are purported to supply up to 80% of the annual hot water requirements. Materials and components used in solar water heating systems vary depending on the expected operating temperature range.

Low-temperature systems are usually uninsulated and produce water at up to 18 F° (10° C) above ambient temperature. They are most often used for heating swimming pool water. Low-temperature collectors are extruded from polypropylene or other polymers with UV stabilizers. Flow passages for the pool water are molded directly into the absorber plate, and pool water is circulated through the collectors with the pool filter circulation pump. Swimming pool heaters cost from $10–$40/square foot [1998].

More than half of the hot water used can be heated by the sun

An ideal match-up

Solar energy is ideal for heating swimming pool water. Here, the timing of available solar energy and heating demand coincides exactly, and no extensive heat storage system is required. In addition, the pool water can be drawn directly through the absorber panel, eliminating the need for a heat exchanger.

range in cost from $40–$90/square foot [1998] of collector area.

High-temperature systems utilize focusing collectors to concentrate sunlight and evacuated tubes around the receiver tube to provide extremely good insulating properties. High temperature systems can be used for higher volume demand or high temperature domestic hot water heating as well as for absorption cooling and electricity generation. Due to the tracking mechanism required to keep the focusing mirrors facing the sun, high-temperature systems are usually very large and mounted on the ground adjacent to a building. Because of economies of scale, large system sizes result in a relatively low cost of $30–50/square foot [1998] whereas smaller systems appropriate for a single-family residence may run $3,000 or more.

Solar hot water heating systems can be further classified by the heat transfer method used:

- Active – requires electric power to activate pumps and/or controls.
- Passive – relies on buoyancy (natural convection) rather than electric power to circulate the water. Thermosyphon systems locate a storage tank above the solar collector, while integrated-collector-storage collectors place the storage inside the collector.
- Direct – heats potable water directly in the collector.
- Indirect – heats propylene glycol or other heat transfer fluid in the collector and transfers heat to potable water via a heat exchanger.

All solar hot water systems must have thermal storage which is generally required to allow for the variation in timing of the solar energy availability with the demand for hot water. In general, 1 to 2 gallons of storage water per square foot of collector area is adequate. For small residential systems, this is usually

Mid-temperature systems produce water 18–129° F (10–50° C) above outside temperature, and are typically used for heating domestic hot water. Mid-temperature collectors consist of flat plates insulated by a low-iron content glazing and polyisocyanurate insulation. In order to reduce radiant losses from the collector, the copper absorber plate is often coated with a black nickel selective surface, which has high absorptivity in the solar spectrum, but low emissivity in the thermal spectrum. Mid-temperature systems

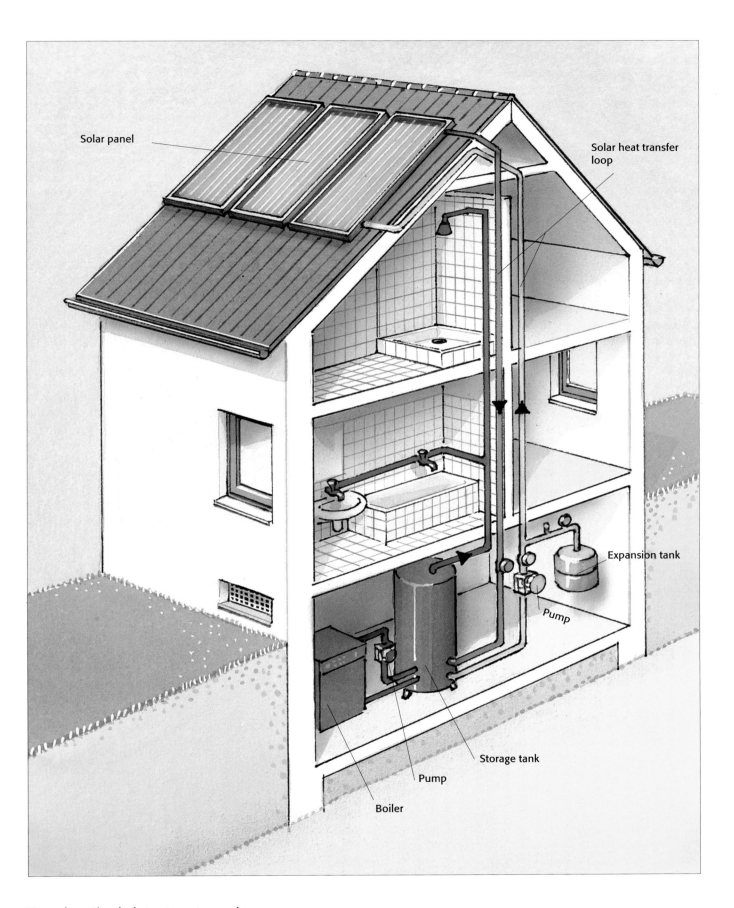

Solar panel

Solar heat transfer loop

Expansion tank

Pump

Storage tank

Pump

Boiler

How a domestic solar hot water system works

The heat produced by the solar collectors is fed via a heat transfer fluid (usually glycol) to heat exchangers in a thermal storage tank installed in the house. If the solar energy is not sufficient to heat the hot water in the storage tank to the desired temperature (usually 100–115° F/38–46° C) the water can be additionally heated to that temperature by means of a conventional boiler or hot water heater. Generally the solar heat exchanger is on the bottom of the storage tank and that of the boiler on top. Although occasionally a long distance may be required for the pipes running to the solar panels, the best position for the storage tank is directly under the roof where they are mounted.

If the system has not been installed properly it may not run efficiently, and its lifespan may be shortened.

Even long-lasting, reasonably priced solar collectors do not pay for themselves at present energy prices. At best they will deliver hot water at about the same price as gas or mineral oil. Only heavy promotion on the part of the manufacturers or perhaps higher taxation of non-renewable energy sources will help these products gain a significant market share. On the other hand, larger systems in which the available energy and the demand for hot water occur at very similar times, such as in hotels and resorts that are used mainly during the summer months, and absorber plate systems for heating the water in open-air swimming pools rapidly pay for themselves.

Active solar heating

Energy demand and supply diverge widely in the case of heating with solar energy. For this reason suitable storage units need to be found that can provide long-term storage of the summer's heat available during the winter. While this has already been put into practice in various experimental buildings, it is not yet economical to accomplish. However, various attempts are being made to supply entire residential estates with common storage devices. In one of the largest systems in Germany, about 31,500 square feet (3,000 square meters) of solar collectors were set up on 124 terraced houses in a solar settlement in Hamburg-Bramfeld. Throughout the year the solar collectors store the heat energy in a large subterranean hot water thermal storage system, with a volume of 1.2 million

Highest efficiency

These tracking vacuum tube collectors are particularly effective in collecting and converting solar energy-efficiently. However, they are also more expensive than conventional flat plate collectors.

Solar heating

In this residential solar development in Germany, solar energy is not just used to produce hot water. Collectors with a total surface area of 31,500 square feet (3,000 square meters) also feeds an underground seasonal storage tank from which energy for space heating can be drawn in winter.

provided by a glass-lined steel water tank. Active systems also have a temperature difference (delta T) controller to start and stop the pumps.

Solar water heaters usually save energy by preheating water to the conventional heater. Solar DHW systems are usually designed to meet 40% to 70% of the water heating load. A back-up, conventional heater is still needed to meet the full demand on cloudy days or when the solar system is down for repairs.

Mid-temperature systems are usually the best solution. They can be installed by anyone with a certain amount of technical skill which further reduces the costs. Ready-made components are available from a range of manufacturers and distributing companies. But if you do it yourself, little technical support is available.

gallons (4,500 cubic meters), raising its temperature to just below the boiling point. In winter the stored heat flows into the households via a low-temperature community heating network. About 50% of the entire demand for heating is said to be met in that way.

Geothermal energy

Geothermal energy is the heat energy contained in underground rocks and fluids; it is the only renewable energy source that does not derive either directly or indirectly from solar energy. It is generated when the earth's crust is heated by the molten rock in the mantle below. According to the National Academy of Sciences, the energy recoverable from geothermal sources could meet US energy needs for 600 to 700 years, but the projected costs of tapping this energy is high. There are, however, many examples in which it has been used economically to heat buildings, generate electricity, produce space heating and cooling, or process heat for industry.

Geothermal energy consists of reservoirs of dry steam (steam with no water droplets), wet steam (mixture of steam and water droplets), and hot water trapped in fractured or porous rock. Other sources include molten rock or magma, which has penetrated the earth's crust, the hot dry rock zones surrounding these penetrations, and low-to-moderate temperature warm rock deposits which can be used for space heating and air-conditioning by providing a heat source for geothermal heat pumps, for example.

In regions where there are geological anomalies, such as hot springs or geysers, geothermal energy has been used for a long time. The Geysers steam field about 90 miles (145 km) northwest of San Francisco, California supplies energy to 28 power plants which furnish 6% of the total electrical power for northern California. Serious efforts are also being made in many areas with geothermal reservoirs, to tap subterranean hot springs and then feed the heat energy into community heating networks.

Although geothermal energy is essentially renewable and abundant it can only be economically harvested in the most concentrated and accessible sources. In some areas geothermal development has been stalled by environmentalist action because it of its potential to destroy or degrade nearby ecosystems. For example in Hawaii, environmentalists were able to prevent construction of a large geothermal project where it threatened the only lowland tropical rainforest left in the United States. Without proper controls, geothermal energy production can cause local environmental problems including, air and water pollution, noise, odor, and local climate changes.

Geothermal power

The only renewable energy source which does not derive from the sun in some form is geothermal heat. It can be readily tapped using deep wells, as shown in the diagram, but natural hot springs can also be used as has been done for some time now in Iceland.

Geothermal power plant

Turbine house with electrical generator

Pumphouse

Cold water

Hot water

Submersible pump

Water circulating through heated rock

Not exactly inconspicuous
The ventilator for this bathroom exhaust system is housed in a rather unsightly box, which would have been better concealed inside the wall or above the ceiling. The important function of removing the damp air to the outside has been accomplished, however, by making use of an old chimney that was no longer needed for other purposes.

VENTILATION

To ensure a pleasant and healthy indoor climate at all times, the air in each room should be changed completely about once every three hours, and even more frequently in the bathroom and kitchen.

Natural ventilation

To do this, the windows should be opened completely, preferably on both the windward and leeward (opposite the wind direction) sides of the building and with a clear passage between to create good cross-ventilation. Of course, all thermostats should be turned off during this time, as only a certain number of electronic thermostats can register open windows and shut off automatically.

However, this does not often work very well in actual practice. Instead, windows are often left partly open all the time, which wastes far too much energy. Often individual unheated rooms are aired constantly, which causes the interior walls to cool off and may lead to an excessive loss of energy as well. Drafts from open windows often make one feel excessively uncomfortable causing that person to turn up the heat even further, exacerbating the problem even more.

Exhaust ventilation systems

The simplest and most cost-effective ventilation systems combine an exhaust air duct and mechanical fan which blows the used air out; vents in the walls or trickle vents incorporated into the windows allow fresh air in to replace it. The vents should be provided with some degree of soundproofing and should be sized according to the capacity of the blower. However, exhaust ventilation including ventilators which draw used, humid air from the kitchen, bathroom and toilet create a low-pressure condition slightly below the outside atmospheric pressure in the entire house. This not only causes fresh air to stream effectively through the vents in the window frames or exterior walls intended for this purpose, but can also cause backdrafting of the flue or chimney which can allow extremely toxic combustion by-products to enter the house.

To make sure that air comes in only at these controllable points and not through poorly fitted air vents, flues or chimneys, buildings have to be airtight, and all exhaust flues must be fitted with backdraft dampers. In principle, these planned ventilation openings replace the earlier unplanned gaps around ill-fitting windows and doors through which energy was lost. In such simple ventilation systems it is also possible to throw the windows wide open occasionally without compromising the entire system. Typically these systems are only used for a few months of the year, because losses caused by ventilating in this fashion are only important during the period when heating is required. In summer it is not a problem if windows are opened wide. On average, a ventilation motor of this type operates on a modest 50–100 W of energy. But if it is used all year round, the total energy consumption could be as much as 900 kWh. The use of trickle ventilators in window frames still has not caught on in the United States and most window manufacturers (other than a few European based companies) do not offer them. An advantage of a ducted intake system is that fresh air can be supplied to rooms which do not have windows.

When a passive or low-energy building includes any of these exhaust ventilation devices it is important that all of them are considered in calculating the proportionate amount of intake vent area. Furthermore, it is always best to provide combustion appliances such as furnaces, water heaters and wood burning stoves with a separately ducted outside air intake and if possible choose systems which do not have a closed flue design which cannot spill over into the inside of the room. This creates a completely closed system.

Supply ventilation systems

In a supply ventilation system a blower forces fresh air through a duct into a central place in the home or preferably through a series of ducts into several rooms, particularly bedrooms and other frequently occupied spaces. A supply system should not be used in a house which does not have a relatively airtight shell or air will penetrate into the exterior walls and result in moisture damage and mold growth.

One way of converting a standard forced-air heating system to a supply ventilation system is by connecting a fresh air intake supply duct to the return air duct before it reaches the central fan. Since the return duct is at a relative negative pressure this will effectively draw outside air into the air supply stream whenever the fan is running and distribute it through the conventional air supply ductwork at very little added cost. Since the ventilation will only occur when the fan is running, it is best to use a fan which runs continuously at low speed and can be switched to high

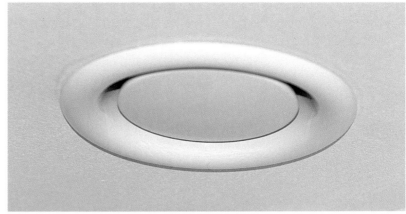

Ceiling grilles
This could be a ceiling vent drawing used air out of a room or a supply register blowing fresh air in. The design is intended to function without creating any noise or unpleasant drafts.

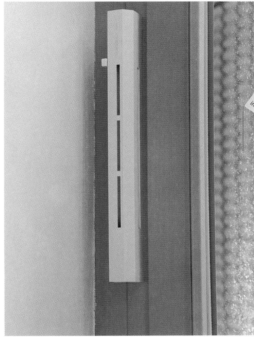

Trickle vent
In exhaust ventilation systems, fresh air can be drawn in through trickle vents like this one.

speed when the heating or cooling system is active. With a single inlet vent the outside air can be filtered before distribution to the rooms which can mean welcome relief for allergy sufferers.

Balanced ventilation systems

Technically a supply system coupled with standard exhaust devices such as range hoods and clothes dryers could be considered a balanced system of sorts; however, normally a balanced system would include two fans of the same capacity: one for blowing fresh outside air into the building and one for exhausting used air. This limits the openings for ventilation to only one inlet and one exhaust port, thereby reducing the amount of unwanted air infiltration when the system is turned off. Balanced systems which operate independently of the heating and air-conditioning system can be turned on and off whenever needed regardless of the heating or cooling requirements and thus provide better ventilation and lower energy consumption. The air intake can be provided with a filter; when outdoor air pollution levels are high the system can even be shut down completely.

Because airing out a building manually is not always possible, a ventilator is usually needed

Heat recovery ventilation

Recovering heat from
exhaust air

To avoid energy losses during ventilation, heat must be recovered from the outgoing air. In a heat recovery ventilation system, the air streams pass through a heat exchanger which extracts both the latent heat (heat energy contained in the moisture of moisture-laden air) and the intrinsic heat (heat energy in the air itself) from the warmer air which is transferred to the cooler air. In winter the heat that would otherwise be expelled with the exhaust air can be used to preheat the incoming air. In summer air-conditioned outgoing air can absorb heat from the incoming air, dehumidify and cool it. With the heat recovery ventilator (HRV) fresh air from outside is admitted at only one point, passed through the core (heat exchanger) and then distributed through the various spaces in a targeted way by small ducts. The warm outgoing air drawn

An HRV system can add as much as $8,000–9,000 to a typical 3-bedroom home and result in energy savings and potential savings on the heating system of between $300–500 per year. In a colder climate the payback period may be as little as 5 to 10 years, whereas in a mild or cooling climate where there is less energy to recover, the payback period can be much longer.

The components of a heat recovery system need to be selected carefully. Until a few years ago, the market was dominated by crossflow heat exchangers where the air streams pass each other in perpendicular fashion. Now a counter-current heat exchanger is available in which the air ducts are arranged parallel to each other like organ pipes. Cold and warm air flow in opposite directions past each other, thus making better

Passive houses don't waste anything
Architect: M. Victor-Ulmke

In a passive house, such as this solar duplex in Münster, Germany it makes good sense to conserve energy wherever possible including recovering the heat from expelled air.

Heat recovery ventilation
systems save considerable
amounts of energy

primarily from the kitchen and bathroom is led through the core where 75% or more of its energy is transferred to the incoming fresh air. For example, if it is 70° F (21° C) inside and 45° F (5° C) outside, a 75% efficient HRV will warm the incoming air up to 55° F (13° C). The reduced heating demand will save considerable amounts of energy and can even result in a smaller heating system being required. Moisture, smells and dust particles are taken outside. In addition, filters in the fresh air intake prevent pollen or other pollutants from entering the building.

Although heat recovery ventilation systems have a higher initial cost than other systems under favorable conditions, they will pay for themselves over time.

use of the laws of thermodynamics. The counter-current heat exchanger has a performance level about a third higher than crossflow heat exchangers and can recover up to 90% of the used air heat.

Besides the heat exchanger itself, the air ducts are the most costly components. The ducts should be as short as possible with no right angles or "t's," and cross-sectional dimensions should be adequate for the intended air flow but not excessive. If the diameter is too small, the air speed will need to be increased which will increase the noise levels and the energy consumption.

The materials typically used for ventilation ducts are steel, aluminum, and spiral ducts made of plastic or

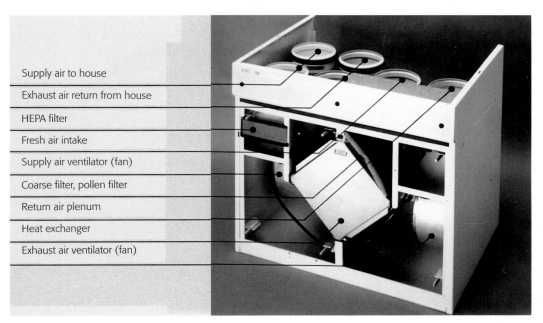

- Supply air to house
- Exhaust air return from house
- HEPA filter
- Fresh air intake
- Supply air ventilator (fan)
- Coarse filter, pollen filter
- Return air plenum
- Heat exchanger
- Exhaust air ventilator (fan)

fiberglass. From an environmental and health point of view, however, galvanized sheet steel is best. The interior walls should be as smooth as possible so that no dust gathers in them and the loss of pressure is minimized. In addition, the air ducts should not be made of materials that absorb water or can hold a static charge, to keep the danger of pollution to a minimum. The air vents have to be planned very carefully so that unpleasant drafts and noise are avoided. The system needs servicing every two or three months to check that dust and moisture have not accumulated and to replace filters if needed. This does not, however, involve a lot of work.

Ventilation systems can also be combined with a forced-air heating system which is, however, not advisable. Forced-air heating systems heat primarily by convection which produces a room climate which is not as pleasant as that of a radiant heating system.

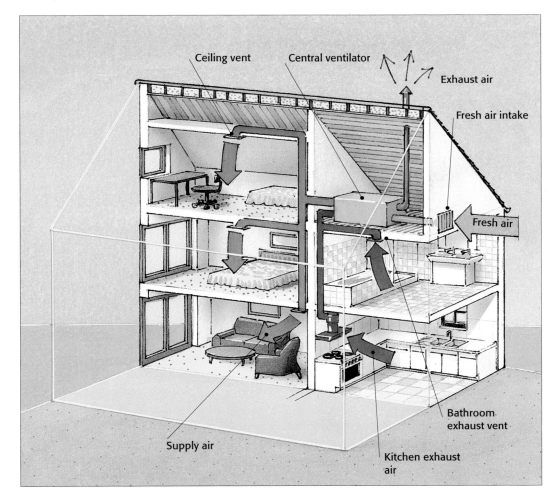

- Ceiling vent
- Central ventilator
- Exhaust air
- Fresh air intake
- Fresh air
- Supply air
- Bathroom exhaust vent
- Kitchen exhaust air

Targeted air distribution

While exhaust ventilation systems usually draw off the used air only from specific locations, controlled ventilation systems such as those with heat recovery usually also have air ducts for fresh air. However, this ductwork requires particularly careful planning.

Air-conditioning systems

Natural cooling
Architect: J. Eble
Artificial watercourses and lots
of plants are effectively used to
assist with natural or passive
cooling in this eco-office building
(above and opposite).

**Air-conditioning systems
can contribute to illnesses
and other health problems**

In Europe air-conditioning systems are used mainly in office and factory buildings, whereas in the United States they are also widely used in homes, and their prevalence is increasing. In 1993 over 42 million homes or 44% of the housing inventory in the US had central air-conditioning. Because of the expedience of combining air-conditioning with forced air heating systems, this has led to a rapid increase in the use of forced-air heating systems as the primary means of home heating (54% of all homes in 1993 up from 26% in 1950) and the steady decline of radiant heating (14% of all homes in 1993 down from 24% in 1950) over the past 50 years. These complex mechanical systems are often referred to as heating, ventilating and air-conditioning (HVAC) systems. Some experts believe that these systems are the most common cause of the health problems known as "sick building syndrome" (SBS).

In the case of air-conditioning systems, the physical disadvantages of using air as a heating medium, already mentioned with respect to forced-air heating systems, lead to drafts or unpleasant variations in temperature. In addition, these systems typically

make a lot of noise. A further disadvantage is the indoor air pollution caused by dust and emissions from a variety of materials in the process of recirculating air. The main danger of air-conditioning systems, however, is that under certain conditions colonies of fungi and bacteria can form in filters and in the corners where condensation tends to gather. In humid conditions microbes thrive in temperatures above 75° F (25° C). The danger posed by *Legionella* bacteria needs to be stressed again at this point. In the best-known outbreaks of Legionnaire's disease (1976 in Philadelphia, and in 1985 in the Stafford Hospital) which both resulted in a significant number of deaths, the pathogens were spread through the air-conditioning systems of the buildings.

Therefore, the use of air-conditioning systems should be considered highly questionable due to health risks alone. This is also true of the countless small room air-conditioning systems used mostly in warm climates. While they are much less likely to spread bacteria to the extent of large mechanical ventilation systems, they still cause the same uncomfortable effects such as drafts, colds caused by extreme changes in

temperature, and noise pollution. Above all, such systems represent an immense waste of energy.

Alternative cooling methods

There are a number of passive and technological cooling methods which can be effective alternatives to mechanical air-conditioning and that do not have the same disadvantages. For example, in multiple-story buildings with open floor plans ventilation openings are provided at or near the highest point of the building, (high indoor air pressure) and low on the building preferably in a shaded location (low internal pressure). The greater internal pressure at the higher vents (or windows) forces the hot air at the upper level to be expelled while the greater external pressure at the lower vents causes cool, fresh air to flow in to replace the outgoing air.

Plants and open water pools and fountains can also provide cooling effects as well as regulate humidity. As air moves over plants and open water, evaporation occurs which has significant cooling potential provided that the moisture-laden air can be expelled and replaced by cool dry air. In a domestic setting, plants and small open surfaces of water can also considerably improve the room climate in summer.

There are also mechanical cooling systems such as absorption refrigeration systems suitable for use in commercial applications such as offices and hotels; the heat source required for their operation can be effectively supplied by using solar energy. Solar collectors can produce hot water at about 200° F (95° C), and this heat energy is used, by the absorption chiller, to produce chilled water at about 48° F (9° C), in a process similar to that used in an older refrigerator. The only energy such a system uses is the electricity required to run the circulating pump. In addition, enough hot water can be produced to supply a significant proportion of the hotel's domestic hot water requirements. Solar cooling is ideal for air-conditioning buildings in hot climates because the periods of solar energy availability and cooling demand coincide. In fact, community cogeneration systems can be used independently or in conjunction with solar hot water systems to provide electrical power as well as heating and cooling throughout the year.

The chilled water produced by these systems can, for example, be used to supply cooling ceilings in which the ceiling of the room is cooled below room temperature, and then kept cool by means of a network of chilled-water pipes. Another new type of cooling system which utilizes chilled water is a radiant cooling system which employs fixtures similar to radiant heating panels but located on or near the ceiling or as a valance or lighting troffer. However, the temperature in these systems must not drop below the dew point, or condensation will occur. Much of the ambient heat can be removed via these chilled ceilings since heat always rises. Such chilled ceilings and radiant cooling panels are also suitable for modernizing old buildings and are already commonly used for air-conditioning computer rooms.

Cool and pleasant in a glass-covered building

The interior of this eco-office building (opposite) shows how in winter, the large glass atrium traps the sunlight, and in summer, plants and water courses ensure that the air is cool and pleasantly moist.

Radiant cooling in the ceiling

Networks of cold water pipes, easily visible here before the ceiling is finished, provide the most comfortable means of cooling a space because the room beneath is air-conditioned in summer without creating cold drafts or allergy problems.

ELECTRICAL INSTALLATION

Technology in the kitchen

Modern kitchens are stuffed with electrical appliances. Here, it is particularly appropriate to start planning the installation at an early stage so that the receptacles are in exactly the right places.

Good planning is the key

Good advance planning is absolutely essential when it comes to wiring a house. This is because you must know the positions, the required amperage and voltage and methods of operation of all electrical appliances that are to be permanently connected or used occasionally so that they can be provided with the proper circuit capacity, gage of wiring and type of receptacle or direct connection. All the necessary ceiling and wall locations for each type of electrical connection or junction box should be included in the rough building plan as well as the size and location of the electrical service entrance, meter, main panel and any subpanels or transformers (for low-voltage systems). Furthermore, the electrical plan should include any on-site power generation equipment such as emergency power systems or PV panels and related components such as batteries, inverters, switches and meters if required at grid connections.

The planning of the interior fixtures, lighting, etc., should also be finalized by the time the electrical installation plan is produced including locations and all types of switches and controls. It is maddening to have to break holes into walls shortly after moving in in order to run additional wires, or to have extension cords, TV cables, and phone cords snaking across the room because you changed your mind about the positioning of the furniture at the last minute. A well-planned electrical installation should also take into account the fact that rooms have different purposes. After all, a small home office needs far more receptacles than a child's bedroom.

The ecological principle that "less is more" also applies here. Electricians often suggest that you fit receptacles and supply points in all corners of the rooms, just in case. But having this much wiring running through all the walls costs more and can also affect your health because it can envelop the whole house in an electromagnetic field. One way out of this dilemma is to install numerous runs of empty conduits or tubing which allow easy expansion in the future.

General tips

It is important to include a heavy copper conductor to act as a ground (earth) and potential equalization line at the perimeter or through the center of the building and connected to a ground stake driven as deep into the earth as practical. Electrical utility companies can provide detailed information on the correct way to install this. The ground conductors of the all electrical equipment and appliances as well as lightning arrestors, television antennas, telephone and computer networks should all be connected to this ground, as should the heating system, gas and water pipes. This cuts down on the possibility of dangerous electrostatic potentials building up between the systems and provides potential equalization throughout the building systems. It is also sensible to add a secondary potential equalization in the bathroom, between the metal drainpipe (if there is one) from the bath and/or shower and any metal water pipes. In many modern homes these pipes are made of synthetic materials which would eliminate the need for this precaution.

To ensure that the wiring is not accidentally damaged by screws or nails when installing interior finishes, it is sensible to run the wiring in specific electrical installation zones along which the receptacles and switches can be placed. Such installation zones are usually:

- 15 inches below the finished ceiling;
- 15 inches above the finished floor;
- 6 inches away from all unfinished wall edges, corners and openings.

The preferred height for fitting switches is 48 inches above the finished floor. Near work surfaces in kitchens or work rooms, receptacles and switches may be fitted at a greater height so that they are not too near the surfaces but for purposes of universal accessibilitiy, switches and controls should never be higher than 54 inches above the finish floor.

Think ahead

It is sensible to fit empty conduits when building, so you can lay wiring into any corner of the room at a later date if you so wish.

All electric wiring is usually insulated by a PVC sheath. If these are beneath the plaster, there is no danger of toxic dioxins being released in the case of a fire. Nonetheless, the use of this plastic is problematic. Alternatives, such as halogen-free wiring or shielded cables that offer protection from electromagnetic fields, have been available but are considerably more expensive and often very difficult to obtain.

No need to carve up your walls

If you don't want to have to make slits in the wall to run wires when changes are made to your plans, consider installing empty conduits right at the start.

Installation zones

These are the areas in which receptacles, switches and cables can be installed safely. They ensure that no electrical wiring will be hit when drilling into the wall.

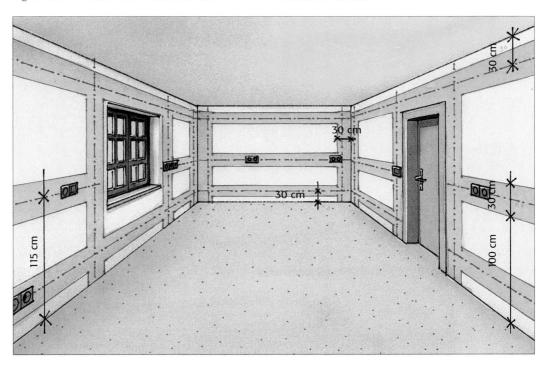

Power-hungry household appliances

The kitchen usually has more electrical appliances than any other room. The most important ones are of course the stove and refrigerator, but there are also many small appliances that are not always necessary. Appliances with standby modes are particularly wasteful, as they consume electricity even when they are not being used.

You could cut your electricity consumption in half

According to a number of surveys, the consumption of electricity in private households (excluding space heaters and domestic hot water) can be broken down as follows:

- 14% for refrigeration;
- 13% for freezing;
- 13% for cooking;
- 11% for lighting;
- 8% for washing;
- 8% for television and hi-fi equipment;
- 4% for dishwashers;
- 3% for dryers;
- 26% for other computers and all other appliances.

Electricity for these purposes accounts for about 14% of the total energy consumption in an average household. You can work out whether you are an average, low or high energy household by consulting the simple table below. It shows electricity consumption per year in kilowatt hours (kWh):

No. of people	low	average	high
1	800	1,640	3,200
2	1,500	2,920	5,800
3	1,900	3,840	7,600
4 or more	2,200	4,470	8,900

If this shows that you are not a particularly economical household in terms of energy consumption, you can try to cut down by altering your patterns of consumption, and buying more economical appliances. The most important single area is refrigeration and freezing. Exchanging an old but functioning appliance for a new one is only worthwhile, given the energy needed to manufacture it, if the new appliance uses at least 0.75 kWh less electricity per day. In the United States as required by the Department of Energy, all appliances are labeled at the point of purchase with an "Energyguide" label. This bright yellow label which gives the annual energy consumption also shows a range of possible energy consumption for that particular appliance group from the most energy-efficient to the least and indicates where on that continuum that appliance falls. The label also gives an average operation cost per year based on current energy prices providing an easy means of comparison. Some manufacturers have made considerable improvements in design, so there can be marked differences in energy consumption between appliances.

Once an appliance is selected further savings can be achieved just by the way appliances are arranged. For example, refrigerators should never be placed next to stoves, heaters or dishwashers, as they will then require about 10–15% more electricity to run. A freezer compartment in a refrigerator increases electricity consumption unnecessarily if there is already a separate freezer. If the freezer is kept in a basement which is 10–15° F cooler, up to 25% can be saved. The freezer should not be too large for your needs, because 18 cubic feet of unused freezer space consumes up to 100 kWh a year. Chest freezers use less electricity than upright freezers because cold air does not escape as readily when the door is opened. In a 1996 study, the most economical refrigerators available used between 1 and 2 kWh/ft.^{3}/month, and the most economical freezers between 2 and 2.5 kWh/ft.^{3}/month.

The best tip for saving energy when cooking is to use a gas stove. It only uses about half as much energy as an electric stove. If you still want to cook with electricity, you can save about 5% compared to ordinary hotplates by using a ceramic top. Modern ovens save about 20% of energy compared to older models because they have double glazing and better insulation. Convection ovens use less electricity than conventional ovens with upper and lower heat. If the oven has an integral microwave, roasting can be done as a combination of the two methods, saving 13% of the energy that would otherwise be required. Cooking with lids on pans saves about 50% of the energy used to cook without lids.

Where washing machines are concerned, most of the electricity is swallowed up in heating the water. If you avoid using the prewash cycle and use cold or warm water instead of hot you can save a third of the energy consumed. Horizontal axis machines use less energy because they require less water per load and they clean better than vertical axis machines requiring less environmentally damaging detergents.

In a study carried out in 1996, the most economical horizontal axis washing machines used about 0.1 kWh/lb./75° F wash while using 5–6 gallons of water per pound of washing. The electricity supplied at the receptacle is generally 110 volts AC. Many appliances, such as computers, television and audio equipment, energy-saving bulbs and various other small electrical appliances, need a current of 12 volts DC or less. These appliances therefore require a transformer which is usually built directly into the appliance or on the end of the power cord. These transformers waste significant amounts of electricity in the form of heat while connected, even when in standby mode (about 60 kWh per appliance annually). They should always be completely disconnected from the receptacle when they are not actually in use.

Standby mode wastes electricity

Ditch that old refrigerator
The bulk of domestic electricity is used for cooling and freezing. This means that it is frequently worth buying a new, more economical refrigerator/freezer. In addition, old appliances often still contain CFCs, which destroy the earth's ozone layer.

Freezing in the basement
Chest freezers which do not constantly need to be opened are best kept in the basement, if you have one. It's cooler down there and the appliance does not need to work as hard. If you don't have a basement, keep it in an unheated room or garage.

Planning lighting

Poor lighting can cause a wide range of physical complaints. Numerous studies have shown that poor lighting can cause headaches and backache, and is one of the most important causes of sick building syndrome. Surveys have found that as many as 98% of all workplaces are poorly lit, even though in many places there are legal requirements governing the provision of lighting in offices and factories. The situation is probably even worse when it comes to lighting in private homes.

The most serious deficit of most lighting arrangements is glare caused by excessive contrasts between the light source and the background or between the light coming through a window and the surrounding wall. Therefore, the living room and all other large common areas should be mainly lit by indirect lighting which basically turns ceilings and walls themselves into light sources eliminating harsh contrasts and deep shadows. Concealed light such as those in a coffered ceiling, uplights in chandeliers, sconces and torchiers as well as lamps with large lamp shades casting a sphere of diffuse light are all suitable for this. Another source of glare is the condition known as a "veiling reflection." This happens when the angle of the light reflecting off a work surface or computer screen to the eye is the same as the angle of light from a source to the surface. The subject matter or task is "veiled from view" by the brightness of the reflection. Glare due to contrast and veiling reflection

can cause severe eyestrain depending on the task being performed. It is always a good idea to diffuse and filter the light whenever possible and to use the appropriate light level for the intended function or task. Standard lamps are quite out of place in a child's room, for example, as they can easily be knocked over. However, a desk where homework is to be done will require additional task lighting such as an overhead recessed or track light.

In terms of light flux, light is measured in lumens. Illumination is measured in footcandles (FC). The footcandle, which is the amount of light from a single candle at a distance of one foot, is equivalent to one lumen per square foot. In order to determine the quantity and intensity of lights in a design the footcandle illumination can be generally translated to watts per square foot (W/ft.²). When using incandescent lamps, these values are given as:

- basements, storerooms:

  | | 5–10 FC | 0.5–1.0 W/ft.² |

- stairs, hallways: 5–15 FC 0.5–1.5 W/ft.²
- living rooms: 10–20 FC 1.0–2.0 W/ft.²
- work rooms, kitchen, bathroom:

  | | 20–30 FC | 2.0–3.0 W/ft.² |

Work surfaces or reading corners should be lit as directly as possible. The rule of thumb is: Every table should have its own direct light. You should not economize when it comes to lighting areas where handicrafts or homework are done. Direct light also structures a room if used to highlight pictures, plants or items of furniture, provided it does not create veiling reflections. This frequently happens with low-voltage quartz lighting systems. Suggested values for accent and direct task lighting are:

- dining table   40–80 FC   4–8 W/ft.²
- cooking, washing dishes 50–70 FC   5–7 W/ft.²
- reading   30–100 FC   3–10 W/ft.²
- lighting pictures or other items

  | | 50–100 FC | 5–10 W/ft.². |

An exception to this is the living room, because it has to fulfill a variety of functions. One evening you may need only discreet background lighting while watching television, but the next you might want to highlight particularly attractive furnishings or pictures for a party. Bright light would be a nuisance if you wanted to eat informally at the dining room table, but the same table would need more light if you wanted to play games at it. One frequently heard solution to these changing lighting requirements is to install several parallel systems which should be switched on in groups from the door, if possible. But this is clearly an attempt on the part of lighting manufacturers to boost their sales. When all systems are on at the same time the electricity bill rises noticeably. For that reason, it should always be possible to switch accent lights on individually.

Another alternative is to adapt the lights to variations in demand by means of dimmers. Solid state dimmers cut down the amount of electricity passing through the bulb, reducing its brightness while at the same time saving electricity. Dimmers do tend to give incandescent light bulbs a reddish tinge while at lower intensities, and turn fluorescent lights a rather unpleasant shade of gray. Some of the energy-saving lamps such as compact fluorescents, cannot be dimmed at all. Also, the lifespan of halogen (quartz) lamps is reduced if they are dimmed too greatly.

In any case, it is possible to install very flexible lighting systems that can be rearranged and redirected according to need. For example, spotlights on tracks and many low-voltage spots can be moved and turned. Swiveling "eyeball" fixtures can provide indirect light when pointed to the wall or across the ceiling, and powerful accent lighting when swiveled toward artwork or where one is working or reading. However, they can often produce glare if precautions are not taken. Low-voltage lights are preferred for lighting valuable artwork because the lower heat output results in less damage to the art.

Flexible/dimmable light fixtures vs. several groups of lights

Types of lamps

Incandescent lamps are the most commonly used sources of artificial light. A tungsten filament in a glass bulb filled with an inert gas such as argon is heated by an electric current, causing it to glow. The radiation from incandescent lamps has an almost continuously rising density of violet to red, peaking in the yellow-red area. While this makes their light seem warmer, they are not particularly suitable for task lighting situations. In addition, incandescent lamps are the least efficient type of lighting, as only 5% of the energy used is transformed into light, giving about 8 lumens per watt and the rest being released as heat energy. In addition, they have a comparatively low lifespan of about 1,000–1,200 hours.

Halogen lamps, also called quartz lamps, work according to the same principle, except that the argon filling also contains a small quantity of a halogen, usually bromine. In addition, the lamp is not made of ordinary glass but of pure quartz with a much higher melting point. The light from halogen lamps is whiter relative to incandescent and closer to the full-spectrum quality of ordinary daylight, but it also contains a comparatively high level of invisible ultraviolet (UV) light. This UV light can contribute to skin cancer or damage to the eyes if it comes from a source closer than 20 inches to the body. A glass plate mounted above the lamp helps screen the harmful UVB rays. The efficiency and lifespan of halogen lamps are about twice that of ordinary incandescent light bulbs. While tungsten lamps give only about 10–12 lumens per watt, halogen produce 20–25 lumens per watt.

Low-voltage systems are commonly required for halogen lamps. They should always be installed by an expert. If the conditions are unfavorable, the transformer used to transform the current can use up to 20% of the amount of energy consumed by the lamps, and if the performance of the transformer and lamps does not match, their lifespan will be drastically reduced. If, on the other hand, mistakes are made when installing a low-voltage system, no electric shocks will result and if there is a short, especially in the system, the circuit breaker will not trip. Instead, however, the transformer will run too hot and could potentially cause a fire.

Fluorescent lamps contain about 4–5 mg of mercury in the form of a vapor. When they are switched on, the mercury atoms are excited and emit UV light which is converted into visible light by the phosphor coating on the inside of the lamp. The brightness and color can be varied widely by the use of different coatings. Fluorescent lamps have an efficiencies rate of as much as 10 lumens per watt – ten times higher than that of incandescent light bulbs, and a lifespan about 10 to 20 times longer – as high as 24,000 hours.

When using fluorescent lamps at the normal alternating current at 60 Hz (50 Hz in Europe), they flicker rapidly in an irritating manner. Combined with a bluish light spectrum, this can lead to discomfort and even health problems for the user. For that reason, the use of fluorescent lamps with electronic (solid state) ballasts is already compulsory or recommended in many sectors (schools, workplaces). These electronic ballasts transform the low-frequency current at 60 Hz into high-frequency current at about 30,000 Hz, thus creating a seemingly non-flickering light. Until 1983, each of the capacitors in fluorescent lamps contained about 200 g of toxic PCBs. Many of these capacitors are still in use. If they become leaky and the honey-colored PCB oil drips out, this can create high levels of localized pollution.

Energy-saving lamps, called compact fluorescent lamps, produce six times the amount of light with eight times the lifespan of conventional incandescent lamps according to manufacturers' figures. This means that an energy-saving bulb rated at 12 W will produce about as much light as an incandescent light bulb rated at 75 W, and will burn for 8,000 hours instead of 1,000 hours before needing to be replaced. In fact, this is the reason how the usually rather high price can be justified. Energy-saving compact fluorescent lamps are most cost-effective when they are used in situations where the lights are usually on for long periods, such as for indirect lighting in living rooms or outdoor entry and security lights. Exchanging incandescent light bulbs for energy-saving lamps is a simple and effective way of saving electricity, and they have even been made available free of charge by a few electrical utility companies in an effort to contain the rising demand and the resulting need for additional power plants.

There are, however, considerable differences in quality between different brands of these energy-saving lamps. In one study, 20% of the lamps tested used more energy than the given wattage would have suggested. The efficacy, mainly in cheaper products, was up to 65% lower than stated. Despite this, surveys by the world market leader in Europe show that 93% of its customers are satisfied with the quality and would buy such a bulb again.

The main point of criticism is the shape of compact fluorescent lamps, which, in fact, takes some getting used to. Manufacturers are now producing rounder lamps that are more similar to incandescent lamps in shape, and do not look out of place in conventional light fittings. Some suppliers have added a glass bulb to give the folded tube the usual bulb or candle shape, but this has a major disadvantage in that it makes it more difficult for the tubes to get rid of their heat, so they produce less light. In addition, compact fluorescent lamps are too heavy for many light fixtures. This demonstrates a further advantage of electronic as opposite to conventional fluorescent lamp ballasts, in that they are only about a third of the weight at around 100 g. Manufacturers recommend that you use the more advantageous combination of adapter and bulb. According to their figures, the adapter lasts about six times as long as the energy-saving bulb. When the bulb quits it can simply be replaced, and the adapter with the integral ballast can continue to be used.

Energy-saving compact fluorescent lamps can cut the electricity used for lighting to one sixth of its former level

Worldwide sale of compact fluorescent lamps (in millions)	
1988	45
1989	59
1990	80
1991	115
1992	139
1993	180
1994	210
1995	240

Source: Worldwatch Institute

Wasteful lamps

Incandescent lamps, usually just called "light bulbs," change just 5% of the energy they use into light, giving off the other 95% as heat. The glow-worm is considerably more economical, as it achieves precisely the opposite, changing 95% of the energy into light.

Daylight

Natural daylight is essential for our well-being. Research has shown that light impulses received by the human eye not only enable us to see, but they also regulate and stimulate our metabolism and hormones. UV light in daylight promotes production of vitamin D, needed for the absorption of calcium. Deprivation of natural light can even lead to nervous system disorders such as seasonal affective disorder (SAD).

Daylight is also superior to artificial light in terms of quality: Twice the light intensity of artificial light is required to achieve the same visual acuity as that afforded by daylight. Coupled with the rotation and movement orbit of the Earth about the sun this creates a gentle transition of color rendition, light intensity, direction, irradiation angle and view. When daylight is perceived inside the building via windows or skylights, we gain information about the time of day and year, the polar orientation (north, south, east and west), not to mention the changing weather on a subconscious level. In addition, the constant change in lighting and view stimulates the nervous system allowing us to remain more alert and be more productive.

This is why it is sensible, both for ecological and health reasons to bathe rooms with copious amounts of natural daylight. The practice known as daylighting does just that. It encompasses a wide range of both passive and active strategies for admitting and distributing light into the building. The three basic rules of good daylighting are:

● Avoid direct sunlight on critical tasks. This can cause glare and visual disability.
● Bring the daylight in high through clerestories and skylights. This allows deeper penetration and better distribution throughout the space.
● Filter the daylight and bounce it off surrounding surfaces. Use trees, plants, draperies, screens or translucent shades and light scattering glazings to soften and diffuse the light and use blinds, baffles, and light shelves to reflect the light onto ceilings and in various directions to prevent shadows.

Although simpler is better in most cases, there are various technically advanced methods which can be employed to daylight buildings. These include solar optic lens films (SOLF) and glazings which are prism-like fresnel lenses imprinted on or molded acrylic.

Daylighting with mirrors

Architect: Frank O. Gehry, Santa Monica, California
This experimental building in Bad Oeynhausen, Germany features daylighting systems that use mirrors to direct light to where it is needed. Daylighting systems are now being incorporated into some office buildings, because nothing can replace the quality of natural light.

Only natural light is "as bright as day"

Let there be light

Arch.: B. Heidbrede, Schwerte, Germany

Natural lighting is cheap, eco-friendly and important for our sense of wellbeing. Lack of light can even cause physical and nervous disorders.

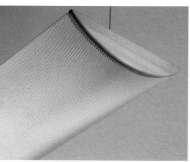

Almost like daylight

Full-spectrum lamps emit light in a broad spectrum which is similar to daylight. They are worth using in workplaces that have to be continually lit, such as offices.

These can be used to change the angle of light more efficiently than standard prisms and mirrors. Then, there are systems of reflectors which track the sun and can transmit it deep into the center of large buildings or holographic diffraction gratings which bend light to any configuration. And there are optical fresnel louver systems which can be used to direct the sunlight deeper into a room and onto the ceiling thereby creating indirect natural illumination. According to studies this method can be used to illuminate rooms up to 25 feet deep with daylight, and to save up to 80% of lighting energy. If daylighting were employed on a widespread basis with only a 40 percent lighting energy savings, it would reduce electricity consumption in the United States by 6 to 9 percent saving 146 to 212 terawatt-hours and avoiding millions of tons of associated CO_2 emissions and other air pollutants.

An alternative to daylighting is to use full-spectrum lights. These are fluorescent lamps with a spectral make-up and color rendition closely matched to natural light but with somewhat lower proportions of damaging UVB light. They are expensive and take some getting used to because of their unvarying cool white light, but in the long term they will guarantee good lighting and pleasant working conditions.

Due to the complicated way in which the fluorescent coatings are assembled, these lamps use more electricity than normal fluorescent lamps, but they have recently also become available in an energy-saving compact fluorescent versions.

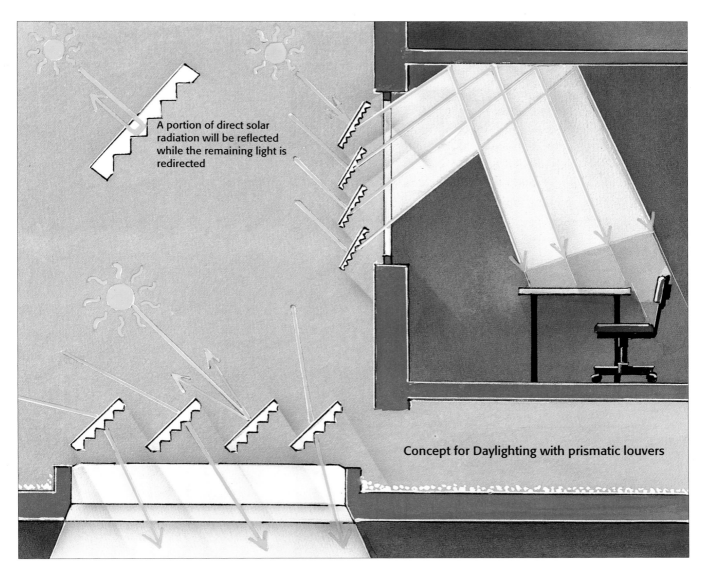

A portion of direct solar radiation will be reflected while the remaining light is redirected

Concept for Daylighting with prismatic louvers

How daylighting systems work

There are various methods available for directing natural light deep into buildings for general accent lighting. Mirrors can be used to direct the light deep into a building lighting areas which would otherwise have no access to natural daylight. With some concepts both protection from direct sun near the window and daylighting is possible through the use of specially designed prismatic louvers or light shelves. These systems not only offer protection from glare, but they also divert part of the light into the room where it is reflected indirectly from the ceiling and gives a pleasant lighting effect.

Concept for a Columnating Daylighting System with dual tracking reflectors

Swiveling columnating mirror

Drive axis

Tracking collector mirror

Electromagnetic smog

There are natural electromagnetic fields (EMF) all around us created by the nervous systems of living organisms where electromagnetic impulses at extremely low intensities stimulate and orchestrate biological processes, and regulate many biological functions by means of very small currents. These intricate natural electromagnetic fields and the sensitive biological functions related to them are, however, being disrupted by the much stronger and coarser

The controversy centers mainly on low-frequency magnetic alternating fields and high-frequency electromagnetic fields. In 1979 a report published in the American Journal of Epidemiology revealed that children living near certain types of electric power lines were at higher risk of developing leukemia. Epidemiological studies among more than 100,000 people living near high-voltage power lines in the USA, Sweden, Canada and Australia have indicated a higher

Computers are setting the standards

The radiation from computer monitors is controlled by standards that are recognized worldwide. If these standards were also applied to other electrical appliances, many of them would have to be redesigned or provided with better EMF shielding.

Electromagnetic fields can cause health problems

electromagnetic fields created by manmade devices. EMFs surround all wires that carry electrical current, electric motors, electric resistance heaters, and any other kind of equipment or appliance that is operated electrically. The resulting types of electromagnetic pollution include:

- low-frequency electrical alternating fields surrounding and produced by the electrical tension in a conductor or appliance (field intensity measured in milligauss and perpendicular to the magnetic flux);
- low-frequency magnetic alternating currents or magnetic flux produced by electrical current flowing through a conductor or appliance (flux density measured in teslas);
- high-frequency electromagnetic waves produced by transmitters of all types such as radar, television, radio, mobile phones (measured in volts/meter and amperes/meter);
- continuous electrical fields surrounding and resulting from the static charge in television screens, artificial fibers and synthetic fabrics;
- continuous magnetic fields created by direct current or magnetism (measured in milligauss).

incidence in these people of cancer, leukemia (in children), nervous problems, heart and circulatory problems, fatigue, migraines, sleep disorders and depression than the normal population once the magnetic flux densities reach levels of 100 to 300 nano-teslas (nT, equal to one billionth of a tesla). The most extensive study so far on the biological effects of power lines was published at the end of 1995 by the US Environmental Protection Agency. This study showed that there are unambiguous signs that even weak electromagnetic fields can damage health if people are exposed to them over a long period and during the human body's rest period when it reacts more sensitively to external environmental influences. A particularly strong influence has been observed in the production of the hormone melatonin, which is responsible for regulating the sleep-wake cycle and also helps govern the body's defense mechanisms.

An official of EPA, Professor Ross Adey, has therefore requested that a limit of 200 nT should be imposed. However, agreement has to date been reached on an international standard of 100,000 nT. This standard is predominantly based on recommendations made

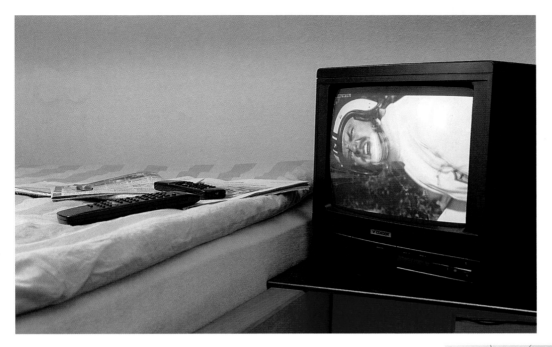

Further away from the bed
The intensity of electromagnetic fields decreases exponentially the further away one is. A distance of 6–7 feet from household appliances is generally enough to reduce the dangerous radiation to almost unnoticeable levels. You should not spend extended periods of time close to electrical appliances, and don't have your television right by the bed!

by the International Commission for Non-Ionizing Radiation Protection (ICNIRP).

The so-called Swedish standards, which are internationally recognized by industry, health and safety authorities and apply to computer screens, require much stricter limits to be observed: 250 nT at a distance of 20 inches or 50 cm (MPR-2 standard) or 200 nT at a distance of 12 inches or 30 cm (TCO standard). The recommended level for continuous exposure is a field density of 100 nT or less and a field intensity of 3 mG or less in sleeping areas. To achieve such field density limitations, the following distances would have to be maintained from high-voltage power lines (the minimum distances refer to the distances within which there is a distinct danger of biological effects during normal operation of the power lines):

- 20 kV power line: 260 feet (min. distance 50 feet)
- 110 kV power line: 310 feet (min. distance 65 feet)
- 220 kV power line: 400 feet (min. distance 100 feet)
- 380 kV power line: 525 feet (min. distance 130 feet)
- overhead railway power lines:
260 feet (min. distance 50 feet)
- underground power lines: 65 feet

It is incumbent upon product manufacturers to consider how they can reduce the EMF pollution created by their appliances. Electrical appliances, such as clock radios and baby monitors, which are typically used in bedrooms or children's rooms, should always be fitted with shielding and a ground. Investigations have shown that many of these devices contribute greatly to EMF pollution, particularly when they are close to heads or bodies. Perhaps the most hazardous source, electric blankets, should not be used at all. The time-honored hot-water bottle is a much better means of warming the bed before retiring.

Power-line nightmare
Houses near to railway lines are subjected not only to noise but to dangerous EMF radiation from the overhead cables.

Dangerous pylons
High-voltage cross-country power lines emit particularly strong electromagnetic fields. It is important to keep as far away from them as possible.

Precautions to take to avoid EMF pollution

The greater the distance from the appliance, the less electromagnetic induction force is produced. This is important to remember when positioning appliances. Electromagnetic fields decrease exponentially the greater the distance. For example, at a distance of 9 inches from one's head, a typical AC clock radio creates the same flow field strength as a high voltage power line, but 3 feet away it can barely be measured. This desirable arm's length distance of a yard applies to almost all electrical appliances. Electric heaters (30 mG), color television sets and fuse boxes, which create induction field strengths of as much as 50 mG, are safe at distances of about 7 feet or more. Another excellent precaution is to arrange a wire-free zone right around the bed with no wiring or appliances whatsoever. Or if it is necessary to install wiring it is a good idea to make use of shielded cables in this location. If this area is connected to an isolated electrical circuit, one can ensure that there is no current left in the wiring by simply tripping the circuit breaker at the main panel.

Electric appliances that you cannot maintain a distance from, such as shavers, toothbrushes, etc., should be used as seldom as possible. Items such as electric shavers and electric blankets create very

Electric blankets as well as water beds are particularly harmful

fairly high field strengths in close proximity. But they are generally used for only a short time and, therefore, present less of a danger than those which are constantly in operation nearby for long periods.

When using older electrical appliances it is important to remember that they should always be operated in phase, i.e. the phase of the appliance should match the phase in the cable. If the opposite is the case, the appliance will still work but will create strong electromagnetic fields. Studies have shown that simply turning a plug around in the socket can reduce the field intensity by 90%. Modern appliances are fitted with plugs which can only fit in the receptacle one way, eliminating this problem, provided the wiring has been correctly installed to begin with.

When buying a new electrical appliance, you should try to make sure that it has a ground conductor (three prong plug). A grounded appliance produces electromagnetic fields several orders of magnitude weaker than an ungrounded one. If your house has an older wiring system without grounded receptacles it is a good idea to upgrade them as soon as possible. You can also reduce electromagnetic stress by grounding large metal surfaces in the house that could act as antennas for ambient EMF radiation.

Disturbed sleep
EMF pollution is believed to have particularly harmful effects when you are sleeping, as your body rhythm changes and you are more sensitive to this interference during the hours of sleep. In addition, the radiation interferes with the production of the hormones that ensure deep sleep.

Keep your distance for less electromagnetic stress

strong electromagnetic fields of up to 100,00 nT (and about 30–40 mG) directly on the skin and should be avoided. They are enough to make an ordinary receptacle tester light up. Fluorescent lamps and dimmer switches also create strong fields (50 mG), as do the transformers used in low-voltage systems such as doorbells (100 mG) and low voltage lighting. Appliances with transformers inside or attached to a power cord should always be disconnected from the receptacle as soon as they are not needed. Other appliances, such as hair dryers and electric ranges, all have

Besides the low-frequency fields surrounding the home wiring network which are relatively low (less than 1 mG), the high-frequency radiation from transmitters has also been regarded as harmful by many experts. Strong transmitters, such as radar equipment and television and radio transmitters, have a warming effect on the body's tissues – similar to a microwave oven. Fatal accidents have been known to occur in the military sector.

In smaller transmitters such as cellular phones, there is typically not enough power for such direct heating

Low-EMF electrical wiring scheme

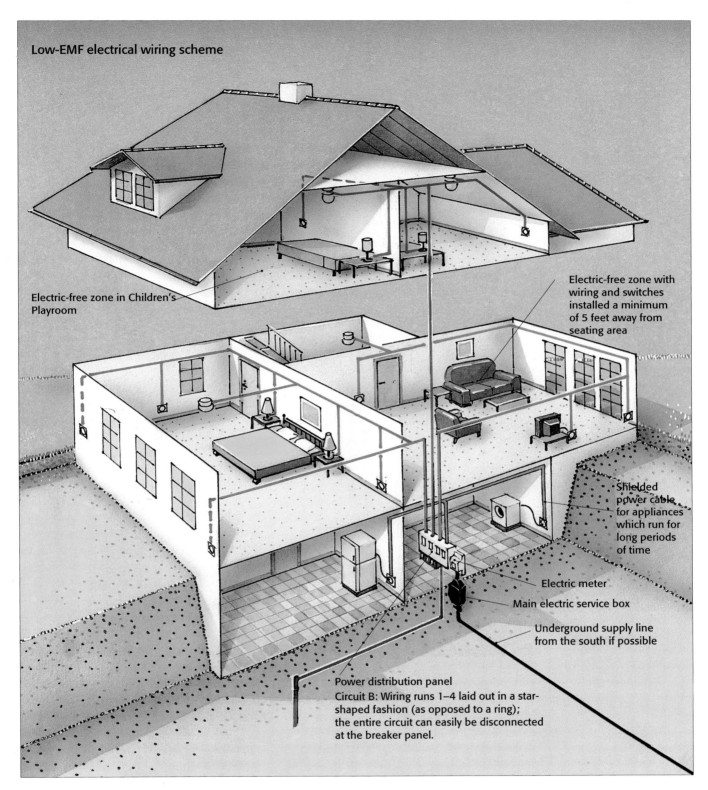

Electric-free zone in Children's Playroom

Electric-free zone with wiring and switches installed a minimum of 5 feet away from seating area

Shielded power cable for appliances which run for long periods of time

Electric meter

Main electric service box

Underground supply line from the south if possible

Power distribution panel
Circuit B: Wiring runs 1–4 laid out in a star-shaped fashion (as opposed to a ring); the entire circuit can easily be disconnected at the breaker panel.

to be observable. This does not, however, mean that the radiation is harmless because the radiation given off by modern D and E network cell phones as well as the digital signal transmission of the new 900 MHz cordless phones work with low-frequency pulsed signals. Scientific research indicates that such pulsed radiation should be viewed rather more critically than non-pulsed digital or analog networks.

Professor Lebrecht von Klitzing, a medical physicist in Lübeck, Germany, was the first to establish that pulsed radiation can affect human brain waves. In the former Soviet Union, extensive experience was gained with the medical use of weak pulsed radiation. According to Wolfgang Maes, a German building scientist (baubiologist), telephoning with the small 2–5 watt mobile phones will affect brain waves to an extent measurable in an EEG even at a distance of 65–300 feet. Just as people with multiple chemical sensitivity (MCS) are hypersensitive to certain chemicals, there have also been recent reports of individuals who are hypersensitive to EMF radiation and cannot tolerate even very low levels (for example, as low as 0.5 mG).

Planning wire-free zones

It's important to ensure that some areas in the house will not be affected by EMF pollution. For example, some walls could be kept free of wiring, or one could use only shielded cables in this location. Circuit breakers can be used to disconnect certain rooms, such as bedrooms and children's rooms, from the power network once all lights are off, thus creating electricity-free areas.

GENERATING ELECTRICITY

Under certain circumstances it is sensible to use renewable energy sources to generate electricity locally on a small scale. Small decentralized systems for using water, wind and solar energy are no longer regarded as eccentricities. Water and wind power has been harnessed for centuries and there are hundreds of small hydroelectric power plants in the United States which have been generating power for decades. While many of these small systems were shut down in the 1970s these small power stations have now been reactivated on a large scale. The United States and

A façade that generates electricity

Architect: T. Holtz, Zurich, Switzerland
A normal office building? Not in the least! Here, photovoltaic modules integrated in the facade are used to generate electricity using sunlight.

Canada have the most hydroelectric capacity at 13 % of the world total each. In 1991, 643,000 megawatts of hydroelectric power generating capacity was in operation worldwide supplying one fifth of the world's electricity and 6 % of its primary energy.

Other renewable technologies include photovoltaics, solar thermal, solar hydrogen, hydrogen fuel cell, geothermal, biomass, and tidal power. Many of these are really not feasible for use in a small scale residential energy generation system, but a few are readily available and worth considering.

Photovoltaics

The photovoltaic (PV) principle has been known for over 150 years, since the Frenchman Alexandre E. Becquerel discovered the photoelectric effect by which light is turned into electricity. But it was not until

1954 that the first solar cell was produced in the United States. Solar cells consist of a semiconductor material (generally silicon) sandwiched in two layers: a relatively thick positive substrate and a very thin negative layer. When the cell is bombarded by electromagnetic radiation (light), paired positive and negative charges are created. An electric field is then created between the metal contacts on the front and back and electricity is produced.

In favorable conditions, a normal 4×4 inch cell will produce 1.5 watts. About 700 cells are required for a nominal output of 1 kW. The individual cells are combined into modules housed in a frame and generally embedded in a protective layer of glass or plastic. Traditional PV cells are made from single crystalline silicon wafers and comprise about 95 % of all installed PV modules. It is by far the most proven PV technology and typically operates at about 13 % efficiency. However, some of the newer products are being tested at efficiencies of over 20 %. Newer thin-film technologies are advancing steadily through applied R&D and promise less costly and lighter weight modules. Although thin film technologies are less proven in terms of long term reliability and production efficiency, they are growing in market share with amorphous silicone (a-Si) the leader in this category at about 31 % of the world PV market in 1990. Depending on the material used, PV cells have different levels of efficiency (values shown are module efficiencies under normal operating conditions):

- Monocrystalline Silicon (Si) 13–17.5%
  (this is the most expensive process which uses grown single crystals and offers the highest efficiencies currently available);
- Polycrystalline Silicon (s-Si) 10–14%
  (also referred to as semicrystalline; this less expensive and less proven process can also involve processing of highly toxic materials, such as cadmium and other heavy metals);
- Amorphous Silicon (a-Si) 7–9%
  (thin film technology made from hydrogenated silicon with a thickness of only 0.008 microns, least expensive process, currently available in form of roof shingles);
- Copper indium Diselenide (CiS) 10–12%
  (polycrystalline thin film process still under development and more costly to manufacture than other thin film modules);
- Gallium Arsenide 17%
  (thin-film technology involving processing of highly toxic materials);
- Cadmium telluride (CdTe) 8%
  (thin film technology now under development).

In addition to the solar modules themselves, a variety of additional components are needed to operate a PV system. Typically referred to as balance-of-systems or

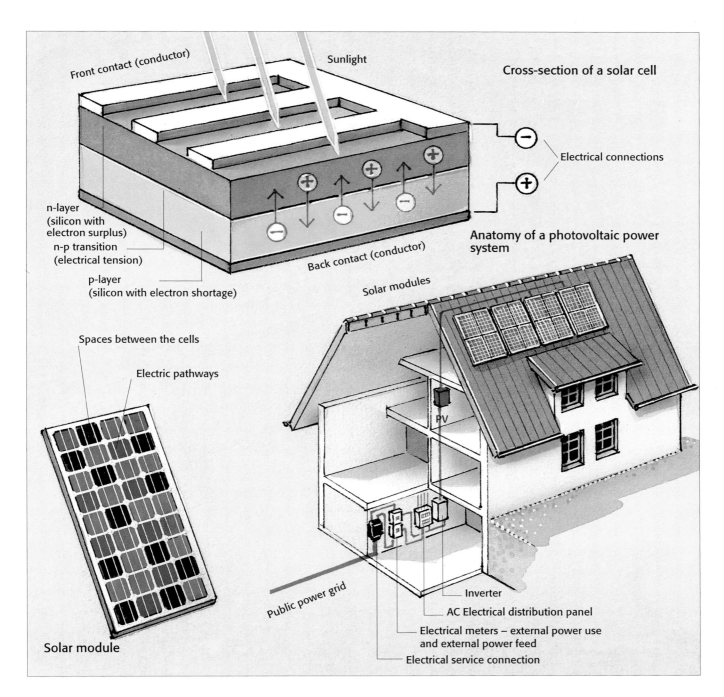

Cross-section of a solar cell

Sunlight

Front contact (conductor)

Electrical connections

n-layer
(silicon with
electron surplus)

n-p transition
(electrical tension)

p-layer
(silicon with electron shortage)

Back contact (conductor)

Anatomy of a photovoltaic power system

Spaces between the cells

Electric pathways

Solar modules

PV

Public power grid

Inverter

AC Electrical distribution panel

Electrical meters – external power use
and external power feed

Electrical service connection

Solar module

BOS, they can amount to about 20–40% of the total cost depending on the size of the system. These components include:

- mounting structures;
- wiring;
- storage batteries;
- battery charge controller;
- direct current converters;
- inverters for converting to alternating current for 110-volt AC appliances;
- if necessary, specially designed inverters for connection to the public power grid or to a conventional back-up power generator.

All unobstructed south-facing roofs are suitable for generating electricity with PV cells. On the continental United States, for example, modules should be rotated within 30° of true or solar south. In addition, a tilt angle (up from the horizontal) equal to the local latitude maximizes year-round solar energy on the panel, however, a tilt angle equal to the latitude *minus* 15° will maximize summer energy production, but reduce winter production and a tilt angle of latitude *plus* 15° maximizes winter production and produces an energy output that is more uniform throughout the year. Some manufacturers of roof tiles supply PV systems that are integrated into the roof, called building integrated PV or BiPV with connections and a variety of trim and covers that match their products. This is a way of saving on expensive mounting systems as well as the roofing replaced by the modules. Other firms offer special BiPV facade elements that are suitable mainly for office buildings and reduce the need for expensive facade cladding materials. In most European countries and in some parts of the US, the installation costs of a PV systems can be underwritten to some extent by state subsidies.

Photovoltaic system

The sun's rays cause the electrons to move from the n-layer consisting of silicon with extra electrons to the p-layer with a shortage of electrons, building up an electric tension in the silicon cell. A large number of these cells are wired together to form a module. This completes the circuit allowing current to flow. The modules can then be ganged together to create an array of any desired area. The direct current generated is conveyed to an inverter and used to supply the household with standard alternating current electricity. Excess electricity can be fed into the public grid, which is why there are two electricity meters.

In principle, you can decide whether you want to use a PV system to provide:

- an isolated solution to supply power to a remote farm, mountain retreat or weekend cottage, RV or boat (the latter if necessary in conjunction with a conventional emergency power generator). To completely supply an economical four-person household one would need a system with an output of about 4 kW. This would require a surface of about 380–420 square feet (36–40 square meters) and at present would cost about $35,000;
- an independent supply for individual appliances (such as emergency phones, weigh stations, fountain pumps and refrigeration or air conditioners);
- a system connected to the power grid in order to partly meet one's own requirements and feed the surplus electricity back into the grid to be purchased and/or used by the local utility. Power can be taken from the network on those occasions when the output from the PV system is insufficient to meet ones own needs.

In the early 1990s there were still many problems with the workmanship, such as loose screws, loose module tracks and rusting clamps, and the inverters were particularly problematic as they were not optimally matched to the output of the systems; but today such problems are no longer occurring.

New developments in solar cells make it likely that the cost of generating solar electricity will, over the next decade, drop from the present $0.20/kWh to as low as $0.10/kWh. Cells with a groove-like surface

Energy for isolated users

Solar power generation becomes quite competitive where an off-grid solution is required, such as the power supplies for boats and recreational vehicles or to power electrical devices along a highway or in an isolated location. These are examples where it would be too expensive or difficult to connect permanently to the grid.

quantities of toxic environmental releases has been shown to be unfounded through extensive life-cycle analyses of these processes.

Silicon is harmless from a toxicological point of view, and according to recent studies the other thin film technologies, such as the cadmium telluride process, actually release smaller amounts of heavy metals than the cleanest conventional electricity generation methods. The argument that PV systems require nearly as much energy to manufacture as they produce during their lifespan has also been disproved. The latest report produced for the European Commission shows that it takes about 2.7 years for a polycrystalline silicon module to produce the amount of energy required for its manufacture. Even taking into account all the other components in the system, a system with a lifespan of about 20 years can be expected to produce at least four times the energy to make it. The pure silicon used for solar cells is largely a waste by-product from the manufacture of electronic circuits, and, therefore, resource-efficient.

Wind power

Windmills have been part of the scenery for centuries. More recently they have been employed more for the generation of electricity than for grinding corn. Between 1982 and 1992 because of state government subsidies, federal tax credits and utility demand side management (DSM) programs, nearly 15,000 wind turbines were installed in California. In 1993

A tradition of wind power

In coastal regions there are still many old windmills that were once used to grind corn. Modern wind turbines produce non-polluting electricity at near competitive prices.

have been developed that raise the level of efficiency by about 20%. As the light is absorbed by reflection on both sides, the light gain can be increased further. Recent tandem modules made of amorphous silicon hold the promise of achieving a particularly favorable balance between efficiency levels, manufacturing costs and the energy used during manufacturing.

The ecological desirability of photovoltaics has now been affirmed by consensus. The fear that mass production of thin film solar cells would cause large

California's wind farms generated nearly 3 billion kWh or 1.2 % of the states electricity consumption. The rising demand for wind turbine production has led to a great increase in the efficiency and reliability of wind machines and a huge drop in their cost. Wind power generated in the United States today yields 3,196 gigawatt-hours (3.2 billion kWh) at an average generating cost of about $0.05 per kWh as compared to $0.04 for coal and natural gas. Worldwide, about 21,000 wind turbine generators are connected to the

Integrated design

Architect: T. Holtz, Zurich, Switzerland
Photovoltaic systems can become an integral part of the architecture, as can be seen at the public works administration in Winterthur, Switzerland.

public grid, producing about 5 billion kilowatt hours of energy annually. Today the favorites are medium-sized plants generating up to 500 kW. In the future increasing numbers of larger plants producing up to 1 MW (megawatt) will make better use of the few favorable sites. Wind turbine generators with a nominal output up to 30 kW can be connected to a low-voltage network (domestic connection). Larger systems require a separate medium-voltage transformer.

Unlike PV systems, it is not sensible to size the system according to your own energy requirements. It can work out cheaper to plan the wind turbine plant according to the amount of wind in the area, as the number of favorable sites is limited and the basic costs such as foundations, access to the site and connection to the grid will have to be met in any case. It is favorable to install numerous wind turbines in wind farms where they are placed close together. In this way they produce electricity at a more constant rate than isolated turbines and there are fewer specific costs associated with installation such as connection to the grid.

In some coastal regions there is a lot of opposition to wind turbine generators because they are rather unsightly, they make considerable noise, and because people feel they pose a danger to wildlife in ecologically sensitive areas. Although they cause a considerable number of casualties, it is almost certain that offshore wind power will be used more and more to generate electricity. Of all renewable energy technologies wind has the lowest present cost of production and one of the largest untapped energy reserves.

PAYMENTS FOR POWER SUPPLY IN VARIOUS COUNTRIES

Country	PV	Wind	Normal Tariff
Austria	1.56 öS	1.28 öS	1.15 öS
Belgium	2.2 BF	2.2 BF	5.6 BF
Germany	0.17 DM	0.17 DM	0.27 DM
Denmark	0.41 DKr	0.58 DKr	1.0 DKr
Spain	11–12 Pts	12 Pts	22.45 Pts
France	0.26 FF	0.29 FF	0.80 FF
Greece	14.2–22.46 Drs	dto.	23.4 Drs
Ireland	0.024–0.064 IRP	dto.	0.0825 IRP
Italy	271–377 LIT	184–233 LIT	230 LIT
Luxembourg	2.95 Flux + 1.0 Bonus	dto.	3.97 Flux
Holland	0.28 NLG	0.163 NLG	0.28 NLG
Portugal	11–12 Esc	11–12 Esc	12–13 Esc
Sweden	-	0.35 SEK + 0.09 Bonus	0.6 SEK
Finland	-	0.1 FIM	0.39 FIM
Great Britain	-	0.042–0.053 £	0.27 PSt
United States	0.20 US$	0.03–0.04 US$	0.01 US$

Source: Solarenergieförderverein 1997; Renewable Energy Project Research Report No. 7, 1999

WORLDWIDE CAPACITY OF WIND AND SOLAR POWER (IN MEGAWATTS)

	Wind power	Solar power
1980	10	6.5
1985	1020	22.8
1990	1930	46.5
1995	4880	81.4

Source: Worldwatch

State subsidies

Many countries in Europe subsidize generating electricity from renewable sources such as solar and wind. In the United States, utilities are required to buy back power from small producers using renewable energy sources. The worldwide renewable energy production capacity is growing at a steady rate.

WATER

Water is cheap. A liter of tap water typically costs less than a penny – about one-hundredth of the price of bottled mineral water. But despite this, tap water is not particularly abundant. Only 3% of the earth's water supply is available as freshwater and 2.997% of that is locked up in ice caps or too deep within the earth's crust to extract. Only 0.003% of the earth's supply of water is available as groundwater, water vapor and surface freshwater. Fortunately there is still enough for our needs provided we do not overload it with contaminants or withdraw it at a rate greater than it can be replenished by the natural hydraulic cycle. In many regions of the world, access to water marks the boundary between the rich and poor. Many regional conflicts have been fought over water supplies and this threatens to increase as water shortages intensify. Even in central Europe, which has plenty of rain, the abundant ground and surface water has to be purified to make it drinkable by means of increasingly sophisticated technologies. The natural hydraulic cycle which collects, purifies and replenishes the supply of usable water has been upset by human intervention. Water is frequently used excessively at precisely those places where it is naturally in short supply, such as urban areas, holiday resorts and irrigation projects in semi-arid regions. 38% of all water withdrawn from surface and groundwater sources in the United States is used for power plant cooling. 41% is used for agricultural use, primarily irrigation. Much of this water is used inefficiently and ground water in agricultural areas is frequently polluted by the careless use of fertilizers and pesticides. Industry uses 11% for the manufacture of goods. Domestic and municipal use account for the remaining 10%.

Municipal water – is it safe?

In most cases the public water supply is suitable for preparing baby food. But in some regions excess fertilizing by agriculture means that nitrate levels in ground water are too high. This can be harmful to infants.

No ideal material

Water pipes can be made of various materials. Old lead pipes are poisonous, and copper pipes can also produce ions that are harmful to infants. Plastic PVC pipes should be rejected on environmental grounds and stainless steel is too expensive.

Drinking water pipes

Tap water is constantly monitored by health authorities to make sure it is safe to drink. Thus, water coming from the municipal water supply is usually moderately free of impurities. However, some underground water mains were made of asbestos cement pipe. These pipes pose a risk that has not yet been properly assessed. In soft water areas in particular, there is a risk that asbestos fibers may be released. Whether the concentrations are high enough to pose a health risk when showering, for example, has not yet been established. The best precaution that can be taken, if asbestos cement pipes are suspected, is the use of a special water filter designed to capture asbestos fibers at any tap used for drinking or cooking water. Drinking water can also be contaminated by raised concentrations of nitrates, which can leach into ground water from fertilizers and other agricultural chemicals. Nitrates are harmful to humans because they are converted by the body into poisonous nitrites and carcinogenic nitrosamines. In sandy soil, in particular, exorbitantly applied fertilizers rapidly reach the ground water table. It is crucial that baby food not be prepared using water with high nitrate levels. In infants up to four months old, drinking water contaminated with nitrates can cause cyanosis. Health experts recommend a limit of 10 mg/l for babies. Water utilities are required to provide information about the nitrate content of their water and if necessary to draw attention to limits that have been exceeded. Sprays used in agriculture and various industrial toxins can also endanger regional water quality. There is a particular danger where the supply comes from private wells, as this water is usually not tested often enough, or it may often be tested by individuals not qualified.

Lead pipes should be replaced immediately to prevent contamination of our environment

The cleansing power of nature

Drinking water from the public water supply is cheap and usually good. But the increasing pollution of ground and surface water supplies with industrial and agricultural pollutants has placed a strain on nature's purifying ability. That's why it's so important for everyone to use this diminishing resource sparingly.

In many countries, portions of the public supply network still consist of old-fashioned lead pipes. Many older houses have water pipes made of either lead, cast-iron or galvanized steel. Of these lead is the most dangerous. They can be recognized by knocking against the pipe with a screwdriver. The sound they make is not metallic but muffled. Lead pipes have a silvery sheen and, unlike steel pipes, they do not have sleeves but are bent round at the corners. Any homes with lead water pipes should have them replaced immediately although, in areas with very hard water, deposits in the pipes can form a natural protective layer preventing lead from dissolving into the water.

In the 1950s and up until the 1970s almost all houses in the United States were built with copper water pipes sweat soldered together at the joints with solder containing a high percentage of lead. Copper is still somewhat common today; however, solder containing lead is now banned for this purpose. Literally millions of homes have copper water pipes which can leach significant amounts of lead into the water because of electrolytic corrosion, especially if it is allowed to stand in the pipes for any period of time. Even in small quantities, lead is a persistent neurotoxin. It impairs the functioning of the nervous system in adults; in children it also impairs cognitive development. The disruption to the immune system creates an increased susceptibility to infection and possibly cancer. Anyone drinking or cooking with water from suspect pipes should always run the water for a few minutes when using the tap after a period of disuse. This will allow water with higher lead concentrations to run out.

The copper pipes themselves can also add poisonous metal ions to the water. Raised concentrations of copper in drinking water are a danger for infants, in particular, as they are not yet able to excrete copper through their gallbladders. For that reason, the first hot water in the morning should be used for showering rather than preparing baby food. In addition, in areas with soft, very acidic water, copper pipes are liable to be affected by pitting and corrosion exacerbating the problem.

There are alternatives in the form of plastic and steel pipes. Plastic pipes are less expensive, easy to install, non-corroding and keep their shape. Plastic pipes are particularly sensible in areas with very acidic or hard water. However, from an environmental point of view, only pipes made of potable grade polyethylene and joined with compression fittings (not cement) can be recommended. They are easy to identify because

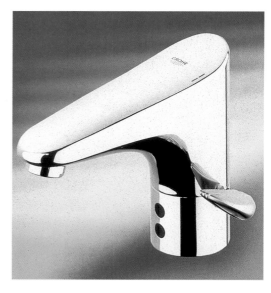

Water conservation

Since 1950 worldwide consumption of water has almost tripled to nearly 40 gallons (150 l) per day. Only a very small proportion of this potable water is actually used for drinking. The largest portion is used for flushing the toilet, washing, doing dishes and bathing. Some of it trickles away due to carelessness: According to estimates by a German water utility, up to 100 billion cubic meters of potable water is lost annually in Germany alone due to dripping faucets and faulty washers. Today there are new types of fittings and appliances which make it easier to save water. For example, if flow restrictors are used, less water flows through the faucet – no matter how fully it is opened. When combined with an aerator, the stream of water from a shower or faucet will feel just as plentiful as before. A typical shower head uses 7 gallons per minute while a water saving model uses 1.5 gl/min. By installing these devices a four-person household will, in effect, save about 3–4 gallons of water per faucet per day, and about 150–200 gallons per day from showers alone. By installing a water saving mechanism inside the toilet tank, the amount of water used per flush can be cut by half. This will save a family of four up to 25 gallons per day. Another alternative is to install a new water-saving toilet, which uses 1.5 gallons per flush instead of the more usual 5. However, some of these systems do not do a good job cleaning the bowl. Still, they can save a family of four about 40 gallons per day.

When buying washing machines and dishwashers make sure you don't opt for water guzzlers. The water-saving models will also use less energy as most of the electricity consumed by dishwashers and washing machines is used for heating the water. It also saves water if you don't have to spend a long time fiddling to adjust the temperature at the faucet or shower. Single-lever faucets or the more expensive thermostatic mixing faucets can remedy this matter. More recently, electronically activated washbasin fittings have become available for domestic use. Here,

they are color-coded red for hot water and blue for cold. Polypropylene tubing, typically a gray color, was used for a period but has been phased out and cannot be recommended. In most areas PVC water pipes can only be used for non-potable water uses such as irrigation. PVC should be rejected in any case because of the well-known objections to this controversial plastic.

The best, albeit the most expensive, alternative is using stainless steel pipes. They have a particularly long lifespan and pose no known health risks. They should not be welded but joined by means of compression fittings as electrolytic corrosion at the welding points could release chrome and nickel into the water. While galvanized steel pipes are much less expensive, they are more difficult to install. They must not be used in a mixed installation with metals such as copper, as electrolytic corrosion will cause zinc and cadmium, a highly toxic metal, to be released from the zinc coating.

the water only flows at the preset temperature when you hold your hands under the faucet. However, there is a wide gulf between the initial expenditure and the return. Considerably more can be achieved by making simple changes to your behavior:

- A shower is more economical than a bath as long as you turn the water off when soaping yourself. A full bath requires about 40 gallons (150 l) of water, but a shower only needs 8–16 gallons (30–60 l).
- Don't shave with running water. It is better to fill the washbasin and clean the razor in it. That saves about 8 gallons (30 l).
- The same applies to washing dishes by hand. About 32 gallons (120 l) more is needed for the rinsing when it is done under running water.
- When brushing your teeth, turn the faucet on only when you actually need the water. This saves up to 5 gallons (20 l).
- Never cool bottled drinks or defrost your food with running water.

- The washing machine and dishwasher should only be used when they are fully loaded.
- The garden should only be watered when it is cool and the sun is not shining, so during the summer it is best to do this during the early evening or early morning. This means that less water will evaporate, so only about half the amount of water will be needed. It is also better for the plants.

WATER CONSUMPTION FOR HOUSEHOLD IN CUBIC METER PER YEAR

Persons	low	average	high
1	37	57	88
2	66	95	146
3	91	131	200
4	113	161	244
5 or more	128	182	277

Thermostat controlled faucets

Modern thermostats like this make it easier to save water. Only water at the preselected temperature is let through, so you don't need to waste water by adjusting the shower before you get in.

Are you wasting water?

You can use the comparative figures on the left to determine whether you have an economical household when it comes to water consumption.

Simple technology

A simple rainwater tank, with the downspout from a small section of roof or a shed leading into it, is all that is needed to harvest rainwater for watering the garden.

Compact construction

Compact domestic waterworks like this one are available for use with rainwater systems. The pump, control mechanism and drinking water refill system are integrated in a compact space in an easy-to-service appliance.

Rainwater harvesting

Rainwater is ideally suited for use in both homes and gardens. It contains low levels of calcium, is already at the correct temperature and can be gathered both cheaply and easily. Toilets use up 30% of our domestic water, and yet they do not need water of drinking quality. If you want to flush them with rainwater, however, you will need to go to a little more technical trouble.

Finally, rainwater is also perfectly suitable for washing clothes – for the prewash and main wash cycles at any rate. As it is particularly soft, one needs less detergent and water softener which further protects the environment from yet another chemical pollution. Some experts believe that the average household could save as much as 13,000

gallons (50,000 l) of precious potable water annually by using rainwater. For rainwater to be the sole or primary source of water to a household, it is recommended that the annual local rainfall be at least 24 inches. With the exception of the southwestern and rocky mountain regions of the United States most areas receive between 30 and 50 inches (750–1250 mm) of precipitation annually. Britain gets around 32 inches (800 mm) of rain a year. One inch of rainfall corresponds to 70 gallons of water per foot of base area (1 mm rain = 1 l/square meter). Projected roof areas must be used to calculate the collecting surface which is roughly equal to the base floor area. If water evaporation and runoff from the roof to the cistern is also taken into consideration, a house with a base of 1,000 square feet will collect about 600 square feet worth of rainwater. That is generally enough to supply the toilet, garden and washing machine. It is estimated that there are as many as 250,000 rainwater harvesting systems in use in the United States – many owned by low-income and often elderly people. In the past, at least in areas with plentiful rainfall, cisterns were only a stopgap measure for dry days or difficult sites, but now they are being promoted in many regions as a means of dealing with water shortages. Increasingly large surfaces are now covered with roofs or hard surfaces so the rainwater has nowhere to go but the drainage system. This means that about half the cost of public wastewater treatment is spent on simple rainwater. After every downpour an enormous torrent of water pours into the sewage plants, overflowing retention ponds and enormous sewer pipes become necessary to deal with this flood.

Numerous small cisterns near homes could take the brunt of this torrent of water and take some of the pressure off the sewage treatment plants. In some regions sewage bills are calculated not merely on the basis of water usage, but also partly based on the amount of the property covered with hard surfaces. In these locations people who use their rainwater or let it drain into porous surfaces do not have to pay this charge for roof areas.

Without any public subsidies, a rainwater harvesting system scarcely pays for itself. Although there may be annual savings on your water bill of roughly $100–200, depending on the price of water and the extent of use, a simple system costs about $4,000 to install while a more sophisticated system with filtering and purification may even cost $15,000 to 20,000, not to mention the electricity required by the pump.

An especially important consideration is the collecting surface, which must be suitable for rainwater that is to be re-used. Green roofs or yard surfaces carry too much biological material which can contaminate the water. Asphalt or bitumen roofs are also entirely unsuitable as they color the water an unpleasant yellow. Asbestos cement roofs can contaminate the water with asbestos fibers, and this equally rules them out from an environmental and health point of view. Certain metal roofs, such as terne and lead, can taint the rainwater with metal ions or lead, which will not only make it unusable for drinking but will even limit its usefulness in the garden and for washing. Wood shingles can leach preservatives and asphalt shingles can leach petroleum products. Moss, leaves and sludge should also regularly be removed from roofs and gutters, as otherwise bacteria growth will be encouraged.

People who only want a little water for their garden will be well served with an outlet from the downspout leading to a water barrel placed in a cool and shady location. Once a larger supply of water is needed, a filter will definitely be required. The particular type of filtration system will depend on the age and type of roof surface and the intended use of the water, in other words, whether it will be used for drinking or merely washing and flushing toilets.

Making every drop count

The diagram shows a rainwater harvesting system where the excess is allowed to permeate into the ground. Here, there is no connection between the rainwater collection system and the wastewater system. Instead of small collection filters in the downspouts, there is a central filter that has to be cleaned occasionally. It is important to calm the water flowing into a concrete cistern so that foreign substances are more likely to settle and sedimentation is not disturbed in any way.

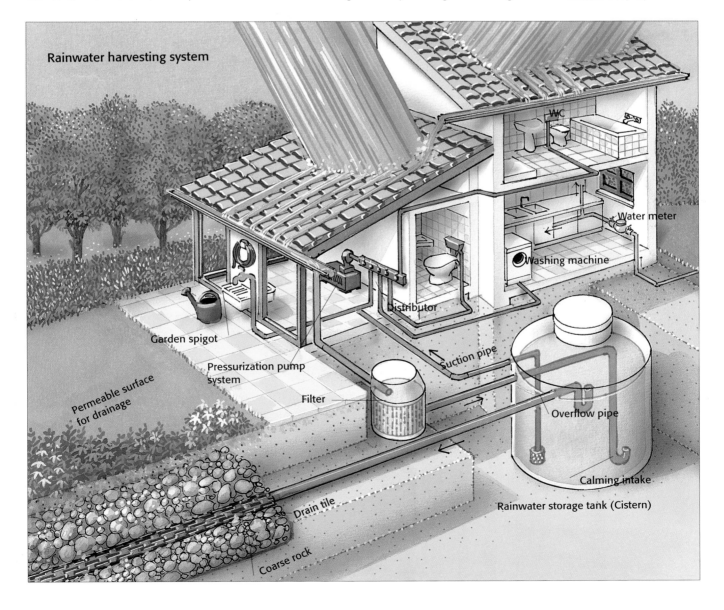

Rainwater harvesting system

WC

Water meter

Washing machine

Distributor

Garden spigot

Pressurization pump system

Suction pipe

Filter

Permeable surface for drainage

Overflow pipe

Calming intake

Drain tile

Rainwater storage tank (Cistern)

Coarse rock

Collection pool for rainwater

Rainwater does not necessarily have to be collected in tanks. In this ecological development in Kiel, Germany, a collection pool serves not only to store rainwater but is also part of the garden's design and a recreational area. It is important to bear in mind, though, that the water will less clear than piped water.

In small systems, a device known as a collection filter – a combination of a collecting system and a filter – has proven decidedly valuable. It makes use of the adhesion property of water, which causes it to run down the inside wall of the downspout. In the collection filter, a cleverly arranged series of slits in the metal ensures that the water is drawn horizontally from the pipe into the storage tank. While doing so, it is directed through a fine-meshed stainless steel wire filter which filters out all the particles larger than 0.17 mm. In this self-cleaning filter, all coarser particles are automatically rinsed into the drainage system as the inner cross-section of the downspout remains clear. The disadvantages of this kind of filtration are that this system still needs to be connected to the drainage system, and for that reason local municipalities may not subsidize these systems, and it does not collect all the water, particularly during a heavy rain.

In larger systems that are fed by several downspouts, a central filter can be used. There are different types available, including those that operate according to the same principle as "vortex" filters connected to the drainage system, or filters filled either with sand, gravel and activated charcoal or filter mats made of artificial fibers. The disadvantage of these filters is the rather extensive maintenance required. For example, leaves have to be picked out regularly if the container is not to overflow.

A very workable solution that does not require a drainage connection is the "porous plate" system. This porous plate lies directly on top of the storage tank and consists of porous concrete that effectively filters the water while it trickles through slowly. This system is also largely self-cleaning, because when the storage tank is full the water pushes out from below, and when rainfall is heavier the dirt on the top is rinsed off into the overflow. The storage tank's overflow should preferably not lead to the drainage system, but to a weir or sloped grassy area in which excess water can soak in without any problems.

Equipment for using rainwater

Roof wash systems are incorporated into some rainwater harvesting systems where the first 10 or 20 minutes of rain are allowed to run off before collection begins thus allowing contaminants which have settled on the roof surface to wash away.

To store and recycle rainwater you will need a suitable storage tank. As a general guideline it should hold at least 400 gallons (1,000 l) for each member of the household, and if you are living in an area where rainfall is typically irregular it should be about 20–50% larger. It is not worthwhile getting too large a tank, because in order for a tank to be

Accessories for rainwater systems

A filter is essential if you want to use rainwater for domestic purposes. A collection filter combines the functions of collecting and filtering by using water's adhesive properties. Rainwater pipes must be carefully marked so that they are not confused with drinking water pipes.

able to clean itself it should, in fact, be able to overflow once or twice a year. There must also be some way of running water from the municipal supply into the tank in order to cope with any additional demand for water during occasional dry spells.

It is best to install the storage tank underground, because this provides the ideal cool and dark conditions for storing the water. If the tank is made of concrete, it will also provide a degree of protection against acid rain. In new buildings, installing such an exterior tank creates few problems. Here, the best solution is a ready-made tank, and these are available from a wide variety of concrete suppliers. The cistern can also be made out of concrete pipe sections such as those used for building sewers. But with these, as with cisterns built on site, there are typically problems with leaks at a later time, and for that reason experts strongly advise against them. Old oil tanks can also be used as rainwater reservoirs, after they have been thoroughly cleaned by qualified experts to avoid any future contamination of the water.

In the tank, the water should then be purified further by means of sedimentation, which means, in effect, that the bacteria and dust particles will settle at the bottom of the tank. In order for this to happen, the tank's intake pipe should be "calmed" so that it does not stir up these sediments continuously. Cisterns are often designed with settling compartments to prevent sedimentation from mixing with the water. If the tank's overflow leads to the drainage system, it needs to be protected against backflow, gases and animals. It is, however, more sensible to allow the surplus to seep away. The predominant way of achieving this is by means of an underground drain field. This is normally only possible with tanks buried in the yard, however. When a rainwater system is to be retrofitted to an existing building, plastic tanks

are often used and installed in the basement. Here narrow, tall tanks are perfectly suitable, because the tank's overflow must be above the height of the wastewater outlet. However, you should always bear in mind that installing such a tank involves introducing quite a large quantity of very cold water into the house. The storage area needs to be very well insulated from the rest of the house so it does not cool down the other rooms, and so that the water is not pointlessly warmed by the heating system which would waste valuable energy. In addition, temperatures above 64° F (18° C) will lead to quite a considerable increase in bacterial growth. Tanks kept in basements should also be made of an opaque material so there is no chance that algae will grow in them. The most reasonably priced tanks are made of recycled polyethylene. PVC and glass fiber reinforced plastic should be rejected on environmental grounds.

Unfortunately it is rarely practical to use a gravity delivery method. In order to achieve adequate pressure and elevation in most cases you will need a pump. The pump is clearly the heart of the system. At the same time, it is also the greatest source of system failure. Cheap automatic pumps are the main culprits when it comes to occasional breakdowns in rainwater harvesting systems. The pump should be of as good a quality as possible and, at the same time, have as low an output as possible. Tried and tested types include pressure-controlled multistage centrifugal pumps or the somewhat more expensive submersible pumps. Whichever is chosen, all parts of the appliance that come into contact with water must be absolutely rustproof – and that normally means paying quite a bit more.

Where rainwater is not the primary source of domestic water, for the sake of expediency, the redundant piping system for rainwater is usually made of plastic and identified as rainwater piping.

Warning signs
Rainwater faucets have to be clearly marked so they are not confused with drinking water – the signs above spell it out: "Non-potable water." Here, the handle can even be removed so that children do not accidentally drink the water.

Concrete Cisterns with filter plate
It is best if a rainwater cistern is made of a single piece of concrete. The one pictured left is just being fitted with a porous plate filtration system. The water can seep into the chamber below through the permeable filter plates, while the dirt stays on top and is washed away.

Vortex filter being installed
A fine vortex type filter is sunk into the earth between the downspout and cistern (far left). The disadvantage of this almost maintenance-free system is that the excess runs off into the house wastewater system.

Gray water

Untreated water from the shower or washing machine should not be used for flushing the toilet. Dirty water stagnates extremely quickly and smells terrible. It also blocks up fittings so they have to be cleaned out at regular intervals. This can only be prevented by adding environmentally damaging chemicals to the water. All experimental plants that have tried to recycle this "gray" water have proved to need servicing far too often. In addition, the dirty water was repeatedly spilled, and large colonies of bacteria and mold developed. It is therefore essential that domestic waste water should be treated before being used in this way. The best way of doing this is by means of a biological purification system. Following initial purification in a sedimentation tank or coarse filter, the waste water is directed through a purification pool containing a substratum of gravel, sand and lime with aquatic plants, such as reeds and rushes, growing in it. Microorganisms living among the roots of the plants ensure that the dirt is biologically broken down. In contrast to sewage treatment plant designed for treating proper sewage from the toilet, also known as "black" water, a biological purification system for treating gray water from the shower only requires a pool surface of about 20–30 square feet (2–3 square meters) per person. This will clean the waste water to the point where it can be used for flushing the toilet or watering the garden. Experiments are already being carried out in which these purification pools are arranged

Biological purification system

If you want to use "gray" water from the shower, bath or washing machine in the garden or toilet, you need to clean it thoroughly beforehand. Biological purification systems, such as the one shown above, are perfectly suitable for this purpose.

Composting toilets save water

These small chamber toilets are suitable for occasional use in vacation homes. The human waste is mixed with bark mulch and composts naturally. This is an ecological way of avoiding the enormous water consumption of a conventional toilet.

All rainwater faucets should also be identified as such and, for safety's sake, it should be possible to remove the handle to prevent children accidentally drinking the water. A sign drawing attention to the rainwater system should also be put up at a central point in the domestic installation. It is frequently recommended that one should install additional finer filters to protect the washing machine or the pump. This is not, however, necessary if the system has been installed correctly. Long-term studies have shown that laundry washed with rainwater is just as bright as if it were washed with water from the regular domestic supply. If this filter is installed in a heated part of the house, and especially if it is transparent to make it easier to check, it will ironically become a breeding ground for all kinds of germs. When the water in the storage tank runs low and the pump is about to run dry, the tank has to be refilled with water to make sure the system continues working flawlessly. When doing this, it is vital to make sure that no connection whatsoever is created between the drinking water and the rainwater pipes. Germs are quite capable of spreading against the direction of the water current and, in that way, can easily contaminate the entire public drinking water system from one illegal connection. For that reason it is best to refill the tank by letting the drinking water pour directly from a spigot into the tank, perhaps controlled by a floating valve or better still by electronic switches.

below one another in a cascade fashion on the outside of buildings, so as to save valuable garden space in cities.

Composting toilets

An equally effective method of saving water is to use a composting toilet. They were developed about 50 years ago by the Swede Rikard Lindström and nowadays there are a number of different types in use, predominantly in Scandinavia. This ingeniously simple invention is promoted by the environmental organization Greenpeace, which considers the worldwide advance of the water closet to be a sign of "civilization going astray." This statement can easily be explained when you keep in mind that the water closet system is first of all responsible for a third of the total domestic consumption of drinking water, secondly it puts a strain on sewage treatment plants, and, last but not least, it means that the important nutrients in human waste, which could potentially be used as fertilizer, are wasted. The principle of composting toilets is based on the natural process of decomposition, similar to that which takes place in soil. A container is installed in the basement with various shafts leading into it. On top of one of them is the toilet, which of course uses no water, and another is used as a disposal chute for kitchen waste and plant matter. Oxygen is drawn into the container, and an exhaust air vent with a built-in ventilator makes sure that gases from the decomposition process are emitted above the roof so that the toilet shaft does not smell. The

The water closet – a luxury we can no longer afford?

Composting toilets for the home

Large systems like this one are only emptied every couple of years. In this time, the human waste rots down to a valuable compost when mixed with kitchen waste, plant matter and wood shavings. Obnoxious odors are drawn off in such a way that they do not create a problem. This system saves enormous quantities of water.

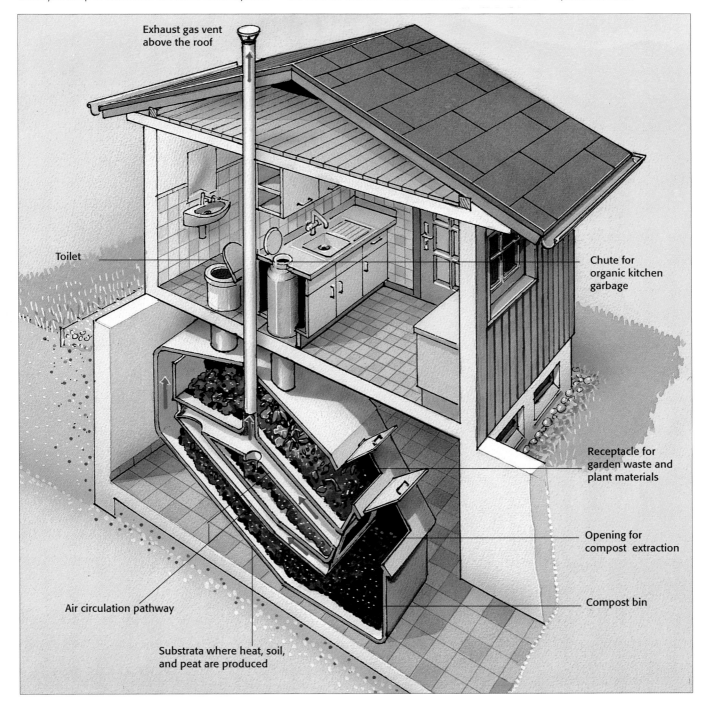

Exhaust gas vent above the roof

Toilet

Chute for organic kitchen garbage

Receptacle for garden waste and plant materials

Opening for compost extraction

Compost bin

Air circulation pathway

Substrata where heat, soil, and peat are produced

toilet itself is constructed in such a way that the waste does not stick to it. During decomposition, the material shrinks to just over 10% of its original bulk. High temperatures created on the inside make sure that bacteria and worm eggs are safely killed off. Within four to eight years the contents change into compost which can safely be used in the garden. For safety reasons, however, this compost should not be used on food plants.

Other small chamber composting toilets are available for houses without basements, vacation homes and places where it is not worth the effort of building a conventional toilet, and the waste products decompose in the open instead of in closed containers. In these systems, bark mulch made from conifers binds urine and accelerates the rotting process. Tannic acids contained in the bark kill germs and reduce the smell. The collection chamber is directly under the toilet seat and is divided into a section for solid waste and a section for urine. Airflow is ensured both by fresh and exhaust air vents.

In this system, however, the waste has to spend another year with kitchen and garden rubbish, composting in an ordinary compost heap. For safety reasons, this compost should not be used for fertilizing food plants either.

These small installations do have a number of disadvantages, the greatest of which is that they need to be emptied every two weeks and cleaned if necessary. The urine in particular smells quite unpleasant and can even disrupt the decomposition process altogether as it kills off bacteria and microorganisms if it is not completely absorbed. To get around this problem you can, of course, install a system that collects urine separately. But this makes the originally simple composting toilet quite a bother to use and maintain.

Finally, composting toilets are still not permitted in most towns and cities in the United States under current health regulations. For now they are more applicable to rural settings; however, as water shortages become more of a problem these regulations can be expected to change.

Purifying drinking water

In hard-water areas deposits form quite easily in pipes and on heating elements which are commonly found in dishwashers, kettles and coffee makers.

Blocked pipes

Calcium deposits can block water pipes and destroy the heating element in appliances. On the other hand, water that is too soft can also be a problem because it can lead to corrosion and pitting. There is no simple solution, because most appliances used to purify domestic drinking water have only a very limited use and, when used incorrectly, could even be harmful to health.

Over time, these calcium deposits damage the appliances, and the water supply eventually proves insufficient due to the narrowing of the openings in pipes. It is also a nuisance when shower heads or aerators in faucets are blocked by calcium deposits. For this reason, devices are frequently used in these regions to soften the entire domestic drinking water supply.

There are three basic systems: chemical, mechanical (filtration), and physical (magnetic). Chemical water softening adds phosphates that bind the calcium and magnesium and dissolve them in the water. The hard elements are then precipitated from 158° F and upwards. However, the salts pollute the houses' wastewater. While mechanical filters with a cationic exchanger remove the magnesium and calcium salts ions are replaced by calcium ions. Anionic exchangers are responsible for removing nitrates and replacing them with chlorine. Activated charcoal is used to filter out poisonous heavy metals and halogenated organic compounds such as pesticides.

There is no filter system that combines all these functions, however. And even if there was, it would be far too complicated to use, and the system would be far too susceptible to the failure of an individual component. In addition, even simple filters do not necessarily operate efficiently all the time. Nitrates are not always completely removed and the filters, especially activated charcoal filters, often develop build-ups of bacteria that can contaminate the filtered water.

Water filters cannot do everything

Cloudy cup
Connoisseurs do not like water containing calcium. It makes tea cloudy and leaves a deposit on cups, and it affects the texture and flavor of boiled vegetables..

very efficiently, they have to be replaced regularly and are relatively expensive. Physical water treatment systems are, for example, intended to alter the structure of the calcium by means of magnets, so that only a powderlike substance remains that can easily be washed away.

Unfortunately, the long term durability and effectiveness of these appliances has not been proven as yet. There are a large number of small water filters available to treat water for drinking and preparing food. In addition, many of these small filters are supposed to be able to remove potentially harmful substances such as pesticides and nitrates from the drinking water. A variety of studies have, however, shown that these filters are not really suitable for general use as they are typically designed to carry out very specialized tasks. Cationic exchangers, for example, sift the carbonates out of the water so that tea stays clear and vegetables remain crunchy. In the process, potassium

In addition, the replacement intervals stipulated by the manufacturers have to be followed religiously as the filter might otherwise, under certain circumstances, give off some of the harmful substances it has collected. This, however, makes filtering water a very expensive convenience. Filters that work by reverse osmosis are not recommended, because they remove many essential minerals that are desirable from a health standpoint.

Distilled water, in other words water that contains no minerals, is decidedly not a healthy alternative because in large enough quantities it can actually be quite harmful to health. Possible consequences of deficiencies in mineral salts include cell damage and functional disorders in important organs, with a variety of symptoms that include fatigue, weakness, headaches and even cardiac disrhythmia and circulatory collapse. It is, in fact, dangerous to drink distilled water while on a diet.

Distilled water can be quite harmful to health

FUNCTIONAL ROOMS

FUNCTIONAL ROOMS

A house has various functional rooms, such as the kitchen, the bathroom and the basement. In the past these rooms were clearly divided from the actual living rooms. Now, however, the trend is to convert them into comfortable living areas in their own right in order to make use of all the available space in the house more efficiently.

The kitchen

Churning butter, slaughtering chickens, curing meat – work in the kitchen used to be so extraordinarily labor-intensive that if you had any spare money at all you employed a number of servants to do the work. They carried on their dirty and often foul-smelling activities in a separate part of the building. At the turn of the twentieth century, however, the era of kitchen staff began to disappear. The kitchen was reorganized from a workplace for many to a workplace for one woman. Then in the 1920s, kitchen designs were streamlined to optimize efficient food preparation, and there was no longer any space for relaxing and socializing.

Today's kitchen appliances and convenience foods make cooking so much faster and easier that the kitchen is no longer considered a workplace. It is now a social center and the heart of the home. The dining table is back in the kitchen area and is now used for homework, hobbies and games, as well as eating. Seating areas and home office centers are becoming standards as the kitchen and the main living area become more integrated. This integration of originally seperated areas clearly follows the ecological principle of not wasting any more space than absolutely necessary.

Use

Because family life is often centered in the kitchen, the kitchen must be designed wisely to allow one to perform a great many specific tasks efficiently and comfortably. When building a new house, it is best to locate the kitchen on the east or northeast side of the house to take full advantage of the morning sun. If you do not want to make a trip through half of the house before you reach the kitchen, a nearby entrance is much more convenient for bringing in heavy grocery bags and taking out the garbage. A second door leading to the back yard or garden provides easy access to the children's play area, any outdoor seating and the compost heap. Windows not only bring welcome light into the kitchen, but they allow parents working in the kitchen to keep an eye on children playing outside. The pantry and the household store room have recently come back into fashion. If possible, they

Living in the kitchen
The kitchen is no longer a place solely for cooking. Now, it is the social center of the home. People often eat as well as cook there.

Solid wood
As a result of a renewed appreciation of solid wood's strength and durability, kitchen units in solid wood are gaining an increasing share of the market.

The right proportions
When planning a kitchen, it is important to provide enough work and storage surfaces around the range and the sink and to make sure that they are far enough away from doors, windows and radiators. The surfaces should be high enough to work comfortably.

A friendly corner

If the kitchen is large enough to include a dining area, the whole family can spend more valuable time together while meals are being prepared.

The secret is in the planning

should be located on the north side of the house and open to the kitchen. The dining table is either in the kitchen or separated from it only by a high, narrow breakfast bar or counter.

Although it is not always possible, homeowners should design their kitchen before the house is built. By doing this they ensure that large appliances such as ranges and freezers do not obstruct doors and windows, connections for water, drainage, electricity and gas are located appropriately and the supply of electricity is adequate to meet increased technological demand (20 kW). Usually at least 2–4 circuits should be run to the kitchen area. A 20 amp circuit for the refrigerator, a 20 amp circuit for other receptacles, a 20 amp circuit for lights and, if necessary, a 50 amp 220 V receptacle for the electric range.

For ease and efficiency, the range or cooktop, for right-handed people, should be to the right of the sink. Experts recommend a minimum of 24 inches (60 cm) of work surface on both sides of the sink and the range. The sink should be near a window to

limit the need for artificial light when cleaning up. The range or cooktop should have either a hood vent fitted with a light or a downdraft vent and overhead task lighting. Window sills in the kitchen work area should be at least 37 inches (95 cm) above the floor so that they do not interfere with the work surfaces. A height of 42 inches (115 cm) is safer so that kitchen appliances and accessories are not in the way when the window is opened and there is adequate space for a back-splash.

When installing wall cabinets (usually 12 to 15 inches or 30 to 40 cm deep) or base cabinets into which you may want to fit a refrigerator or an oven (usually 24 inches or 60 cm deep), you will need to leave a distance of between 20 and 30 inches (50 and 75 cm) between the cabinets and the window or door.

Living in the kitchen does require a certain degree of tidiness. Nobody wants to have to sit and look at piles of dirty dishes and other kitchen clutter. Yet one needs to be broadminded enough to overlook the natural chaos that arises in lived-in places.

Pleasures of the table

The dining table is not just a place for eating. It is also very often used for work, hobbies and informal gatherings.

A lot of light

Because the dining area has so many functions, it should be well lit. The best place for it is by a southeast-facing window in order to take advantage of the cheering effect of the morning sun.

Kitchen units

Individuality is practical

Decor: Fern Mehring, Dortmund
You can save a lot of money by putting together your own kitchen out of separate items of furniture instead of opting for stock cabinetry. Then you can simply take them with you if you move. Depending on the state of your finances, you can add new pieces as you go along.

Ergonomics is important

Kitchen units in particular have to be ergonomic. The most hotly debated subject here is the height of the work surfaces. The ideal height of work surfaces should allow one to work standing upright or bent to a maximum of 20 degrees The standard countertop in the United States is 36 inches. While this is a comfortable height for the "average person," not everyone is of average height.

The newest trend in kitchen design is to incorporate work surfaces of different heights to accommodate the needs of all family members. The cooking surface, for instance, is set low to make it easier to look in the saucepans, and the sink and the food preparation work top are placed a little higher. There are even electrically operated moveable fittings to raise or lower worksurfaces. These fittings, however, are very expensive and are really intended for kitchens for the disabled. A less expensive alternative is to put the refrigerator and the oven at eye level and store the pots under the cooking surface. This alternative has the added advantage of being safer for children.

The cooking island, once seen only in large kitchens and smart restaurants, is now a standard in many kitchen designs. These islands are not only very convenient for cooking, but they also allow the cook to communicate easily with family and friends while preparing meals. Lavish use of high-grade steel makes these islands both decorative and substantial while suggesting a certain professionalism. The cooking island does need a great deal of space, and

buying the equipment and installing it in the middle of the room is an expensive venture.

A few manufacturers now offer an economy version of the island: the mobile kitchen. Cabinets incorporating work surfaces, refrigerators and freezers and even cooktops are on rollers. While the cord linking these islands to the electrical supply limits their mobility, they do have advantages. When families need more space, they can wheel the island in a corner. The mobile kitchen is also excellent for dinner parties. The island becomes a mobile serving table where the amateur chef can prepare dishes right at the table.

As homeowners become increasingly ecologically oriented, more natural materials appear in the kitchen. These natural materials are not only healthy and environmentally friendly but also stylish and practical. Ceramic tiles are more durable than plastic laminates and just as easy to clean. Although very expensive, granite work surfaces last forever, are scratchproof, heat-resistant and insensitive to moisture. Unlike marble or travertine, they are also resistant to acid, and sprays of vinegar or slices of lemon leave no marks. A work surface made of good ash or pear wood, or even simple beechwood, which has been thoroughly impregnated with olive oil and polished several times, is just as esthetically pleasing and almost as durable, but it must be protected from heat, food remains and standing water. Lacquered wood is not recommended for work surfaces. Water quickly gets in through cuts and scratches and mildew sets in.

Kitchen appliances

The most important ecological kitchen appliance is a gas range. Not only does a gas range save a household of three around $26 a year, it also, more importantly, uses only half the primary energy of an electric range. Because gas ranges are more expensive to buy, the user notices the financial difference only after about five years. But the environment profits immediately from the lower consumption of energy. Despite its environmental benefits, many Americans who are connected to a main supply of gas and use it for heating do not use it for cooking. They may have an irrational fear of an open flame or falsely assume that gas is less convenient. Modern gas ranges are as safe as electric ranges and as easy to use. They have pilotless ignition and a reliable security shut-off system. Nearly all master chefs prefer to use gas ranges because gas ranges react quicker to temperature changes and produce much better results.

Most gas cooktops have several burner sizes. There should be a small burner for smaller saucepans and for simmering. The metal grille on which the pans sit should be removable for easy cleaning, e.g. in a dishwasher. Finally, the burners should always be sealed to keep spills away from gas jets and from seeping below the cooktop.

Gas ranges and cooktops are available with glass ceramic cooking surfaces. Professionals, however, to not have a high opinion of these cooking surfaces and prefer to work with the traditional range top with a grid and open burners. While the ceramic cooking

All set for the island
Cooking islands or freestanding work surfaces enable you to use space economically. They are also more sociable because they allow the cook to work without having to turn his or her back on everyone else in the room.

surface is easier to clean than the traditional cooktop, it uses almost a third more energy than the open gas cooking surface. Because the flame does not warm the pan and its contents directly, it takes about two minutes longer to boil a liter of water; a waste of energy which had better be avoided. If you do not use the residual heat in the ceramic cooking surface,

Different heights
If work surfaces are higher than the cooktop, you'll find that cutting and looking down into saucepans is easier.

Why not use gas?

Architect: B. Heidbrede, Schwerte, Germany

A gas cooktop is significantly better for the environment and also much more economical than an electric one.

it continues to give off unused energy just like an electric cooktop. In the past, the gas oven did not perform as well as the electric oven. However, that has changed by now and there are now gas ranges on the market with ovens that can compete with the best electric ovens. They can be switched to heat from the top (using an additional burner in the upper side of the pipe) to brown and grill food. The new ovens can also be switched to work with circulating air so that roasts and cakes can be cooked at the same time on different shelves. Although they offer more features, these ovens do not use more energy. They just use it more efficiently.

Even food storage can be organized in a more ecologically sound way. The most important instrument of change here is the newly rediscovered pantry: an unheated store room next to the kitchen. Preferably located on the north side of the home, the pantry keeps food fresh without wasting energy. The refrigerator is reserved for food that spoils quickly and for drinks that need to be ice-cold.

Because a cabinet that produces cold in an artificially heated room when it is cold outside seems contradictory, scientists have developed a totally new kind of refrigerator. Although it is not yet available in the shops, this refrigerator is designed to be built directly into a north-facing wall and to use the cold of the house walls to good effect to cool the food. In winter a blower brings cold air from outside, and in summer a refrigeration unit cools the air.

This type of refrigerator is a fixed component of the house. Since it needs no casing, there is a saving on raw materials and transportation. It is insulated with environmentally friendly materials like cork or expanded concrete. This insulation is more effective than the ecologically questionable foam materials used in moveable refrigerators. The refrigeration unit is installed separately from the refrigerator, so it can be replaced at reasonable intervals when new developments in environmentally sound technology come along. The doors curve outwards, the optimal form for the largest interior possible, with a small and, therefore, energy-saving exterior. The interior dimensions were calculated to accommodate a large pie plate and a bottle of champagne. There are three rather than two degrees of cold: the freezing compartment, the cool compartment, and the pantry compartment. Each compartment can be put in and taken out singly from outside. The temperature is regulated separately, so you do not have to open the door. Even if such advanced technology is not available in your area, there are still acceptable alternatives. Most US manufacturers have responded to enticements such as the "golden carrot" (a 30 million dollar prize awarded by a consortium of electric utilities to the first manufacturer who could develop an affordable refrigerator that would require only 350–550 kilowatt-hours of electricity per year) and have introduced energy saving models. By selecting an Environmental Protection Agency (EPA) *Energy Star* labeled refrigerator you will save at least 30% in electrical operating costs from a conventional model.

Conventional stock kitchen cabinetry is usually made from varnished or veneered chipboard panels. Even in so-called "real wood" or "solid wood" kitchen cabinets the doors are usually the only solid wood items.

The rest of the "wood" is usually chipboard or MDF with a 1 mm veneer of wood on top. Such cabinets cannot be moved and often end up in a landfill after ten years of use. They are particularly sensitive to humidity and temperature changes and cannot be repaired or resurfaced. Due to the substances they contain, they are also potentially harmful to health. On top of all that, in some places it is difficult to dispose of manmade surfaces containing formaldehyde resin, chrome handles and plastic drawer-racks.

All in all, the stock kitchen cabinetry so heavily promoted by the manufacturers is only for homeowners who never change their taste. For everyone else, flexibility is the key word.

Since stock cabinetry is usually not easy to rebuild to suit a different layout, why not have a kitchen made up of single units which you can change according to your taste and resources? This way you can combine that wonderful Italian designer range with an antique kitchen cabinet and an inexpensive garden table. Woodwork manuals can give directions for converting an inexpensive set of shelves and louvered doors into a serviceable kitchen cabinet.

Top chefs
With gas you can control the heat precisely, so that the food is "done to a turn." This is why top chefs use gas.

Conventional stock kitchen cabinetry is often impractical whereas a collection of simple units can easily be changed

A refrigerator in the wall
This refrigerator has been developed by the German designer Ursula Tischner. Built directly into a north-facing wall it is a fixed component of the house. In winter it uses the cold air from outside the building to good effect which makes it particularly economical.

Kitchen gadgets

In the case of most electrical kitchen gadgets there is a simpler, more traditional way of getting the job done. Electrical can-openers are, in fact, superfluous, and coffee makers are vastly inferior to a gas range and a heat-retaining coffeepot in terms of energy consumption. Dishwashers compare to washing up by hand only under very special circumstances.

The same applies to the microwave oven so often touted as a great energy saver. Tests have shown that there is no direct danger from radiation leaking out of modern microwaves, and microwaves certainly consume much less energy than an electric range. But these machines are primarily used to defrost and cook deep-frozen convenience foods which provide little nutritional value yet required a great deal of energy to prepare in the first place.

One sensible, money-saving kitchen gadget that does also reduce environmental clutter is the soda fountain. Americans who consume bottled water and carbonated beverages should consider the soda fountain which the German water authority recently featured in a campaign to encourage its customers to switch from bottled water to tap water. Soda fountains developed from the classic siphon which released carbon dioxide from a steel cartridge into a bottle of water. This produced carbonic acid and a lot of waste, since the little disposable cartridges only made one liter of soda water. The new table-top soda fountains have a compartment in which you place a refillable bottle of carbon dioxide sufficient for many liters of water. Depending on the make, the manufacturers promise 50–200 squirts per bottle. A button

Practical wastebins

Kitchen waste has to be sorted: Compost materials go in the garden; paper to the waste-paper collection point; bottles to the bottle bin, and so on. Only a small amount of waste is left to go to the dump or to be taken away by the garbage collectors. Having separate wastebins in the kitchen makes it easier to sort.

The right tools

Simple kitchen gadgets get the job done without fuss and can look so stylish that you want to display them.

Soda fountain

Mineral water is popular and healthy. If you do not want to cart heavy bottles home from the store, you can use a soda fountain to inject carbon gas into ordinary tap water. Most people cannot taste the difference!

Garbage-separating systems are increasingly important to help save our environment

releases the desired amount of carbon dioxide into a plastic bottle of water or directly into the glass. Since tap water generally tastes reasonably good and is often as pure as bottled water, consumers can not only save money with this machine but they can save energy and help the environment.

Some users found that in early versions of the soda fountain the plastic bottles had a rather unpleasant smell. Although the bottles are mostly made from polyester, which is an odorless manmade substance, the rubber linings in the caps contained potentially harmful softening chemicals as well as toxic toluol-isocyanate. Manufacturers have since then solved these problems with far better linings which do not constitute a hazard to the consumers' health. Now the only causes for concern are the PVC bottles and caps sold with some soda fountains and the potentially allergenic sweeteners or preservatives in the juice concentrates some manufacturers provide to flavor the fizzy water.

One indispensable kitchen aid is a garbage-separation system. Many kitchen manufacturers have designed home recycling centers for separating waste into organic material, packaging, glass, plastics, cans and newspapers without filling the kitchen with multi-colored bins. So there are systems of drawers, round garbage cans sectioned like pies, stacking bins and a line of narrow rectangular containers. They swing out or tip forward invitingly as the cabinet door opens. According to the New York State Department of Environmental Conservation, recycling requires only a 3×3 foot area. If kitchen space is limited, consider an alternative location in a utility room, a storage or broom closet, or an attached garage if it is associated with or near the kitchen.

In Europe some sink manufacturers provide a garbage-pipe which is right next to the sink to send vegetable remains directly into the appropriate bucket – possibly even into the storage-container for the composting bin.

In the United States garbage disposals are built into sinks to grind up organic waste so that it can be disposed of effortlessly via the drainage system. These gadgets are definitely not environmentally friendly. Because they overload water-purification plants with additional organic material, several countries have banned them. From an ecological point of view, it is far better to dispose of vegetable waste on the compost heap where it turns into natural fertilizer. In addition, for under $100, one can select from a wide range of composting devices which take much of the hassle and the untidyness out of composting in the home garden. The value of nutrient rich home-made compost easiliy derived from kitchen and yard wastes to a healthy garden cannot be overstated.

THE BATHROOM

Only a couple of generations ago indoor bathrooms were a rarity in many parts of Europe and the United States. Today, however, households without baths and toilets are almost unknown. The bathroom is no longer simply a functional room for the care of the body. It is also a room for living, a place to relax and escape life's stress and demands. Indeed, homeowners want bathrooms that are attractive, convenient, comfortable, and even luxurious.

Consequently, bathrooms have moved to the top of the home-modelers' list. In the past people tended to economize on the bathroom. Now homeowners are busier and more prosperous, and they are remodeling and building bathrooms to reflect their particular lifestyle. They are opting for sunnier spaces, barrier-free designs, more storage space, and improved lighting. In addition, many want to include whirlpool tubs, luxurious showers and two washbasins in the bathroom of their dreams. Depending on the amount of renovating you have in mind, remodeling the bathroom can cost $5,000 to $15,000. More luxurious renovation can cost five times that amount.

Living in the bathroom

The first sign of the growing trend to make the bathroom more livable was the increasing use of colorful tiles and bathroom suites in the 1970s and 1980s. These tiles and designs are so distinctive that just by looking at the bathroom, you can tell with reasonable accuracy in what year it was built.

However, fashions and preferences are constantly changing, and people quickly got tired of looking at those once highly fashionable colors. When things have to last a long time, fashion should play a secondary role. Otherwise the user's finances and the environment are sacrificed to design. The worst excesses of the color boom seem to be over, and the fashion nowadays is for tiles and fixtures in light, more or less timeless color schemes, which have the added advantage of making the room look bigger. People are beginning to realize that all-over tiles are not a criterion of quality. Putting tiles only where they are really needed as splash protection saves money, allows more wall space for other things and creates a more comfortable and inviting atmosphere.

Beautifully economical

Fittings should not only look beautiful but also help save water. Devices to limit water flow, and durable ceramic washers are gradually gaining in popularity. The Axor range of fittings is made not of the more conventional brass but of durable and eco-friendly high-grade steel.

Status-conscious consumers are following the general decor trends and are investing in expensive and often superfluous bathroom furniture. Once content with a mirror-fronted cabinet, a laundry basket and perhaps a few shelves and clothes hooks, they now want storage units of every possible kind for bath accessories and supplies and for a homey but uncluttered look. In color, form and materials, this new bathroom furniture is a long way from the clinical no-frills whiteness of earlier models. It is beginning to look more like kitchen furniture or the wall of storage units in the living room. New buildings at the top of the market feature enormous luxurious bathrooms that reflect those of stately houses in an earlier era or even Roman-style bathrooms. Enormous bathtubs with room for two, whirlpool tubs, saunas and steam rooms are an invitation to linger and squander water and energy.

There is usually a shower for those in a hurry, but it doesn't bear much resemblance to the water-saving variety. In some of the new systems, the overhead shower is supplemented by various lateral showers that massage the body and produce a relaxing, tingling sensation. Instead of a washbasin there are elegant freestanding wash-fountains reminiscent of the old bedroom washstand. The aspects driving this movement can be divided into three categories: The desire for comfort, the desire for convenience and the desire to make improvements which will attract homebuyers when the property is sold at some point in the future. In making plans for the bathroom, health and environmental issues should not be ignored and the potential dangers (*legionella*) of whirlpools and spas should not be forgotten. Convenience is really just a matter of good design and not of excessive spaciousness.

The wave of luxury has reached the bathroom

Handsome cross-shaped faucets

These old-fashioned faucets look good in old houses, but they are not very practical in terms of saving energy and water.

Function over form

Today's bathroom fittings and accessories are just as trendy as those elsewhere in the home. Before buying anything for your bath, you should always consider whether it is functional. Does the soap-saver really save soap, and are the elegant fittings really durable and economical?

Washing at the fountain

Washbasins such as this one shaped like a drinking fountain are popular with style-conscious customers. They are not very practical, however, especially when more than one person is using the bathroom.

which also takes up all wires and piping. This frame extends from the actual wall and is fastened to it and tiled to match. Usually all that can be seen of it is a "step," which can be used to rest things on. This system makes it particularly easy to install thermal and sound insulation.

False walls do need more space because the pipes do not disappear into the wall, but you can build free-standing ones which allow you to make the most of the available space. For example, the toilet and bidet could be built against a low wall which would separate the bathtub from the rest of the room. To increase the spectacular effect still further, the bathtub could be set on a pedestal.

In new buildings it may even make sense to do without a shower cubicle and let the water from the shower flow away down a hole in the floor like it does in the public showers at swimming pools. This creates more living space because the shower area can be used in a variety of ways. Elderly and disabled people especially appreciate the easy barrier-free access of floor-level showers. Floor-level showers are costly, however, because the sealing is more expensive, and drainage at floor level is more complicated in terms of construction and technology.

Sanitary fixtures and fittings

Enamel bathtubs and ceramic washbasins and toilet bowls are the most durable and thus the most desirable choices from an ecological point of view. Acrylic baths and basins are available in many colors and unusual styles, but they scratch more easily and become rather fragile over time. Take care to choose washbasins with built-in metal brackets for attaching them to the wall. The joint can be tiled over, so that no water seeps in. This joint will last much longer than a joint sealed with silicone, and is also preferable since silicones contain materials that are harmful to health and the environment.

A fixed shower-wall at the edge of the bath is a far better value than an inexpensive shower curtain. All in all, the wall is more pleasing esthetically, easier to clean and does not cling to the body whenever there

When space is very restricted

Older bathrooms are usually quite small. When converting one, there may not be enough room for everything you want. Moveable washbasins can help solve this problem. You can store them over the shower or the bath when not in use and gain space for an extra toilet.

Ideas for the small bathroom

Just because a bathroom is small, it does not have to be uncomfortable or spartan. The manufacturers of sanitary ware have developed numerous ideas for incorporating fashionable bathroom accessories such as bidets or an additional shower into the smallest space. There are bathtubs that narrow toward the bottom, swiveling washbasins and ingenious ways of fitting everything together. An important element in creating flexible bathrooms is the "false wall." The washbasin and toilet are not fixed to the bathroom wall, but to a metal frame,

is a draft. In addition, shower curtains are generally made from environmentally unsound PVC.

Fittings should be water-saving and sound-deadening. Mixer faucets with a single handle and thermostatic heat regulation are a good idea. They swiftly adjust the temperature so you don't have to run the water for several minutes just to get it to the right temperature. Fittings should be entirely covered in chrome or enamel. These finishes are much more durable than lacquer, which quickly scratches and becomes unsightly. High-quality steel fittings are better than the usual brass fittings since steel has a more favorable energy balance. Flow regulators can be put in afterwards. If you have an instantaneous water heater, however, make certain that it is safe to use a flow regulator with that water heater. You should use the water-saving stop-buttons that go in shower hoses because the rapid build-up of pressure often makes the hoses burst.

Light in the bathroom

Bathrooms are often placed in the interior of buildings to save space, but like all rooms bathrooms are best lit by natural light. Not only is natural light more pleasing from an esthetic point of view, but it is important for many typical bathroom activities, such as applying makeup. More importantly, daylight counteracts depression and claustrophobia. A window to the exterior is also the most effective way of ventilating a damp bathroom.

If a bathroom has no possibility for a window, consider putting in sky lights. Sunlight streaming into the space can be a great way of warming a ceramic tile floor in the morning and can actually help to control mold and mildew growth because of the antiseptic effect of UV light. The warmth of sunlight can be far more effective and pleasing than wasteful heat lamps or electrically heated floors. Even if there is a source of natural light, all bathrooms require plenty of artificial light which is very focused but not blinding. The space around the mirror, in particular, needs several light sources for even illumination and to prevent distracting shadows. This is where one should be sure to avoid cold conventional fluorescent light. Full spectrum fluorescents combined with full-spectrum incandescent lamps can provide pleasing light and visual comfort at all hours of the day.

Thrifty tiling
There is no point in tiling a bathroom up to the ceiling. If you only put tiles where they are needed you save money, and the bathroom does not look so clinical.

The awkward bathroom
Modern technology can help provide economical and esthetically pleasing design solutions even for tall narrow bathrooms like this one (above).

Installing false walls
Installations like this one not only make it easier to fit or convert a bathroom, they also make it possible to place baths, toilets, etc., in a freestanding position to make better use of space.

THE BASEMENT

Considering basements

In many cases it is questionable whether putting in a basement is worthwhile. However, on a slope, basement rooms can also be used as living rooms without much additional expense. These basements do, of course, require much better waterproofing and insulation than storage basements.

In the past the basement was usually cold and damp and was typically used to store food supplies and wine. Then it became warm and dry and was used to supply heating to the house and to store heating materials like wood, coal, and finally tanks of fuel oil. When modern gas and electric heating finally deprived the basement of this function, it became a hobby area, store room or even a rented apartment in many cases. People building a new house, therefore, naturally ask themselves whether the additional investment of around $10,000–20,000 in a basement is actually worthwhile. Whenever extra space is needed, for example, for storing supplies the addition

of an outhouse or shed is an excellent and less costly alternative which does not necessarily entail any wasteful use of land.

When does a basement make sense?

Whether you should add a basement to your building or not depends first of all on the nature of your building site. If you want to build your house near a lake or a river and the ground water level is so high that it would cost a fortune to make the basement watertight, then you should definitely think twice about building a basement.

The same applies to a rocky piece of land where the basement would have to be laboriously hacked or blasted out of the rock; the manpower needed to prepare the ground will greatly add to your expense. If, however, your site is in a colder climate where frost footings must be at least three or four feet below grade it is not that much additional expense to excavate the few extra feet required for a basement. It is good to keep in mind that, when building on a slope, normal foundations will be almost as expensive to put in as a basement. In addition, the basement rooms lower down the slope will have full access to natural light and can be turned into living rooms without too much expense. In this case, it makes sense to build a basement to provide additional living areas for your family or to build an extra apartment which can be rented by another person.

A second important consideration is the basement's planned function. Nobody likes carrying bikes up basement steps. It is better to keep these out of the elements in an unheated shed or garage. It is also better to store old furniture or clothes in a dry, airy, unheated attic rather than in a basement. Finally, basements do not usually have enough light for a workshop, so a better place for that is usually an annex or a garage.

Provided it is not indispensable for heating, there are actually only a few functions for which a basement is really suited. The first is as a cool, dark storage area for food supplies. For example, anyone with a large vegetable garden needs a basement. Stored in a dark, unheated area of a basement, vegetables and fruit stay fresh a long time, potatoes do not sprout, and home-made canned goods

The basement is best suited for storing wine and food supplies or for use as a laundry room

Storage and wine cellars

Basement rooms are ideally suited for storing food and maturing wine. They do not need to be heated or insulated, but should be cool and somewhat damp. This means, though, that you have to thoroughly insulate the floor of the rooms above.

will keep without preservatives. Additionally, a basement provides the ideal conditions for storing wine, and it enables new wine to ferment gently in barrels or even bottles. It also keeps beer at the perfect temperature.

The basement is also a particularly good place for a laundry room, especially in wooden houses and light constructions in general. A thundering washing machine upstairs can set the whole house rocking and quickly crack plaster and tiles.

Finally, the basement is a useful place for noisy activities such as music practice or woodwork.

Light and air

This picture shows the interior of the basement in the house shown opposite. Part of the basement was converted into a living room, and this corner has been opened up to allow plenty of light to enter. The extra space can, for example, be used as a guestroom. The rooms behind are used for storage.

Vaulted cellar
Cellars like this cannot be used for living in, unless you are prepared to spend a fortune to adapt them. They are ideal, however, for food storage as the food stays fresh longer in the cool, damp atmosphere. Old limestone cellars are ideal for this purpose. The trodden clay floor is not sealed against radon infiltration, but this is a problem only in a few areas.

Construction methods

The vaulted cellar of earlier times usually had sandstone walls and a floor of tamped clay or natural stone paving. The damp atmosphere was ideal for storing all kinds of food supplies, as long as there was minimal ventilation.

Too much warm fresh air is not good for this kind of basement because the water in the air condenses on the cool walls and provides a perfect environment for mold. It is still possible, of course, to build an old-fashioned cellar without a man-made floor as a cool damp storage place for food, but it is essential to ensure that its ceiling is well isolated from the rooms above and that the dampness does not travel upwards. Modern basements generally serve other purposes as well, including providing living spaces at least from time to time. These spaces do not have to be heated, but they do have to be insulated in such a way as to maintain the best possible interior climate. Building a separate root cellar off the garden may make sense. It can be in the style of a prehistoric underground store or be a ready-made cement vault which you simply place over a hole and cover with at least 31 inches (80 cm) of soil.

The floor can be loosely covered with natural stone slabs or ecologically sound paving. The door of the ready-made "bio-cellar" is insulated against heat and has slits for ventilation. This "bio-cellar" is apparently condensation-free and remains at roughly the same temperature and atmospheric humidity all the time. Old, uninsulated basements are susceptible to radon, a radioactive gas. The radon results from the decay of naturally occurring uranium and thorium and is most prevalent in areas where there is a great deal of granite or deposits of uranium ore. This very mobile gas gets into the upper layers of the soil and, then, finds its way through cracks into the basement and accumulates there. Radon problems are typically confined to certain regions and can be mitigated by creating ventilated cavities between the exterior basement walls and interior spaces. Basement floors can be protected by setting the floor over a bed of large gravel or building a false floor with an air space below and evacuating radon gas by means of a mechanical ventilator exhausting the gas up a vent stack through the roof. In new construction soils should be tested for radant prior to construction.

The normal dry basement is somewhat insulated against radon since it is well-sealed against penetration of the gas through the walls and floor. To remain dry a basement must be adequately protected against dampness coming up from the ground and rising ground water and must have proper heat insulation to prevent moisture in the air from condensing on the cold basement walls.

One problem with basements is that water sometimes seeps down a slope, collects against the walls building up considerable hydrostatic pressure and threatens to undermine them. To counteract this, you can install a simple drainage system which can also be used to treat damage that has occurred during the course of building. Installing such a drainage system entails removing the soil from the outside of the basement wall down to the footing and filling the space with coarse gravel.

A special drainpipe or drain tile channels the collected water into the stormwater drainage system or often simply into a drainage ditch or weir. A durable layer of manmade fibrous material called filter fabric placed between the gravel and the ground prevents the gravel from settling and filling with sediment. The same material is generally used to wrap the drain tile so that it does not become clogged with soil. The wall of the basement is lined with bituminous dampproofing or, better still, a solid waterproof layer or drainage matting is laid next to the soil in a procedure known as perimeter waterproofing. From an environmental point of view, the most suitable material for this purpose is fiberglass insulation boards.

In addition to the current building methods using reinforced concrete, there are various systems involving prefabricated basements which are within the capability of do-it-yourself builders. First, lay a footing of cast-in-place concrete, then build walls on this base using either prefabricated expanded concrete blocks or stacking up the molds supplied by the manufacturer and filling them with concrete. You do not need specialized bricklaying skills to do this.

Since concrete is almost impervious to water, it is in some ways a very suitable material for basement walls. However, if you plan to use even a part of the basement for living or for doing anything that requires you to be there for any length of time, unfinished concrete walls are not advisable. Concrete cannot absorb water, so the atmosphere will be unpleasantly clammy. Since basement walls have to be particularly well insulated and waterproofed in any case, it is much better to use calcareous sandstone and mortar rather than concrete. In addition, the basement area is actually a very good place for putting down large trestles to speed the building work.

Basement rooms are particularly economical to build. They usually cost less than half of the amount per square foot that the rest of the house costs to build. If you put in extensive perimeter waterproofing and radon mitigation systems, the cost rises. Nonetheless, you should definitely do this if you plan to develop your basement space for more intensive use and can afford the extra expense of insulation, lighting and heating.

Basement rooms are inexpensive to build

Keeping the basement dry
A vertical barrier and drainage help to prevent water from coming in from the outside. Coarse gravel allows the water to seep away quickly, and it is then carried away through a drainage pipe. In addition, the basement wall is reinforced by so-called perimeter waterproofing. To further protect the basement against rising moisture, the exterior wall has to be provided with two horizontal barriers.

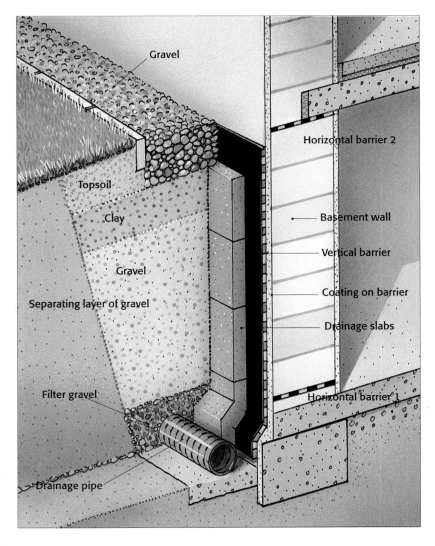

Gravel

Topsoil

Clay

Gravel

Separating layer of gravel

Filter gravel

Drainage pipe

Horizontal barrier 2

Basement wall

Vertical barrier

Coating on barrier

Drainage slabs

Horizontal barrier 1

A PLACE TO PARK

Open or closed?

Open carports are the most environmentally friendly places to put your car. With some greenery on the roof, they blend particularly well into their surroundings. On the other hand, you can use a closed garage for a lot of other purposes besides parking your car.

Most new houses are usually equipped with garages or parking spaces for the "essential" car even though group parking for several houses saves money and frees the space taken up by driveways for better things. But attached garages also have their advantages. Not only are they convenient for bringing in groceries, but they are a good location for recycling storage, workshops and storing garden equipment. Anyone who actually can do without a car can use the garage simply for hobbies or storage and as a safe shelter for the family bicycles and seasonal yard furnishings.

Garage and carport

A carport is the most environmentally friendly option when it comes to providing parking. Although the car is in the open, it is under a roof and relatively well protected against any damage incurred by the weather, such as hail, for example, could inflict. Because the ground under a carport does not have to be sealed, and you can easily cover the simple roof with greenery, it has little impact on the scenery. Carports are also inexpensive to build. On the other hand, their uses are limited. They provide only a place to park a car and store firewood. Anything more valuable stored there is not protected against theft.

A garage can be used to store all sorts of things. It can also act as a weather-shield for the main house or block off an unattractive view. It can be the boundary to a courtyard or occupy the space under a terrace. Garages do not have to be ugly, windowless units. There are prefabricated garages with rainwater cisterns built under them, low-profile garages that can be sunk in the ground so that they do not intrude on the landscape, and even garages with roof gardens.

Bicycle racks

Whether the bicycle is adopted as an alternative mode of transport will depend to a large extent on the infrastructure provided for it. This infrastructure must include the construction of well-designed shelters in front of public buildings and residential complexes to keep bikes safe from theft, vandalism and weather. In the United States bicycle shelters are less common than they are in Europe. While many of the larger cities in the United States have installed fiberglass or plexi-glass bicycle shelters in their downtown area, few residential complexes have provided such facilities. In Europe, however, Dutch suppliers are rushing to fill this neglected market niche. An exotic but stylish example is the so-called "bicycle trunk" which looks like an oversized cylindrical plexiglass breadbin with room for five bikes. It has a single, simple lock and is probably best suited to a small family with their own home in a quiet suburb. It also converts easily to a sandpit with a lid. Although on the bulky side, bicycle garages provide effective protection against theft. Dutch firms have also developed a bicycle safe that can be produced in various forms for housing complexes and public places. German manufacturers have also produced various types of bicycle stores. Many consist of single lockable boxes with a groove in which to stand the bike. The makes differ in material and construction, but the design is usually horrible but will hopefully improve in the not too distant future. They range from simple metal boxes to kennel-like lockups and little houses made of wood or concrete with trellis and plant pots to create a garden effect. Numerous firms make larger lockup sheds which will take from ten to thirty bikes. The price of these generally uninspired, self-assembly bicycle racks varies enormously depending on their particular size and fittings. The racks come in a wide variety of materials, such as wood, sheet-metal or concrete. Wood is not necessarily the most environmentally sound choice here, as some makers use tropical hardwoods. Streets in most European apartment blocks have lockable stands in front. These stands take ten to twelve bikes, and some of them even rotate so you can reach any bike easily from the door.

Shelter

A basic bike shed like this one can easily be put up against any house. It is also a very good place for drying wood.

Taking a bike into town

Cyclists cannot really enter congested city areas unless there is an adequate infrastructure for them. This means bicycle stands that do not damage tires, have locking facilities to secure the bikes, and a covered parking area. Bike shelters like this one are a cyclist's dream.

PESTS

PESTS

Household pests are a painful topic for many people. No one likes to admit to having roaches in the kitchen, mice in the pantry, moths in the closet or wood-boring beetles in the rafters. Fear and ignorance often make people use any type of pesticide just to get rid of their unwanted guests as quickly as possible. But this can endanger the whole family and contaminate the environment.

Pesticides are generally not necessary, and certainly not as a preventative measure. Load-bearing wooden beams are no longer treated with toxic pesticides as a matter of course.

Pests that attack wood

Pests can cause serious damage in wooden buildings, to the point of endangering the structure. While the wood-eating larvae of various beetles are responsible for this damage in Europe, termites and carpenter ants cause the bulk of serious damage to structures in the United States. The most common reasons for various kinds of infestation are:

● The use of insufficiently seasoned wood
● The use of low-grade or damaged wood
● Excessive moisture caused by defective ventilation
● Building defects and warm-air conduits which allow the wood to get wet and mold to form.

When conditions are right, the insects lose no time in starting their destructive work. Long-horned beetles, which carry their feelers bent backwards when at rest so that they resemble goat's horns, are blackish-brown and relatively large. The female is almost an inch (25 mm) long. She lays up to 400 eggs in cracks and holes in the wood. A few weeks later the larvae hatch and bore straight into the wood, where they chew away for between three and ten years without any exterior sign of what is happening. They bore almost up to the exterior but not quite. A thin layer of wood, therefore, hides their activities. They can grow to about an inch (3 cm) long and almost a quarter of an inch (5 mm) thick, and can do great damage to load-bearing parts of the building. In some countries, as in Germany, an outbreak must be reported to the local authorities.

Because the larvae take so long to develop into beetles, the infestation is often only discovered when the beams are so riddled with holes that an additional load causes them to collapse. Homeowners usually only discover the infestation when someone notices the flight-hole through which the adult beetle has escaped after pupation. This hole is less than half an inch (5–10 mm) across and is usually found on the underside of a beam. You can uncover an infestation earlier if you "listen" regularly to the roof-beams. When you knock on them, they ring hollow. On a warm day you can even hear larvae gnawing if you use a stethoscope.

Since they need temperatures over 77° F (25° C), long-horned beetle larvae generally only feel at home in the rafters on the warm southerly side of a wooden house. They only attack unseasoned, damp softwood. They do not like valuable deciduous woods like oak or beech, or the hard inner wood of the larch, or properly seasoned, dry wood.

The least toxic and most effective way of ridding oneself of these and other wood-damaging pests is the hot-air treatment. Insects in general cannot survive a temperature of over 131° F (55° C). Accordingly, if the wood is heated to this level for a long enough period, the larvae should be eliminated. Special equipment is used to heat all the rafters until a temperature of 131–140° F (55–60° C) is reached in the center of the thickest beam, and this temperature is maintained for an hour.

The best-known wood beetle is the death-watch beetle. The name comes from the mating behavior of the mature insect, which knocks its hard thorax against the wood to attract a mate. This sound can only be heard when everything is "as silent as a tomb." These beetles are less than half an inch long (3–9 mm), depending on the individual species, and live only a few weeks, but their larvae, familiarly known as "woodworm," survive for two to eight years. While the death-watch beetle afflicts wooden buildings and oak beams after the wood has been weakened by fungus, its near relation, the anobium (which does no knocking) specializes in wooden furniture and picture frames.

The favorable temperature for death-watch beetles is around 73° F (23° C). They prefer damp wood, so they cannot survive in places where relative humidity is below 55% and the corresponding wood moisture content is below 12%. An active woodworm infestation shows itself by a trickle of sawdust, except in the case of the exotic bark beetle, which has become more prevalent recently. It belongs to another species, but looks very much like the anobium and bores the same sort of 1 mm holes. The larvae take only a year to develop and prefer tropical woods or sap wood from the outer parts of oak or elm.

A woodworm infestation does not normally endanger the loading capacity of beams. Getting rid of the cause of the trouble, usually excessive moisture, normally deals with the problem. It is a good idea to consult an expert for advice on how to do this. Hot-air treatment in a sauna or a mobile hot-box is used to rid furniture of woodworm. Houses can be protected against termites either by a metal termite shield between the concrete or masonry foundation and any wood framing members or by constructing the building entirely of materials which these pests do not attack, such as concrete, brick, stone, or steel.

The hot-air treatment will effectively eliminate all insect larvae

Unlike the long-horned beetle's damage, the woodworm's damage does not make the house likely to fall down

Endangered by woodworm
Insects that attack wood can cause severe structural weakening and even collapse. These insects, however, only attack wood that is always damp or weakened by dry rot. Woodworms do not infest dry, well-insulated and well-sealed houses.

PESTS IN THE HOUSE

Rats, roaches and moths are currently increasing in number after a temporary reversal due to campaigns to control them. The reason for this, besides the growing resistance of these pests to chemical extermination methods, is the extravagant Western lifestyle. We throw away more food than ever before. As a result, we provide pests with an inexhaustible supply of food.

In addition, modern building methods, better heating and greater comfort contribute to the spread of these unwanted guests. The cool underground cellars, dry pantries and drafty attic store rooms of the past were not only better for storing food than the humid warmth of modern over-heated and poorly ventilated kitchens, but pests found them less inviting for building nests. On the other hand, the motors of today's refrigerators and freezers are both inaccessible and warm and provide ideal breeding grounds for pests. Old-fashioned glass jars and tin

Rats, roaches and moths are on the increase

Rats and mice

The rat population is increasing both in cities and in rural areas. Rats are shy animals, yet sightings in daylight are becoming more frequent. One rat sighting is a good indication that there are many more rats nearby. In large cities there may be as many as one rat per inhabitant. The brown rat is particularly widespread. It can weight over a pound (500 g) and grow up to 19 inches (50 cm) long including the tail. Rats are very fertile and have a litter of 8–12 young 4–6 times a year, and the young rats can start breeding at just three months of age.

Brown rats like moist conditions, eat all kinds of food, and have a large range within which they travel searching for food. They can swim very well and are just as at home in sewers and on riverbanks as they are in garbage dumps and in food storage areas, where they can find plenty to eat. The somewhat smaller house rat is less common in Europe. It is an expert climber, and

Humane traps
The problem with these traps is what to do with the rodents once they are caught. Simply letting them out somewhere else is not a viable solution.

cans withstood the attacks of vermin far better than today's plastic bags and cardboard boxes. Fitted carpets that are only occasionally cleaned with a vacuum cleaner offer a better home for dust-mites than rugs that can be aired and beaten on the line.

Needless to say, custom kitchens with their tightly enclosed cabinets make pest control somewhat more difficult. In addition, decades of unsuccessful attempts at extermination with toxic sprays have unfortunately made many creatures resistant to chemical pesticides.

prefers houses and stables. The house mouse is the smallest of the rodent pests, reaching a weight of less than an ounce (20 g). It makes up for its diminutive size by being a good climber and prefers to live in lofts, heating shafts or grain stores.

The first signs of a rat or mouse infestation are gnaw marks and droppings, as well as the strong smell of urine with which they mark their territory. As rodents normally only become active in the evening, the noise they make sometimes gives them away. Rats are the natural hosts for many dangerous bacteria

Rats are the natural hosts for a great many dangerous bacteria

that cause diseases like typhoid, diarrhea, cholera, TB, leprosy, plague, jaundice, trichina and salmonella.

To guard against rodent infestation, you had better reduce food sources. Store food in glass jars or sealed containers, do not use the toilet as a waste-bin, keep garbage in tightly covered cans or bins, throw food remains and animal waste onto the compost heap, and remove pet food and water as soon as the pet is through eating or drinking.

The best mousetrap is still a cat. A single cat can kill up to 3,000 mice a year. To avoid hindering the cat in its hunting, all inside doors, including those to the basement and the attic, should be left open. Animal lovers who abhor traps that kill rats and mice by breaking their necks can buy more humane traps in pet shops, hardware stores, drugstores and even some supermarkets. It is unclear, however, what should be done with the animals caught in these non-lethal traps. Simply releasing them in the garden or street does not exactly solve the problem.

If you prefer not to use a trap, you can place a smooth, straight-sided wastepaper basket near a chair, and put the rodents' favorite food inside. Put some crumpled paper in the basket to tempt the mice, which are not stupid, to risk the jump. Once lured into the wastepaper basket, they are too small to climb up the smooth sides and get out. When dealing with any traps you should wear thick gloves and high boots to protect yourself against dangerous bites. Professional pest-control technicians recommend boxes made of folded paper with poisonous bait inside. The active ingredient in such baits, e.g. difenacoum, slowly destroys the blood vessels. After consuming the bait, the mice typically become

claustrophobic, rush into the open and die there. The advantage is that they do not decay in hidden corners or behind baseboards. Unfortunately, what is deadly for mammals like mice cannot be good for humans, pets or the environment. The effectiveness of ultrasound anti-rodent devices has not yet been conclusively proven but they are gaining in popularity. Good baits for mice are chocolate or peanut butter; for rats, sweetened mashed potato. Set out several baited traps, and watch them for at least eight weeks to be sure that the descendants of your unwanted guests have also been removed. To prevent more mice from entering the house, seal all cracks in the wall, the baseboard and the floor. Mouse-proof basement windows with quarter inch hardware cloth. Mice can make themselves very small and come in through tiny holes.

Roaches

Roaches have been on the earth for millions of years, but in recent times they have shown an increased fondness for human company. They like the warmth of central heating, ovens and electric motors. Because they are omnivorous, they will always find plenty to eat. In restaurants, big kitchens, hospitals, bakeries and shopping malls they have already become a plague, and once established they can easily take over a large area. The roach's flat body enables it to get into any crack without any problems. They are sensitive to light. During the day they conceal themselves in hiding places, so it is difficult to discover them before they have multiplied to an alarming degree. They are very hardy and have proven resistant to many methods of control. They protect their sack of eggs with a strong layer of chitin. Roaches can run fast, but not swim. The roach most commonly encountered in Europe is relatively small, but it can still jump up to 4 inches (10 cm). The larger American cock roach (up to 1.5 inches or 3.8 cm), which is also spreading on the continent, can even fly – which it normally does at night.

Cock roaches are not only disgusting; they are a health hazard. They scramble around in dirt and in human food, and they can carry germs like salmonella, tuberculosis and anthrax as well as pinworms. While in some European countries you are required to report an infestation of roaches, there are no such regulations in the United States. Health departments, however, routinely inspect food establishments for roaches as well as other disease-carrying pests. The best means of combating the obstinate cock roach are pheromone traps. A tablet of sexually attractive material is placed in a cardboard box. The males go onto the sticky material in the expectation of mating and die. It is important to know with what species of roach you are dealing with (there are 3,500 worldwide) in order to choose the right bait. Even with the right bait, you eliminate only the male roaches; the females live on for a while.

An intelligent beast

Rats are very adaptable and highly intelligent (left). They also multiply extremely rapidly under favorable conditions.

Roaches are best combatted with pheromone traps

Food is a pest magnet

Food that is stored in bags or cartons or simply left lying around attracts pests like roaches and weevils. Tin cans or tightly closing bottles are better for storage, since pests cannot get into them.

Pest control experts

People presenting themselves as "pest exterminators" may no longer spray just any pesticide. It is advisable not to let things get to that stage, but if you are inundated by pests, you may have to call in a pest control professional. They at least operate under government regulation and should have the necessary specialist knowledge.

An innovation, which has not been tested as yet, is roach control through growth regulators. These hormones, which the creatures absorb from bait or an edible spray, inhibit their growth. They are reportedly harmless to humans and other vertebrates, but they are still rather controversial because they could very well kill a number of useful insects as well. Another common method of control is electric shocks. The roaches are attracted by sweet-smelling substances, walk into a contraption, which resembles a shoebox, and immediately receive a slight but lethal electric shock.

If you are still battling the roaches after about eight months, it may be time to call in a pest-control expert. Do not try to apply insecticides yourself. Some of the products sold in drugstores and home and garden stores are highly toxic. Make certain that the pest-control technicians are certified and well

Seldom seen

If you see one or two roaches running around, your house is very likely infested by thousands of the creatures (above). They tend to hide in the day and do their dirty work by night, and for every one you see there are many more in hiding.

trained. Following their diagnosis, it may turn out that it is not just the kitchen that has to be treated but the rooms above, below and next to it.

There is an increasing trend now to use natural pyrethrum for pest control. Pyrethrum is derived from a species of chrysanthemum. Although it is toxic for people and animals if it gets into the bloodstream, it is fully biodegradable and disappears from the environment within a day of its application. It is probably preferable to use natural pyrethrum for pest control, rather than the more dangerous synthetic versions called pyrethroids.

Mites and moths

Dust mites are small members of the spider family that live in places such as mattresses, pillows, upholstered furniture and carpets. They are somewhat dependent on us in that they feed primarily on cast-off scales of human skin and on minute funguses. The average person sheds about on half ounce (1.5 g) of skin per day, enough to feed 100,000 mites. Mites occur in virtually every home and will multiply rapidly when conditions are favorable. Ideal temperatures for mites are between 68° and 87° F (20° and 30° C) and they do best when relative humidity is over 65%. However, they can tolerate much lower temperatures and relative humidity as low as 35%. They prefer to live in fibrous materials, such as carpet underfelt, fluffy pillows and mattresses. More and more people are developing allergic reactions to the waste products of these mites, especially in autumn when there is more of their excreta and more decaying dead mites in the home. Allergy symptoms include shortness of breath, coughing, a constantly running nose, asthma attacks and watering eyes.

Although you can never be entirely free of dust mites, simple measures will go a long way toward reducing their numbers and thus the severity of the problem. If possible, install smooth floor surfaces such as tiles, linoleum or hardwood flooring; reduce humidity levels in the home to less than 40% by frequent ventilation or mechanical dehumidification if necessary; and vacuum all possible dust-catchers, including mattresses and furnishes, as often as possible. In order to reduce the amount of shed skin in bedding, do not undress or comb your hair right next to the bed. Air beds every day in summer to allow moisture from perspiration to dissipate, and store bed linen perfectly dry and under a cover or in a linen-box. You can rid fluffy toys of mites by putting the toys in the freezer periodically. If you do not have a central vacuum system, the best vacuum cleaner to use is one with especially fine filters such as hepa filtration. Another common place for mites to reside is under beds and couches where all those "dust bunnies" accumulate. Vacuum these locations frequently or purchase a bed which has a solid base which goes all the way to the floor so that dust cannot accumulate. Persons who know they are allergic to dust mite wastes should take extra precautions. Special mattress covers and pillow cases which protect against dust mites can be obtained from medical supply companies specializing in products for allergy sufferers. Remove any older carpets and replace them with rugs which can be commercially cleaned. Eliminate upholstered furniture and opt for removable cushions and pillows which are also easier to clean. The caterpillars of the clothes moth attack not only textiles and carpets with at least a 20% wool content, but also furs and feathers. It is relatively easy to detect the presence of moths. In addition to moth

holes, which are uneven and have frayed edges, moths leave behind tubular webs. You do not have to treat the fabrics with toxic chemicals to prevent any damage. Strong smells, light and movement will repel moths. Lavender bags, cloths soaked in essential oils, strong-smelling soap, and clothes hangers or little balls made of cedarwood drive away moths, but perspiration laden, dirty clothing attracts them. Since moths do not eat cotton, putting the clothes you need to protect into a sack made by sewing up an old cotton sheet will also protect them from moths. The traditional cedar chest is also very effective in controlling moths as are cedar lined closets. Hot ironing or a few days in the freezer will kill moths entirely. Hanging your clothes outdoors overnight in the winter when there is a sharp frost several nights running will also eliminate them.

Roach traps

These traps (top) attract roaches with sexual markers known as pheromones. If the male roaches crawl inside they get trapped on the sticky floor.

Smells repel moths

Strong odors like lavender or cedarwood keep moths out of the closet (above). A simple lavender bag or little balls made of cedarwood will often do the job.

DECOR

The retail furniture trade has been booming since the 1980s. Today people are concentrating their buying power on creating comfortable, stylishly furnished homes. Nevertheless, they often find that ten years after furnishing a house the contents all need renewing again. Craftsmanship has been left behind in the price war between suppliers. The furniture field is dominated by substitutes: chipboard instead of solid wood; foam instead of proper stuffing; glue instead of nails; screws and staples instead of traditional joining methods; chemically treated fabric and imitation or colored leather instead of good quality natural materials. A few furniture manufacturers dominate the market, and the handful at the top account for a major part of all the furniture sold by retail outlets.

The general desire for a return to healthier, more natural practices has, however, finally reached the furniture trade. Small suppliers, emphasizing fine craftsmanship and solid wood furniture in more fashionable styles, are leading this trend. Big manufacturers are recognizing that the chipboard culture is a dead end, and they are trying other routes. Today stylish solid wood furniture can be found even in conventional furniture stores.

Ecology in furniture means above all durability. Not only must material and construction be durable, but also design. Classic forms and proportions are timeless and remain up-to-date even when taste changes. Natural surfaces grow old gracefully and do not go out of fashion the way colors do. Quality is always in style, but quality has its price.

If buying quality new furniture is beyond your means, try renovating furniture that has lost its appeal. Valuable antiques are not the only furniture worth restoring. Provided they are basically sound, many old pieces of ordinary furniture are worth brightening up with a bit of color and imagination.

The living room

The days of the three-piece suite and of having everything precisely arranged and coordinated are fortunately over. Nowadays, the need for flexibility in the living space and the desire for better quality are making people reexamine the way they furnish their living rooms. Instead of buying complete suites of furniture, people now tend to opt for good-quality single items that will serve as many purposes as possible. Massive fitted cupboards and wall units are out of fashion. Not only are they difficult to move, but they usually do not fit in another house which may have an altogether different layout or where the rooms may be much smaller. They take up an enormous amount of wall

space, which is very limited in modern open-plan houses. Monstrous corner sofas have given way to smaller, much more flexible couches that can easily be moved around and even used as guest beds now and then.

Furniture for storage

Sets of shelves, cupboards and glass-fronted cabinets are suitable not just for the living room, but the kitchen, bedroom and children's rooms as well. Chipboard cupboards, whether they are veneered or coated with synthetic material, are not a good choice for any of these rooms. Even slight damage is irreparable, and the joints do not last. It is the limited lifespan of such furniture that first caused "solid wood" to be recognized as a hallmark of quality. Consumers looking for durable, attractive furniture want solid wood. Economical softwoods such as Scots pine, spruce and fir, and less expensive hardwoods like beech or birch as well as the highly prized cherry or pear wood and the fashionable ash and maple are all part of the trend.

The ecologists claim it is extravagant to use valuable solid wood for storage items. Because all-wood furniture shrinks and expands more than artificial material, they point out that in centrally heated rooms solid wood is more likely to get cracks and distortion — defects that are particularly visible in angular items of furniture. Chipboard, they say, is easier to make from wood products and has the added advantage that lower-grade wood can be used. It is, therefore, an acceptable choice at least in cases where there is not much wear and tear. A further argument is that there must be some ecologically sound products for the

smaller budget. Nonetheless, the antiques of tomorrow are made of solid wood. A classic, timeless design suits the long life of such furniture better than faddish trends. This is why going back to traditional forms and workmanship makes sense. The quality of any metalwork, hinges and moveable parts should match that of the basic material. You must also consider whether you want a cupboard or wall unit that you can take apart when you move to another house, or whether you prefer a combination of small units with doweled and tenon joints that stay permanently in one piece.

Even solid wood furniture must meet certain criteria. There should be no bark, no horizontal or vertical cracks, no discoloration through red rot or blue fungus, no loose knots, no flaws oozing resin, no glued-together joints on visible surfaces. Solid wood furniture should either be left untreated or simply oiled or waxed with natural products.

Solid workmanship

Good craftsmanship is essential when it comes to making solid furniture. Today there is increasing interest in traditional methods of production and a great demand for pieces made by skilled craftsmen. These items of furniture will continue to give pleasure far into the future.

The antiques of tomorrow

Items of furniture in solid wood and natural materials are tomorrow's antiques. Instead of losing value, they become more precious with each passing year.

Upholstered furniture

Ecologically sound upholstered furniture in natural materials is indistinguishable at first sight from elegant traditional furniture. With the exception of custom-made furniture and a few very expensive pieces, however, the use of natural material in American upholstered furniture is limited. While solid hardwood frames are standard and down feather cushions and natural fabric display covers are common, most sofas have metal springs and are filled with foam and polyester batting. Furnature, a chemical-free furniture company in Boston, Massachusetts, produces sofas and chairs using solid rock maple for frames, steel bases and cores for seats, backs and cushions, and only 100% organic cotton batting, canvas and filling. In Germany, on the other hand, there are manufacturers who emphasize not only solid workmanship but also completely natural materials. A sofa of this kind will have solid hardwood, such as beech, for the frame and all the other wooden parts. Jute webbing or loose wooden slats attached by rubber hinges for the seat and back and cushions stuffed with duck feathers assure comfort. The frame is often made without screws or other metal parts. Instead traditional joinery methods like wooden dowels or butt joints reinforced with wooden splines and held with formaldehyde- and solvent-free glue are used to join the arms and legs to the seat. The upholstery is made from sustainable natural materials, for instance a "sandwich" of sheep's wool, latex, coconut fiber and sisal. Finally, the covers are made from untreated cotton, linen, wool, or leather tanned with vegetable substances, and can be removed for cleaning.

In making such upholstered furniture, one German manufacturer has gone so far as to use rye stalks (which was not unusual in past times) surrounded by flax and sheep's wool to make it comfortable. To stop it pricking or rustling when you sit down, the long rye stalks are laid crosswise, then stitched together and

Environmentally friendly upholstery stuffing has no artificial foam or fibers

Fashionable loose covers
These loose-fitting covers can be thrown over chairs, armchairs and sofas, transforming their appearance at very little cost. They are also easy to remove and wash.

Timeless design
Environmentally friendly furniture should be attractive as well as ecologically sound, so that you really want to have it around.

Easy eco-decor
Upholstered monsters are out, small two- and three-seat sofas are in. Their proportions are more pleasing, and they are easier to blend in with existing decor.

finally covered with woven jute. The straw is so firmly packed that no depressions form where people have been sitting. For those who prefer a softer seat, the straw can be combined with a layer of natural latex.

If you visualize a lumpy mouse-gray sofa when you think of upholstered furniture in natural materials, you are in for a pleasant surprise. These pieces are now available in a wide choice of contemporary fabrics, including many small geometric patterns and durable plain fabrics with textured weaves. Sofas, chairs, stools and sofabeds come in modern designs. Heavyweight upholstered furniture is definitely a thing of the past. Today's fashion is for small, neat two- and three-seat sofas that can be moved around in various attractive combinations.

The intelligent use of detail ensures a durable exterior. Many linen and furniture manufacturers are making simple loose covers for upholstered furniture. You put these covers over the sofa like a coat. You can put light colors on in summer, dark ones in winter, or vice versa. The covers not only offer protection and an inexpensive way to change the room's color scheme, but good quality covers are easy to clean. You simply take the cover off, put it in the washing machine, iron it and put it on the sofa or chair again. You can even buy covers fastened simply with Velcro.

Long-lasting upholstered furniture must be well designed on the inside. Parts such as arms, seats, backs, and cushions that are most subject to wear should be replaceable. To make them easy to replace,

Simple loose covers offer protection and are easy to clean

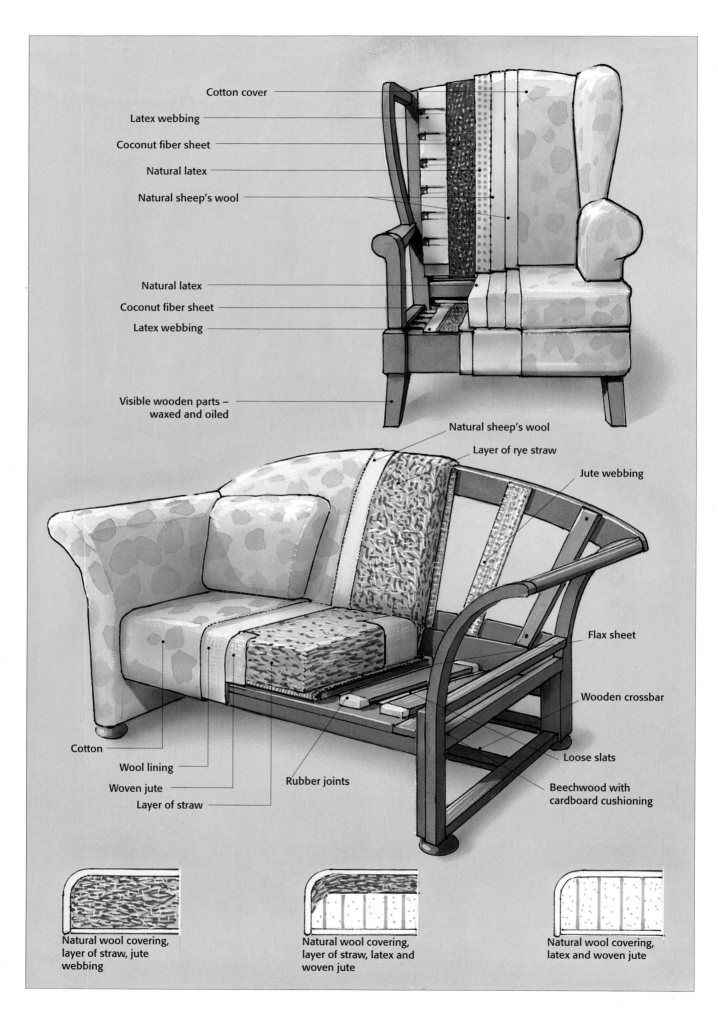

Cotton cover

Latex webbing

Coconut fiber sheet

Natural latex

Natural sheep's wool

Natural latex

Coconut fiber sheet

Latex webbing

Visible wooden parts – waxed and oiled

Natural sheep's wool

Layer of rye straw

Jute webbing

Flax sheet

Wooden crossbar

Loose slats

Beechwood with cardboard cushioning

Rubber joints

Cotton

Wool lining

Woven jute

Layer of straw

Natural wool covering, layer of straw, jute webbing

Natural wool covering, layer of straw, latex and woven jute

Natural wool covering, latex and woven jute

the most sensible manufacturers have given up using staples and glue in favor of methods like clamping the material in a groove.

A sofa that collapses can be taken apart step by step and repaired. When a good furniture piece reaches the end of its life, the parts are easier to detach. Many furniture workshops even guarantee that they will take things back once the furniture is beyond repair or you simply want to exchange your old pieces against something new.

Even conventional furniture manufacturers are putting their money on quality. Apart from observing the legal restrictions on CFC foam, formaldehyde and wood preservatives, some are going green of their own free will. For instance, more and more firms are changing to water-soluble varnish and glue without formaldehyde. To protect the environment and for economy, they are also using recycled materials. The arms of a chair or a sofa are reinforced with old cardboard and the seat padding and cushions filled with secondhand foam. In the US, government regulations often restrict recycled materials in upholstered furniture. There are companies that do use recycled wood products

and Mitchell Gold in Taylorsville, North Carolina uses recycled soda-bottle fabric for chair covers.

That is only one side of the picture. Whole ranges of harmful ingredients still go into the making of armchairs and sofas. Practically every piece of upholstered furniture contains polyurethane foam, which is produced from toxic isocyanates. Artificial substitutes, such as *waterlily* foam, are not much better.

Covers are usually made from synthetic fibers: Polyacrylic *(Dralon, Dolan, Leacryl, Dunora)*, Polyamide *(Perlon, Nylon)*, Polyester *(Trevira, Dacron, Diolen)*, and chemically altered fibers of natural origin like Viscose *(Reyon, Danufil, Lenzing)* and Rayon. They normally come in wool or cotton mixtures.

Environmentally harmful finishes are not uncommon. Many suppliers consider softeners and treatments to make fabric water-, oil- and dirt-proof essential. Fabric may even be colored with carcinogenic azo dyes.

High-quality craftsmanship

Anyone can nail two pieces of wood together. Sometimes you even see wood that has been joined with staples. The traditional joints illustrated below ensure lasting quality.

A healthy inner life

This eco-friendly furniture (opposite) is made out of all natural materials: jute webbing and loose wooden slats for sitting on; a core of straw, latex, feathers, cotton and wool as padding; and a cotton cover treated with natural dyes.

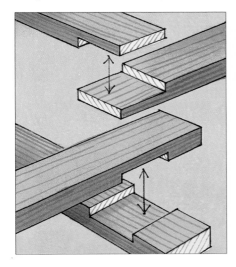

Half lap joints

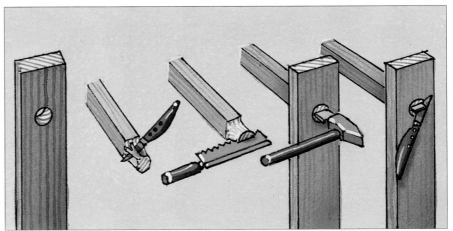

Doweled joints

Splined butt and miter joints

Round mortice and tenon joints

Old furniture need not
be tossed on the dump

Renovating old furniture

If price dictates your choice of furniture, you probably will not be keeping it for a very long time. More
than likely you will tire of it long before it wears
out. Fashions change so quickly that if things are
too trendy and up-to-the-minute they soon begin
to look outdated.

As a result, thousands of sets of perfectly serviceable
shelves, tables, cupboards and upholstered furniture
are thrown out each year. Several charities have set up
a regular trade in secondhand furniture. They repair
the furniture where necessary and then sell it, or give it
to the needy.

With a little patience and imagination, it is possible to
lengthen the short life of a great deal of furniture
yourself. Often you may only need to put new
handles on a bureau or to remove damaged feet or to
replace the feet with casters.

Restored with love

With a little color and a lot of imagination, you can create a
beautiful child's room with a pleasant atmosphere although you
have been using old furniture.

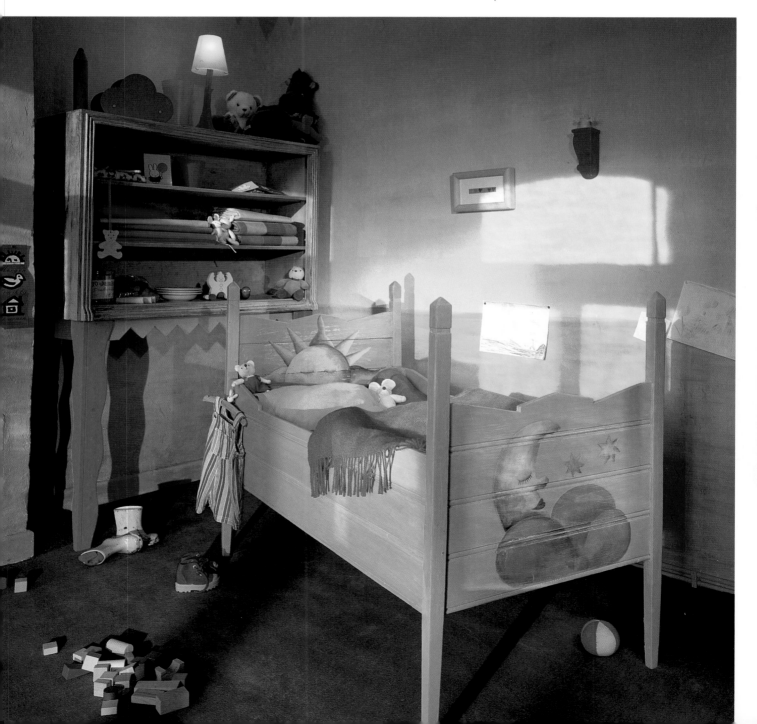

A table as good as new
A multi-colored glaze gives the old dining room table a new lease of life.

New ideas for old favorites
An original technique using swishes of paint gives new allure to an old cupboard.

With a new top, a table can become the showpiece of the home. Conversely an old table top will get a new lease on life when supported by the trestles from an old workbench, or the stand from an old hand sewing-machine, or even by worn-out car tires. An old fruit-picking ladder makes a good frame for a set of shelves. Placing glass shelves on this frame will create a really distinctive unit. Chairs covered in something unexpected, like leather, take on a whole different personality. An ungainly armoire can be transformed into a work of art by adding decorative borders or stylish fabric on the doors, or by covering it with wallpaper. Home-made covers are a good solution for the living room armchairs. You could make two sets: one for everyday use and one for special occasions. If you are not a seamstress, you can solve the problem of threadbare upholstery by hiding your couch under a colorful throw.

If you feel these measures are not enough to transform your rather worn furnishings, you will need to invest a little more patience and craftsman-ship. Painting an object is, of course, the easiest solution. Provided the existing coat of paint is reasonably sound, all you need to do is roughen the surface with sandpaper and paint over it. Before painting shabby waxed or oiled furniture, you should wash the surface with soapy water or a 10% solution of ammonia; this way you can ensure that the surface area is reasonably clean and free of dust, and the new layer of paint will be smooth and even overall.

If you want to ensure the durability of your finish, it is better to spend more time and money. The old paint will tend to flake off unless it is completely removed. This can only be done with paint stripper. However, any kind of paint remover is unhealthy and stays behind in the environment, so it is best to call in a firm of commercial strippers, who will use a concentrated corrosive preparation and get rid of the paint in an environmentally friendly way. Once the old paint is finally off, you can start on the improvements. You can replace defective legs, glue on loose parts, round corners and oil creaking hinges. All in all, solid wood furniture is the most rewarding to repair. It is very easy to sand away blemishes and reattach wobbly legs with dowels, screws or glue. With the addition of a supporting sheet of wood, you can put old sofas on their feet again. Re-upholstery is not something you can do yourself, however. Replacing environmentally unfriendly foam with stuffing made of kapok or wool fiber, straw or rubber is clearly a job for the professional. Professionals can also repair wicker chairs and fraying rattan (cane) furniture. Although there are not many people around any more with expertise in wickerwork, thanks chiefly to the rising demand for authentic restoration the craft is enjoying a resurgence.

Once you have refurbished the piece, it will only need oil or wax to enhance the natural charm it lends to the home. People wanting to restore and repair wooden objects themselves can now get pro-fessional hard wax without harmful solvents or arti-ficial additives.

BEDROOMS

Blissful sleep

Enjoy pure relaxation in a solid wood bedroom where there is no metal in the bed to interrupt your sleep.

The bedroom is one of the most important rooms in the house. After all, you spend about a third of your life there. When the body relaxes in sleep, it is particularly sensitive to external influences. For this reason, you should locate the bedroom in the quietest area in the house. You should also avoid electromagnetic smog and emissions from building materials. Finally, the room you sleep in should be easy to air, so the atmosphere in the room does not get stale and stuffy.

Beds

You've made your bed, so lie in it!

Do not hesitate to spend a little more on a bed. Ecologically minded cabinetmakers build beds using traditional craft skills. The parts are not only screwed together but also firmly locked together with tenon joints, which will withstand several removals. These beds do not creak or squeak because the materials are carefully matched. The cabinetmaker uses only solid wood and blockboard. Chipboard and synthetic materials are taboo in specialist interior design shops. Instead, they favor the distinctive qualities of solid woods: beech, maple, ash, cherry, pine, elm, hawthorn, birch and pear wood. Treated only with oil and wax, the wooden beds are available in every shade from light beige to dark brown. Even department stores and large furniture retailers are promoting solid wood beds. Their beds often have only a solid wood frame; hidden inside is cheap chipboard. Ecologically minded cabinetmakers are cutting down on the amount of metal in the beds they make. Pride in their craft is not the only reason they are doing this. There is a suspicion that metal may disturb sleep. If steel is artificially magnetized, either during production or in later manufacturing processes, or if it interacts with the electromagnetic fields of clock radios or television sets, the natural magnetic field of the earth can, in fact, become distorted. This change may be passed on to people, and doctors have observed that it can lead to a number of psychosomatic illnesses, such as sleep disturbances, headaches, blood pressure problems and mood swings. None of this, however, has been conclusively proven, but if you recognize yourself as having some of the above-mentioned symptoms you may want to check up on this.

The highly popular innerspring mattress is full of metal. A simple test will show whether the springs are magnetized. If you pass a compass over the mattress and the needle wobbles and no longer finds the north, the springs are magnetized.

The base can also contain metal in the form of springs or spiral mesh. But the metal is not the only drawback that these mattresses have. They are also bad for your back because your spine is constantly slipping and sliding. Fortunately, beds with a slatted wooden base that is much healthier for the spine are becoming more popular.

There are various types of slatted bases ranging enormously in price. In the simplest models the lattice is firmly anchored in a frame or sewn into a fabric strip. The cheapest bases are hard, however, and do not adapt particularly well to the natural curvature of the body. There are two types of flexible lattices. In one, a single row of slats are held in place with elastic moveable rubber or manmade hinges. In the second, the slats lie in two rows: The top row is elastic, the lower row firm. These more expensive models usually have adjustable bed-ends.

A green firm has recently introduced a new base in which the slats go lengthwise instead of crosswise. This arrangement is intended to support you as you roll from your back onto your side while you sleep. The lattice has three different zones of elasticity: The torso, the diaphragm and the legs all sink into the bed to a different depth. Naturally the bed is completely metal-free with strips of natural rubber and latex blocks for support.

Your choice of base does not depend solely on comfort and price. The frame must fit the mattress — which you may already have. As a general rule, a hard, relatively inflexible base is best combined with a firm mattress. This combination prevents the sleeper from feeling the slats. A flexible base, on the other hand, demands a softer mattresslike latex. This softer mattress will best transmit the springiness of the frame.

A metal-free sanctuary

This bed-frame with loose slats attached by rubber joints can be adjusted for comfort. It has no metal, so it promotes healthy sleep. This type of frame needs a soft mattress.

Peace, perfect peace

Good quality, solid wood beds like these are not just timelessly elegant, they also aid relaxation because they contain no metal and the surfaces are oiled and waxed only with natural substances. Mattress and frame need to suit each other, hence the current fashion for selling them as a pair. Although they may prove costly, this expense may well be worth it.

Mattresses

It is not easy to find the right mattress. Because we all have different preferences when it comes to the most comfortable bed for us, it is important to "nap test" any mattress before buying it. Almost every material has its drawbacks. Health-conscious people prefer to sleep on natural latex, derived from the sap of the rubber tree. But this material, like sheep's wool, horsehair, coconut fiber or sisal, can emit fumes of the banned, highly toxic, anti-mildew treatment PCP. Recent investigations have shown that this substance is being used less and less now. But on the other hand independent researchers have been finding a lot of the carcinogenic nitrosamines, which may

be produced during the processing of the rubber. Many manufacturers have stopped using this danger-ous substance. However, the latest investigations detected sulfur disulfide in almost all latex nuclei. This highly toxic chemical can damage nerves, kidneys and liver, cause heart disease and is suspected of harming the unborn child. Experts are certain that this material, which is given off during the production process, can be greatly reduced in the factory. There are other dubi-ous mattress materials. Interior springs can affect the earth's natural magnetic field and rob sensitive people of a good night's rest. The manufacture of foam causes pollution and unhealthy isocyanates

Romantic bedrooms

A fairytale canopy and a profu-sion of pastel-colored materials in the bedroom create a romantic atmosphere.

emissions. In sheep's wool increased levels of the anti-moth product naphthalene, a suspected carcinogen, have been found. The cotton underlay of one model had even been polluted with pesticides containing arsenic. Waterbeds are definitely not recommended. The body sinks too deeply into the mattress. This position is a sure recipe for lower-back pain. In addition, the necessary electrical heating causes the worst kind of electromagnetic smog.

Another frequent problem occurs when the different layers of the mattress are glued together. Since glue can prevent air from getting through, patches of mildew may form underneath the mattress. In addition, glue can even introduce harmful solvents into the mattress. To make matters worse, the glue attaches the materials so firmly to each other that they are impossible to recycle.

In order to banish the widespread concern about unhealthy mattresses, several firms in Germany, for example, test regularly for injurious substances, and can supply certificates. Some ecologically aware interior design firms require manufacturers to supply a full list of all auxiliary materials used and the mattresses to undergo a pollution test. In addition, the manufacturers have to document the source of their raw materials.

In the United States each mattress component must meet government standards, and each new mattress must have a "do not remove" tag. This tag lists the percentage of each material used, where the mattress was made, and the warranty code. While they do not issue labels, consumers groups, like the Consumers Union, evaluate mattresses for durability and value and publish their findings.

Innerspring and latex mattresses are the most popular types. You can often see from the label whether artificial substances have been used in their manufacture. For the most part, these mattresses are inferior because they do not absorb the pint (half liter) of sweat every sleeper gives off at night. On the other hand, natural fibers, especially wool, can absorb moisture very well. Mattresses with woolen padding under the cotton cover are thus very comfortable, particularly in summer. Many linen shops and department stores in the United States sell a wool mattress pad to place between the mattress and sheet, and some manufacturers of innerspring mattresses now attach a "pillowtop" stuffed with wool on their innerspring mattresses. A good mattress supports the body in such a way that heavy parts of the body like the pelvis and the shoulders can sink in deeper than the lighter parts.

This variable elasticity is easy to check. If you press your knee into the mattress, it should not leave a large dent. Mattresses made of natural latex are very elastic and can be softer or harder according to the proportion of other substances in them. If a mattress is too hard, your pelvis sticks up. Very hard mattresses also make you toss and turn constantly.

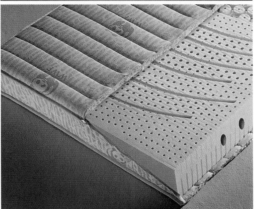

Are you getting magnetized?

Today most mattresses have inner springs, even if they are occasionally supported by a layer of latex. In fact, such mattresses can have a negative effect on sleep. Because most springs are capable of being magnetized, they pick up and magnify electromagnetic radiation.

Latex mattresses are not always OK

Latex mattresses are a healthy and natural alternative to inner-spring mattresses. But they must be manufactured with care because inferior latex can leave toxic residue.

The mattress determines the quality of sleep

Poorly made innerspring mattresses have so much give in them that you tend to lie spreadeagled in bed to stop yourself from bouncing around all night. Mattresses that are entirely made of natural materials and contain no latex are generally rather hard; for that reason not many people like them. Good horsehair mattresses are relatively elastic, and, above all, almost no chemicals are used in their manufacture. If a new mattress smells unpleasant, the likely cause is glue, but it can also be the latex or the natural fibers. In any case it is a good idea to air a new mattress for two weeks before using it. Anyone who suffers from an allergy to latex should not buy a mattress made of natural rubber, just in case. Synthetic latex causes no problems for allergy sufferers.

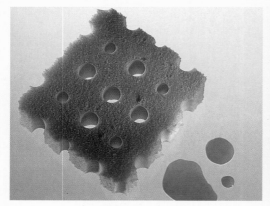

Latex

Coconut fiber treated with latex

Natural materials for healthy sleep

Latex, coconut fiber, horsehair, hemp, flax, cotton or wool — these are the most important components of a natural mattress. They are combined to produce a filling with the right balance of warmth, softness, firmness, absorbency and coziness. The diagrams on the next page show the composition of two high-grade mattresses.

Horsehair

Horsehair

Hemp

Hemp fiber

Sheep's wool

Sheep's wool

Individual cross-sections

On pages 420–421 you can see cross-sections of mattresses made with natural materials. They represent only a small selection of the many possible combinations.

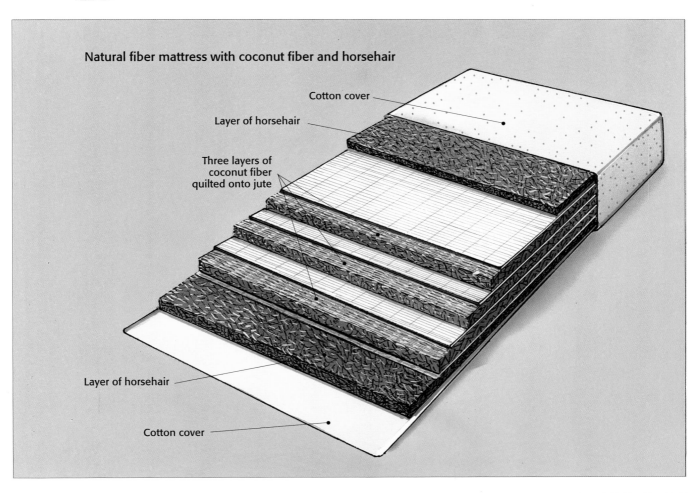

Natural fiber mattress with coconut fiber and horsehair

Cotton cover

Layer of horsehair

Three layers of coconut fiber quilted onto jute

Layer of horsehair

Cotton cover

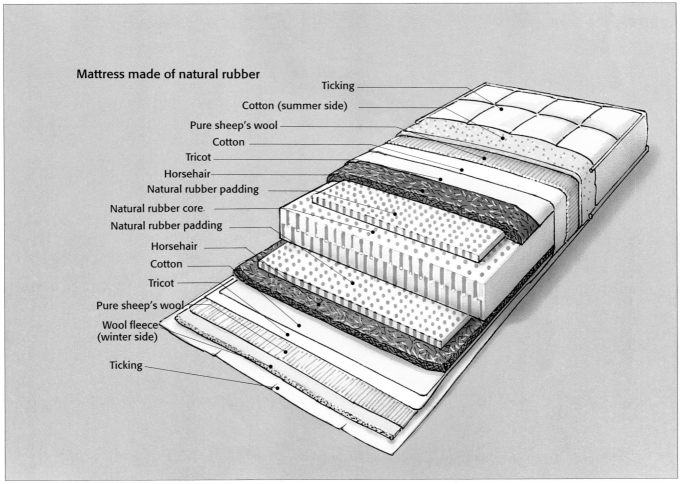

Mattress made of natural rubber

Ticking

Cotton (summer side)

Pure sheep's wool

Cotton

Tricot

Horsehair

Natural rubber padding

Natural rubber core

Natural rubber padding

Horsehair

Cotton

Tricot

Pure sheep's wool

Wool fleece (winter side)

Ticking

Cotton futon with jute core

Latex mattresses of varying strengths

Cotton futon with a core of latex-treated coconut fiber

Latex mattress with jute core

Three-layer mattress with layers of latex, horsehair and latex-treated coconut fiber stuffing

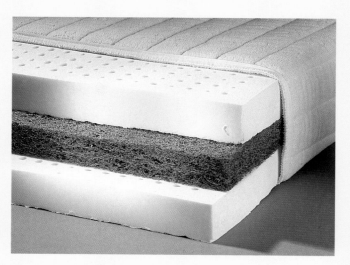

Latex mattress with latex-treated coconut fiber

Cotton futon with natural latex core

Cotton futon with horsehair core

Mattress made of three layers of latex with jute stuffing

Mattress made of sheep's wool, natural latex and latex-treated coconut fiber

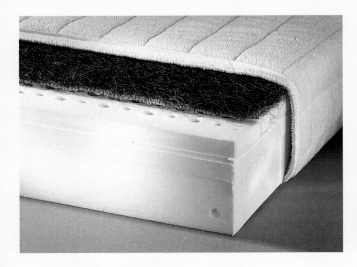

Latex mattress topped with horsehair

Mattress with sheep's wool and latex-treated coconut fiber

More room to play

The children's room is normally the smallest in the house, so it makes sense to place the bed high enough to take advantage of the space underneath it, providing the child with a larger play area. This creative design is reminiscent of a wigwam.

CHILDREN'S ROOMS

The children's room is usually the smallest in the home, but it is the most intensively used. Children devote more than 15,000 hours to play in their first six years. Most of that play takes place in their own rooms because the living area is often not an inviting area for play. In addition, safe play areas outside the home are not always within easy reach. The average space available for play in a room shared by two children is around 24 square feet (2.16 square meters). For this reason, it is especially important to make the most of the space available for each child to provide them with the best opportunities for satisfying their play instinct.

Children's furniture

Particular care should be taken when it comes to choosing furniture for children. Children's furniture should not be a copy of what goes typically in an adult "sitting room" but, instead, be suited to the children's natural need to play. The contents of children's rooms will have to stand a lot of rough use. They must be stable, sturdy, and have no sharp angles or places where a child can get caught and hurt itself in any way. Above all they should be free of domestic toxins. Not even the use of E1 chipboard, which is low in formaldehydes, guarantees safety. The chipboard is tested under particular conditions that may not be at all similar to those in a child's room. In a room that is often very small and full of furniture, it is easy to exceed the permitted level of formaldehyde in the air.

Many furniture manufacturers have tried to meet the need for good quality, non-toxic children's furniture. Even the large firms are now using solid pine or birch wood, water-based sealant or water-soluble stain, glue without formaldehyde, and metal-free joints on the beds. Despite these positive beginnings on the part of big manufacturers, it is still the small ones that work to the most stringent criteria.

The most important single purchase for a child's room is a bed. Since it is usually the parents who choose the bed, many children's beds are designed to suit their taste. Newborn babies are bundled up in cozy cribs with canopies and little bells or in frilly indoor strollers that can be pushed from room to room. These pretty items are expensive, and not just in terms of price. As early as five months, a child will be kicking and bouncing around so much that he or she can easily overturn a fragile crib.

It makes more sense to start out with a proper child's bed. It should be at least 23 inches (70 cm) wide and 55 inches (140 cm) long; children grow out of anything smaller too soon. Many models can be adapted to various stages of the child's development. These beds have side rails to stop children in the first years from falling out or wandering round the house. Good models are equipped with detachable latticed sides which parents can simply remove later to provide an "emergency exit" for the toddler, who is beginning to climb and might otherwise topple over the side rail.

In an infant's bed, the height of the slatted base should also be adjustable. The first to benefit from this is, of course, the mother. Raising the base to a comfortable height will protect the mother's back in the first few months when she is constantly lifting the baby out of the bed.

When the child is about three years of age, parents can lower the base as far as it will go and remove the latticed safety sides and then have a regular child's bed. Because the high headboards look odd if left standing, in some models each end consists of two interlocking parts. To reduce the height of the end you simply take off the top half.

At around age six, the child usually outgrows this bed. At that point you need a youth or junior bed. The fashion at the moment is for play-bunks. City children in particular value the many possibilities afforded by ladders and slides that can be turned into lifeboats or racetracks. Girls seem more enthusiastic about beds with two curtains on one side. Here they can open a shop or a puppet theater. When the child reaches this stage, it is important to let him or her have some input in the type of bed you buy.

An intelligently constructed bed meets the child's changing needs. A ten-year-old may refuse to sleep in the pirate ship that he adored at six. So you have to be able to remove play elements such as a steering wheel or a climbing rope. If a child of ten now thinks the bunk he once loved is silly, his parents should be able to lower it, unscrew the now-superfluous safety rail, and make a plain bed. However imaginative the designs of the producers, all children's beds must conform to government safety standards. In the United States, cribs can have no more than 2⅜ inches (6 cm) of space between slats or spindles. There must be 9 inches (23 cm) between the top of the side rail and the mattress support when the mattress support is at the highest position and 26 inches (66 cm) when the mattress support is at the lowest position. These safety standards protect the child from accidental falls and possible entrapment and strangulation.

Children's beds and bunks should be as versatile as possible

Solid wood but playful too
Solid wood is ideal for furnishing the children's room. It provides a healthy atmosphere for them, and the furniture can generally be changed to suit different ages. The child's bed with built-in cave or puppet theater is easily converted into a normal bed for an older child or adult.

Take care that edges and corners are rounded, and there must be no slits or places where threads or cords can get caught and strangle the child. To prevent a child from falling off a bunk bed the safety rail on bunk beds must be at least 10 inches (26 cm) high, and there must be no space greater than 3½ inches (9 cm) between the mattress and the top of the safety rail.

Furniture that grows with the child

A wicker crib that grows up with the child

Because children grow out of their furniture almost as quickly as their clothes, intelligent manufacturers are going for quality furniture that is adaptable for different ages. This piece of solid-wood and wicker furniture starts out as a crib, then becomes a toddler's bed, and finally turns into an attractive seating arrangement for a young child.

Furniture must grow too

If you purchase high-grade solid wood furniture for your children's room, you naturally want to be able to use it as long as possible, especially since you can keep sanding out any bangs and nicks which may occur over time. This is why nearly all manufacturers have been thinking of ways to make furniture grow with the child. However, the space-saving sleeping platform which is a big hit with four-to-ten-year-olds must be capable of being turned into an ordinary bed when the child decides it is not so great any more. Flexible-use bunk beds are now standard, and more adventurous ideas are coming along all the time. A crib that turns into a bed with wooden rails finally turns into a desk. Sets of shelves are eminently transformable. An Austrian firm, for example, produces an especially successful range of furniture that grows with the child. Its solid maple furniture would be equally prized by an adult and could very well be used in a living room or an office.

For many parents, the purchase of such high-grade expensive furniture is out of the question. Young families in particular often only have enough money to equip the kitchen and the living room. They mistakenly skimp on children's furniture. They either buy a cheap set from a catalog or discount store,

or they make do with old bits of adult furniture. Even if this old furniture is still in good condition, it does not always serve a child's needs. While an old table with sawn-off legs and rounded corners may work well in a child's room, a little child does not feel protected in an adult bed. The alternative is do-it-yourself. A lot of very versatile pieces are available in kit form. For example, there is the high-chair that comes apart into a table and chair and can be used for play right through to school age. There is also the set consisting of a little seat and a stool, a bench and a table. Another versatile piece is the highchair with a seat that can be inserted at different heights. Parents who are good with their hands can carry out these quick-change ideas inexpensively. In addition they can ensure that the materials used are not harmful to health. Do-it-yourselfers have to be especially careful when putting together furniture for children. Because children are so active and adventurous and tend to be more accident-prone than adults, furniture for them must be very sturdy and very stable and all surfaces must be smooth and free of dangerous angles. In spite of this, you do not need to complete an apprenticeship as a carpenter before you can make good-looking furniture for your child.

New roles

When a child outgrows the bed (top), it can quite easily be converted into a table for painting and crafts and for doing homework later on (left).

To build yourself

This versatile piece of furniture can serve not only as a little chair but also as a stool or a table. Depending on which side is up, it will be the right height for sitting or play. Do-it-yourselfers can easily make a simple item of child's furniture like this.

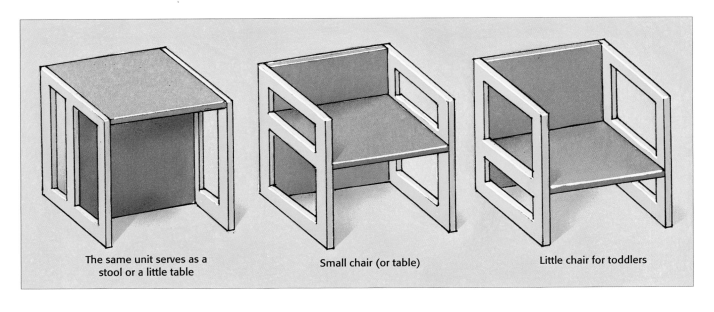

The same unit serves as a stool or a little table

Small chair (or table)

Little chair for toddlers

OFFICE

White-collar workers can spend up to 60,000 hours of their lives in the office. Up to half of all office workers often feel below par and incapable of performing at their best. This may have something to do with the office furniture. Desks made of chipboard and then covered with synthetic materials, shelves that give off formaldehyde vapors and chromed steel office chairs upholstered with foam and covered in manmade fabrics still dominate today's business premises. This is even truer of a home office, which is frequently furnished with castoffs from the workplace. Relying on such pieces may seem like an inexpensive way to

60,000 hours in the stench created by unhealthy office furniture

furnish your home office, but this is false economy at the cost of your health. You do not have to put in a bulk order to an office furniture store to have a healthy, ecological workplace at home.

Ergonomics and ecology

Office chairs from the German company Grammer, for example, are a positive exception. For several years this company, the largest manufacturer of chairs in the world, has been working on the concept of ecologically sound desks and conference

and tables made of 100% renewable cork and finished with a light natural wax. HAG, Inc. in North Carolina produces an award-winning line of chairs made of natural beechwood with an innovative flexible internal seat and back mechanism that encourages movement for increased comfort and reduced fatigue. Office furniture manufacturers like these are adopting the basic standards used in other ecological furnishings. They are emphasizing solid homegrown woods with formaldehyde-free glue, sound craftsmanship, sensitive treatment of surfaces with natural colors and waxes, and the most sparing use of metal.

Even solid wood desks, however, can lead to solid health problems if they are not ergonomic: If you cannot sit and work comfortably at them. The basic rule for a good desk is that everything that can be adjustable should be. This includes the height (and possibly slope) of the work surface and the height of the "third plane" over the work surface where the computer screen can be installed. A good desk should have at least 35 inches (90 cm) of work surface.

When buying office chairs, green building methods and disposability are not the only factors. The chairs should be built to suit the human body. Just because you are sitting down, you are not necessarily relaxed. Sitting puts 80% more weight on the spine than standing, and sitting badly can decrease your productivity by 40%.

An office chair must be constructed in such a way that the spine is stretched while you are sitting down, but no additional strain is placed on your muscles. This is achieved when the seat is padded in such a way as to keep the diaphragm in an upright position. The chair back should be adjustable to support that posture even when you are leaning forward or back. The height of the seat should also be adjustable, so that

So many choices
Today there is a dazzling array of eco-friendly office furniture on the market which do not contain any hazardous substances (left).

An office chair should relax the spine by stretching it

The "Natura" office chair by Grammer
This award-winning chair is a model of ecological design. It combines a careful choice of materials with versatility of use and ease of repair.

chairs. Equal emphasis is placed on timeless design, on longevity and comfort, and on a green attitude to materials and energy. The result is a chair that has won many prizes, and stands as a model of ecological design, both on the grounds of materials, and because every part can be repaired. Only a few exclusive furniture producers are on this level. In the United States more and more manufacturers are subscribing to a green philosophy. Their concern for the environment is an important factor in their designs and choice of materials. The ICF Group in New York produces a line of sturdy, durable chairs

A second level

This desk stands out because of its ergonomic form and the introduction of a second level. A computer screen could be placed on the small platform instead of a telephone.

your arms form a 90° angle on the work surface. Because it is not good for your back to sit down all the time, you should try to complete some tasks while standing. The good old-fashioned tall desk, which is currently enjoying a renaissance due to modern ergonomic considerations, is ideal for this.

Office furniture should be capable of as many combinations as possible. A table system allows much more flexibility than a traditional desk. For example,

the table system can consist of elements that can be arranged in different ways. A writing desk, a table for a monitor, a filing cabinet and a desk at which you can stand can each be moved to meet various requirements or to perform different functions.

Ecology and care for health are not always a question of price. You can get an all-wood table top in untreated pine and four legs that can be adjusted for different heights inexpensively at a building supply store. Unvarnished filing cabinets are available, though you will have to find your own environmentally friendly finish for them. Do-it-yourself experts can put together a whole office.

A number of office furniture manufacturers are making furniture component parts from recycled material. For example, Studio, Inc. in California makes modular office furniture from 98% recycled materials: cardboard, newsprint, and rubber from recycled tires. It is not only recyclable without any problems but also perfectly suited for easy disassembly. HAG, Inc. uses recycled bottle-caps in the production of back and seat shells for some of its office chairs. While recycling can save tons of waste from ending in landfills one has to keep in mind, however, that not all recycling is totally green. Some recycling is really a form of down-cycling to a different throwaway material, and more energy has to be used in washing, drying and re-forming the material. Such recycling is, of course, not part of a self-sustaining cycle.

On your knees – but not in front of the boss

This office chair produces an upright posture, in which you are kneeling rather than sitting.

Cutting table
The height is variable, the table mobile.

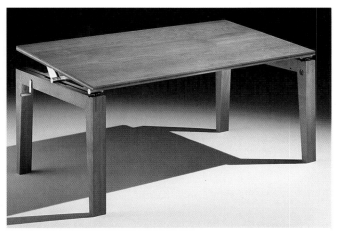

Table with moveable top
A work surface that can be inclined reduces strain when drawing.

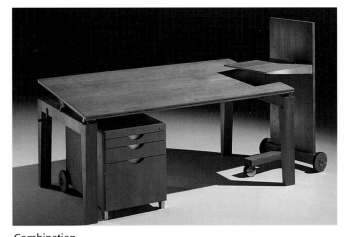

Combination
This elegant combination gains much of its distinction from the use of naturally treated solid wood.

Partition
These elegant solid wood shelves are free standing and can be used to divide working space from living area.

A typical work corner
Furniture for the home office should not consist of rejects brought home from the workplace. You cannot use castoffs to come up with inspired solutions for a limited workspace like this.

YARD AND GARDEN

Green spaces have become rare in many cities, where up to 90% of the ground is paved. The price of land in most cities is so high that few can afford a large yard. Back yards are often covered in asphalt and used for cars, bikes and garbage cans. Gray concrete vistas like these spoil city life for many people. Yet a dreary back yard can be turned into a green oasis without too much expense.

If you do have a yard, it can be much more than just a plain stretch of lawn that resembles a putting green. Indigenous hedges, a little pond, a heap of rocks, dead wood and dry walls provide a habitat for rarer types of plant and animal life. A flowering field is not only a joy to the eye, but it provides a vital toehold for nature. You can grow all the herbs you need for the kitchen on an "herb spiral," and a small vegetable patch will show children that peas do not always come out of cans. You can also make valuable fertilizer by composting kitchen waste.

Making more of your garden

Layout

If you have a large yard that you can landscape as you please, it is easy to create several zones to suit different types and levels of use and to plant whatever you like. Although the size of yards in the United States varies greatly depending upon whether the property is in a city, suburb, or rural area, the average yard is between 5,000 and 10,000 square feet. Even a small

A natural oasis
The stylish garden furniture and the natural layout of the garden itself provide an oasis in the middle of the city.

yard, however, affords enough space for creating an esthetically pleasing habitat for a diverse variety of plants and small animals.

Zoning the garden

The first and most important step in landscaping is to determine exactly what functions your yard will serve and divide it up accordingly into zones. A zone for intensive use, with a sun terrace, a play area for the children, and the compost heap, can adjoin a quieter zone needing more cultivation. Here you can lay out various biotopes. The vegetable garden should always be separated from the first two zones. Landscaped mounds, dry walls, hedges and trees are not

only suitable for separating the zones, but they also offer a habitat for many creatures and form an adventure playground for children to explore.

The second step in designing your yard is analyzing your plot thoroughly. Does the soil have a lot of sand, or clay? Which part is damp, which dry and warm? This analysis will decide which plants are most suitable for which location. The relationship of your yard to its surroundings is also an important consideration. When and where do neighboring houses or trees cast shadows? Where is the yard most visible, and where is it more private? Where is disturbance from traffic or the neighbors to be expected? Where are the interconnecting paths likely to be? These are decisive questions when determining where to locate each zone and where to place a windbreak or block off a view. Finally, you need to consider where and how to separate each zone with the least expense. While the house is still being built you can watch for suitable materials such as excavated earth, rocks or old beams and store them for use later on when you are dividing the yard into zones.

Greening the yard

Green back yards add to the quality of city life. If you can get out with a deckchair and enjoy the shade of a tree, the rustling of leaves and the twittering of birds in your own yard, you no longer have to get into the car every weekend for a drive into the country.

When landscaping a small city yard, you must take into account the immediate surroundings and the habits of the people who will be using the yard. Identify what is especially disturbing in the yard and determine how you can make the best of it. For instance, climbing plants can be used to conceal an ugly wall, the area where the garbage cans are kept, or the entrance to the cellar.

The location of paths depends on where the residents walk most. The paths should be made of tough material that will let water drain through. Even though it is easy to plant a lawn, you do need to consider whether it will be trodden bare in a short space of time. For sitting you can place an inviting wooden seat between the flowerbeds or you can even use the tops of walls for seats.

There are many questions that have to be answered before you can begin landscaping. Where will you store the garden tools? What is the most suitable location for a secluded spot to allow people to sit down and relax for a while without the neighbors or any passer-by to disturb you? Is there enough space for a pergola and play equipment for the children? Do you want to grow some fruit: Do you want an

Filling the courtyard with greenery
Green courtyards are good for cities. They provide coolness, moisture, and a much needed foothold for nature.

apple tree, or red currant bushes, or an espalier pear on the wall? How big are the trees planted now going to be in 20 years? Are there any allergy sufferers in the family who might be bothered by particular trees or shrubs? And, last but not least, who is going to water the flowers, prune the plants in autumn and rake up the leaves?

Landscaping can be an expensive project. Even if you do the work yourself, you will still have to pay for plants and for rubble removal.

Often you can use materials that cost nothing but the effort of collecting them and bringing them to your yard. It is not too difficult to find sandstone dug out of a building site, remains of old plaster, or wooden beams from a demolished house or barn.

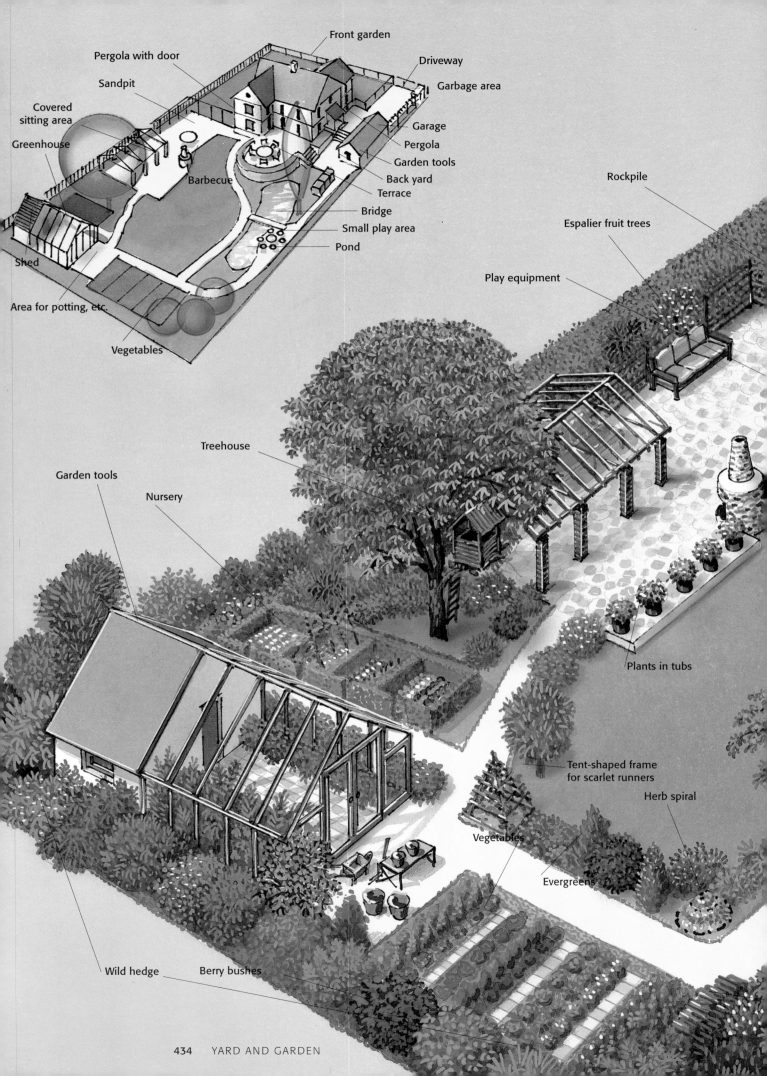

Front garden

Pergola with door

Sandpit

Driveway

Garbage area

Covered
sitting area

Garage

Greenhouse

Pergola

Garden tools

Back yard

Barbecue

Terrace

Bridge

Shed

Small play area

Area for potting, etc.

Pond

Vegetables

Rockpile

Espalier fruit trees

Play equipment

Treehouse

Garden tools

Nursery

Plants in tubs

Tent-shaped frame
for scarlet runners

Herb spiral

Vegetables

Evergreens

Wild hedge

Berry bushes

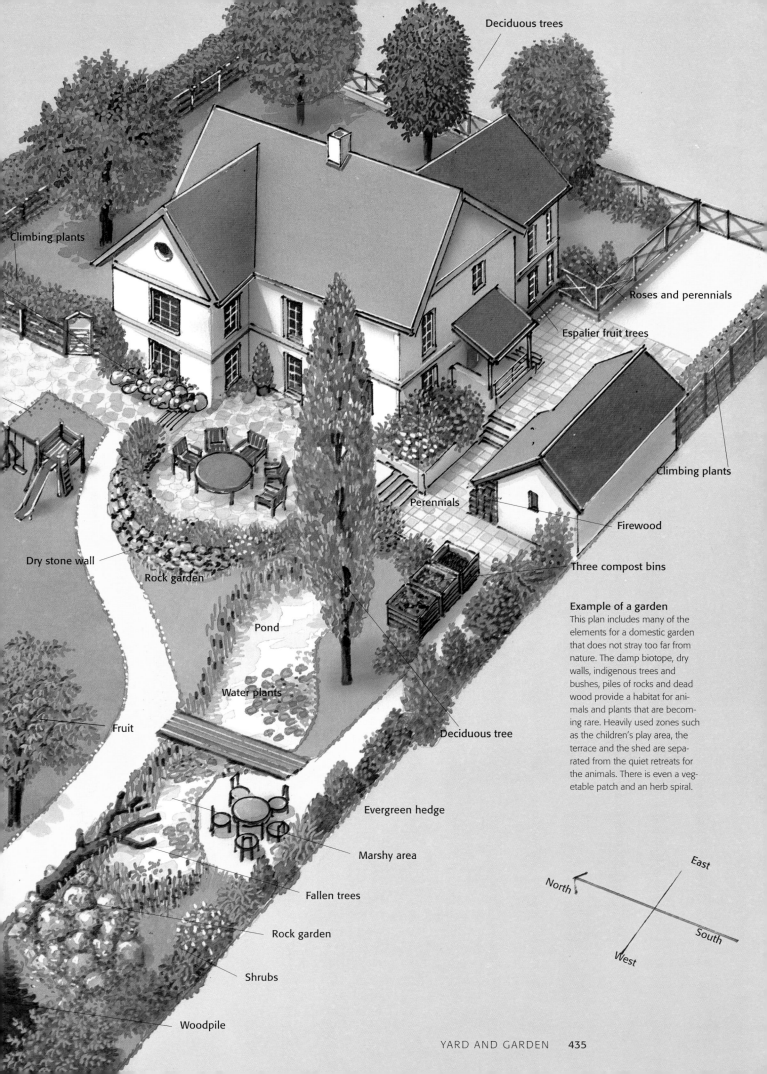

Deciduous trees

Climbing plants

Roses and perennials

Espalier fruit trees

Climbing plants

Perennials

Firewood

Three compost bins

Dry stone wall

Rock garden

Pond

Water plants

Fruit

Deciduous tree

Example of a garden
This plan includes many of the elements for a domestic garden that does not stray too far from nature. The damp biotope, dry walls, indigenous trees and bushes, piles of rocks and dead wood provide a habitat for animals and plants that are becoming rare. Heavily used zones such as the children's play area, the terrace and the shed are separated from the quiet retreats for the animals. There is even a vegetable patch and an herb spiral.

Evergreen hedge

Marshy area

Fallen trees

Rock garden

Shrubs

Woodpile

East

North

South

West

GETTING RID OF PAVING

Paths, yards and driveways should not be covered with concrete or asphalt. In contrast to unpaved areas, rain flows straight off these surfaces and into the drains, overloading the sewerage system and indirectly causing floods. Paved surfaces also prevent ground water reservoirs from filling up. This, in turn, leads to the destruction of animal and plant habitats. In addition, the dense surface prevents oxygen from getting into the soil, so microorganisms cannot survive and eventually the soil dies.

Paving kills the soil

Independent studies have shown that the paving could be removed from at least half of the open spaces in built-up areas. Not every garden path needs to be paved. You can cover a path with wood chips. In some cities you may be able to get the wood chips free from the city maintenance department or you can produce them from your own garden waste with the help of a mechanical shredder or chipper. Wood chips decay more slowly than farm straw and have to be renewed

offer a wide variety of systems. These systems enable you to create a hard surface that also remains porous. For instance there is the gravel lawn, composed of a mixture of soil and small stones, and the patented precast concrete lawn system where grass grows in the typically honeycomb-shaped gaps between the blocks. There are also paving blocks that can be laid with gaps between them where grass and plants can grow. The best of these systems have spacers attached to the blocks. These are generally of a far better value and are much more stable than those with loose spacers made of synthetic material or wood. In addition, there is regular paving where the narrow space between the stones is filled with grit.

Some firms offer porous paving, which is said to have such a coarse particle structure that water and air can get through the stone. The manufacturers are making amazing claims about these porous stones. For example, some of them are supposed to let through

A green car park
Cars do not necessarily have to be parked on asphalt. There are many special types of paving that let the rainwater drain away and the grass grow.

only once a year. Wooden boards last a long time if they are laid on a bed of sand and gravel.

Natural stones or brick pavers also make attractive garden paths. All you need to do is lay them in a bed of sand so that water can seep through. It is important, too, to lay out paths in an imaginative way. Curving, meandering paths are far more appealing than straight paths. With driveways it is often enough to put a hard surface just where the car wheels go.

For terraces or parking spaces where a hard surface is essential, garden centers and cement manufacturers

850 gallons (3,300 l) of water per 2½ acres (1 hectare). At that rate the wonder paving would cope even in the worst tropical storm. Experts, however, are not convinced. For the most part, the results are based on laboratory tests and do not give a true picture of what would happen in practice. Furthermore, the firms test their products as they leave the factory. They are less interested in whether they will still be porous in five years. Measurements taken in the open air over a long period show that the effectiveness of all the systems drops sharply because dust gets into the

pores. After five years at the most, the porous stone becomes watertight.

Even paving blocks with gaps between them clog up over the years, no matter how wide the gaps are. This is due partly to the mixture of clay and inorganic silt used to fill the cracks and allow grass to take root, and partly to the grass roots themselves, which eventually form a barrier against rainwater. This barrier effect is also a problem in the concrete lawn systems. Nonetheless, such ground coverings are preferable to smooth concrete and asphalt or to seamless paving. The right ground covering is not the only factor affecting drainage. If the ground underneath the covering is dense clay or loess, rainwater collects on top of it and makes it soft. If the ground is sandy, rainwater drains away with no problems.

It is expensive to get rid of paving. In addition to the cost of breaking up the old paving and disposing of it, there is the expense of getting new stones. In water-protection zones it is sometimes prohibited to remove the paving in traffic areas such as parking places because they have to be proofed against the possible spillage of oil or gasoline.

An economical solution is to provide drainage gullies so that the water from paved areas can simply flow away. You can easily build these gullies yourself. They do require space, however, as they will take up at least a tenth of the paved area.

Eco-friendly alternatives to paving

The type of surface you choose will depend primarily on degree of use. Paths that are not heavily used can be surfaced with a gravel lawn (top picture). Precast cement lawn-blocks are good for car parks but not very good for walking paths. Paving with spaces for grass looks attractive but needs maintenance.

THE NATURAL GARDEN

Geometrically clipped thuja hedges, exotic decorative bushes, pseudo-cypresses and blue firs border many front and backyards. Yet these exotic woody plants are incapable of maintaining the ecological balance because they do not provide a suitable habitat for local birds and butterflies. There are, however, alternatives to these exotic hedges that do provide natural habitats. If they are regularly pruned, freely growing wild hedges will fit into even a small garden. Native woody plants can even be clipped into formal hedges, just like thuja.

The ecological solution – which is also an esthetically pleasing one, since the bushes flower at different times – is to combine different species, e.g. hornbeam, dogwood, virburnum, yew, spice bush, privet, witch hazel, and buckthorn, to name just a few. It is always a good idea to plant three to five of the same kind of bushes next to each other so that fast-growing

An almost-natural hedge
Easily maintained but lifeless thuja hedges are not the only way to enclose your property. Many indigenous bushes are just as suitable, and they also provide food and shelter for animals.

bushes do not crowd out the others. Native wild roses are a particularly beautiful sight, and they also make excellent hedges. Around 40 varieties have been developed and propagated in recent years. Indigenous hedges and bushes provide food and a habitat for dozens of different species of mammals, depending on the area. Witch hazel bushes alone are a feeding ground for 70 different sorts of insects, whitethorn for an astonishing 150.

Strictly speaking, you should plant only bushes that are indigenous to the region. They have adapted to the local climate and are most resistant to local pests and diseases. The only trouble is that indigenous plants have almost ceased to exist in many areas. This may not be an issue where you are planting a domestic garden because you can safeguard vulnerable plants. Nonetheless, in many regions, "green" gardeners are adopting a policy of reintroducing indigenous woody plants.

Even if you live in a row of houses with very small front yards, you need not give up on the idea of having a hedge. A fence woven out of willow twigs after the frosts are over and stuck in the ground and watered well comes to life as soon as the first spring sun warms the yard. Experienced gardeners keep on weaving the shoots back into the hedge to keep it neat and compact. It will soon become as dense as a wooden fence and will be the first port of call for the earliest bees in spring.

If you have a bit of space in your yard, you should definitely have a heap of twigs and dead wood. You can pile sawn-off branches and twigs onto it, as well as the remains of perennials that have been around a few years, old rotting boards and broken fruit-boxes. This dead wood provides a habitat and hiding place for many useful insects and reptiles, as well as a place for hedgehogs to spend the winter and birds to build their nests. The cut wood breaks down surprisingly fast, so you can add new material every year without the pile getting any bigger.

A heap of dead wood is also an ideal place for strawberries, since it imitates their natural growing conditions. Another biotope that is readily adopted by many creatures is a heap of stones. Piled against a sunny house wall, the stones offer a home to insects and the many kinds of plants that prefer a dry location. Lizards use sun-warmed stones to restore their body heat. In a shady place, various mosses will quickly settle on the stones. In addition, the stone heap provides food and a shady hiding place during the day for worms and toads.

A particularly handsome addition to a yard, and without doubt its most useful biotope, is a dry stone wall. In the past these stone walls were everywhere: bordering fields, shoring up terraces in hilly areas. Today walls in such places are made of concrete or of stones stuck together with mortar. They no longer offer a habitat to plants and animals.

You can use a dry wall to shore up a sloping garden or as a boundary or a seat in a level one. Because it takes an astonishing number of stones to build a dry wall, it is best to gather stones from your own garden or nearby land. You may even be lucky enough to find a farmer who is glad to rid his field of unwelcome rocks. If you build a low wall – up to 23 inches (60 cm) – it will not need any foundation.

For higher walls or walls that are to be built on sinking ground, you need to dig an 8 to 16 inch (20–40 cm) ditch and fill it with gravel. Place the largest and flattest stones on the gravel. Then add layers of smaller stones and fill the spaces between them with earth and sand to make it easier for plants to take root.

The wall must have a 15° incline relative to the slope on which it is built. If it is a freestanding wall, both sides must slope inwards by that same amount. The ditch and the layer of gravel should have the same incline to ensure stability. Only low walls with a height of up to 20 inches (50 cm) can be built vertically.

As a rule of thumb, the width of the wall at its foot should be about a third of its height. Dry stone walls are held together by the weight of the stones. If you place uneven stones with the broadest side facing outwards, the incline will form almost on its own. Every so often you must put in a layer of large stones running through the whole breadth of the wall. These are the so-called "binders" which keep the wall stable.

Various levels

An effective trick for making a small garden more interesting is to build it on different levels. For instance, growing plants on a heap of stones like this one adds variety and also provides a habitat for animals.

Dry stone wall

The cracks and spaces in a wall made of loose stones provide a habitat for animals and plants.

Habitat

Living things find a congenial home in the gaps in a dry stone wall, which uses no mortar to hold the stones together.

How to build a dry stone wall

Use uncut stones, stacked up without mortar (i.e. "dry"), and life will develop in the gaps. Begin the dry stone wall with a good foundation of sand and gravel. Be sure to insert flat stones deep in the wall at intervals to ensure stability. Low walls up to 20 inches (50 cm) high can be vertical, but if the wall is any taller it must slope back at an angle of 15°. Fill the gaps between the stones with earth and sand. If you also use natural stones for paths, the gaps between them should be wide enough to let the rain through.

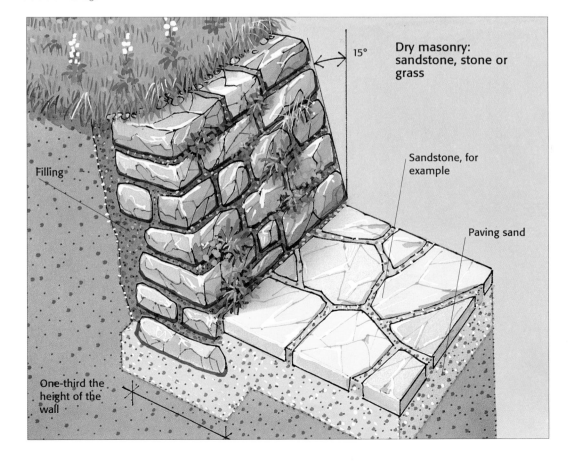

15°

Dry masonry: sandstone, stone or grass

Filling

Sandstone, for example

Paving sand

One-third the height of the wall

THE GARDEN POND

Glorious water lilies

Beautiful indigenous water plants like this water lily will thrive in a garden pond.

Water holds a particular attraction for human beings, and it is associated with relaxation and recuperation. Humans, however, are not the only animals that enjoy a garden pond. A garden pond provides a habitat for a wide variety of plants and animals – a habitat that is more sorely needed now than ever before because village ponds, puddles, water meadows and marshes are vanishing. Yet, do not expect too much from a small garden pond: A peaceful biotope of fish and amphibians you can observe from the immediate proximity of your terrace will not be easy to establish. You should not introduce any fish into the pond, but let nature take its course in stocking the water with animal life. Frogs will not go near water harboring a lot of fish, and dragonflies will hatch out only where fish are not going to eat their larvae. Do not expect to see frogs and other amphibians appearing overnight. These creatures and rare species, in particular, are naturally shy and avoid people if they can.

Planning

The nature pond should be located away from the bustle of the house, but close enough for you to arrange a quiet spot where you can sit and observe the life in and around the pond. There should be no trees along the edge. Leaves could fall in and over-load the water with rotting matter, and tree roots could also damage the pond's waterproofing.

The amount of sunlight the pond receives is an important factor. The pond should not be in deep shade, nor should it be in direct sunlight for long periods. Of course, the plants and animals living in it need a certain amount of sunlight, but too much strong sunlight will overstimulate the growth of plants and algae. To help you determine the best location, you could lay a piece of string or flexible garden hose on the ground in the shape of the future pond and then observe for a while how much sunlight the spot gets in the course of the day.

Controversial goldfish

Although fish are nice to look at in a garden pond, they can easily disturb the ecological balance. They are the natural predators of such pond-dwelling species as frogs and other amphibians that need protection.

Mare's-tail in water

This dainty swamp-growing plant proliferates readily in natural ponds. In winter it often stays green under water providing oxygen for underwater life.

Spectacular dragonflies

Often the first to settle in a new pond, these beautiful creatures add a touch of splendor to the natural garden.

In principle, you can make a natural pond of any size or depth. However, there are a few limitations: Small ponds less than 23 inches (60 cm) deep will certainly grow over and fill up quickly and freeze during the winter in cold areas. This inevitably means that the small creatures that spend the winter in the water cannot survive.

While a pond does not need to fill your entire property, a surface of at least 108 square feet (10 square meters) is essential and 270 square feet (25 square meters) is preferable. The pond must also be at least 31 inches (80 cm) deep. Over the years, the pond will develop a stable balance. It will not require much looking after, and a growing range of species will inhabit it. Even if you do not have enough space for a pond, a small patch of water, like a simple birdbath or a mortar trough buried in the ground and half-filled with stones and sand, fulfills an ecological function.

The bank of the pond should be flat so that animals can drink safely. The edge is the most populated part of the water. Most of the plants, insects and amphibians live in this boggy area, so it really should not be narrower than 20 inches (50 cm), and preferably considerably wider, and only about an inch deep at the edge. The shore zone of the pond should be no deeper than 8 inches (20 cm). After that the bed should go down in steps to the deepest part. The steps should be quite broad, and the angle of the slope should not be more than 40 degrees; this way you can easily ensure that the waterproofing does not slide down into the substratum.

Directly in front of the observation area, the edge of the pond can go up more steeply; you can possibly reinforce it with a dry stone wall, so that you can enjoy the pond even more directly. But even here there should be a way out of the water for any creatures that may fall in.

Every bit of water in a garden, however small, fulfills an ecological function

Construction

Building a pond starts with digging the hole from the deep end to the shallow end. Because you have to take into account the layer of waterproofing and the substratum in which the aquatic plants will grow, you must dig the hole deeper than you want the pond to be. The humus-rich topsoil from the hole can be used elsewhere in the yard (e.g., for a mound-shaped flowerbed), but the infertile soil from the bottom of the hole is suitable only for mixing with sand, clay and gravel to make the floor of the pond.

If the soil on your property is rich in clay, you can do without a pond liner and create an entirely natural pond. To do this you need to get a load of fresh clay or unfired bricks and stamp them into the hole to create an eight-inch (20 cm) layer of natural waterproofing. Needless to say, a natural pond is a lot of work, and it is not particularly cheap. Although they are less expensive, ready-made ponds in acrylic butadiene styrene, fiberglass-reinforced plastic or PVC should be avoided because these materials cause too many environmental problems both in producing and in disposing of them. In addition, these ponds are generally too small, and their walls are so steep and slippery that they are deathtraps for hedgehogs, birds and lizards. A near-natural pond should have zones that merge gradually into each other, and it should suit the site. Pond liners made of plastic sheeting are generally the best for producing this effect. Although most pond liners on sale are made from environmentally harmful PVC, less harmful polyethylene and rubber compounds are available.

The pond liner must be protected underneath by a layer of sand about 2 inches (5 cm) deep. If the ground is rocky, you will need to protect the liner with a special mat. While you are digging, it is a good idea to spread the liner out on the yard where it can warm up and become more pliable. It is vital that the liner extends above the level of the water, or the surrounding ground will drain the pond dry. You can use stones or coconut matting, which will very soon be covered by plants, to keep it in place at shore level. A mixture of stones and gravel along the edge will make the pond look less artificial. In addition, it is perfectly possible to build the stones unearthed during the excavations into a "castle" on the shore, where little animals will be able to hide.

As an overflow in case of heavy rainfall, you can construct a marshy bed at a slightly lower level or have an

An extended marshy zone

It is important for a pond to have an extensive marshy rim in order for it to be self-purifying. This rim provides a habitat for many kinds of decorative plants and makes it easier for the animals to get in and out of the water.

A good pond cleans itself

overflow pipe which leads into a regular drainage ditch, lined with stones and gravel. Both of these must be far enough from the pond, so that the overflow does not undermine it.

You can put pond plants directly into the mud at the bottom or in baskets, which have the advantage of keeping their growth within bounds and making it easier to control. Every type of plant prefers a particular depth of water. The greatest variety is in the marsh-growing plants. These include the various types of rushes and cattails, marsh marigolds, water irises, cypress grass, arrowleaf and water trefoil. A bit further away from the pond where the ground is drier water meadow plants will grow. Yarrow, cotton grass or meadowsweet, as well as ornamental ferns, are good choices for this area.

For deep water, the usual favorite is the spreading water lily, which can grow up from as deep as 58 inches (150 cm). There are, however, many other useful plants that grow above or below the surface of the water. Like the spreading water lily, they also generate oxygen and are important in controlling algae and purifying the water. Waterfringe and the yellow water lily are attractive examples. In addition, the hornnut and even the humble duckweed are particularly good for purifying the water, and water aloe and water soldier serve as breeding grounds for a rare sort of dragonfly. Both the star-headed chickweed and water milfoil are very decorative species which will turn every pond into a veritable showpiece.

The natural pond does not require any technology to help it along. On the other hand, if you want to make it an even more pleasant place and increase its oxygenation, you could include an artificial spring. A little pump – solar-powered, of course – propels the water via an underground pipe to a manmade outlet among the stones. You could even add an artificial rivulet which would provide ideal conditions for the growth of watercress, mint or crowfoot.

No artifice
This beautiful garden pond, with plants growing out into the water, looks as though it has always been there. A foundation of plastic sheeting is the best way of achieving this natural look.

Building a pond with plastic sheeting
The sheeting, which keeps in the water, must lie in a protective bed of gravel and sand. Water plants can be rooted in boxes or baskets to make it easier to control their growth. While it is important to control this growth, it is even more important to control the amount of nutrients lying on the floor of the pond.

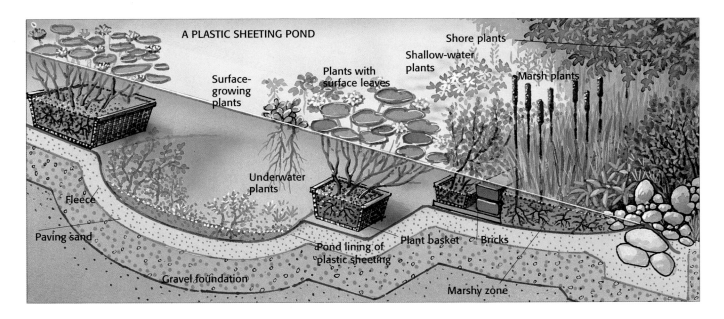

A PLASTIC SHEETING POND

Shore plants

Shallow-water plants

Plants with surface leaves

Marsh plants

Surface-growing plants

Underwater plants

Fleece

Paving sand

Pond lining of plastic sheeting

Plant basket

Bricks

Gravel foundation

Marshy zone

The bathing pond

Anyone who has the room and the extra money does not need to restrict their enjoyment to a garden pond. Instead you can put in a bathing pond , creating a natural, private, bathers' paradise. Rather than the bleak tiles and chlorinated water of the typical swimming pool, you can enjoy soft clear water without worrying about algae and water plants. This is because such ponds have their own highly sophisticated self-purifying system copied from nature.

A pond for bathing needs at least 648 square feet (60 square meters) of surface area and should be more than 6½ feet (2 meters) deep for half of its length so that children and adults can do their serious swimming there. The other half, which could be screened off by a water-permeable dam (e.g. made of gravel), should be shallow. This area has the task of

keeping the water clean in a natural way as well as making the pond look more natural by giving it an irregular shape and a sprinkling of vegetation. A strong pump insures the necessary circulation of water, at least every few hours. You can give the pond a totally individual, but natural and appropriate shape, according to the layout and size of your yard.

When water is more than 5 feet (1.5 meters) deep even water lilies cannot take root, so if your pond is 6½ feet (2 meters) deep it should remain free of plants. You can keep algae away by removing the substances they live on. Just introduce certain types of duckweed and other "regenerating" plants that are used in sewage purification. You can purchase these plants at garden centers specializing in water plants. Naturally occurring bacteria also effectively remove

the substances which algae live on by swiftly breaking down any organic material that gets into the pond. You can provide a supporting environment for them by coating the floor of the pond with a thin layer of zeolite, a clay-like substance that spreads easily. Additionally, chalky pebbles provide a buffer against acidic sediment.

To keep these natural processes going, the pond should have a total volume of about 5,295 cubic feet (150 cubic meters) of water. It should also be as deep as possible, so that there is a gradation in temperature to combat the development of algae and prevent organic matter from rotting in the water and depriving it of oxygen. Algae are most likely to strike just after the pond begins to function and in spring because their natural enemies have not yet

managed to establish themselves. But a short bloom of algae quite often dies away on its own. Once the nitrates in the water have been broken down, the unicellular organisms have nothing to feed on.

Many bathing ponds are built in such a way that the overflow channel catches the leaves and pollen from flowering trees. There must be a layer of coarse gravel around the edge of the pond so that heavy rain does not wash too much earth or vegetation into it. You should put a net over the pool in autumn to prevent leaves and bits of dead foliage getting into the pool when the growing season is over. Unfortunately animals can get caught in these nets.

The sludge that collects in the deepest part of the pool has to be removed at regular intervals with a water vacuum cleaner. Many systems

Luxurious bathing pond

If you have some extra money and would like to enjoy the comfort of a swimming pool combined with the beauty and naturalness of a pond, you can install a lovely bathing pond like this one above. No more than half of the pond should be deep enough for swimming. The other half should be a shallow-water zone where plants can purify the water naturally. No chlorine is needed.

Castles in the water

A bathing pond straight out of most nature-lovers' fantasies: Enjoy the magic of nature all the year round and refreshing water almost on your doorstep in summer.

Bathing ponds are a better value than pools

have a pump at the deepest point which regularly sucks off the cold, relatively unoxygenated water together with the sludge, but this is an expensive enterprise. It is even possible to heat the pond with solar power. Although a warm bathing pond is certainly inviting, heating the pond cannot be entirely recommended. Warm water might encourage organic matter in the pond to rot. The shallow water area in a bathing pond operates in a way similar to a biological water-purification plant. Rushes, reeds, irises and other marsh plants clean the water with the help of the bacteria that are active in their roots. These plants are also very attractive, and they provide a habitat for lots of small creatures. Since a bathing pond is not nearly as dirty as the waste water from the house, there should be no unpleasant smells.

Because the pond lining, which holds in the water, is very slippery, a wooden path generally is used to provide access to the water. Steps made from tree trunks or even a little sandy beach are more natural looking but less durable. The pond lining is necessary to keep in the water and to stop the pond from silting up too quickly. As with the decorative pond, this lining should not be made of environmentally harmful PVC. There are alternatives made from polyethylene and rubber compounds.

Despite the higher cost, building the bathing pond out of concrete guarantees its stability. Concrete may, for this reason, be a better choice. Quite apart from its greater esthetic appeal, a bathing pond of this kind is still cheaper to build and maintain than a conventional swimming pool.

Professionally built

If you want a pool large enough in which to row a boat, you should hire professional help. There are a number of firms that will install bathing ponds. The installation is no more expensive than for a tiled swimming pool, and the upkeep is, in fact, significantly cheaper.

Not for the do-it-yourself builder

Like a garden pond, a bathing pond is lined with plastic sheeting to give it its natural shape. You should not try your hand at this yourself, however. Installing a bathing pond like this is impossible without any professional help because it requires quite heavy equipment like an earthmover and a crane.

The principle of the bathing pond

The pond in this drawing is fitted with a gravel-bed filtering system which purifies the water. It also has a pump to keep the water circulating. Yet bathing pools can remain clean even without this technology. Such pools simply need a large shallow-water area where plants do the work of purifying the water.

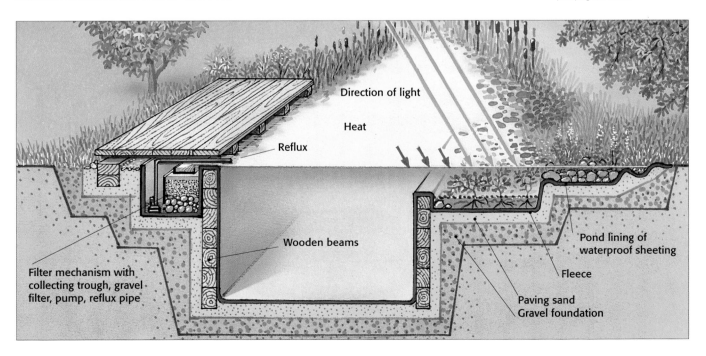

Direction of light

Heat

Reflux

Wooden beams

Filter mechanism with collecting trough, gravel filter, pump, reflux pipe

Pond lining of waterproof sheeting

Fleece

Paving sand
Gravel foundation

THE VEGETABLE GARDEN

Many garden owners banish their vegetable patch to the most distant corner because they think the plants are not decorative enough to be on display. But it is perfectly possible to plant vegetables and herbs in a visually attractive way. There is no reason for the kitchen garden to look like a farmyard.

A good example of an attractive kitchen garden is the typical old cottage garden. This garden is laid out geometrically with four symmetrical little garden areas separated by paths in the form of a cross. Each of the individual garden areas is sown in yearly rotation with plants and herbs making varying degrees of demand upon the soil. The same geometrical pattern is repeated with each sowing, and the plants are mixed in pleasing combinations. The pattern and combinations, along with the white gravel path and decorative flowers or little hedges bordering the beds, make a most attractive picture.

In spite of its careful design, there is nothing artificial about the cottage garden. Mixed cultivation is very close to what happens in nature. Particular plants benefit each other. For instance, planting leeks, which grow tall but have shallow roots, with carrots, which have long roots and shorter foliage, makes better use of space because the roots thoroughly penetrate the soil. Onions have properties that protect carrots from the carrot-rust fly, and the smell of carrots drives away

The vegetable patch can be decorative too

Not hidden

You do not need to hide all the useful plants in the garden. A well-designed vegetable and herb garden can also be esthetically pleasing.

The classic kitchen garden
This traditional kitchen garden, with paths crossing in the center, has a long history. There is no reason not to have one like it today. Plants are juxtaposed not just out of individual preference or for decorative reasons, but because mixed cultivation provides very effective natural protection against pests.

Rich harvest
The work put into a vegetable garden is rewarding not just because it is meaningful and satisfying, but because it will yield a rich harvest.

the onion fly. Marigolds not only add color to the garden, but they also deter harmful nematodes that could injure vegetables. Whole books have been devoted to the secrets of the cottage garden and companion planting.

The herb spiral

An herb spiral is not only a very esthetic addition to your garden, but it also allows you to grow many fresh herbs of varying origin and from different climates in your own garden. To build an herb spiral, first select a sunny spot about 8 feet (2.5 meters) across. Then build a dry stone wall into a spiral-shaped hill that is about 3 feet (1 meter) from the ground at its highest point. Dig out the ground at the lowest point to form a shallow ditch and line that with clay so that the moisture will stay in.

Next, fill the lower level with humus-rich soil fortified with compost. As you move up the spiral, the soil should become thinner and stonier, so that the top is dry, sunny and poor in soil nutrients. The dry stone wall is perfectly suited to retain heat, which helps the plants to grow; in addition, the wall will give them a certain amount of protection.

The raised bed

A bed in the form of a little mound is also an attractive feature in a yard because there is always something to see. A raised bed is a bit like a compost heap with plants on it. It is generally about 31 inches (80 cm) in height, with terraces running north to south to make the best use of the sunlight. There is such a good supply of nutrients that even plants that require a lot of feeding do well in this bed. The raised bed actually has five layers:

Not a wilderness

A vegetable garden full of useful plants can be designed in such a natural way that the result of all the planning and care can still look almost like a wilderness.

Right at the top level of your herb spiral you can put a variety of typical Mediterranean plants, such as lavender, oregano, rosemary and thyme. In the middle zone plants like basil, tarragon, marjoram, balm and sage will thrive exceptionally well. Finally, in the rich soil at the bottom you can easily grow parsley, dill, chives, mint and chervil. Quite incidentally, herb spirals provide a much needed habitat for a great many small creatures.

In a small space
You do not need a lot of space for a vegetable patch. You can grow herbs and a few vegetables in a very small area.

Vegetables and herbs – too beautiful to be banished into a distant corner of the garden

- at the very bottom, branches and thicker twigs;
- next, lumps of turf, root side outwards;
- above these, leaves and smaller twigs;
- then, kitchen garbage and lumpy compost;
- on top, soil with fine compost.

In a raised bed you can work in a lot of lumpy organic material that would be out of place on a compost heap. A raised bed will enlarge the space available for planting by almost 30%.

Variety on a spiral
The various levels of the herb spiral (above) offer quite different habitats for culinary herbs from different climatic zones.

This type of bed is extremely easy to cultivate and care for, and it provides plants with optimal living conditions. The decay taking place inside the mound generates heat that further encourages plant growth, even between seasons.

The compost area

It makes sense to construct a compost area with three bins. The middle one receives new kitchen garbage. In the left one, the kitchen garbage is mixed with lawn clippings, finely chopped twigs and other coarse material to form a compost heap. In the right one, layers of prepared compost mature undisturbed.

Most kitchen waste can be used to fertilize the garden

Most household waste can be composted. Garden waste, dead flowers and mown grass can all be turned into valuable fertilizer on the compost heap. Even the leftover vegetable and fruit peels, tea leaves and coffee filters, eggshells, wood ash and bits of wood and hair clippings can be composted. There are a few things, however, that should not be composted. You should put cooked food, bones, and animal waste into the garbage can. Otherwise, these wastes will attract rats if you put them on the compost heap.

The best way of making compost is to have three rectangular containers, each about 27 inches (70 cm) square. You can easily make these containers yourself or buy suitable ones at a garden shop or a building supply store. You start the composting cycle with putting new waste material in the first container, and then transfer it to the second one approximately every six to eight weeks. It is important to mix the waste material with coarser material from the garden or with straw. The coarser material ensures that enough oxygen gets into the compost and that it does not ferment. For the same reason, you should also put a lid on the container or bin, so that the compost does not get too wet. You can improve the consistency of the compost by adding chalk, bonemeal or sand. When the bin is full, it will take a year or two before the rotting process is complete, and

worms, bacteria and other inhabitants of the soil have turned the green waste into sweet-smelling compost. This is why you need the third container to fill with new compost while you are waiting.

You can purchase quick-composting containers made out of recycled material. These containers have insulating properties which manufacturers claim speed up the composting process. But despite the makers' assurances to the contrary, you cannot put any leftover food in them. Rats are intelligent enough to find a way into them even when they are sealed.

Heat-retaining composters can certainly be useful in a small garden, though they often do not provide enough ventilation. Nor do they work miracles. The process of decay takes time, even in these containers. Even a small household will need two, so one can be left to mature at its own pace.

The compost area must always be in shade and out of the wind so that the compost does not dry out. It should also not be too difficult to get to in all kinds of weather, so that the compost bucket in the kitchen can be emptied regularly. This requires having a hardened surface on the path because the area around the compost bin gets muddy quickly. Planting hedges around the compost area will screen it from the wind as well as from view.

What the soil needs

Compost is not only the best soil conditioner; it also supplies all the multitude of nutrients that garden plants need. Decayed matter from green plants and mulch provide the ground with humus, nitrogen and minerals. They suppress the growth of weeds, prevent nutrients from being washed away by rain and generally protect the soil from drying out. Only poor soils or plants requiring a lot of nutrients should need any additional organic manure.

Decorative plants need only a little organic manure. Bushes and fruit trees are satisfied with mulch or fresh compost. Many indigenous wild bushes and plants do not even like manure. Lawns flourish if they are strewn with sieved compost. Grass clippings from mown grass should be left lying. In time soil organisms will break the clippings down into much needed humus.

A cultivator or a hoe are excellent tools for loosening and aerating the soil. However, you must be careful not to dig too deeply – say, up to the shaft of the spade – or you may dig the nutrients in so deep that the roots can hardly reach them in the spring which would have quite a detrimental effect on the growth of your garden.

You do not necessarily need a chemical analysis to know about the composition of your garden soil. You can often learn more about your soil from the type of wild plants that move in without invitation. Corn camomile and sorrel, for example, prefer a soil without much chalk. Field horsetail and coltsfoot, on the other hand, indicate a soil that is insufficiently aerated. Where birthwort and wild camomile grow, the earth is rich in humus. Stinging nettles and galinsoga signal a soil with a high nitrogen content.

A sheltered place

Compost should be well protected from the wind, and it should be in partial shade so that it does not smell unpleasant or dry out. In addition, it should be fairly close to the kitchen.

Quicker with a thermal composter

Heat-insulated plastic compost barrels keep the temperature high enough during the winter period to continue the rotting process all year long.

The greenhouse

Increasingly, a greenhouse is the first item on a true gardener's wish list. With a small greenhouse in the garden, you can successfully defy the weather and prolong the various seasons of the garden, harvesting leaf lettuce and spinach, for example, until late autumn. A frost-free greenhouse is also an ideal winter home for oleander bushes and other heat-loving tropical plants that decorate the patio in summer.

The most economical way to have your own greenhouse is to make one yourself with wood and plastic sheeting. With some basic carpentry, you can construct a simple wooden frame and then stretch the sheeting over it. To prevent the greenhouse from turning into an oven in summer, you need to provide good ventilation. This does make building the greenhouse a bit more difficult. In addition, you need to carefully secure the frame so that it is stable even in windy conditions. The easiest type of greenhouse to build is an inexpensive tunnel made of plastic sheeting, which is supported by featherweight steel rods bent into a half circle and anchored in the ground. A long rod running along the top keeps the frame stable at all times. The sheeting is laid over this frame, stretched with the help of wooden strips, and simply stuck into the ground.

While plastic sheeting made of environmentally harmful PVC is still available for greenhouses, the sheeting you most often find now is made of poly-ethylene (PE), a fairly sustainable, green substance. This material comes in different grades and even reinforced with a woven nylon mesh. This nylon mesh allows the sheeting to be cut, sewn, or nailed without ripping. You should not use ordinary builder's sheeting because the sun will destroy it in a short time. PE sheeting is treated with stabilizers to make it last longer, but some of these have their dangers. If the sheeting is slightly yellow, that could mean that it has been treated with environmentally unsound nickel-based stabilizers.

Although PE sheeting lets in a lot of sunlight, it also lets out a lot of heat. This heat loss can lead to frost damage on cold, clear spring nights. Special additives, however, will hinder the escape of heat. Sheeting with these additives is marked IR: "impermeable by infra-red." If you want to prevent condensation running down the plastic, look for sheeting with the "no drop" mark. Water will form a film over this sheeting and not drip down and damage the plants. Sheeting with a component of ethylvinylacetate (EVA) lets out less heat than PE sheeting, is more elastic and less liable to tear, but it is also more expensive.

A residential greenhouse should be as attractive when viewed from a distance as when you are enjoying the quiet beauty inside the structure. Glass is the best solution for this. It does not discolor, fog, or fade over time, is easier to keep clean and lasts significantly longer. There are a number of small, inexpensive glass greenhouses available for the amateur gardener from $300 to $2000 which vary in size from a small patio greenhouse of 12 square feet (1 square meter) to 64 square feet (6 square meters). Regardless of the size, it is cheaper to make a glass greenhouse yourself. The self-builder has a choice of wood or metal for the frame. Wood certainly looks classier, but it distorts easily where there are strong fluctuations in temperature and humidity. The beams are also thicker and cast more shadow in the greenhouse than the narrower metal strips. An aluminum frame is lighter, does not rust and is easier to handle because the panes can be held in place with special clamps rather than with glue. On the other hand, metal parts are heat conductors, so some solar energy is lost at night.

The standard roof covering for greenhouses is simple panes of glass or, even better, heat-insulating double cellular sheets in various strengths. Plexiglas or polycarbonate last long, but PVC panes turn yellow and become fragile after a few years. If you do not mind spending a lot, you can install insulating glass.

Small unheated greenhouses, however, do not need expensive materials. Ordinary glass will do. You should purchase this glass at a garden center or building supply store rather than from a glazier because glass for gardens is of a slightly lower quality than window glass but is more than adequate. You can prevent plants from getting "sunburned" by using frosted glass. It is also possible to put together a greenhouse using old sash windows, but you have to take great care that there are no gaps in the construction that will allow the heat to escape.

Adequate ventilation and shade are crucial to the success of any greenhouse. While in spring, autumn and winter you want as much sun as possible to reach the greenhouse, in summer you have to protect the plants from excessive heat. The greenhouse should have operable windows or louvered openings in the sides and, most importantly, in the roof. Full-length roof vents combined with cross ventilation are ideal. You can also hang straw mats and canvas blinds on the inside to provide shade or use a special type of plastic sheeting with a built-in mesh. Another alternative is to make the glass semi-transparent by painting it with whitewash, which you wash off again at the end of the summer. Automatic window openers with flaps that spring open when a certain temperature is reached are not just for the professional; cheap and simple ones are available for the amateur as well.

If you want to use a greenhouse all year, the question of heating arises. In order to grow fresh vegetables and protect your tropical plants, the structure must be warm enough to keep frost out in winter. In most regions of the United States, this requires a heater of some kind. Because the heat loss from a heated greenhouse is tremendous, the only green solution

Plants are always in season in a greenhouse

Double glazing makes a difference

There are many advantages to "glassing" in your greenhouse with double cellular plastic. The material is unbreakable, long-lasting and retains heat. This heat retention is particularly useful in between the seasons when cold snaps can damage the plants.

for part time gardeners is nevertheless an unheated greenhouse. You can improve insulation with the double cellular sheets described above or with sheeting, which has tiny air cushions to lessen heat loss. This sheeting can be placed on the inside or on the outside of the greenhouse. Another means of prolonging the season is to place plastic water-filled tubes on the ground inside the greenhouse. These tubes store solar energy during the day and release it at night when heat is needed.

Made from old windows

It is not easy to build a greenhouse like this one with old single-glazed windows. Nonetheless, it is very original, and the materials cost next to nothing.

EQUIPPING THE GARDEN

A shady walk, roofed in leaves

An idyllic leafy walk like this one, overgrown with roses or climbing plants, is ideal for linking the main house to outbuildings or for providing shade for rooms that get too hot.

The garden is not just a source of vegetables and herbs or a little natural oasis for contemplation. Above all, it is an ideal place for recreation. Because children are protected from the danger of traffic, the backyard garden is the perfect spot for children to play safely. With the addition of some play equipment, the area becomes even more attractive for the children. Adults can switch off everyday stress on a garden seat among the greenery or rock away their cares on a porch swing. For shade, a pergola covered in climbing plants and creepers is ideal and pleasant to look at. A foliage-covered utility shed or a lean-to can house the garden tools, the lawnmower and possibly the bicycles, and, given the proper insulation and light, it can also serve as a home for non-hardy plants during the winter.

You can also let wood grow old gracefully

The pergola

You should not simply place a pergola or a rose-covered arbor in the open yard. Instead, use these structures to divide or to connect elements within the yard. A pergola can furnish shade or cut off an unsightly view around a sitting area or a terrace, or even provide a green arch over a path between the utility shed and the house. Wild roses growing on the pergola will give plenty of shade and protection. Fast-growing Virginia Creeper is ideal for making a thick roof, and Dutchman's pipe forms an opaque wall of green, making it an excellent screen. The climbing plants will cover the pergola

quicker and more thoroughly if you put in some additional struts between the supports and the beams.

The sitting area by the pergola and the path under the green arches should always be hardened with some water-permeable material; otherwise, your garden furniture will sink into the ground. You can place stone chips, porphyry for example, in a bed of sand or gravel that will allow the water to drain through and keep your feet dry. Since pergolas are going to be exposed to the weather, it is advisable to protect those made of pine or spruce against decay and fungus. These woods are generally treated by the pressure-impregnation method, where a watery solution of inorganic salts, generally chromium or copper, is forced into the pores under high pressure. The procedure is especially suitable for pine, where the solution sinks in well. Although this treatment does hinder decay and fungus, it creates a host of other problems. Compounds of fluoride and arsenic, which are still sometimes used in the treatment, can be harmful to humans, and chromium compounds harm the environment as the rain gradually washes them out. Woods treated in this way cause still more problems when you want to dispose of them. In many areas they are categorized as special garbage and must not be burned or composted.

One alternative might be to use weather-resistant woods. Apart from tropical wood, which usually comes from questionable sources, the most promising woods are redwood, cedar, and cypress but even these species have been heavily harvested and could become endangered from irresponsible cutting. You can use exotic, foreign wood, such as teak, when it is has the label from the FSC (Forest Stewardship Council) or some other recognized certification verifying that the wood has been harvested from a forest managed according to internationally agreed social and environmental standards. These exotic woods are very expensive and more suitable for prestigious uses. Another option is to treat the wood yourself with harmless wood preservatives and paint it in weather-resistant natural colors. You do have to remember, though, that this coat of paint cannot be renewed once the pergola is covered with vegetation. Only this vegetation will make the pergola really pleasant and functional.

Since a pergola is not exposed to any static or mechanical loads, a third option is to simply let it grow old gracefully and renew the whole structure only when it is no longer stable. Weathered wood is handsome because it takes on so many shades, and it will blend in well with the natural environment of your garden. Regardless of which option you choose, when installing the pergola, the supporting posts should not be simply stuck into the soil. They must be set into a concrete base that protrudes slightly above ground level and be kept in place with a simple steel peg or a special casing cemented into the base. You could simply dig a hole in the ground and fill it with cement, but ground frost will take its toll on it over the years. It is better to make a mold out of wood or an old bucket, let the cement base harden with the peg in it, then sink them in a bed of gravel. Screws and pegs should be galvanized so that they will not rust and prevent you from making necessary repairs.

Pergolas give shelter

A leafy pergola is as much appreciated for the protection it affords from sun and wind as it is for its ability to block out an unsightly view. The wood used in its construction does not necessarily have to be treated with harmful chemicals.

A pleasant place to sit

A secluded sitting area like this, on a foundation of planks, will last you a long time a long time and be a source of great pleasure, provided the wood is not in constant contact with a source of moisture and can always dry out on all sides.

Lasting garden furniture

The wood of the locust tree makes garden furniture that is both sturdy and weather resistant. You can quite safely leave it outside in bad weather. The wood, however, is difficult to work, and the furniture correspondingly expensive.

Garden furniture

Put it down and forget about it. That is the usual attitude toward benches, tables and chairs meant for the garden. Most people find it too much of an effort to drag the garden furniture into the house or garage every time the sky clouds over. Not doing this, however, does limit the choice of materials. For smaller budgets, plastic furniture may be the only option. Surprisingly enough, this sort of furniture does not have any particular ecological disadvantages, if it is made out of something like recyclable polypropylene. But the cheap variety of dazzling white, easily scratched furniture does not suit a natural garden. Those who can afford it are selecting handsome teak furniture in classic designs. These purchasers are usually given

the oily wood, you need to use a type of adhesive that is very harmful environmentally in order to join the parts. For this reason, it is much better to join the wood of the locust tree with screws or tenon joints. Manufacturers give locust wood furniture a ten-year guarantee against rot. Beautifully crafted collections of chairs, tables, benches and even porch swings are available in this wood. These pieces very often follow classical models like the deckchairs of the great old ocean liners. On the negative side, however, they are at the top of the price range, and often only available from specialist firms and mail-order companies.

Just as resistant and highly suitable for garden furniture is our native western red cedar, but this wood also poses problems for the carpenter. Cedar has a tendency to split, so the design of any furniture must take this characteristic into consideration. But the extra work will definitely be worth it: Well-designed cedar furniture, which is properly finished and maintained, will deliver decades of trouble-free service.

Although it is widely used because of its strength and durability, oak cannot really be considered ideal for garden furniture. Its surface weathers easily and becomes unsightly if left in the open.

If you are put off by the elevated prices of wooden garden furniture that may be as dubious from an ecological point of view as plastic, you might consider lowering your sights a little. You can purchase a garden lounge or settee with wheels, and tables and chairs that fold up. You can easily store them under cover and only bring them out when the weather tempts you into the garden. You do not even have to bother putting them in the basement if you have a garden shed, a garage near the sitting-area or a rainproof lean-to attached to the house (you could store firewood in this too).

All-metal garden furniture is on the uncomfortable side. It is also not particularly durable if it is made solely of painted iron. There are alternatives to solid painted iron furniture, which perform better. These include chairs with frames of high-grade steel, aluminum or galvanized iron, and garden tables with metal feet. These pieces do take a lot of energy to manufacture, but they can be very durable and easy to repair. The wooden surfaces on these chairs and tables must be suitably varnished or painted, and you must be able to unscrew the surfaces so that they can be replaced when they become too weathered.

Cushions for garden furniture are usually made of synthetic fabrics that are rather uncomfortable to the skin and are quite often filled with environmentally harmful polyurethane. There are, however, some smaller manufacturers who do offer alternatives. Their cushions may be stuffed with horsehair, sheep's wool, or the fibers of the Asiatic kapok plant. Unfortunately these cushions do not react well to rain. Here is another argument in favor of folding and putting away your garden furniture.

Garden furniture should be put away when it rains

Folded up and put away
Wooden garden furniture should not be left outside all the time. When the weather is bad, it should be protected. For this reason, it is more convenient if chairs and tables can be folded.

the impression that the trees were not illegally felled in forests but obtained from teak plantations in places like the Indonesian island of Java.

Experts only believe these claims when a recognized certificate backs them up. Even the opinion among ecologists is very divided about the plantation system itself. Weather-resistant redwood is also used to make garden furniture, but here too there are doubts about the way that it is harvested.

Another wood with weather-resistant properties similar to teak's, but which is indigenous, is the locust tree, or false acacia. This wood is very hard and difficult to work, however. The trees often grow in a twisted shape, and because glue does not stick to

Play equipment

Metal playground equipment is as unimaginative today as it has been for decades. There is still the same old swing hanging in a two-colored steel frame next to a rocking boat or a seesaw with two ordinary ladders to satisfy the older children's desire to climb. In more expensive models, you can purchase additional parts like a loop to swing in or a climbing rope for a greater variety of active games. All this equipment is modeled on the dreary equipment of 1970s public playgrounds we are all familiar with.

Domestic models, however, are noticeably less durable. Though safety tests show that swing frames have by now become safer and more stable, this is only a recent development. As late as the mid-1980s there were still some climbing frames with hidden metal tubes and sharp edges, and many frames had a tendency to tip over when rocked. Regardless of whether you have a simple swing or an adult home gym, if you do not want to run the risk of an abrupt end to your child's or your gymnastics, you need to make certain that any steel-framed apparatus is firmly anchored in the ground before being used. The manufacturers suggest that you set the base of any piece of play equipment in concrete.

The frames made of wood are far more pleasant to the touch than those made of thin cold metal. Wood has the advantage of being strong, naturally attractive and "user friendly" for youngsters. Like the metal equipment, wooden play centers come in home-assembly kits. A simple one could cost under $100, but for that you only get a swing and two steep ladders. A good starter set will cost between $350–$550. Some firms make so-called "adventure centers" that cost considerably more. Yet you can add on many extra pieces, and adults as well as children can enjoy themselves on these centers. The main attraction is a double swing in which two small children can swing together. Those with more time and talent can design and construct a unique play set or build one following any number of plans for play equipment which are available in books.

To insure that the equipment is safe for children, the pine and spruce of which it is made has to be thoroughly pressure-impregnated in the way described earlier. When using treated wood, it is important to make sure the wood carries the American Wood Preservation Bureau approval. The advantage of this type of treatment is that the toxic substances have sunk so deep into the wood that there is no danger to the children's health involved because their hands do not come into contact with hazardous material. The disadvantage is that your yard now has a heap of

Nature offers greater opportunities for games than a swing on a frame

Natural materials as play equipment

Building huts and caves, hiding, or swinging through the air like Tarzan does not require any expensive play equipment. Natural materials do the job just as well and can even provide more fun in a healthy environment.

Adventures in a tree house

A tree house is every child's dream. Nothing comes close to the excitement of having your own little home away from adult eyes, where you can let your imagination run riot.

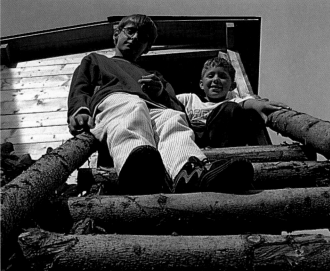

Not a dreary old sandpit

A homemade wooden sandpit like this one is much more fun than the lifeless plastic shells you can buy in toyshops.

Lag bolts

Cross bar

Carrying beam

Four-post
upright beam

Brace

Four-post
upright beam

Binding coated
with bitumen

Concrete foundation

Wooden spacers

Brace

Strut

what may one day be "special" garbage, which, in addition, cannot be put on a bonfire or simply taken away with other wood-based trash.

One solution would be to use rot-resistant woods that survive for years without any chemical protection. Leaving aside tropical woods such as teak, which cannot be recommended without reservations because it is extremely slow-growing and very difficult to replace, oak and locust tree wood are both very suitable. Although it is not readily available in all regions of the United States, some manufacturers are experimenting with larch, which is simpler to work with and cheaper. If you construct the equipment so that the wood does not come into contact with the ground, it will not need chemical protection to remain solid enough for children to play on safely. To combine the advantages of various types of wood, a few firms in Europe are experimenting with

wood from the locust tree for the legs and larch for the superstructure.

Garden play apparatus needs quite a lot of space. A simple swing needs a surface of around 140 square feet (13 square meters); a frame with a swing and a rocking boat needs up to 269 square feet (25 square meters). An alternative to larger items like the boat is a climbing net made of rope ladders on which a child can both swing and climb. These nets are inexpensive and can be hung on trees or stable rails.

All children love rocking, whether in a boat, on a seesaw, or a simple board. But swinging alone is not enough to satisfy their play instinct. The more rigid and less adaptable a piece of equipment, the less children enjoy playing with it. Children will soon tire of a plain garden swing because it can only be used in one way and does not offer them any creative possibilities. A climbing frame does not lend itself

Swing made with wooden poles

Swings are always popular and doubtless fulfill a basic need in all children. Using this simple method, you can build a stable swing using wooden poles. It is important to make the base properly and to be sure the foundations are weatherproof.

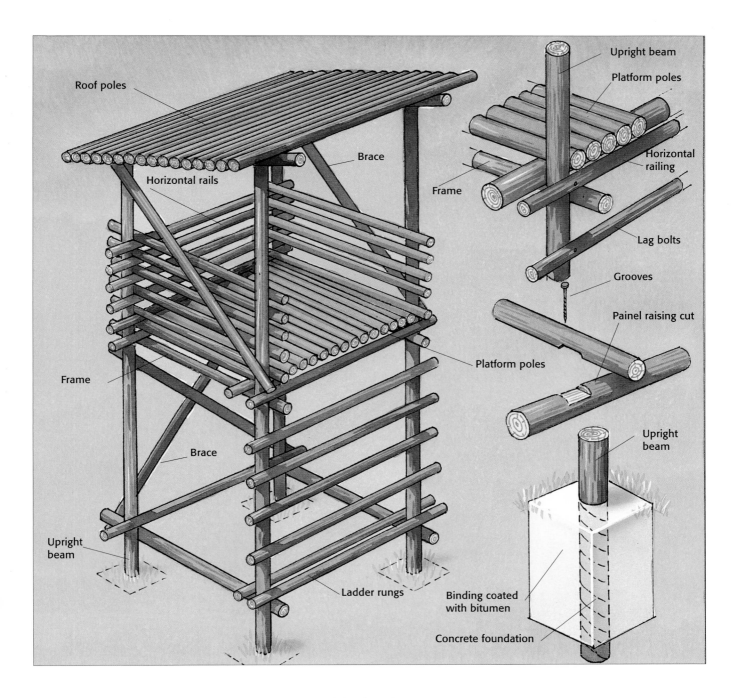

Roof poles

Horizontal rails

Brace

Frame

Frame

Brace

Upright beam

Ladder rungs

Platform poles

Upright beam

Platform poles

Horizontal railing

Frame

Lag bolts

Grooves

Painel raising cut

Upright beam

Binding coated with bitumen

Concrete foundation

to role-playing in the same way as a sandpit or a tree house. There the children can organize, discuss, decide and make their own designs and alterations. If you leave the children some creative freedom in their play, they will not get bored so quickly; in addition, you will save a lot of money.

With simple materials like boards, old car tires, ropes and poles children can build all sorts of different things that will keep them amused for hours.

The amount of fun children can have in the yard depends not only on the equipment, but also on the play potential of the yard itself. Shrubs and bushes serve as hiding places or an exciting maze. Trees are as good as any climbing frame. Future bakers and engineers may discover their vocation in the sandpit. The only requirements for creating a yard full of play potential are adults who do not mind a degree of disorder and a large yard.

A good view from the tower

A refuge for pirates, knights, or jungle-dwellers, a tower like this can sometimes be built where a tree house is out of the question.

That large yard does not have to be your own bit of land. Building regulations in many cities prescribe that an area be set aside for a playground in all major residential developments.

Smaller modern housing developments frequently have a communal space that belongs to all the homeowners. Installing a playground collectively can strengthen community feeling. In addition, if parents have control over the design of the playground they can build a play area that is best suited to their children's needs.

ENCLOSURE

Fences and walls can be justified in certain places. For instance, they are necessary to prevent grazing animals from getting out of the pen and wild animals from getting into gardens and destroying laboriously cultivated crops.

They also have a function in marking the limits of the road. In modern built-up areas, however, they generally have no other purpose than to mark people's territorial claims. But be careful what actually belongs to your property before you fence it in. Unless the property is surveyed and clearly delineated, a fence can easily end up on adjacent land and lead to frequent quarrels between neighbors. Many terrace house dwellers remove party walls to enlarge the space available for children and wildlife. If you want some form of enclosure, an indigenous hedge will provide an ideal habitat for wild creatures, and it is a lot more attractive than a fence. The disadvantage is that it takes up a relatively large amount of space. A ditch with water in it is also a good boundary. While it is easier and cheaper to create than a pond, it does not act as a screen. A ditch may also take up quite a lot of space and, depending on its width, may still not be able to keep out larger animals, such as dogs, that could easily jump across it.

The garden fence

If a fence is needed, the easiest and most space-saving solution is a fence of plastic coated or galvanized wire mesh fastened to concrete posts or to steel supports anchored in concrete. This is the least attractive kind of fence whether viewed up close or from a distance. More importantly, it does not suit a natural garden. If you get a wide mesh you can at least allow berry bushes, trumpet vine or morning glories to grow over it, but this might not be to everyone's taste.

The usual wooden fence, whether of the cheap, unattractive lattice variety or the more respectable picket fence, is made of pressure-impregnated wood. Although this wood is longlasting, it is a problem to dispose of when it reaches the end of its life. When building any fence, you have to sink the posts in a gravel bed or set them in concrete foundations in order to make the fence halfway secure for the 10 to 15 years you can expect it to last. If you fail to do this and the posts are in contact with the earth, the fence will last only about three years.

Instead of using precut toxic wooden boards, it is better to use spare planks to make your own fence boards. You can go to a sawmill and get a load of offcuts for very little money. These are the irregular, partly rounded pieces that fall off the sides of a log as it is being sawn. You simply nail these boards horizontally to wooden posts for an unusual fence.

If you have plenty of time on your hands, you can easily make your own picket fence using poles from

The best-looking boundary
Wooden fences are the most beautiful way of marking boundaries. The old-fashioned picket fence can easily be made at home with ordinary poles from the forest, and the wood does not need to be protected. Otherwise, a wooden fence is relatively expensive to maintain.

You can make a garden fence yourself out of waste wood

branches and hedges that have been trimmed. You can also hammer in stakes close to each other and interweave them with pliable branches and twigs. This ancient form of fencing is not treated with any form of wood protection and will only last a few years. It must be replenished regularly with new material, but there should be no shortage of that in a natural garden.

The palisade is an especially handsome fence. It is made out of round or square poles stuck in side by side. It too must be set in a bed of gravel, so that it does not rot from below. You can get palisades that have not been pressure-treated, but they do need treating with environmentally sound wood preservatives available from suppliers of natural colorants.

Even though you sometimes find them being used in children's playgrounds, it is definitely not advisable to use old railroad ties. These ties have been treated with tarry substances that leave dirty marks and are very damaging to one's health. They contain a high level of polycyclic aromatic hydrocarbons, including the dangerous carcinogen benzoapyren.

Undisturbed by fences
Good neighbors get along fine without fences. If they each have only a small piece of ground, they will end up with far more playing space if they simply allow one yard to flow into the next without any barriers to separate them.

Garden walls

To make garden walls that face out onto the street, you can get ready-made units that are easy to put up and to join with cement. These walls bear a certain resemblance to brick or natural stone and are practical because they are quick and easy to erect, look neat and do not take up much room.

In environmental terms, however, they are a dead loss. In addition, they take a great deal of energy to manufacture. On the other hand, a dry wall made of layers of ordinary stones provides a habitat for plants and animals, and though it may be regarded by some as "untidy," at least it testifies to the willingness of the owner to give something back to nature.

A good neighborhood
There are no unsightly fences in this neighborhood either, but the residents still have their own enclosed, sheltered areas. The layout of the vegetation and the individual details of each house divide the area sufficiently to make each house unique.

WHAT IS ECOLOGICALLY SOUND BUILDING?

The solar house: the house of the future

Architect: H. v. Kilian, Stuttgart
Modern, unpretentious architecture, all directed toward the use of solar power. This house in Stuttgart, Germany, shows a viable alternative to traditional, wasteful energy consumption.

This book has given a whole spectrum of answers to that simple question. Many individual problems have been addressed and a wealth of tentative solutions put forward. But all the individual facets have a single common denominator: Ecological building creates room for living.

The object of ecologically sound building is to enable people to live in a healthy way without damaging the environment and spoiling the legacy they will leave future generations.

Some people believe that the whole concept of ecological building is irrelevant. For them "there is only good building and bad building." But every age has a new definition of what good or bad building is, and today good building is ecological building. Ecologically sound living is not an ideology or a closed system that shuts its doors to new insights and new developments. On the contrary, these are exactly what make the concept thrive and grow.

For that reason, this book can only be a temporary inventory; a distillation of the knowledge which we at *ÖKO-TEST* and *ÖKO-HAUS,* two ecologically-minded consumer magazines in Germany, have gained through our work, viewed in the light of current scientific knowledge.

Of course, we cannot give any definitive answers. Even as we were working on this book, new developments occurred that made it necessary to correct individual statements. This in itself is a sign of how dynamic the ecological movement is. It is to be expected that in the near future further technological advances will help in bringing us ever closer to the goal of creating living spaces which will both answer the needs of human beings and avoid the destruction of our environment.

We hope that there will be a wealth of reactions to this book and that it will give people plenty of ideas on how to make their homes and lifestyles more ecologically friendly. This process knows no national boundaries. The book has originally been written from a German standpoint – not because we believe that we are on the cutting edge of ecological progress, but because we could draw upon the German experience that was all around us. Ecological behavior must, however, be defined anew in every country depending on the prevailing conditions there. For the English publication of our book, therefore, we have been assisted by researchers with ample knowledge of the current ecological developments in other countries, especially the United States. Some

of the topics that we dealt with in this book may still be unfamiliar to people living outside of Germany. It was our intention that the examples and information provided will show the reader in the UK, US and elsewhere outside of Europe new and viable alternatives for sustainable, ecological building.

We hope this book has proven that green behavior in general and ecological building in particular are certainly not synonymous with discomfort, inconvenience and self-denial. The opposite is the case. Anyone who builds according to ecological principles will have a warm, well-insulated house. Their home technology will be modern and their decor welcoming. The materials used during the construction of their building will be non-hazardous to their health and provide a pleasant and comfortable atmosphere. All that has been renounced is extravagance, laziness and sheer lack of imagination.

The photos in this volume show all that. They also show that a green lifestyle brings esthetic enrichment. Ecological design does not mean stepping back from the achievements of industrial society, but rather recognizing its boundaries.

Ecological design must, however, compete successfully in the marketplace if it is to survive and thrive. We recognize that green ideas are being translated into products in an ever more professional way and that these products are already satisfying the needs of a healthier sector of society with green ideals. Tomorrow such products will become an undeniable component of the quality of life in industrial societies. The day after that we will see whether or not the culture of sustainability is, as accepted, a model for the rest of the world as the consumer society of today has effectively been. Once the market has been established, there will be a cheap version and a luxury version of every ecological product. Because ecology in building has less to do with expensive technology than with durability and quality, an ecological house and its decor need not be more expensive than a "normal" house. It should simply last longer and present fewer problems to its residents.

This is what people want. While the finishing touches were being made to this book, a major building society published the results of an extensive survey on the question: Where would you like to live? Around three-quarters of those questioned replied that they would like to live in an ecologically friendly house and a healthy environment. We are confident that this book will effectively contribute to this goal.

RESOURCES

GREEN BUILDING MATERIAL DIRECTORIES AND GUIDES

- **Guide to Resource Efficient Building Elements (GREBE)**
  Center for Resourceful Building Technology, Missoula Montana
  PO Box 100, Missoula, MT 59806
  (406) 549 7678
- **REDI Guide**
  Iris Communications, Inc.
  PO BOX 5920, Eugene, OR 97405-5920
  (541) 383-9353

RECYCLING AND REUSE OF BUILDING MATERIALS

- **Construction Materials Recycling Guidebook**
  Minnesota Office of Environmental Assistance
  (800) 877-6300
- **The Harris Directory of Recycled Content Building Materials**
  BJ Harris, 522 Acequia Madre, Santa Fe, NM 87501
  (505) 955-0337
- **RCRA - Recycled Content Goods Guidelines**
  RCRA Information Center Hotline
  (800) 424 9346

CONSUMER GUIDES AND ADVISORY SERVICES

- **Consumer Research Council**
  1424 16th Street NW, Suite 604
  Washington, DC 20036
- **The Safe Shopper's Bible: A Consumer's Guide to Nontoxic Household Products, Cosmetics and Food**
  by David Steinman & Samuel S. Epstein, M.D.
  Macmillan USA
  1633 Broadway, New York, NY 10019
- **Solar Living Sourcebook - 8th Edition**
  Real Goods Trading Corporation
  (800) 762 7325

ENERGY RELATED RESOURCES

- **EPA Energy Star Programs hotline**
  US Environmental Protection Agency
  (888) 782-7937, (888) STAR-YES
- **NFRC Certified Products Directory**
  National Fenestration Rating Council
  1300 Spring St., Suite 120, Silver Spring, MD 20910
  (301) 589-NFRC
- **1995 Model Energy Code (MEC)**
  Contact Council of American Building Officials (CABO)
  (800) 245-2691
- **Residential, Regulatory and Information Programs**
  Canadian Office of Energy Efficiency
  (613) 947-2000 Fax: (613) 943-1590

GRANTS, SUBSIDIES AND FINANCING

- **GMACM National Solar Loan Program**
  (888) 290-4622
  For the location of a GMACM solar loan specialist in your area call Elizabeth Keane, Assistant Vice President for GMACM
  (203) 876-8686

SUSTAINABLE WOOD RESOURCES

- **1996 Good Wood Directory**
  Certified Forest Products Council
  14780 SW Osprey Drive, Suite 285, Beaverton, OR 97009-8424
  (406) 590-6600
- **Woods of the World Database**
  Forest World (Tree-Talk Inc.)
  PO Box 426, Burlington, VT 05402
  (802) 865 1111

LIGHTING AND DAYLIGHTING

- **EPA Green Lights (Energy Star) Hotline**
  (888) 782-7937

LOW-ENERGY HOUSES

- **Energy Design Update**
  Cutter Information Corp.
  37 Broadway, Arlington, MA 02174-5552
  (781) 641-5118

ORGANIZATIONS

- **Energy Efficient Building Association (EEBA)**
  (715) 675 6331
- **Building Environmental Science and Technology (B.E.S.T.)**
  P.O. Box 1007
  Upper Marlboro, Maryland 20773 USA
  (410) 867-8000; Fax: (301) 889-0889

REFERRALS TO ECOLOGICALLY MINDED ARCHITECTS AND BUILDERS

- **American Institute of Architects - Environment PIA (COTE)**
  contact: Christopher Gibbs
  1735 New York Ave NW, Washington, DC 20006
  (800) 365-ARCH
- **American Society of Interior Designers (ASID)**
  (202) 675-2344
- **Ecological Design Association**
  Slad Road, Stroud, Glos GL5 1QW, UK
  +44 453 765575

- **Energy Efficient Building Association (EEBA)**
  490 Concordia Ave.
  St. Paul, MN USA 55103-2441
  (651) 994-1563
- **Green Builder Program and Sustainable Sources**
  Contact: Mark Richmond-Powers
  City of Austin Environmental & Conservation Dept.
  206 E 9th St., Suite 17.102, Austin, TX 78701
  (512) 499 3029

ADVICE ABOUT ECOLOGICAL ARCHITECTURE AND LIFESTYLES
- **Center of Excellence for Sustainable Development**
  US Department of Energy
  Office of Efficiency and Renewable Energy
  Denver Regional Support Office
  16 A Cole Boulevard
  Golden, CO 80401
  (800) 363-3732; Fax (303) 275-4830
- **Environmental Building News**
  28 Birge St, Brattleboro, VT 05301
  (802) 257-7300

WATER CONSERVATION AND RAINWATER HARVESTING
- **Texas Guide to Rainwater Harvesting**
  Texas Water Development Board
  PO Box 13231, Austin, TX 78711-3231

INDOOR AIR QUALITY, CERTIFICATION AND TESTING
- **EPA Indoor Air Quality Information Clearinghouse**
  US Environmental Protection Agency
  401 M Street, SW
  Washington, DC 20460-0003
  (202) 260-2090
- **The Healthy House Institute**
  430 North Sewell Rd., Bloomington IN 47408
  (812) 332-5073
- **Indoor Air Bulletin**
  Indoor Air Information Service
  PO Box 8446, Santa Cruz, CA 95061-8446
  (408) 426-6624

SOLAR ENERGY AND OTHER RENEWABLE ENERGY SOURCES
- **American Solar Energy Society**
  2400 Central Avenue, G-1,Boulder, CO 80301-2843
  (303) 443-3130
- **Center for Renewable Energy Technology (CREST)**
  1200 18th Street NW #900
  Washington, DC 20036
  (202) 530-2202; Fax: (202) 887-0497
- **1998 List of Manufacturers of Collectors and Distributors of Systems Certified by the Solar Rating and Certification Corporation**
  Florida Solar Energy Center
  1679 Clearlake Road, Cocoa Florida 32922
  Office Hours: Mon – Fri 8:00 am to 5:00 pm
  (407) 638-1000; Fax: (407) 638-1010
- **Passive Solar Design Strategies: Guidelines for Home Builders with Builderguide software and Designing Low Energy Buildings with ENERGY 10 Software**
  Passive Solar Industries Council (PSIC)
  1511 K St NW, Washington, DC 20005
  (202) 628-7400
- **Renewable Energy Policy Project**
  16 K St. NW, Suite 410, Washington, DC 20006
- **Solar Energy Industries Association (SEIA)**
  Solar Energy System Manufacturers
  202-383-2611

ENVIRONMENTAL ORGANIZATIONS
- **The Envirolink Network**
  5808 Forbes Ave., 2nd Floor
  Pittsburgh, PA 15217
  (412) 420-6400; Fax: (412) 420-6404
- **Rocky Mountain Institute (RMI)**
  1739 Snowmass Creek Rd., Snowmass, CO, 81654-9199
  (303) 927-3851
- **U.S. Green Building Council (USGBC)**
  (301) 657 3469

EXPERIMENTAL LIVING
- **The Cohousing Network**
  P.O. Box 2584, Berkeley, CA 94702
  (510) 549-9980
- **Habitat for Humanity International**
  Donor Response
  121 Habitat St
  Americus, GA 31709
  (912) 924-6935, ext. 2551 or 2552

BIBLIOGRAPHY

- Abraham, Loren E. et al. Sustainable Building Technical Manual (Chapter 9 Daylighting). Public Technology, Inc., 1996.
- Abraham, Loren E., Athens, Bernheim, Burke, Gottfried, Reed, et al. Sustainable Building Technical Manual. Public Technology Inc., United States Department of Energy, 1996.
- Abraham, Loren E. The Gap Corporate Campus Cost Benefit Analysis. William McDonough + Partners, PLC, Architects, 1995.
- American Institute of Architects. AIA Environmental Resource Guide. AIA and the United States Environmental Protection Agency, 1993.
- American Society of Heating Refrigerating and Air-conditioning Engineers. "Energy Efficient Design of New Low-rise Residential Buildings." ASHRAE 90.2-1993.
- ANSI. American National Standard Specifications for Making Buildings and Facilities Accessible to and Usable by Physically Handicapped People. ANSI A117.1-1980.
- Ballast, David Kent. Architect's Handbook of Formulas, Tables, & Mathematical Calculations. New Jersey: Prentice Hall, 1988.
- Birren, F. Light, Color, and Environment. New York: VanNostrand Reinhold, 1969.
- Bower, John. Healthy House Building; a design & construction guide. The Healthy House Institute, 1993.
- Bower, John. Understanding Ventilation: How to design, select and install residential ventilation systems. The Healthy House Institute, 1995.
- Breyer, Donald E. Design of Wood Structures. 2nd Edition. McGraw-Hill, Inc., 1988.
- Brown, G.Z. Sun Wind and Light: Architectural Design Strategies. Wiley & Sons, 1985.
- Brown, Lester. State of the World. Worldwatch Institute, 1994.
- Brown, Lester. State of the World. Worldwatch Institute, 1995.
- Brown, Lester. State of the World. Worldwatch Institute, 1996.
- Browning, Evans, Franta, Ander, Selkowitz, Sprunt, et al. Greening of the White House Feasibility Report and Phase One Action Plan. American Institute of Architects and United States Department of Energy Federal Energy Management Program (FEMP), 1993.
- Caldicott, Helen. If you Love this Planet: A Plan to Heal the Earth. W.W. Norton & Co., 1992.
- Callender, John Hancock. Time-Saver Standards for Architectural Design Data. 7th Edition. McGraw-Hill, Inc., 1990.
- Carmody, Selkowitz, Heschong. Residential Windows, A guide to new technologies and energy performance. Norton, 1996.
- Colborn, Theo, et al. Our Stolen Future. Dutton, 1996.
- Collins, B.L., R.T. Ruegg, R. Chapman, and T. Kusada. A New Look at Windows. Center for Building Technology, National Bureau of Standards, January 1978.
- Collins, Belinda. "Windows and People," An anthology of studies and surveys. 1988.
- Cook, Billman, Adcock. Photovoltaic Fundamentals. National Renewable Energy Laboratory and United States Department of Energy, 1994.
- Council of American Building Officials. 1995 Model Energy Code. CABO, 1995.
- Demkin, Joseph (ed.). Environmental Resource Guide. Revised Edition. John Wiley & Sons, 1996.
- Denver Water. Xeriscape Plant Guide: 100 Water-wise Plants for Gardens and Landscapes. Fulcrum Publishing, 1996.
- Ellison, Donald C., Whitney C. Huntington. Building Construction: Materials and Types of Construction. 6th Edition. Wiley & Sons, 1987.
- Environmental Building News. Insulation Materials: Environmental Comparisons. EBN Volume 4, No. 1 -- January/February 1995.
- EREN, "The Borrower's Guide to Financing Solar Energy Systems: A Federal Overview US Department of Energy, EREN website" (Document Available in PDF format).
- Evans, Benjamin H. Daylight In Architecture. New York: McGraw-Hill, 1981.
- Flavin, Christopher and Nicholas Lenssen. Power Surge. Guide to the Coming Energy Revolution. Norton, 1994.
- Flavin, Christopher. A New Power Base: Renewable Energy Policies for the Nineties and Beyond. Worldwatch Institute, 1995.
- Flavin, Christopher. Worldwatch report. Worldwatch Institute, 1998.
- Florida Solar Energy Center. Manufacturers of Collectors and Distributors of Systems Certified by the Solar Rating and Certification Corporation. FSEC, 1998.
- Gore, Al. Earth in the Balance. Houghton Mifflen, NY, 1992.
- Hanson, Chris. The Cohousing Handbook. Building a Place for Community. Vancouver, B.C.: Hartley and Marks, 1996.
- Hawkin, Paul. The Ecology of Commerce: A Declaration of Sustainability. Harper Business, 1993.
- Hopkinson, R.G. and J.D. Kay. The Lighting of Buildings. New York: Praeger, 1960.

- ICBO. Allowable Structural Design Stresses from Uniform Building Code Table 25-A-1 and 25-E. International Conference of Building Officials, 1992.
- Illuminating Engineering Society of North America. Recommended Practice of Daylighting. New York, 1979.
- Industry Standard for exterior wood windows. National Wood Window and Door Manufacturers Association (NWWDA).
- Institute for Local Self Reliance. Manufacturing from Recyclables, 24 Case studies of Successful Recycling Enterprises. US Environmental Protection Agency, 1995.
- International Energy Agency. New Method for Measuring the Efficiency of Solar Air Collectors Developed, Solar Update. IEA, August 1998.
- Levin, Hal (ed.). Indoor Air Bulletin – Technology, Research, and News for Indoor Environmental Quality. 1994.
- Liberman, Jacob. Light – Medicine of the Future. Santa Fe, NM: Bear and Company, 1991.
- MacDonald, O.S., Matts Myhrman. Build it with Bales: A Step-by-step Guide to Straw-bale Construction. Version Two. 1997.
- Maine Bureau of Banking Consumer Outreach Program. A Consumer's Guide to Home Mortgage Financing In The 1990s. Maine Bureau of Banking Consumer Outreach Program, 1998.
- Mazria, Edward. The Passive Solar Energy Book, A complete guide to passive solar home, greenhouse and building design. Rodale Press, 1979.
- McVeigh, James, Dallas Burtraw, Joel Darmstadter, Karen Palmer. "Winner, Loser or Innocent Victim: Has Renewable Energy Performed as expected," REPP Research Report No. 7, Renewable Energy Policy Project. Washington, D.C., March 1999.
- Means Residential Cost Data. R.S. Means, 1997.
- Miller, G. Tyler, Jr. Living in the Environment. 9th Edition. Wadsworth Publishing, US, 1996.
- Nevalainen, Aino. Microbial Contamination in Buildings, Proceedings of the Sixth Annual Conference on Indoor Air Quality and Climate. Vol. 4. Helsinki, Finland, 1993.
- NIRS (Nuclear Information Resource Service).
- Olkowski, William, Sheila Daar, Helga Olkowski. Common-sense Pest Control: Least-toxic solutions for your home, garden, pets and community. The Taunton Press, 1991.
- Passive Solar Design Strategies: Guidelines for Builders with BuilderGuide Software. Passive Solar Industries Council, 1996. Contact PSIC, 1511 K Street NW, Ste. 600, Washington, D.C., 20005.
- Passive Solar Industries Council. NavFac Whole Building Design Guidelines. U.S. Department of the Navy Naval Facilities Administration, 1996.
- Pearson, David. The New Natural House Book. Revised Edition. Simon & Schuster, 1998.
- Prowler, Donald, William Bobbenhausen, Adrian Tulucca, Michael Nicklas, Robert Erwin. Designing Low Energy Buildings with Energy 10 Software v.1.2. Passive Solar Industries Council, 1996. Contact PSIC, 1511 K Street NW, Ste. 600, Washington, D.C., 20005.
- Ramsey, Charles George. Ramsey/Sleeper Architectural Graphic Standards. John Wiley & Sons, 1988.
- Renewable Resource Data Center (RReDC).
- Rocky Mountain Institute, Alex Wilson. Green Development: Integrating Ecology and Real Estate. John Wiley & Sons, 1998.
- Rousseau, David, James Wasley. Healthy by Design: Building and Remodeling Solutions for Creating Healthy Homes. Hartley and Marks, 1997.
- San Martin, Robert. U.S. Department of Energy "Environmental Emissions from Energy Technology Systems: The total Fuel Cycle." Washington, D.C., 1989.
- Schaeffer, John (ed.). Solar Living Sourcebook. Real Goods Trading Corporation, 1994.
- Schaeffer, John. Solar Living Source Book, The Complete Guide to renewable Energy Technologies and Sustainable Technology. 8th Edition. Real Goods, 1994.
- SETAC. A Technical Framework for Life-cycle Assessment. Society for Environmental Toxicology and Chemistry and the SETAC Foundation. Washington, D.C., 1991.
- U.S. Bureau of the Census. Census Data 1990. 1995.
- U.S. Department of Energy. Passive Solar Design Handbook. New York: Van Nostrand Reinhold Company, Inc., 1984.
- United States Green Building Council. Local Governments Sustainable Buildings Guidebook. Public Technology Incorporated, Washington, D.C.
- Upton, Christopher, Stephen Bass. The Forest Certification Handbook. St. Lucie Press, Inc., 1996.
- US Department of Energy – Energy Information Administration (EIA). Annual Electric Generator Report. Washington, D.C., 1995.

INDEX

ACKNOWLEDGEMENTS

The author and publishers would like to thank Ms. Marianne Dedekind, certified architectural engineer, Institut Energie und Bau, Hamburg, Germany for technical advice.

The author would like to thank the following authors for giving permission to reproduce their contributions to the magazine *ÖKO-TEST:* Martina Arnold, Stefan Becker, Marcus Brian, Rolf Gramm, Gabi Haas, Peter Hermes, Martina Keller, Wolfgang Langeneck, Jochen Paulus, Eva Roth, Annette Sabersky, Birgit Schumacher, Jürgen Stellpflug.

The publishers would like to thank the following for the support they have provided to the photographer and picture researchers: BASTA Baubüro, Anne Mense and Burkhard Bürger, Dortmund; BAUFRITZ, Erkheim im Allgäu; Bernd Heidbrede, Architect, Schwerte; Walter Hösel, Europäisches Design Depot, Klagenfurt; Klaus W. König, Architect, Überlingen; Manfred Kuhr, Forestry Office, and Josef Heer, Bergweide Sauerland, Olpe; Bernd Küpper, Isafloc, Altenkirchen; MUTA GmbH, Öko Baumarkt, Dortmund; Peter Patt, Flammersfeld; Sandler Solar, Kaufbeuren; Hans H. Stamer, Möhnsen, Marianne Stöcker, Oedingen – and Benito Barajas, Emanuel Bloedt, Annette Hudemann, Claus Langer, Tobias Mense, Ralf Müller, Andreas Roters, Elke Stollmeier.

We would like to thank the following for their help with the picture credits: Aicha Becker, Andreas Bodden, Iris Heinen, Thomas Ristow.

PHOTOGRAPHIC CREDITS

Most of the illustrations, not credited here individually, are new photographs taken by
Karin Heßmann, Architectural Photographer, c/o Centrum Studio für Fotografie, Dortmund.
Assistants: Nicole Alheidt and Petra Warrass.
Picture research: Hans-Jürgen Wolf, Frauke Steinhoff-Balz, Karin Heßmann.

The graphics were created by Dietmar Lochner, Hamburg
(except: p. 319, back boiler from Brunner + Rosai GmbH, Unterschließheim).

The author and publishers would like to thank the following companies and photographers,
as well as the architects mentioned in the captions, for providing photographs and giving permission for their reproduction.
Despite all our efforts, it has not proved possible to contact all the architects concerned.
Holders of existing rights are therefore requested to contact the publishers.

Auro, Brunswick
p. 289 t.
Arge Holz Arbeitsgemeinschaft Holz e. V., Düsseldorf
p. 202; p. 203
Arbeitsgemeinschaft Ziegeldecke e.V., Brunntal
p. 112 t.r.; p. 113 t.l.; p. 113 r.

Barajas, B., Dortmund
p. 176; p. 241 t.; p. 272; p. 295 t.;
p. 295 b. r.
Baufritz GmbH & Co., Erkheim/Allgäu
p. 79 b.; p. 113 b.; p. 390
Berger Biotechnik GmbH, Hamburg
p. 368
Bionova, Munich
pp. 444/445; p. 446 t.; p. 446 r.; p. 447 2nd row
B&O Holzbau GmbH, Hamburg
p. 119 t.; p. 164; p. 165 t.; p. 172 c.
Brunner + Rosai GmbH, Unterschließheim
p. 313; p. 314 b.l.; p. 315; p. 316; p. 317 t.;
p. 318; p. 319 (illustration)
Bruderus Heiztechnik GmbH
p. 307 b.
Böttger, Ulrich, Cologne
p. 83 t.

Claytec, Viersen
p. 194 b.l.
Cortex Kork-Vertriebs-GmbH, Fürth
p. 274

Dedekind, C., Hamburg
p. 70 t.; p. 112 b.l.; p. 120 b.; p. 123 c.;
p. 176 t.l.; p. 176 r.; p. 183 t.; p. 306 t.; p.
328 b.; p. 330 t.; p. 333 t.
Dennert KG, Schlüsselfeld
p. 197 c.
Deltau, G., Haiger Weidelbach
p. 367 b.r.
Deutsche Heraklith GmbH, Simbach/Inn
p. 179
Deutsche Pittsburgh Corning GmbH, Haan

p. 219 4th row; p. 219 b.
Doppelmayer, Kempten
p. 324 b.l.
Duravit Aktiengesellschaft, Hornberg
p. 387 l.

EuroCeramik GmbH, Viersen
p. 249 b.r.; p. 249 l.

Faist GmbH & Co. KG, Krumbach
p. 183 b.; p. 215 b.; p. 227 c.b.
Flachglas AG, Gelsenkirchen
p. 259 t.; p. 262; p. 263 b.l.; p. 263 r.
Forbo, Pirmasens
p. 261

Giacomini-Opel Armaturen GmbH, Waldbröl
p. 339
Gutex GmbH & Co., Waldshut-Tiengen
p. 180 t.; p. 121 t.; p. 212 b.; p. 213
Grammer Bürostühle GmbH, Amberg
p. 427 b.
Grohe AG, Hemer
p. 362 t.; p. 363; p. 386 b.r.; p. 387 r.c.; p.
387 r.b.

Halotech Lichtfabrik GmbH, Innsbruck (A)
p. 345
Hansgrohe GmbH & Co KG, Schiltach
p. 386 t.; p. 387 r.t.
Heidelberger Zement, Heidelberg
p. 200
Heiermann, Dorothea, Cologne
p. 286 (artist: Henrike Müller, Gut Horbell, Cologne)
Heinemann GmbH, Schondorf
p. 335 t.
Heraklith GmbH, Simbach/Inn
p. 179
hiwo-Holzindustrie Waldburg zu Wolfegg GmbH & Co. KG, Wolfegg
p. 209 t.l.; p. 209 r.; p. 211 t.
Hoesch Design, Düren
p. 45 b.; p. 288; p. 325
Hornitex, Horn-Bad Meinberg

p. 210 t.
Isofloc, Hessisch Lichtenau
p. 180 b.l.; p. 120 t.; p. 124 t.; p. 220 t.l.; p.
220 b.l.; p. 221
Isocotton, Augsburg
p. 227 t.c.

JAB, Bielefeld
p. 408
Kambium Möbelwerkstätte, Lindlar
p. 429 1st row; p. 429 2nd row
KK Public Relations, Münster
p. 121 b.
König, K. W., Überlingen
p. 132 t.l.; p. 132 b.; p. 226 b.; p. 227 l.; p.
367 t.; p. 389 b.
Kottmeier, C., agenda, Hamburg
p. 57 b.; p. 223 t.
KSB AG, Pignitz
p. 364 b.

Landschaftsverband Rheinland, Xanten
p. 320
Lange, Peter, Bexbach
p. 225 b.r.
Langer, Claus, Hagen
p. 132
Levermann, Münster
p. 31; p. 70 b.
Lias Leichtbaustoffe, Tuningen
p. 218 t.; p. 219 t.l.
Lignotrend, Weilheim-Bannholz
p. 209 t.r.
Lindström Systeme, Elstorf
p. 206 b.; p. 207

Mallbeton, Donaueschingen
p. 367 b.l.
Mac Bett, Dortmund
p. 227 t.r; p. 227 b.r.; p. 418; p. 420; p. 421;
p. 422
Moll, Schwetzingen
p. 123 t.; p. 124 b.

Öko-Test-Verlag, Frankfurt
    p. 225 b.r.; p. 296 b. (Bio Pinn); p. 368 b.;
    p. 437
Osram GmbH, Munich
    p. 346; p. 347 b.l.; p. 347 b.r.
Origo, Schwäbisch-Gmünd
    p. 415 t.

Paradigma, Karlsbad
    p. 322 b.l.
Perma-Trade, Leonberg
    p. 370
P.O.S. Bauer+Köhler AG, Neu-Isenburg
    p. 303
Picea, Unterthurheim
    p. 224
Puren-Schaumstoff GmbH, Überlingen
    p. 215 c.

Ross, Hamburg
    p. 350 l.
Rockwool, Gladbeck
    p. 217 t.r.
Ruckstuhl, Langenthal (CH)
    p. 41 b.; pp. 278/279 m.; p. 281
Rimmele, Ehingen
    p. 193 t.l.; p. 193 3rd row; p. 193 2nd row l.
    p. 193 4th row r.

Schlipphak GmbH, Stuttgart
    p. 388
Schlüter, Stadthagen
    p. 405, p. 409

Schulz, Expo-Stadt, Kassel
    p. 98; p. 99
Schütz GmbH, Lichtenfels
    p. 422
Sembella Liegekomfort GmbH, Bochum
    p. 417 t.; p. 417 c.
Senertec GmbH, Schweinfurt
    p. 305
Simonsen, Kai, Cabinet Maker, Oetzen
    p. 269 b
Solar Diamant, Wettringen
    p. 84; p. 334
Sterflinger, Kirchweiach
    p. 225 c.r.; p. 225 c.l.
Sto AG, Stühlingen
    p. 201 1st row; p. 201 2nd row; p. 280; p.
    284; p. 285 4th row
Strobel, Peter, Cologne
    p. 148; p. 153; p. 173; p. 184 b.; p. 311; p.
    331; p. 355; p. 410; p. 436; p. 464; p. 465

Team 7 Natürlich Wohnen GmbH, Ried (A)
    p. 375 t; p. 382; p. 414; p. 415 b.; p. 415 c.;
    p. 423; p. 425; pp. 426/427; p. 428 t.; p.
    429 b.
Tischner, U., Dip. Design, Cologne
    p. 381 b.
Thüringer Waid Verarbeitungs-GmbH,
Neudietendorf
    p. 206 t.r.; p. 206 c.l.

Villeroy & Boch, Mettlach
    p. 304; p. 384; p. 385

Vrogum, Oksbol (DK)
    p. 266; p. 267

Wagner & Co Solartechnik GmbH., Cölbe
    p. 366 c.; p. 366 b.
Wassmuth, J., Dortmund
    p. 201 3rd row; p. 219 c.l.
Weber-Haus, Rheinau-Link
    p. 144 t.
Wienerberger Ziegelindustrie GmbH & Co,
Hanover-Lahe
    p. 192; p. 193 t.l.; p. 193 b.l.; p. 193 c.t.r.
Wirus-Bauelemente GmbH, Gütersloh
    p 268; p. 269 2nd row; p. 269 3rd row; p.
    269 4th row
Wools of New Zealand, Düsseldorf
    p. 278 l.; p. 279 r.; p. 280

Ytong AG, Munich
    p. 197 t.; p. 197 l.b.

Zagan, H.-G., Ludwigsburg
    p. 322 t
Zehnder-Beutler GmbH, Lahr
    p. 322 b.r.; p. 323; p. 324 t.
Zimmer & Rhode, Oberursel
    p. 416

Key: t.l. = top left; c.r. = center right; 2nd row b.
= 2nd row bottom.